Manchu

A Textbook for Reading Documents

second edition

NFLRC
monographs

NFLRC Monographs is a refereed series sponsored by the National Foreign Language Resource Center at the University of Hawai'i under the supervision of the series editor, Richard Schmidt. NFLRC Monographs present the findings of recent work in applied linguistics that is of relevance to language teaching and learning, with a focus on the less commonly-taught languages of Asia and the Pacific.

Research among learners of Chinese as a foreign language
Michael E. Everson, & Helen H. Shen (Eds.), 2010
ISBN 978–0–9800459–4–9

Toward useful program evaluation in college foreign language education
John M. Norris, John McE. Davis, Castle Sinicrope, & Yukiko Watanabe (Editors), 2009
ISBN 978–0–9800459–3–2

Second language teaching and learning in the Net Generation
Raquel Oxford & Jeffrey Oxford (Editors), 2009
ISBN 978–0–9800459–2–5

Case studies in foreign language placement: Practices and possibilities
Thom Hudson & Martyn Clark (Editors), 2008
ISBN 978–0–9800459–0–1

Chinese as a heritage language: Fostering rooted world citizenry
Agnes Weiyun He & Yun Xiao (Editors), 2008
ISBN 978–0–8248328–6–5

Perspectives on teaching connected speech to second language speakers
James Dean Brown & Kimi Kondo-Brown (Editors), 2006
ISBN 978–0–8248313–6–3

ordering information at nflrc.hawaii.edu

Manchu

A Textbook for Reading Documents

second edition

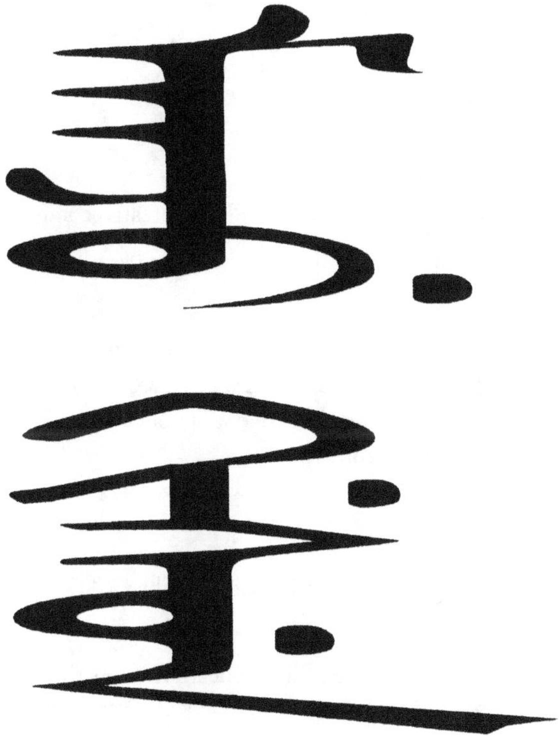

Gertraude Roth Li

NATIONAL FOREIGN LANGUAGE RESOURCE CENTER
University of Hawai'i at Mānoa

Manufactured in the United States of America.

The contents of this publication were developed in part under a grant from the U.S. Department of Education (CFDA 84.229, P229A060002). However, the contents do not necessarily represent the policy of the Department of Education, and one should not assume endorsement by the Federal Government.

ISBN: 978–0–9800459–5–6
Library of Congress Control Number: 2009943695

The paper used in this publication meets the minimum requirements of the American National Standard for Information Sciences–Permanence of Paper for Printed Library Materials.
ANSI Z39.48–1984

distributed by

National Foreign Language Resource Center
University of Hawai'i
1859 East-West Road #106
Honolulu HI 96822–2322
nflrc.hawaii.edu

To

Joe Fletcher

Manchu: A vanishing rainbow

by Chang Ming

Learning to read these unfamiliar symbols
My soul is lighter than a flower awaking to spring,
Lighter than a seagull winging to ocean,
Lighter than a rainbow arching to sky.
  I find my long lost rainbow.

Trying to write these unfamiliar symbols
My heart lies heavier than mountains on earth,
Heavier than a volcano on lava,
Heavier than a tree on roots.
  I stand by my long lost root.

Dedicated to Dr. Gertraude Roth Li
Honolulu, 2004

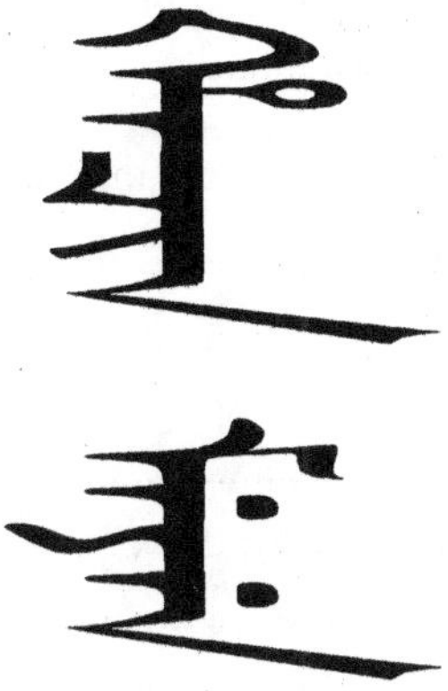

Contents

Part II: Reading Selections

Part III: Study Aids

Acknowledgments

Support for publication of the first edition was provided by the Walter & Elise Haas Chair in East Asian Studies, University of California at Berkeley, and by the National Foreign Language Resource Center at the University of Hawai'i at Manoa, funded by a grant from the United States Department of Education, CFDA 84.229A P229A6007.

Many people helped me during the preparation of the book: At a crucial stage in the writing process of the first edition, Frederic Wakeman, Jr., invited me teach Manchu at Berkeley giving me an opportunity to refine the notes for the reading selections. Other individuals provided answers to various questions and thereby helped make the book better than it otherwise would have been: Pamela Crossley, Mark Elliott, Jiang Qiao, Tatiana Pang, Giovanni Stary, Stephen Wadley, Alexander Vovin, Cheng Zhi, and Wu Hsiao-ting.

The second edition benefits enormously from the contribution by David Holm, Professor of Chinese at the University of Melbourne, who with the help of Tong Leisheng produced the accompanying audio recordings which are accessible online. Formerly a schoolteacher in Chabchal, Xinjiang, Mr. Tong is a native speaker of Sibe. My heartfelt thanks go to both of them. Over the years various users of the book have provided valuable feedback. Among them I feel particularly indebted to Sigrid Lambert, an enthusiastic and diligent student of Manchu, who helped me discover many inadequacies in the text. I also appreciated Randy Alexander's questions and suggestions which led me to restructure the first reading selection.

I am grateful to Richard Schmidt, director of the National Foreign Language Resource Center at the University of Hawaii, for making the second edition possible and to Deborah Masterson for shepherding the revision through the publication process. I also say thank you my husband Yuan-Hui Li for his moral and emotional support over the many years it took to complete the work and to Chang Ming for sharing his sense of joy over the book through a poem.

Part I

Introduction

Introduction

The purpose of this book

This textbook is designed as a tool to acquire a basic knowledge of written Manchu by studying a variety of texts. Manchu was the language of a group of people, the Jurchens, who in the sixteenth century lived to the northeast of China and later became known as Manchus. After building alliances and establishing a new state in the southern part of Manchuria in the early seventeenth century, they conquered China and ruled as the Qing dynasty until 1911. The swift development of the Manchu script, undoubtedly connected to the Manchus' concept of Manchu identity and state power, allowed them to readily follow Chinese dynastic precedent of historic record keeping. Millions of Manchu records—along with records in Chinese and Mongolian—were created during the Manchus' nearly three hundred years in power. Most of the existing Manchu documents are located in Chinese and Taiwanese archives.

Contemporary Qing historians increasingly urge students to learn Manchu and to include Manchu sources in their research. However, students interested in following their teachers' advice have difficulty gaining access to a formal class. Manchu is taught at only a few universities and generally at highly irregular intervals. Nor is there an appropriate Manchu textbook for the English-speaking student. Several grammars, some with reading selections, have been published in the People's Republic of China within the last two decades. More recently a Manchu textbook came out in Japan and a Manchu Grammar (in English) in Europe. These works demonstrate a rising interest in Manchu studies worldwide.

This book seeks to fill the need by providing an English-language tool which allows students to study Manchu without or with minimal support from a teacher. Because it was written primarily for students of Chinese history, it does not focus on linguistic analyses, though it does include sufficient grammatical information to insure a full understanding of the reading selections. Building on that foundation, students of history and students of linguistics will be able to continue with texts of their own choosing.

Why study Manchu?

During the course of the Qing dynasty, missionaries and sinologists busied themselves studying Manchu primarily to gain access to the imperial court and its influence or to use it as a crutch towards a better understanding of the Chinese classics. Manchu was easier to learn and seemed to have fewer ambiguities than Chinese. Though Manchu certainly has its share of ambiguous sentence structures, a knowledge of the language can indeed be helpful with bilingual Manchu-Chinese texts. Nonetheless, with an imperial Manchu court out of the picture, few scholars study Manchu today as a crutch to Chinese. The resurgence of interest in Manchu studies, in and outside of China, stems in good part from a new accessibility of Manchu documents, which in turn has led to a better understanding of the types of Manchu documents available. The new interest in Manchu also reflects a growing awareness among Qing scholars that current Qing historical research may be an unbalanced account due to the scholars' lack of using Manchu documents.

For linguists, the Manchu language offers an excellent medium through which to study issues related to Altaic languages and to examine linguistic influences between Manchu and the northern Chinese dialects. Manchu is the only Tungusic language with a significant body of written historical literature and the Manchus' close and extensive relationship to China's Mandarin speakers has led to extensive mutual linguistic give and take between the two languages.[1]

There is also a contemporary dimension to Manchu studies, partially due to a resurgence of ethnic identities that is sweeping the world. Relatively free to express their ethnic identity, people of Manchu ancestry in the People's Republic of China (PRC) and in Taiwan are increasingly interested in learning about their language and culture which they have all but lost. In Taiwan, a group of about two hundred ethnic Manchus founded the Republic of China's Manchu Association in 1981. In the PRC, the number of people claiming Manchu ethnicity is up from over two million in the 1950s to over ten million in 2001. Whereas many people in China register, if possible, as minority in order to take advantage of certain "affirmative action" programs, there is also a true interest in acknowledging and learning about one's own ethnic background. When in 1985 Manchu descendants established a Manchu language school in Beijing, organizers hoped to attract about twenty students, but found that they had to resort to an entrance examination in order to select students from among over 150 applicants.[2]

Manchu sources

Since the opening of China in the 1980s, international scholars have gained access to library collections in the People's Republic of China. As for Manchu sources, Beijing's First Historical Archives contains the largest number of Manchu documents. Other repositories, such as the Liaoning Archives in Shenyang and the Dalian library, also contain Manchu archival materials and printed books.

While many Manchu documents in the PRC are accessible to international scholars, some documents are still waiting to be catalogued and are said to be deteriorating. In

---

[1] For a study on the interrelationship between Manchu and northern Chinese dialects see Mantarō Hashimoto 橋本萬太朗 *Beifang Hanyu de jiegou fazhan* 北方漢語的結構發展, *Yuyan yanjiu* 語言研究 1, No. 4 (1983): 88–99.

[2] Huang Xiang, "School saves Manchu language," *People's Daily*, 16 July 1987.

1987, an article in the *Renmin ribao* 人民日報[3] reported that at the current pace the sorting and cataloguing work of Manchu documents in the Peking archives would take at least four hundred years and that insects were destroying the documents at about the same speed.

Taiwan's Manchu collections in the Palace Museum and in the Academia Sinica are in good storage, though not all are catalogued and accessible. Other Manchu collections are scattered amongst libraries around the world: Manchu documents are preserved in Japan, Denmark, Great Britain, Germany, Russia, India, and Mongolia. In the U.S., repositories with Manchu collections include Harvard, Princeton, the Library of Congress, the Newberry Library in Chicago, and the New York Public Library.

Bibliographies: In the past, scholars with Manchu language skills have concentrated on producing catalogues, bibliographies and bibliographic essays to tell colleagues about Manchu materials in the various places. The following list—far from complete—gives a sense of the extent of this effort:

Boettcher, Cheryl M. "In Search of Manchu Bibliography." C.A.S. thesis, University of Illinois, 1989.

Chen Jiexian (Ch'en Chieh-hsien). *Manchu Archival Materials*. Taipei: Linking, 1988.

———. *The Manchu Palace Memorials*. Taipei: Linking, 1987.

Elliott, Mark. "An Outline of the Manchu Holdings of the Grand Secretariat and Imperial Palace Archives at the No. 1 Historical Archives, Beijing." Translated by Akira Yanagisawa. *Tōhōgaku* 東學 85 (January 1993): 147. (Text in Japanese.)

Fletcher, Joseph. "Manchu Sources." In *Essays on the Sources for Chinese History*, edited by D. D. Leslie et. al., 141–46. Canberra: Australian National University Press, 1973.

———. Review of *Manchu Books in London: A Union Catalogue of Manchu Language*. London: British Museum, 1977. Compiled by Walter Simon and Howard G. H. Nelson. *Harvard Journal of Asian Studies* 42, No. 2 (1981): 653–63.

Fuchs, Walter. "Beiträge zur mandjurischen Bibliographie und Literatur" (Contributions to Manchu bibliography and literature). *Mitteilungen der Deutschen Gesellschaft für Natur- und Völkerkunde Ostasiens*, 1936.

———. "Verzeichnis der manjurischen Bücher in der Universitätsbibliothek zu Cambridge" (A catalogue of Manchu books in the Cambridge University Library), edited by Martin Gimm. *Aetas Manjurica* 2 (1991): 14–41.

Fuchs, Walter and Martin Gimm. "Die manjurische Sammlung der königlichen Bibliothek zu Kopenhagen" (The Manchu collection of the Royal Library in Copenhagen). *Aetas Manjurica* 2 (1991): 42–116.

[3] Mao Weihui 毛維會, "Jicheng Manwen de renmen" 繼承滿文的人們. *Renmin ribao* 人民日報, Overseas ed., 15 Sep. 1987.

Giles, Herbert Allen and Thomas Francis Wade. *A Catalog of the Wade Collection of Chinese and Manchu Books in the Library of the University of Cambridge*. Cambridge: Cambridge University Press, 1898.

Gimm, Martin. "Zu den mandschurischen Sammlungen der Sowjetunion, I" (On the Manchu collections in the Soviet Union, I). *T'oung Pao* 54, nos.1–3 (1963): 147–79.

Guan Xiaolian 關孝廉. "Qing Kangxi chao Manwen zhupi zouzhe chuyi" 清康熙朝滿文硃批奏摺芻議 (Manchu language memorials to the throne with vermilion comments during the reign of Kangxi). *Lishi dang'an* 歷史檔案 1 (1994): 84–90.

Huang Run-hua 黃潤華et al. *Quanguo Manwen ziliao lianhe mulu* 全國滿文資料聯合目錄 (A national union catalogue of Manchu sources). Peking: Shumu chubanshe, 1992.

Jia Ning (Chia Ning). "The Manchu Collection in the Johns Hopkins University." *Central & Inner Asian Studies* 6 (1992): 36–43.

Jin Ning. *A Catalogue of Sibe Manchu Publications 1954–1989*. With an introduction and indices edited by Giovanni Stary. Wiesbaden: Harrassowitz, 1990.

Laufer, Berthold. "Skizze der mandjurischen Literatur" (Overview of the Manchu literature). *Keleti Szemle* 8 (1908): 1–53. Reprinted in Hartmut Walravens, ed., *Kleinere Schriften von Berthold Laufer*. Wiesbaden: Franz Steiner, 1976.

———. *Descriptive Account of the Collection of Chinese, Tibetan, Mongol and Japanese Books in the Newberry Library*. Chicago: Newberry Library, 1913.

Li Deqi (Li Teh-ch'i) 李德起. *Guoli Beiping tushuguan gugong bowuguan Manwen shuji lianhe mulu*. 國立北平圖書館故宮博物館滿文書籍聯合目錄 (Union catalogue of Manchu books in the National Library of Peiping and the Library of the National Palace Museum). Beijing: National Library of Beiping and Library of the National Museum, 1933.

Li Xuezhi (Li Hsüeh-chih). "Manchu Sources on Taiwan." Translated by Jerry Norman. *Ch'ing-shih wen-t'i* 1, no. 5 (April 1967): 2–6.

Matsumura Jun. "A Catalogue of the Manchu Books in the Library of Congress." *Tōhō gakuhō* 東洋學報 57, nos. 1–2 (1976): 230–53.

Mish, John Leo. *The Manchus: A List of References in the New York Public Library*. New York, 1947.

Naquin, Susan. "The Grand Secretariat Archives at the Institute of History and Philology, Academia Sinica, Taiwan." *Late Imperial China* 8, no. 2 (December 1987): 102–7.

Pang, Tatiana A. "Manchu Rare Manuscripts at the St. Petersburg Branch of the Institute of Oriental Studies." *Manuscripta Orientalia*, 1, no. 3 (1995): 33–46.

———. "Mandschurische Sprachführer aus der Sammlung der Leningrader Abteilung des Orientalischen Instituts der Akademie der Wissenschaften" (Manchu textbooks in the collection of the Oriental Institute of the Leningrad Academy of Sciences). *Central Asiatic Journal* 32, nos. 1/2 (1988): 91–97.

———. *A Catalogue of Manchu Materials in Paris: Manuscripts, Block-prints, Scrolls, Rubbings, Weapons*. Wiesbaden: Harrassowitz, 1998.

Poppe, N. N, Leon Nahum Hurvitz, and Hidehiro Okada. *Catalogue of the Manchu-Mongol Section of the Tōyō Bunko*. Tokyo, Seattle: University of Washington Press, 1964.

Puyraimond, Jeanne Marie et al. *Catalogue du fonds Mandchou*. Paris: Bibliothèque Nationale, 1979.

Qu Liusheng 屈六生. "Qingdai junjichu Manwen dang'an congshu." 清代軍機處滿文檔案叢書 (Collection of Manchu documents from the Qing Grand Council). *Lishi dang'an* 歷史檔案 1 (1989): 124–49.

Sinor, Denis. *Introduction a l'étude de l'Eurasie Centrale* (Introduction to the study of Central Eurasia). Wiesbaden: Harrassowitz, 1963.

Stary, Giovanni. *Manchu Studies: An International Bibliography*. Wiesbaden: Harrassowitz, 1990.

Walravens, Hartmut. "Some Notes on Manchu Bibliography." *Central Asiatic Journal* 33, nos. 3/4 (1989): 254.

———. *Buddhist Literature of the Manchus: A Catalogue of the Manchu Holdings in the Raghu Vira Collection at the International Academy of Indian Culture*. New Delhi: Academy, 1981.

———. *Mandjurische Bücher in Russland: Drei Bestandskataloge, in deutscher Fassung* (Manchu books in Russia: Three catalogues, in German). Hamburg: Bell, 1986.

———. *Vorläufige Titelliste der Mandjurica in Bibliotheken der USA* (Preliminary list of Manchu sources in U.S. libraries). Wiesbaden: Harrassowitz, 1969 (i.e., 1976): 552–613.

Wu Yuanfeng 吳元豐 "Junjichu Manwen yuezhebao ji qi zhengli bianmu 軍機處滿文月摺包及其整理編目" (The memorials in Manchu language, packed monthly by the Grand Council, and their catalogue). *Qingshi yanjiu* 清史研究 2 (1991): 61–64.

Archival collections: Among the various types of Manchu sources, archival materials are probably of greatest interest to the Qing historian. Some of these collections have been published.

For example, documents written between 1607 and 1636, were published as *Jiu Manzhou dang* 舊滿洲檔 (Old Manchu archives).[4] A Qianlong revision of these early documents was romanized and translated into Japanese.[5] Additional pre-1644 documents that were not included in the *Old Manchu Archives* were published in *Qing Taizu chao lao Manwen yuandang* 清太祖朝老滿文原檔 (Original archives in Old Manchu of the Qing Taizu reign),[6] which romanizes and translates the Manchu documents into Chinese, in *Kyū Manchūtō tensō kyūnen* 舊滿洲檔天聰九年 (The Old

[4] (Taipei: Taiwan National Palace Museum, 1969).

[5] Kanda Nobuo et al., *Mambun rōtō* 滿文老檔. *Tongki fuka sindaha hergen i dangse*, The Secret Chronicles of the Manchu Dynasty (Tokyo: Tōyō Bunko, 1955–63).

[6] Guang Lu (Kuang Lu) 廣祿 and Li Xuezhi (Li Hsüeh-chih) 李學智, comp. and trans., 2 vols. ([Taipei:] Institute of History and Philology, Academia Sinica, 1970).

Manchu archives: The ninth year of Tiancong),[7] and in *Ming Qing dang'an cun zhen xuanji* 名青檔案存真選輯 (Selected materials from the Ming–Qing archives).[8] Manchu documents from 1636 to 1644 preserved in the First Historical Archives in Beijing were published in Chinese translation—unfortunately without accompanying Manchu texts—as *Qingchu neiguoshiyuan Manwen dang'an yibian* 清初內國史院滿文檔案譯編 (Translation of Manchu documents from the Palace Historiographic Academy).[9] These various pre-1644 Manchu documents were the primary sources for the *Yargiyan kooli/Shilu* 實錄 (Veritable records) of the first two Qing emperors, Nurhaci and Hong Taiji.

During the Qing dynasty Manchu documents were routinely translated into Chinese. There were, however, many exceptions, because Manchu was also used to deliberately keep certain information inaccessible to non-Manchu speaking officials. Thus, a set of Kangxi period Manchu materials, which was published as part of *Gongzhongdang Kangxi chao zouzhe* 宮中檔康熙朝奏摺 (Memorials from the Kangxi reign in the Palace Archives),[10] contains numerous notations indicating that a particular memorial or the attached imperial response should not be translated. The collection published as *Gongzhongdang Qianlong chao zouzhe* 宮中檔乾隆朝奏摺 (Secret palace memorials of the Qianlong reign)[11] also includes Manchu documents.

Another set of Manchu documents has become available with the Japanese publication of the *Jōkōkitō* 鑲紅旗檔 (Archives of the Bordered Red Banner) of the Yongzheng and Qianlong reigns.[12] The majority of Manchu documents, however, are not published and remain in archival form, though some have been translated into Chinese. For example, the imperially endorsed Manchu memorials from the Kangxi period—about five thousand are stored in the First Historical Archives in Beijing—have been translated into Chinese and published as *Kangxi chao Manwen zhupi zouzhe quanyi* 康熙朝滿文硃批奏摺全議 (Complete translation of the Manchu palace memorials of the Kangxi reign).[13] These memorials, which were sent directly to the emperor, served as a tool for secrecy and control, and as such were the precursors of the later secret palace memorials.

---

7 Kanda Nobuo et al., eds., 2 vols. (Tokyo: Tōyō Bunko, 1972).

8 Li Guangtao (Li Kwang-t'ao) 李光濤 and Li Xuezhi (Li Hsüeh-chih) 李學智, comp. (Taipei: Institute of History and Philology, Academia Sinica, 1973).

9 Wang Wei 王蔚, ed. (Beijing: Guangming ribao, 1986).

10 Vols. 8 and 9 (Taipei: Taiwan National Palace Museum, 1977).

11 9 vols. (Taipei: National Palace Museum, 1975–77).

12 *Jōkōkitō—Yōseichō* (Archives of the Bordered Red Banner—Yongzheng reign) and *Jōkōkitō—Kenryūchō 1* (Archives of the Bordered Red Banner I—Qianlong reign), comp. and trans. by Kanda Nobuo et al. (Tokyo: Tōyō Bunko, 1983).

13 Guan Xiaolian 關孝廉, Qu Liusheng 屈六生, ed. and comp. (Beijing: Dang'an chubanshe, 1984–85). Guan Xiaolian 關孝廉, "Qing Kangxi chao Manwen zhupi zouzhe chuyi" 清康熙朝滿文硃批奏摺芻議, *Lishi dang'an* 歷史檔案, 1 (1994): 87.

Many documents that were created by or transmitted through the Grand Council (Ma. *cooha i nashūn i ba*; Chin. *junjichu* 軍機處), a high level policy making body of the Inner Court created in 1729, were written in Manchu only. Unlike the regular administrative offices of the Outer Court, officials of the Inner Court were not bound by regulations that required palace memorials to be submitted in more than one language. When filed, palace memorials, often with imperial responses appended, were grouped into packets called *lufu zouzhe* 錄副奏摺 for storage. Those related to military affairs—most of them from Qianlong's campaigns before 1760—make up about 80% of the Manchu packets from 1724 to 1910 and were collected separately into military affairs bundles (*junwubao* 軍務包). Documents from the Grand Council's Manchu division deal with appointments, promotions, dismissals of banner personnel, escapees from exile, etc. According to Bartlett, even many of the eighteenth and early nineteenth century documents relating to the Imperial Household Department (Ma. *dorgi baita be uheri kadalara yamun*; Chin. *neiwufu* 內務府) exist only in Manchu.[14]

Some documents created by the Court of Colonial Affairs (Ma. *tulergi golo be dasara jurgan*; Chin. *lifanyuan* 理藩院) were meant for Manchu speaking audiences only. This organization, which had started as the Mongolian Bureau and became the Court of Colonial Affairs in 1638, was in charge of diplomatic communication and other matters relating to the administration of Mongol, Turkic, and Tibetan regions. In some cases its jurisdiction extended to Russian matters. Its president was by statute Manchu or Mongol and the language of communication was largely Manchu. Given the potential importance of the Manchu archival materials created by the Court of Colonial Affairs, it is unfortunate that there is as yet no detailed description of this specific historical source.

The Shenyang collection of *heitu* documents (*heitu* 黑圖 from Manchu *hetu* 'horizontal') covers communication between the Shenyang and Beijing palaces between 1662 to 1861. Before 1732 these documents were written in Manchu. After a transitional period of bilingual documentation, later communication was conducted in Chinese only.

Official publications: The Qing emperors commissioned many bilingual or trilingual (Manchu, Chinese, and Mongolian) compilations.
General government publications:
Yargiyan kooli/Shilu 實錄 (Veritable records)
Da hergen i bithe/Benji 本紀 (Basic annals)
Daicing gurun i uheri kooli bithe/Da-Qing huidian 大清會典 (Collected statutes)
Enduringge tacihiyan/Shengxun 聖訓 (Sacred instructions)
Dergi hese/Shangyu 上諭 (Edicts)

14 Described in Beatrice Bartlett, *Monarchs and Ministers: The Grand Council in mid-Qing China, 1723-1820* (Berkeley: University of California, 1991): 222–25.

Jakūn gūsai tung jy bithe/Baqi tongzhi 八旗通志 (General history of the banner system)
Hesei toktobuha Daicing gurun i fafun i bithe kooli/Da Qing lüli 大清律例 (Regulations of the Qing Dynasty)

Precedents and regulations for administrative offices:
Hesei toktobuha Daicing gurun i uheri kooli i kooli hacin bithe /Qinding Da Qing huidian zeli 欽定大清會典則例 (Regulations of the officially commissioned collected statutes of the Qing Dynasty)
Dorolon i jurgan i kooli hacin i bithe/Libu zeli 禮部則例 (Regulations of the Ministry of Rites)
Hafan i jurgan i faššan be baicara fiyenten i kooli/Libu jixun si zeli 吏部稽勳司則例 (Regulations of the Ministry of Personnel Bureau of Merit Titles)
Tulergi golo be dasara jurgan i kooli hacin i bithe/Lifanyuan zeli 理藩院則例 (Regulations of the Court of Colonial Affairs)
Jakūn gūsai kooli hacin i bithe/Baqi zeli 八旗則例 (Regulations of the Eight Banners)

Military campaign reports:
Daicing gurun i fukjin doro neihe bodogon i bithe/Huang Qing kaiguo fanglüe 皇清開國方略 (Records of the founding of the Qing Dynasty)
Beye dailame wargi amargi babe necihiyeme toktobuha bodogon i bithe/Qinzheng pingding shuomo fanglüe 親征平定朔漠仿略 (Official history of the campaign against Galdan)
Jungar i babe necihiyeme toktobuha bodogon i bithe/Qinding pingding Zhungaer fanglüe 欽定平定準噶爾方略 (Record of the pacification of the Dzungars)

Biographies:
Tulergi Monggo hoise aiman i wang gung sai iletun ulabun/Waifan Menggu huibu wang gong biaozhuan 外藩蒙古回部王公表傳 (Imperially commissioned genealogical tables and biographies of the princes of the Mongols and Muslims of the outer entourage)
Hesei toktobuha gurun i suduri i ambasai faidangga ulabun/Qinding guoshi dachen liezhuan 欽定國史大臣列傳 (Imperially commissioned ordered biographies of the high officials of the Qing Dynasty)

Another Manchu text, accessible through a recent publication is the *Huang Qing zhigongtu* 皇清職貢圖, a collection of illustrations and descriptions (text in Manchu script and romanization, with Chinese translation) of foreign tribute bearers to the Chinese court.[15]

---

15 Zhuang Jifa (Chuang Chi-fa) 莊吉發, ed. *Xie sui «Zhigongtu» Manwen tu shuo jiao zhu* 謝遂«職貢圖»滿文圖說校注 (The Manchu texts to Xie Sui's 'Drawings of tribute bearers') (Taipei: Palace Museum,1989).

Non-official sources: There are many other known Manchu language materials, such as translations from the Chinese classics and Chinese literature, translation of Buddhist literature, genealogies of important Manchu clans, and travel reports. Two well-known, and now also easily accessible documents are Tulišen's report of his travels to the Torghut in 1712–15[16] and the *Tale of the Nisan Shamaness.*[17] Chances are that there are also untold unknown or less well-known documents, even from later periods. When doing his field research in Manchuria during the early twentieth century, the Russian scholar Shirokogoroff reported seeing clan lists, some of which included legendary accounts of clan leaders.[18] It would seem possible, if not likely, that some of these genealogies, perhaps along with some personal correspondence, are still preserved in boxes or closets somewhere in China.

The value of Manchu documents

Building on available inventory information and preliminary examinations of Manchu records, scholars have challenged the previously prevalent view that Manchu documents are nearly all translations from Chinese and that little would be gained from reading the Manchu versions. Moreover, they have made a convincing case that these documents hold high potential value to researchers of Chinese history. The late Joseph Fletcher pointed out in 1981 that "Qing scholars who want to do first-class work in the archives must, from now on, learn Manchu and routinely compare the Manchu and Chinese sources for their topics of research."[19] Other scholars with Manchu language skills have supported this view. Several have made good cases for the study of Manchu by presenting excellent and useful details on the value of Manchu sources:

Bartlett, Beatrice. "Books of Revelations: The Importance of the Manchu Language Archival Record Books for Research on Ch'ing History." *Imperial China* 6, no. 2 (1985): 25–33. See also the section on the Grand Council Manchu Division in Bartlett's *The Grand Council in Mid-Ch'ing China, 1723–1820.* Berkeley: University of California, 1991, 222–25.

Chen Jiexian (Ch'en Chieh-hsien). *Manchu Archival Materials*. Taipei: Linking, 1988. Especially chapters 2, 4, and 7.

Crossley, Pamela K. and E. S. Rawski: "Profile of the Manchu Language in Qing History." *Harvard Journal of Asian Studies* 53, no. 1 (June 1993): 63–102.

---

16 Zhuang Jifa (Chuang Chi-fa) 莊吉發, ed. and trans., *Lakcaha jecen de takuraha babe ejehe bithe* (Report of Tulišen's travels to the outer regions) (Taipei: Wenzhe chubanshe, 1983).

17 *The Tale of the Nisan Shamaness*, A Manchu Folk Epic, introduction and interpretation by Margaret Nowak, translation and transcription by Stephen Durrant (Seattle: University of Washington Press, 1977).

18 S. M. Shirokogoroff, *Social Organization of the Manchus: A Study of the Manchu Clan Organization*, Extra Vol. 3 (Shanghai: Royal Asiatic Society [North China Branch], 1924): 33-34.

19 Joseph Fletcher, review of *Manchu Books in London*, by W. Simon and H. G. Nelson, in *Harvard Journal of Asian Studies* 41, no.2 (1981): 655–56.

Zhuang Jifa (Chuang Chi-fa 莊吉發), *Gugong dang'an shuyao* 故宮檔案述要 (Overview of the archives in the National Palace Museum). Taipei: National Palace Museum, 1983. See pages 63–93 on the value of Manchu memorials in the collection.

———. *Qingdai shiliao lunshu* 清代史料論述 (A discussion of Qing historical sources). Taipei: Wenshizhe, 1979.

The importance of Manchu sources depends, of course, on the topic. For example, Manchu documents are unlikely to make much of a contribution to issues related to Chinese language examination systems or to studies of local Chinese administrations. On the other hand, topics concerning frontier matters, banner garrisons, and imperial household affairs which included the ginseng, jade, and other government monopolies, almost certainly require at least some consultation of Manchu documents. Bartlett found that even after the Grand Council began to record its recommendations in Chinese, many of its discussion memorials (*yifu zouzhe* 議覆奏摺), including those based on Chinese language memorials, were still written in Manchu. In her "Books of Revelations"[20] she suggests that the use of Manchu did not substantially decline during the nineteenth century and that Manchu materials possess previously unsuspected advantages in that they, compared to their Chinese counterparts, were less raided, weeded, or lost over the years and that therefore a run of Manchu archival records would be likely to be more complete.

Work to be done

Now that Manchu collections are accessible, inventories have been compiled, and the case has been made attesting to the value of Manchu documents, it is time to move on to actually using Manchu sources and incorporating the knowledge gained from them into scholarly studies. Japanese scholars have made a great start, but so far only a few works of Western scholars have made significant use of Manchu sources. A number of excellent studies by Giovanni Stary (University of Venice, Italy) are based on Manchu sources. My own dissertation, written over thirty years ago, and a related article on the Manchu-Chinese relationship prior to 1644 draw heavily on the *Old Manchu Archives*.[21] In his book *The Manchu Way: The Eight Banners and Ethnic Identity in Late Imperial China*,[22] Mark C. Elliott," shows what is possible when research on Qing history incorporates knowledge from Manchu documents. I look forward to seeing students who use this text forge ahead and undertake analytical research projects that make meaningful use of original Manchu materials.

---

[20] Beatrice Bartlett, "Books of Revelations: The Importance of the Manchu Language Archival Record Books for Research on Ch'ing History," *Imperial China* 6, no. 2 (1985): 33.

[21] Gertraude Roth Li, "The Rise of the Early Manchu State," diss., Harvard, 1975. Also, "The Manchu-Chinese Relationship," in *From Ming to Ch'ing: Conquest, Region, and Continuity in Seventeenth Century China*, edited by Jonathan D. Spence and John E. Wills, Jr. (New Haven and London: Yale University Press, 1979): 3–37.

[22] Stanford: Stanford University Press, 2001.

There is much to be done. We need to find out what is in those text that exist in Manchu versions only. We need scholarly comparisons of bilingual texts looking out for differences and omissions. And we need more good linguistic analyses, especially studies of Manchu verbs.

About the Manchu language

Manchu belongs to the Tungusic language family which spreads from Western Siberia to the Pacific. Its southern branch consists of about a dozen languages, which include Manchu, Ewenki, Ewen and Nanai. Manchu, as well as other Tungusic languages bear a remarkable similarity to languages belonging to language families found in Central and East Asia (Turkic, Mongolic, Korean, and Japonic) that used to be called Altaic. Though linguists have debated whether Altaic languages are genetically linked or whether their similarities merely reflect borrowings from one another, most specialists in Altaic languages now believe that these similarities are the result of centuries of extensive contact.

History of the Manchu language: When the predecessors of the Manchus, the Jurchens, ruled North China as the Jin dynasty (1115–1234) they developed two scripts of their own, the so-called big and small scripts. Both looked like, but were different from, Chinese characters. Over time, these scripts fell into disuse, and the last known Jurchen inscription dates from 1526. As their own scripts disappeared, the Jurchens substituted written Mongolian whenever they had a need for documentation.

In 1599, Nurhaci, the founder of the Manchu empire, commissioned two scholars, Gagai and Erdeni, to modify the Mongolian script so that it would be suitable for writing Manchu. The origin of the Mongolian script lay in the Middle East: The Mongols had adapted their script from that of the Uyghurs, who got theirs from the Sogdians (who lived in the area of modern-day Uzbekistan and northern Iran). Originally this script was written horizontally like Arabic, from right to left. However, the Uyghur script that inspired the Mongols was already written vertically in columns from left to right. The result of Nurhaci's 1599 initiative was the creation of the Old Manchu script (*tongki fuka akū hergen* 'script without dots and circles'). Most of the pre-1644 Manchu documents, now known as the *Old Manchu Archives*, are recorded in that script. Beginning in the 1620s, the script was further refined by adding dots and circles to eliminate certain ambiguities of the Mongolian script.[23] This modified Manchu script (*tongki fuka sindaha hergen* 'script with dots and circles') remained in use throughout the Qing dynasty.

---

[23] The process of modifying the script occurred over at least a decade and was not, as some Chinese sources make it appear, carried out singlehandedly by Dahai in 1632. For a discussion of the issue, see the following: Michael Weiers, "Zur Registratur der mandschurischen Holztäfelchen," *Aetas Manjurica* 6 (1988): 251–313; Carsten Näher, "On the periodization of written Manchu," *Saksaha: A Review of*

Following the establishment of the Qing dynasty in 1644, most Manchus lived either in Peking, or in walled garrisons throughout the empire. For a while they were able to maintain their language, especially within the garrisons and civil examinations could be taken in either Manchu or Chinese. Initially it was a great distinction for a Manchu to have qualified under the Chinese examinations, an accomplishment worthy of a special memorial to the emperor. But already by the end of the seventeenth century the emperor felt a need to compliment the Hangzhou garrison bannermen for their accomplishments in spoken Manchu, thereby acknowledging that good spoken Manchu could no longer be taken for granted. By the mid-eighteenth century, Chinese had become the dominant language among the Manchus, leading the emperor to embark on a major campaign to maintain Manchu as a spoken and written language.

In 1753, Qianlong proclaimed that Manchu speech was to be "the foundation of the Manchus and every bannerman's foremost duty." In line with his wishes that all bannerman should "speak Manchu, ride well, shoot straight and drill regularly,"[24] schools were established, along with government incentive programs for students of Manchu. All banner officers assigned to duty in Peking were required to be able to speak Manchu. However, a 1791 imperial injunction that "every single man has a responsibility to written Manchu" bears further witness that the battle for spoken Manchu was being lost. Though government documentation continued to be recorded bilingually or trilingually (including Mongolian), an ever smaller number of Manchus possessed usable Manchu language skills.

The trend was hastened by the fact that toward the end of the dynasty, but especially after the 1911 revolution, the Manchus became targets of Chinese persecution, creating a situation which made those who could still speak Manchu ill inclined to publicize that fact. Outside China proper the Manchu language survived somewhat longer. Researcher S. M. Shirokogoroff noted that in 1917 almost all men in Aigun, the northernmost part of Manchuria, could still read Manchu.[25] Similarly, Owen Lattimore, a well-known scholar of China's border areas, reported that officials of the Chahar Mongols during the early 20th century occasionally still spoke Manchu in order to keep the common people from eavesdropping on their conversations. They also wrote official documents, such as passports, in Manchu, not Mongolian.[26]

Several Manchu publications continued to be published in the Northeast during the Republican period: *Sahaliyan ula erindari boolara hoošan* (in Tsitsihar, supplementing

---

Manchu Studies, no. 3 (Spring 1998): 22–30; also Giovanni Stary and Tatiana A. Pang, *New Light on Manchu Historiography and Literature* (Wiesbaden: Harrassowitz, 1998).

24 Pamela Crossley, *Orphan Warriors* (Princeton: Princeton University Press, 1990): 78.

25 *Social Organization of the Manchus: A Study of the Manchu Clan Organization*, Extra Vol. 3 (Shanghai: Royal Asiatic Society [North China Branch], 1924).

26 Owen Lattimore, *Inner Asian Frontiers* (Boston: Beacon Press, 1940): 135, 138.

the *Heilongjiang ribao* 黑龍江日報 from around 1925); *Ice donjin i boolabun* (in Hailar from 1925 to 1930); and *Hulun buir ice donjin afaha* (about 1930). Some materials from the Republican era are preserved at the Hoover Institution.[27]

A survey done in the People's Republic of China (PRC) in the 1950s found that quite a few elderly Manchus who lived in the more remote regions of Manchuria could still speak Manchu. Those over thirty years old were likely to understand it, while the younger generation could neither speak nor understand it.[28] Since then, anthropologists and linguists doing research in northern Manchuria have been reporting on a rapidly dwindling number of Manchu speakers. By now Manchu speakers have become nearly non-existent.

Because of the demise of Manchu as a spoken language among the Manchus, it is all the more interesting to find that a modern version of Manchu, Sibe (Chin. *Xibe* 錫伯), is still the language of daily communication among about twenty thousand people living in the Sibe Cabcal Autonomous County in the Ili region of Xinjiang. These Sibe, whose language is closely related to Manchu but who appreciate being recognized as a group distinct from the Manchus, are descendants of about three thousand Sibe who were moved by the Qianlong emperor in 1764 from Manchuria to Ili. Whereas the Sibe who stayed in China's Northeast subsequently lost their language and culture, those who resettled in Ili have maintained—at least to a moderate degree—both until today. Some Cabcal elementary schools continue to use Sibe as the medium of instruction at least in the early grades. Others offer Sibe as a second language. Magazines, numerous books—many translations from Chinese, and a newsletter, the *Cabcal serkin*, provide adult Sibe readers with native language reading material.[29]

Still, even though the 1982 PRC constitution provides that people of all nationalities have the freedom to use and develop their own spoken and written languages, the Sibe language situation is precarious. Not only is modern Sibe's vocabulary heavily inundated with Chinese words, but many expressions, verb forms, and even grammatical structures also reflect a strong Chinese influence (see Reading Selections D). After recovering from the effects of adverse policies during the cultural revolution, during which time only Chinese instruction was allowed in Sibe schools, there is now a renewed emphasis on coining new Sibe words and on maintaining the spoken and written language.

---

[27] For more details on these publications, see Giovanni Stary, "Manchu Journals and Newspapers. Some Bibliographical Notes," in *Proceedings of the XXVIIIth Permanent Altaistic Conference*, ed. G. Stary (Wiesbaden: Harrassowitz, 1989): 217–32.

[28] *Manzu shehui lishi diaocha* 滿族社會歷史調查 (Survey of the history of Manchu society) (Shenyang: Liaoning People's Press, 1985).

[29] The *Cabcal serkin* (Cabcal news) has been published since 1972, when it succeeded a previous publication, the *Ice banjin* (New life) (1946–72). Additional publications are listed in Stary, "Manchu Journals and Newspapers" (Wiesbaden: Harrassowitz, 1989): 220.

Alphabet: Some scholars consider the Manchu script to be a syllabic one. Others see it as having an alphabet with individual letters, some of which differ according to their position within a word. Thus, whereas Denis Sinor argued in favor of a syllabic theory,[30] Louis Ligeti preferred to consider the Manchu script an alphabetical one.[31] Students of Manchu in the People's Republic of China usually start their studies by learning hundreds of syllables, whereas Westerners generally study the script as an alphabet. Though I take no stand on the merits of either interpretation, I have chosen to join the alphabetic camp for the purpose of this text because I believe that it is easier to learn the script as individual letters than as a multitude of syllables. The Chinese approach, however, has the advantage of requiring students to spend a considerable amount of time up front on the script, an excellent investment of time in view of the fact that the script tends to remain a challenge for most students for a good long while.

As an alphabet, Manchu has six vowels (*a, e, i, o, u, ū*) which fall into two categories: *a, o, ū* are considered back vowels, *e* and *u* are front vowels, while *i* is considered neutral. A few scholars (e.g. Erich Haenisch, *Mandschu-Grammatik*, Leipzig 1961, p. 33) take both *u* and *i* to be neutral. Some prefer to use the terms hard and soft instead of back and front. Manchu has the following consonants: *b, p, s, š, l, m, c, j, y, r, f, w, n* (*ng*), as well as front and back versions of the letters *k, g, h, t*, and *d*. In addition, there are ten elements to represent Chinese sounds. Some of these letters exist in the regular Manchu alphabet, but as such are subject to restricted use. For example, because the regular Manchu front *g* or *k* cannot occur before *a* and *o*, a new letter was designed to transcribe Chinese words starting with *ga, go, ka*, or *ko*.

Romanization: Dictionaries, scholarly articles, and books employ a number of different romanization systems for transliterating the Manchu alphabet (e.g., H. C. von der Gabelentz, P. G. von Möllendorff, Louis Ligeti, Jerry Norman). For this text I have chosen to follow Norman's system. I have done so because English speaking students of Manchu are likely to start out using Norman's dictionary as a first reference tool, and also because once familiar with Norman's romanization students will have little difficulty recognizing other romanizations. Ligeti's romanization, has the advantage of distinguishing between front and back *k, g*, and *h* (back *k, g*, and *h* are represented by *q*, *γ*, and *χ*, respectively; front *h* is written as *x*), thus more accurately reflecting the Manchu alphabet. Though I do not make these distinctions in this text, I suggest students use Ligeti's forms for their personal use.

For ease of typing romanized Manchu texts it has become common practice among Manchu enthusiasts to substitute the letter *v* for *ū* and *x* for *š*.

---

[30] Denis Sinor, *Introduction to Manchu Studies,* Research and Studies in Uralic and Altaic Languages, no. 104 (Washington: ACLS, 1963).

[31] Louis Ligeti, "A propos de l'écriture mandchoue" (On the Manchu script), *Acta Orientalia* (Academia Scientarium Hungaricae) 2 (1952): 235–98.

Pronunciation: The audio recordings (go to: http://hdl.handle.net/10125/6050) for the Sample Words listed at the end of this Introduction (p. 28-30) and for Reading Selections A-1 and A-2 offer a guide to pronouncing Manchu. Given the fact that there are now no longer any native speakers fluent in Manchu, the recordings represent the pronunciation used for reading literary Sibe.

The following descriptions of pronunciation, generally agreed upon by earlier western scholars of Manchu, are only approximations.

a, i, o, u	As in German.
e	As in English *bed.* After labials *b*, *p*, *m*, and *f*, *e* is usually pronounced like a short *o*. In contemporary Sibe all *e* sound like the *e* in bed.
eo	Pronounced *ou.*
oo	Long *ō*, used in Manchu words and for *ao* in Chinese words.
ū	Pronounced like u. The most important function of *ū* is to distinguish back *k*, *g* and *h* (uvulars) from their front (velar) counterparts before the letter *u*. The letter *ū* was also used to transliterate the Chinese sound of *ü*, as in *jiangjun* 將軍 (Ma: *jiyanggiyūn*).
c	As *ch* in *cheers.*
j	As *j* in *just.*
š	As in *shell.*
s + i	In initial position the *si* is pronounced like English *she.* In modern Sibe all *si* are pronounced like *she.*
ši	Like Chinese *shi* 石.
y	As in *yonder.*
ž	Like the French *j* in *jardin*; or like *r* in Chinese *ri* 日.
h (*x*)	Front *h*, like the German *ch* in *ich.*
h (*χ*)	Back *h*, like the German *ch* in *Bach.*
w	Like *v* in English *vase;* sometimes also like *w* in English *we.*

According to linguist Jerry Norman[32] front and back *k*, *g* and *h* represent two separate series of consonants: before the vowels *a*, *o* and *ū* they are pronounced as uvulars while before *e*, *i* and *u* they are velars. However, the Korean scholar Hui Lie believes it is also possible that Manchu, unlike Mongolian, had basically only one sound each for *k*, *g* and *h* and that the orthographic differentiation may have been simply copied along with the Mongolian alphabet. He points out that the letters were not differentiated by Koreans who transcribed early Qing dynasty Manchu texts into Korean.[33]

---

[32] Jerry Norman, review of *Manchu: a Text for Reading Documents*, by Gertraude Roth Li, in *Saksaha: A Review of Manchu studies*, no. 5 (2000): 41-42.

[33] Hui Lie, *Die Mandschu-Sprachkunde in Korea* (Research on the Manchu language in Korea), Uralic and Altaic Series, vol. 114 (Bloomington: Indiana University, 1972): 64.

Modern Sibe makes no noticeable differentiation between front and back *d*, or between front and back *t*. The distinction was not present in the Old Manchu alphabet and does not exist in Mongolian. The fact that the two letters were differentiated when the Old Manchu script was modified points to a possible difference in pronunciation at the time. When *y* and *w* separate *i*, *ū*, and *u* from the following vowel, the two syllables are pronounced as one; examples: *hūwa-liya-sun* 'harmony,' or *niyeng-niye-ri* 'spring.'

Over time, scholars of Manchu have held contradictory views regarding the stress in a Manchu word.[34] Contemporary Sibe speakers reading Manchu texts out loud appear to generally stress the last syllable of a word. Whereas this stress is quite prominent in words ending in the letter *n*, in many other words all syllables seem to receive nearly equal stress. A different stress does not alter the meaning of the word.

Language characteristics: Manchu words cannot begin with the letter *r*, *ū*, or with consonant clusters, and they generally end in *n*, *ng*, or a vowel.

Vowel harmony: Vowel harmony, meaning that the vowels within a given word must harmonize, is the best-known characteristic of Altaic languages.[35] According to vowel harmony each word can only contain either front or back vowels. Manchu follows the rule generally, but does not adhere strictly to vowel harmony. In Manchu the letters *u* and *i* are considered neutral and may combine with either front vowel *e* or back vowels *ū*, *o*, and *a* .

Examples:

monggorombi
bahanarambi
hergen
selgiyembi
gisurembi
yargiyan kooli

Vowel harmony affects various suffixes that may be attached to the stem of the word. Many suffixes have more than one version, one for front vowel words, and another for back vowel words. For example, suffix *-kan*, *-ken*, *-kon* conveys the meaning of "somewhat"; *amba-kan* therefore means 'somewhat large' and *olho-kon* 'somewhat dry.' Some suffixes, such as *de* ('in' or 'at') and *ci* ('from') have only one form.

---

[34] For example, P. G. von Möllendorf, *Manchu Grammar with Analyzed Texts*, (Shanghai: American Presbyterian Mission Press, 1892): 1. Also see Nicola Di Cosmo, "Alcune osservazioni sull'accento mancese" (Some observations on the accent in Manchu), *Aetas Manjurica* 1 (1981): 1–14.

[35] See J. Ard, "Vowel Harmony in Manchu: A Critical Overview," *Journal of Linguistics* 20 (1984): 57-80; and D. Odden, "Abstract Vowel Harmony in Manchu," *Linguistic Analysis* 4 (1978): 149–65.

In some cases front and back vowels designate masculinity and femininity; for example: *ama* 'father' and *eme* 'mother'; *haha* 'man' and *hehe* 'woman'; *naca* 'brother in-law' and *nece* 'sister-in-law'; *emile* 'hen' and *amila* 'rooster'; *ganggan* 'strong' and *genggen* 'weak.'

Agglutination: Agglutination means that inflection and word formation occur by adding suffixes to word stems. The stem of the word does not change. Vowel changes, as in the English verb *sing*, *sang*, *sung*, do not occur.

In Manchu a multitude of syllables can be added to verb stems. For example, *ara-* is the verb stem of the verb 'to write.' Most dictionaries list verb stems with the finite verb ending *-mbi*; for example, *arambi* 'to write.' Verbs may also take other mid-position syllables, which follow vowel harmony rules and convey additional meaning. The following syllables are commonly used to create verbal derivatives:

-la-, *-le-*, *-lo-*:	*ejelembi* 'to rule' (*ejen* 'ruler')
-da-, *-de-*, *-do-*:	*jalidambi* 'to cheat' (*jali* 'crafty')
-na-, *-ne-*, *-no-*:	*acanambi* 'to meet' (*acan* 'union')
-ra-, *-re-*, *-ro-*:	*gisurembi* 'to speak' (*gisun* 'word')
-ša-, *-še-*, *-šo-*:	*adališambi* 'to be similar' (*adali* 'similar')

Syllables which convey additional meaning:

To cooperate with someone: *-nu-*, *-ndu-*; or *-ca-*, *-co-*, *-ce-*.
injendumbi 'to laugh together' (*injembi* 'to laugh')
eficembi 'to play together' (*efimbi* 'to play')

To come to do something: *-nji-* from *jimbi* 'to come'
afanjimbi 'to come to fight' (*afambi* 'to fight')

To go to do something: *-na-*, *-no-*, *-ne-*.
alanambi 'to go to report' (*alambi* 'to report')

To send (someone) to do something: *-nggi-* from *unggimbi* 'to send'
alanggimbi 'to send (someone) to report'

To do frequently or repeatedly, or to denote action or movement:
-ca-, *-ce-*, *-co-*; *-nja-*, *-nje-*, *-njo-*; *-ta-*, *-te-*, *-to-*; *-ša-*, *-še-*, *-šo-*.
fekucembi 'to jump back and forth' (*fekumbi* 'to jump')
halanjambi 'to keep changing' (*halambi* 'to change')
anatambi 'to push together' or 'to push repeatedly' (*anambi* 'to push')
bulekušembi 'to look into the mirror' (*buleku* 'mirror')

To cause someone to do something: *-bu-*.
arabumbi 'to make someone write' (*arambi* 'to write')

Some of these syllables can be strung together.

Examples:

tacimbi	to learn
tacibumbi	to cause to learn, to teach
tacibubumbi	to make someone teach
aranabumbi	to make someone go to write
arabunambi	to go to cause someone to write

Manchu verbs have many forms to express aspect, tense, and mood and can distinguish many shades of meaning. The forms will be pointed out in the reading selections.

Foreign language influence: The traditional Manchu language contains many words of Turkic and Mongolian origin. Turkic loan words probably came through Mongolian, because most of these words also occur in Mongolian and because Mongolian was the primary cultural contact for the early Manchu speakers. Nicholas Poppe estimates that 20 to 30 percent of the entire Manchu vocabulary are words of Mongolian origin.[36]

Standard Manchu adopts many Chinese words without change; for example, gung 'duke' or wang 'prince' from Chinese gong 公 and wang 王. It may do so even when a Manchu word exists; for example, using funghūwang 'phoenix' from Chinese fenghuang 鳳凰 instead of garudai. In other cases a slight change may occur, as in ginggulembi 'to honor' from Chinese jing 敬. Some words are ancient loan words; for example, fi 'brush' from Chinese bi 筆, fafun from fa 法, dulefun from du 度 Words starting in r or ending in m, l, or t are foreign; e.g., Tsewang Raptan, a personal name.

The Manchu script

Manchu is written from top to bottom, with lines following from left to right. Strokes for individual letters generally start at the top and move down, move from the right to the left and from the spine toward the left. Strokes, dots and circles on the right side of the spine are written after the word is completed.

For punctuation, Manchu uses two kinds of markers, two dots to indicate a strong break (similar to a period) and one dot to indicate a weaker pause (similar to a comma). A series of parallel nouns—often names of people or places—are quite reliably separated by a dot, but otherwise punctuation is inconsistent, leaving the reader well advised to not rely too heavily on it for understanding the text.

---

36 Nicholas Poppe, *Introduction to Altaic Linguistics* (Wiesbaden: Harrassowitz, 1965): 160–61.

Writing peculiarities: Writing conventions differ depending on the type of document and the time of the writing. Not only are there differences between Old Manchu (OM), Standard Manchu (SM), and Sibe or modern Manchu (MM), even documents within the same category may exhibit differences. Some documents contain numerous writing errors, suggesting that the particular writer was no longer thoroughly familiar with the language. In general, however, the differences are not dramatic and pose no great difficulties, though they add to the challenge presented by what already is a "less than perfect" alphabet.

- When the letter *i* follows a vowel, it is doubled, written with two long strokes in Old and Standard Manchu. In Sibe it is written like the initial *i*. When *o* is followed by a double-stroke *i*, it is *oi*, not *ūi*. The combination *ūi* exists only in final position.

- The letters *f* and *w* are distinguished only when followed by the vowels *a* or *e*. For these cases *f* is written with a long stroke. Because there are no words with the combination *wi*, *wo*, and *wu*, the short-stroke *f* (i.e., *w*) is used for *fi*, *fo*, and *fu*. Some Sibe texts follow the above SM rules, others distinguish the letters *f* and *w* regardless of which vowel follows.

- The letter *n* has a dot only when occurring before a vowel. There is no dot before consonants. A final *n* looks like a final *a*, but it cannot be confused with that letter because a final *n* is always preceded by a vowel. In Chinese loanwords the final *n* may be marked with an underdot if there exists an identical Manchu word; e.g., *han*, Manchu word for 'emperor'; or *haṇ* 漢 as a Chinese loanword.

- When *i* is followed by another vowel, a *y* is inserted, e.g., *biya*. When *u* is followed by another vowel, *w* is inserted, e.g., *suwe*.

- There are two forms (front and back, or hard and soft) for the letters *d* and *t*. The front letters are used before vowels *e* and *u*, and the back letters before back vowels and before neutral vowel *i*. A dot distinguishes the letters *t* and *d*. Because the kind of consonant—front or back—determines whether the following vowel is *e* versus *a*, or *o* versus *u*, no dot is necessary for the vowels in this case.

- Front *k* and *g* precede front and neutral vowels (*e*, *i*, *u*), while back *k* (*q*) and *g* (*γ*) precede back vowels. Therefore, a dot is not needed to mark the following vowels *e* or *u*. If a dot is present, its function is to distinguish front *g* from front *k*, or back *g* (*γ*) from back *k* (*q*).

- Note that in the syllables *ke, ge*, and *he* the front consonants *k*, *g*, and *h* do not include the first tip or "tooth." In the syllables *ka*, *ga*, and *ha*, however, the first tooth is part of the back consonant.

- When *k* occurs at the end of a syllable (either at the end of the word or before another consonant), the following rules apply: Back *k* (*q*) with two dots is used when the letter is preceded by *a*, *o*, *ū*, *u* (but not *ku*, *gu*, *hu*, or *hū*), or *te* (but not *e*). Front *k* is used when the letter is preceded by *ku*, *gu*, *hu*, *hū*, or *e* (but not *te*). Though these rules may be difficult to remember, they only pose a challenge when writing Manchu. Recognizing the letter is rarely a problem.

- In Standard Manchu back *k* (*q*) has two teeth with two dots on the left side. In modern Sibe it also has two dots, but only one tooth.

- Printed and handwritten letters differ somewhat. Though all of the selections used in this book employ square bracket versions for final *e*, *a* and *n*, prominent in many handwritten texts are the long rounded tails.

Printed final *a* ᠠ; handwritten final *a* 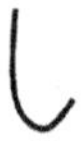

Printed final *n* ᠨ ; handwritten final *n* 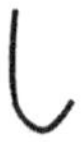

Printed final *e* ᡝ ; handwritten final *e* 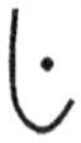

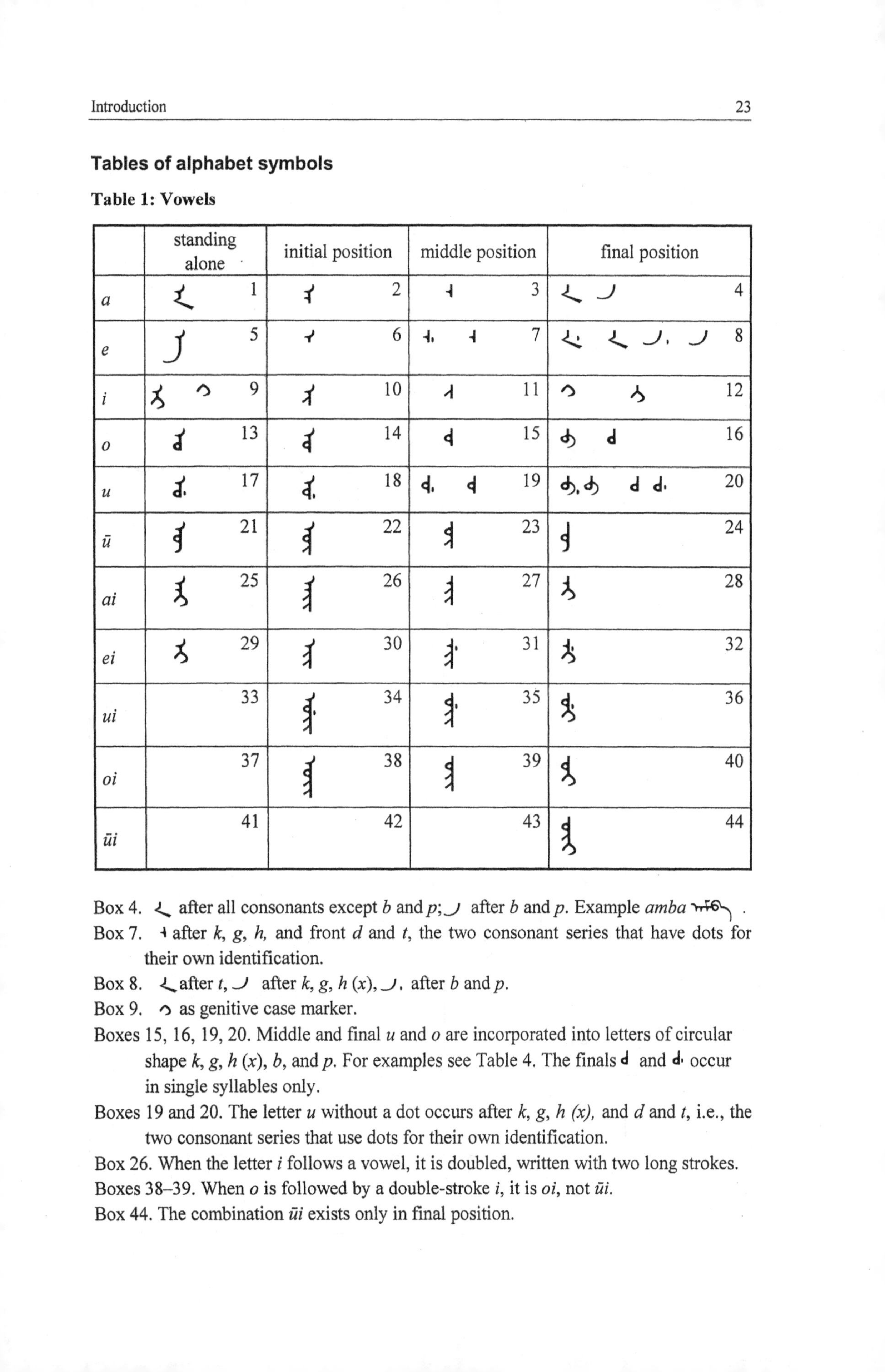

Tables of alphabet symbols

Table 1: Vowels

	standing alone	initial position	middle position	final position
a	1	2	3	4
e	5	6	7	8
i	9	10	11	12
o	13	14	15	16
u	17	18	19	20
ū	21	22	23	24
ai	25	26	27	28
ei	29	30	31	32
ui	33	34	35	36
oi	37	38	39	40
ūi	41	42	43	44

Box 4. after all consonants except *b* and *p*; after *b* and *p*. Example *amba* .

Box 7. after *k, g, h,* and front *d* and *t*, the two consonant series that have dots for their own identification.

Box 8. after *t*, after *k, g, h* (*x*), after *b* and *p*.

Box 9. as genitive case marker.

Boxes 15, 16, 19, 20. Middle and final *u* and *o* are incorporated into letters of circular shape *k, g, h* (*x*), *b*, and *p*. For examples see Table 4. The finals and occur in single syllables only.

Boxes 19 and 20. The letter *u* without a dot occurs after *k, g, h (x),* and *d* and *t*, i.e., the two consonant series that use dots for their own identification.

Box 26. When the letter *i* follows a vowel, it is doubled, written with two long strokes.

Boxes 38–39. When *o* is followed by a double-stroke *i*, it is *oi*, not *ūi*.

Box 44. The combination *ūi* exists only in final position.

Table 2: Consonants

	initial	middle	final	
n		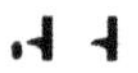	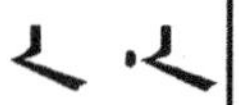	Before a vowel mid-position *n* has a dot. Before a consonant mid-position *n* has no dot. Final *n* has a dot only in certain words of Chinese origin.
k (*q*)		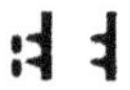	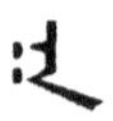	Before *a*, *o*, *ū*. Before a consonant mid-position *k* has two dots. Before a vowel mid-position *k* has no dots. Final k is preceded by *a*, *o*, *te*, *ū*, or *u* (but not *ku*, *gu*, *hu*, *hū*).
g (*γ*)				Before *a*, *o*, *ū*.
h (*χ*)				Before *a*, *o*, *ū*.
k		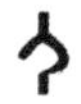	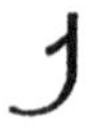	Before *e*, *i*, *u*. Occurs after *ku*, *gu*, *hu*, *hū*, or *e* when followed by a consonant. Final *k* is preceded by *i* or *e* but not *te*.
g		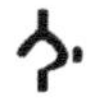		Before *e*, *i*, *u*.
h (*x*)		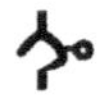		Before *e*, *i*, *u*.
b				
p		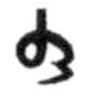		
s				
š				

Consonants (continued)

	initial	middle	final	
t (back)		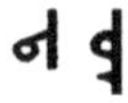	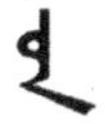	Before *a, o, ū, i*. Before another consonant *t* is written as .
d (back)				Before *a, o, ū, i*.
t (front)	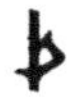	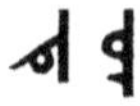	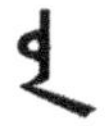	Before *e, u*. Before another consonant *t* is written as .
d (front)	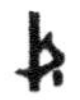	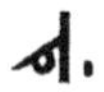		Before *e, u*.
l				
m				
c				
j				
y				
r				Initial *r* occurs only in foreign words/names.
f	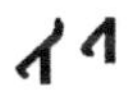	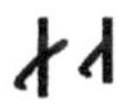		Before *a* and *e* the letter *f* is written with a long stroke. Before *o, u, i, ū* a short stroke is used (*w* does not occur before these vowels).
w				Occurs only before *a* or *e*.
ng		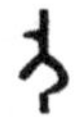	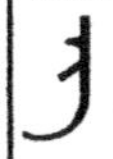	

Table 3: Symbols for transcribing Chinese words

initial	middle	final	alone	Norman	Hauer	Chinese	
ᠺ	ᠺ			*k'*	*k'*	開	Before *a*, *o*.
ᡬ	ᡬ			*g'*	*g'*	蓋	Before *a*, *o*.
ᡭ	ᡭ			*h'*	*h'*		Before *a*, *o*.
ᡮ	ᡮ			*ts*	*z'*	蔡	Before *a*, *e*, *o*, *u*.
ᡮᡟ	ᡮᡟ	ᡮᡟ	ᡮᡟ	*ts*	*z'e*	詞	Before *i*.
ᡯ	ᡯ			*dz*	*z*	祖	Before *a*, *e*, *o*, *u*.
ᡯᡟ	ᡯᡟ	ᡯᡟ	ᡯᡟ	*dz*	*ze*	子	Before *i*.
ᡷ	ᡷ			*ž*	*j*	熱	Before *a*, *e*, *o*, *u*.
ᡷᡳ	ᡷᡳ	ᡷᡳ	ᡷᡳ	*ži*	*ji*	日	Before *i*.
ᠵᡟ	ᠵᡟ	ᠵᡟ	ᠵᡟ	*jy*	*j'i*	知	Before *i*.
ᠴᡟ	ᠴᡟ	ᠴᡟ	ᠴᡟ	*cy*	*c'i*	吃	Before *i*.
ᠰᡟ	ᠰᡟ	ᠰᡟ	ᠰᡟ	*sy*	*se*	四	Before *i*.
ᡧᡳ	ᡧᡳ	ᡧᡳ	ᡧᡳ	*ši*	*ši*	石	Before *i*.

Though the letters *s* and *š* are part of the regular Manchu alphabet, in combination with *i* they transcribe Chinese characters with the pronunciation of *si* and *shi*.

Introduction

Table 4: Writing conventions and peculiarities

Because the letters *b, p, k, g,* and *h (x)* do not include the tooth at the bottom, some vowels are incorporated into the circular shape of the letter. This is not so for the letters *k (q), g (γ),* and *h (χ)* which do include the bottom tip. The letter *p* follows the same rules as *b*.

	initial	middle	final			initial	middle	final
ba		Not	Not		ka (qa)			
be		Not	Not		ga (γa)			
bi		Not	Not		ha (χa)			
bo		Not	Not		ko (qo)			
bu		Not	Not		go (γo)			
ke		Not	Not		ho (χo)			
ku		Not	Not		kū (qū)			
ki		Not	Not		gū (γū)			
ge		Not	Not		hū (χū)			
gu		Not	Not					
gi		Not	Not					
he		Not	Not					
hu		Not	Not					
hi		Not	Not					

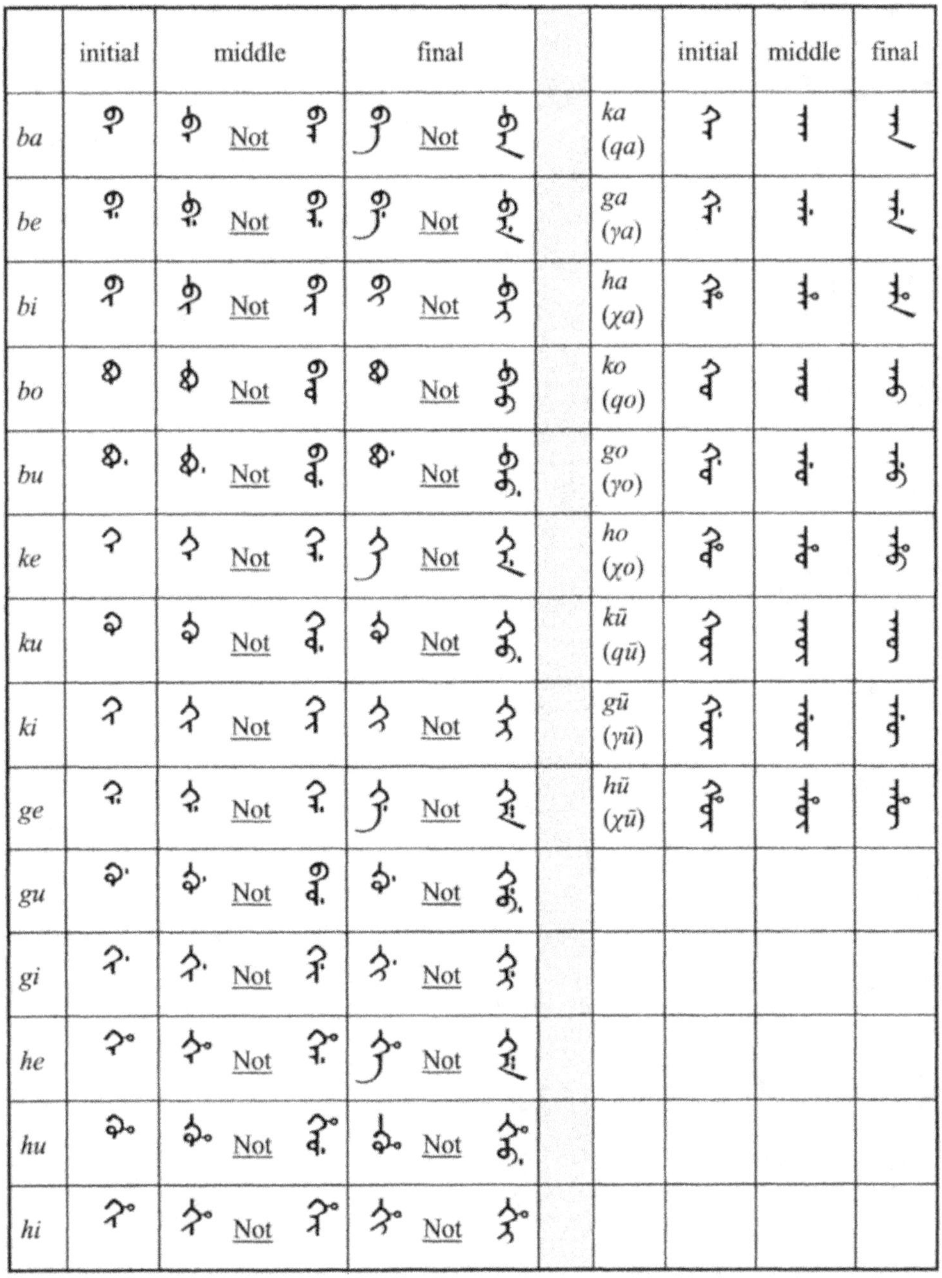

Reading exercise – Sample words

ᠮᠠᠨᠵᡠ	*manju*	Manchu
ᠮᠣᠩᡤᠣ	*monggo*	Mongolian
ᠨᡳᡴᠠᠨ	*nikan*	Chinese
ᡤᡠᡵᡠᠨ	*gurun*	country
ᡤᡳᠰᡠᠨ	*gisun*	language
ᠪᡳᡨᡥᡝ	*bithe*	script
ᠮᠠᠩᡤᠠ	*mangga*	difficult
ᠨᡳᠶᠠᠯᠮᠠ	*niyalma*	person
ᡳᠨᡠ	*inu*	also
ᡤᡝᠮᡠ	*gemu*	all
ᡠᠯᡥᡳᠮᠪᡳ	*ulhimbi*	understand
ᠰᠠᡵᡴᡡ	*sarkū*	not know
ᡤᡳᠰᡠᡵᡝᠮᠪᡳ	*gisurembi*	speak
ᡩᠠᡥᠠᠮᡝ	*dahame*	because

For audio recording of Sample Words go to: http://hdl.handle.net/10125/6050

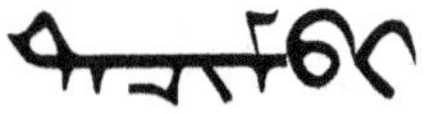	*tacimbi*	learn
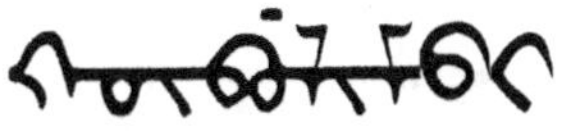	*kūbulimbi*	change
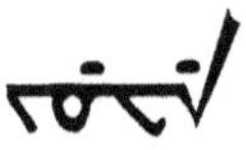	*juwe*	two
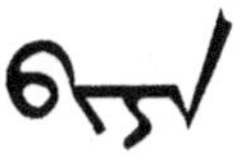	*biya*	month
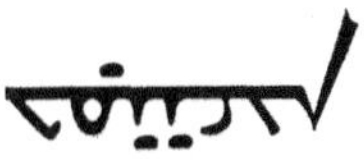	*fukjin*	origin
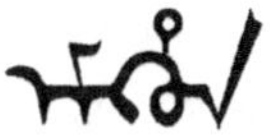	*emhun*	alone
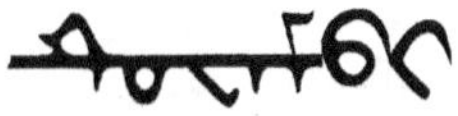	*tuwambi*	look
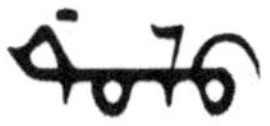	*dolo*	within
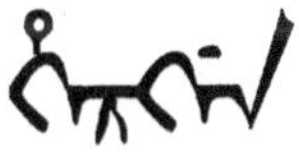	*hergen*	letter
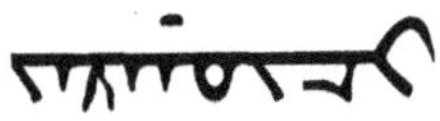	*jargūci*	judge
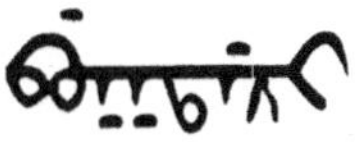	*bukdari*	memorial
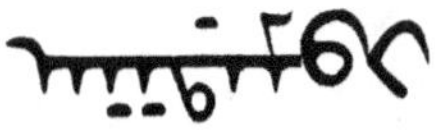	*akdambi*	trust
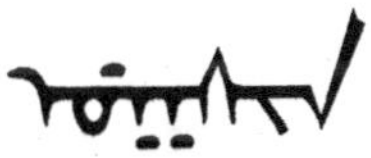	*uksin*	armor, soldier
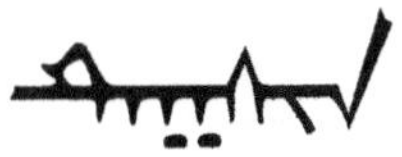	*teksin*	straight
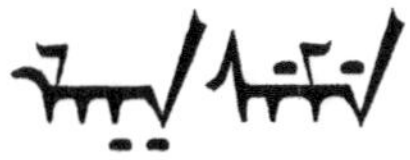	*lak seme*	just right

For audio recording of Sample Words go to: http://hdl.handle.net/10125/6050

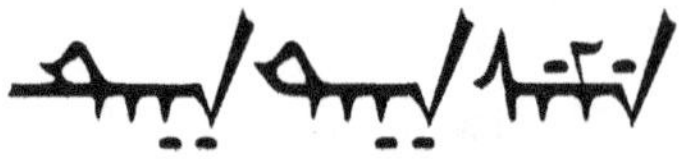	*tek tak seme*	sound of shouting
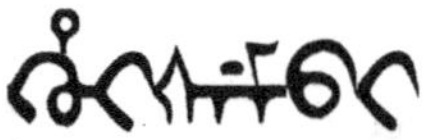	*hukšembi*	carry on the head
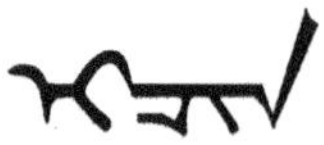	*ekcin*	river bank
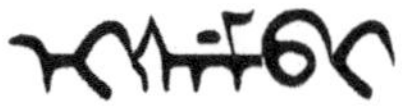	*ekšembi*	hurry
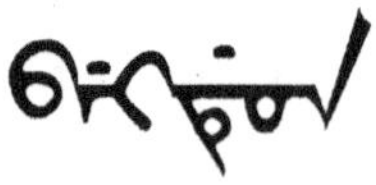	*bekdun*	debt
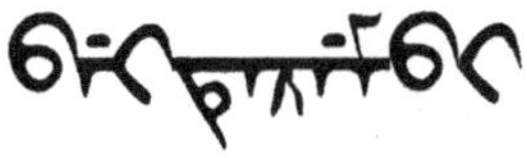	*bekterembi*	frozen in one's track
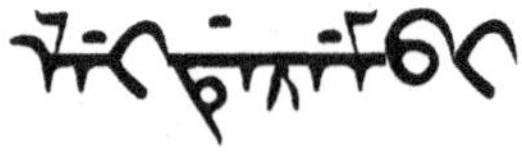	*lekderembi*	be unkempt
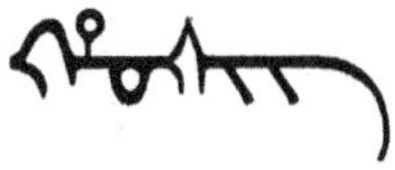	*Hošik*	(personal name)
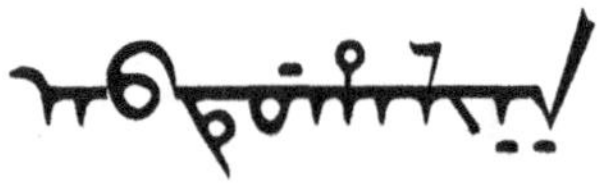	*Abduhalik*	(personal name)
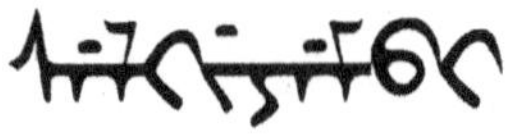	*selgiyembi*	disseminate
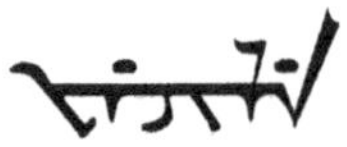	*fejile*	under
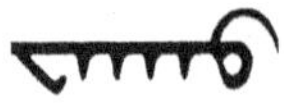	*wakao*	is it not?
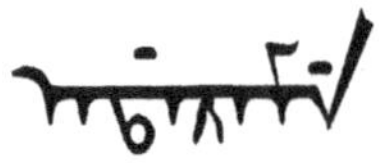	*adarame*	why

For audio recording of Sample Words go to: http://hdl.handle.net/10125/6050

Part II

Reading Selections

Reading Selections

How to use the texts

For students who want to gain a good grounding in the Manchu language, this book offers a selection of various types of documents from different time periods. If studied in its entirety, the material represents the approximate equivalent of a three-semester course (one year and a half). Before tackling the actual texts, it is a good idea to become familiar with the information about the Manchu language and script presented in the Introduction and also spend some time going over the Grammatical Points in Part III. Doing so provides an overall picture of the language before plunging ahead. While the notes to the individual reading selections cover the grammatical points encountered in the text, the grammatical section in Part III offers a handy tool for reference and review.

Because the Manchu alphabet is not particularly "user-friendly," it will present a challenge to the student for some time. A good strategy for mastering the script involves 1) repeatedly rereading the texts that have been studied, 2) writing the romanized text in Manchu script and then checking yourself against the Manchu text for accuracy, and 3) memorizing as much vocabulary as quickly as possible. It is beneficial to study the vocabulary prior to reading a selection. When you know a word, it is easier to recognize it in script. Therefore the larger your vocabulary is, the less troublesome the alphabet tends to be. In the beginning it may also be helpful to xerox a given selection in enlarged form to see the individual letters more clearly.

Most of the selections in this book relate to frontier areas. Whereas it does not mean that a reading knowledge of Manchu is only important for this topic, staying within one general subject area allows a student to more easily become familiar with the basic terminology and benefit from a growing familiarity of the subject matter. A brief sketch of the Qing Dzungar campaigns in Part III of this book provides a historical background to the biographies, as well as to Reading Selections C–2 through C–6.

Section A consists of narratives, a short excerpt from the *Veritable Records*, and five biographies. The biographies offer the beginning student a considerable amount of repetition in format, vocabulary, sentence structure, and general content and therefore help consolidate the knowledge gained as the student progresses. All of these pieces are written in Standard Manchu and in a relatively clear script. The Manchu texts in sections B, C, and D are written in various styles and with differing degrees of clarity. Some are easier to decipher than others. They reflect the challenge researchers encounter when using Manchu materials.

Each reading selection consists of several parts: the original Manchu text, a romanized transliteration, a vocabulary list (for Reading Selections A–1 to A–5), explanatory notes, and a review of grammatical points with some translation exercises. In order to encourage students to study each selection thoroughly, there are no keys to the translation exercises. Instead, the phrases and sentences in the exercises are taken directly from the lesson text, occasionally substituting a particular word, but always leaving the structure of the phrase or sentence intact. In this way, students who have studied the text well before doing the exercises will have no problem, and there is always the possibility of reviewing the lesson in order to find the answer.

In contents and form the Old Manchu narratives in section B are similar to those in section A. Anticipating that not all students will be interested in studying the differences between Old and Standard Manchu scripts, I have provided the text in both versions. In this way, students have the option of reading pre-1644 materials for content and practice without being intimidated by the script, which is considerably more difficult because of the lack of diacritics.

A student whose primary goal is to read memorials may choose to read the short pieces in section A first, and then start with the memorials in section B. Once familiar with the format of memorials, these pieces present no significantly higher degree of difficulty than the narratives. However, for the purpose of consolidating the knowledge gained, it is a good idea to slowly continue with the narratives in section A. In this way, there will be some variety, the delight of finishing several short pieces, but also the challenge and the accompanying sense of accomplishment when eventually finishing longer pieces, including A–6. Students who want more practice reading memorials can find additional Manchu memorials in the published volumes of Kangxi and Qianlong memorials.

Unfortunately, some scholars in the past have called Manchu "an easy language." Personally, I think that such statements tend to lead to unrealistic expectations. There is no need to be discouraged by the script, but, like other languages, learning Manchu does require an investment of time.

About the reading selections

The reading materials in section A were selected and used by Professor Joseph Fletcher for his first Manchu class, taught at Harvard in 1968 to two intrepid souls. I have chosen to retain these texts for several reasons: Written in Standard Manchu, these mid-Qing materials generally contain few writing errors, are relatively easy to read and interesting in content. Making these texts part of this book also allows me to pay tribute to my teacher and mentor. Notes, exercises, translations, and grammatical points, however, are my creations and any mistakes therein are my own.[1]

---

[1] A Fletcher translation of Reading Selection A–2 (Hošik) has been published as chapter VIII, "The Biography of Khwush Kipäk Beg (d. 1781) in the *Waifan Menggu huibu wang gong biao zhuan*," in

Reading Selections A–2 to A–6 are biographies from the *Qinding waifan Menggu huibu wang gong biao zhuan* 欽定外藩蒙古回部王公表傳 (Imperially commissioned genealogical tables and biographies of the Mongols and Muslims of the outer entourage). The Chinese translations of these narratives can be found in the *Qinding siku quanshu* 欽定四庫全書 (Imperially commissioned Four Treasuries).

Reading selections in section B are Qing archival documents which follow formats typical of Chinese official communications of the time. Selection B–1 is taken from a 1905 collection of memorials which may have served as samples for memorial writers who had become increasingly unfamiliar with the Manchu language. An official report on weather conditions in Mukden (B–2) shows the detailed reporting of local conditions by officials during the Qianlong reign. Selections B–3 through B–6 are communications written from the northwestern front during the Kangxi emperor's Dzungar campaigns in the late seventeenth century.

Section C consists of excerpts from the *Old Manchu Archives.* These documents, many written on scrap paper obtained by the Manchus from China and Korea, reflect the novelty of the Manchu script and bear witness to the transition from Old to Standard Manchu.

Section D introduces two pieces from twentieth-century Sibe. "Dead Horses Obstructing the Road" comes from a 1987 Sibe book of jokes and funny stories. The story "Mr. Mouse Moves" is one of the lessons contained in a 1954 Sibe fourth grade reader, part of a textbook series called *Niyamangga gisun* (Mother tongue). It reflects the language and content of Sibe elementary school teaching material in the People's Republic of China until recently. The second edition of *Niyamangga gisun*, printed in twelve booklets in 1983–84, is only slightly less dogmatic than its 1954 predecessor. However, if the first two booklets of a third edition are indicative, this latest set of Sibe readers maybe a bit less blunt in its political rhetoric.

The translations of official titles and governmental organizations follow Charles O. Hucker, *A Dictionary of Official Titles in Imperial China* (Stanford, Ca.: Stanford University Press, 1985). They are marked in the vocabulary with (H). I have made an exception to this rule and use Grand Council instead of Council of State, because this term is commonly used by scholars today. A few terms that are not listed in Hucker are taken from H. S. Brunnert and V. V. Hagelstrom, *Present Day Political Organization in China* (Foochow, China: 1911). They are noted with (BH). Also, when Chinese character equivalents are given for non-Chinese proper names, keep in mind that there may be more than one version. Many names were written inconsistently.

Joseph F. Fletcher, *Studies on Chinese and Islamic Inner Asia* (Brookfield, Vt.: Ashgate Publishing Co., 1995).

References for the reading selections:

A–1: *Manju i yargiyan kooli/Da Qing Manzhou shilu* 大清滿洲實錄 (Qing Manchu veritable records) (Taipei: Huawen shuju, 1969): 108–10. [Entry for Tianming 8, 5th month (1623)].

A–2 through A–6: *Hesei toktobuha tulergi Monggo hoise aiman i wang gung sai iletun ulabun. Qinding waifan Menggu huibu wang gong biaozhuan* 欽定外藩蒙古回部王公表傳 (Imperially commissioned genealogical tables and biographies of the princes of the Mongols and Muslims of the outer entourage) (Peking: Wuying Dian, 1795).

A–2 through A–5: Chapter 117, 101st biography.

A–6: Chapter 118, 102nd biography.

B–1: *Zouti* 奏題 (Topics for memorials) (n.p., 1905): 7. Manuscript in Manchu and Chinese, located in the Harvard Yenching Library (Ma 4664.8/3232).

B–2: *Gongzhong dang Qianlong chao zouzhe* 宮中檔乾隆朝奏摺 (Secret palace memorials of the Qianlong period). *Qing Documents at National Palace Museum* Vol. 75 (Shilin, Taipei: National Palace Museum, 1988): 800–802.

B–3 to B–6: *Gongzhong dang Kangxi chao zouzhe* 宮中檔康熙朝奏摺 (Secret palace memorials of the Kangxi period). *Qing Documents at National Palace Museum* (Shih-lin, Taipei: National Palace Museum, 1977).

B–3: Vol. 8: 447–8; 460–62.

B–4: Vol. 8: 777–81.

B–5: Vol. 8: 782–85.

B–6: Vol. 9: 35–39.

C–1 through C–4: *Jiu Manzhou dang* 舊滿洲檔 (Old Manchu archives). 10 vols. Taipei: Palace Museum, 1969. A Qianlong revision of these documents was transliterated and translated into Japanese as *Mambun Rōtō* 滿文老檔 (MR), trans. by Kanda Nobuo et al. Tokyo, Tōyō Bunko, 1955–63.

C–1: Vol. III: 1254–59. MR II: 555–56.

C–2: Pages 253-55 (262-64): Vol. II: 830–32; MR I: 422.
Page 256 (265): Vol. II: 1053–54; MR II: 559.
Pages 257-58 (266-67): Vol. II: 1080–81; MR II: 575–76.
Pages 259-61 (268-70): Vol. III: 1242–45; MR II: 609–10.

C–3: Vol. III: 1585–87; MR II: 771.

C–4: Vol. X: 5293-96; MR VII: 1438–40.

D–1: *Injekungge gisun* (Funny stories) (Urumchi: Sinkiang People's Press, 1987): 45–46.

D–2: *Niyamangga gisun* (Mother tongue), Vol. 8 (Urumchi: Sinkiang Education Press, 1954): 44.

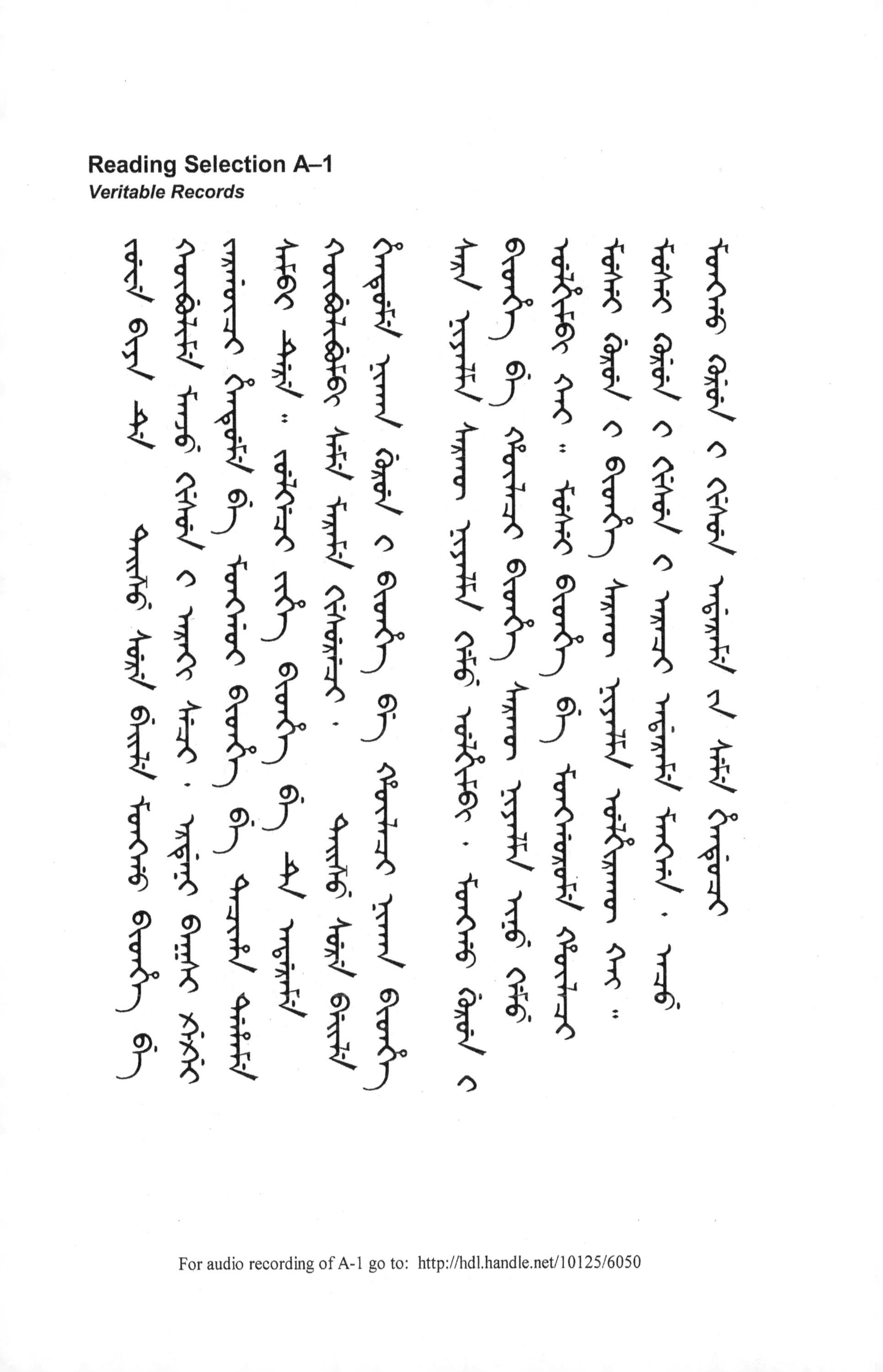

Reading Selection A–1

Veritable Records

[illegible]

For audio recording of A-1 go to: http://hdl.handle.net/10125/6050

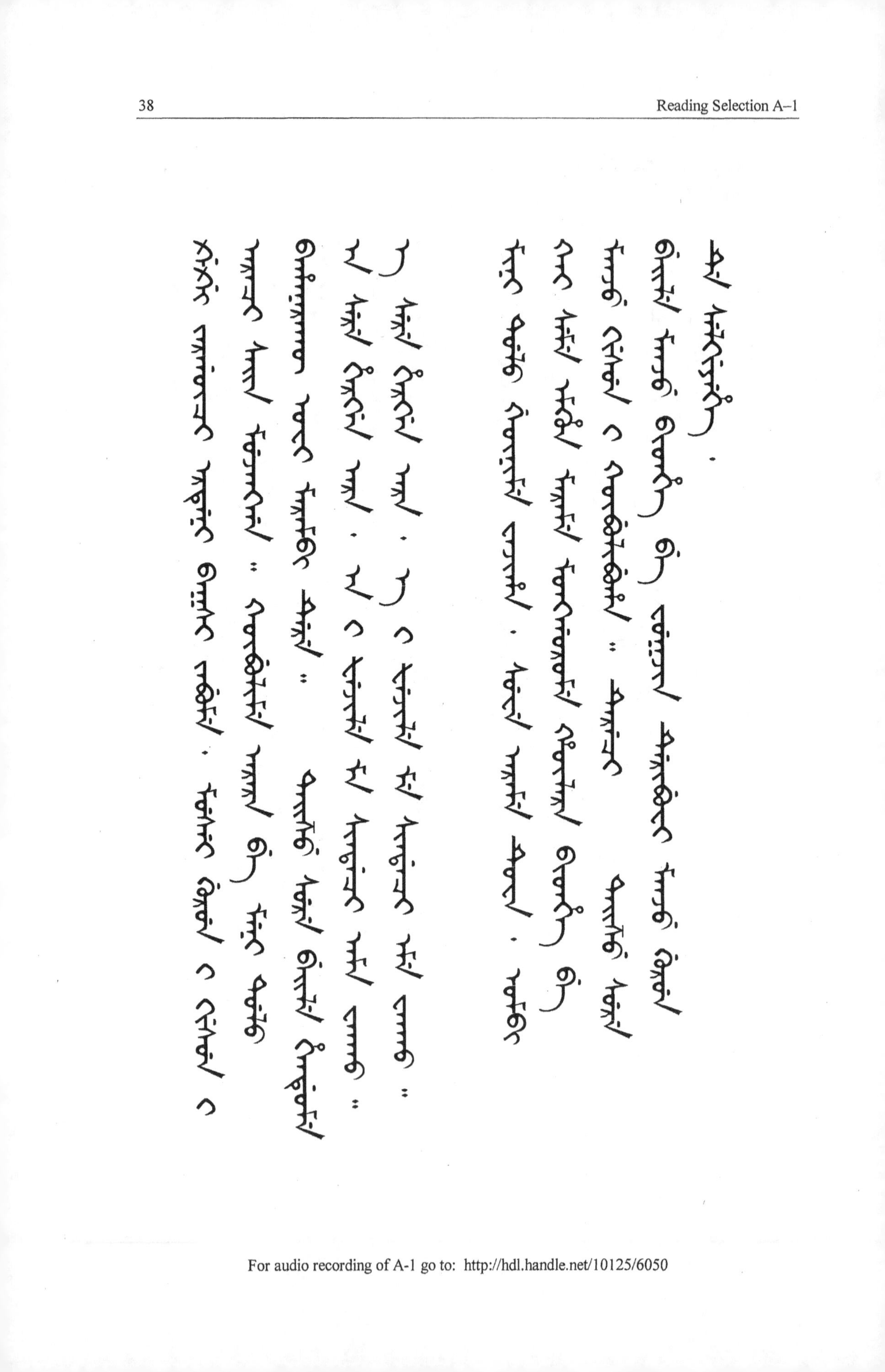

[illegible]

[illegible]

Transliteration

(37) *juwe biya de* [1] *Taidzu sure beile* [2] *«monggo bithe be kūbulime* [3] *manju gisun i araki» seci, Erdeni baksi G'ag'ai jargūci hendume «be monggoi bithe be taciha dahame sambi dere. julgeci jihe bithe be te adarame kūbulibumbi» seme marame gisureci, Taidzu sure beile hendume: «nikan gurun i bithe be hūlaci nikan bithe*

sara niyalma sarkū niyalma gemu [4] *ulhimbi. monggo gurun i bithe be hūlaci, bithe sarkū niyalma inu gemu ulhimbi kai. musei bithe be monggorome hūlaci, musei gurun i bithe sarkū niyalma ulhirakū kai. musei gurun i gisun i araci adarame mangga. encu* [5] *monggo gurun i gisun adarame ja» seme henduci,*

(38) *G'ag'ai jargūci Erdeni baksi jabume, «musei gurun i gisun i araci sain mujangga. kūbulime arara* [6] *be meni dolo bahanarakū ofi marambi dere.»*[7] *Taidzu sure beile hendume: «a sere hergen ara. a i fejile ma sindaci ama wakao.*[8] *e sere hergen ara. e i fejile me sindaci eme wakao.*

mini dolo gūnime wajiha.[9] *suwe arame tuwa.*[10] *ombi kai» seme emhun marame; monggorome hūlara bithe be manju gisun i kūbulibuha. tereci Taidzu sure beile manju bithe be fukjin deribufi manju gurun de selgiyehe.*

Vocabulary

(verb stem)	imperative
adarame	how, why
akū	there is not, there are not
ama	father
ara	write (imperative)
arambi	to write
bahanambi	to be able
baksi (Chin. *boshi* 博士)	scholar, learned man
be	accusative particle
be	we (exclusive)
beile	prince, *beile* (title)
bi	I
bimbi	to be
bithe	language, book, letter, script
biya	month
-bu-	causative
bumbi	to give
-ci	conditional and temporal converb (if, when)

For audio recording of A-1 go to: http://hdl.handle.net/10125/6050

ci	ablative/elative case marker
dahame	because
de	dative, locative particle
dere	probably, likely (sentence particle of doubt)
derimbi	to enter
dolo	inside, the inside
eme	mother
emhun	alone
encu	different, other, alone
Erdeni	(pers. name)
fejile (w/genitive)	under
-fi	subordinative converb (after, because)
fukjin	beginning, origin
fukjin deribumbi	to originate
G'ag'ai	Gagai (pers. name)
gemu	all
gisun	language, speech
gisurembi	to speak, say
gūnimbi	to think
gurun	country
-ha, -he, -ho	perfective participle; perfective finite verb
-hakū, -hekū, -hokū	negative perfective participle and finite verb
hendumbi	to say, to speak, to answer
hergen	alphabet letter
hūlambi	to read aloud, to shout
i	genitive particle
inu	also, too, correct
ja	easy
jabumbi	to answer
jargūci	judge
jimbi	to come
julge	antiquity, ancient times
juwe	two
kai	sentence particle denoting emphasis
-ki	future and desiderative verb ending
kūbulimbi	to change (something); to become altered
mangga	difficult
manju	Manchu
marambi	to refuse, to be obstinate
-mbi	imperfective finite verb (present and future)
-me	coordinative converb

meni	our
mini	of me, my
monggo	Mongol
monggorombi	to act or speak Mongolian
mujangga	indeed (sentence particle denoting certainty); true, correct; truly
muse	we (inclusive)
nikan	Chinese
niyalma	person, human being
-o	interrogative suffix
ofi	because (lit. 'having become')
ombi	to become; to be, to be permissible
-rakū	negative imperfective participle and converb
-re, -ra, -ro	imperfective participle and converb
sain	good
sambi	to know
sarkū (= sara+akū)	do/does not know
selgiyembi	to disseminate
sembi	to say
sindambi	to put
sure	wise
suwe	you (plural)
tacimbi	to learn
Taidzu (Chin. *taizu* 太祖)	appellation for Nurhaci
te	now
tere	that; he, she, it
tuwambi	to look, to examine; (preceded by *–me* converb) to try to (do something)
ulhimbi	to understand
wajimbi	to finish
waka	sentence particle that negates nominal predicates

The Manchu sentence: Some basic components and rules

Subjects

In Manchu sentences the subject, especially personal pronouns, may be left out. Though generally the meaning can be understood from the context, there are cases when the absence of a stated subject creates ambiguities.

niyalma ulhimbi	the people understand
taciha	[he, one] learned

Case markers

Like German and other languages Manchu has case markers. These may be written as separate words (as particle) or be attached to the noun (as suffix).

Suffix/particle	Case	Function
(none)	nominative	subject indefinite object compound words
i (*ni* after *-ng*)	genitive instrumental	possessive means, cause
de	dative locative direction	indirect object location in space or time direction towards
be	accusative	direct object
ci	ablative	point of departure comparison

Personal pronouns with case markers

Nominative	**Genitive**	**Dative**	**Accusative**	**Ablative**	**English**
bi	*mini*	*minde*	*mimbe*	*minci*	I
si	*sini*	*sinde*	*simbe*	*sinci*	you
i	*ini*	*inde*	*imbe*	*inci*	he/she/it
muse	*musei*	*musede*	*musebe*	*museci*	we (incl.)
be	*meni*	*mende*	*membe*	*menci*	we (excl.)
suwe	*suweni*	*suwende*	*suwembe*	*suwenci*	you
ce	*ceni*	*cende*	*cembe*	*cenci*	they

The inclusive *muse* means that the speaker includes the person(s) spoken to. The exclusive pronoun is *be*. Case markers after personal pronouns are usually written in attached form.

It is not unusual for a case marker to be left out, especially (but not only) for expressions that may be understood as a compound, such as *manju gisun* 'Manchu language' instead of *manju i gisun*, or *monggo gurun* 'Mongol country' instead of *monggoi gurun*. However, there is no firm rule on this, as we see from the fact that both *monggo bithe* and *monggoi bithe* occur in this text.

Examples:

manju gisun	the Manchu language
monggo gurun	the Mongolian country
sini gisun	your language
musei bithe	our script
gurun i gisun	the language of the country
manju gisun i arambi	to write in (by means of) Manchu
bithe be kūbulimbi	to change the script
bithe be suwende bumbi	[one] gives the book to you
monggoi bithe be tacimbi	[we] learn the Mongolian writing
manju bithe be fukjin deribumbi	[he] creates the Manchu script
nikan gurun de genembi	to go to China
bithe be gurun de selgiyembi	to disseminate the script in the country
juwe biya de	in the second month
monggo gurun ci	from the Mongolian country
manju gisun ci nikan gisun mangga	Chinese is more difficult than Manchu

Postpositions

Instead of prepositions, so common in European languages, Manchu uses postpositions. Those that express location usually follow the genitive. Postposition *dahame* 'because' often, but not always, occurs with the accusative '*be*.'

mini dolo	inside (of) me
meni dolo	inside ourselves
a i fejile ma sindambi	to put a *ma* under the *a*
monggoi bithe be taciha dahame	because [we] learned the Mongolian script
manju gurun de jihe be dahame	because [he] came from the Manchu country

Common verb endings

1. *-mbi* imperfective finite verb (basic dictionary form)
This form expresses present or future and is used for general statements. The negative form is *–rakū*.

arambi	to write (dictionary form)
niyalma gemu ulhimbi	the people all understand
niyalma ulhirakū	the people don't understand
Erdeni jaburakū	Erdeni does not answer

2. *-ha, -he, -ho* perfective finite verb and perfective participle

The particular form is variable and depends on the vowel in the final syllable of the verb root. The root is the verb minus *–mbi* (and minus any suffix that may precede *-mbi*, such as the causative *–bu-* that is introduced in this selection).

-ha: verbs with back vocalic roots (*a*, *o*, *ū*) and *i*;
-he: verbs with front vocalic roots (*e*, *u*);
-ho: verbs with *o* in all syllables.

The negative equivalent is also variable: *-hakū*, *-hekū*, and (rarely) *-hokū*. These forms are contractions of *-ha* + *akū*, *-he* + *akū*, and *-ho* + *akū* .

Not all verbs adhere to the above rules for their perfective form. For example, many *o*-verbs have perfective participles ending in *-ha*. Some verbs have perfective forms of *-ke* and *-ka*. Most dictionaries include these irregularities in their listings.

Examples of the perfective finite verb (the verb ends the sentence)

G'ag'ai jabuha	Gagai replied
Erdeni gisurehe	Erdeni spoke
G'ag'ai jabuhakū	Gagai did not reply
Erdeni gisurehekū	Erdenie did not speak

Examples of the perfective participle (the verb modifies a noun). As a modifier the participle may be translated as a relative clause.

araha bithe	the script that [he] wrote
gisurehe gisun	the words [one] spoke
tacibuha gisun	the language [one] has taught
julgeci jihe gisun	the language that has come to us as of old
tere gurun ci jihe niyalma	the people who came from that country
tacihakū gisun	the language [one] has not learned
gurun de selgiyehekū bithe	the script that was not disseminated in the country

2. *-ra, -re, -ro* imperfective participle

The particular form depends on the vowel in the final syllable of the verb stem (the verb minus *–mbi*).

-ra: verbs with *a* in final syllable of stem;
-re: verbs with *e, i, u, ū* in final syllable of stem;
-ro: verbs with stems containing only the vowel *o*.

The negative equivalent *-rakū* is invariable, though irregularities exist, as in *sarkū*, the negative form of *sambi* 'to know.'

sara niyalma	the people who know
tacibure gisun	the language [he] teaches
a sere hergen	the letter that is called *a*
monggorome hūlara bithe	the script that [we] read in the Mongolian manner
sarkū niyalma	the people who do not know
taciburakū bithe	the script [one] does not teach
ulhirakū gisun	the language [one] does not understand

4. Imperative

The imperative is formed by the verb stem (dropping the *–mbi*).

jabu, hendu	answer
selgiye	disseminate
sinda	put down
hūla	read out loud
gisure	speak
bithe be tacibu	teach the script

5. *-ki* desiderative and polite imperative

This form, consisting of the verb stem plus *-ki* , expresses a) a desire or intent to do something ('let me' or 'let us'), and b) a polite imperative ('please do'). When followed by *sembi*, as in this text, it means 'to want to';

araki	let [me] write; please write
tuwaki	let [us] look; please look
manju gisun be taciki	let [me] learn Manchu
bithe be gurun de selgiyeki	let [us] distribute the script in the country
monggo bithe i araki sembi	[he] wants to write in the Mongolian script

Overview of verb functions

verb ending [negative form]	verbal noun	modifier	finite verb
-mbi [-rakū (bi)]	no	no	yes
-ra, -re, -ro [-rakū]	yes	yes	rare
-ha, -he, -ho [-hakū, -hekū]	yes	yes	yes
-me [-rakū]	no	modifies verbs (adverbial usage)	no

Regular and irregular verb forms

Examples of regular verbs:

present/future	perfective participle	imperfective participle	English
sambi	*saha*	*sara*	know
sembi	*sehe*	*sere*	say
marambi	*maraha*	*marara*	refuse
gisurembi	*gisurehe*	*gisurere*	speak
hendumbi	*henduhe*	*hendure*	answer
hūlambi	*hūlaha*	*hūlara*	read aloud
arambi	*araha*	*arara*	write
bahanambi	*bahanaha*	*bahanara*	be able
selgiyembi	*selgiyehe*	*selgiyere*	disseminate
ulhimbi	*ulhihe*	*ulhire*	understand
sindambi	*sindaha*	*sindara*	put
tacimbi	*taciha*	*tacire*	learn

Examples of irregular verbs:

jimbi	*jihe*	*jidere*	come
kūbulimbi	*kūbulika*	*kūbulire*	change

Modifiers precede that which is modified

The general rule in Manchu is that that which modifies precedes that which is modified. Thus the object comes before the verb that governs it and adjectives, demonstrative pronouns, nouns and participles precede the noun they modify.

sain bithe	a good book
tere gisun	this language
gisun sara niyalma	people who know the language
nikan bithe sarkū niyalma	the people who don't know the Chinese script
gurun i ejen	the leader of the country
monggo gurun	the Mongol country
a sere hergen	the letter that is called *a*
gurun i gisun	the language of the country

Converbs

A converb modifies a finite verb or another converb which means that the subordinate clause in which it occurs must precede that which it modifies. In English we can say "After I finished my homework, I went to a movie," or we can say "I went to a movie after I finished my homework." In Manchu the second position is not possible.

1. Coordinative converb *–me*

The most common converb is the coordinative converb which consists of the verb stem (the dictionary form minus the *–mbi*) and *–me*. This converb usually refers to a simultaneous action or state and can be translated as 'by doing,' or adverbially; e.g., to speak "laughingly". Sometimes we can just translate it with 'and.'

Examples

hendume sehe	[he] answered and said
bithe be kūbulime araki	let us write by changing the script
monggorome hūlaha	[he] read in Mongolian
gūnime wajiha	[I] have finished thinking
kūbulime ara	write by changing
arame tuwa	try to write
marame bithe be kūbulibuha	objecting, he had them change the script

In some cases, especially with verbs of motion, the coordinative converb may also express the purpose of the subsequent verb (translated as 'in order to').

Example: *manju gisun be tacime jihe* 'he came in order to learn Manchu.'

2. Subordinative converb *-fi*

Another very common converb is the subordinative converb *-fi* which refers to an action that occurs prior to that of the finite verb.

Examples

monggo bithe be kūbulifi, manju bithe be gurun de selgiyehe	after [he] changed the Mongolian script, he disseminated it in the country
Taidzu marafi bithe be kūbuliha	after Taizu objected, he changed the script
bithe be fukjin deribufi gurun de selgiyehe	after [he] created the script, [he] disseminated it in the country

3. Conditional/temporary converb –*ci*

The conditional/temporal converb is formed by the verb stem plus *–ci.* It specifies the time when an action occurs or defines the condition under which an action occurs. Example

seci	if/when [he] said
nikan gurun i bithe be hūlaci	if/when [one] reads the Chinese script
a i fejile ma sindaci	if/when [you] put a *ma* under the *a*
musei gurun i gisun i araci	if/when [we] write in the language of our country

Manchu sentences typically contain a string of converbs, which can produce very long sentences, particularly if they also include direct speech which is often the case. Usually such structures need to be divided into several sentences for an appropriate English translation.

Direct speech

Quotes are usually introduced by coordinative converbs derived from a verb of speaking and they end with a finite form of another verb of speaking. There are numerous variations. For example:

Erdeni hendume (quote) *sehe*	Erdeni answered by saying (quote)
Erdeni hendume (quote) *seme henduhe*	Erdeni said (quote)
Erdeni hendume (quote) seme marame gisureci	when Erdeni spoke by objecting saying (quote)

Except for the last two lines, the entire text in this selection is one sentence: *Taidzu … araki seci, Erdeni G'ag'ai hendume* (quote) *seme marame gisureci, Taidzu hendume* (quote) *seme henduci, Erdeni G'ag'ai jabume* (quote) (*seci* is omitted here!), *Taidzu hendume seme marame…kūbulibuha.*

Notes

1. ***juwe biya de*****:** 'in the second month.' Cardinal numerals are used with months, ordinal numerals with years. Example: *juweci aniya* 'the second year' or 'in the second year.' Note that the latter expression does not use *de*.

2. ***Taidzu sure beile*****:** Common appellation for Nurhaci, first emperor of a dynasty (cf. Chinese *taizu* 太祖). The word Taidzu is a posthumous title and therefore does not occur in the Manchu documents created before 1644. It probably came into use during the Shunzhi period (1644–61). Following Chinese tradition, Manchu words referring to the emperor are preceded by a space or elevated in a new line to express respect.

3. ***-bu-*****:** Causative verbal suffix, which is inserted between the verb stem and the verb ending, conveys the meaning that someone makes someone else do something.

kūbulimbi	to change	*kūbulibumbi*	to cause to change
sambi	to know	*sabumbi*	to cause to know
tacimbi	to learn	*tacibumbi*	to cause to learn (= to teach)
tacibumbi	to teach	*tacibubumbi*	to cause to teach

4. ***gemu*****:** 'all.' Follows the noun, like Chin. *dou* 都.

5. ***encu*****:** 'different.' Here it might also be translated as 'on the other hand.' In Manchu there is no clear delineation between the functions of adjectives, adverbs, and nouns.

6. ***arara*****:** 'the act of writing.' The imperfective participle functions here as a verbal noun.

7. ***marambi dere*****:** The dictionary meaning of *marambi* is "to refuse, to be obstinate." In this context it appears to refer to the situation as being "obstinate", i.e. difficult. Hence the Chinese text in the Veritable Records translates *marambi dere* as *nan er* 難耳 'difficult.' The final quotation marker, e.g., *sehe* or *seci*, is omitted.

8. ***waka-o*****:** 'is it not?' *Waka* + question particle *o*. *Waka* 'is not' means 'A does not equal B.'

9. ***mini dolo gūnime wajiha*:** 'I have finished thinking within myself.' Meaning: 'I have already figured it out' or 'my mind is made up.'

10. ***suwe arame tuwa*:** 'write and see, try to write it.' Comp. Chin: *ni xie kan.kan* 你寫看看.

Review

1. Expressions of time

juwe biya de	in the second month
juwe biya	two months
juweci aniya	in the second year
juwe aniya	two years

2. Verbal nouns

arara be bahanarakū	I can't do the writing
tacire be bahanarakū	I can't do the learning
tacibure be bahanambi	I can do the teaching

3. *adarame* 'why?'

adarame mangga?	why is it difficult
adarame sarkū?	why don't you know
adarame sain?	why is it good
adarame sure?	why is (he) wise

4. *waka* 'is not'

manju gisun monggo gisun waka	Manchu is not Mongolian
manju niyalma nikan niyalma waka	a Manchu person is not a Chinese person

5. Write in Manchu script and translate into English: a) *bithe be kūbulime araki*; b) *bithe be taciha dahame sambi dere*; c) *julgeci jihe bithe*; d) *marame gisureci*; e) *bithe sarkū niyalma ulhimbi*; f) *musei gurun i gisun i araci sain mujangga*; g) *arara be meni dolo bahanarakū*; h) *mini dolo gūnime wajiha*; i) *bithe be fukjin deribuhe*.

6. Translate into Manchu: a) Why is it difficult? b) put a *ma* under the *a*; c) he disseminated the Manchu script throughout (in) the country; d) he alone objected; e) is it not *ama*? f) the language one has learned; g) the prince who has come from the Manchu country; h) the letters one does not know.

Reading Selection A–2

Hošik

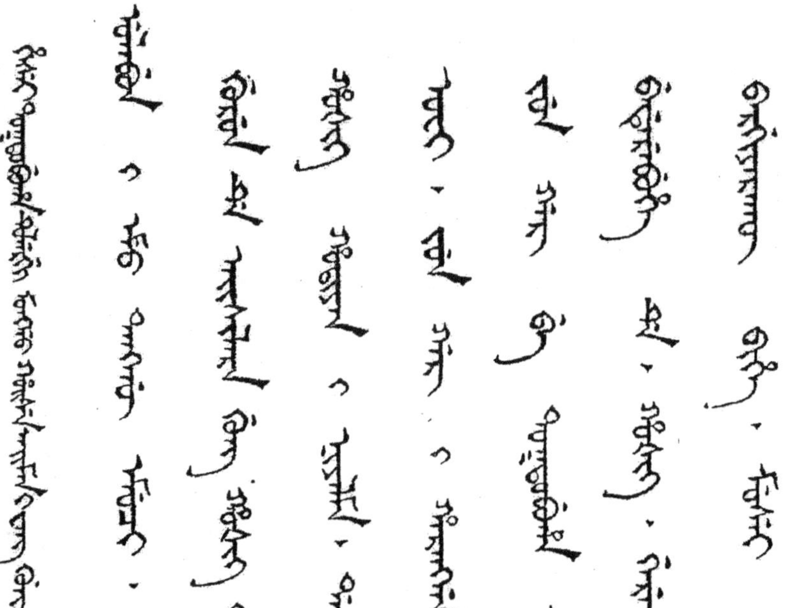

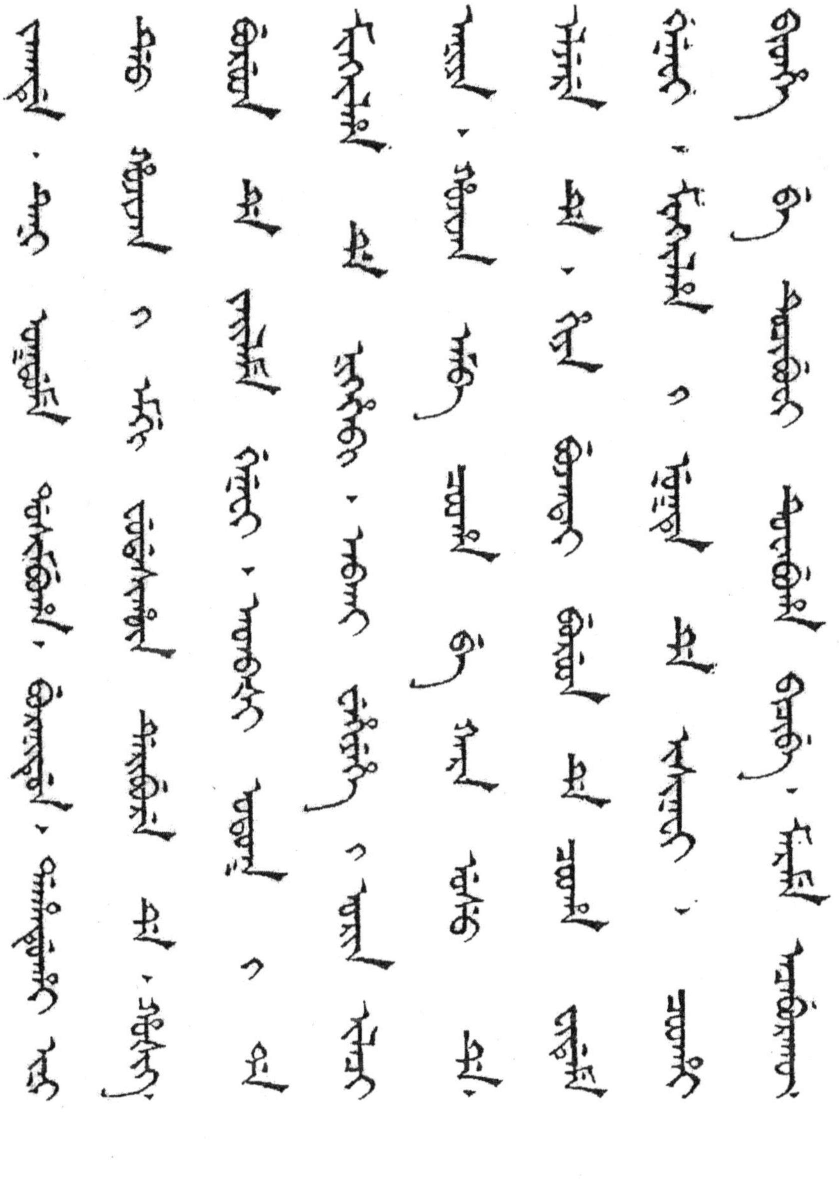

For audio recording of A-2 go to: http://hdl.handle.net/10125/6050

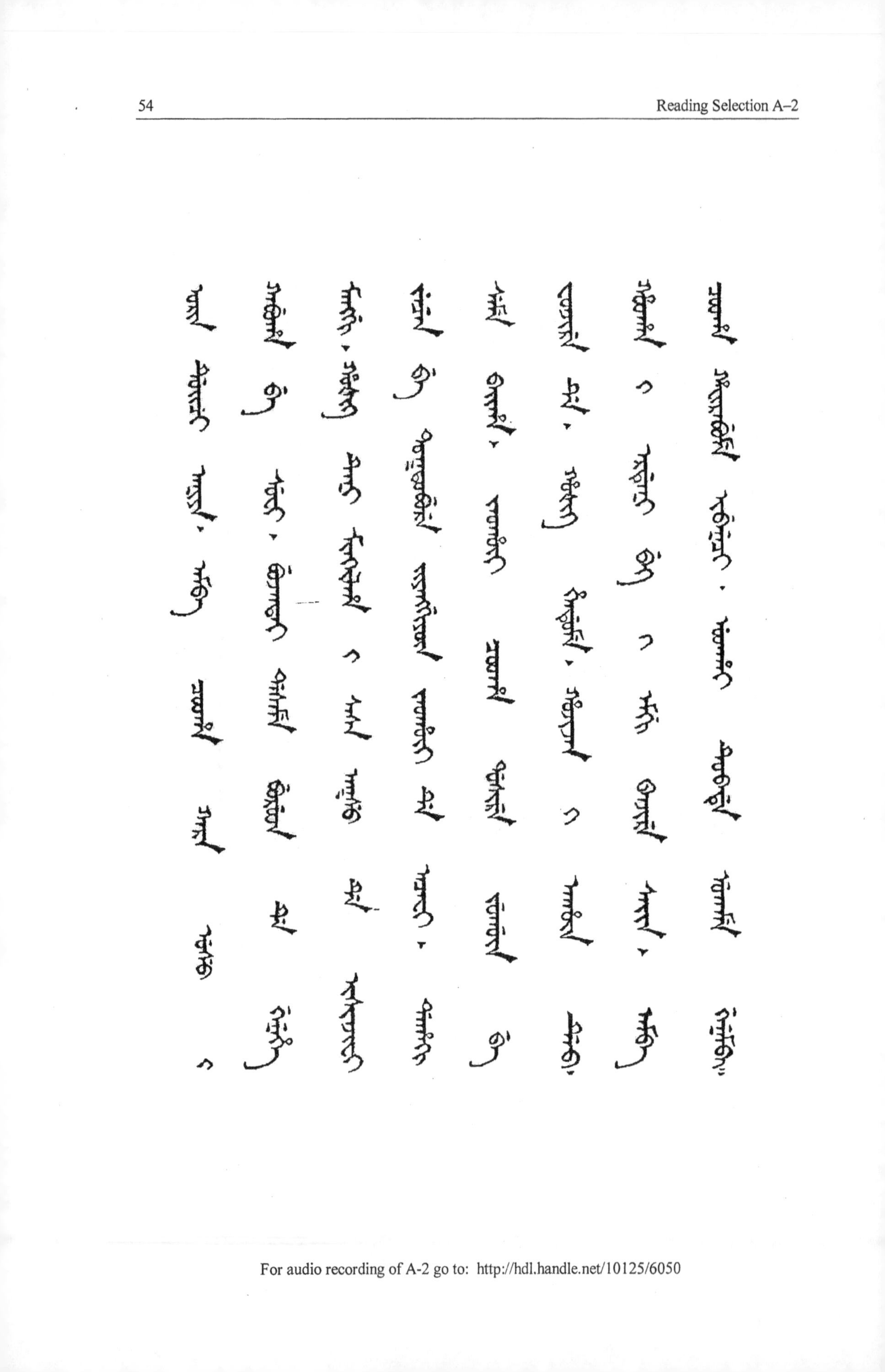

For audio recording of A-2 go to: http://hdl.handle.net/10125/6050

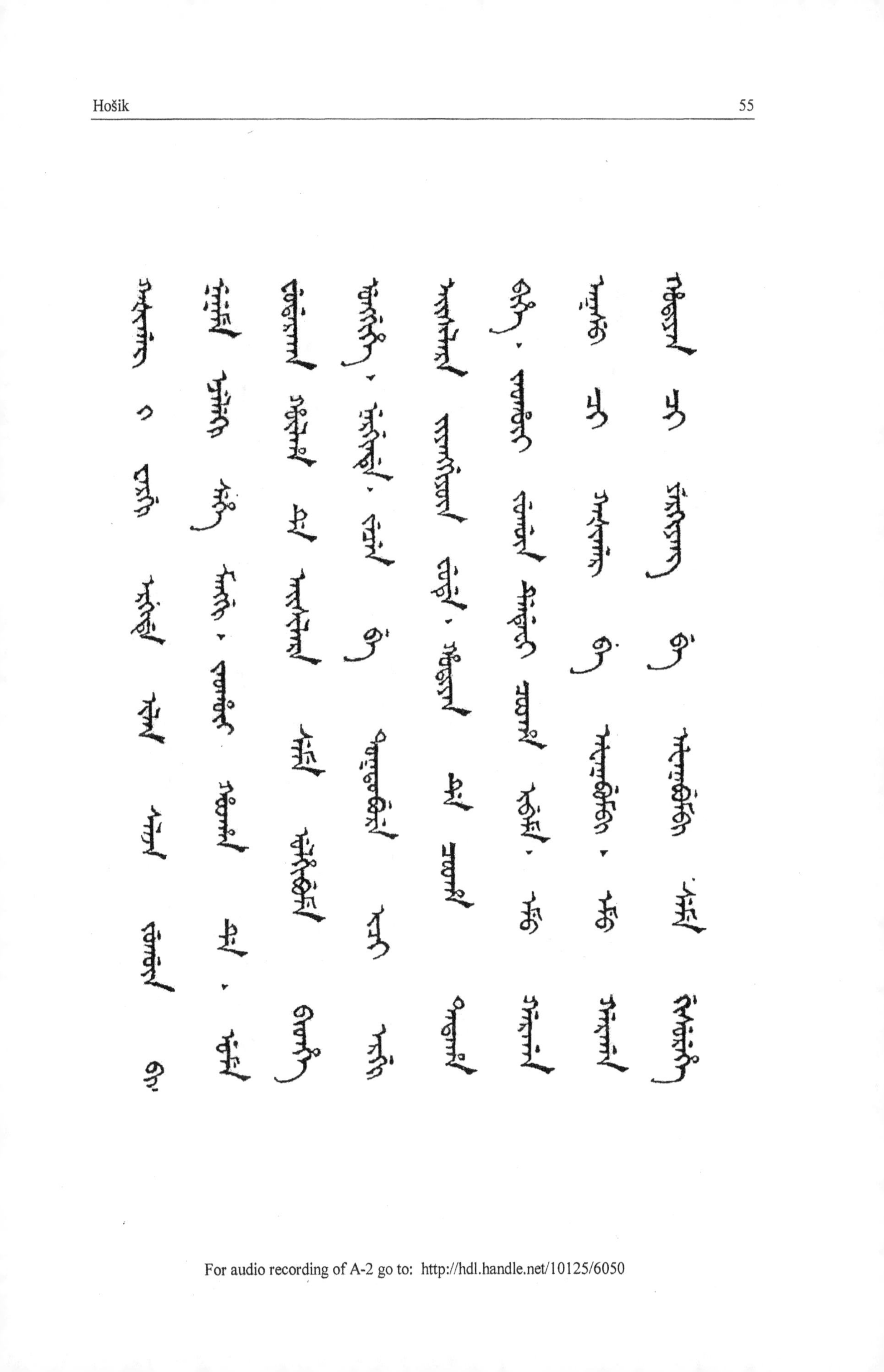

[illegible]

[illegible]

[illegible]

[illegible]

[illegible]

[illegible]

[illegible]

[illegible]

For audio recording of A-2 go to: http://hdl.handle.net/10125/6050

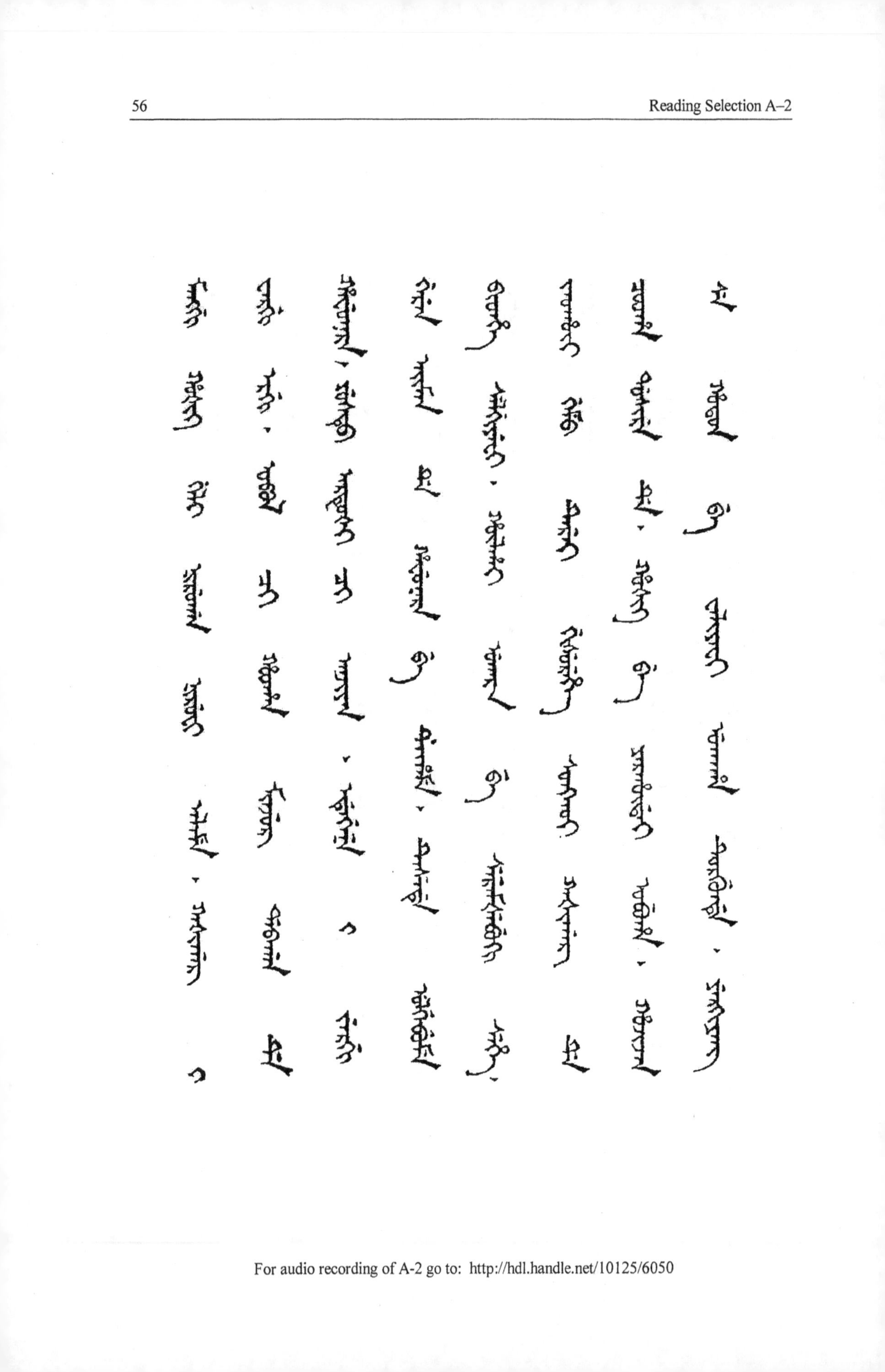

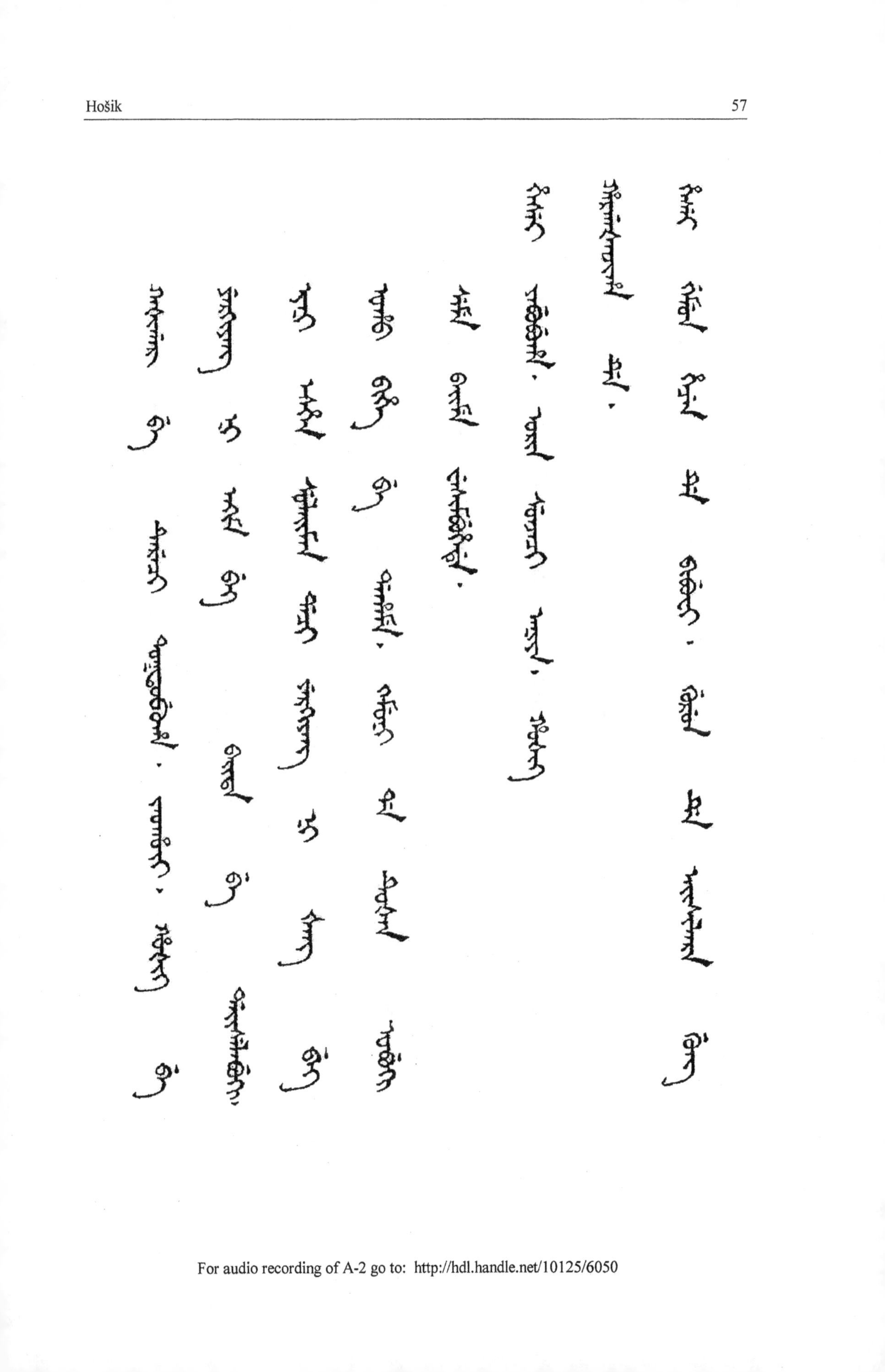

[illegible]

[illegible]

[illegible]

[illegible]

[illegible]

[illegible]

[illegible]

[illegible]

For audio recording of A-2 go to: http://hdl.handle.net/10125/6050

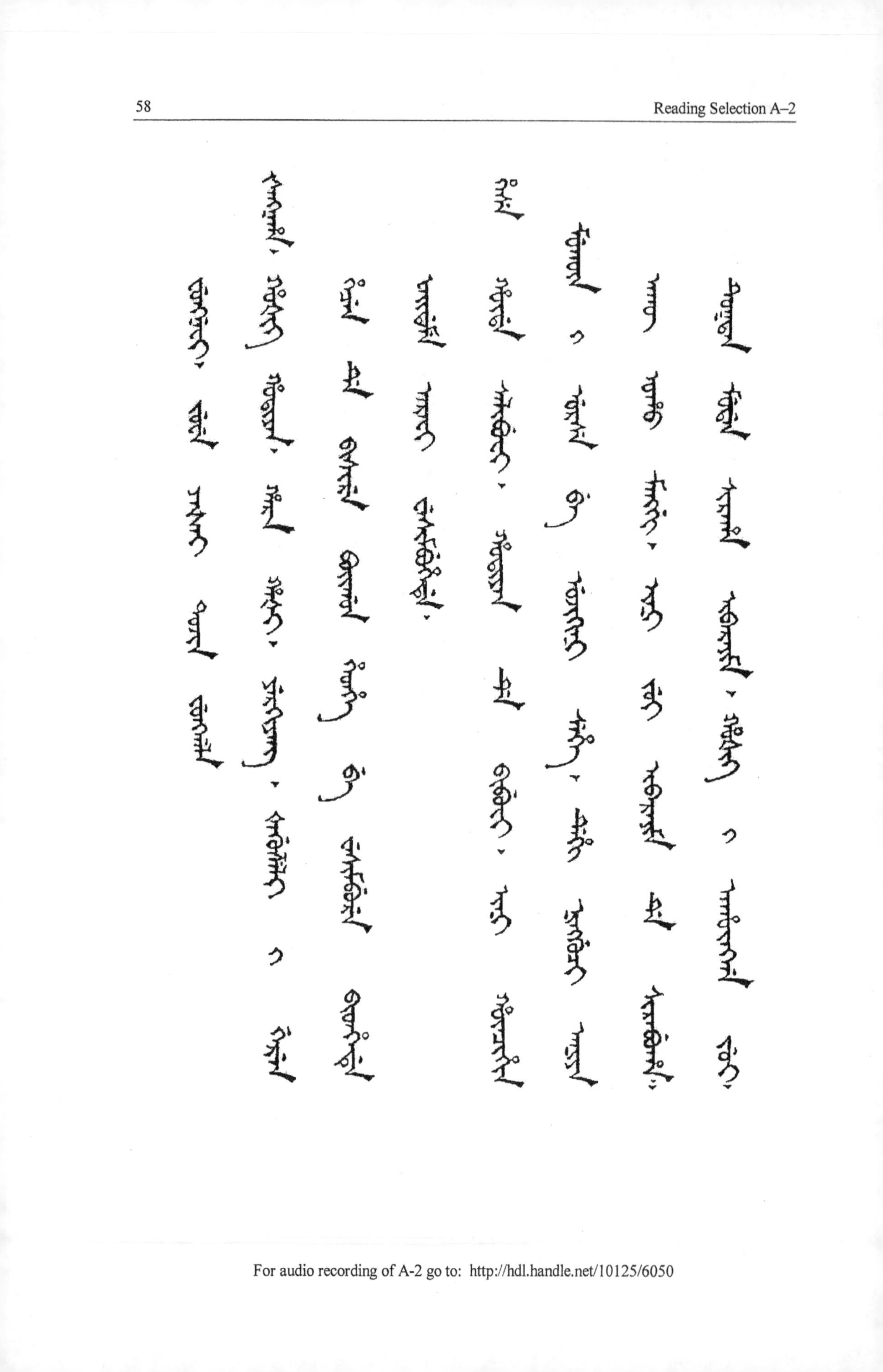

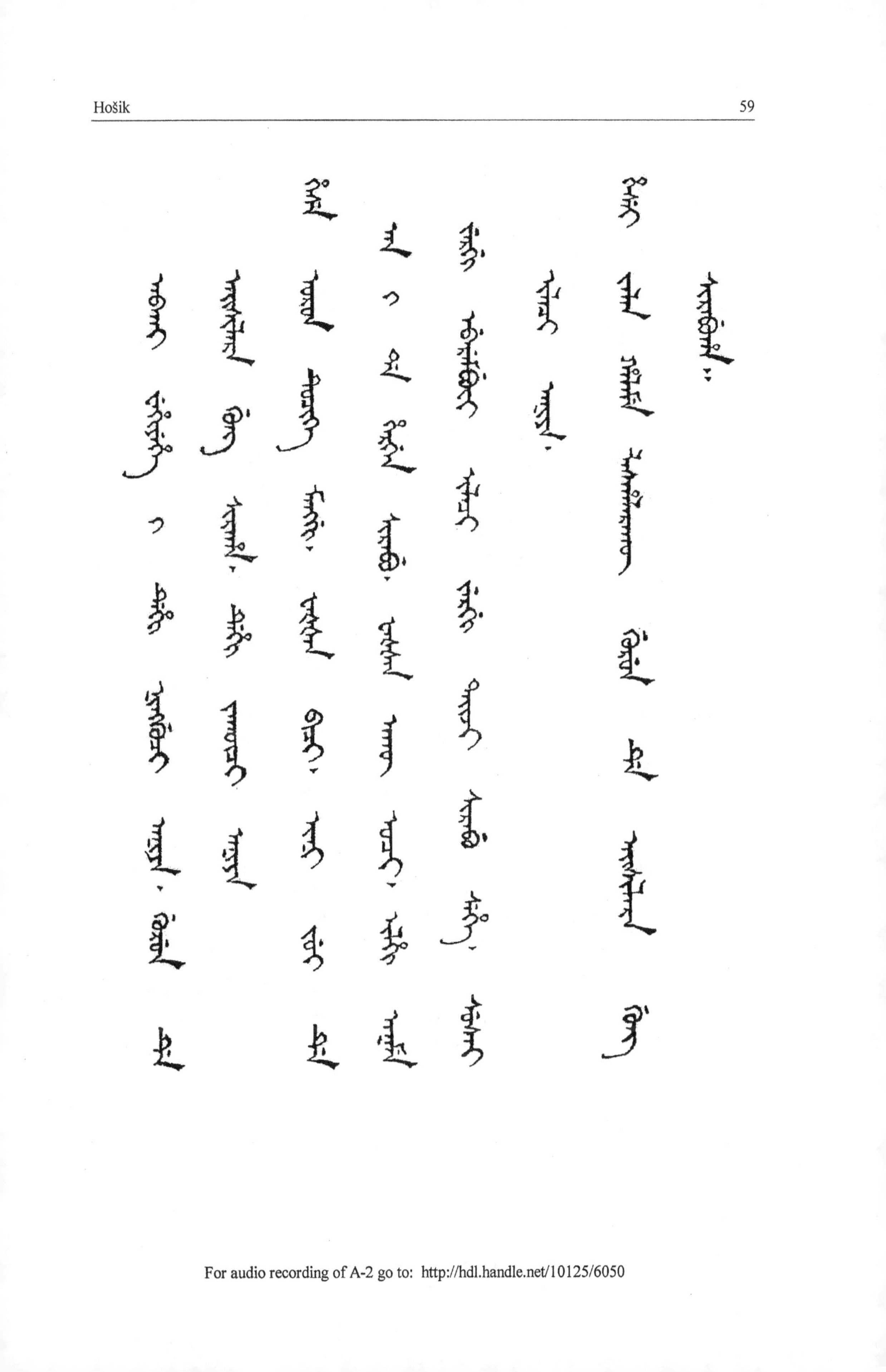

For audio recording of A-2 go to: http://hdl.handle.net/10125/6050

Transliteration

(52) *hesei toktobuha tulergi monggo hoise aiman i wang gung-sai iletun* [1] *ulabun i emu tanggū juwan nadaci* [2] *debtelin. ulabun i emu tanggū emuci. gurun de aisilara gung* [3] *Hošik i faidangga ulabun. gemun hecen de tehe hoise hergen inu. Hošik Hotiyan i niyalma, dade Kašigar i akim bek* [4] *ofi, Jun gar i harangga oho bihe.*[5] *amba cooha Jun gar be toktobuha manggi, Buranidun be Ili ci bederebuhe de, Hošik geren bek i sasa gemu bargiyarakū bihe. musei cooha isinaha be donjire*

(53) *jakade,*[6] *teni okdome dosimbuha. Buranidun dahanduhai ini deo Hojijan i emgi fudasihūn deribure de, Hošik, Burut* [7] *de jailame genefi, Atbaši* [8] *otok i da Ming'ilha* [9] *de nikehebi.*[10] *abkai wehiyehe i orin ilaci aniya, Hojijan amba cooha be Kara Usu de eljere de, hiya Bujantai Burut de cooha fideme genefi, Ming'ilha i nukte de isinafi, coohai bithe be tucibufi tuwabuha bicibe, marame acaburakū.*[11]

(54) *orin duici aniya, amba cooha Kara Usu i kabuha be sufi,*[12] *Bujantai dasame Burut de genehe manggi, Hošik teni Ming'ilha i sasa Aksu de isinjifi jecen be toktobure jiyanggiyūn Jaohūi de acafi, dahaki seme baiha.*[13] *Jaohūi cooha dosire jugūn be fonjire de,*[14] *Hošik hendume, «Hojijan i ahūn deo Hoohan i Erdeni bek i emgi banjire sain, amba cooha hafirabume ibeneci uthai tubade ukame genembi.*

(55) *Kašigar i wargi ergide ilan salja jugūn bi. neneme ejeleki» sehe manggi, Jaohūi Hoohan de «ume fudaraka hūlha de aisilara»*[15] *seme ulhibume* [16] *bithe unggihe. nerginde jecen be toktobure ici ergi aisilara jiyanggiyūn Fude Hotiyan de cooha tataha bihe. Jaohūi jugūn dendefi cooha ibeme emu gargan Aksu ci Kašigar be afanabumbi, emu gargan Hotiyan ci Yerkiyang be afanabumbi seme gisurehe*

(56) *manggi, Hošik geli nirugan nirufi alame, «Kašigar i wargi ergi, Opol ci Hoohan Minjur dabagan de hafunara, Yustu Artuši ci Anjiyan, Edegene i jergi geren aiman de hafunara be dahame,*[17] *tesede ulgebume bithe selgiyefi, hūlhai ukara be seremšebuki»* [18] *sehe. Jaohūi gemu* [19] *terei gisurehe songkoi Kašigar de cooha dosire de, Hošik be yarhūdai obuha. Hojijan se hoton be waliyafi ukaha turgunde, Yerkiyang*

(57) *Kašigar be tereci toktobuha. Jaohūi, «Hošik be Yerkiyang ni akim bek baita be daiselabuki. ini eshen Sulaiman daci Yerkiyang ni šang bek oho bihe be dahame, kemuni da tušan obuki»*[20] *seme baime wesimbuhede hesei yabubuha.*[21] *orin sunjaci aniya Hošik hargašanjiha de hesei gemun hecen de bibufi, gurun de aisilara gung*

(58) *fungnefi, juwe yasai tojin funggala šangnaha.*[22] *Hošik Hotiyan Hara Haši, Yerkiyang, Šagudzeli i geren hecen de bisire boigon hethe be wesimbure bithede faidame arafi wesimbuhede, hese «hūda salibufi, Hotiyan de bibufi,*[23] *ini hūncihin*

mukūn i urse be ujikini[24]*» sehe, dehi ningguci aniya akū oho manggi, ini jui Ibarayim de sirabuha. tuktan mudan siraha Ibarayim, Hošik i ahūngga jui.*

(59) *abkai wehiyehe i dehi ningguci aniya gurun de aisilara gung siraha. dehi jakūci aniya hese «oron tucike* [25] *manggi, faššan bici, ini jui de an i da hergen sirabu.*[26] *faššan akū oci, ilhi aname jergi eberembufi* [27] *ilaci jergi taiji sirabu» sehe. susai ilaci aniya hesei jalan halame lashalarakū gurun de aisilara gung sirabuha.*[28]

Vocabulary

abka	heaven, emperor, sky
abkai wehiyehe	Qianlong reign (1736-1796)
acambi	to meet with, to come together; to be in agreement; to be appropriate
afambi	to fight
afanambi	to go and attack
ahūn	elder brother
ahūngga	eldest
aiman	tribe
aisilambi (w/dative)	to help
akim bek	(local) governor (BH 863)
Aksu	(geogr. name)
akū ombi	to die
alambi	to inform
amba	great
an	usual, ordinary, common
an i	original, as customary
anambi	to move
aniya	year
Anjiyan	Andijan (geogr. name)
Atbaši	Atbash (geogr. name)
baimbi	to request
baita	matter
banjimbi	to live
banjimbi sain	to be on good terms
bargiyambi	to receive
bederembi	to return
bek	*beg* (Turkish title)
bi	there is, there are
bimbi	to be, to remain
bisire	imperfective participle of *bimbi*

boigon	household
Bujantai	(pers. name)
Buranidun	(pers. name)
Burut	Kirghiz
-ci	suffix for ordinal numerals
-cibe	although (concessive converb suffix)
cooha	army
cooha dosimbi	to invade
coohai bithe	call to arms
da	leader, head, origin; original
dabagan	mountain pass
daci	from the beginning, originally, formerly
dade	in the beginning, originally
dahambi	to follow, to submit
dahanduhai	subsequently
daiselambi	to administer in an acting capacity
dasame	again
de	if, when
debtelin	chapter
dehi	forty
dendembi	to divide
deo	younger brother
deribumbi	to begin, to let begin, to conjure up
donjimbi	to hear
dosimbi	to enter
duici	fourth
duin	four
eberembi	to diminish
Edegene	name of a Kirghiz tribe
ejelembi	to occupy, to rule
eljembi	to oppose, to resist
emgi (w/genitive)	with
emu	one
ergi	side
eshen	father's younger brother
faidambi	to enumerate, to list
faidangga	arranged in order
faidangga ulabun (Chin. *liezhuan* 列傳)	biography, collected biographies
faššan	effort
fidembi	to enlist
fonjimbi	to ask
fudarambi	to rebel

fudasihūn	rebellion, rebellious
fudasihūn deribumbi	to become rebellious, to start a rebellion
Fude (Chin. *Fude* 富德)	(pers. name)
funggala	feather
fungnembi	to appoint, to enfeoff
gargan	detachment
gašan	village
geli	again, then, also
gemu	in every case, even
gemun	the imperial capital
gemun hecen	capital
genembi	to go
geren	numerous, the various
gisurembi	to discuss, to speak
gung (Chin. *gong* 公)	duke
gurun de aisilara gung (Chin. *fuguogong* 輔國公)	bulwark duke, prince of the sixth degree (H 2075)
gurun de aisilara jiyanggiyūn (Chin. *fuguo jiangjun* 輔國將軍)	bulwark-general of the state, noble of the tenth rank (H 2073)
hafirambi	to pinch, to pressure, to threaten
hafirabumbi (trans. and intrans.)	to put into a difficult situation, to pressure someone; to be put into a difficult situation; to be pressured
hafunambi	to connect with another place
halambi	to change
Hara Haši	Hara Hash (geogr. name)
harangga	subject
hargašambi	to have an audience
hecen	city, town
hergen	rank
hese	edict
hethe	property
hiya	guard, aide
hoise	Muslim
Hojijan	(pers. name)
Hoohan	Kokand (geogr. name)
Hošik (Chin. *Heshike* 和什克)	(pers. name)
Hotiyan	Khotan (geogr. name)
hoton	town, city
hūda	value
hūda salibumbi	to appraise the value
hūlha	bandit, rebel

hūncihin	relatives by marriage
Ibarayim	Ibrahim (pers. name)
ibembi	to go forward
ibenembi	to go forward, to advance
ici	right (not left)
ilaci	third
iletun	genealogical table
ilhi	next, subsequent
Ili	(geogr. name)
ini	of him, it, her
inu	is, was; also; so
isinambi	to arrive
jailambi	to escape
jakade (w/imperfective)	because, when; in front of, up to, near
jalan	generation
Jaohūi (Chin. *Zhaohui* 兆惠)	(pers. name)
jecen	border
jecen be toktobure jiyanggiyūn (Chin. *dingbian jiangjun* 定邊將軍)	pacifier of the frontier (H 6740)
jecen be toktobure ici ergi aisilara jiyanggiyun (Chin. *dingbian you fujiangjun* 定邊右副將軍)	right pacifier of the frontier
jergi	kind of, grade
jiyanggiyūn (Chin. *jiangjun* 將軍)	military general
jugūn	road, route
jui	son
Jun gar	Dzungars
juwan	ten
kambi	to block, to surround
Kara Usu	(geogr. name)
Kašigar	Kashgar (geogr. name)
kemuni	likewise, still, yet
kimulembi	to harbor enmity, to seek revenge
-kini	let him, let them; may you (verbal suffix)
lashalambi	to interrupt
manggi	after
Ming'ilha	Ming Ilha (pers. name)
Minjur	(geogr. name)
mudan	time, occurrence
mukūn	clan, extended family
-na-, -ne-, -no-	to go (verbal suffix)
nadaci	seventh

neneme	beforehand
nerginde	on that occasion
nikembi (w/dative)	to put oneself under the protection of
ningguci	sixth
ninggun	six
nirugan	picture, sketch
nirumbi	to draw, to sketch
-nji-	to come (verbal suffix)
nukte	(nomadic) territory
okdombi	to go to meet, to welcome
Opol	Opal (geogr. name)
orin	twenty
oron	place
otok	tribal territory, tribal unit
-sa, -se, -so	plural suffix
Šagudzeli	(geogr. name)
salibumbi	to estimate the price
salja	branch, crossroads
salja jugūn	crossroads, intersection of three roads
šang bek	(Turkish official title)
šangnambi	to bestow, to grant
sasa (w/genitive)	with, together
seremšembi	to be on guard, to defend against
sirambi	to succeed, to inherit
songkoi	in accordance with
Sulaiman	Sulayman (pers. name)
sumbi	to free, to sever
sunja	five
susai	fifty
taiji	(Mongolian official title)
tanggū	hundred
tatambi	to halt
tembi	to reside
teni	then
tereci	thereafter
tese	those
tojin	peacock
toktobumbi	to pacify, to fix
toktombi	to fix, to determine
tuba	there, that place
tucimbi	to come out, to go out
tuktan	first; at first, originally

tulergi	outer
turgunde	because
tušan	office, duty
tuwabumbi	to show
ujimbi	to feed, to support
ukambi	to escape
ulabun	biography
ulgimbi	to understand
ume (w/imperfective)	don't
unggimbi	to send
urse	people
uthai	immediately, then
waliyambi	to abandon
wang (Chin. *wang* 王)	prince
wargi	west
wehiyembi	to support
wesibumbi (trans. and intrans.)	to lift; to promote, to cause to go up; to select
wesimbi	to go up, to advance (in rank)
wesimbumbi	to memorialize, to present to the emperor; to cause to go up, to promote
yabumbi	to carry out, to go
yarhūdai	guide
yasa	eye
Yerkiyang	Yarkand (geogr. name)
Yustu Artuši	Yustu Artush (geogr. name)

Notes

1. ***hese i toktobuha iletun*:** 'the tables which one established by edict' (Chin. *qinding* 欽定, 'imperially commissioned'). As translated above, the word *hese i* is taken as an instrumental genitive. However, it is also possible to view *hese i toktobuha* as a phrase which modifies *iletun* (equivalent to a relative clause in English). When a subject-verb phrase modifies a noun, the subject of the phrase usually appears in the genitive: *hese i toktobuha iletun* 'the tables which an edict established' or *tere i gisurehe gisun* 'the words which he spoke'.

2. ***emu tanggū juwan nadaci*:** 'the 117th'.

Cardinal numerals

			10	*juwan*	20	*orin*
1	*emu*		11	*juwan emu*	21	*orin emu*
2	*juwe*		12	*juwan juwe*	22	*orin juwe*
3	*ilan*		13	*juwan ilan*	23	*orin ilan*
4	*duin*		14	*juwan duin*	24	*orin duin*
5	*sunja*	**but:**	15	*tofohon*	25	*orin sunja*
6	*ninggun*		16	*juwan ninggun*	26	*orin ninggun*
7	*nadan*		17	*juwan nadan*	27	*orin nadan*
8	*jakūn*		18	*juwan jakūn*	28	*orin jakūn*
9	*uyun*		19	*juwan uyun*	29	*orin uyun*

30	*gūsin*	70	*nadanju*	101	*tanggū emu*
40	*dehi*	80	*jakūnju*	200	*juwe tanggū*
50	*susai*	90	*uyunju*	1,000	*minggan*
60	*ninju*	100	*tanggū*	10,000	*tumen*

Ordinal numerals

Ordinals are formed by adding the suffix *-ci*. Except for *juwanci* 'tenth' and *tumenci* '10,000th', the final *n* of the cardinals is dropped before *-ci*.

1	*emuci*	7	*nadaci*	13	*juwan ilaci*
2	*juweci*	8	*jakūci*	14	*juwan duici*
3	*ilaci*	9	*uyuci*	15	*tofohoci*
4	*duici*	10	*juwanci*	16	*juwan ningguci*
5	*sunjaci*	11	*juwan emuci*	etc.	
6	*ningguci*	12	*juwan juweci*		

20	*orici*	50	*susaici*	100	*tanggūci*
21	*orin emuci*	60	*ninjuci*	101	*tanggū emuci*
30	*gūsici*	70	*nadanjuci*	200	*juwe tanggūci*
40	*dehici*	80	*jakūnjuci*	1,000	*minggaci*
		90	*uyunjuci*	10,000	*tumenci*

3. *gurun de aisilara gung*: Chin. *fuguogong* 輔國公 'bulwark duke, prince of the sixth degree'. According to Brunnert and Hagelstrom (#27A), this title is an honor reserved for people of Manchu or Mongolian descent; the imperfective participle *aisilara* modifies *gung*.

4. ***akim bek*****:** The word *beg* is a pre-Muslim term for chiefs in Inner Asia. It occurs in Orkhon inscriptions and is believed to be a loan word, based on the Chinese *bo* 伯. Brunnert and Hagelstrom (# 863) lists six classes of *begs*:

a. Ak'im Beg (Ma. *akim bek*)	(local) governor
b. Ishhan Beg (Ma. *isigan bek*)	assistant governor
c. Shang Beg (Ma. *šang bek*)	collector of revenues
d. Katsonatch'i Beg (Ma. *gadzanaci bek*)	collector of revenues
e. Hatsze Beg (Ma. *hadzi bek*)	judge
f. Mirabu Beg (Ma. *mirabu bek*)	superintendent of agriculture

5. ***oho bihe*****:** 'it was a fact of having become,' i.e., 'it had become'. When combined with other verbs, the various forms of the irregular verb *bimbi* express the process of an action that is just concluding or that already has concluded. For more information refer to Grammatical Points, Verbs, p. 364-66. Also see Review 5.

6. ***cooha isinaha be donjire jakade*****:** 'when/because he heard that the imperial army had arrived'. Indirect speech: (subject) (verb) *be donjifi*. The postposition *jakade* 'when' or 'because' follows the imperfective participle.

7. Burut: Another name for Kirghiz.

8. Atbaši: *-ši* is the closest Manchu can come to a final *sh* sound.

9. Ming'ilha: Note that in this proper name the *i* in *ilha* is written as an initial *i*, indicated here by an apostrophe. This spelling is not to be confused with the Chinese *g'* which occurs only before *a* and *o*. Also note that if *ng* is followed by a vowel in Manchu words, another *g* is inserted; compare *jiyanggiyūn* on the next page.

10. ***nikehe-bi*****:** 'he had put himself under the protection'. Compare Note 5. There are different shades to these tenses in Manchu. More literally, one might translate it here as "it was a state (fact) of him having put himself under the protection.'

11. ***coohai bithe be tucibufi tuwabuha bicibe, marame acaburakū*****:** 'even though he sent out a call to arms and showed it to Ming Ilha, Ming Ilha (note change of subject) refused and did not make (troops) come together'.

12. *amba cooha Kara Usu i kabuha be sufi*: 'after the imperial army cut through the blockade (lit. 'having-been-surroundedness') of Kara Usu'. Note the nominalization of the passive verb *kabuha.*

13. *dahaki seme baiha*: lit. 'requested saying let me submit', i.e., 'requested to submit'. The grammatical structure leaves it unclear whether Hošik and Ming Ilha both submit, or whether only one of the two does so.

14. *cooha dosire jugūn be fonjire de*: 'when he asked which road the army was to enter'.

15. *ume...aisilara*: 'don't help'. *Ume* takes the imperfective verb form.

16. *ulhibume*: Modifies *bithe unggihe*, not only *bithe*; the *-me* coordinative converb has only an adverbial function. It cannot serve as an adjective. Meaning: 'one sent a letter letting them understand that they should not help the rebels'.

17. *be dahame*: Relates to each of the two *hafunara.*

18. *tesede ulgebume...hūlhai ukara be seremšebuki*: lit. 'let us make them guard against the escaping of bandits by making them understand'. *ulgebume* should be *ulgibume.*

19. *gemu*: 'in every case'.

20. *ini eshen Sulaiman...kemuni da tušan obuki*: 'because (Hošik's) father's younger brother, Sulayman, had formerly been *shang beg* of Yarkand, (Jaohūi)) requested to let Sulayman remain in that office'.

21. *hesei yabubuha*: 'it was carried out by edict'.

Passive: The causing agent is designated through *de*. For example, *hecen hūlha de kabuha* 'the city was besieged by the rebels'. Some causative/passive verbs may have a new dictionary meaning that varies from the original verb. Examples:

tacimbi	to learn	*tacibumbi*	to teach
salimbi	to be worth	*salibumbi*	to appraise
wesimbi	to go up, ascend	*wesibumbi*	to promote

Causative (with *be*)**:** *bithe be kūbulibumbi* 'to cause the script to change'.

22. ***tojin funggala šangnaha*:** Awarding a peacock feather was a means for the emperor to convey distinction to persons of merit.

23. ***Hotiyan de bibufi*:** Could mean 'one had it (the property) remain in Khotan' or 'one had him remain in Khotan'; the judgement on which is correct needs to be made on the basis of other available information (e.g., he was one of the Muslims residing in the capital). This sentence is an example of inherent ambiguities in Manchu and it shows the translator's need to fill in missing information.

24. ***uji-kini*:** 'may it/he support the people'. The verb suffix *-kini* expresses a wish that somebody may do something. In most cases *-kini* refers to the third person.

25. ***tuci-ke*:** Some perfective participles are irregular and take *-ke* instead of *-he*, *-ka* instead of *-ha*. Cf. *fudaraka*.

26. ***ini jui de an i da hergen sirabu*:** 'the same rank is to be inherited by the son'. Imperative and passive. Official ranks were often lowered by one grade upon inheritance.

27. ***ilhi aname jergi eberembufi*:** 'the rank having been diminished by moving to the next step'. Here *ilhi* 'next' or 'subsequent' is used adverbially, meaning 'nextward'.

28. ***jalan halame lashalarakū gurun de aisilara gung sirabuha*:** lit. 'it (the rank) was inherited generations changing without interruption as bulwark duke, prince of the sixth degree'. The verb form *lashalarakū* is the negative counterpart to the converb *lashalame* and to the imperfective participle *lashalara*. Therefore two grammatical structures are possible: as a converb *lashalarakū* modifies *sirabuha*, but as an adjectival modifier, *lashalarakū* can modify *gung*.

Review

1. Numbers and dates

emu tanggū juwan nadaci debtelin	the 117th chapter
orin ilaci iletun	the twenty-third genealogical table
emu tanggū emuci aniya	in the 101st year
orin sunjaci aniya	in the twenty-fifth year
juwe biya de	in the second month
susai emu aiman	fifty-one tribes
abkai wehiyehe i orin ilaci aniya	in the twenty-third year of Qianlong

2. *-ci* 'if' or 'when'

manju gisun i araci	if/when one writes in the Manchu language
hafirabume ibeneci	if/when one advances pressing them
ukame geneci	if/when one goes to escape
Kašigar de cooha dosici	if/when they attacked Kashgar
baime wesimbuci	if/when one memorialized requesting
cooha fideme geneci	if/when he went to enlist troops

3. *de* 'when'

Jaohūi cooha dosire de	when Jaohūi attacked
hafirabume ibenere de	when one advances pressing them
ukame genere de	when one goes to escape
baime wesimbuhe de	when one memorialized requesting
bithe (be) unggire de	when one sent a letter

4. *(be) dahame; turgunde; jakade* 'because'

ibenere be dahame	because one advanced
bithe unggihe (be) dahame	because one sent a letter
ukame genehe turgunde	because he went to escape
baime wesimbuhe turgunde	because one memorialized requesting
marame cooha be acaburakū jakade	because he refused and did not bring any troops together

5. *-ha*, *-he*, *-ho* + *bihe* 'one had'

cooha tataha bihe	one had halted the troops
harangga oho bihe	he had become a subject
dade akim bek oho bihe	originally he had been governor
gung de nikehe bihe	he had put himself under the protection of the duke

6. *bicibe* 'although'

ibenehe bicibe	although one advanced
bithe be tuwabuha bicibe	although one showed the letter
ukame genehe bicibe	although he went to escape
baime wesimbuhe bicibe	although one memorialized and requested
akū oho bicibe	although he died

7. *-fi* and *manggi* 'after'

nukte de isinafi	having arrived in the nomad territory
nukte de isinaha manggi	after he arrived in the nomad territory
hafirabume ibenehe manggi	after one advanced and pressured them
ukame genehe manggi	after he escaped
ulhibume bithe unggihe manggi	after one sent a letter alerting them
baime wesimbufi	having memorialized and requested
kabuha be sufi	having broken the siege

8. Imperatives

ume fudaraka hūlha de aisilara	don't help the rebellious bandits
ume hecen de genere	don't go to the town
ume bithe selgiyere	don't disseminate the letter
ukara hūlha be seremše	guard against escaping bandits
gisurehe songkoi yabu	act according to what he said

9. Coordinative converb *-me*

baime wesimbuhe	he memorialized and requested
ukame genembi	they will go to escape
marame cooha be acaburakū	he refused and did not bring troops together

ulhibume bithe unggihe	one sent a letter alerting them
cooha ibeme afanambi	the army will advance and go to fight

10. Causative

adarame kūbulibumbi	why have it changed
Hotiyan de bibufi	after one had him remain in Khotan
da tušan obuki	let us make it the original office
Hošik be yarhūdai obuha	he made Hošik the guide

11. Passive

hesei yabubuha	it was carried out by edict
hergen ini jui de sirabuha	the rank was inherited by his son
hūlha cooha de gidabuha	the bandits were defeated by the army

12. Causative and Passive

arabubu	cause it to be written, let it be written
bithe be arabubuha	one caused the letter to be written
Jaohūi Hošik de arabubuha	Jaohūi had it written by Hošik
Jaohūi bithe be Hošik de arabubuha	Jaohūi had the letter written by Hošik

13. Translate into English: a) *terebe jecen ci bederebure jakade*; b) *hesei toktobuha debtelin; c) hecen de tere niyalma*; d) *faidangga ulabun*; e) *Hošik i sasa jailame genehe*; f) *geneki seme baiha*; g) *jailaki seme henduhe*; h) *dosire jugūn be fonjire de*; i) *ilhi aname jergi eberembufi*; j) *hesei yabubuha*; k) *ume jihe hūlha de aisilara*; l) *Hojijan se tubade ukaha turgunde*; m) *emu gargan Kašigar be afanabumbi*; n) *nirugan be tuwabure jakade*; o) *wargi ergi dabagan de hafunambi.*

14. Write in Manchu script and translate into English: a) *terei gisurehe songkoi cooha dosire de*; b) *hoton be waliyafi ukaha*; c) *akim bek baita be daiselabuki*; d) *jiyanggiyūn baita be daiselaha bihe*; e) *gemun hecen de hargašanjiha bihe*; f) *hecen de bisire boigon*; g) *Kašigar de bisire hethe*; h) Chicago *de bisire niyalma*; i) *urse be ujikini*; j) *gemun hecen de bibukini*; k) *ini jui de sirabukini*; l) *gurun de aisilara gung siraha*; m) *jalan halame akim bek sirabuha*; n) *ini jui de jalan halame akim bek sirabuha.*

15. Translate into Manchu: a) biographies determined by edict; b) because one pacified the Dzungars; c) after one let the bandits return from Ili; d) I will receive him in Beijing; e) Hošik put himself under the protection of the leader of the nomadic territory; f) although one showed him the letter; g) after he went out to meet him and let him enter; h) Hojijan, together with the bandits, started a rebellion; i) after one broke the blockage of Kara Usu; j) when one asked by which road one might enter; k) having divided the route, Jaohūi advanced; l) one detachment will free the blockage; m) Hošik reported to the imperial army; n) the west side provides access to the Minjur mountain pass; o) because one pacified the tribes thereafter; p) don't bestow a double-eyed peacock feather; q) list the property in a letter; r) one had him live in the capital; s) a rank that is not interrupted for generations; t) after Hošik died he was succeeded by his oldest son; u) if there is no effort; v) in accordance with what one had discussed.

Reading Selection A–3
Husayn

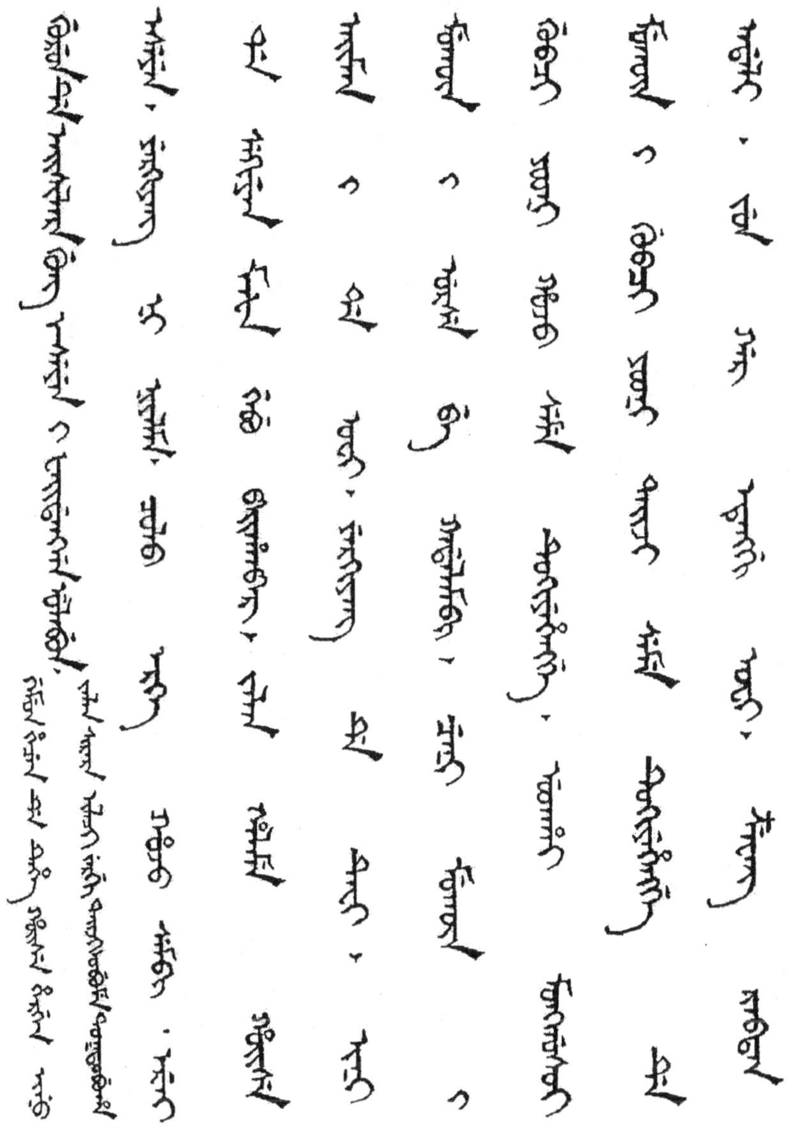

ᠠᠪᡴᠠᡳ ᡝᠵᡝᠨ [illegible] [illegible] ᡩᡝ [illegible] [illegible]᠈ [illegible]
[illegible] ᠪᡝ [illegible]᠈ [illegible] [illegible] ᡳ [illegible] ᠪᡝ
[illegible] ᡳ [illegible] [illegible]᠈ ᡨᡝᡵᡝ [illegible] ᡳ [illegible]
[illegible] ᠪᡝ [illegible] [illegible]᠈ [illegible] [illegible] [illegible] [illegible]᠈
ᡨᡝᡵᡝ ᠠᠪᡴᠠᡳ ᡝᠵᡝᠨ ᡩᡝ [illegible]᠈ [illegible] [illegible] [illegible]
[illegible] [illegible] ᡳ [illegible]᠈ [illegible] [illegible] [illegible]᠈
[illegible] ᡳ [illegible] ᠪᡝ [illegible] [illegible] ᡩᡝ [illegible]᠈
[illegible] ᠪᡝ [illegible]᠈ [illegible] [illegible] ᠪᡝ [illegible]᠈ [illegible]

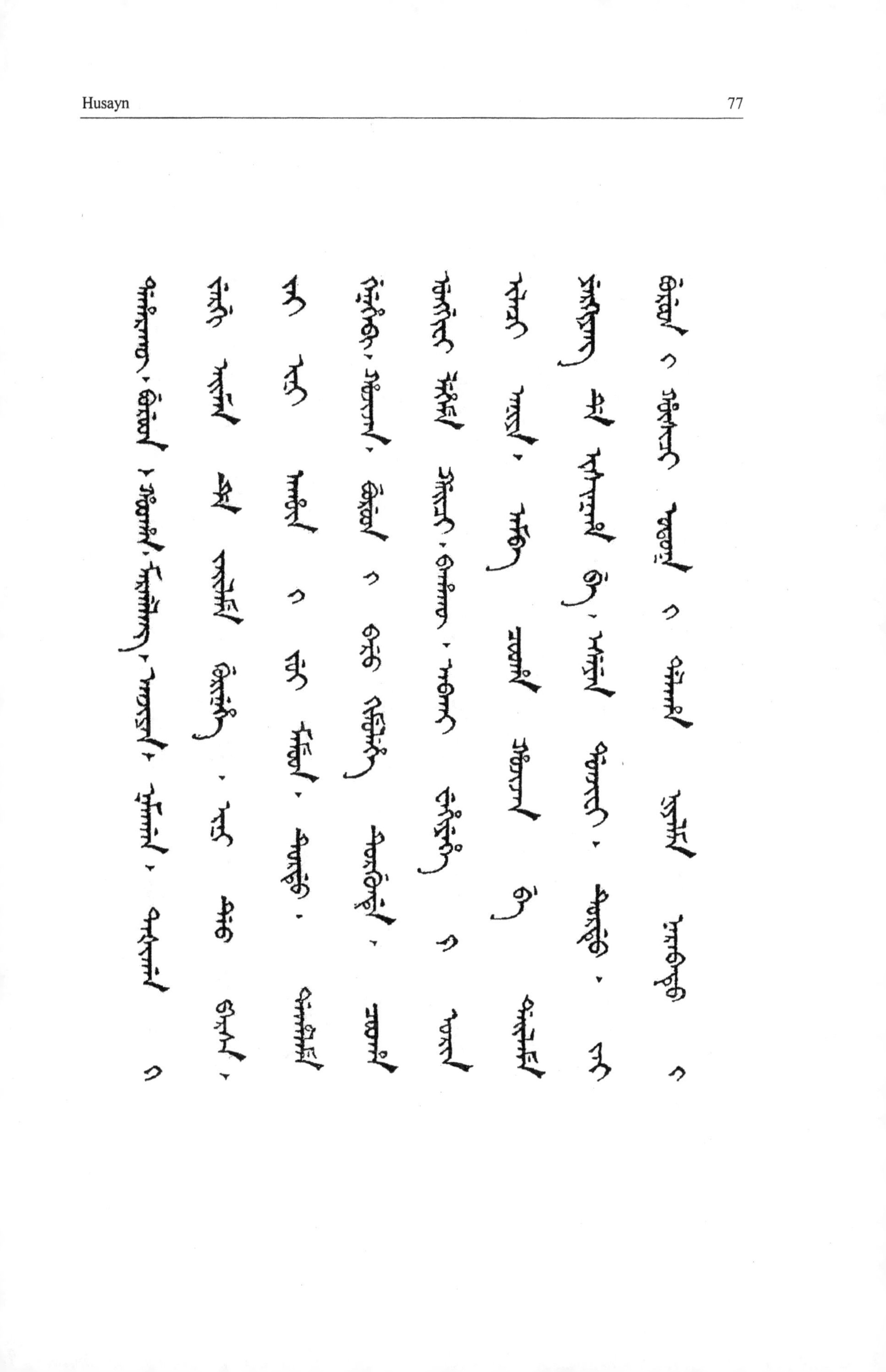

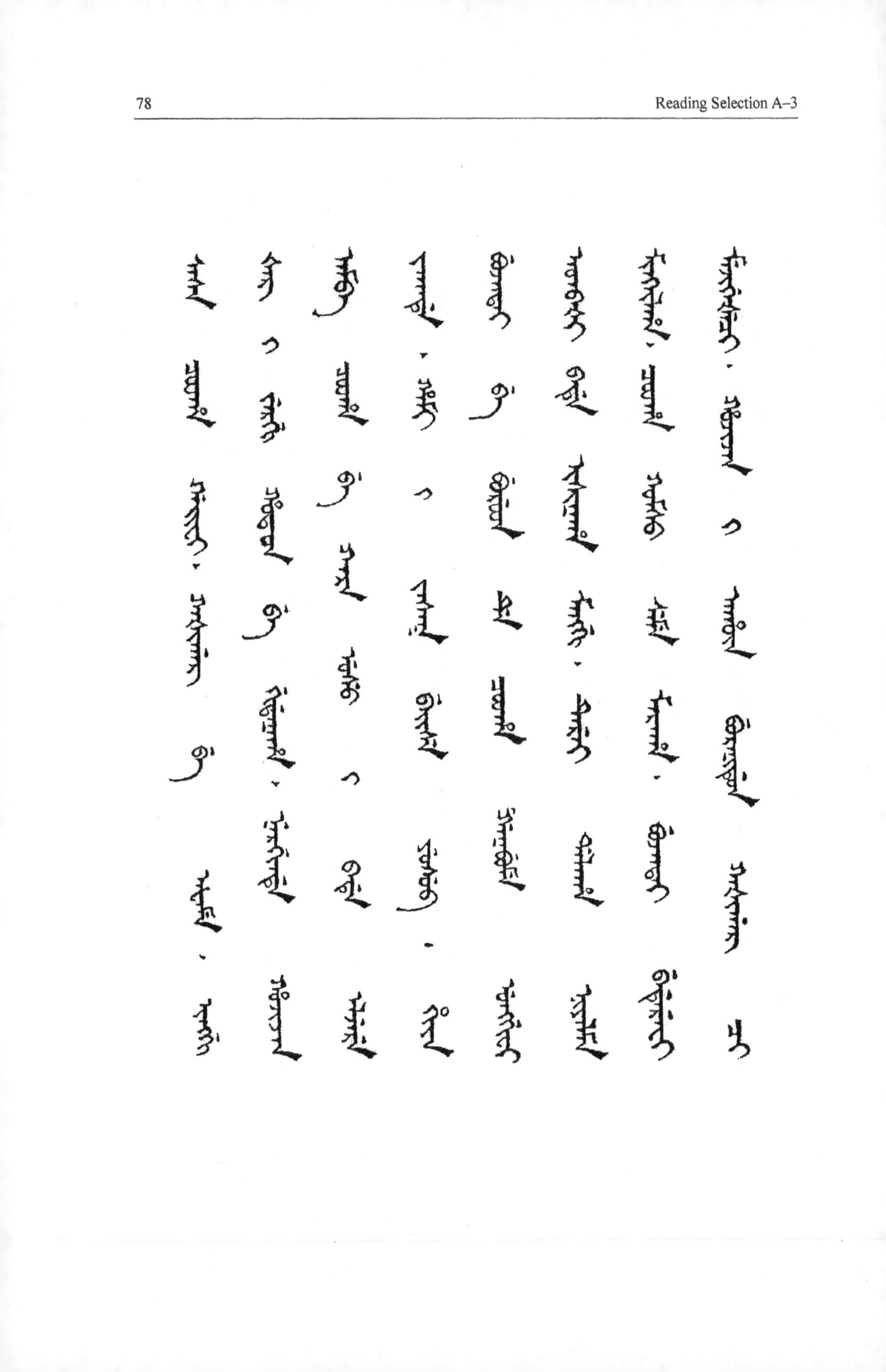

[illegible]

[illegible]

[illegible]

[illegible]

[illegible]

[illegible]

[illegible]

[illegible]

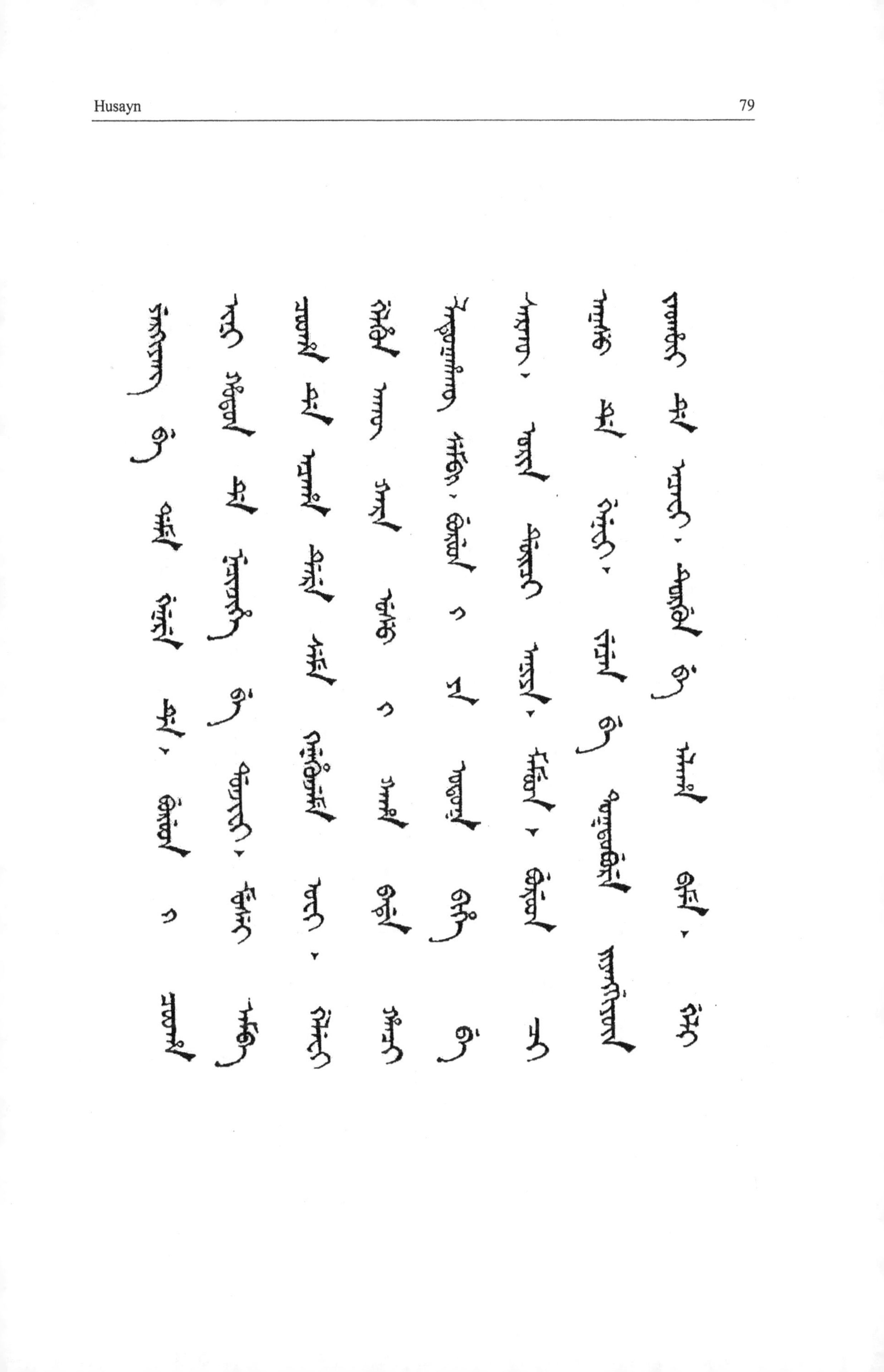

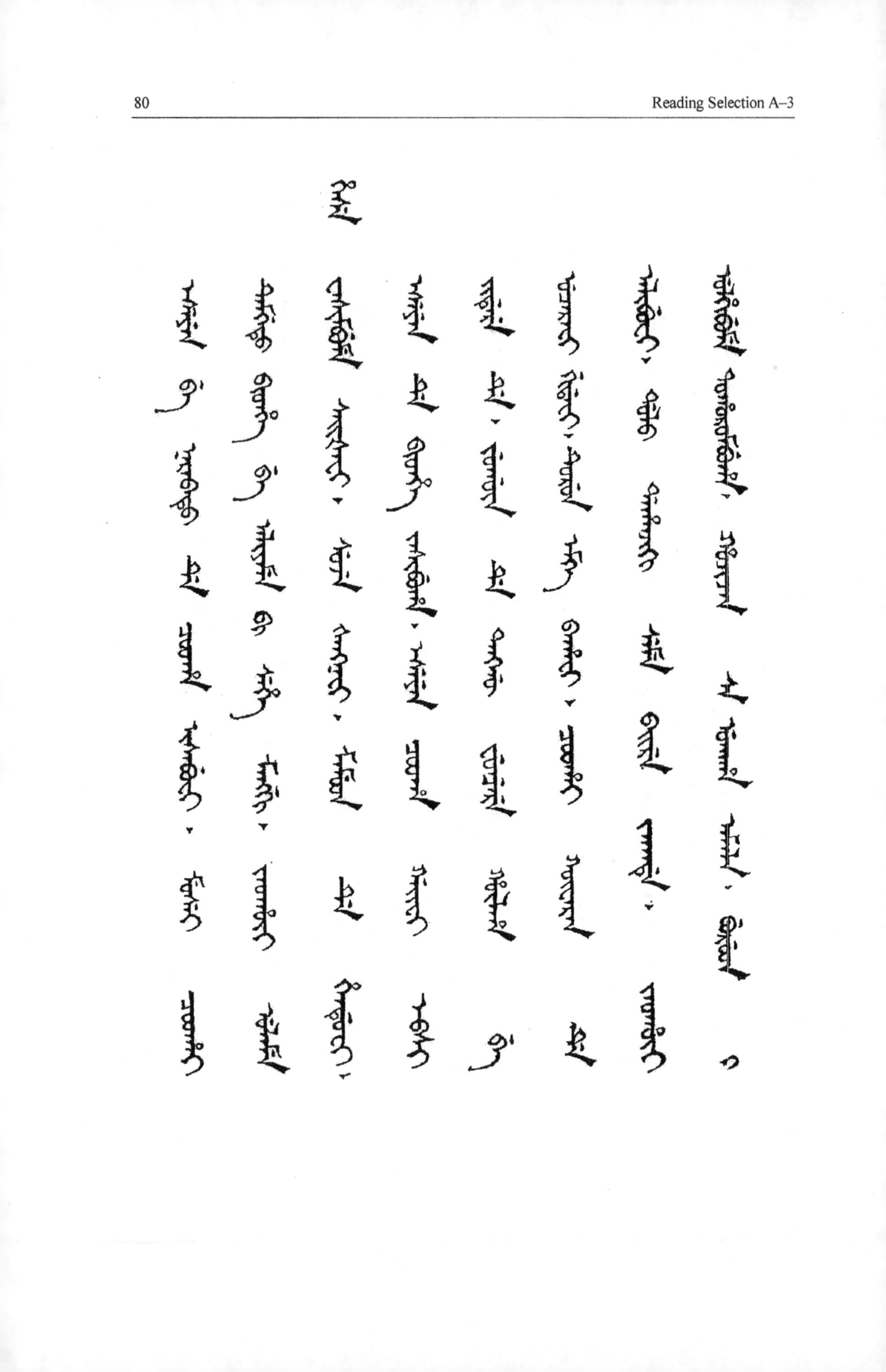

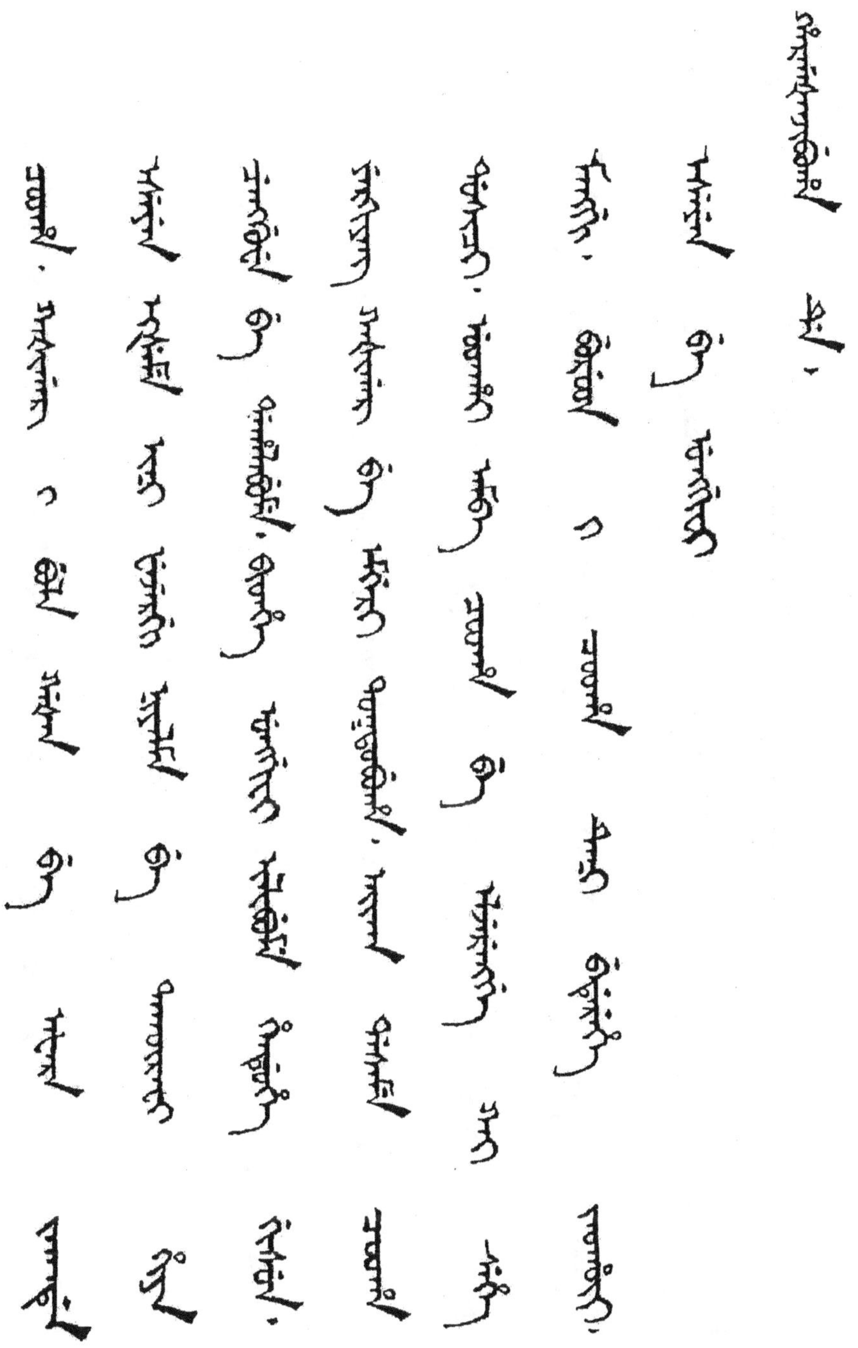

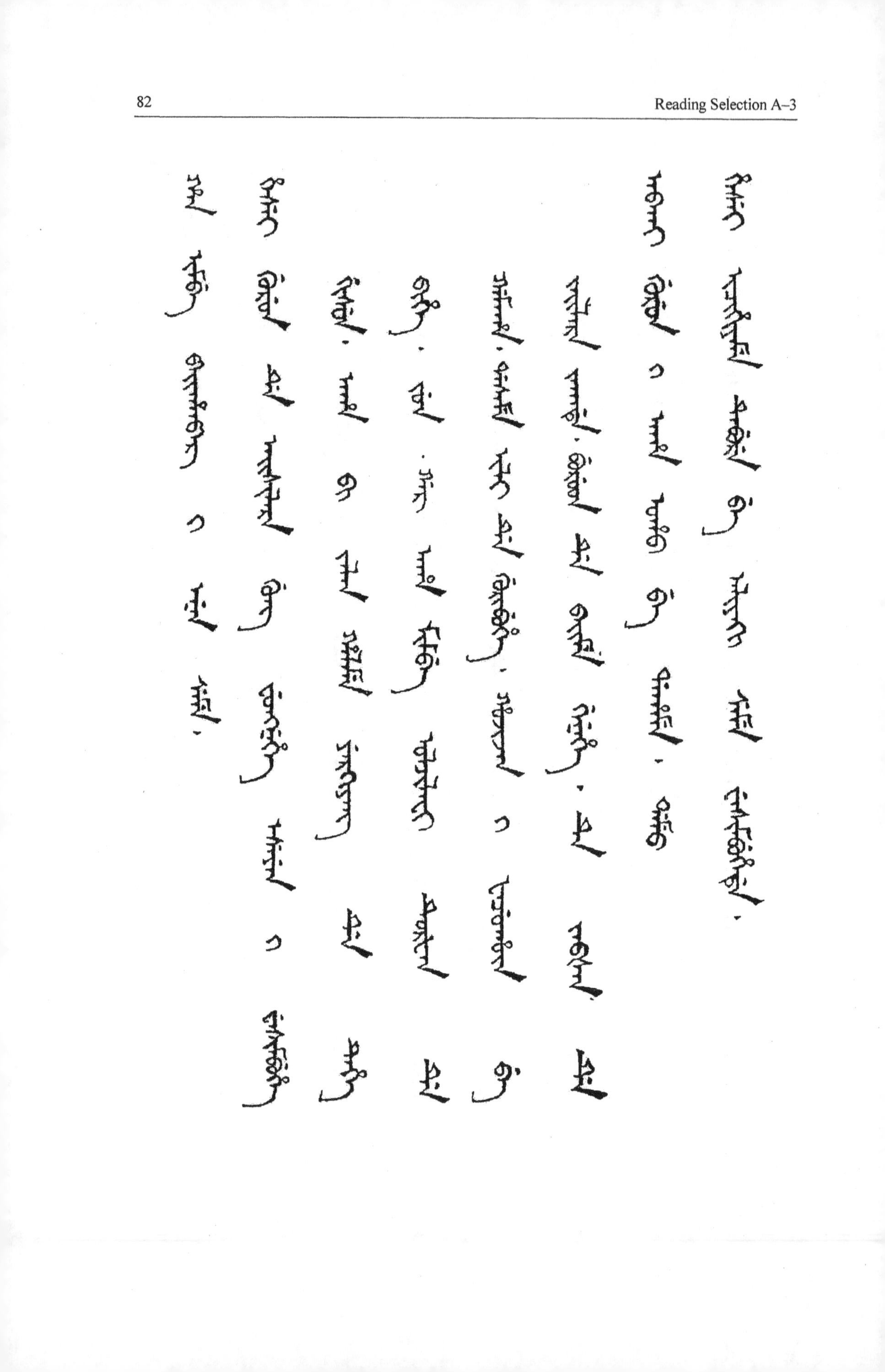

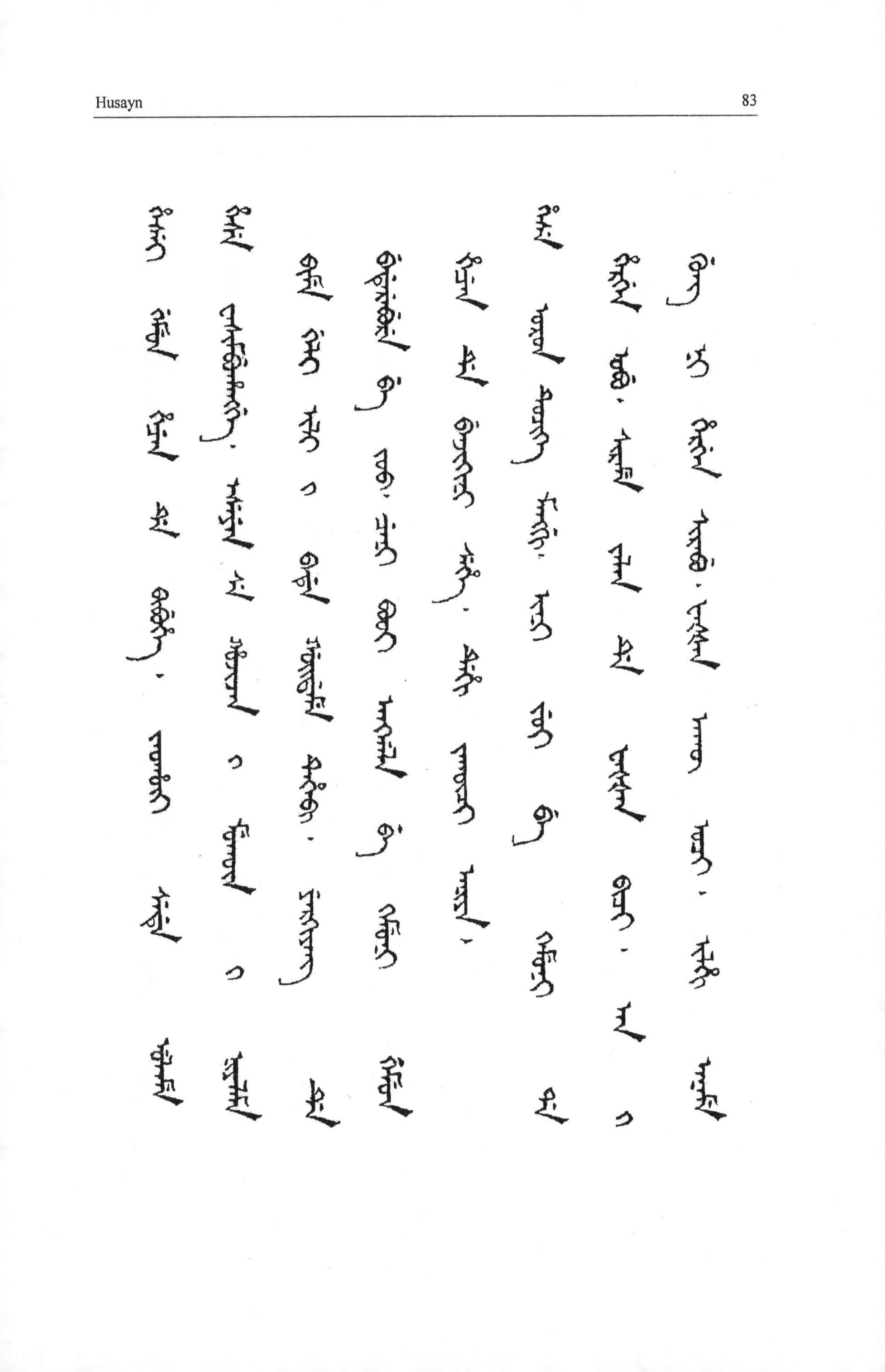

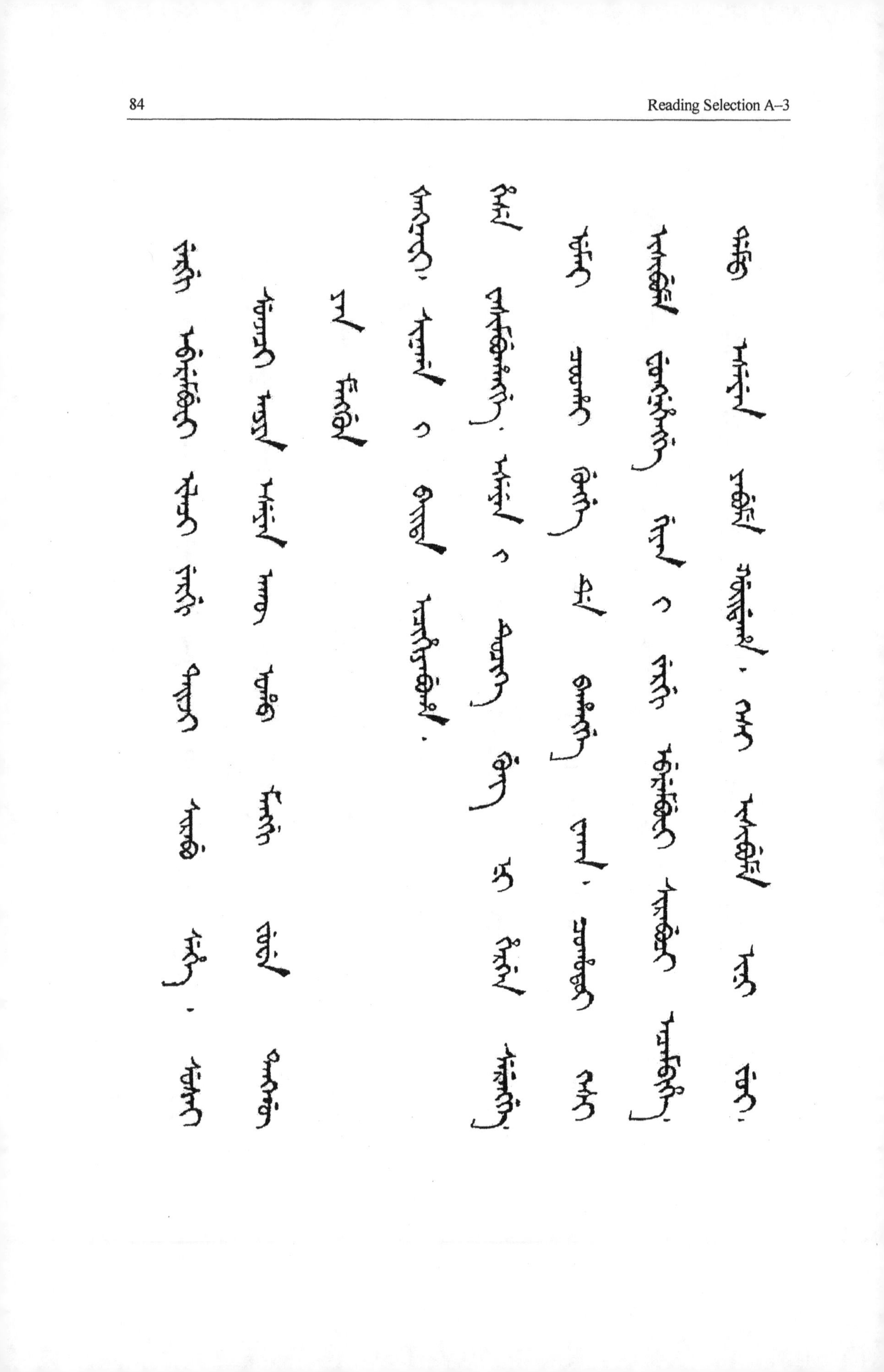

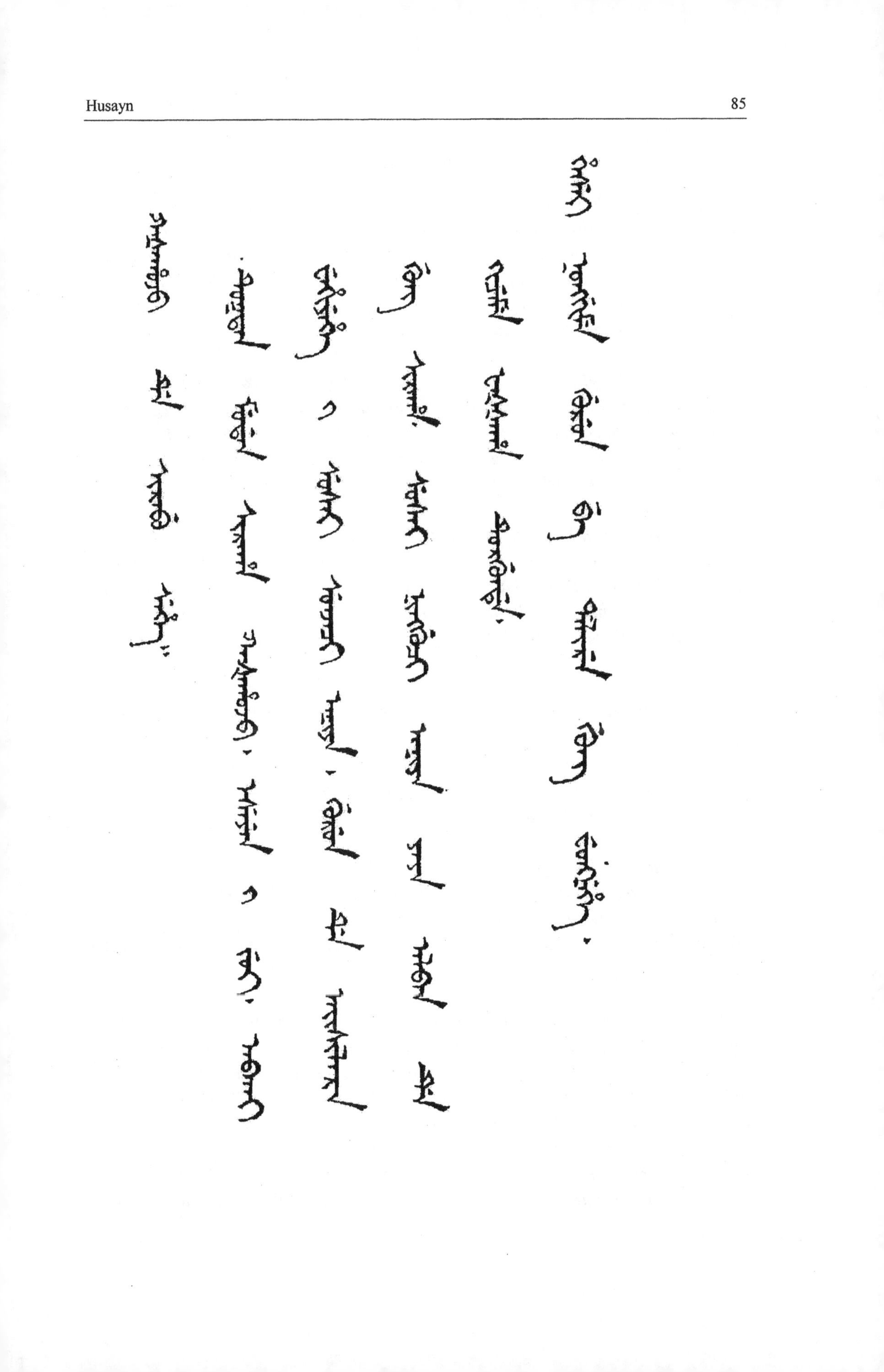

[illegible]

[illegible]

[illegible]

[illegible]

[illegible]

[illegible]

Transliteration

(75) *gurun de aisilara gung Eseyen i faidangga ulabun. gemun hecen de tehe hoise hergen inu. jalan sirara ilaci jergi taiji obume toktobuha.*[1] *Eseyen Yerkiyang ni niyalma. colo Erke hojo sembi. erei da sekiyen mafa gebu Paihanpar.*[2] *jalan halame hoise aiman i da ofi, Yerkiyang de tefi, ini mukūn i urse be kadalambi.*[3] *ceni mukūn i gubci yooni hojo seme tukiyehengge,*[4] *uthai Monggosoi mukūn i gubci yooni taiji seme tukiyehengge de adali. Jun gar etenggi ofi, Tsewang Rabtan*

(76) *Yerkiyang be gidanafi, hojo Ahamat be nakabufi, ini mukūn i urse be oljilafi Turfan de tebuhe. dahanduhai Turfan i urse dolo dahanjiha turgunde, geli ergeleme Ili de guribuhe. amba cooha Jun gar be toktobuha manggi, Eseyen se dahanjiki sembihe.*[5] *Ahamat i jui Hojijan geli Amursana i facuhūraha nashūn be amcame ini mukūn i urse be ergeleme Ili ci Yerkiyang de bedereki serede, Eseyen*

(77) *daharakū, Burut, Hoohan, Margalang, Anjiyan, Namagan, Tašigan i jergi aiman* [6] *de jailame gurinehe. ini deo Parsa, jai ini ahūn i jui Mamut, Turdu,*[7] *dahalame genehebi. Hojijan, Burut i baru kimulehe turgunde, cooha unggifi leheme gaici bahakū.*[8] *abkai wehiyehe i orin ilaci aniya amba cooha Hojijan be dailame Yerkiyang de isinaha be, Eseyen donjifi,*[9] *Turdu, jai* [10] *Burut i Hūsici otok i dalaha niyalma Narabatu i*

(78) *sasa cooha gaifi, Kašigar be afame Inggi Šar i jergi hoton be gidanaha. nerginde Hojijan, amba cooha be Kara Usu i bade eljere jakade, Hami i jasak beise Yusub, hiya Bujantai be Burut de cooha ganabume unggifi Atbaši bade isinaha manggi, terei dalaha niyalma Ming'ilha, cooha komso seme maraha. Bujantai bederefi mejigešeci,*[11] *«Hojijan i ahūn Buranidun Kašigar ci*

(79) *Yerkiyang be dame genere de, Burut i cooha ini hoton de necinjihe be donjifi, musei amba cooha de acaha dere seme kenehunjeme ofi, gelefi gelhun akū Kara Usu i kaha bade hanci latunahakū»*[12] *sembi. Burut i ya otok bihe be sarkū. orin duici aniya, Mamut, Burut ci Aksu de genefi, jecen be toktobure jiyanggiyūn Jaohūi de acafi, turgun be alaha bime,*[13] *geli*

(80) *Eseyen be Narabatu de cooha isabufi, musei coohai temgetu bithe be aliyame bi sehe*[14] *manggi, Jaohūi ulame hese wasimbume saišafi, suje šangnafi, Mamut de hendufi, Eseyen de bithe jasibuha. Eseyen cooha gaifi ebsi jidere de, jugūn de tanggū funcere hūlha be ucarafi gidafi, turun emke* [15] *bahafi, coohai kūwaran de alibufi, dolo dahanjiki seme baire jakade, Jaohūi ulhibume tohorombuha. Hojijan sa ukaha amala, Burut i*

(81) *cooha Kašigar i Bula gašan be afara jakade Eseyen ekšeme ini fejergi niyalma be takūrafi hiya Cengguwe be dahalabume, bithe unggifi ilibume henduhe gisun,*[16]

«Yerkiyang Kašigar be emgeri toktobuha. aika dasame cooha dosici, uthai amba cooha be eljerengge kai» sehe manggi, Burut i cooha teni bederehe. Jaohūi, Eseyen be unggifi, hargašanjibuha de,

(82) *han imbe Paihanpar i enen seme, hesei gurun de aisilara gung fungnehe. Eseyen i wesimbuhe gisun, «aha bi* [17] *jalan halame Yerkiyang de tehe bihe. Jun gar aha mimbe oljilafi Turfan de gamaha. dasame Ili de guribuhe. Hojijan i facuhūn be jailara jakade, Burut de baime genehe. te jabšan de abkai gurun i aha oho be dahame, damu hesei icihiyame tebure be aliyaki» seme wesimbuhede,*

(83) *hesei gemun hecen de bibuhe. Jaohūi sede ulame hese wasimbuhangge:*[18] *«Eseyen se Hojijan i mukūn i niyalma bime geli Ili i bade goidame tehebi. Yerkiyang de bederebure be joo.*[19] *ceni booi anggala be kemuni gemun hecen de benjikini» sehe. dehi jakūci aniya, hese «oron tucike manggi, ini jui be kemuni da hergen obu. sirame jalan de faššan bici, an i gung ni hergen sirabu. faššan akū oci, ilhi aname*

(84) *jergi eberembufi ilaci jergi taiji sirabu» sehe. susai sunjaci aniya Eseyen akū oho manggi, juwe tanggū yan menggun šangnafi, sinaga* [20] *i baita icihiyabuha. hese wasimbuhangge, «Eseyen i tucike gung ni hergen serengge, umai coohai gungge de bahangge waka.*[21] *cohotoi kesi isibume fungnehengge. giyan i jergi eberembufi sirabuci acambihe.*[22] *damu Eseyen yabume goidaha, kesi isibume ini jui*

(85) *Kašahojo de sirabu» sehe. tuktan mudan siraha Kašahojo, Eseyen i jui. abkai wehiyehe i susai sunjaci aniya, gurun de aisalara gung siraha. susai ningguci aniya yaya alban de kiceme faššaha turgunde, hesei nonggime gurun be dalire gung fungnehe.*

Vocabulary

adali	similar
aha	slave, servant
Ahamat	Ahmad (pers. name)
aika	if
alban	service, obligation (to a superior)
alibumbi	to present, to offer (to a superior)
alimbi	to receive
aliyambi	to wait
amala	after
amcambi	to take advantage of, to pursue
Amursana	(pers. name)
an i	same, continued
aname	in sequence, in order

anggala	individual, person
ba	place
baha	perfective participle of *bahambi*
bahambi	to obtain
baimbi	to request, to seek refuge
baru	toward, opposite
beise	Manchu title
benjimbi	to bring
bi	I (first person singular)
boo	house, family
Bula	(geogr. name)
Cengguwe	(pers. name)
ceni	their
-ci acambi	if…, it would be appropriate, should
-ci ombi	it is permissible to, one may
cohotoi	especially, particularly
colo (Chin. *hao* 號)	courtesy name, title
da	leader; original; same
da sekiyen	origin, source
da sekiyen mafa	founder of the lineage, progenitor
dahalambi	to accompany
dailambi	to attack, to fight
dalambi	to rule, to be chief
dambi	to aid, to help
damu	however, nevertheless, only, but
dolo dahambi	to submit
dolo dahanjimbi	to come to submit
eberembumbi	causative/passive of *eberembi*
ebsi	hither
ekšembi	to hasten, to hurry
emgeri	once, already
emke	one
enen	descendant
ere	this
ergelembi	to coerce
Erke	(pers. name)
Eseyen	Husayn (pers. name)
etenggi	strong
facuhūn	rebellion
facuhūrambi	to be in disorder, to be in confusion
faššambi	to exert oneself, to make a great effort
fejergi	under

funcembi	to be in excess of
gaimbi	to take
gamambi	to take to another place
ganambi	to go to take, to go to raise
gebu	name
gelembi	to fear
gelhun	fear
gidambi	to oppress, to press
giyan i	on principle, appropriately
goidambi	to last for a long time
gubci	entire, universal, all
gungge	merit, accomplishment
gurimbi	to move
gurun be dalire gung (Chin. *zhenguo jiangjun* 鎮國將軍)	defender-general of the state (H 382)
Hami	(geogr. name)
han	emperor, *khan*
hanci	near
Hojijan	(pers. name)
hojo	*khoja* (Muslim title)
Hūsici	name of Kirghiz tribal subdivision
icihiyambi	to arrange, put in order; prepare a body for funeral
ilimbi	to stop
imbe	him, her, it
Inggi Šar	Yanggishar (geogr. name)
isambi	to assemble
jabšan	fortune
jai	second, next, again, still
jailambi	to avoid, to get out of the way
jakūci	eighth
jasak	hereditary chief (Mongol title, H 35)
jasak beise	(official title)
jasimbi	to send
jergi	rank; sequence; layer; and so forth
jidere	irregular imperfective participle of *jimbi*
joombi	to cease, to stop
jui	son
kadalambi	to rule, to govern
Kašahojo	(pers. name)
kenehunjembi	to doubt, to suspect
kesi	favor, grace

kesi isibumbi	to bestow a favor
kicembi	to be diligent
kimulembi	to habor a grudge against
komso	few
kūwaran	camp
latumbi	to incite, to provoke; to glue; to attach
latunambi	to go to attack, to go to incite
lehembi	to demand
mafa	ancestor, grandfather
Mamut	Mahmut (pers. name)
Margalang	Marghiland (geogr. name)
mejigešembi	to spy
mejigešeci ... sembi	to find out by spying
menggun	silver
mimbe	me
Monggoso	Mongols
nakabumbi	to dismiss
nakambi	to stop, to leave a post
Namagan	(geogr. name)
Narabatu	(pers. name)
nashūn	opportunity, occasion
necimbi	to attack
-ngge	nominalizing verbal suffix
ni	genitive case marker (after *-ng*)
nonggimbi	to add, to increase
oljilambi	to take prisoner
oron	place, vacancy
Paihanpar	(pers. name)
Parsa	(pers. name)
saišambi	to commend
sekiyen	origin, source
sinagan	mourning
sinagan i baita	funeral
sirame	next
suje	silk
sunjaci	fifth
takūrambi	to send, to dispatch
Tašigan	Tashkent (geogr. name)
temgetu	seal
temgetu bithe	certificate, manifest, license
tohorombi	to calm down, become calm
toktobumbi	to decide,to determine; pass. of *toktombi*

Tsewang Raptan	(pers. name)
tukiyembi	to hold up, to honor
Turdu	(pers. name)
Turfan	(geogr. name)
turgun	situation; reason, motive
turun	military banner, standard
ucarambi	to meet, to encounter
ulambi	to transmit, to pass to, to pass on
ulame hese wasimbumbi	to transmit an edict
umai	at all (with negative)
wambi	to kill
wasimbi	to descend, to come down, to sink
wasimbumbi	to send down (order, edict); causative of *wasimbi*
ya	which (interrogative adjective)
yabumbi	to be active, to serve at a post
yan	tael (monetary unit)
yaya	whatsoever, ever
yooni	complete, altogether
Yusub	Yusuf (pers. name)

Notes

1. ***taiji obume toktobuha*:** 'it was determined to make him *taiji*'.

2. ***erei da sekiyen mafa gebu Paihanpar*:** 'as for the founder of his line, the name was Paihanpar'. This sentence consists of a subject (without a topic marker) and a predicate which is a noun.

3. ***kadalambi*:** 'were/had been governing'. Note the imperfective verb form.

4. ***ceni mukūn i gubci yooni hojo seme tukiyehengge uthai...gubci yooni taiji seme tukiyehengge de adali*:** lit. 'The honoring by the entire clan all saying *khoja* is like the entire Mongol clan all honoring (people) by saying *taiji*'. Invariable *-ngge*, added to the imperfective or perfective participle, nominalizes the verb (which then usually serves as sentence subject or topic). The verb nominalized with *-ngge* has several meanings: For example, *arahangge* can be translated as a) the writing, b) that which is written, c) that which he has written, d) the case of writing. Frequently, as is the case here, a sentence has a set of *-ngge* verbs, meaning A equals/does not equal B. See Review 4.

5. *dahanjiki sembihe*: 'he had been wanting to submit'. Combinations of a verb with a form of *bimbi* (e.g., *seme* + *bihe*) provide a means to express various nuances of aspects or tenses. Cf. Notes 13 and 14, and Review 8.

6. *Burut...Tašigan i jergi aiman*: 'Kirghiz tribes, such as those of Kokand...and Tashkent'.

7. *ini ahūn i jui Mamut, Turdu*: 'his elder brother's sons, Mahmut and Turdu'. Plural suffixes are commonly omitted.

8. *leheme gaici bahakū*: lit. 'demandingly he could not obtain', meaning that when he asked to have the *khoja*s sent back, the Kirghiz did not comply. The verbs *ombi* 'to be able to' and *acambi* 'it is appropriate' combine with *-ci* for similar constructions. With *mutembi* and *bahanambi*, both meaning 'to be able to', the preceding verb takes the coordinative suffix *-me*. Also see Review 7.

araci ombi	one can write, one may (is allowed to) write
araci acambi	one should (ought, must) write
araci acarakū	one should (ought, must) not write
arame mutembi	one is able to write
arame bahanambi	one is able to write

9. *amba cooha Yerkiyang de isinaha be Eseyen donjifi*: 'upon hearing that the imperial army had arrived in Yarkand, Husayn...'. The entire sentence is put into the accusative, as the object of *donjifi*. Note the differences between direct and indirect speech:

Direct speech: (subject) (predicate) *seme gisurehe*. Example: *cooha afanambi seme gisurehe* 'he said: "the troops will go to fight."' Often this structure is best translated into English as indirect speech: 'he said (that) the troops would go to fight'.

Indirect speech: There are two structures for indirect speech:

1. (subject) (predicate) *be* (*seme*) (finite verb);
2. (subject) *be* (predicate) (*seme*) (finite verb).

Examples:

1. *cooha isinaha be seme alaha.*
2. *cooha be isinaha seme alaha.*

Both sentences translate as 'he reported that the troops had arrived'.

10. ***jai*:** 'and'. Connects two equal nouns. 'Husayn together with Turdu and Narabatu'.

11. ***mejigešeci…sembi*:** 'when one spied… they said', i.e. one found out through spying. See Review 3.

12. ***gelefi gelhūn akū…latunahakū*:** lit. 'fearing did not strike without fear', meaning 'did not dare to attack'.

13. ***turgun be alaha bime…sehe manggi*:** 'having reported on the situation he said that…' *bime* is a converb to *sehe*.

14. ***Eseyen be…bithe be aliyame bi sehe*:** 'he said that Husayn was waiting for a letter'. *aliyame bi* is the present progressive form. Contracted it becomes *aliyambi*.

15. ***emke*:** *turun emke = emu turun.*

16. ***ilibume henduhe gisun*:** 'the words spoken to make them stop'.

17. ***aha bi*:** 'I, your slave'. Usually said by Manchus and Mongols when addressing the emperor. Husayn was a Muslim, but might also have been of Mongol descent since many Mongols in the region of the former Chagatai empire had converted to Islam. However, it is also possible that the members of the non-Mongol, Islamic elite enjoyed a status vis-a-vis the emperor that was similar to that of the Mongols and that they, too, used the term *aha*.

18. ***Jaohūi sede ulame hese wasimbuhangge…sehe*:** lit. 'that which one issued as an edict by transmitting it through Jaohūi said'. *hese wasimbuha* is substantivized and becomes the subject of *sehe*. The word *sede* is miswritten as *seden*.

19. ***bederebure be joo*:** 'don't make him return'.

20. ***sinaga i baita*:** should read *sinagan i baita*.

21. ***Eseyen i...hergen serengge umai cooha i gungge de bahangge waka*****:** lit. 'that which is called the rank of prince which Husayn has vacated is not at all something that he has obtained through military merit'. The word *de* here is used instrumentally, 'by merit'. Another example: *ejen i hese de* 'by order from the leader'.

22. ***giyan i sirabuci acambihe*****:** lit. 'if it is inherited it will have been appropriate'. Meaning: 'it should be inherited'. The word *giyan i* is not necessary, but often occurs with *-ci acambi*, adding emphasis, such as 'technically should'.

Review

1. Direct speech (Subject) (predicate) (*seme*, *gisurehe*, etc.)

Hošik geren hoton de «amba cooha isinjiha» seme bithe unggihe	Hošik sent a letter to the various towns saying: "The imperial army has arrived"
hese «hūda salibufi, mukūn i urse be ujikini» sehe	an edict said: "Appraise the value (of the property) and let it/him support his relatives"
Erdeni baksi hendume «julgeci jihe bithe be te adarame kūbulibumbi?» seme maraha	Erdeni Baksi refused and said: "Why now change the language that has come to us from ancient times?"

2. Indirect speech

A. (Subject) (predicate) *be* (*donjiha*, *sehe*, etc.)

Jaohūi geren hoton be toktobuha be niyalma donjiha	the people heard that Jaohūi had pacified all the towns
Burut i cooha ini hoton de necinjihe be donjifi	having heard that Kirghiz troops had come to his town to attack
Buranidun amba cooha isinaha be donjifi ukaha	upon hearing that the imperial army had arrived, Buranidun escaped
Hojijan amba cooha be eljere be donjire de	when he heard that Hojijan was resisting the imperial army

B. (Subject) *be* (predicate) (*sehe*, *donjiha*, etc.)

Hošik be akū oho donjiha	he heard that Hošik had died

Jaohūi Eseyen be yabume goidaha seme wesimbuhede	when Jaohūi memorialized saying that Husayn had served for a long time
Mamut Eseyen be bithe be aliyame bi sehe	Mahmut said that Husayn was waiting for a message

3. Direct and indirect speech with *-ci* + (*sehe*, *donjiha*, etc.)

tuwaci hoton etenggi sehe	he saw that the town was strong
donjici hoton i niyalma ukaha sehe	one heard that the people of the town had escaped
donjici ini ahūn hūlha de wabuha sembi	one heard that his brother was killed by bandits
Bujantai mejigešeci cooha isinaha be donjiha	Bujantai found out by spying that the troops had arrived

4. *-ngge*

hojo serengge taiji serengge de adali	saying *khoja* is similar to saying *taiji*
hese wasimbuhangge booi anggala be hecen de benjikini sehe	that which was issued as an edict said: "let him bring his family to the capital"
amba cooha be eljerengge kai	it will be a matter of taking on the imperial army
Eseyen i tucike hergen serengge cooha i gungge de bahangge waka	the rank which Husayn has vacated is not one he earned through military merits

5. *gelhūn akū*

gelhūn akū Kara Usu de latunahakū	he did not dare go and strike at Kara Usu
gelhūn akū amba cooha be eljerakū	he did not dare oppose the imperial army

6. Passive/causative

taiji obume toktobuha	one decided to make him *taiji*
Turfan de tebuhe	one had him reside in Turfan
urse be Ili de guribuhe	he made the people move to Ili
ini ahūn hūlha de wabuha	his brother was killed by the bandits

7. *-ci ombi, -ci acambi, -me mutembi, -me bahanambi*

geneci ombi	you can go, you may go
geneci ojorakū	you must not go
sirabuci acambi	he should be succeeded
bithe unggici acarakū	you should not send a letter
manju hergen be arame mutembi	he is able to write Manchu letters
Turfan de isiname mutehekū	they were unable to reach Turfan
ini mukūn i urse be kadalame bahanambi	he is able to rule the people of his clan
manju gisun i arame bahanarakū	we don't know how to write in Manchu

8. Compound tenses

bithe be aliyame bi	he is waiting for a letter
Eseyen dahanjiki sembihe	Husayn had wanted to submit
hecen de tehe bi	he had been living in the capital
Burut be dalaha bihe	he used to be chief of the Khirgiz
bargiyarakū bihe	he had not received (them)
turgun be alaha bime	having reported on the situation
ini deo jai ini ahūn dahalame genehebi	his younger and older brother had gone along with him

9. Write in Manchu script and translate into English: a) *Eseyen hoise hergen inu*; b) *colo Erke hojo sembi*; c) *ini mukūn i urse be kadalambi;* d) *tere be ume nakabure*; e) *Burut i baru kimulehe turgunde*; f) *han imbe Paihanpar i enen seme gurun de aisilara gung fungnehe*; g) *hese i nonggime gung ni hergen fungnehe*; h) *oron tucike manggi*; i) *sirame jalan de faššan bici*; j) *tere hergen cooha i gungge de bahaburakū*; k) *yaya alban de kicehe*; l) *suje be šangnafi bithe jasibuha*; m) *facuhūn be jailara jakade*; n) *Bujantai be Burut de cooha ganabume unggifi*; o) *Hošik be afaha Narabatu Burut i otok i dalaha niyalma*; p) *donjici Eseyen isinaha be sehe.*

10. Translate into Manchu: a) because Husayn did not go along; b) Hojijan returned to that place; c) he had been ruling the people of his clan for generations; d) using (saying) the title *hojo* is like using (saying) the title *taiji*; e) because the Manchu language is easy; f) because his family had been leaders for generations; g) when he requested to submit; h) fortunately I have now become a subject of your country; i) let him bring the people of his household to the capital; j) he should come for an audience; k) the same rank may be inherited; l) after Husayn died the funeral was arranged; m) he was granted one hundred and fifty taels of silver; n) one did not know which Kirghiz tribe it was; o) having met with Jaohūi, he reported on the situation; p) don't take advantage of the rebellion.

Reading Selection A-4

Hasim

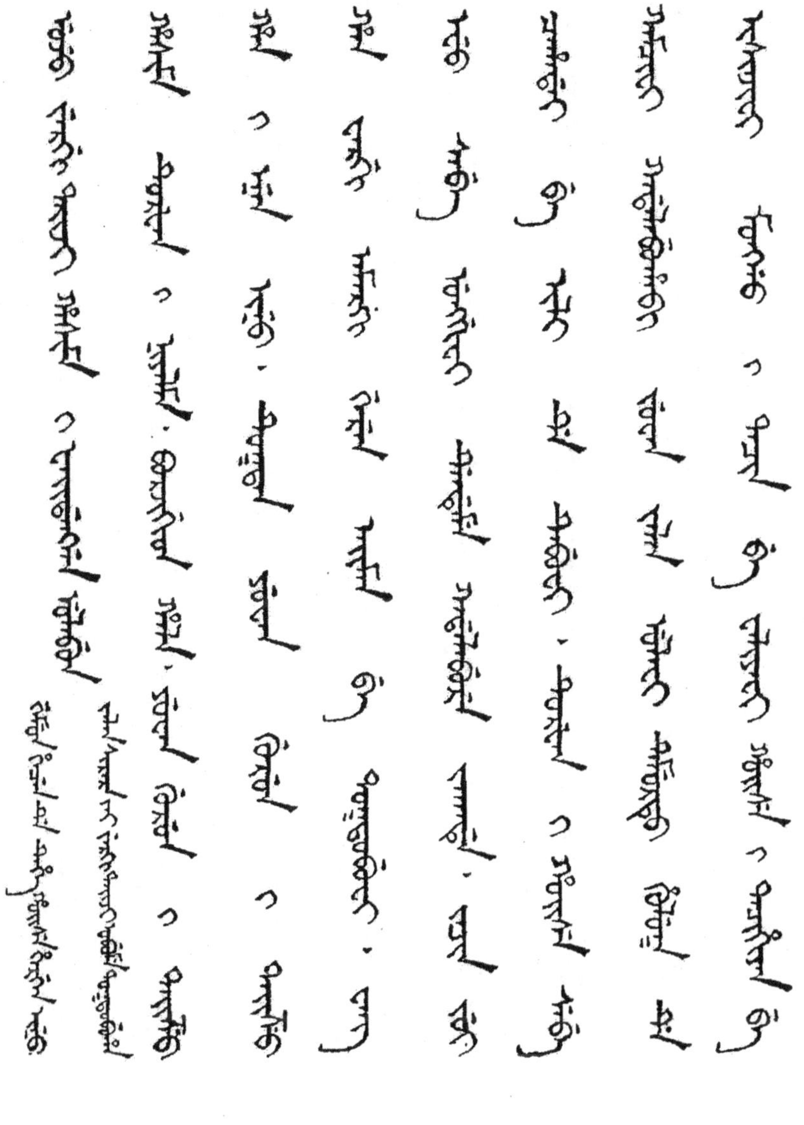

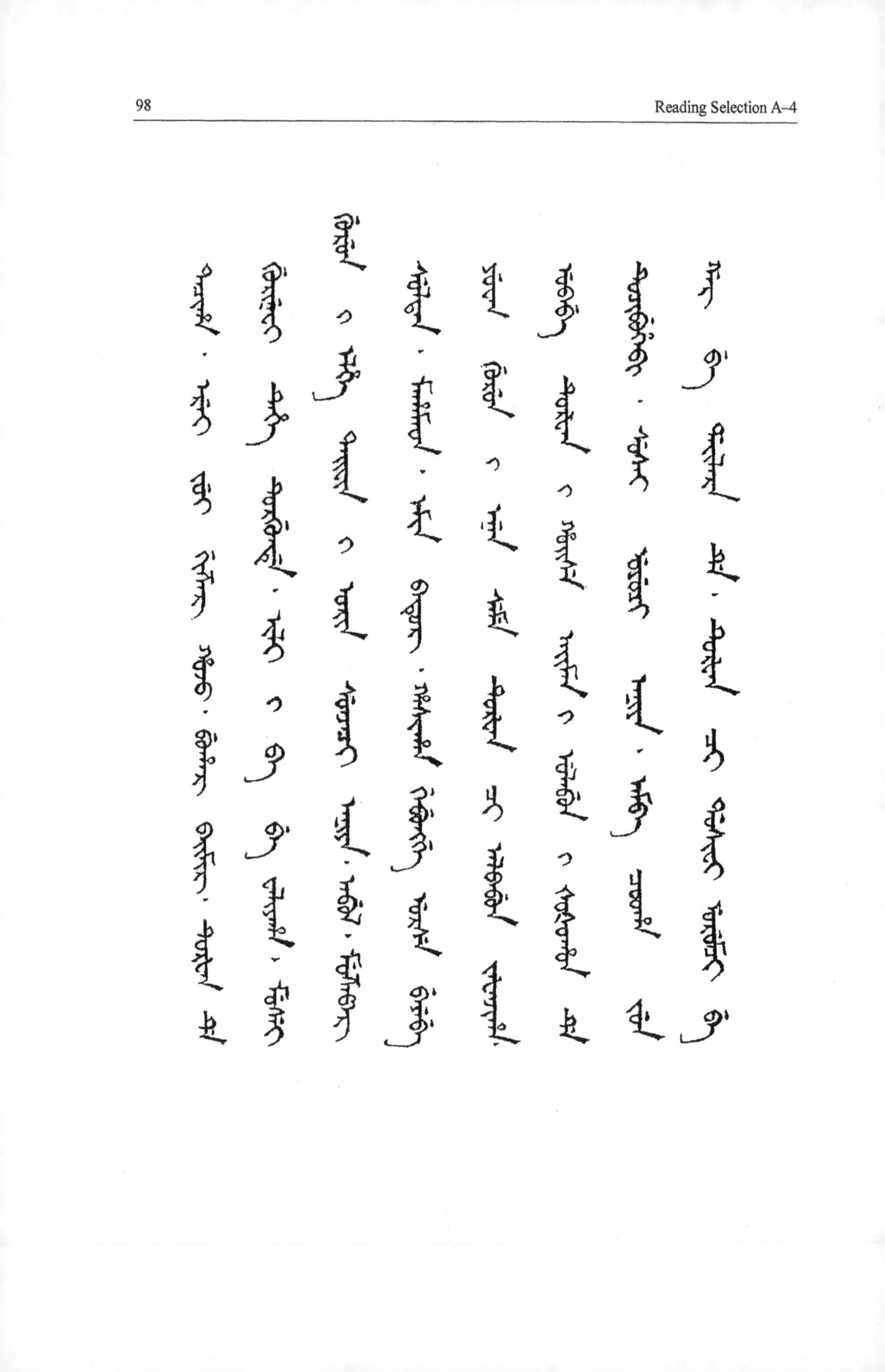

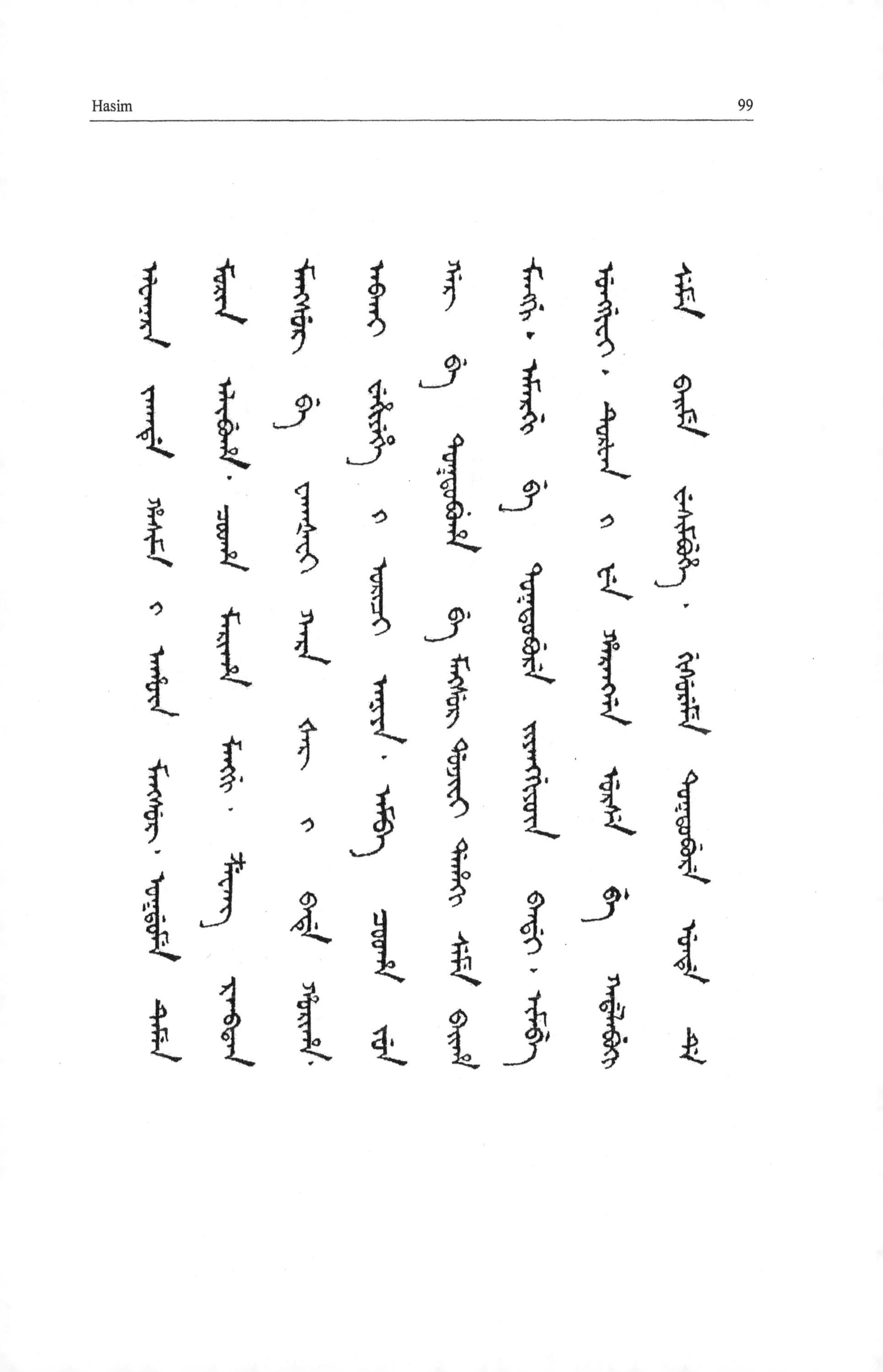

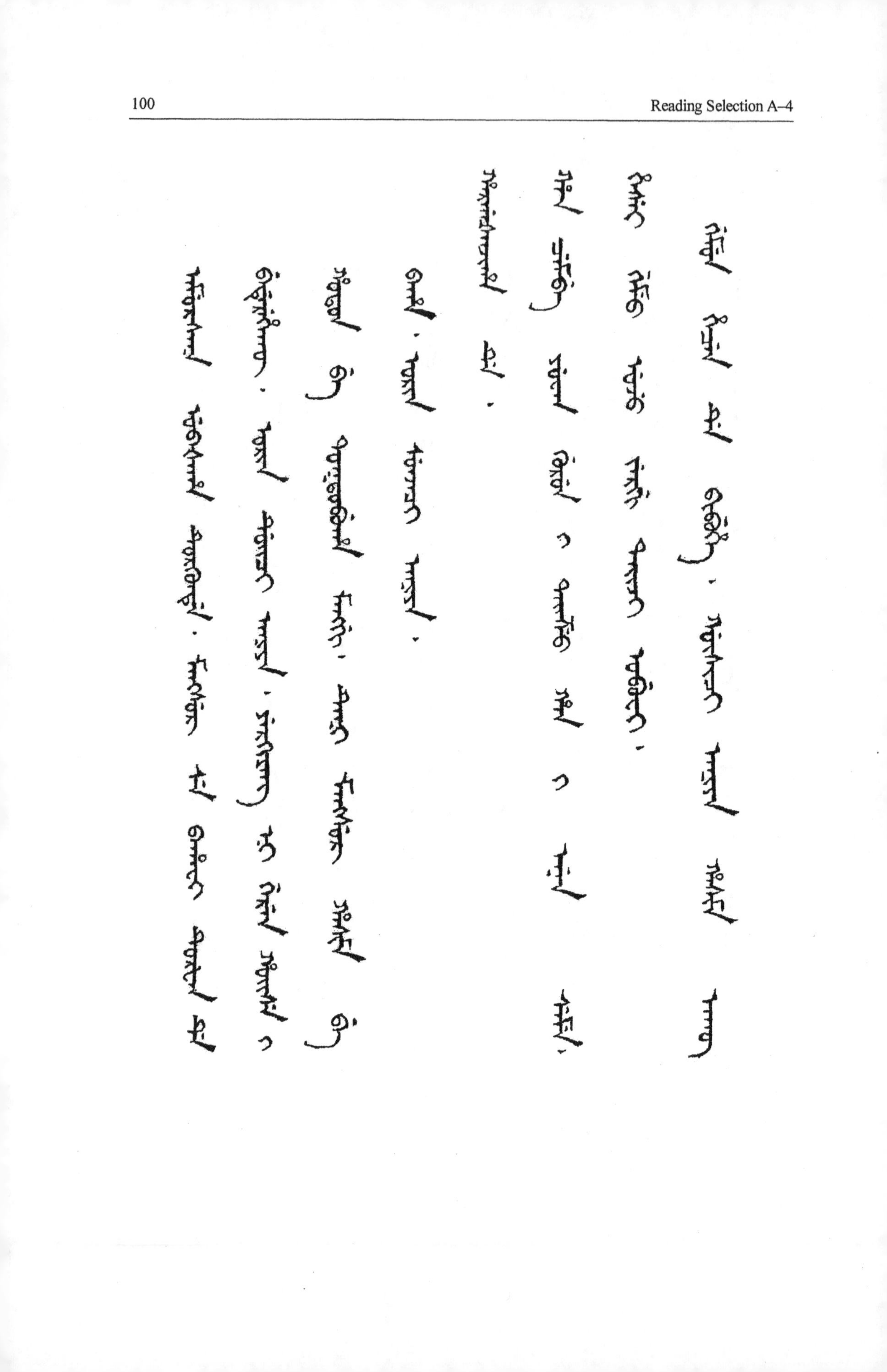

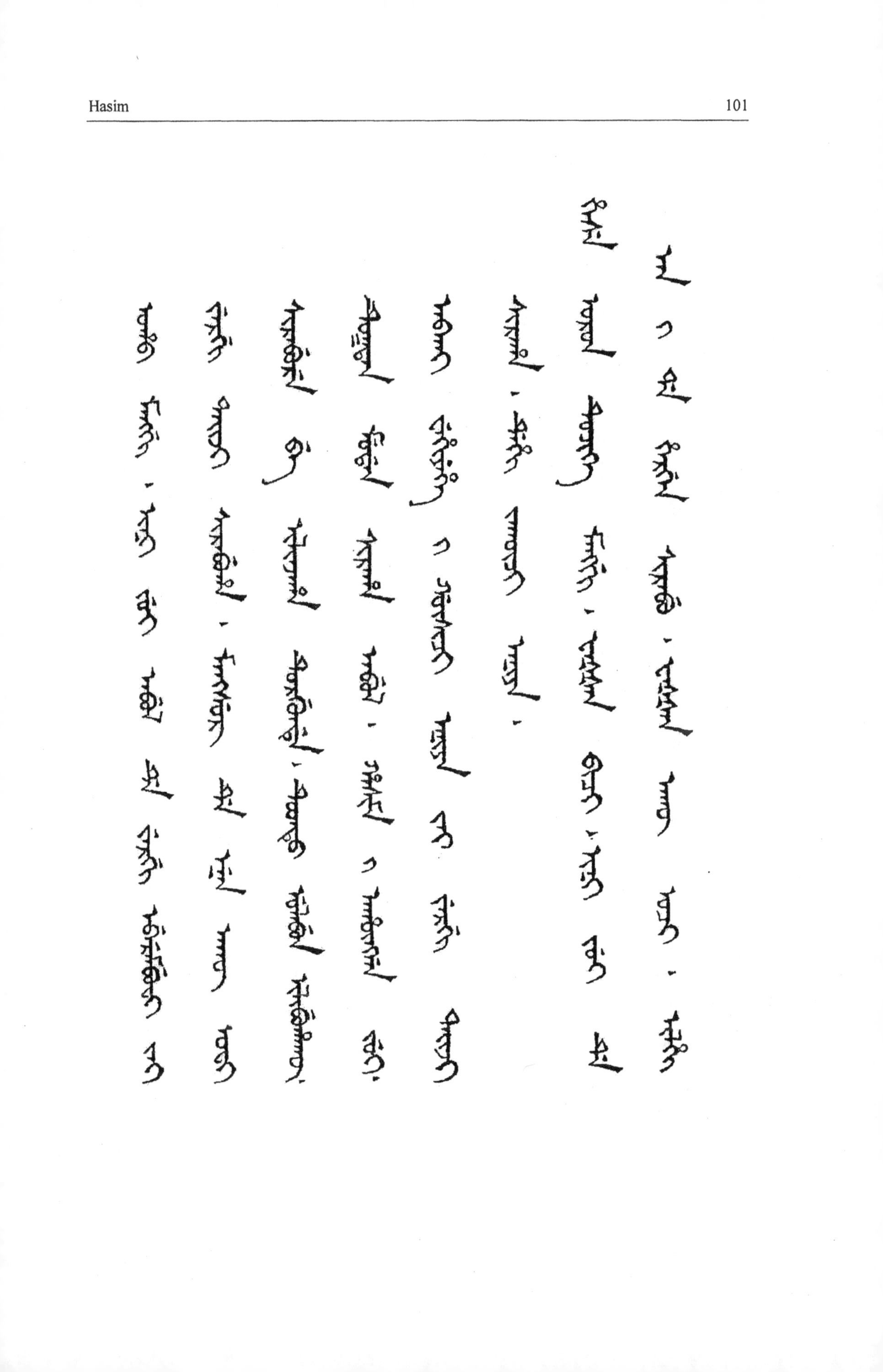

[illegible]

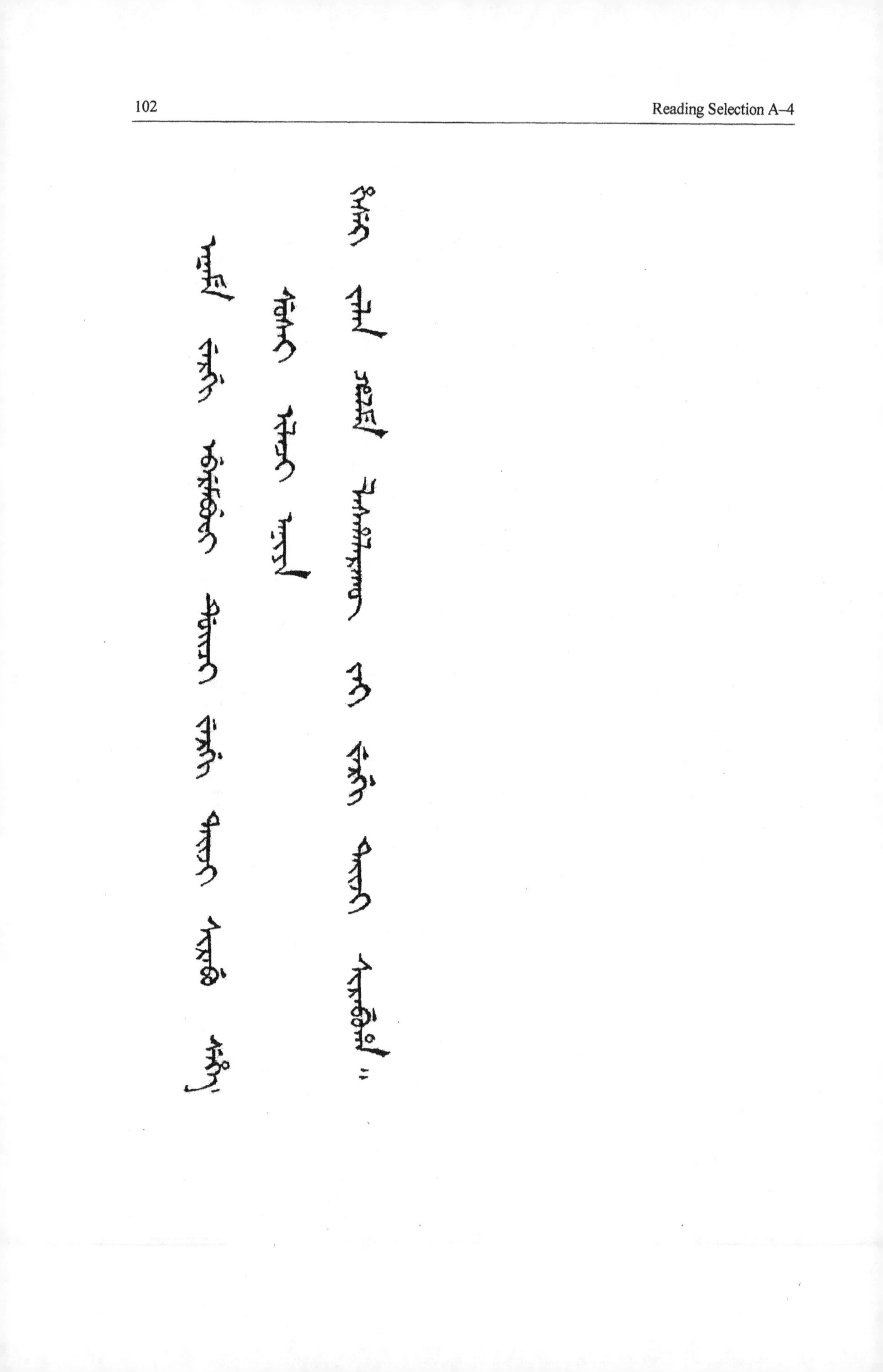

Transliteration

(97) *uju jergi taiji Hasim i faidangga ulabun. gemun hecen de tehe hoise hergen inu. jalan sirara jai jergi taiji obume toktobuha. Hasim Turfan i niyalma. Borjigit hala. Yuwan gurun i taidzu han i enen inu. tuktan Yuwan gurun i taidzu han wargi amargi* [1] *geren aiman be toktobufi, wang efu sabe unggifi dendeme kadalabure jakade, jacin jui Cahadai be Ili de tebufi, Turfan i hoise sebe kamcifi kadalabuhabi.*[2] *juwan jalan ulafi Temurtu Huluk de isinjifi, Monggo i tacin be waliyafi hoise i tacihiyan be*

(98) *taciha. ѐrei jui Gidzar Hojo, Buhar Baimir, Turfan de gurinefi tehe turgunde, Ili i ba be waliyaha. musei gurun i elhe taifin i orin sunjaci aniya, Abul, Mudzapar, Sultan, Mahamat, Emin Batur, Hasihan gebungge urse* [3] *beyebe Yuwan gurun i enen seme* [4] *Turfan ci albabun jafanjiha. ubabe Turfan i hoise aiman i ulabun i šošohon de tucibuhebi.*[5] *susai uyuci aniya amba cooha Jun gar be dailara de, Turfan ci dosifi Urumci be*

(99) *afanara jakade Hasim i ahūn Mangsur, okdome temen morin alibuha. cooha mariha manggi, Tsewang Rabtan Mangsur be wakašafi Kara Šar i bade horiha. abkai wehiyehe i orici aniya, amba cooha Jun gar be toktobuha be Mangsur donjifi* [6] *dahaki seme baiha manggi, amargi be toktobure jiyanggiyūn Bandi, imbe unggifi, Turfan i fe harangga urse be kadalabuki seme baime wesimbuhe. gisureme toktobure unde de*

(100) *Amursana ubašaha turgunde, Mangsur se bahafi Turfan de bederehekū.*[7] *orin duici aniya, Yerkiyang ni geren hoise i hoton be toktobuha manggi, teni Mangsur Hasim be baha. orin sunjaci aniya, hargašanjiha de han cembe Yuwan gurun i taidzu han i enen seme hesei gemu uju jergi taiji obufi, gemun hecen de bibuhe. gūsici aniya Hasim akū*

(101) *oho manggi, ini jui Abul de jergi eberembufi jai jergi taiji sirabuha.*[8] *Mangsur de enen akū* [9] *ofi sirabure be ilinjaha turgunde, tuttu ulabun ilibuhakū. tuktan mudan siraha Abul, Hasim i ahūngga jui. abkai wehiyehe i gūsici aniya jai jergi taiji siraha. dehi jakūci aniya, hese «oron tucike manggi, faššan bici, ini jui de an i da hergen sirabu. faššan akū oci, ilhi*

(102) *aname jergi eberembufi duici jergi taiji sirabu» sehe. susai ilaci aniya, hesei jalan halame lashalarakū jai jergi taiji sirabuha.*

Vocabulary

Abul	(pers. name)
albabun	tribute
albabun jafambi	to bring tribute
alibumbi	causative of *alimbi*; to present, to offer

amargi	north; back, behind
amargi be toktobure jiyanggiyūn (Chin. *dingbei jiangjun* 定北將軍)	general for pacifying the north, general (name), pacifier of the north
Bandi (Chin. *Bandi* 班第)	(pers. name)
beye	self
bira	river
Borjigit	Borjigid (name of Chinggis Khan's clan)
Buhar Baimir	(pers. name)
Cahadai	Chaghadai (pers. name)
cembe	them
dergi	east, eastern; top, above, upper
efu (plural *–te*)	husband of imperial princess, husband of elder sister or of wife's elder sister
elhe	peace
elhe taifin	Kangxi period
erin	time, season
Emin Batur	(pers. name)
fe	old
gebungge	named
Gidzar	(pers. name)
gūsici	thirtieth
hala	clan, family, family name
Hasihan	(pers. name)
Hasim	(pers. name)
horimbi	to imprison
ilimbi	to stand, to set up
ilinjambi	to stop (v.t.)
isinjimbi:	to arrive, to reach
jacin	second, other
jafambi	to take
julergi	south; front, in front of
kamcimbi	to place close together; to serve concurrently; to do at the same time
kamcifi kadalambi:	to rule or administer concurrently
Kara Šar	Karashar (geogr. name)
kemuni	still, yet; often
kemuni unde	not yet, still not
Mahamat	(pers. name)
Mangsur	(pers. name)
marimbi	to return, to go back
morin	horse
Mudzapar	Musaffar (pers. name)

okdombi	to go out to meet; to greet; to engage the enemy
orici	twentieth
se bahambi	to become old
Sultan	(pers. name)
šošohon	compilation, summary
tacihiyan	religion; teaching, training
tacin	customs; religion; learning, skill
taifin	peace
temen	camel
Temurtu Huluk	Tughluk Temur (pers. name)
tucibumbi	to cause to come out; to publish
tuttu	thus
uba	this place
ubašambi	to rebel, to turn against
uju	head, first
unde (w/imperfect)	not yet, before
Urumci	Urumchi (geogr. name)
uyuci	ninth
wakašambi	to accuse, to blame
wargi	west; under, underneath; right (side)
wargi amargi	northwest, northwestern
Yuwan gurun	Yuan dynasty

Notes

1. ***wargi amargi geren aiman***: 'all the northwestern tribes'. Directional words can function as modifiers (as is the case here), postpositions or nouns. See Review 2.

2. ***Turfan i hoise sebe kamcifi kadalabuhabi***: 'had him concurrently govern the Turfan Muslims (besides Ili)'.

3. ***Abul, Mudzapar, Sultan, Mahamat, Emin Batur, Hasihan gebungge urse***: Punctuation seems to indicate that six people are involved. However, unless names and identities are known, one cannot be certain.

4. ***beyebe Yuwan gurun i enen seme***: 'saying that they were descendants of the Yuan dynasty'. Indirect speech with subject (*beyebe*) in the accusative.

5. *ubabe Turfan i hoise aiman i ulabun i šošohon de tucibuhebi*: lit. 'one has caused this place to come out in the summary of biographies of the Turfan Muslim tribes'. Meaning: 'this place has been dealt with in the general section of the biographies of the Turfan Muslim tribes'.

6. *amba cooha Jun gar be toktobuha be Mangsur donjifi*: 'after Mangsur heard that the imperial troops had pacified the Dzungars'. Indirect speech, with the entire sentence in the accusative.

7. *Mangsur se bahafi Turfan de bederehekū*: 'Mangsur and his people were unable to return to Turfan'. This is a special construction in which *bahambi*, usually in the *-fi* form, precedes the finite verb to express the meaning of 'to manage', or 'to be able to'. See Review 1. In another context this sentence could mean 'Mangsur having gotten old, could not return to Turfan'. See Review 1.

8. *ini jui Abul de jergi eberembufi jai jergi taiji sirabuha*: 'he was succeeded by his son Abul as a second rank *taiji*, the rank having been reduced by one grade'; or, 'the rank of second rank *taiji*, having been reduced by a grade, was inherited by his son Abul'.

9. *Mangsur de enen akū*: lit. 'there were no descendants to Mangsur'. Meaning: 'Mangsur did not have any descendants'.

Review

1. *bahafi* + finite verb 'to be able, to manage'

bahafi ukafi bederehe	he managed to escape and return
si adarame bahafi ubade jihe?	how did you manage to come here?
tere erinde bahafi tuwanjihakū	at that time he was unable to come and see (you)
Mangsur se bahafi Turfan de bederehekū	Mangsur and his people were unable to return to Turfan

2. Directionals

amargi jugūn	the northern route
amargi ergi de hafunacibe	though it connects to the northern side

hoton i dergi julergi ergi	the southeastern side of the town
bira i dergi	the east (side) of the river
amargi be toktobure jiyanggiyūn	the general who pacifies the north

3. *(kemuni)* … *unde* 'not yet', ***unde de*** 'before'

tere isinjire unde	he has not yet arrived
tere kemuni jidere unde	he has not yet come
emu biya ojoro unde	less than a month ago
toktobure unde de	before it was determined

4. Write in Manchu script and translate into English: a) *wargi amargi geren aiman be toktobuha*; b) *wang efu sabe unggifi*; c) *dendeme kadalabumbi*; d*) jakūn jalan ulafi*; e) *hoise i tacihiyan be taciha*; f) *Mangsur be wakašafi horiha*; g*) gisureme toktobure unde de*; h) *Mangsur bahafi Turfan de bederehekū*; i) *jergi eberembufi taiji sirabuha*; j) *sirabure be ilinjaha*; k) *jalan halame lashalarakū taiji sirabuha.*

5. Translate into Manchu: a) the twenty-fifth year of Kangxi; b) he abandoned the capital; c) the people of Turfan came to bring tribute; d) Mangsur went to meet (them) and offered horses; e) because Mangsur had no descendants; f) a biography was established; g) the Muslim tribes of Turfan said they were descendants of the Mongol dynasty; h) Turfan is dealt with in the summary of the biographies of the Muslim tribes; i) by decree the hereditary rank of second degree *taiji* was inherited; j) he requested to submit; k) after Amursana rebelled Mangsur was unable to return to Turfan (use *bahambi* construction).

Reading Selection A–5

Abdurman

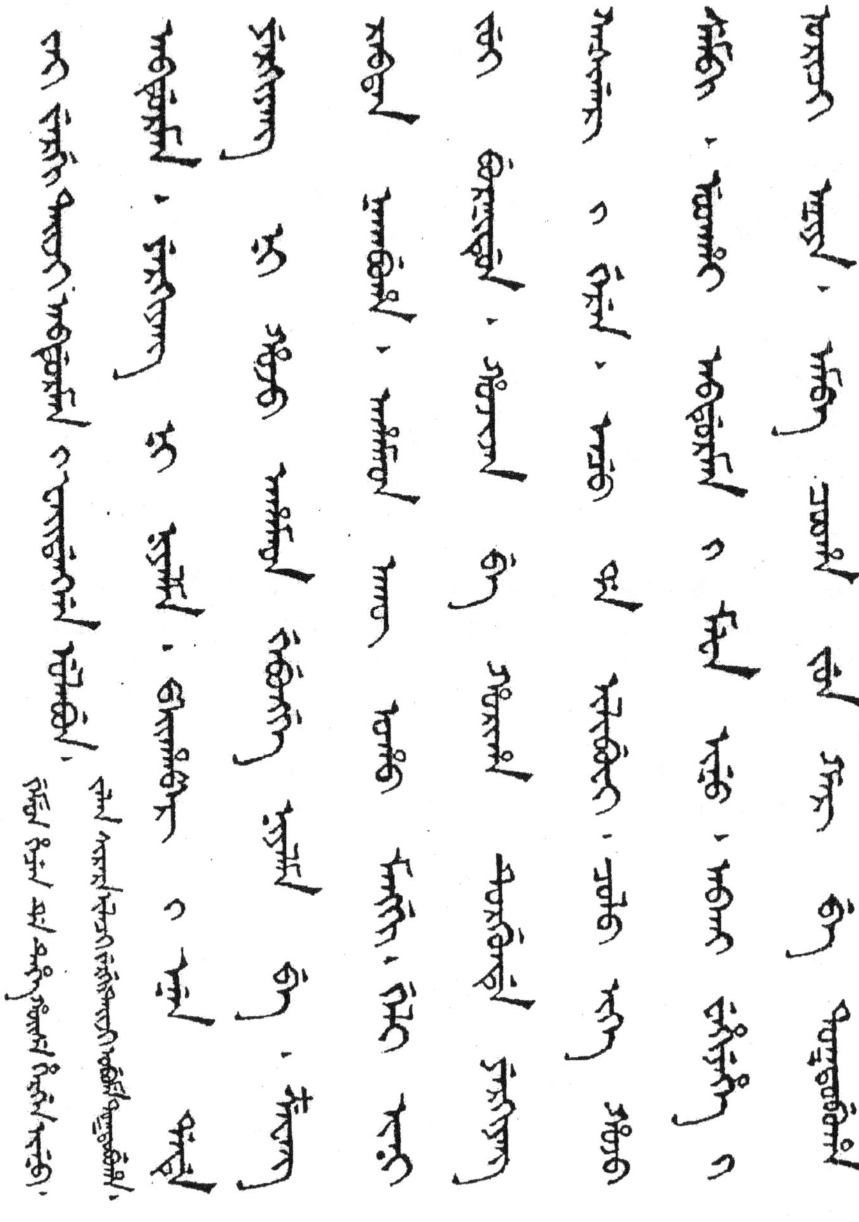

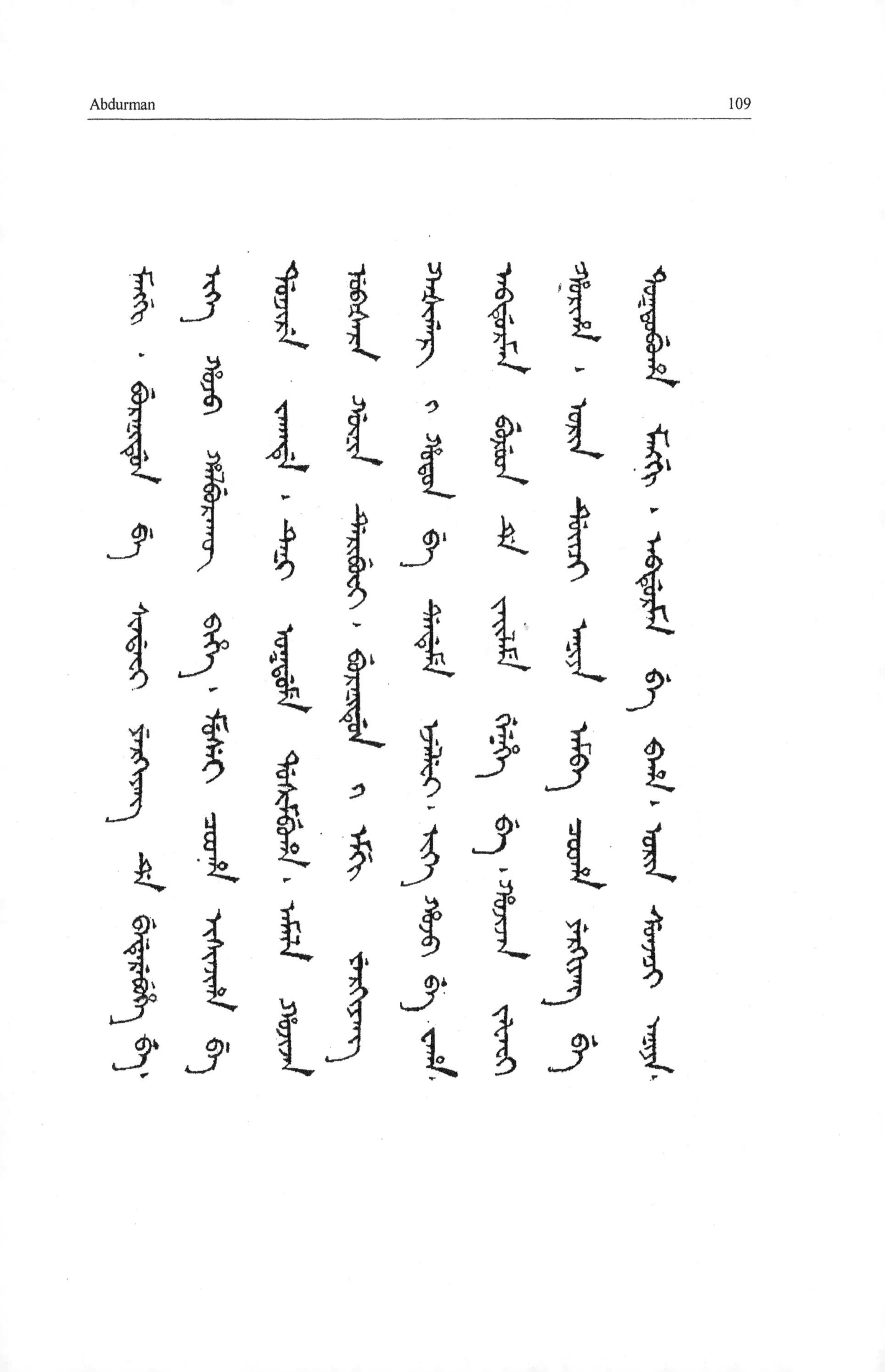

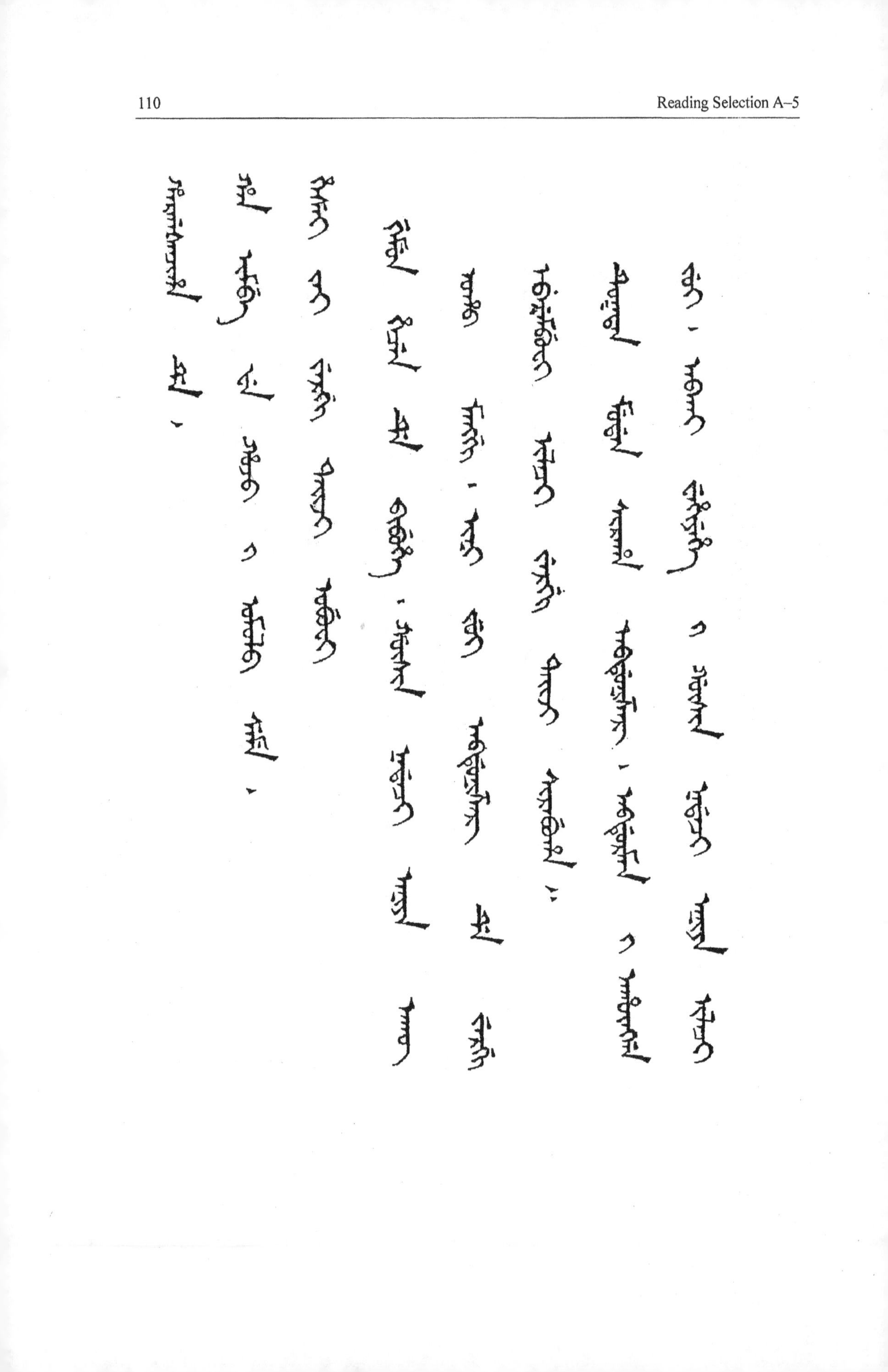

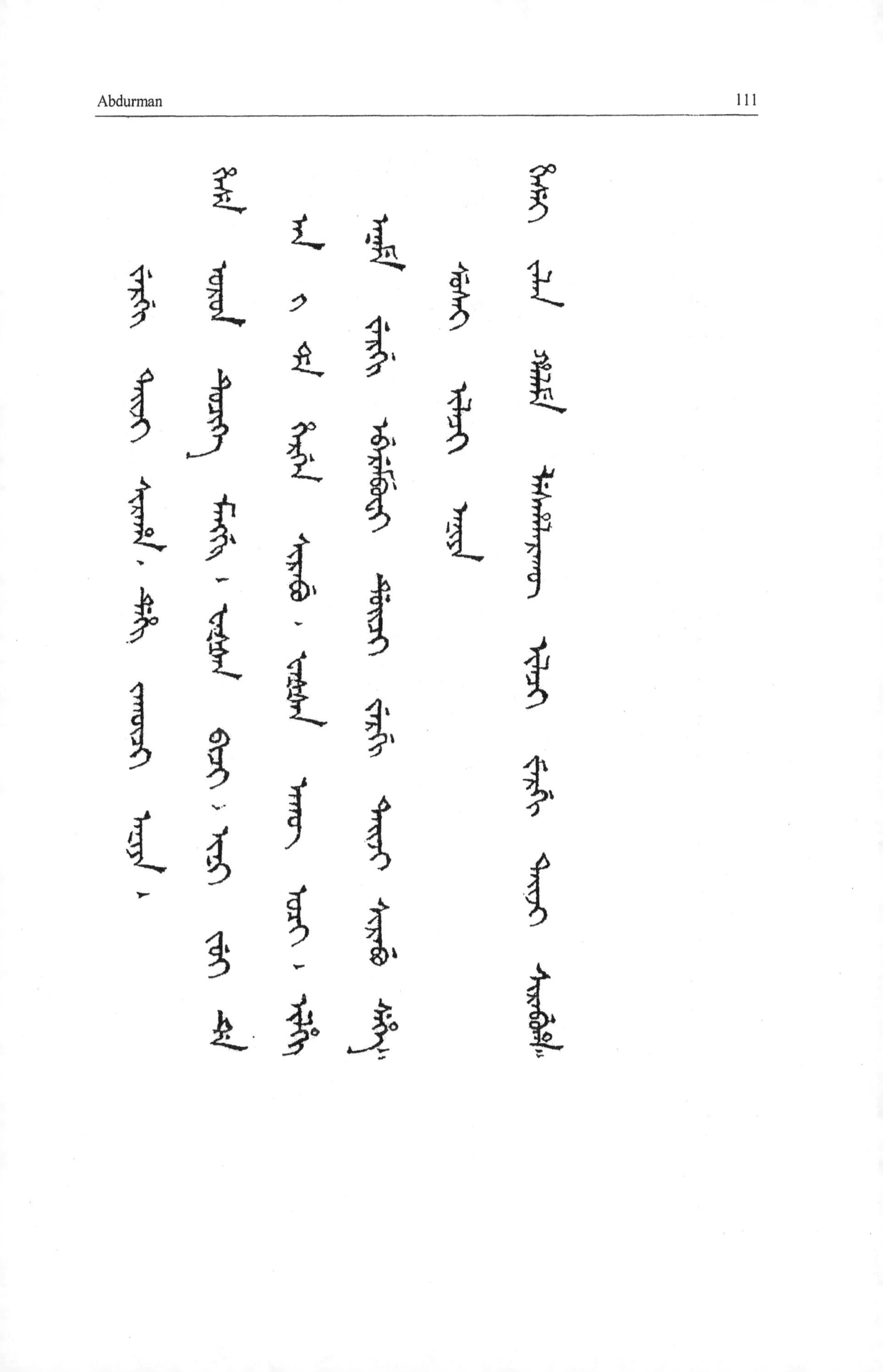

Transliteration

(108) *jai jergi taiji Abdurman i faidangga ulabun: gemun hecen de tehe hoise hergen inu. jalan sirara ilaci jergi taiji obume toktobuha. Abdurman, Yerkiyang ni niyalma. Paihanpar i enen. dade Yerkiyang ni hojo Ahamat gebungge niyalma be, Tsewang Rabtan nakabuha. Ahamat akū oho manggi, geli ini jui Buranidun, Hojijan be horiha turgunde, Yerkiyang Kašigar i geren encu da ilibufi, colo Ike hojo sembi. uthai* [1] *Abdurman i mafa inu. abkai wehiyehe i orici aniya, amba cooha Jun gar be toktobuha*

(109) *manggi, Buranidun be sindafi, Yerkiyang de bederebuhe be Ike hojo halburakū bihe.*[2] *musei cooha isinjiha be donjire jakade, teni okdome dosimbuha. amala* [3] *Hojijan ubašara gūnin deribufi, Buranidun i emgi Yerkiyang Kašigar i hoton be dendeme ejelefi, Ike hojo be waha. Abdurman Burut de jailame genehe be Hojijan jafafi horiha.*[4] *orin duici aniya amba cooha Yerkiyang be toktobuha manggi, Abdurman be baha. orin sunjaci aniya*

(110) *hargašanjiha de han imbe fe hojo i omolo seme* [5] *hesei jai jergi taiji obufi gemun hecen de bibuhe. gūsin nadaci aniya akū oho manggi, ini jui Abdunidzar de jergi eberembufi ilaci jergi taiji sirabuha. tuktan mudan siraha Abdunidzar, Abdurman i ahūngga jui. abkai wehiyehe i gūsin nadaci aniya ilaci*

(111) *jergi taiji siraha. dehi jakūci aniya, hese «oron tucike manggi, faššan bici, ini jui de an i da hergen sirabu. faššan akū oci, ilhi aname jergi eberembufi duici jergi taiji sirabu» sehe. susai ilaci aniya hesei jalan halame lashalarakū ilaci jergi taiji sirabuha.*

Vocabulary

Abdunidzar	(pers. name)
Abdurman	(pers. name)
amala	after; later; behind
dendeme	separately, by dividing
ejelembi	to rule, to establish control over
geren	people, multitude; the various
gūnin	intention
gūsin	thirty
halbumbi (w/accusative)	to give entrance to, to give shelter to
horimbi	to imprison
Ike	(pers. name)
ilibumbi	to set up; to stop
jafambi:	to arrest; to seize, to grip; to collect (taxes)
omolo	grandson
sindambi	to release

ubašambi	to rebel, to turn against
wambi	to kill

Notes

1. ***uthai*:** 'then, immediately'; often used as equivalent to Chinese *jiu.shi* 就是.

2. ***Buranidun be sindafi Yerkiyang de bederebuhe be Ike hojo halburakū bihe*:** 'Ike *khoja* did not give entrance to Buranidun whom one had released and allowed to return to Yarkand'. *Buranidun...bederebuhe be* can be considered either the topic for the sentence or the object to *halburakū*. See Review 1.

Note that titles, like *taiji* and *khoja*, may occur either before or after the name. In this piece Abdurman is referred to as *jai jergi taiji Abdurman* and Ike as *Ike hojo*. In Reading Selection A–3 we encountered *hojo Ahamat* and *Erke hojo*. It is not clear what determines the position of the title.

3. ***amala*:** 'later, after, behind'. In the meaning of 'later' *amala* is an adverb and may occur at the beginning of a sentence. As 'behind' *amala* is a postposition, taking the genitive. Example: *booi amala* 'behind the house'.

4. ***Abdurman Burut de jailame genehe be Hojijan jafafi horiha*:** 'Hojijan captured Abdurman (who was) on his way to escape to the Buruts and imprisoned him'. *Abdurman...genehe be* is the topic of the sentence or the object to *jafafi*.

5. ***han imbe fe hojo i omolo seme*:** Though this type of *seme* construction is indirect speech, it comes close to the meaning of 'because'. Meaning: 'The *khan* made him *taiji* because he was the grandson of the former *khoja*'. See Review 2.

Review

1. Topic marker or object

Abdurman Burut de jailame genehe be Hojijan horiha	Hojijan imprisoned Abdurman who had escaped to the Kirghiz
Fude isinjiha be Ūdui ini jui be takūrafi okdobuha	Ūdui sent his son to meet Fude who had arrived

Hojijan hoton be dosika be musei cooha sarkū	our army did not know that Hojijan had entered the town
Buranidun juwe tanggū hūlha be gaifi Kašigar de dosika be amba cooha gidaha	the imperial army defeated Buranidun who had taken 200 rebels and entered Kashgar

2. *seme* 'because'

han imbe fe hojo i omolo seme taiji obuha	the *khan* made him *taiji* because he was the grandson of the former *khoja*
Abul, Mudzapar beyebe Yuwan gurun i enen seme Turfan ci albabun jafanjiha	Abul and Musaffar came to bring tribute from Turfan on the grounds that they were descendants of the Yuan dynasty
han cembe Yuwan gurun i Taidzu han i enen seme hesei gemu uju jergi taiji obuha	the *khan* by edict made both of them first rank *taiji* on the grounds that they were descendants of the Taizu emperor of the Yuan dynasty

3. Write in Manchu script and translate into English: a) *encu da be ilibuha*; b) *colo Ike hojo sembi*; c) *han imbe fe hojo i omolo seme gemun hecen de bibuhe*; d) *Hojijan ubašara gūnin deribuhe*; e) *Kašigar i hoton be ejelefi Ike hojo be waha.*

4. Translate into Manchu: a) because he heard that our army had arrived; b) they divided the towns (between themselves) and ruled them; c) because he was the grandson of the former *khoja*; d) the same rank shall be inherited by his son; e) he was succeeded as second degree *taiji.*

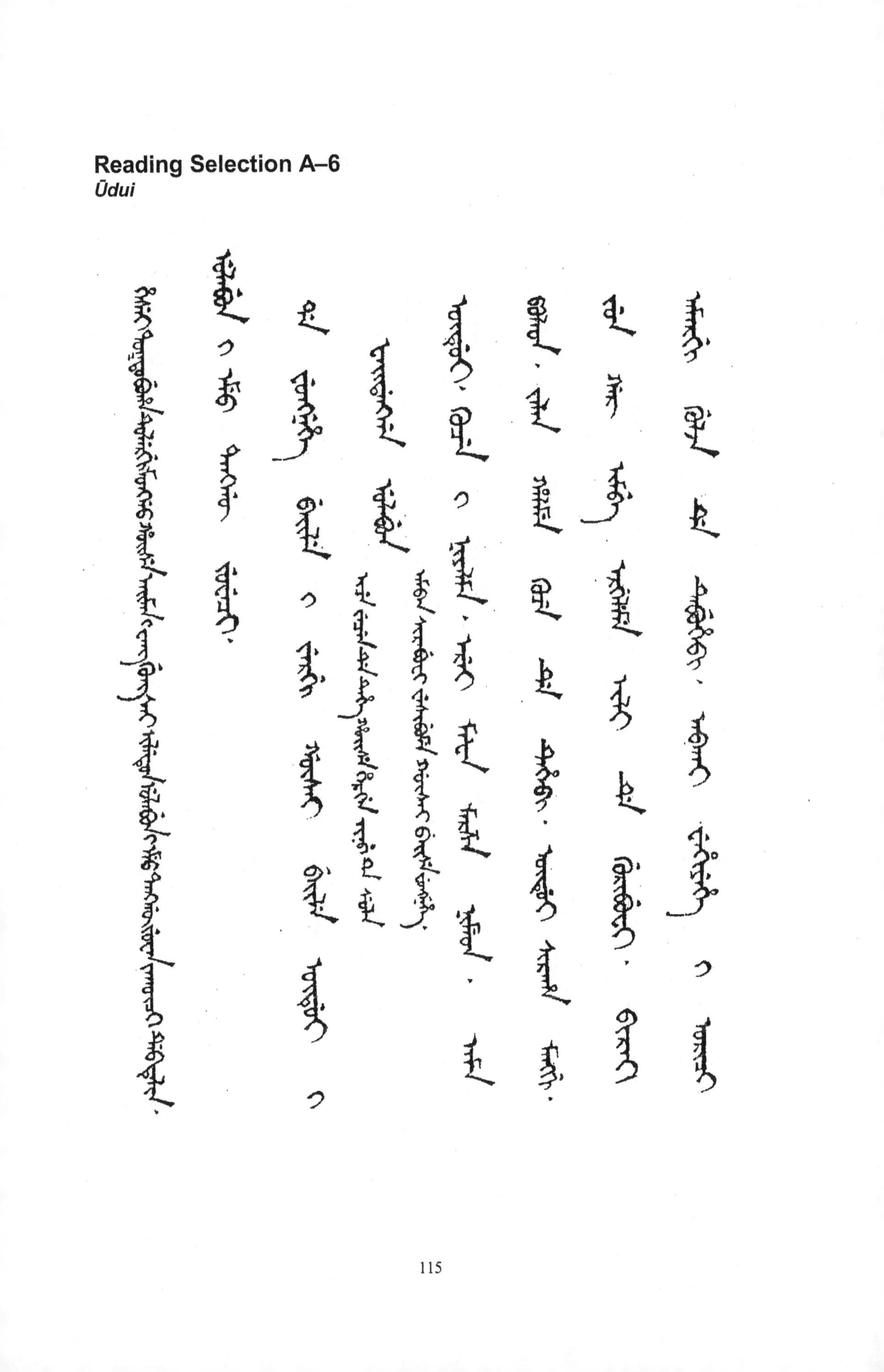

Reading Selection A–6

Ūdui

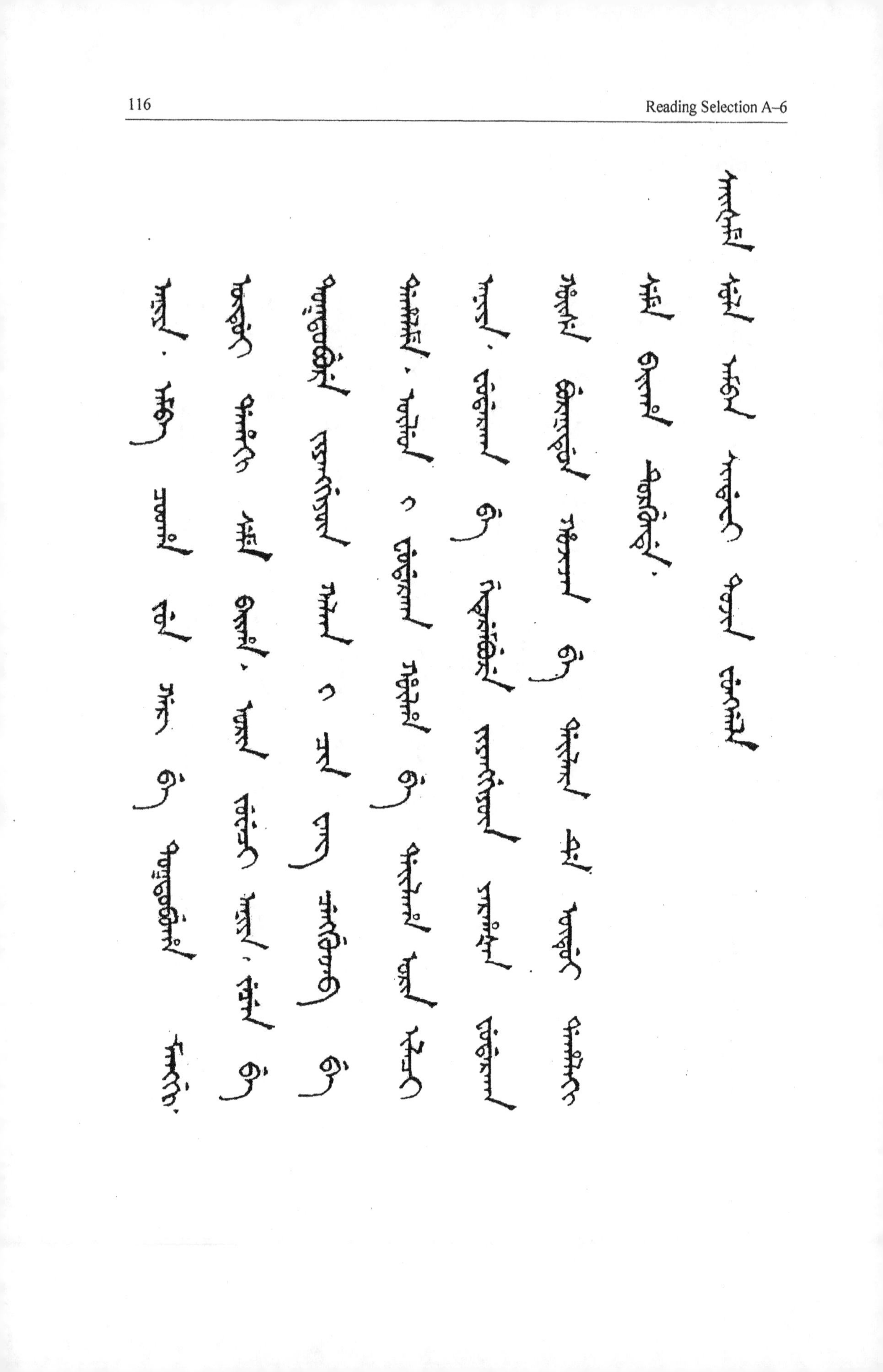

[illegible]

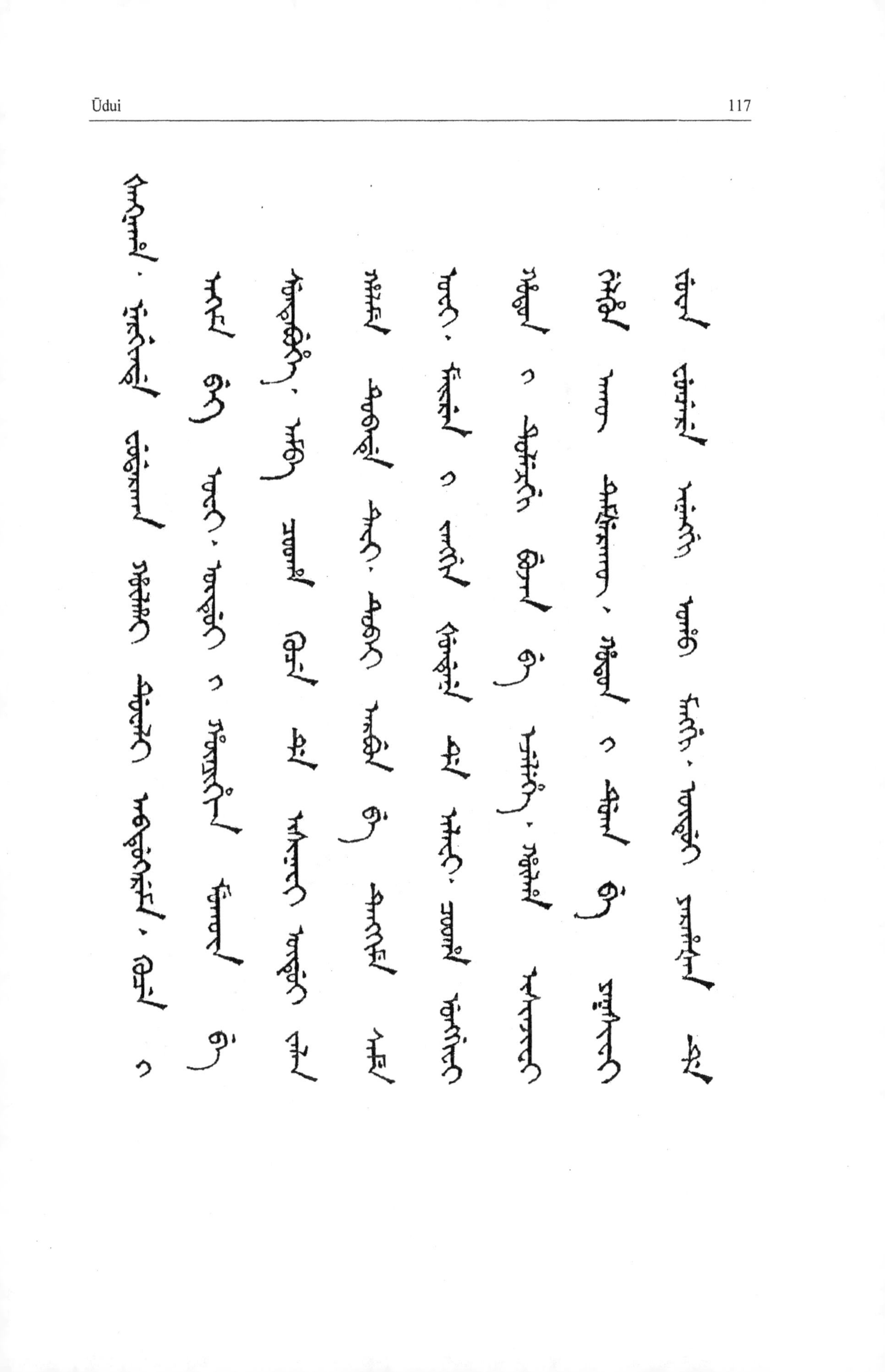

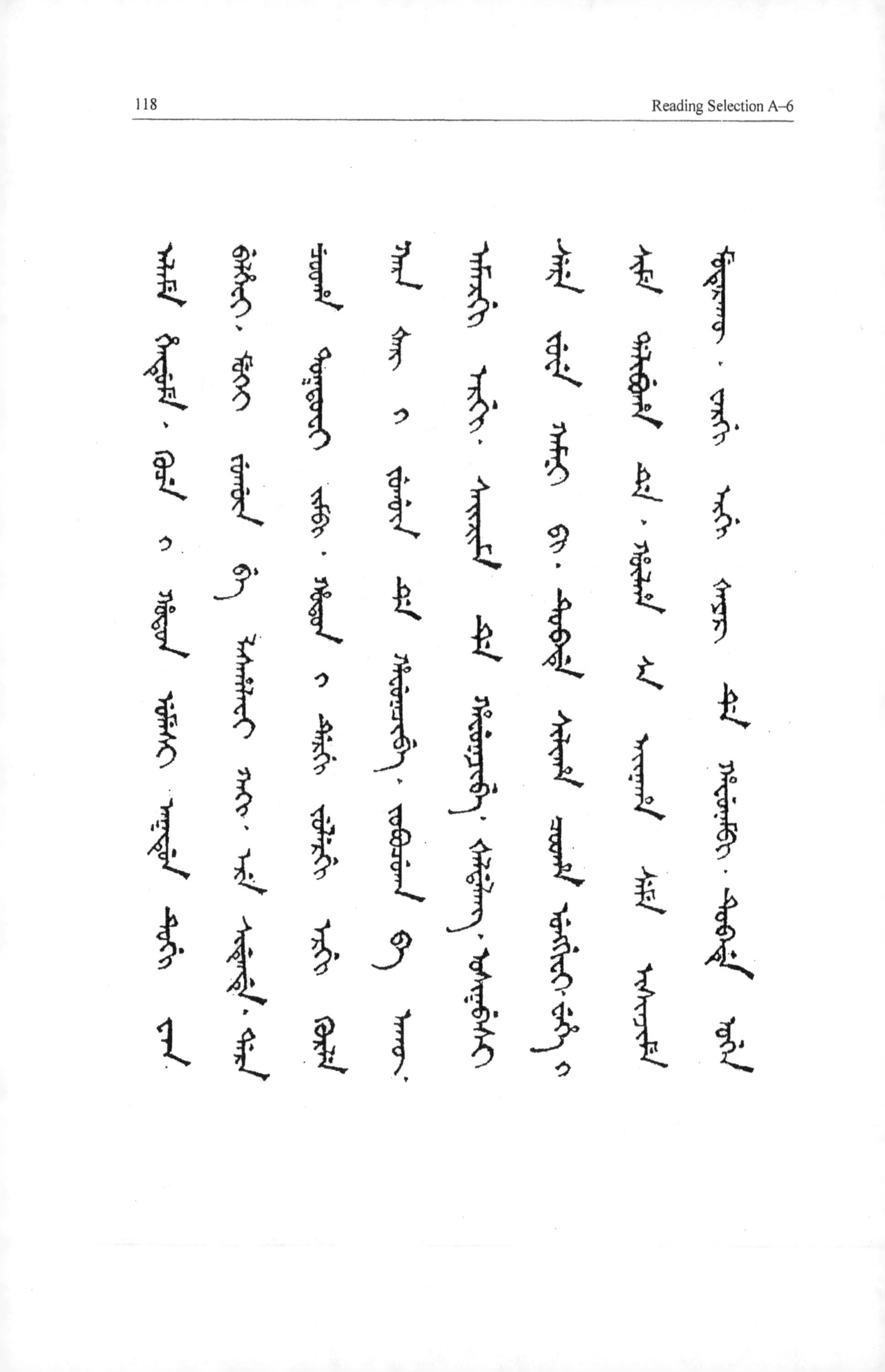

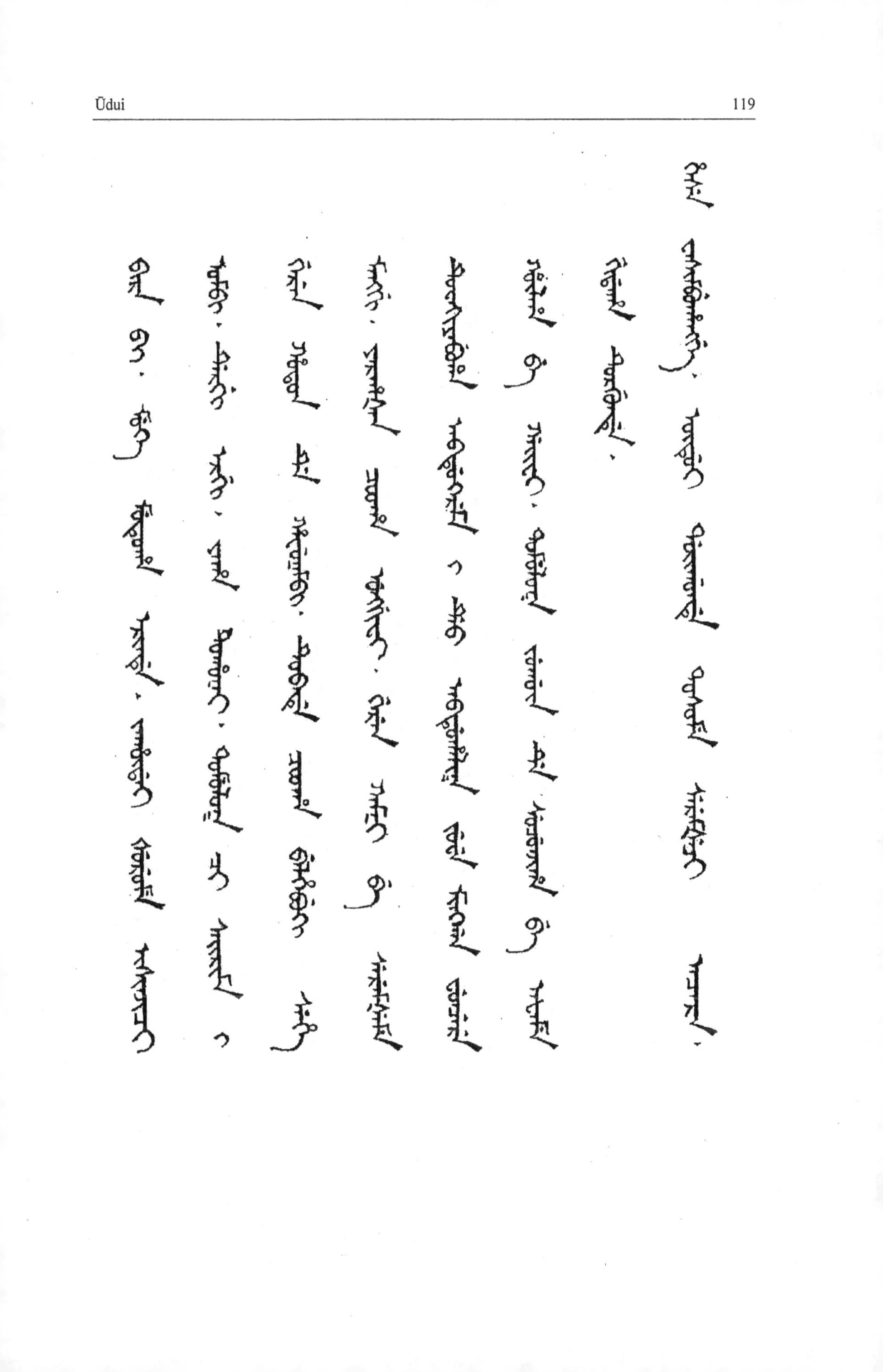

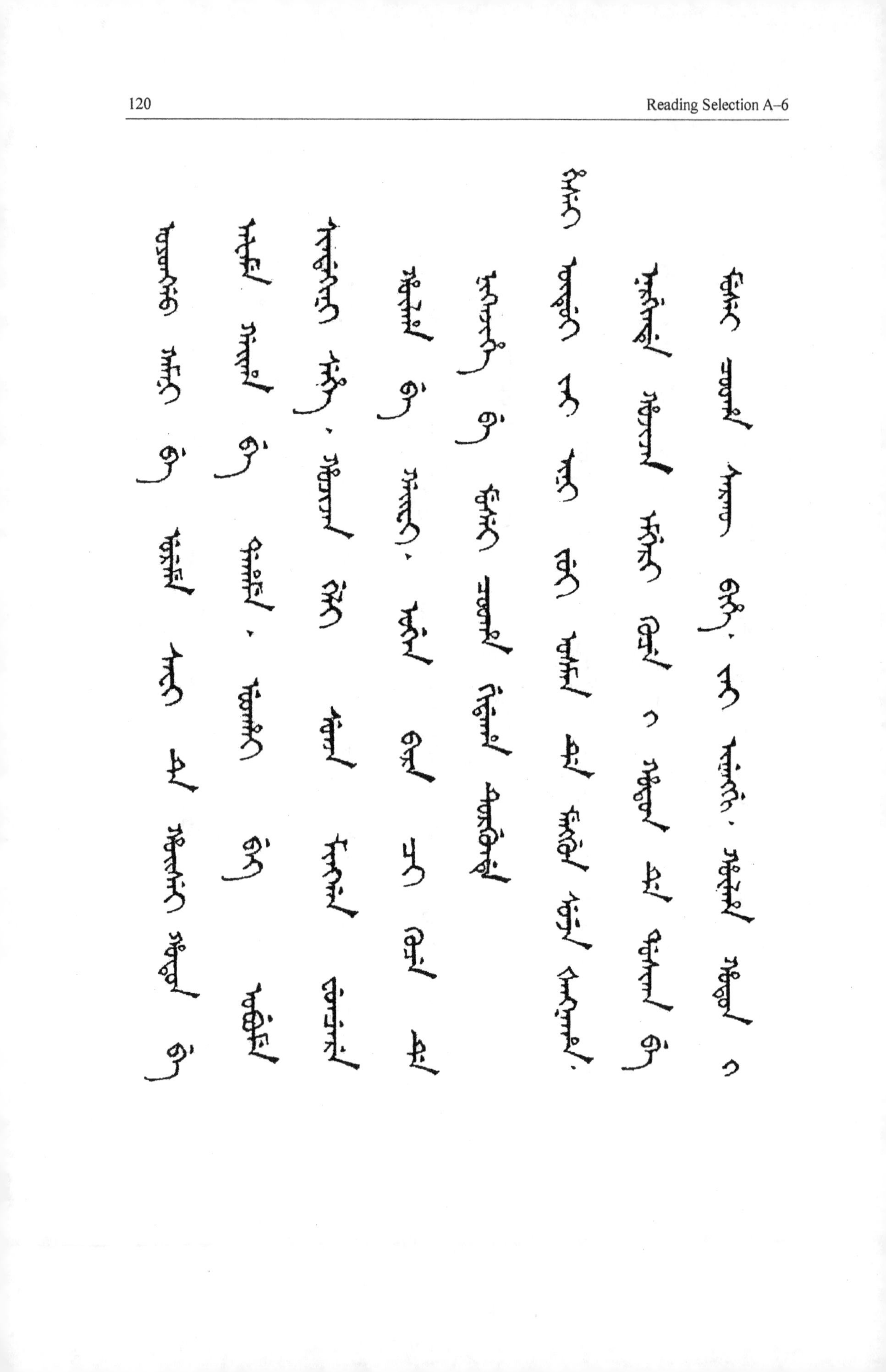

[illegible]

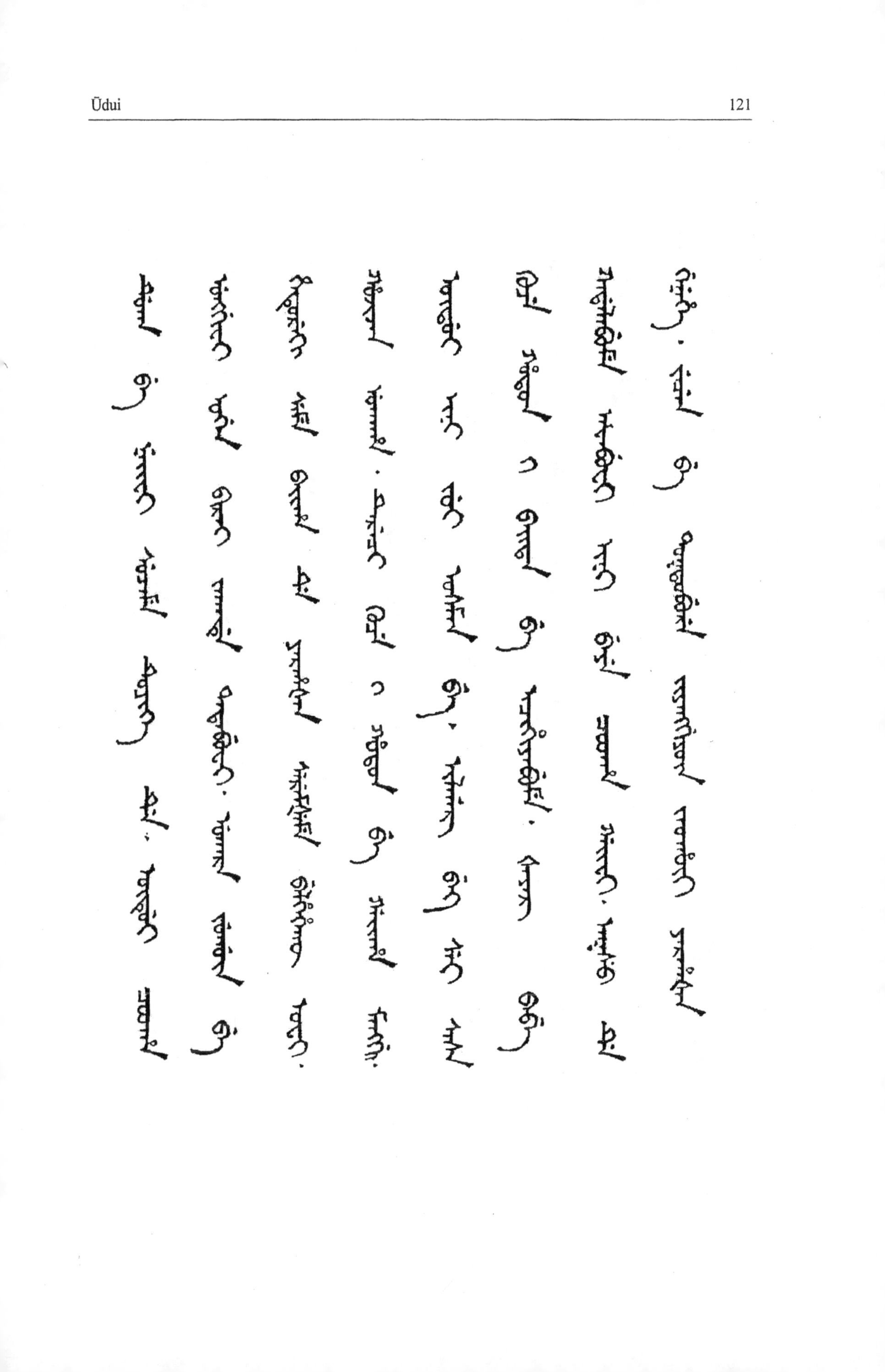

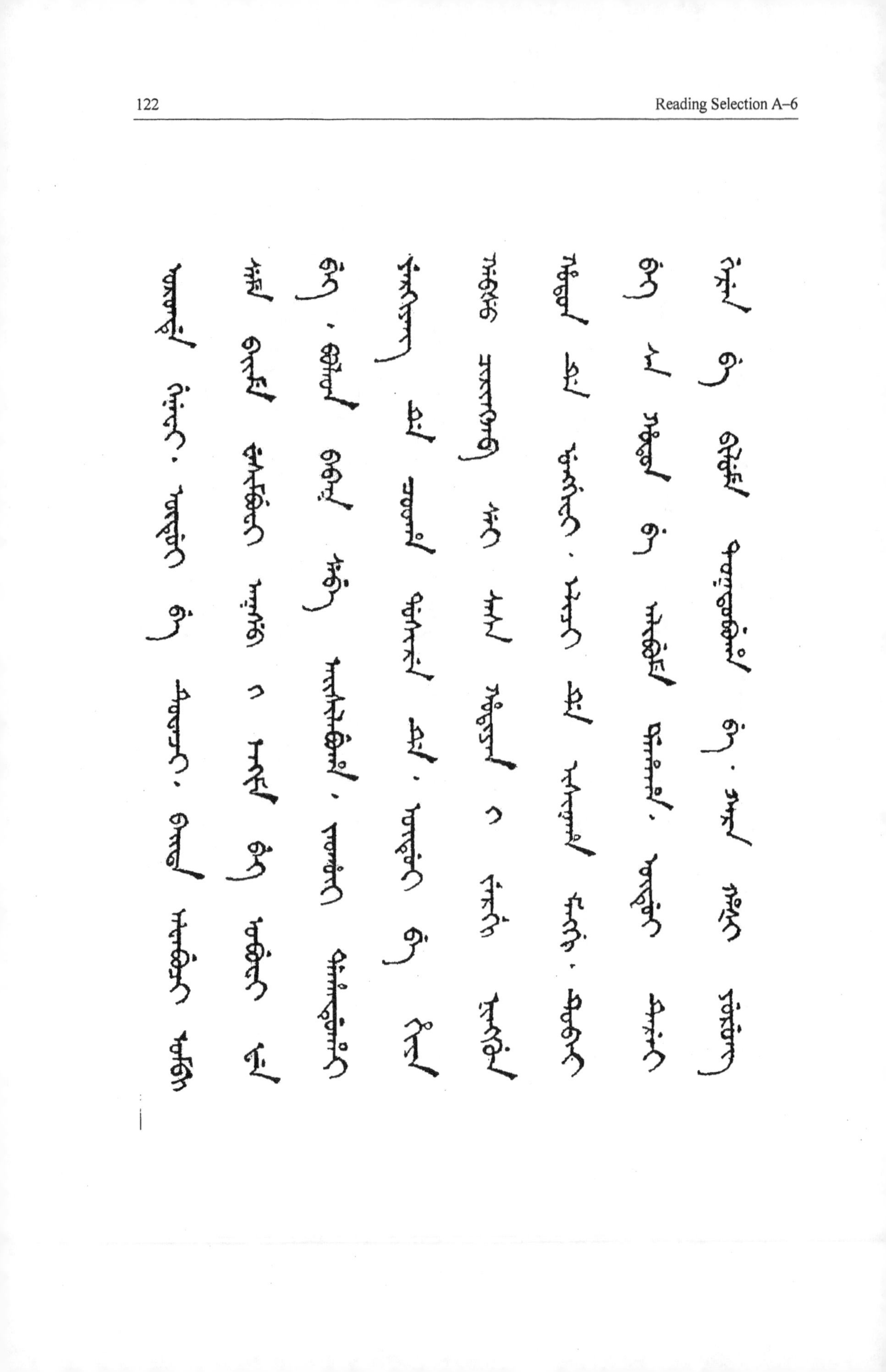

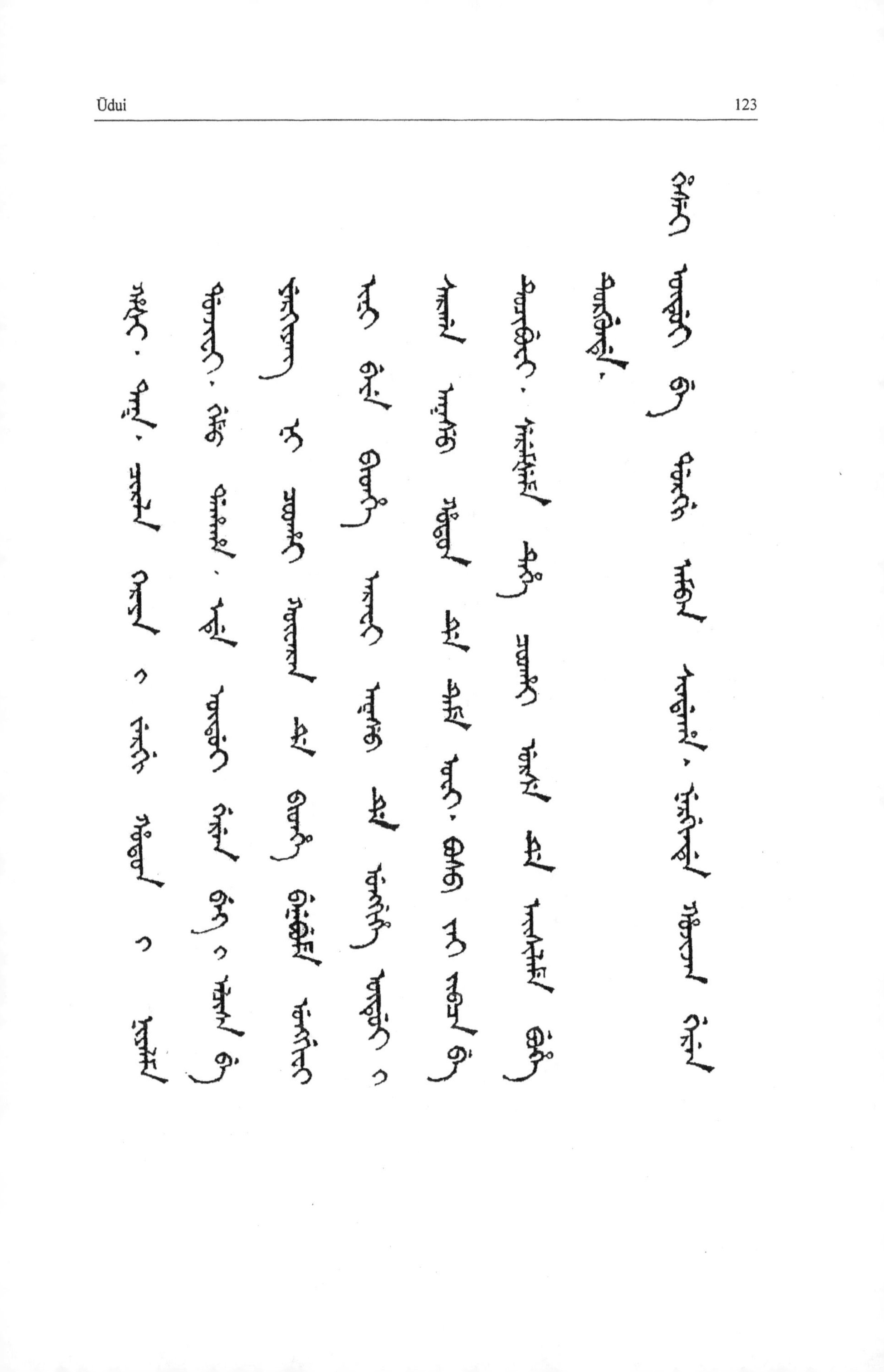

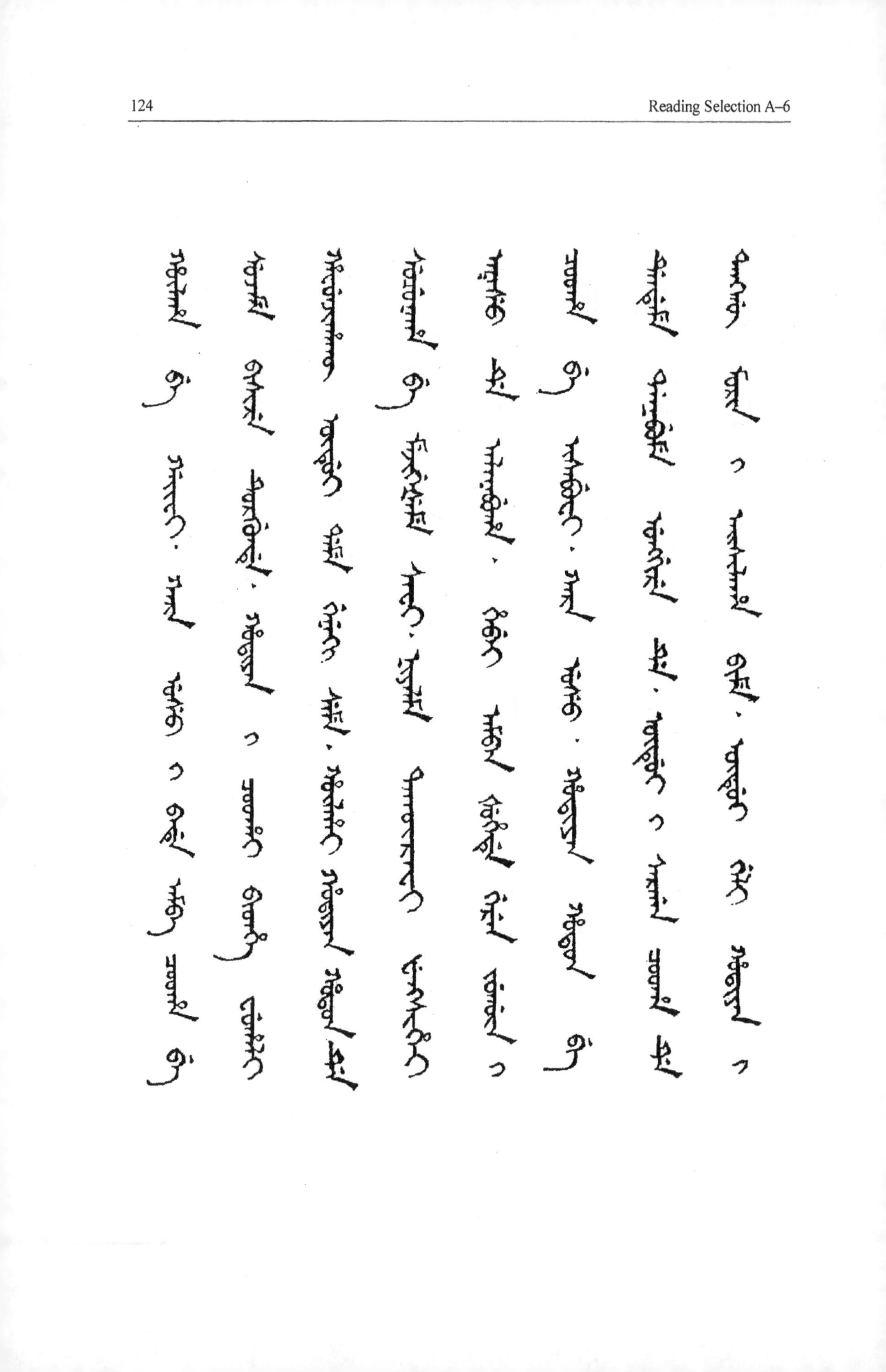

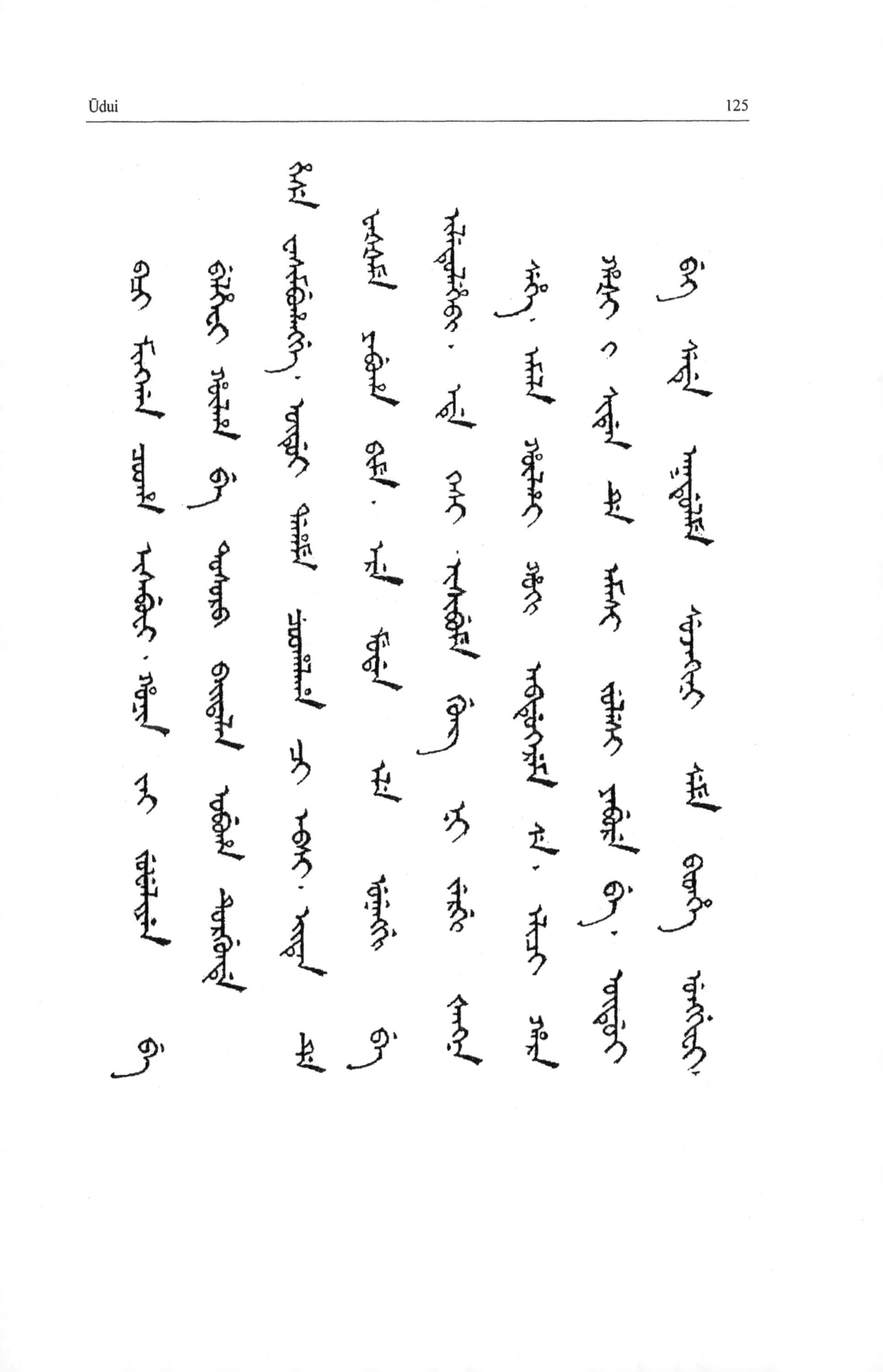

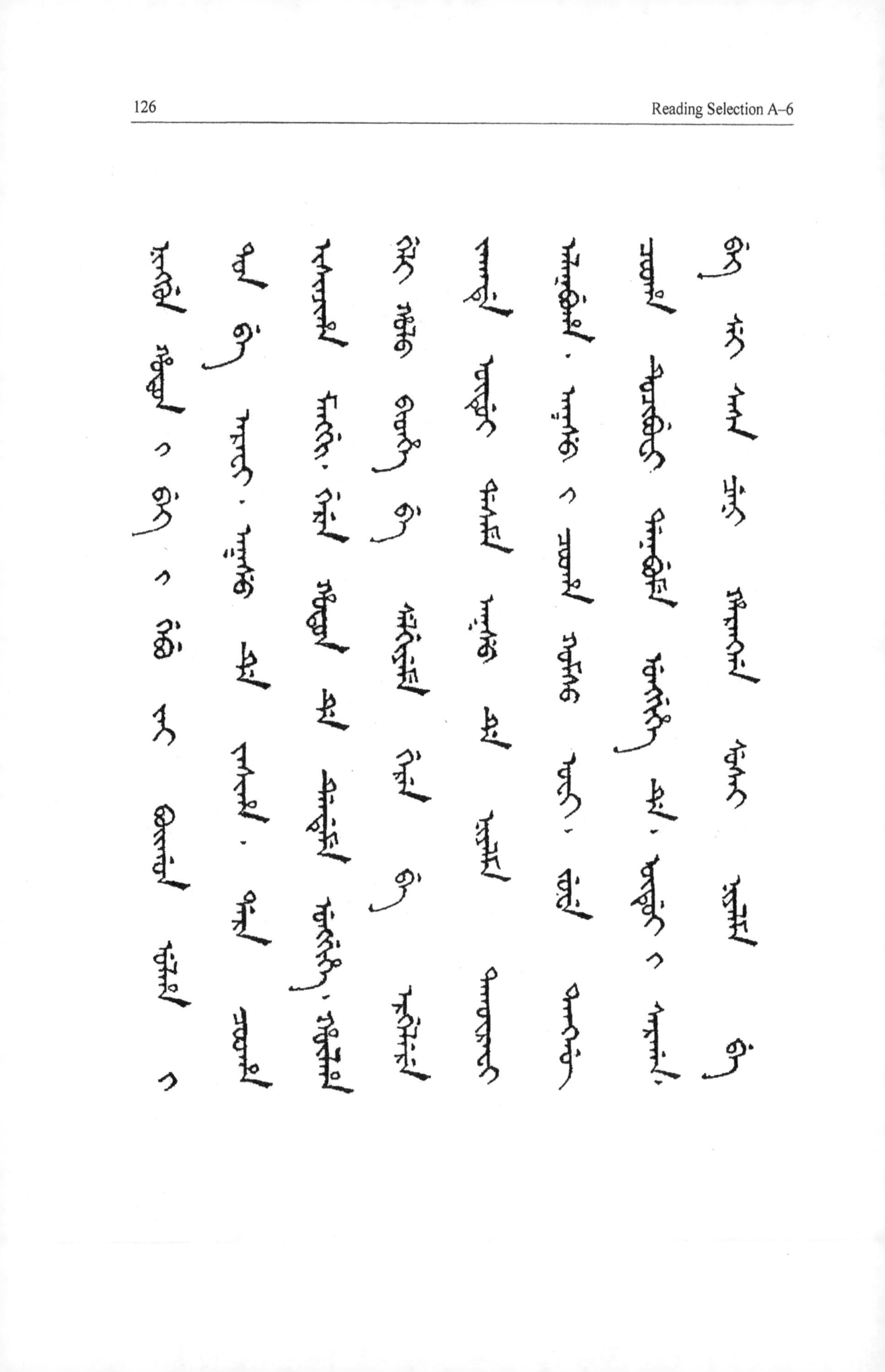

[illegible]

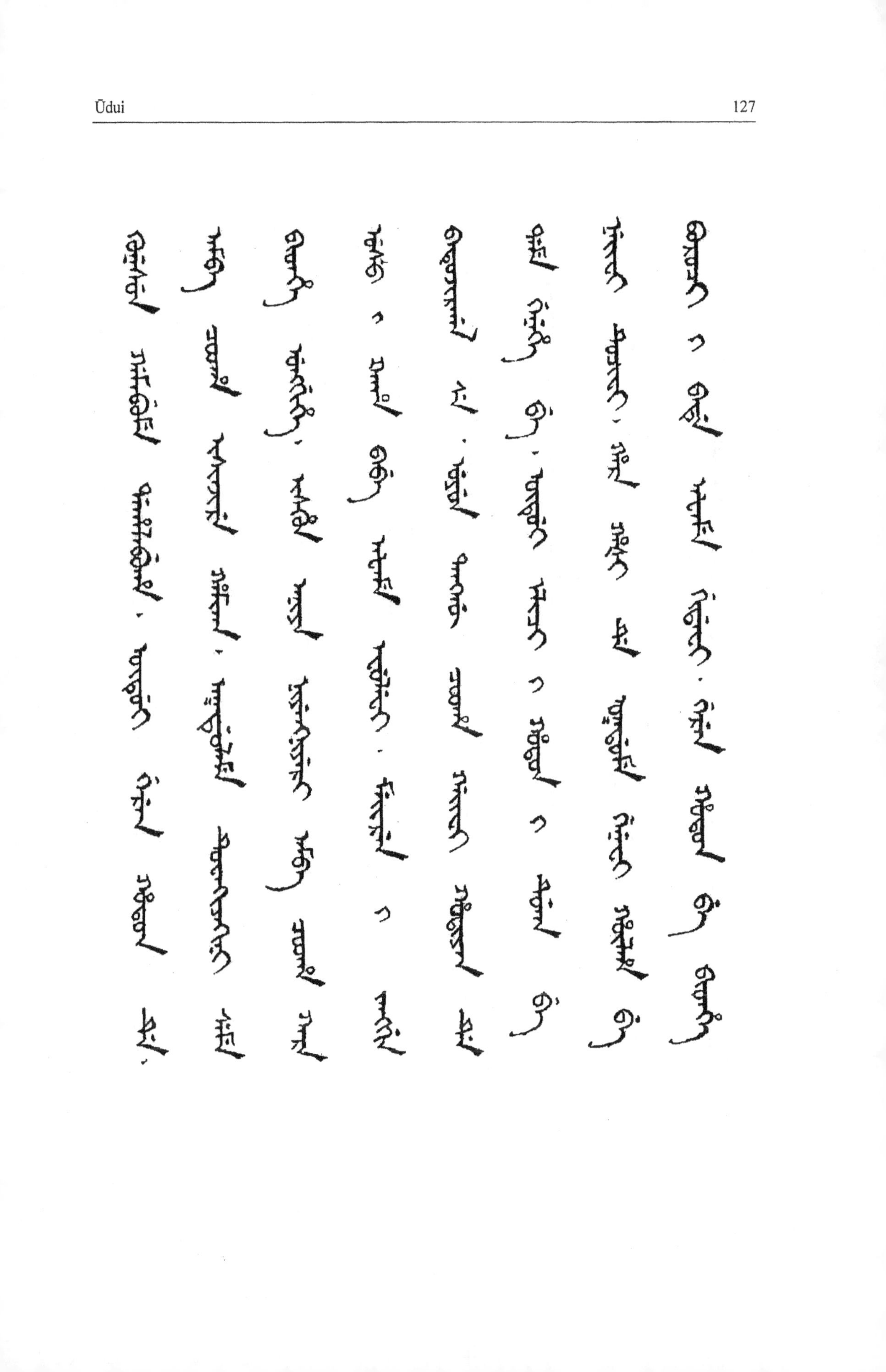

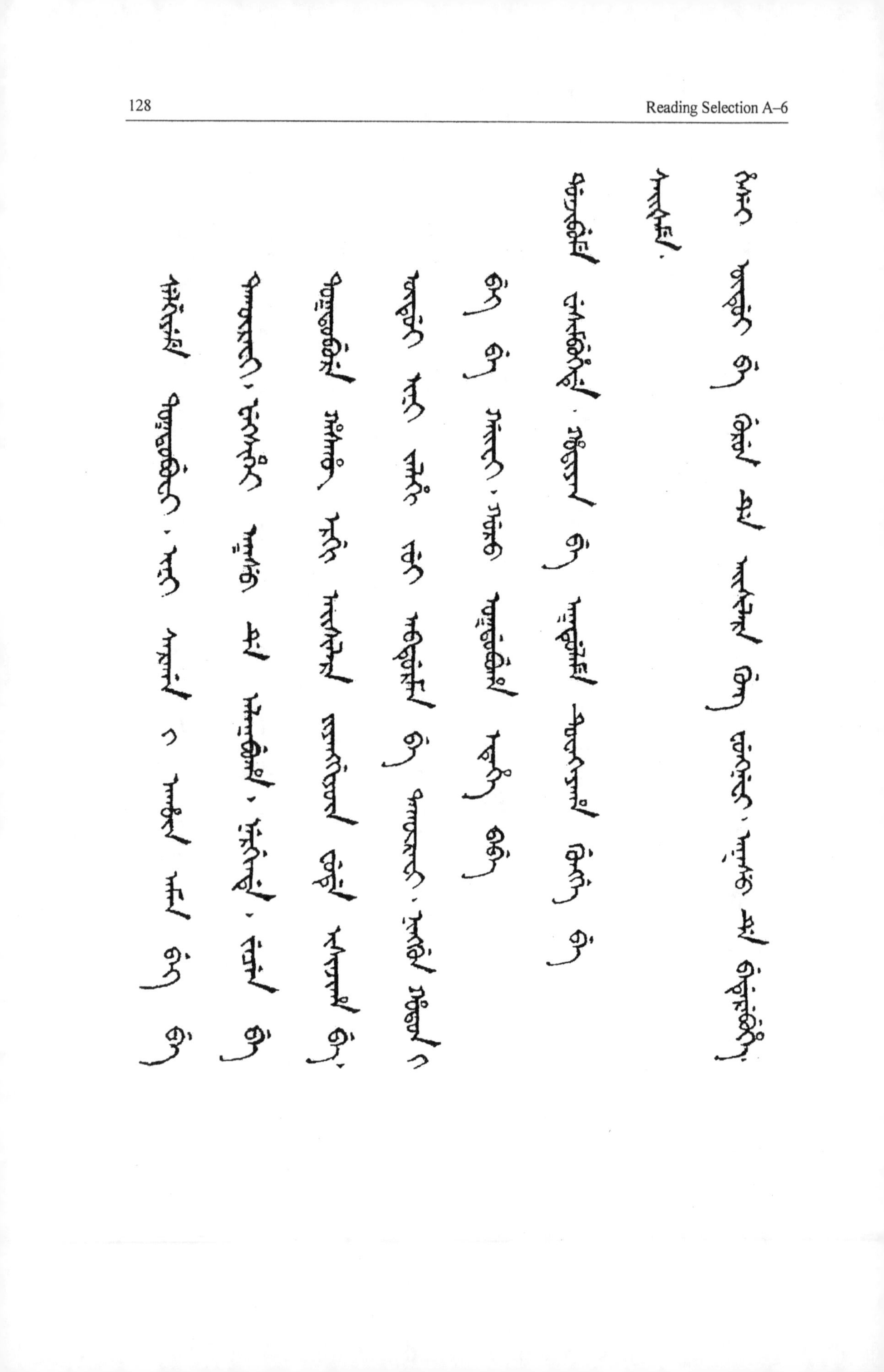

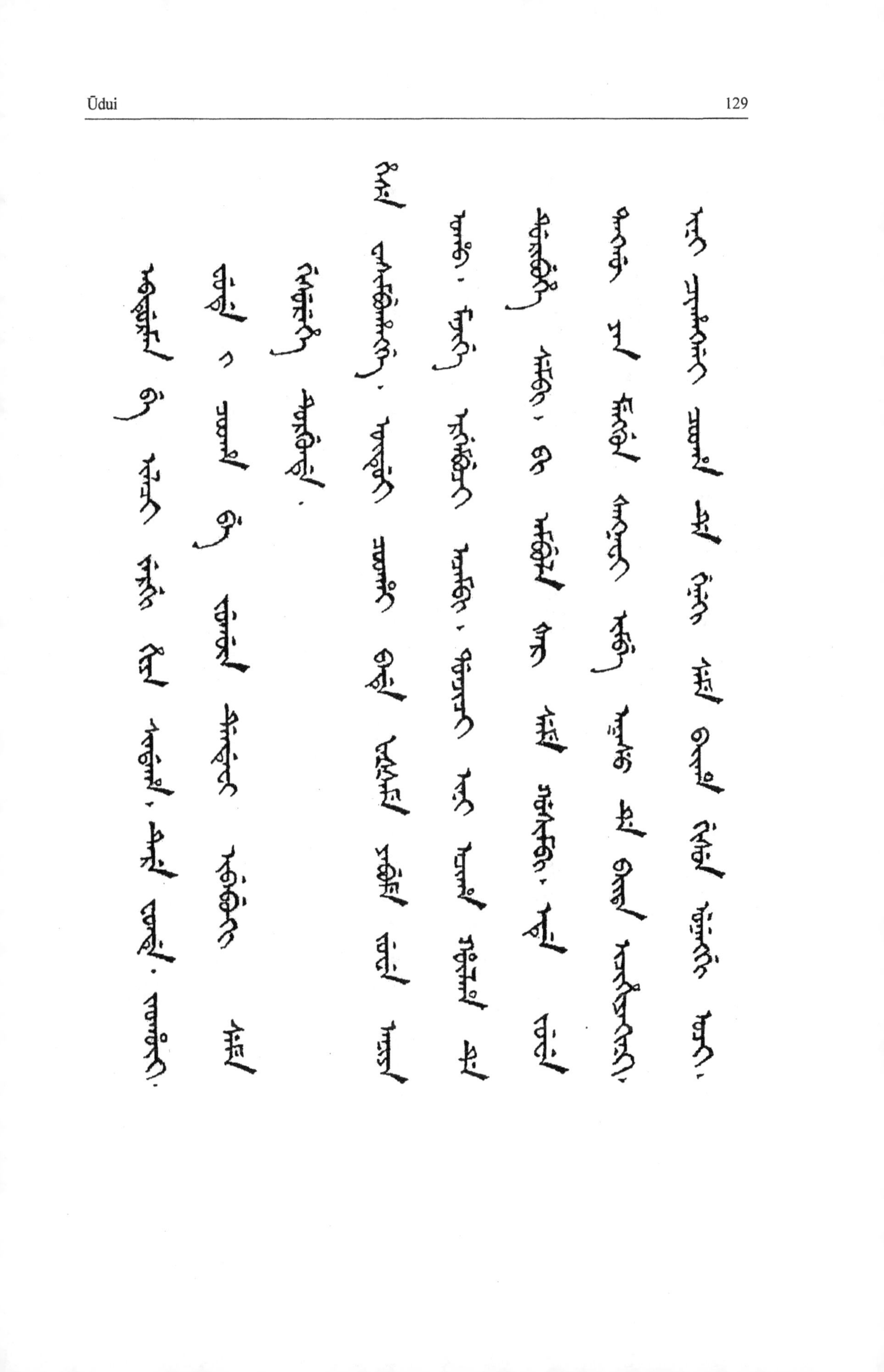

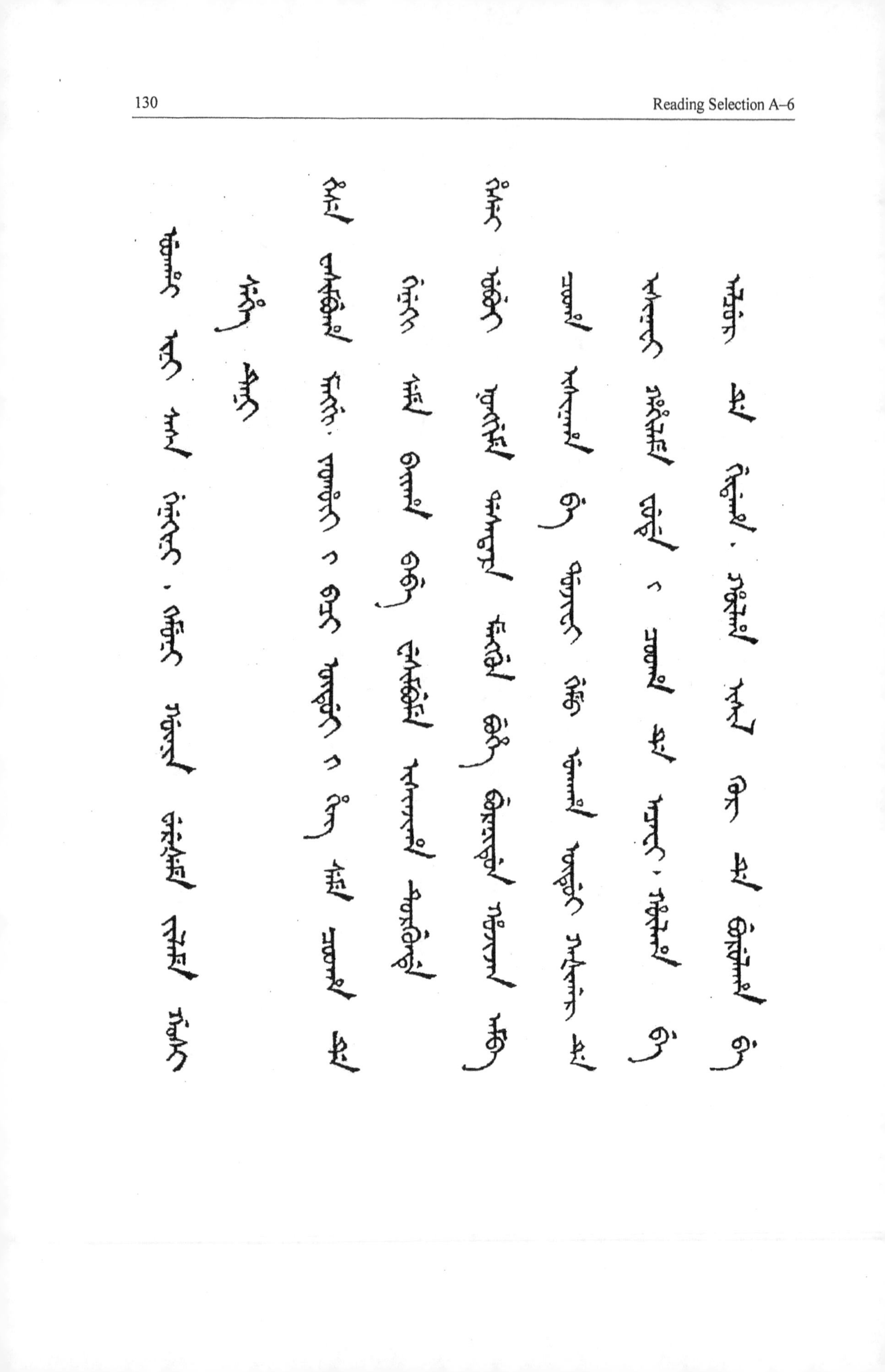

[illegible]

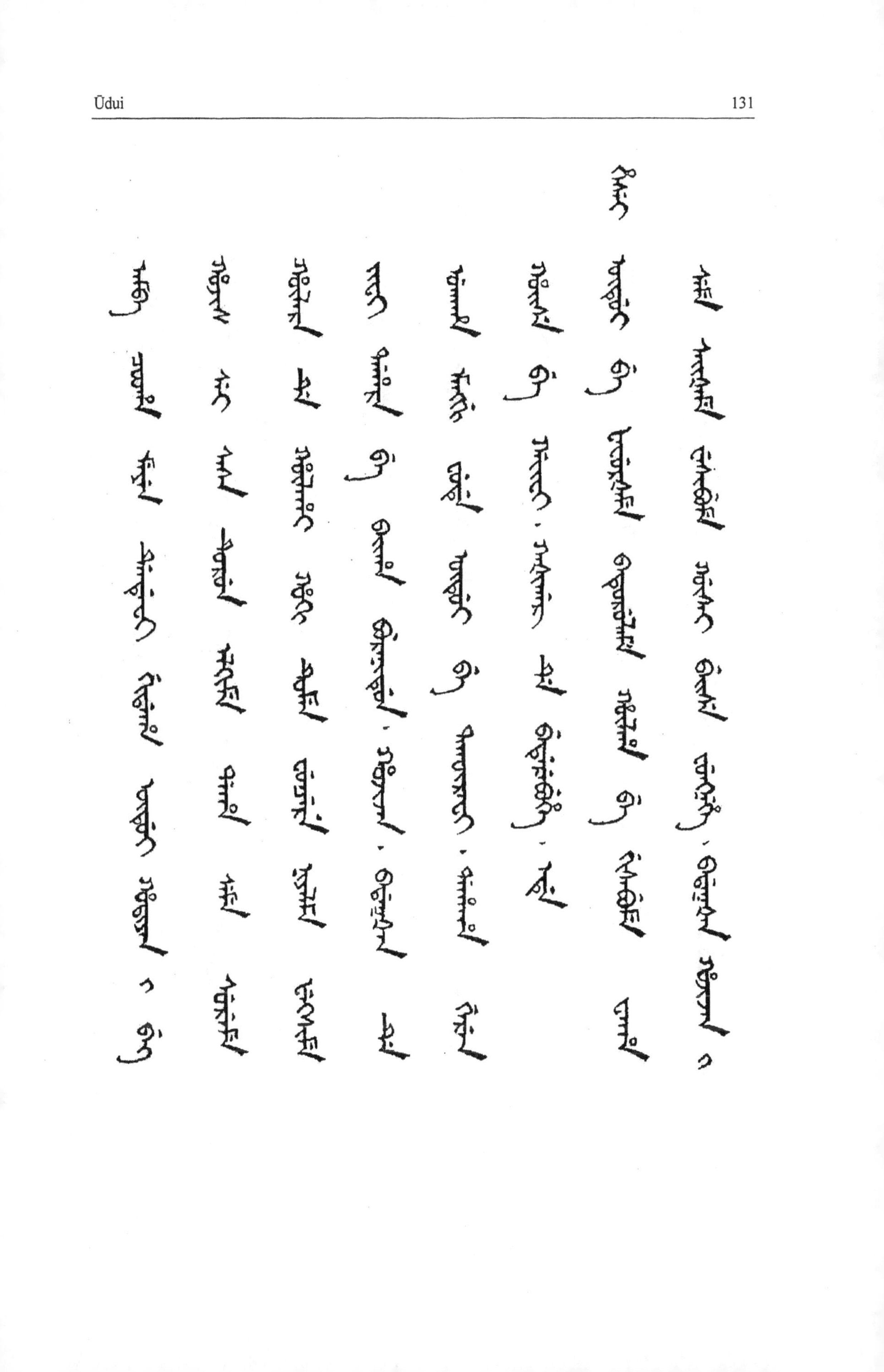

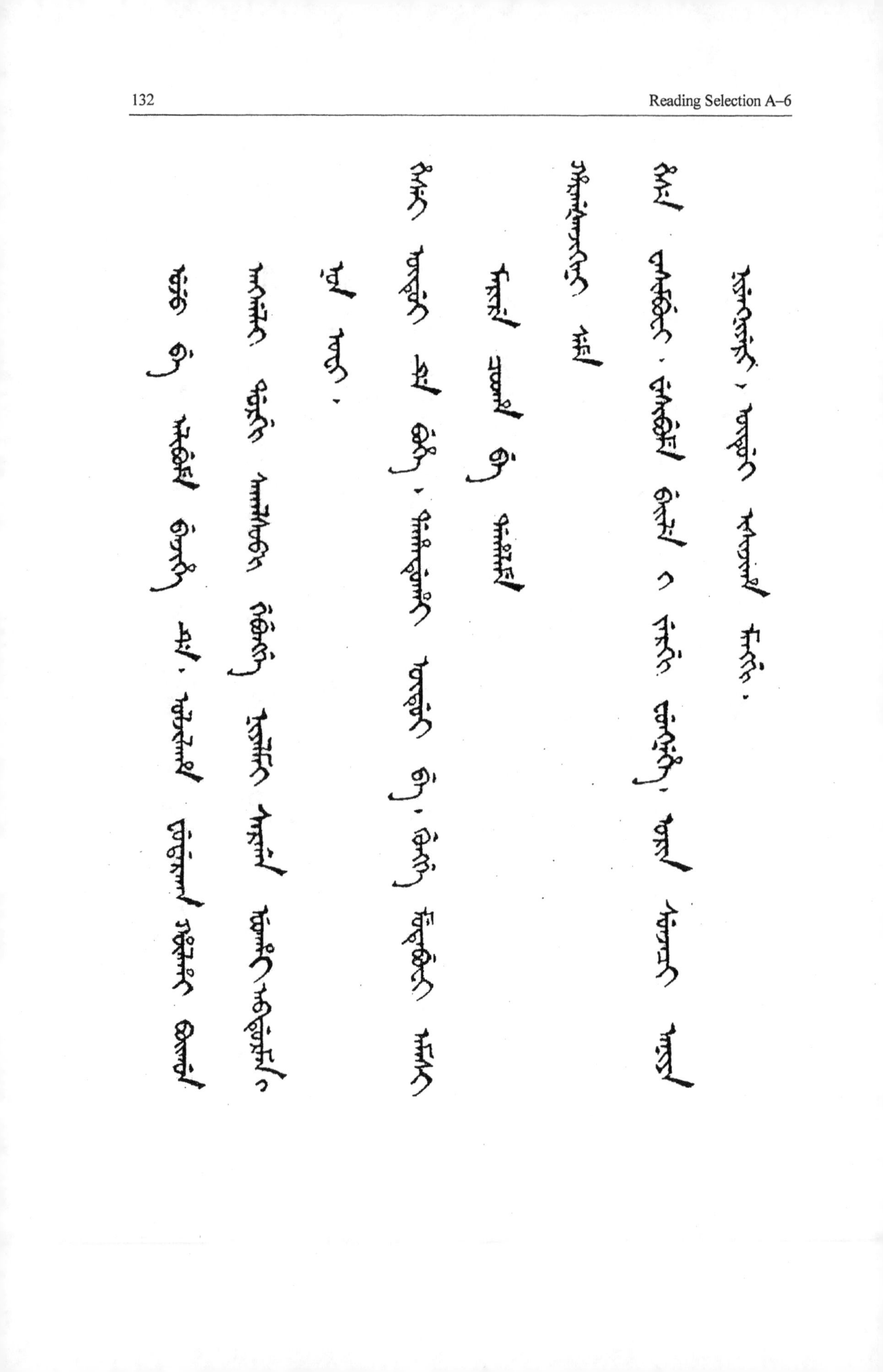

[illegible]

[illegible]

[illegible]

[illegible]

[illegible]

[illegible]

[illegible]

[illegible]

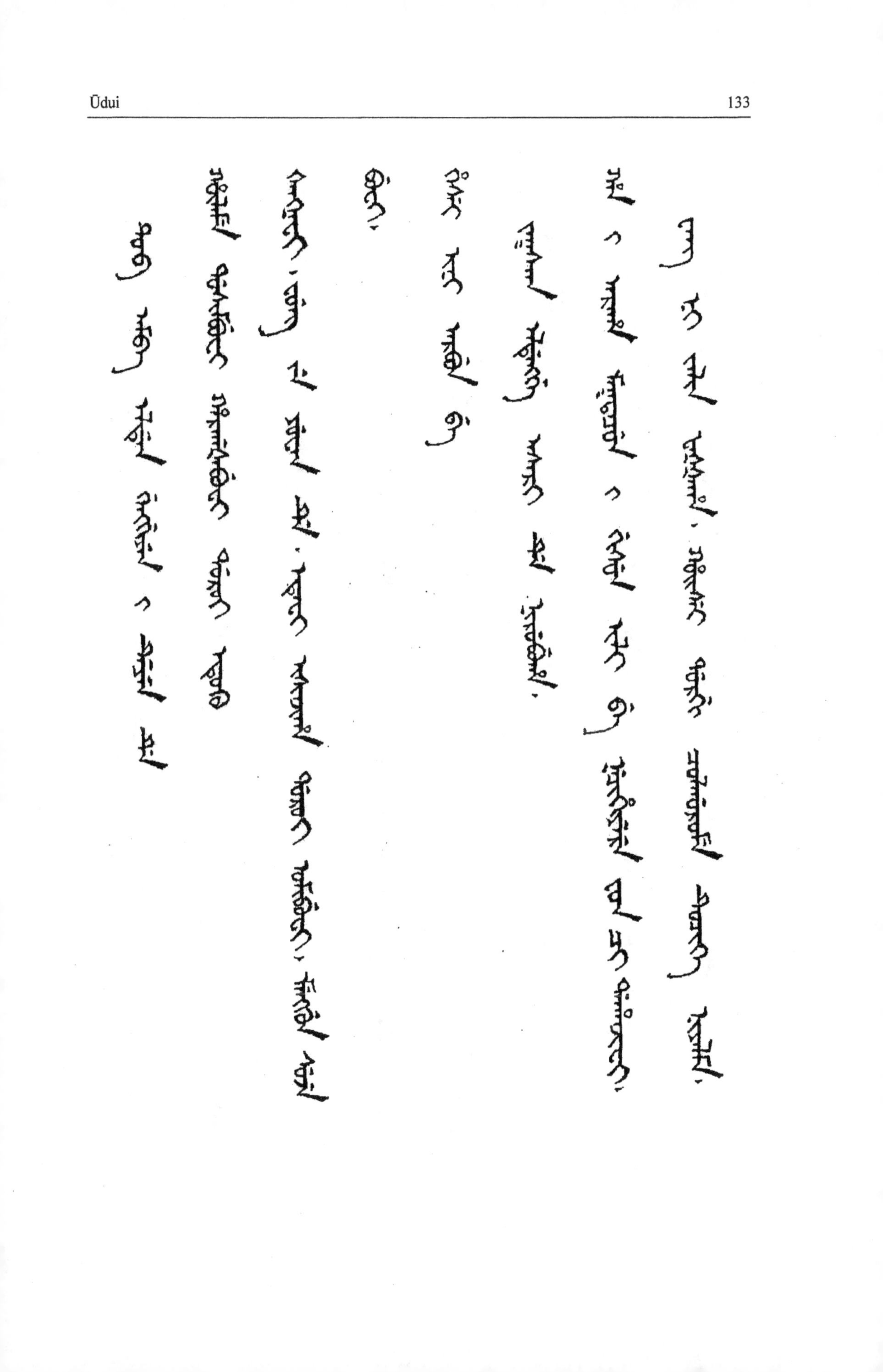

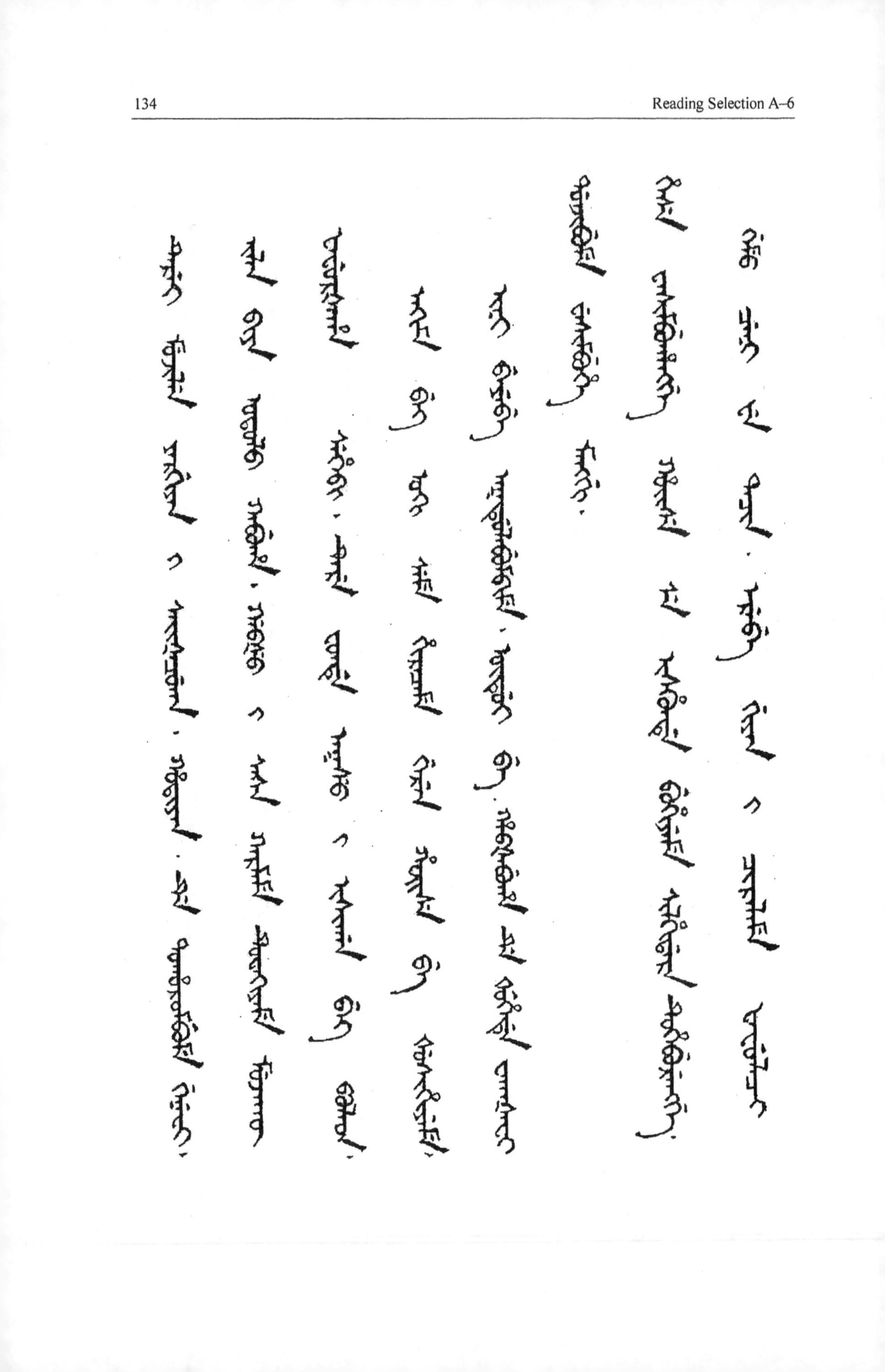

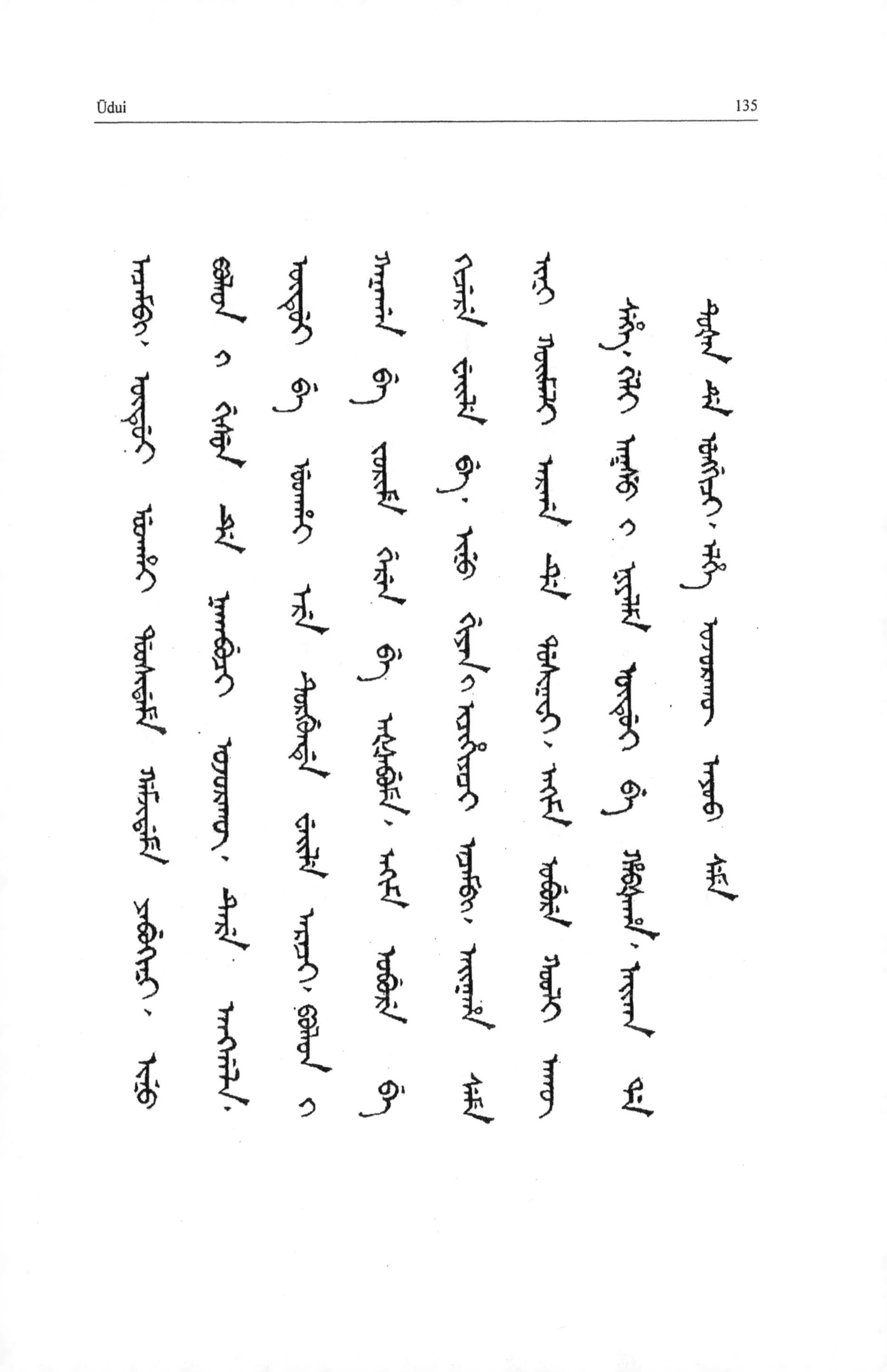

[illegible]

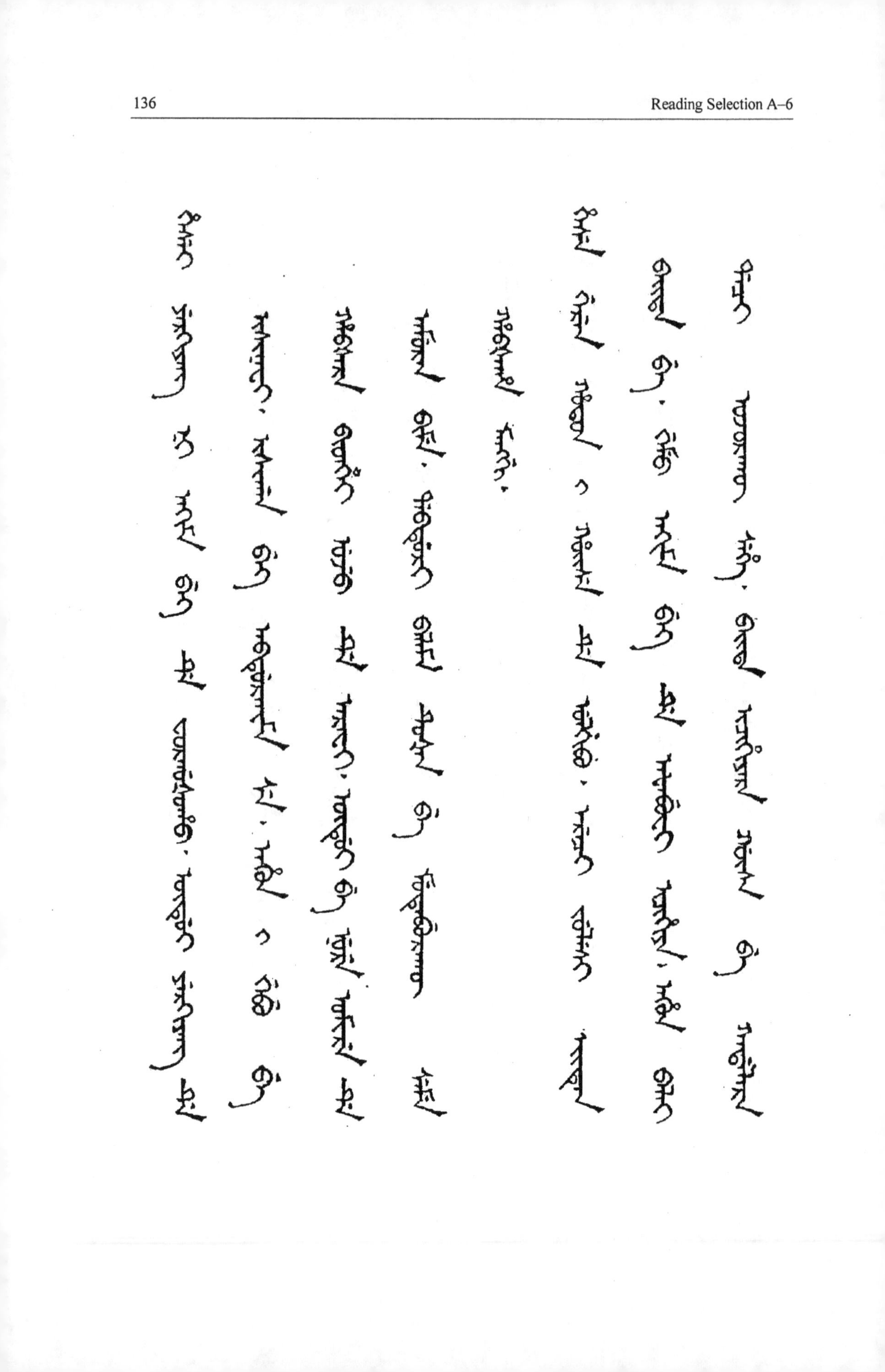

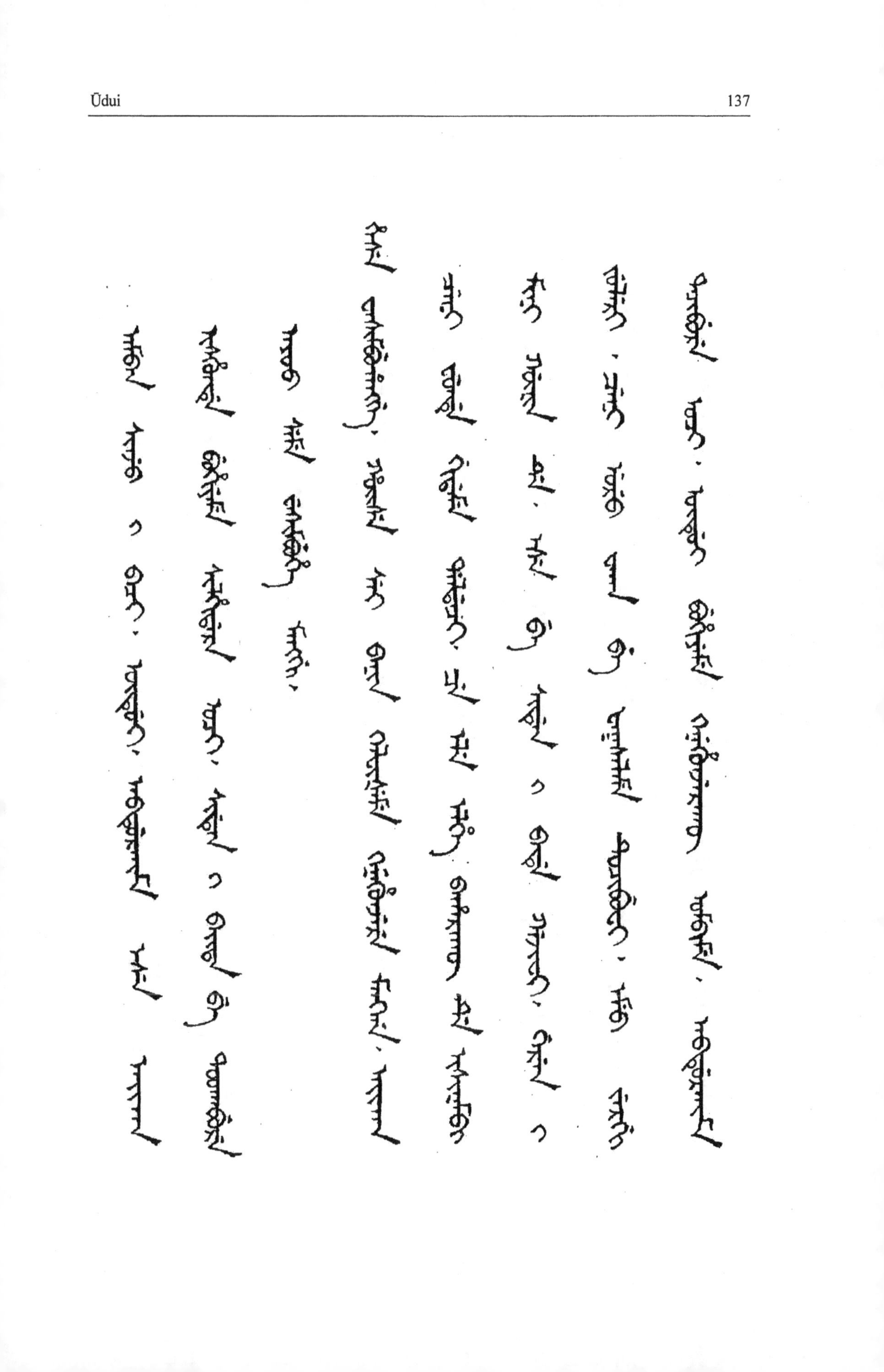

[illegible]

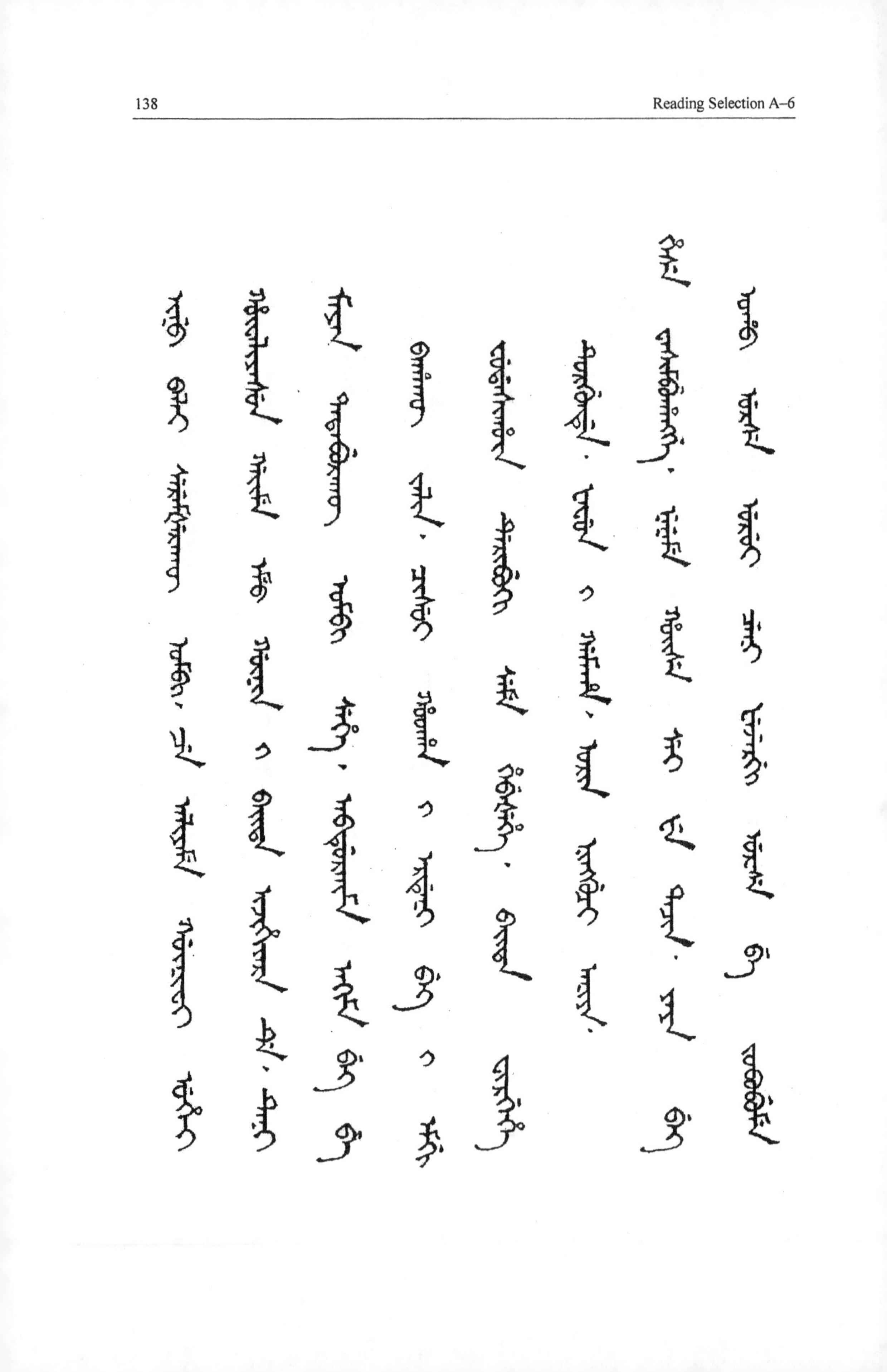

[illegible]

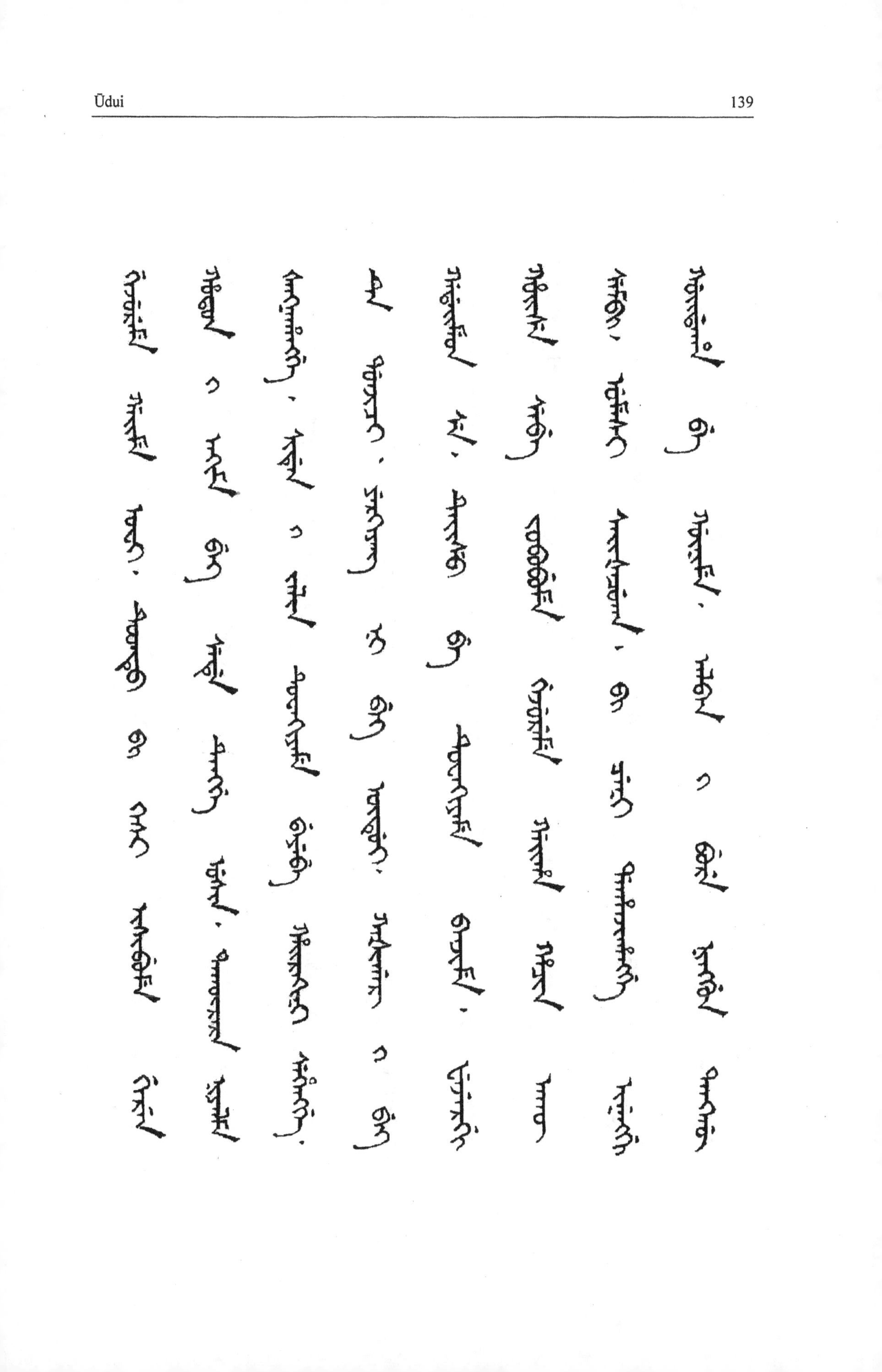

[illegible]

[illegible]

[illegible]

[illegible]

[illegible]

[illegible]

[illegible]

[illegible]

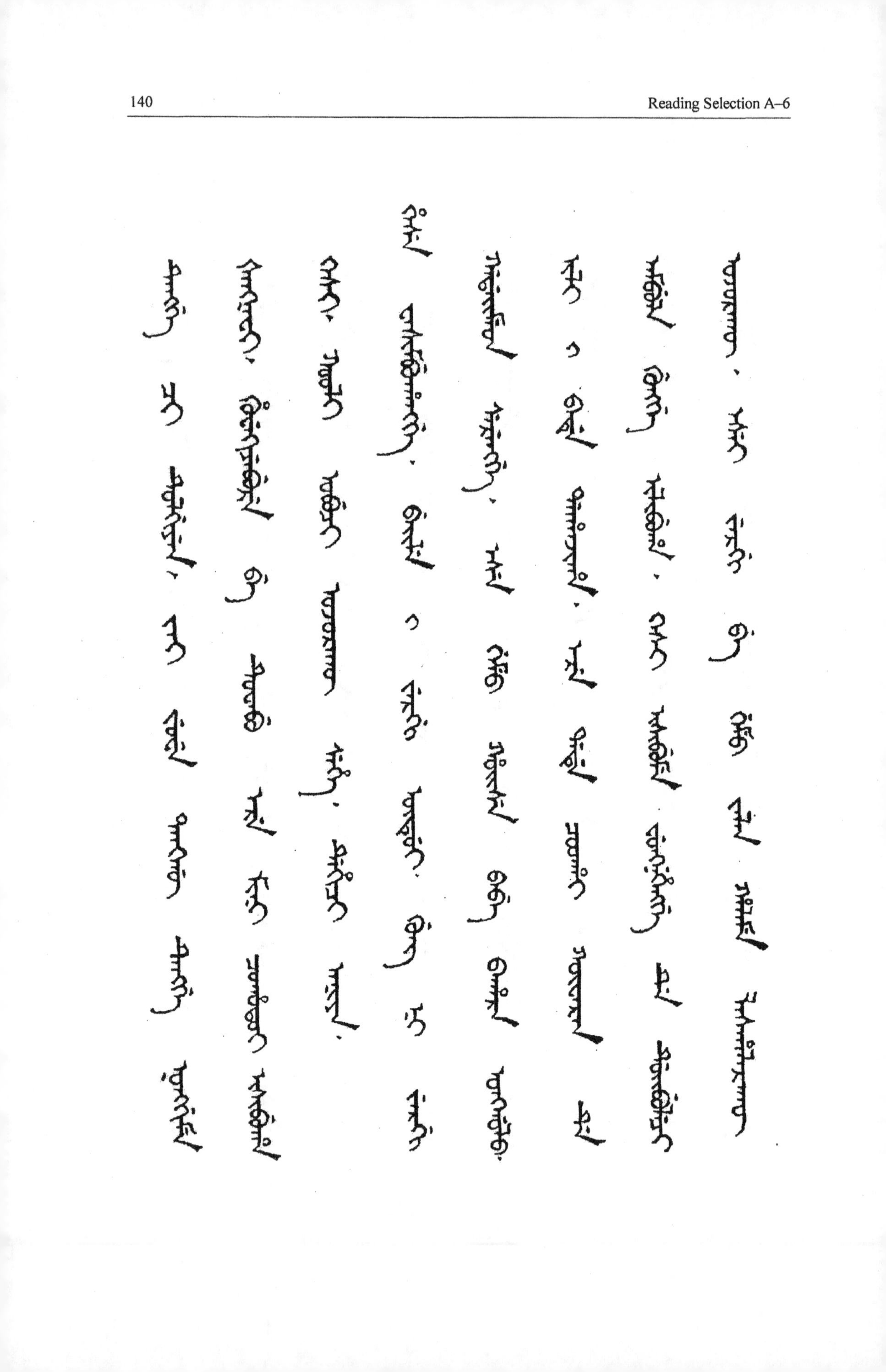

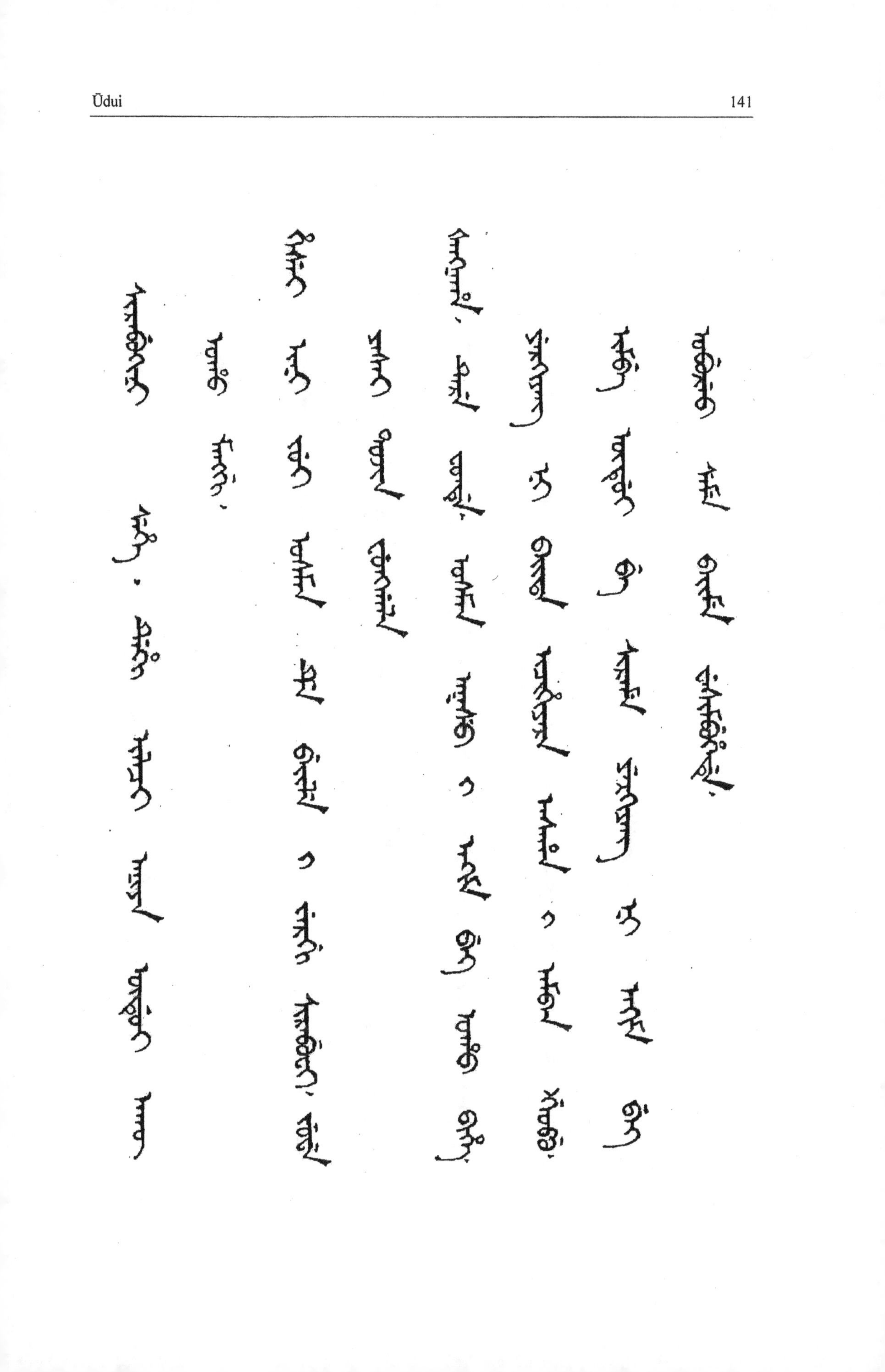

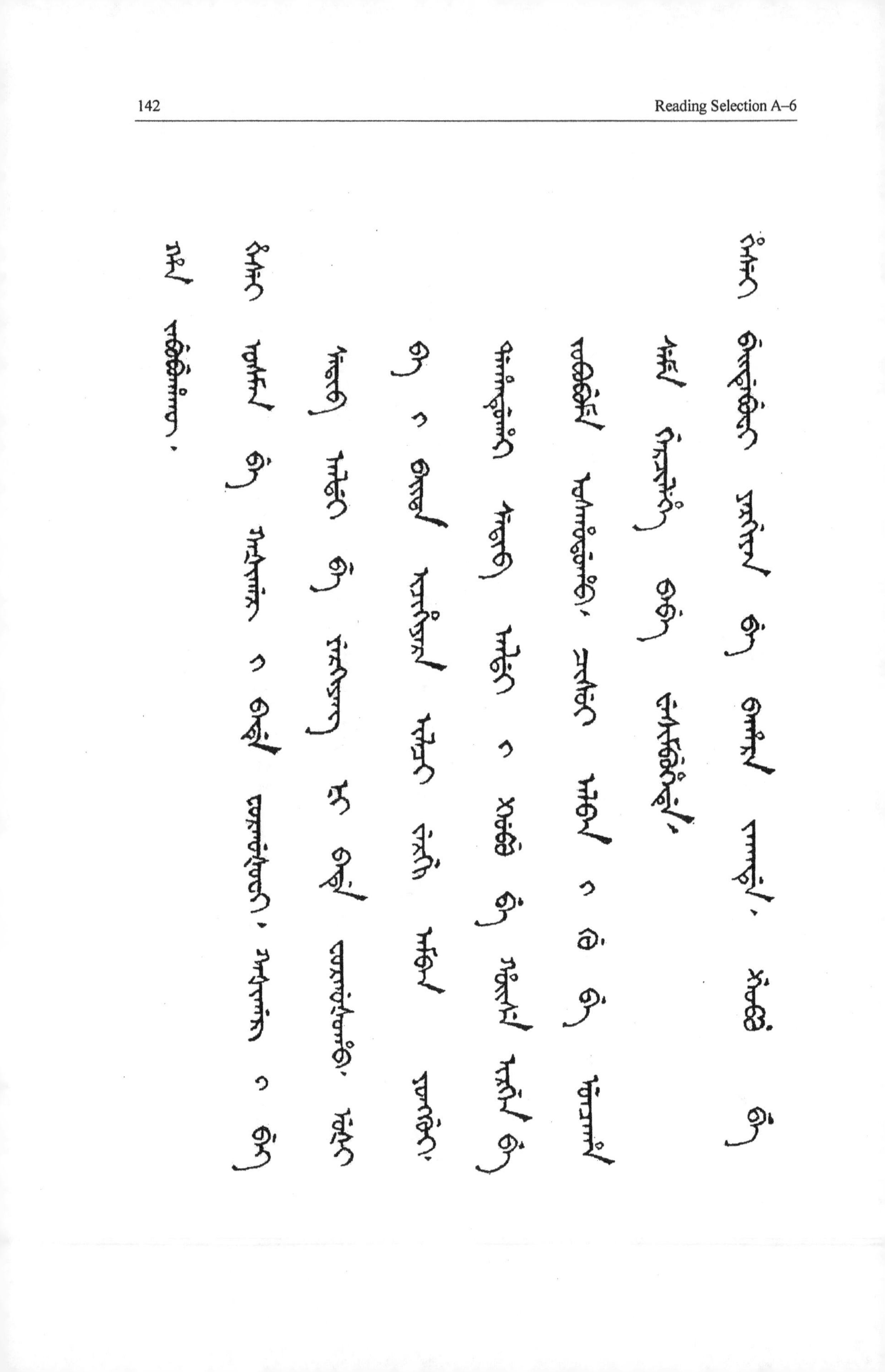

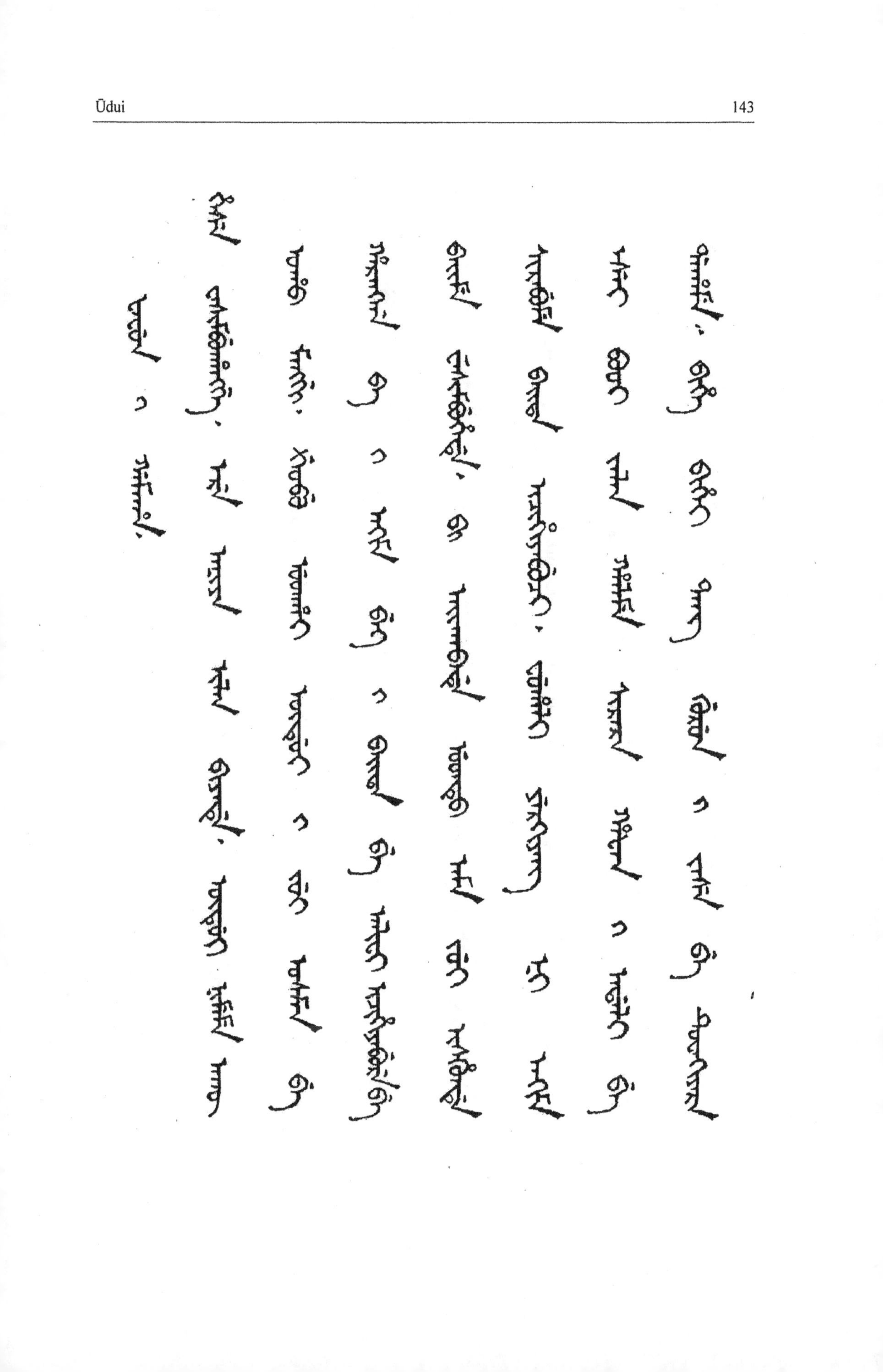

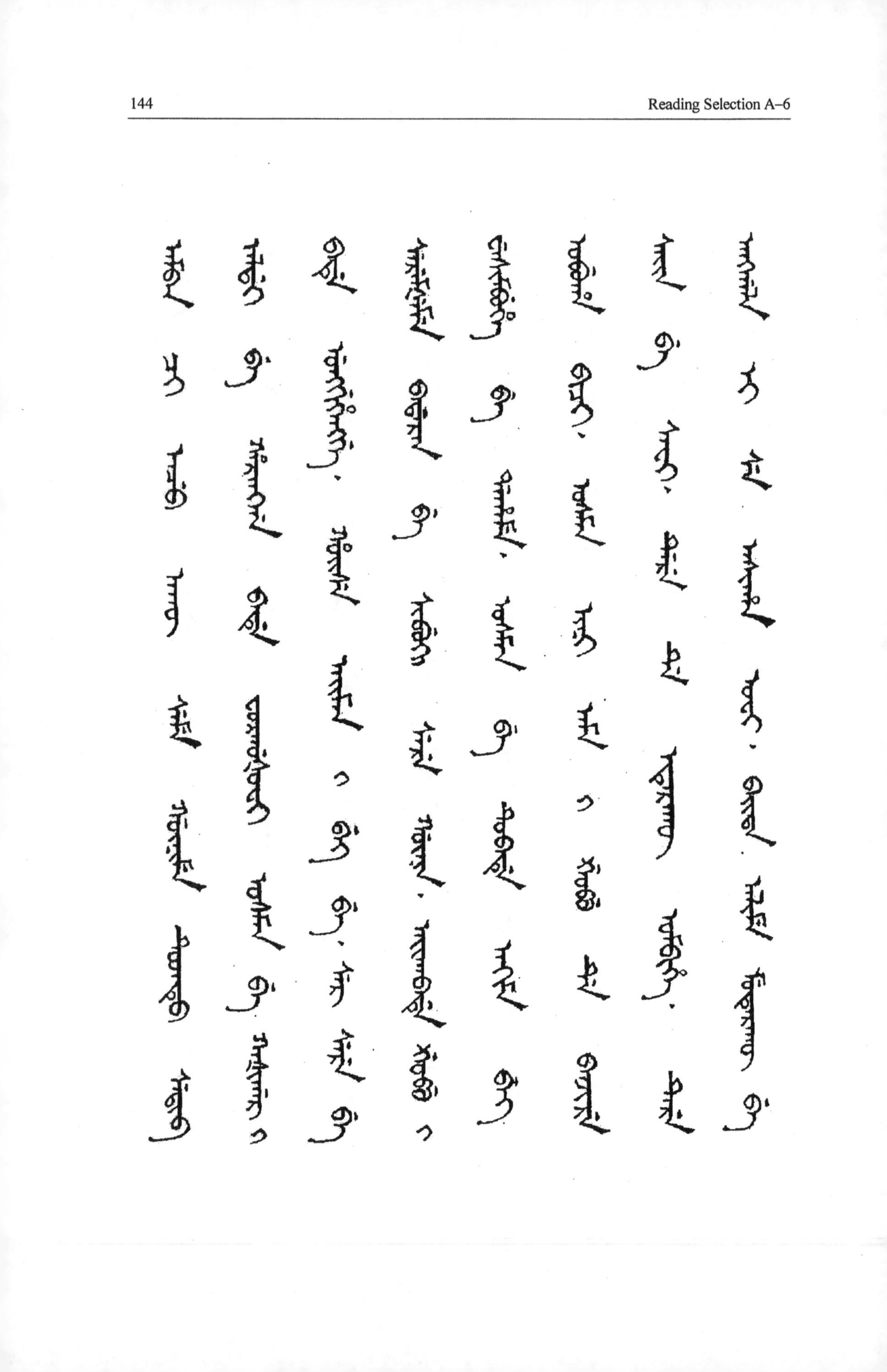

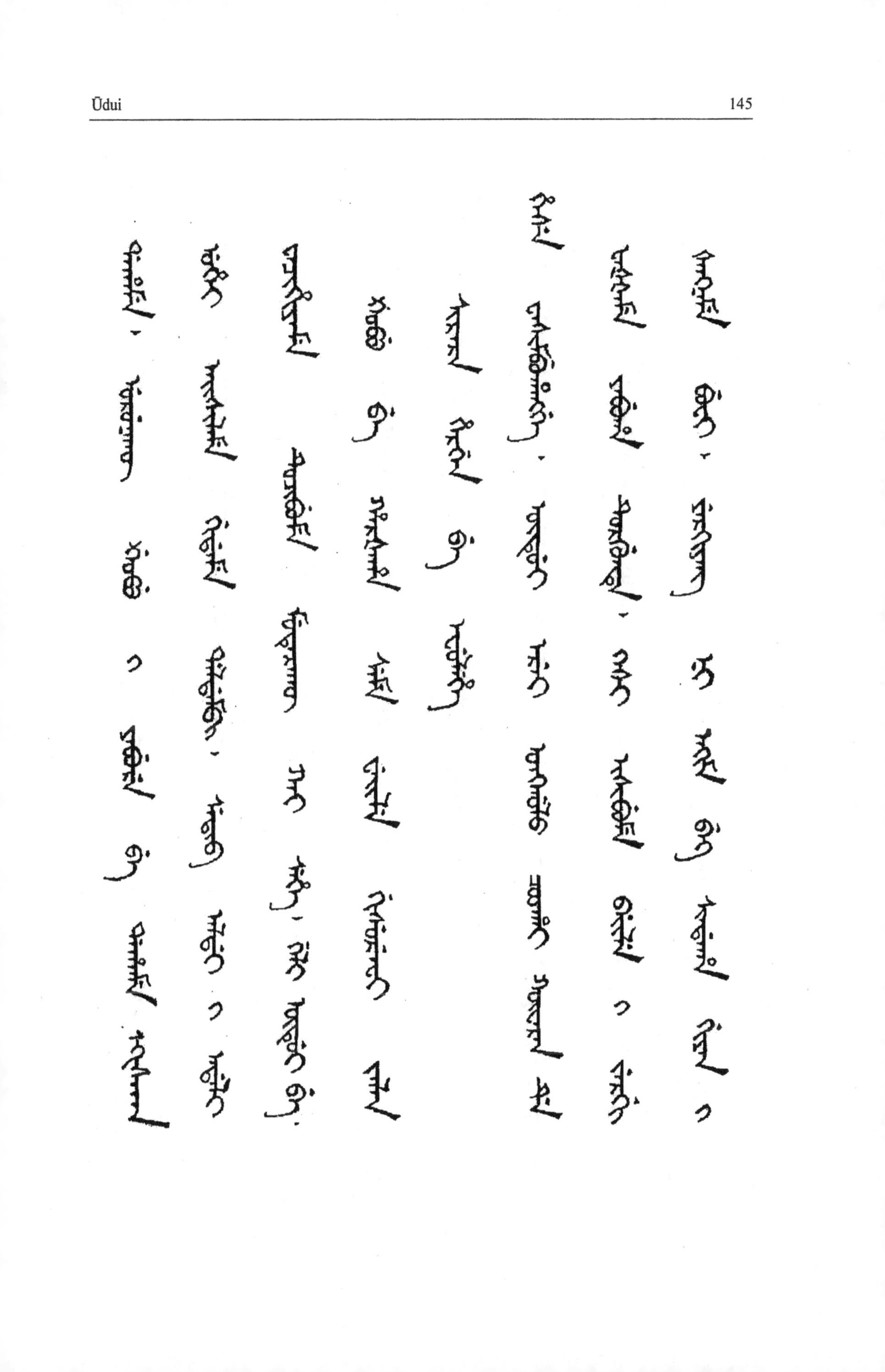

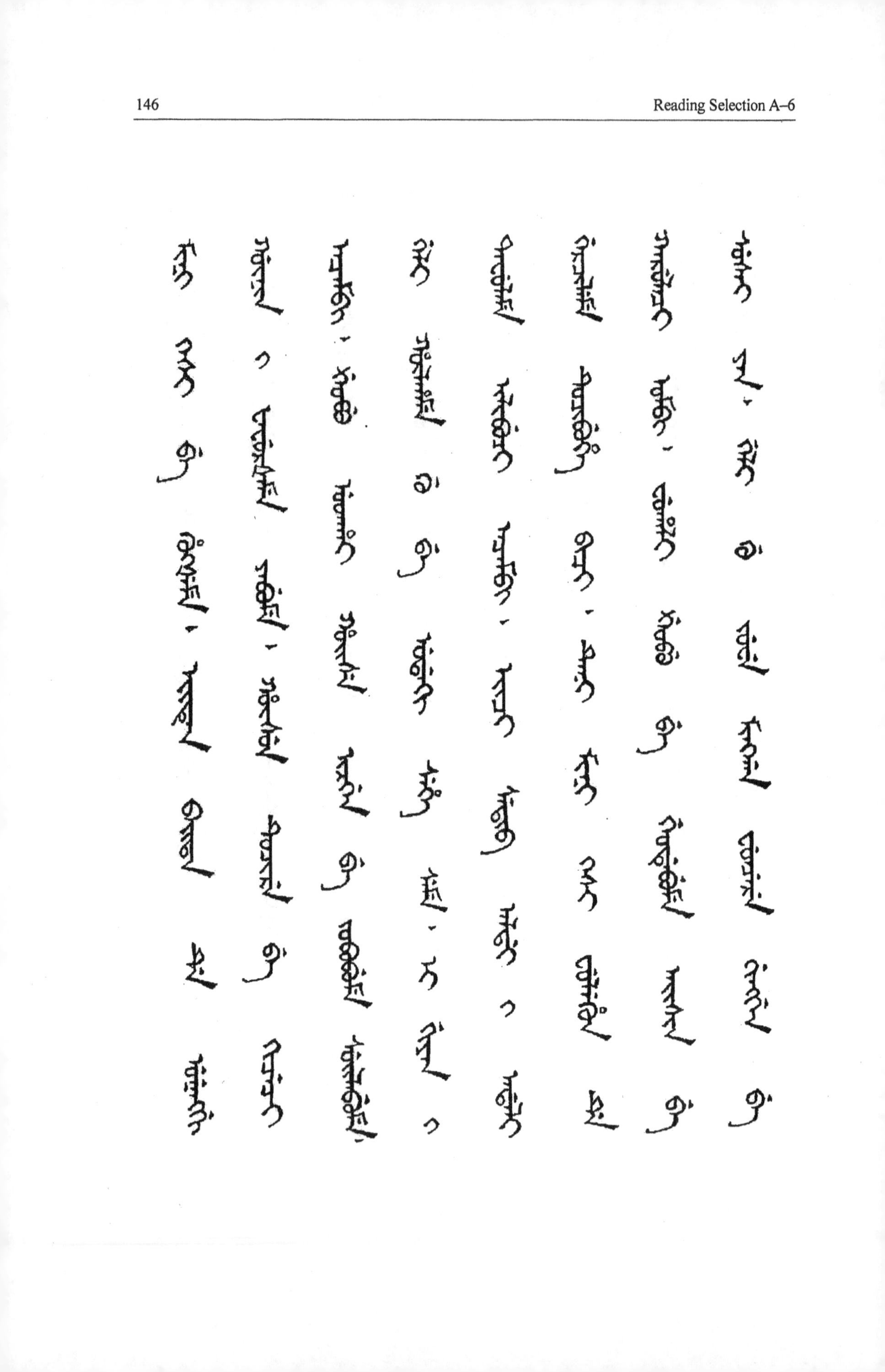

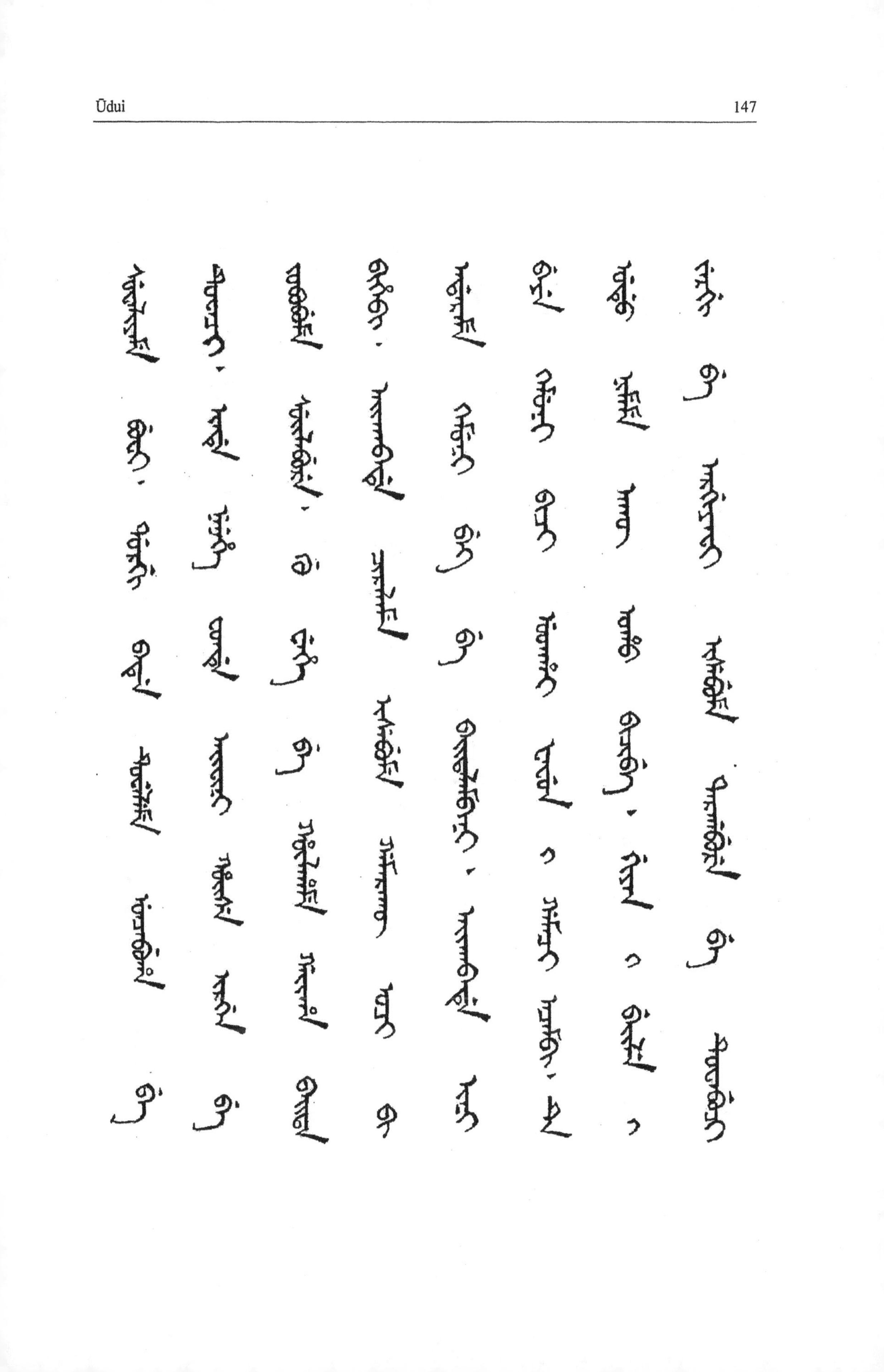

[illegible]

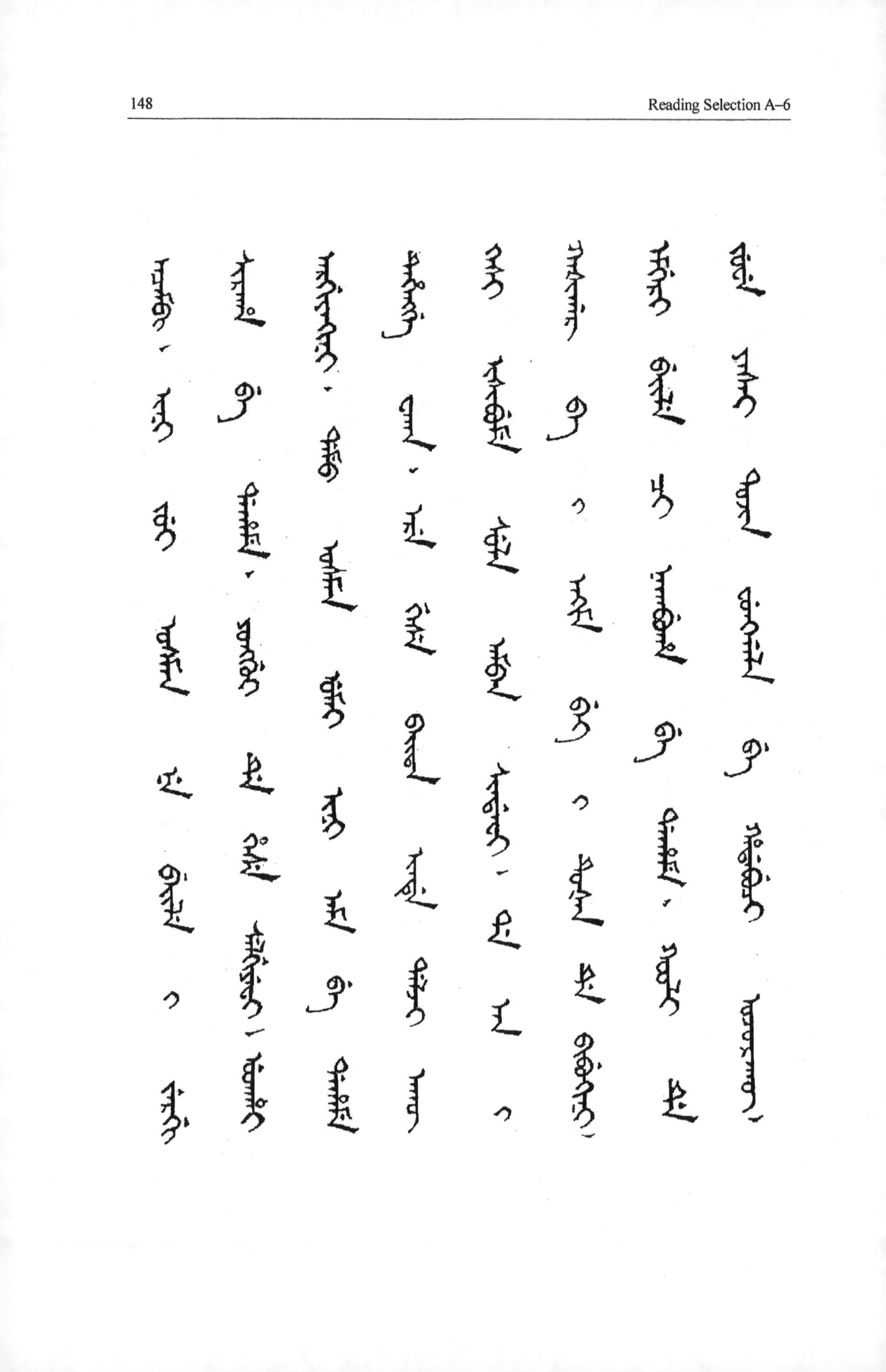

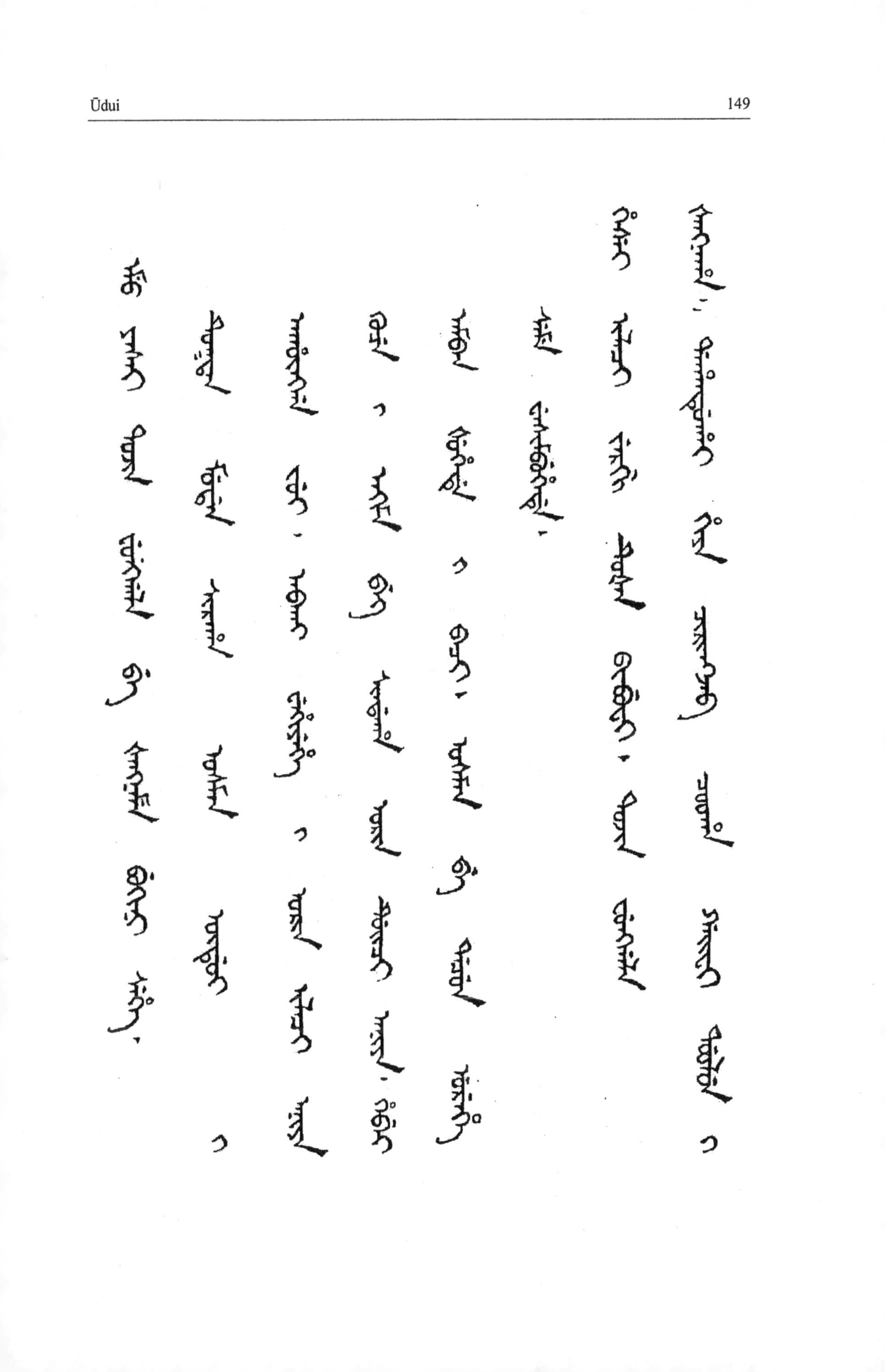

[illegible]

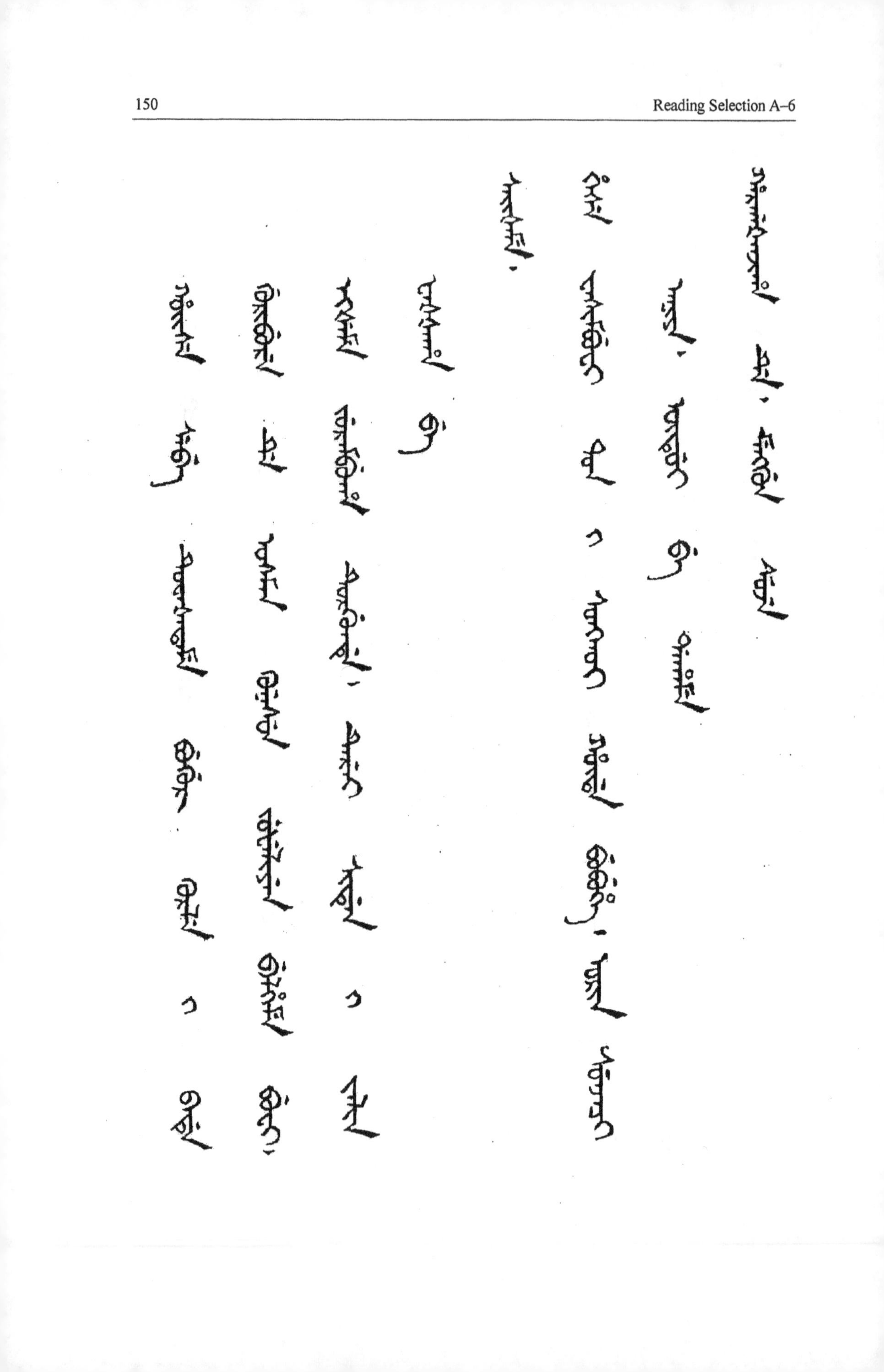

[illegible] [illegible] [illegible] [illegible] [illegible] ᡳ [illegible]
[illegible] ᡩᡝ [illegible] [illegible] [illegible] [illegible] [illegible]
[illegible] [illegible] [illegible] [illegible] [illegible] ᡳ [illegible]
[illegible] ᠪᡝ
[illegible]᠉
[illegible] [illegible] [illegible] ᡳ [illegible] [illegible] [illegible] [illegible] [illegible]
[illegible]᠈ [illegible] ᠪᡝ [illegible]
[illegible] ᡩᡝ᠈ [illegible] [illegible]

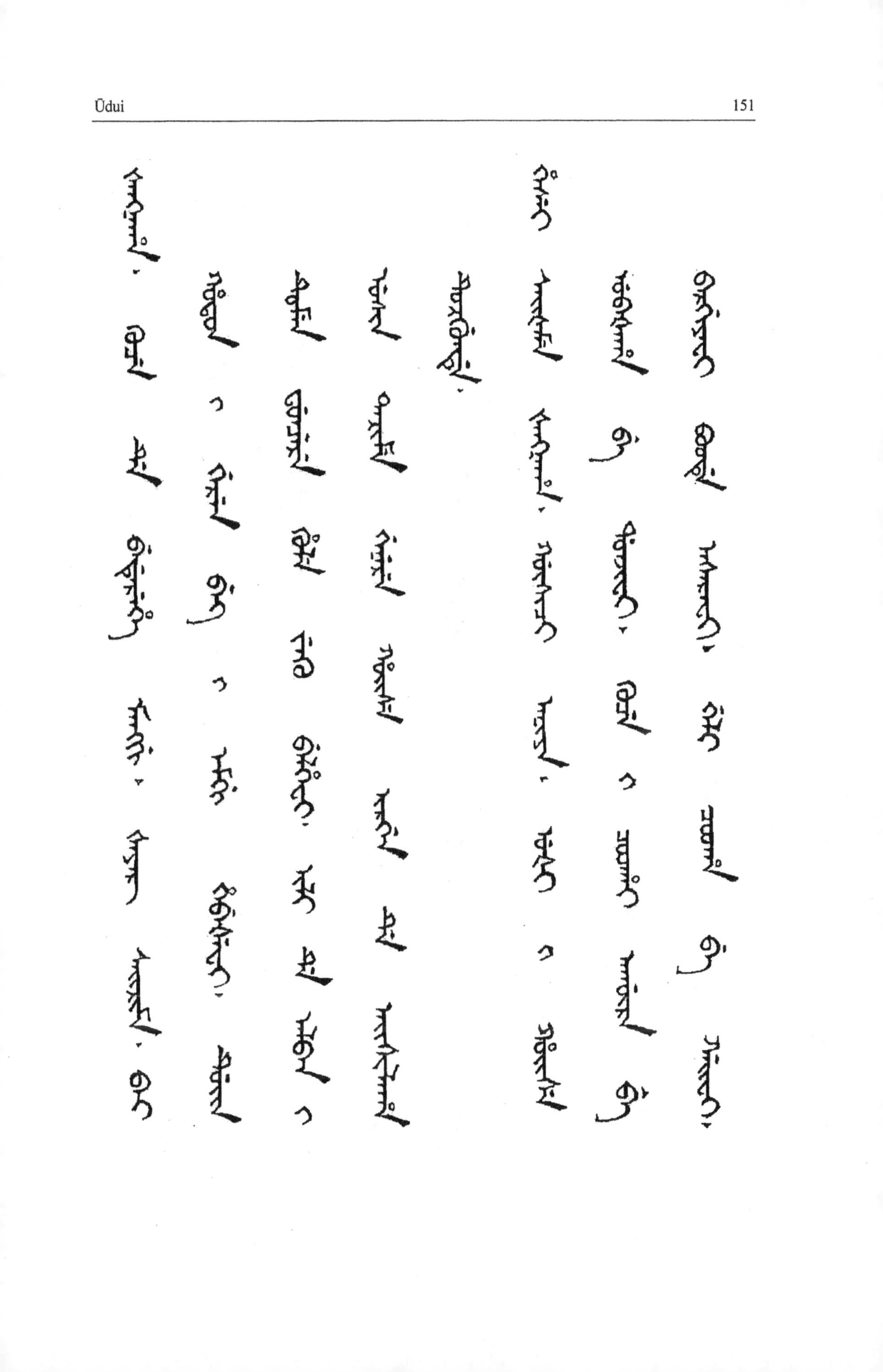

[illegible]

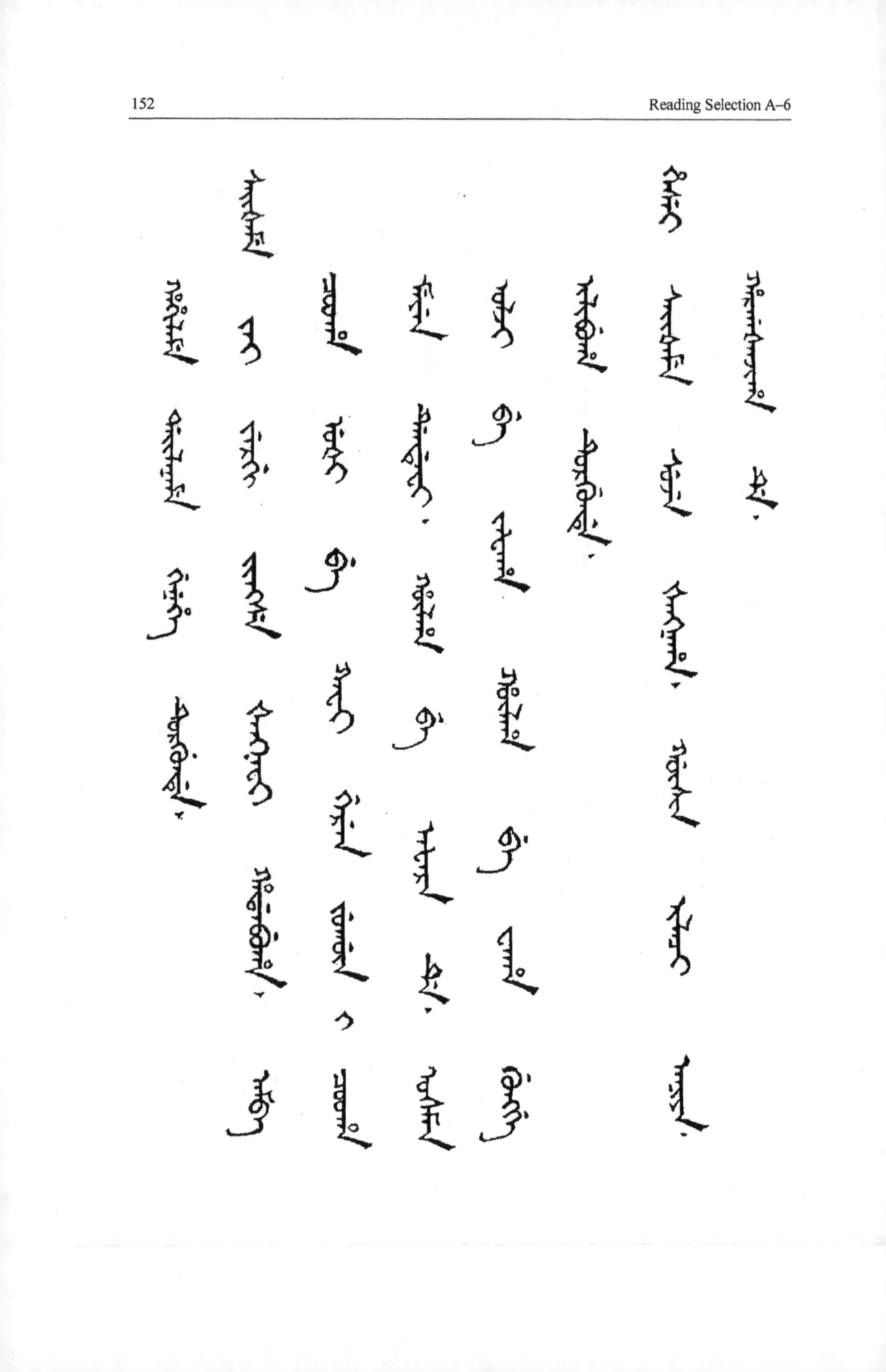

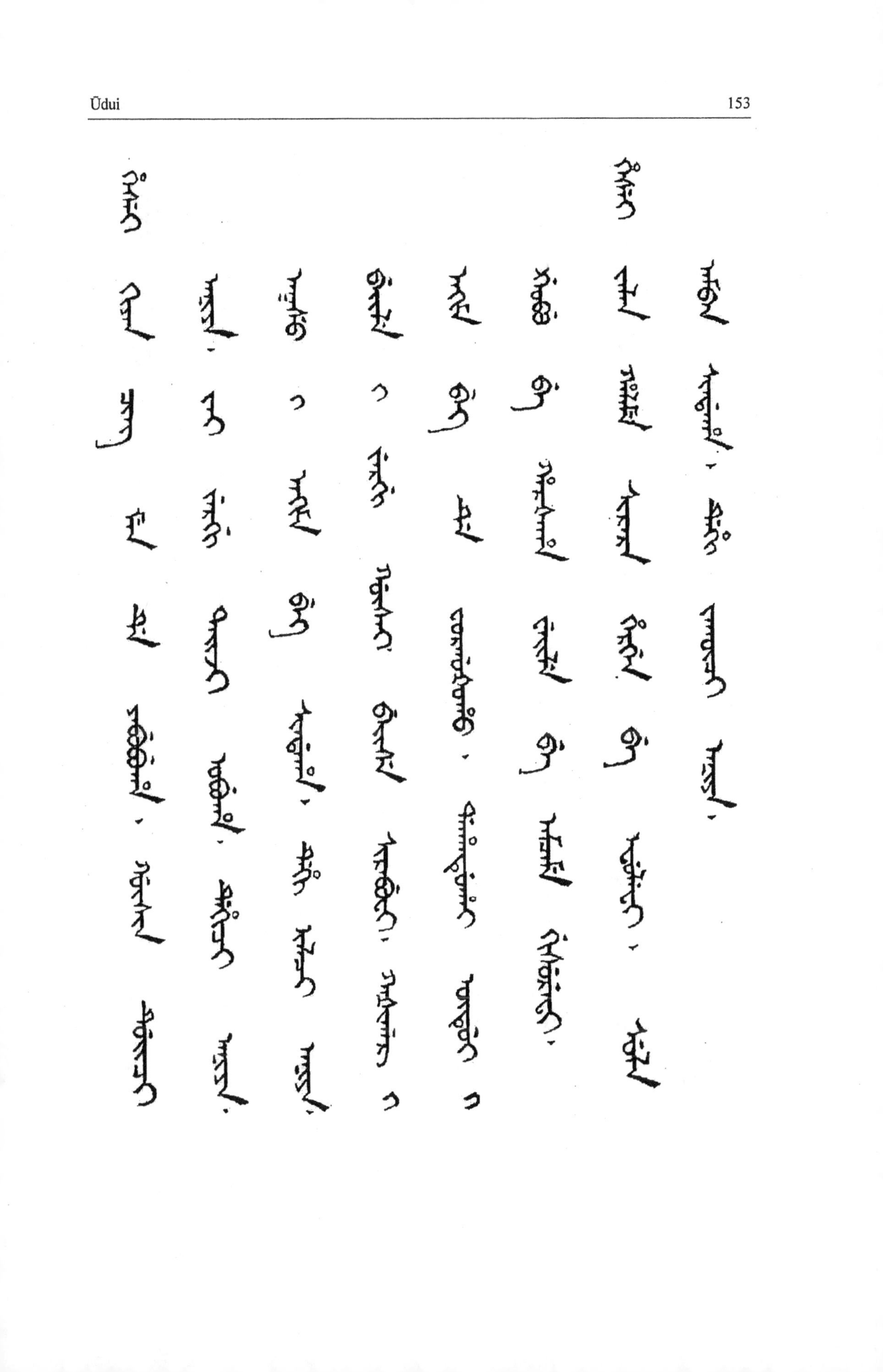

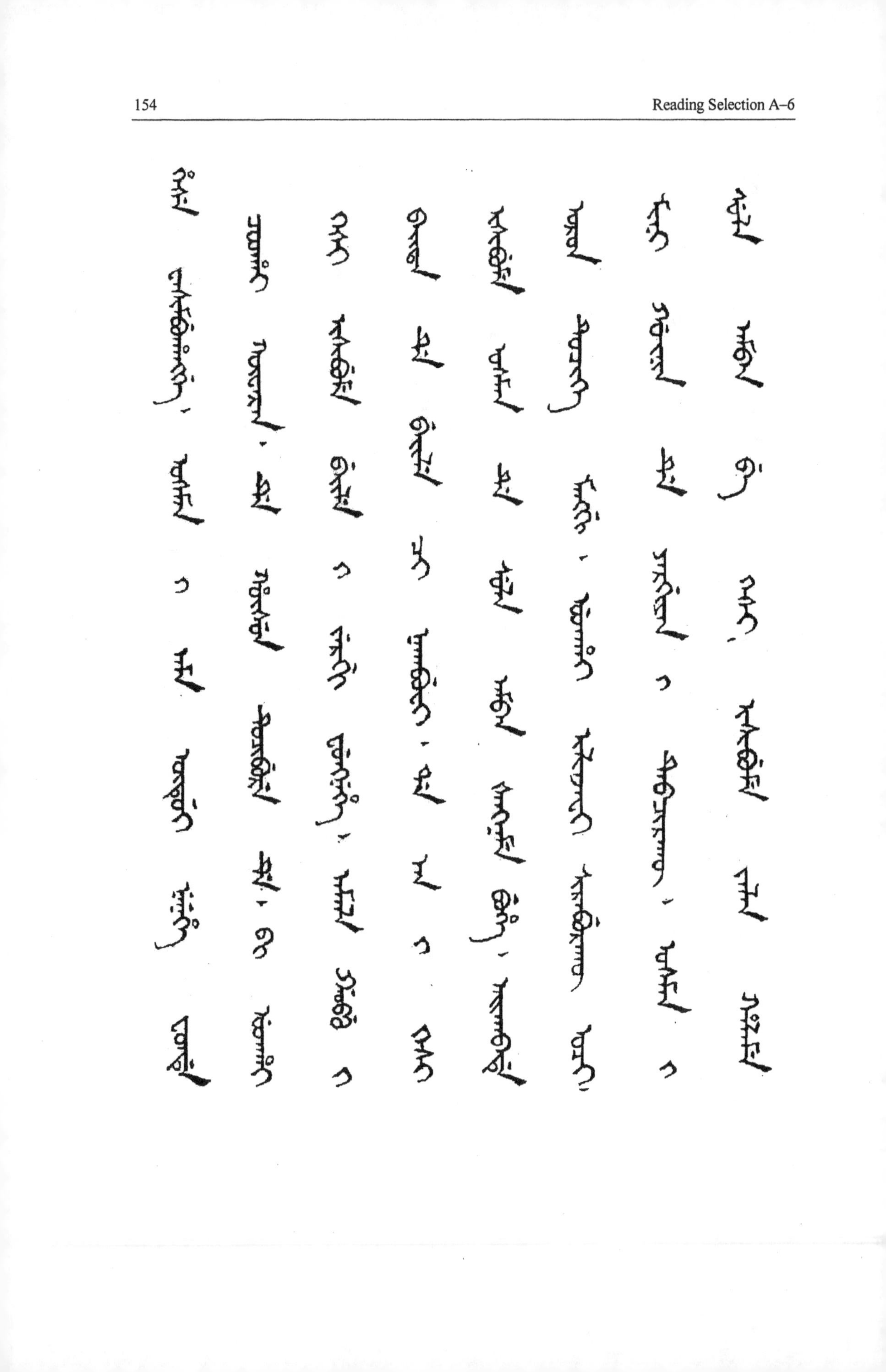

[illegible]

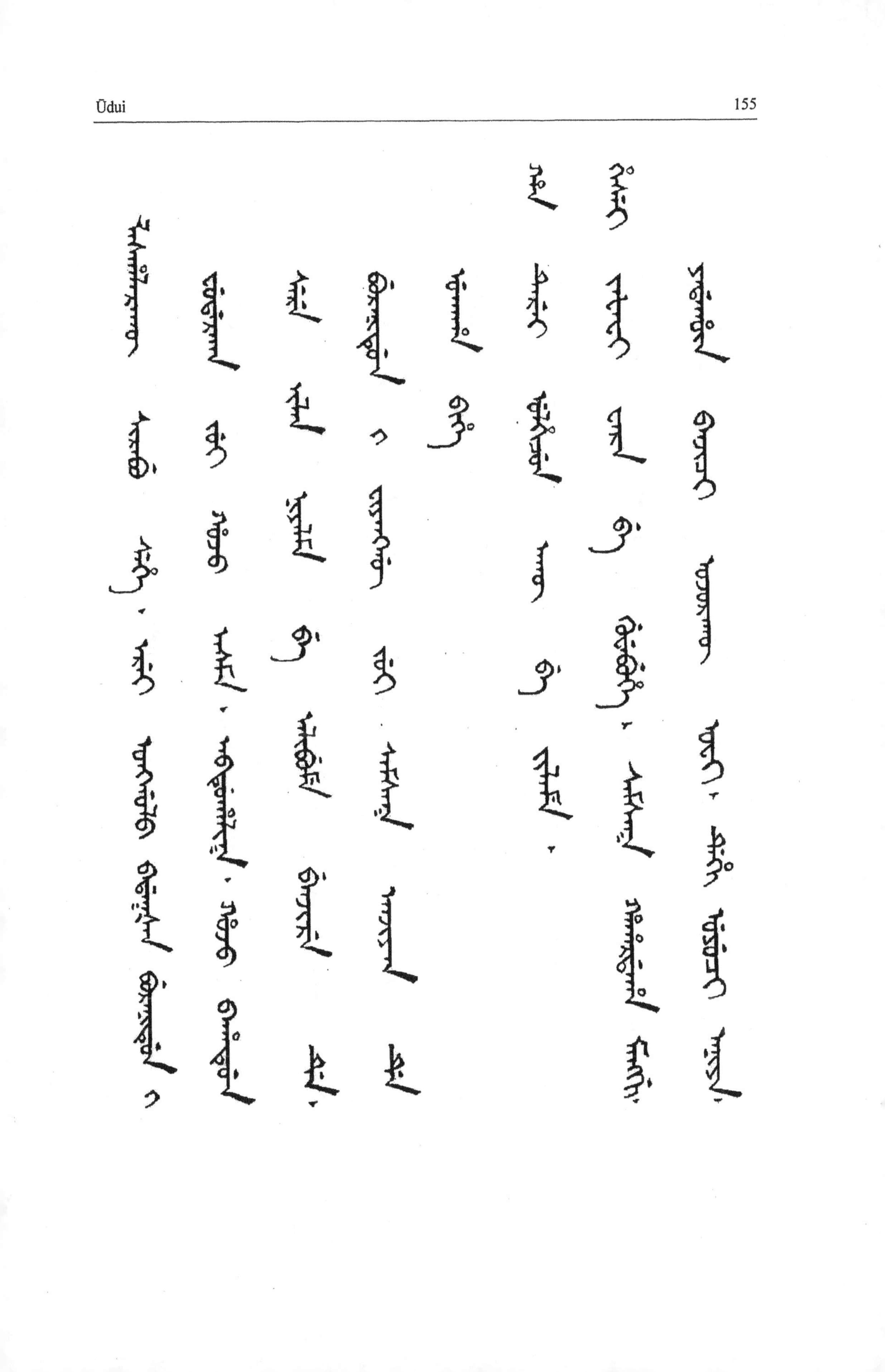

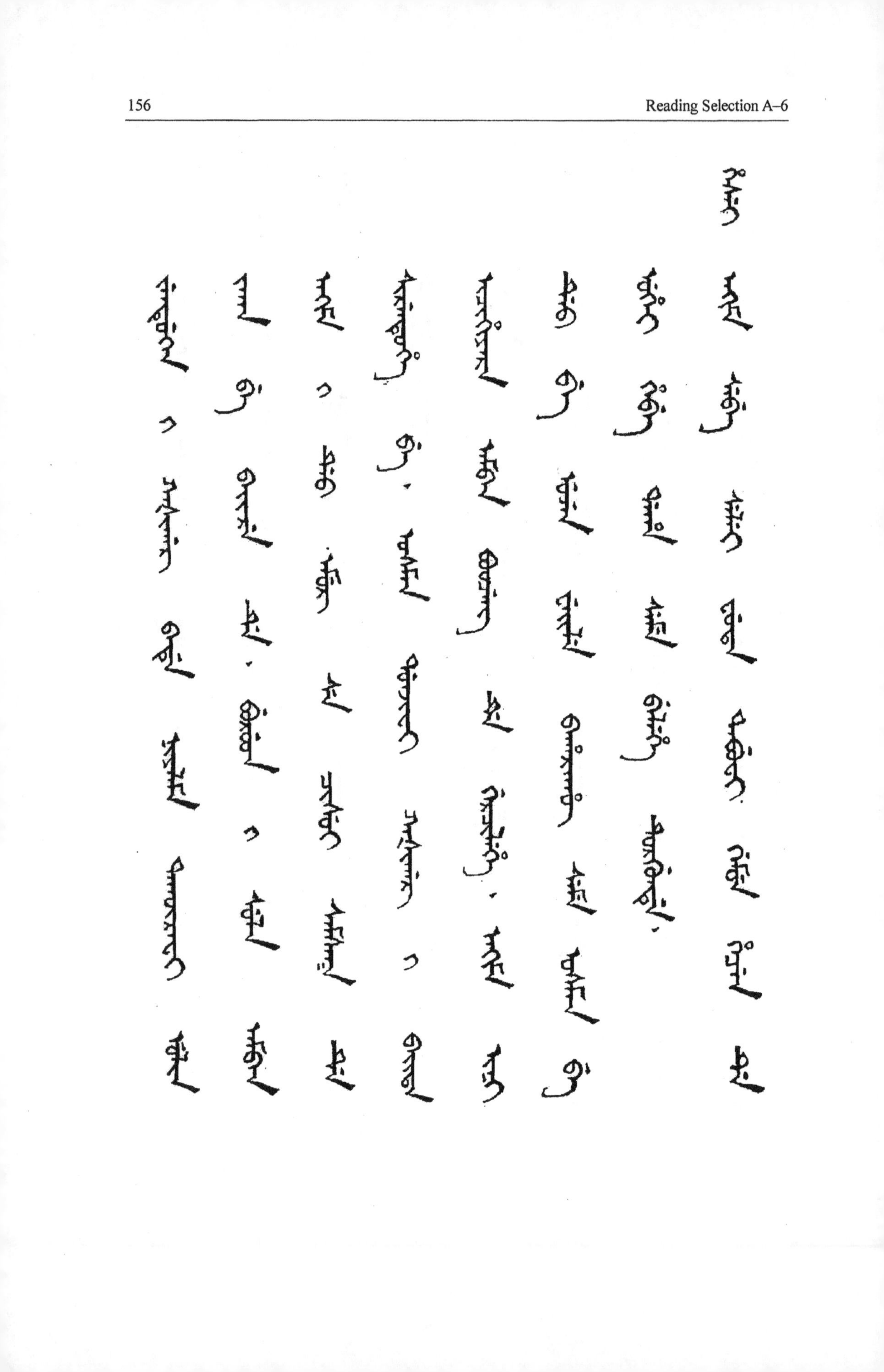

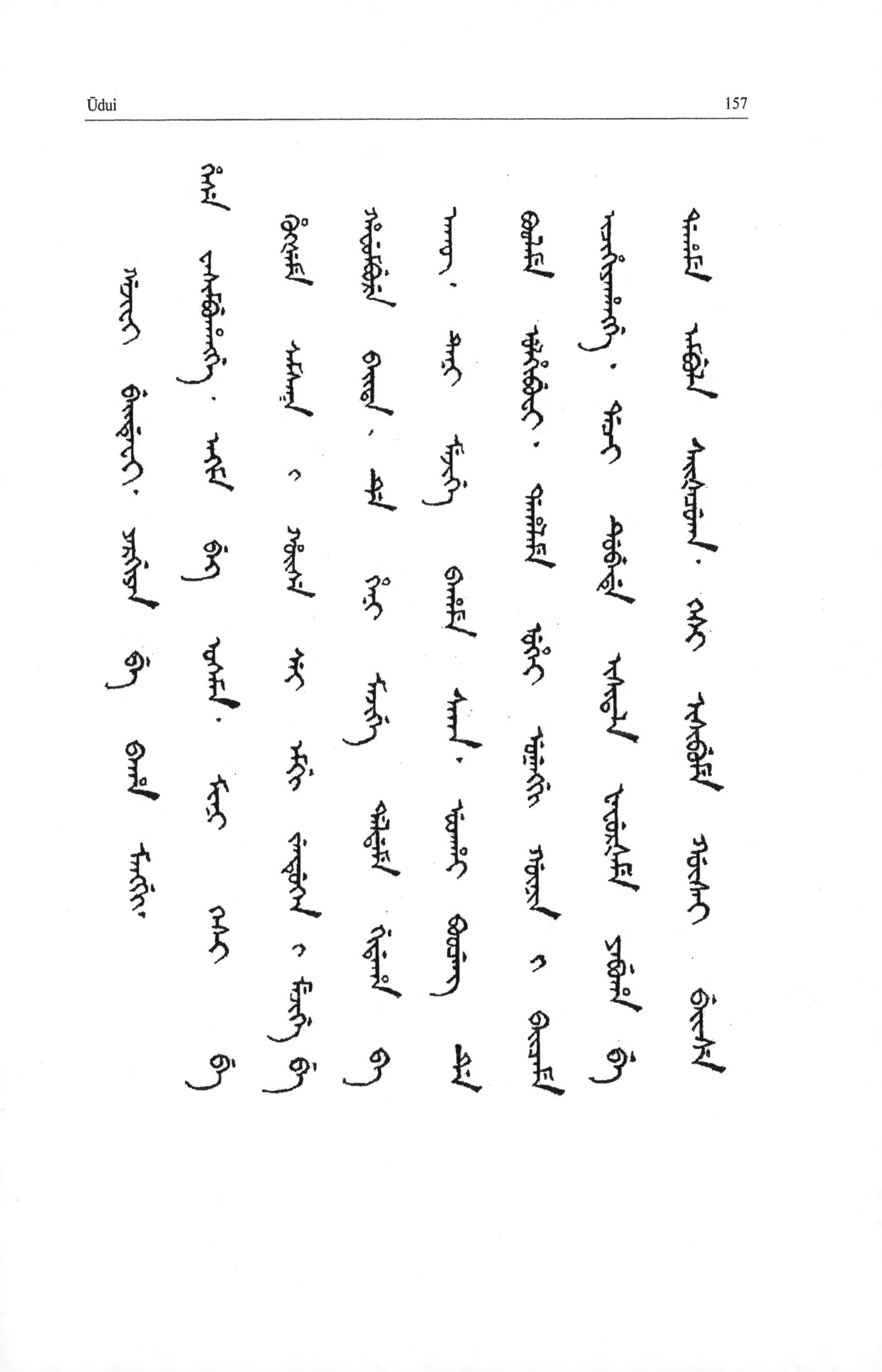

[illegible]

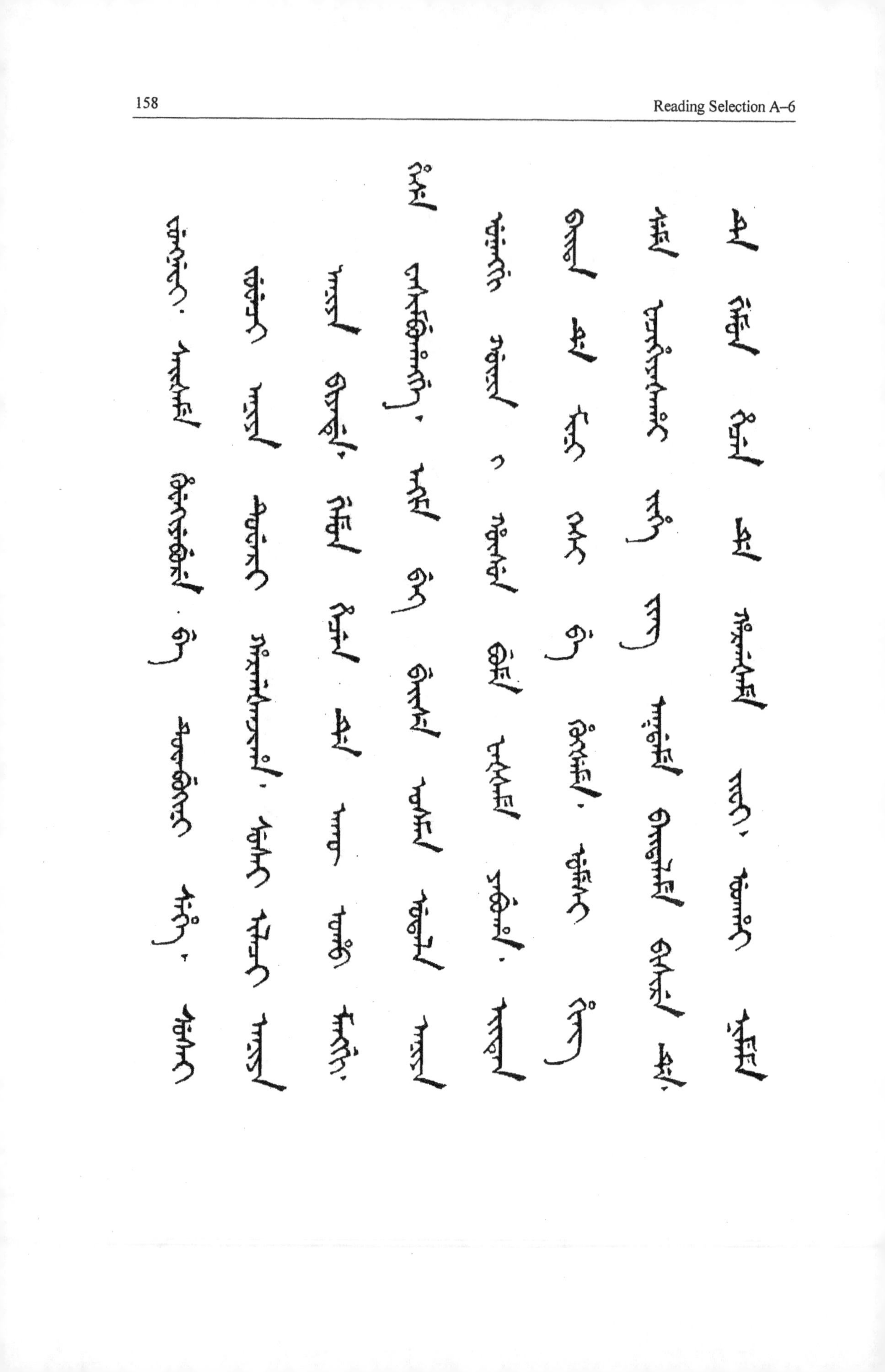

[illegible]

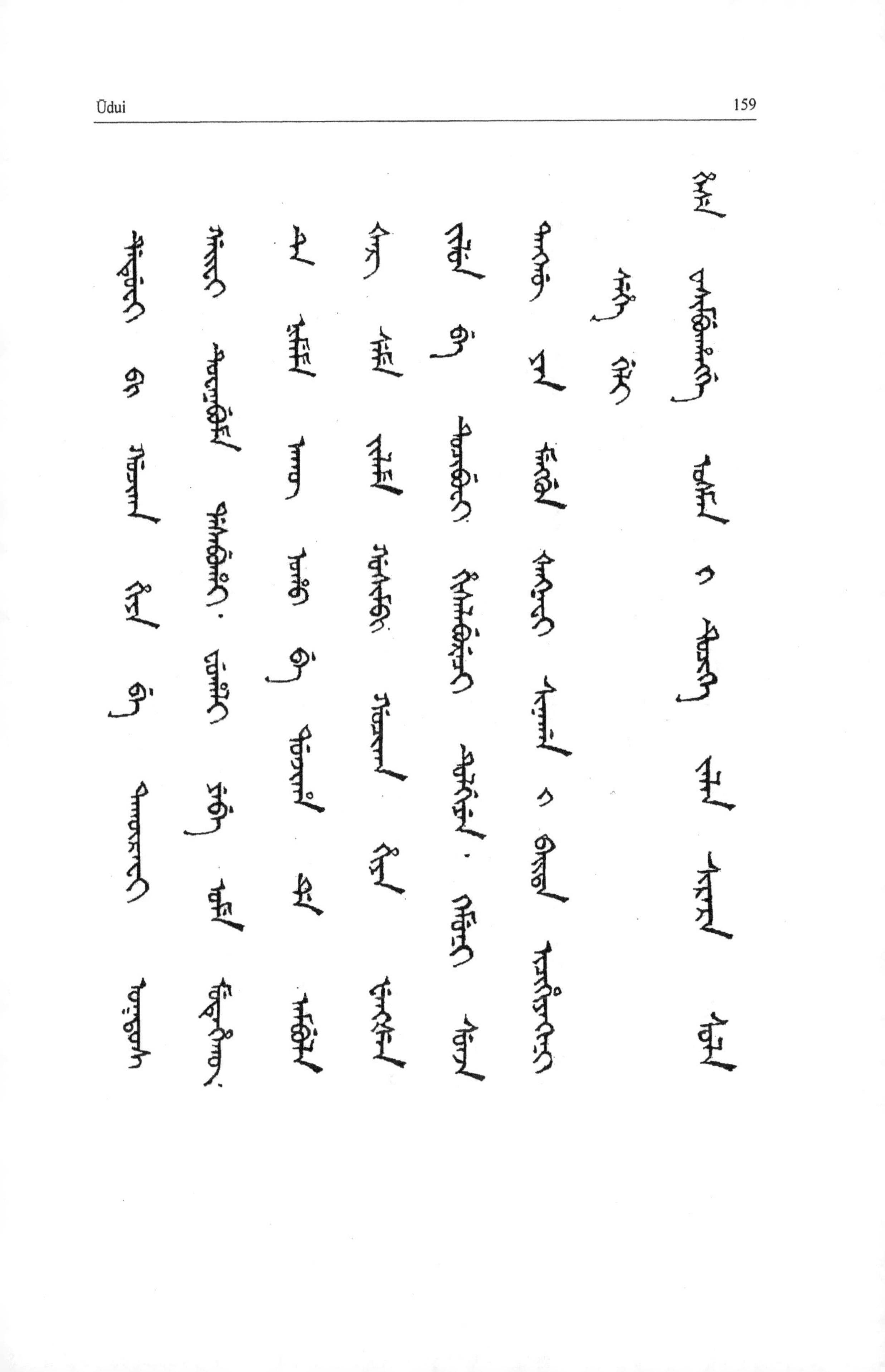

[illegible]

[illegible]

[illegible]

[illegible]

[illegible]

[illegible]

[illegible]

[illegible]

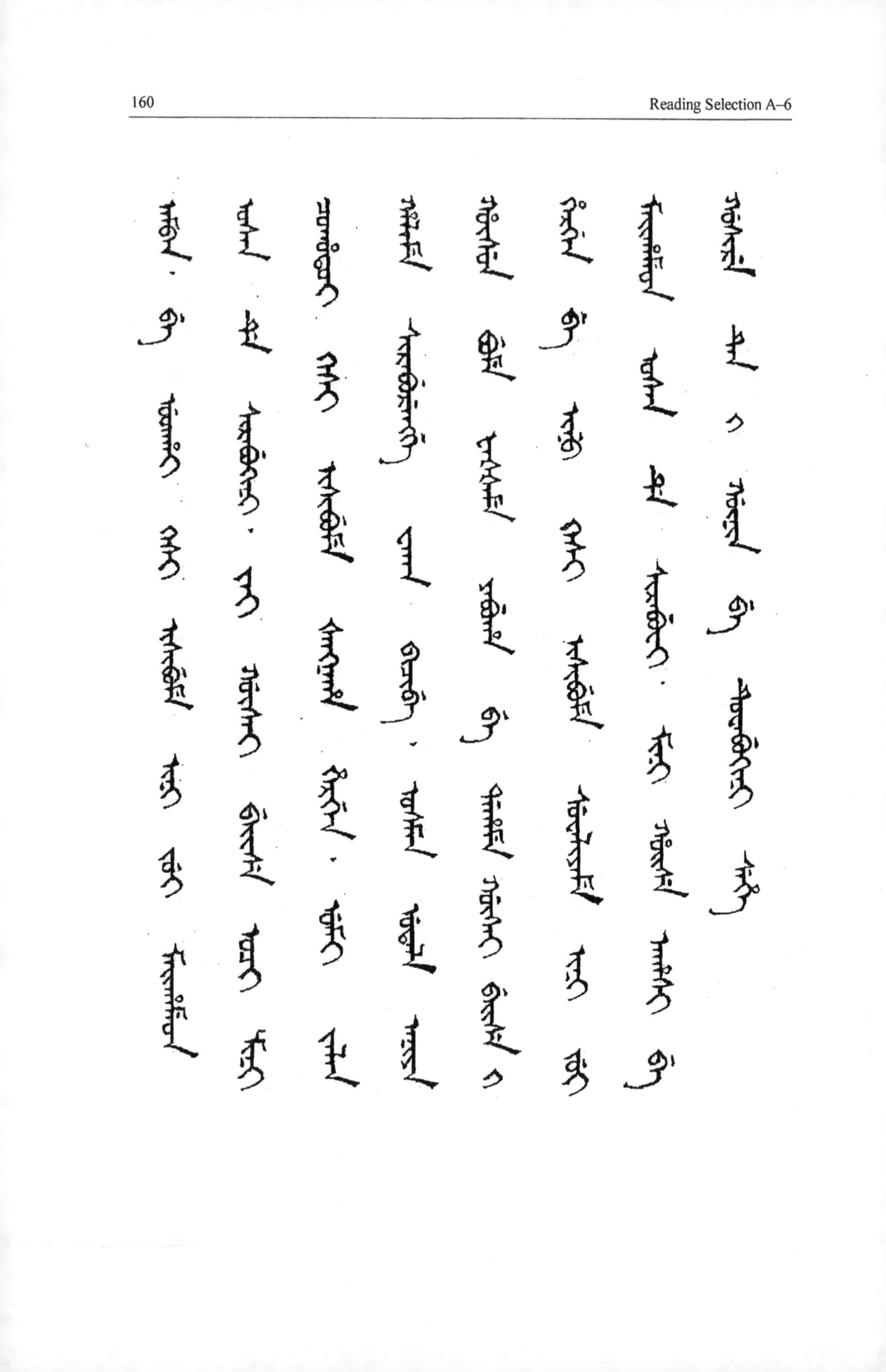

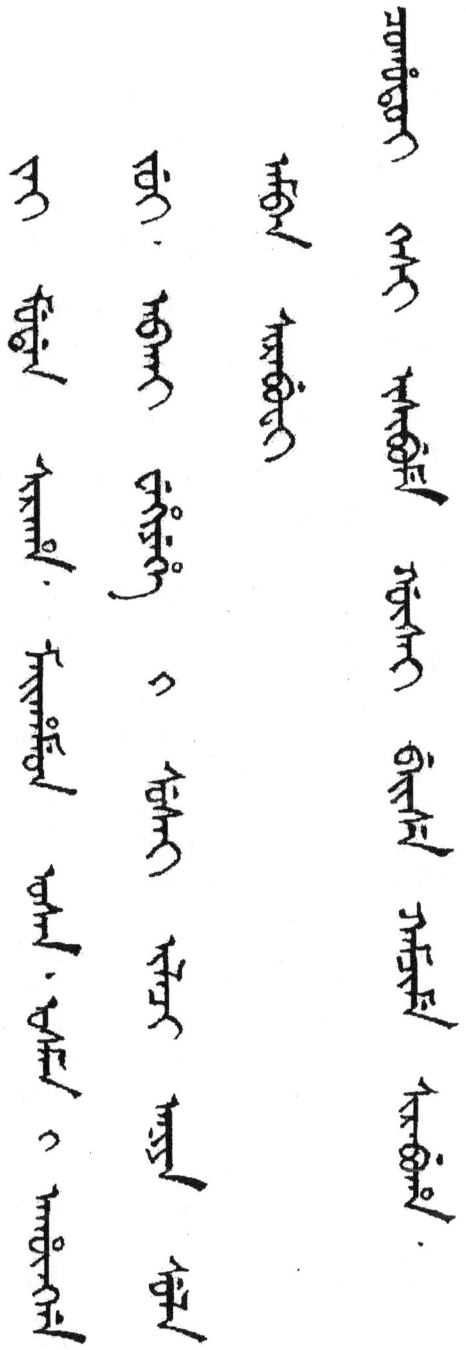

Transliteration

(115) *hesei toktobuha tulergi* [1] *Monggo hoise aiman i wang gung sai iletun ulabun i emu tanggū juwan jakūci debtelin. ulabun i emu tanggū juweci: da fungnehe beile i jergi* [2] *gūsai beile Ūdui i faidangga ulabun: ice jecen de tehe hoise hergen inu. te sula amban sirabufi wesibume gūsai beise fungnehe. Ūdui, Kuce i niyalma. erei mafa Mardza Nimet. ama Polat. jalan halame Kuce de tehebi. Ūdui siraha manggi, Jun gar imbe ergeleme Ili de guribufi, birai amargi Gulja de tebuhebi. abkai wehiyehe i orici*

(116) *aniya, amba cooha Jun gar be toktobuha manggi, Ūdui dahaki seme baiha. orin juweci aniya jecen be toktobure jiyanggiyūn Kalka i cin wang Cenggunjab be dahalame Ūlet i fudaraka hūlha be dailaha.*[3] *orin ilaci aniya, fudaraka be geterembure jiyanggiyūn Yarhašan fudaraka hoise Buranidun Hojijan be dailara de Ūdui dahalaki seme baiha turgunde, saišame sula amban sindafi tojin funggala*

(117) *šangnaha. nerginde fudaraka hūlhai duwali Abdukerem, Kuce i akim bek ofi, Ūdui i hūncihin mukūn* [4] *be suntebuhe. amba cooha Kuce de isinafi Ūdui jalan halame tubade tefi, tubai arbun be tengkime same ofi, meiren i janggin Šundenen de alafi, cooha unggifi hoton i tulergi bujan be ejelehe. hūlha isinjifi gelhun akū temšerakū. hoton i duka be yaksifi, juwan funcere inenggi oho manggi, Ūdui Yarhašan de*

(118) *alame hendume, «Kuce i hoton umesi akdun. tugi wan belhefi, mukei jugūn be lashalafi kaki. ere sidende dara cooha toktofi jimbi. hoton i dergi julergi ergi Kurle Kara Šar i jugūn de hafunacibe, jobocuka ba akū. amargi ergi Sairim de hafunacibe, Šaldalang, Osikbesi sere juwe kamni bi. tubade siliha cooha unggifi, wehe i sime dalibuha de,*[5] *hūlha sa ainaha seme isinjime muterakū. wargi ergi Šayar de hafunambi. tubade Ogen*

(119) *bira bi. muke mutuha erinde jahūdai šurume isinjici ombi.*[6] *dergi ergi, Yaha Tohonai, Tomulok ci Sairim i geren hoton de hafunambi. tubade cooha belhebuki» sehe manggi, Yarhašan cooha unggifi, geren kamni be seremšeme tuwakiyabuha. Abdukerem i deo Abduhalik juwe minggan funcere hūlha be gaifi, Tomulok jugūn de sucunjiha be afame gidaha* [7] *turgunde, hese wasimbuhangge: «Ūdui doigonde tosome seremšeci acara,*

(120) *oyonggo kamni* [8] *be ureme safi te hoisei hoton be afame gaiha be dahame, uthai bek obume sindakini» sehe. Hojijan geli sunja minggan funcere hūlha be gaifi Ogen bira ci Kuce de nikenjihe be* [9] *musei cooha gidaha turgunde, hesei Ūdui jai ini jui Osman de menggun suje šangnaha. nerginde Hojijan emgeri Kuce i hoton de dosika be musei cooha sarkū bihe.*[10] *jai inenggi hūlha hoton i*

(121) *duka be neifi sujame tucike de, Ūdui «cooha unggifi Ogen birai jakade tatabufi ukara jugūn be hetureki» seme baiha de Yarhašan seremšeme belhehekū*

ofi, Hojijan ukaha. tereci Kuce i hoton be gaiha manggi, Ūdui ini jui Osman be, Ilgar bek sei sasa Kuce hoton i baita be icihiyabume Šayar babe kadalabume afabufi ini beye cooha gaifi Aksu de genehe. jecen be toktobure jiyanggiyūn Jaohūi, Yarhašan

(122) *oronde genefi,*[11] *«Ūdui be tuwaci, baita afabuci ombi»*[12] *seme baime wesimbufi Aksu i akim bek obufi fe bek, Polat Babak sebe aisilabuha. Jaohūi dahanduhai Yerkiyang de cooha dosire de, Ūdui be hiya Gabšu Ciringjab sei sasa Hotiyan i jergi ninggun hoton de unggifi Elici de isinaha manggi, tubai bek se hoton be alibume dahaha. Ūdui terei geren be bilume toktobuha be, Kara Haši, Yurung*

(123) *Haši, Tak Cirla, Kerya i jergi hoton i niyalma donjifi, gemu dahaha. ede Ūdui geren bek i elcisa be, Yerkiyang ni coohai kūwaran de bithe benebume unggifi, ini beye bithe arafi Aksu de unggihe. Ūdui i sargan Aksu hoton de teme ofi, boso jai jibca be tucibufi, seremšeme tehe coohai urse de aisilame buhe turgunde, hesei Ūdui be dorgi amban sindaha. nerginde Hojijan geren*

(124) *hūlha be gaifi, Kara Usu i bade amba cooha be sujame bisire* [13] *turgunde, Hotiyan i coohai bithe fuhali hafunjihakū. Ūdui dame geneki seme* [14] *hūlhai Hotiyan hoton de sucunaha be mejigešeme safi,*[15] *niyalma takūrafi feksihei* [16] *Aksu de alanabuha. hebei amban Šuhede geren jugūn i cooha be isabufi, Kara Usu Hotiyan hoton be dendeme danabume unggire de, Ūdui i sargan cooha de tanggū morin i aisilaha bime, Ūdui geli Hotiyan i*

(125) *baci minggan cooha isabufi, honin jai jufeliyen be belhefi hūlha be tosoro baitalan* [17] *obuha turgunde hese wasimbuhangge: «Ūdui dahame coohalaha ci ebsi, eiten de faššame yabuha bime, ere mudan ele unenggi be iletulehebi. ede kesi isibume gung ni jergi šangna» sehe. amala hūlhai hoki Abdukerem se, Elici Hara Haši i siden de amasi julesi yabure be, Ūdui bek sede akdulame sujakini seme bithe unggifi,*

(126) *ninggun hoton i bek i gebu jai boigon ulha i ton be arafi, Aksu de jasiha. dara cooha isinjiha manggi, geren hoton de dendeme unggihe. hūlha geli holo bithe be selgiyeme geren be ergelere jakade* [18] *Ūdui dasame Aksu de niyalma takūrafi alanabuha. Aksu i cooha komso ofi, juwe tanggū cooha tucibufi danabume unggihe de, Ūdui i sargan, bek sei sasa ceni harangga susai niyalma be*

(127) *kunesun gamabume dahalabuha. Ūdui geren hoton de, «amba cooha isinjire hamika. akdulame tuwakiyakini» seme bithe unggihe. ishun aniya niyengniyeri, amba cooha Kara Usu i kaha babe afame efulefi, meiren i janggin Batujirgal se uyun tanggū cooha gaifi Hotiyan de dame genehe be, Ūdui Elici i hoton i duka be neifi tucifi, Hara Haši de okdome genefi* [19] *hūlha be Boroci i bade afame gidafi, geren hoton be bithe*

(128) *selgiyeme toktobufi, ini sargan i ahūn Aman bek be takūrafi, feksihei Aksu de alanabuha. nerginde jecen be toktobure hashū ergi aisilara jiyanggiyūn Fude isinjiha be,*[20] *Ūdui ini jalahi jui Abdurman be takūrafi, ninggun hoton i bek be gaifi, goro okdobuha. etehe babe donjibume wesimbuhede, Hotiyan be akdulame tuwakiyaha gungge be saišame, hesei Ūdui be gurun de aisalara gung fungnefi, Aksu de bederebuhe.*

(129) *Abdurman be ilaci jergi hiya sindaha. tere fonde, Jaohūi, Fude i cooha be* [21] *jugūn dendefi ibebuki seme gisurehe turgunde, hese wasimbuhangge: «Ūdui coohai bade faššame yabume juwe aniya oho, majige ergembuci acambi. donjici ini aciha hūlha de duribuhe sembi.*[22] *bi ambula šar seme gosimbi. ede juwe tanggū yan menggun šangnafi imbe Aksu de baita icihiyakini. ini cihanggai cooha de geneki seme baiha gisun unenggi oci,*

(130) *uthai ini sasa* [23] *genekini. kemuni gūnin werešeme jilame gosi»*[24] *sehe. teni hese wasimbuha manggi, Jaohūi i baci Ūdui i hing seme cooha de geneki seme baiha babe wesimbume isinjiha* [25] *turgunde, hesei ubui i nonggime dasatara menggun buhe. Buranidun Hojijan amba cooha isinaha be donjifi gemu ukaha. Ūdui Kašigar de isinafi hahilame Fude i cooha de acafi, hūlha be Alcur de gidaha. hūlha Isil Kur de burulaha be*

(131) *amba cooha meyen dendefi gidaha.*[26] *Ūdui Hotiyan i bek Hojis sei sasa turun elkime daha seme sureme hūlara de, hūlhai hoki tumen funcere niyalma feksime jifi dahara be baiha.*[27] *Buranidun, Hojijan, Badakšan de ukaha manggi, Fude Ūdui be takūrafi, dahaha geren hoise be gaifi, Kašigar de bederebuhe. ede hesei «Ūdui be fafuršame baturulame hūlha be gisabume waha» seme saišame wesibume, gūsai beise fungnehe. Badakšan Hojijan i*

(132) *uju be alibume benjihe de, oljilaha fudaraka hūlhai boigon anggalai dorgi Sakalsopi gebungge niyalmai sargan uthai Abdurman i non ofi, hesei Ūdui de buhe. dahanduhai «Ūdui be, gungge mutebufi amasi marire cooha* [28] *be dahalame hargašanjikini» seme, hese wasimbufi, wesibume beile i jergi fungnehe. orin sunjaci aniya niyengniyeri, Ūdui isinjiha manggi*

(133) *tob amba elden genggiyen i deyen de hūlame dosimbufi hargašabufi doroi etuku šangnafi, fung je yuwan de etefi isinjiha doroi omibufi,*[29] *menggun suje bufi, hesei ini arbun be jaksaka eldengge asari de nirubuha. han i araha maktacun i gisun «Ili be necihiyere fon ci dahanjifi, wang ni jalin faššaha. hoisei dorgi colgorome tucike niyalma.*

(134) *terei mujilen yargiyan i saišacuka. Hotiyan de tohorombume genefi, ilan biya otolo* [30] *kabuha. Gabšu i sasa karmame tuwakiyame mujakū fafuršaha» sehebi. tere fonde Aksu i isigan bek Polat, akim bek oki seme hiracame geren hoise be šusihiyeme, ini beyebe akdulabumbime, Ūdui be habšabuha* [31] *de Šuhede wakašafi donjibume wesimbuhe manggi, hese wasimbuhangge «hoise se ishunde buhiyeme silhidara tuheburengge, gemu ceni fe tacin. erebe giyan i ciralame fafulaci*

(135) *acambi. Ūdui uthai doosidame gamjidame yabukini, inu* [32] *Polat i gisun de nakabuci ojorakū.*[33] *tere anggala, Ūdui be uthai ere turgunde weile araci, Polat i kanagan be jorime geren be aššabume, akim obure be kicere weile* [34] *be, inu giyan i icihiyaci acambi. ainaha seme ini koimali arga de dosinafi, akim obure kooli akū»*[35] *sehe. geli Aksu i niyalma Ūdui be habšaha. aika da tušan de unggici, elhe ojorakū ayoo seme*

(136) *hesei Yerkiyang ni akim bek de forgošoho. Ūdui Yerkiyang de isinafi, isigan bek Abdura'im* [36] *se ahun i gebu be habšara bithei uju de arafi, Ūdui be nure omire de amuran bime, dabduri balama tušan be muteburakū seme habšaha manggi, hese «geren hoton i hoise de ulgibu. ereci julesi eiten baita be, gemu akim bek de afabufi, icihiya. ahun balai daci ojorakū» sehe. baita icihiyara gūsa be kadalara*

(137) *amban Sinju i baci, «Ūdui, Abdura'im ese aika ishunde buhiyeme silhidara oci, siden i baita be tookabure ayoo» seme wesimbuhe manggi, hese wasimbuhangge: «hoise sei banin kelfišeme kenehunjere mangga.*[37] *aika ceni funde gidame daldaci, ce ele elhe baharakū de isinambi. mini gūnin de ese be siden i bade gajifi, geren i juleri ceni uru waka be faksalame tucibufi, emu jergi tacibure oci,*[38] *Ūdui buhiyeme kenehunjerakū ombime,*[39] *Abdura'im*

(138) *inu balai seremšerakū ombi. ce aliyame gūnifi uhei hūwaliyasun gaime emu gūnin i baita icihiyara de, teni mayan tataburakū ombi» sehe. Abdura'im akim bek be bahakū jalin, cisui Hoohan i Erdeni bek i emgi fudasihūn deribuki seme hebešehe. baita firgehe turgunde, fafun i gamaha. orin ningguci aniya, hese wasimbuhangge: «neneme hoise sei fe tacin, yaya bek oho urse,*[40] *urui ceni fejergi urse be jobobume*

(139) *gejureme gaime ofi,*[41] *tuttu bi kesi isibume geren hoton i akim bek sede tengge usin takūrara niyalma šangnahangge, siden i jalin tuwakiyame* [42] *beyebe hairakini sehengge.*[43] *te donjici Yerkiyang ni bek Ūdui, Kašigar i bek Gadaimet se, teisu be tuwakiyame banjime, fejergi hoise sebe jobobume gejureme gaiha hacin akū sembi. umesi saišacuka. bi ceni dahanjihangge inenggi goidaha be gūnime, alban i bure* [44] *ninggun tanggū*

(140) *tengge ci tulgiyen, jai juwe tanggū tengge nonggime šangnafi, huwekiyebure be tuwabu. ere mini cohotoi isibuha kesi. kooli obuci ojorakū» sehe. dehici aniya hese wasimbuhangge; «beile i jergi Ūdui gung ni jergi Gadaimet serengge, ese gemu hoise babe bahara onggolo, Ili i bade dahanjiha. ere dade, coohai kūwaran de ambula gungge ilibuha. kesi isibume fungnehengge de duibuleci ojorakū. esei jergi be gemu jalan halame lashalarakū*

(141) *sirabukini» sehe. dehi ilaci aniya Ūdui akū oho manggi, hesei ini jui Osman de beile i jergi sirabufi, juwe yasai tojin funggala šangnaha. tere fonde Osman Aksu i akim bek oho bihe. Yerkiyang ni baita icihiyara ashan i amban G'aopu, «imbe Ūdui be sirame Yerkiyang ni akim bek obureo* [45]*» seme baime wesimbuhede*

(142) *han jabubuhakū. hesei Osman be Kašigar i bade forgošofi, Kašigar i bek Setib Aldi be Yerkiyang ni bade forgošoho. Uši ba i baita icihiyara ilaci jergi amban Yonggui, dahanduhai Setib Aldi i «G'aopu be hoise irgen be jobobume oshodoho. cisui alban i gu be uncaha» seme gercilehe babe wesimbuhede,*[46] *hesei beidebufi yargiyan be bahara jakade, G'aopu be*

(143) *fafun i gamaha. hese wasimbuhangge: « ere aniya ilan biyade, Ūdui nimeme akū oho manggi, G'aopu uthai Ūdui i jui Osman be harangga ba i akim bek i baita be alifi icihiyabure be baime wesimbuhede,*[47] *bi aikabade uttu ama jui ishunde sirabume baita icihiyabuci, fuhali Yerkiyang ni akim* [48] *esei booi jalan halame sirara hafan i adali be dahame, bihe bihei Tang gurun i jase be tuwakiyara*

(144) *amban ci encu akū seme gūnime,*[49] *tuttu Setib Aldi be harangga bade forgošofi, Osman be Kašigar i bade unggihengge hoise aiman i bek be ser sere be seremšeme badaran be sibuki sere gūnin.*[50] *aikabade G'aopu i wesimbuhe be dahame, Osman be tubade akim bek obuha bici, Osman ini ama i G'aopu de banjire sain be safi, dere de eterakū ombihe. tere anggala i se asihan ofi, baita alime muterakū be*

(145) *dahame, urunakū G'aopu i yabure be dahame ekisaka uhei aisilame gidame daldambi. Setib Aldi i adali wacihiyame tucibume muterakū kai» sehe. geli Ūdui be, G'aopu be haršaha seme weile gisurefi* [51] *jalan sirara hergen be efulehe. hese wasimbuhangge: «Ūdui erei onggolo coohai kūwaran de faššame yabuha turgunde, kesi isibume beile i jergi šangname bufi, Yerkiyang ni akim bek sindaha. giyan i*

(146) *mini kesi be hukšeme, eiten baita de unenggi gūnin i fafuršame yabume, hūsun tucire be kiceci acambi. G'aopu uthai hoise irgen be jobobume suilabume, geli hūlhame gu be udaki sehe seme,*[52] *i giyan i tafulame ilibuci acambi.*[53] *eici Setib Aldi i adali gercileme tucibuhe bici, teni mini kesi fulehun de karulaci ombi.*[54] *fuhali G'aopu be geodebume aisin be susai yan, geli gu juwe minggan funcere ginggen be*

(147) *suwaliyame bufi, dorgi bade tuweleme uncabuha be tuwaci, inde nenehe fonde aifini hoise irgen be jobobume suilabure, gu wehe be hūlhame gaiha baita bihebi.*[55] *aikabade ciralame isebume gamarakū oci bi adarame kemuni bek be baitalambini. aikabade ini beye kemuni bici,*[56] *uthai fafun i gamaci acambi. te udu nimeme akū oho bicibe, giyan i beile i jergi be argiyafi isebume targabure be tuwabuci*

(148) *acambi.*[57] *ini jui Osman ne beile i jergi siraha be dahame, Yonggui de hese selgiyefi, uthai argiyakini. damu Osman umai ini ama be dahame tehengge waka.*[58] *ere gese baita inde dalji akū. kesi isibume sula amban sindafi, da an i Kašigar ba i akim bek i tušan de bibukini. emgeri beile ci nakabuha be dahame, kooli de juwe yasai tojin funggala be hadabuci ojorakū.*

(149) *emu yasai tojin funggala be šangname bukini» sehe. tuktan mudan siraha Osman Ūdui i ahūngga jui. abkai wehiyehe i orin ilaci aniya Kuce i akim bek sindaha. orin duici aniya, hebei amban Šuhede i baci, Osman be dacun urehe seme wesimbuhede, hesei ilaci jergi tušan bibufi, tojin funggala šangnaha. dahanduhai hiya Ciringjab cooha gaifi Doolun i*

(150) *hoise sebe tuwašatame Bugur Kurle i bade guribure de Osman kunesun jufeliyen belheme bufi, ekšeme jurambuha turgunde, terei siden i jalin faššaha be saišame, hese wasimbufi ton i songkoi hūda bubuhe. orin sunjaci aniya, Ūdui be dahame hargašanjiha de, menggun suje*

(151) *šangnaha. Kuce de bederehe manggi, Šayar Sairim, Bai hoton i geren bek i emgi hebešefi, duin tumen funcere hule jeku belhefi, Ili de alban i usin tarime genere hoise irgen de aisilaha turgunde, hesei saišame šangnaha. gūsici aniya Uši i hoise ubašaha be donjifi, Kuce i coohai agūra be bargiyafi boode asarafi, geli cooha be gaifi,*

(152) *hahilame dailaname genehe turgunde, saišame jai jergi jingse šangnafi hadabuha. amba cooha Uši be kafi, geren jugūn i cooha meyen dendefi, hūlha be afara de, Osman olji be jafaha hūlha be waha gungge ilibuha turgunde, hesei saišame suje šangnaha. gūsin ilaci aniya hargašanjiha de*

(153) *hesei kiyan cing men* [59] *de yabubuha. gūsin duici aniya, jai jergi taiji obuha. dehici aniya, Aksu i akim bek sindaha. dehi ilaci aniya, beile i jergi gūsai beise sirabufi, Kašigar i akim bek de forgošoho. dahanduhai Ūdui i G'aopu be haršaha weile be amcame gisurefi, hesei jalan halame sirara hergen be efulefi, sula amban sindaha. dehi jakūci aniya,*

(154) *hese wasimbuhangge: «Osman i ama Ūdui nenehe fonde coohai kūwaran de hūsun tucibure de, bi uthai kesi isibume beile i jergi fungnehe. amala G'aopu i baita de beile ci nakabufi, da an i kesi isibume Osman de sula amban šangname buhe. aikabade oron tucike manggi, uthai ilinjafi siraburakū oci, mini gūnin de yargiyan i tebcirakū. Osman i sula amban be kesi isibume jalan halame*

(155) *lashalaraku sirabu» sehe. erei onggolo Badakšan Buranidun i fudaraka jui hojo Asma, Abduhalik, hojo Bahadun sere ilan niyalma be alibume benjire de, Buranidun i fiyanggū jui Samsak Anjiyan de ukaha bihe. han terei ulhicun akū be jilame, hesei jafafi wara be guwebuhe. Samsak hahardaha manggi, yadahūn banjici ojorakū ofi, dehi uyuci aniya,*

(156) *jenduken i* [60] *Kašigar bade niyalma takūrafi ulin jaka be baire de, Burut i sula amban Akim i deo Emur se cisui Samsak de sirentuhe be, Osman donjifi, Kašigar i baita icihiyara amban Booceng de gercilehe. Akim ini deo be ujen weile baharahū seme* [61] *Osman be uhei hebe daha seme belehe turgunde, hesei Akim sebe selei futa tabufi gemun hecen de*

(157) *gajifi beidefi, yargiyan be baha manggi, hese wasimbuhangge «akim bek Osman mini kesi be hukšeme Samsak i hoise sei emgi jenduken i mejige be hafumbure baita de heni majige daldame gidaha ba akū.*[62] *teni mejige bahame saka, uthai Booceng de boolame ulhibufi, dahalame uhei unenggi gūnin i baicame icihiyahangge. daci dubede isitala fafuršame yabuha be dahame ambula saišacuka. kesi isibume gūsai beise*

(158) *fungnefi, saišame huwekiyebure be tuwabukini» sehe. susai juweci aniya tuweri hargašanjiha. susai ilaci aniya aniya biyade, gemun hecen de akū oho manggi, hese wasimbuhangge: «akim bek beise Osman utala aniya unenggi gūnin i hūsun bume faššame yabuha. eiten baita de mini kesi be hukšeme umesi hing seme facihiyašahai jihe.*[63] *jing akdame baitalame bisire de,*[64] *te gemun hecen de hargašame jifi, uthai nimeme*

(159) *dedufi bi gocika hiya be takūrafi oktosi gaifi tuwanabume dasabuhai fuhali yebe ome mutehekū.*[65] *te nimeme akū oho be donjiha de ambula šar seme jilame gosimbi. gocika hiya Fengšen Jilun be tucibufi, hisalabureci tulgiyen, kemuni sunja tanggū yan menggun šangnafi sinagan i baita icihiyakini» sehe. geli hese wasimbuhangge: «Osman i tucike jalan sirara sula*

(160) *amban be uthai kesi isibume ini jui Maihamet Osan de sirabukini. jai gūsai beise oci* [66] *mini cohotoi kesi isibume šangnaha hergen umai jalan halame siraburengge waka bicibe, Osman utala aniya hūsun bume faššame yabuha be dahame gūsai beise i hergen be inu kesi isibume suwaliyame* [67] *ini jui Maihamet Osan de sirabufi. mini hoise ahasi be gosira ten i gūnin be tuwabukini»* [68] *sehe.*

(161) *jai mudan siraha Maihamet Osan, Osman i ahūngga jui. abkai wehiyehe i susai ilaci aniya sula amban sirabufi cohotoi kesi isibume gūsai beise kamcime sirabuha.*

Notes

1. ***tulergi*****:** *tule* 'outside' + *ergi* 'side'. The word *tulergi* 'outer' here refers to the outer entourage or outer retainers of the dynasty (Chin. *waifan* 外藩). It is not to be confused with Outer Mongolia. See Joseph F. Fletcher, Jr., "The Biography of Khwush Kipäk Beg (d. 1781) in the *Wai-fan Meng-ku hui-pu wang kung piao chuan*," *Studies in Chinese and Islamic Inner Asia* (Great Yarmouth: Variorum, 1995), p. 252.

2. ***jergi*****:** *da fungnehe beile i jergi gūsai beile Ūdui* 'Ūdui, a *beile* prince of the class of the originally appointed *beile'*. The word *jergi* has a number of different meanings and functions as noun or modifier. See Review 1.

3. *dai-la-ha*: Adding the syllable *-la* (*-le*, *-lo*) to nouns or adjectives often creates a verb. Examples: *dain* 'war' vs. *dailambi* 'to make war', *ejen* 'ruler' vs. *ejelembi* 'to rule'. Note that the final *n* is dropped in these cases. See Review 2.

4. *mukūn*: The Qianlong translation of Ūdui's biography translates *hūncihin mukūn* with the Chinese term *qishu* 戚屬 'relatives by marriage'. The dictionary definition of the Manchu term *hūncihin* is 'relatives by marriage', and *mukūn* is 'clan, lineage' (Chin. *zu* 族). Another Manchu term for clan, one that is more encompassing than *mukūn*, is *hala* 'clan, family, family name' (Chin. *xing* 姓; the Chinese equivalents may not be an accurate fit). According to S. M. Shirokogoroff, both units may have been exogamic units at one time. He argued that as political and social changes dispersed the members of the group, new, smaller units may have emerged. A *mukūn* does not have a name of its own. For more information see S. M. Shirokogoroff, *Social Organization of the Manchus: A Study of the Manchu Clan Organization*, extra volume III (Shanghai: Royal Asiatic Society [North China Branch], 1924):16-19; Pamela K. Crossley, "*Manzhou Yuanliu Kao* and the Formalization of the Manchu Heritage," *Journal of Asian Studies* 46, no. 4 (Nov 1987): 767; and Chen Wenshi, "The Creation of the Manchu *Niru*," *Chinese Studies in History* 14, no. 4 (Summer 1981): 11-46; and Li Xuehong, ed., *Qingdai quanshi* 清代全史 (Shenyang: Liaoning renmin chubanshe, 1991): 31-38.

5. *wehe i sime dalibuha de*: 'when we have them protect the pass by sealing it off with boulders'. For different functions of *de* see Review 3.

6. *isinjici ombi*: lit. 'if one arrives it will do'. Meaning: 'one can arrive'. Review Reading Selection A-3, note 8 and A-3, Review 7.

7. *Abduhalik...Tomulok jugūn de sucunjiha be afame gidaha*: '(the imperial army) having fought off Abduhalik who had come to launch an attack on the Tomuluk road'. For a review of the construction see Reading Selection A-5, Review 1.

8. *seremšeci acara oyonggo kamni*: 'important defiles one should protect'. Here the *-ci acambi* construction is used as a modifier, parallel to the adjective *oyonggo*.

9. *Hojijan geli sunja minggan funcere hūlha be gaifi Ogen bira ci Kuce de nikenjihe be*: The entire sentence is a topic marker or object of *gidaha*. Compare Note 7.

10. *Hojijan emgeri Kuce i hoton de dosika be musei cooha sarkū bihe*: 'our army did not know that Hojijan had entered the town'. Same structure as in Notes 7 and 9 above.

11. *Jaohui, Yarhašan oronde genefi*: lit. 'after Jaohūi had gone into Yarhašan's position'. Meaning: 'after Jaohūi had replaced Yarhašan'. Yarhašan was recalled from the Ili campaign for poor performance. He was subsequently executed.

12. *Ūdui be tuwaci baita afabuci ombi*: 'if one looks at Ūdui, one can entrust him with matters'. Meaning: 'I think we can entrust matters to Ūdui'.

13. *sujame bisire*: 'was resisting'. *bisire* is the imperfective participle of *bimbi.* The various forms of *bimbi* combine with participles and converbs of other verbs. These derived or compound tenses generally express various shades of progressive action.

arame bi (=arambi)	I am writing
arame bihe (=arambihe)	I was writing, I used to write
arame bicibe	although I am/was writing
arame ofi	because I am/was writing
arame bisire	just as I am/was writing
arambime	while I am/was writing

As is true for other verb forms, the English translation of these verbs depends on the tense or aspect of the finite verb in the sentence. Cf. Reading Selection A-3, Review 8.

14. *Ūdui dame geneki seme*: 'Ūdui wanting to go to the rescue'.

15. *hūlhai Hotiyan hoton de sucunaha be...safi*: 'having found out about the rebels' attack on the town of Khotan'. The logical subject of the clause, *hūlha,* occurs in the genitive. For further examples of this construction see Review 4. Also cf. A-2, Note 1.

16. *feksihei*: 'by way of galloping, quickly'.Verb stems with endings *-hai*, *-hei*, *-hoi* are durative converbs which describe actions or events that occur or continue at the same time as the action of the main verb. In translation this construction comes close to the *-me* coordinative converb. See Review 5.

17. *hūlha be tosoro baitalan*: 'tools that prepare for (fighting) bandits'.

18. *hūlha holo bithe be selgiyeme geren be ergelere jakade*: 'because the rebels coerced people by means of distributing a spurious letter'.

19. *Batujirgal...Hotiyan de dame genere be, Ūdui...Hara Haši de okdome genefi*: 'Ūdui went to Hara Hash to welcome Baturjirgal who had gone to Khotan to help'.

20. *Fude isinjiha be...Ūdui Abdurman be okdobuha*: 'Ūdui had Abdurman welcome Fude who had arrived'.

21. *Jaohūi, Fude i cooha be...ibebuki seme gisurehe turgunde*: 'because one proposed to divide Jaohūi and Fude's troops and have them advance along two different routes'.

22. *donjici ini aciha hūlha de duribuhe sembi*: 'I hear that his baggage was seized by the rebels'. Lit.: 'if I listen, they say'.

23. *ini sasa*: 'together with it (the army)'.

24. *kemuni gūnin werešeme jilame gosi*: 'yet, be sensitive and compassionate'.

25. *Jaohūi i baci Ūdui i hing seme cooha de geneki seme baiha babe wesimbume isinjiha*: lit. 'one arrived from Jaohūi's office memorializing the fact that Ūdui had earnestly requested to go on the campaign'. The phrase *Ūdui i...baiha* modifies *ba.* Compare Note 15.

26. *hūlha Isil Kur de burulaha be amba cooha...gidaha*: 'the imperial army defeated the rebels who had fled to Isil Kur'. Here the subject of the phrase (*hūlha*) is not in the genitive form.

27. *dahara be baiha*: 'requested to submit'. More commonly: *dahaki seme baiha.*

28. *gungge mutebufi amasi marire cooha*: lit. 'the troops who after having achieved merit were returning home'.

29. *etefi isinjiha doroi omibufi*: lit. 'after having him drink in the manner of the having-arrived-after-having-been-victorious-ceremony'. The genitive in *doroi* is instrumental, meaning 'in or with this kind of ceremony'; *etefi isinjiha* modifies *doro*.

30. *otolo*: *o-* verb stem of *ombi* + *-tolo*. The suffix *-tolo,* (or-*tele, -tala*) marks a terminative converb, meaning 'up to' or 'until'. The ending may also be added to words other than verbs, e.g., *uttu* 'like this', *utala* 'so many as this'. See Review 6.

31. *ini beye be akdulabumbime Ūdui be habšabuha*: 'accused Ūdui in order to make people recommend him (for office)'.

32. *uthai...-kini, inu*: 'even if/though...still'. See Review 7 for other ways to express the meaning of 'even if/though...still'.

33. *Polat i gisun de nakabuci ojorakū*: 'one cannot (should not) dismiss him on the basis of Polat's words'. See Review 3 for functions of *de*.

34. *Polat i kanagan be jorime geren be aššabume, akim obure be kicere weile*: 'Polat's crime of striving to be governor by stirring up the people and by availing himself of the pretext'. The phrase *kanagan...kicere* modifies *weile*.

35. *akim obure kooli akū*: 'there is no such principle as (falling into his cunning trap and) making him governor'.

36. *Abdura'im*: The letter *i* is written as an initial *i,* with one short and one long stroke.

37. *hoise sei banin kelfišeme kenehunjere mangga*: lit. 'as for the nature of Muslims, their being irresolute and distrusting is strong'.

38. *tacibure oci*: same as *tacibureci* 'if we teach'.

39. *kenehunjerakū ombime*: 'he will not be suspicious'. This is another example of a compound tense expressing progressive action. See Note 13.

40. ***yaya bek oho urse*:** lit. 'the whosoever-had-become-*beg* people'. Meaning: 'whosoever had become *beg*'.

41. ***gaime ofi*:** 'because they were taking'.

42. ***siden i jalin tuwakiyame*:** 'watching out on behalf of the public good'.

43. ***šangnahangge...sehengge*:** 'my bestowing (something) is a way of saying (that...)'. Two parallel nominalized verbs, meaning A equals B.

44. ***alban i bure tengge*:** 'the money one officially gives'.

45. ***obureo*:** imperfective *–re*, *-ra*, *-ro* plus interrogative suffix *o* 'will you please, 'may you please'. Polite request to a superior.

46. ***Setib Aldi i...gercilehe babe wesimbuhede*:** 'When (Yonggui) memorialized Setib Aldi's accusation'. See Note 15 and Review 4.

47. ***G'aopu...Osman be harangga ba i akim bek i baita be alifi icihiyabure be baime wesimbuhede*:** 'when Gaopu requested that one have Osman handle the mattters of the governor's office of the said place'. The sentence ending in *icihiyabure be* is the object of *baiha*. Compare A-3, Review 2, indirect speech.

48. ***Yerkiyang ni akim*:** 'the office of governor of Yarkand'. Titles are commonly used to refer to the office.

49. ***seme gūnime*:** 'thinking that'.

50. ***Osman be Kašigar i bade unggihengge hoise aiman i bek be ser sere be seremšeme badaran be sibuki sere gūnin*:** lit. 'sending Osman to Kashgar reflects my intent of wanting to protect the small and stop the powerful among the Muslim leaders'. The converb *seremšeme* is converb to *sibuki*, and *sibuki sere* modifies *gūnin*.

51. ***Ūdui be G'aopu be haršaha seme weile gisurefi*:** 'having accused Ūdui saying he covered (up for) Gaopu'.

52. ***G'aopu uthai...gu be udaki sehe seme*:** lit. 'although Gaopu then wanted to buy jade'.

53. ***i giyan i tafulame ilibuci acambi*:** 'he should advise/have advised and stop/stopped him'. In English the context requires the past tense.

54. ***tucibuhe bici fulehun de karulaci ombi*:** 'if he had brought it out, he could have repaid my favor'. One might have expected to see *ombihe*.

55. ***irgen be...suilabure...gu wehe be gaiha baita bihebi*:** 'there have been cases of him (Ūdui) making people suffer and of having taken jade'.

56. ***aikabade ini beye kemuni bici*:** lit. 'if his body was still here', 'if he were still alive'.

57. ***giyan i...targabure be tuwabuci acambi*:** lit. 'one should show the warning'. The word *giyan i* meaning 'appropriately' often goes together with *-ci acambi* 'should'.

58. ***Osman umai ini ama be dahame tehengge waka*:** 'it was not at all a case of Osman residing with his father'. The entire sentence from *Osman* through *tehengge* is the subject or topic.

59. ***kiyan cing men*:** An audience hall in the Forbidden City where foreign dignitaries were feasted.

60. ***jenduken i*:** 'rather secretly'. Other adjectives/adverbs may be similarly formed with the suffix *-kan*, *-ken*, or *-kon*. Words ending in the letter *n* drop *n* before the suffix. See Review 8.

61. *Akim ini deo be ujen weile baharahū seme*: 'because Akim feared that his younger brother might have committed a serious crime'. The apprehensive (also temeritive) converb suffix *-rahū* is but one way to express fear. For additional constructions see Review 9 and A-3, Review 5. Also note that *seme* 'saying' often conveys the meaning of 'because'. See Review 10.

62. *Samsak i hoise sei emgi jenduken i mejige be hafumbure baita de...gidaha ba akū*: 'there was no cover-up in the matter of reporting Samsak's secret communication with the Muslims'. The imperfective participle *hafumbure* modifies *baita* and *Samsak i jenduken i mejige be* is object to *hafumbure* 'to give a detailed account of'.

63. *hing seme facihiyašahai jihe*: 'he has been applying himself earnestly'. The durative converb (*-hai*, *-hei*, *-hoi*), when followed by *jimbi* 'to come' or *yabumbi* 'to go', indicates that the action or state of the main verb is continuous. See Review 5.

64. *akdame baitalame bisire de*: 'just as I was relying (on him)'.

65. *oktosi gaifi tuwanabume dasabuhai fuhali yebe ome mutehekū*: lit. 'he was not able to become better at all by having a doctor come to examine him and treat him'.

66. *jai gūsa i beise oci*: *gūsai beise* (160, line 1) and *gūsai beile* (115, line 3) are interchangeable here. In the Chinese translation both are translated as *gushan beizi* 固山貝子 'banner prince'. Originally, *beise* was simply the plural of *beile*, but already during the early Qing dynasty the rank *beise* was a degree below that of *beile*.

67. *suwaliyame*: 'adding, in addition'. Commonly used as meaning 'also'.

68. *mini hoise ahasi be gosire ten i gūnin be tuwabukini*: lit. 'Show my deep concern for my Muslim subjects'. *ahasi be* is object to *gosire*; both *gosire* and *ten i* modify *gūnin*.

Review

1. *jergi* (1) ordinary; (2) kind of, various; (3) time; (4) rank, grade; (5) layer; (6) sequence

(1) *jergi niyalma*	ordinary people
(2) *da fungnehe beile i jergi beile*	a *beile* of the rank of the originally appointed *beile*s
(2) *Ingi Šar i jergi hoton*	the (various) towns of Yanggishar
(2) *ai jergi jaka*	what kind of thing
(3) *emu jergi, emu mudan*	one time
(3) *emu biya de juwe jergi tucike*	they came out twice a month
(3) *emu jergi edun*	a breeze (of wind)
(4) *jergi be tuwame*	depending on rank
(4) *beile i jergi sirambi*	to succeed as *beile*
(5) *etuku juwe jergi*	two layers of clothing
(6) *jergi ilhi*	sequence

2. Verb formation: Noun or adjective + *-la-, -le-, -lo-*

ejen	leader	*ejelembi*	to rule
dain	war	*dailambi*	to make war
cooha	troops	*coohalambi*	to make war
okto	poison	*oktolombi*	to poison
ahūn	elder brother	*ahūlambi*	to act like an older brother
olji	captive, booty	*oljilambi*	to take prisoner
akdun	strong	*akdulambi*	to make strong
iletu	clear, open	*iletulembi*	to be clear, to reveal
uju	head, first	*ujulembi*	to head up, to be in charge

3. *de* (1) dative; (2) locative; (3) direction; (4) temporal; (5) agent in passive construction; (6) instrumental

(1) *Ūdui beksede bithe unggihe*	Ūdui sent a letter to the *begs*
(1) *ama de juwe jui bi*	the father had two sons
(2) *Aksu de tembi*	to reside in Aksu
(3) *tubade siliha cooha be unggimbi*	to send select troops there
(4) *juwe biya de*	in the second month
(4) *orin aniya hargašanjiha de*	when he came for an audience in the 20th year

(5) *bata de wabuha*	he was killed by the enemy
(6) *ejen i hese de*	by edict from the ruler
(6) *Polat i gisun de nakabuci ojorakū*	one should not dismiss him on the basis of Polat's words

4. Genitive form of the subject in the subordinate clause

hūlha i Hotiyan hoton de sucunaha be mejigešeme saha	one found out through spying that the rebels had gone to Khotan to attack
Setib Aldi i gercilehe babe wesimbuhe	one memorialized the matter of Setib Aldi's accusation
hesei wasimbuha gisun	the words that one sent down by edict
Eseyen i tucike hergen serengge	as for the rank that Husayn vacated
Ūdui i cooha de geneki seme baiha babe wesimbuhe	one memorialized the fact that Ūdui wanted to join the campaign
hūlha i ukara be seremšeki	let us watch out for rebels escaping
Samsak i mejige be hafumbure baita de gidaha ba akū	nothing was covered up in the matter of Samsak's communication
Ūdui i G'aopu be haršaha weile be amcame gisurehe	one reviewed Odui's crime of covering up for Gaopu

5. Coordinative converb *-me* (emphasis on manner) and durative converb *-hai, -hei, -hoi* (emphasis on duration)

teme aliyambi	he sat and waited
tehei aliyambi	he sat while he waited
feksime alanabuha	he had someone go and report quickly
feksihei alanabuha	he had someone go and report quickly
dasabuhai yebe ome mutehekū	he could not become better while being treated
yabuhai boode isinaha	he arrived home by having walked
ebsi ukame jihei isinjiha	they escaped and arrived here
hing seme facihiyašahai jihe	he has been applying himself earnestly

6. Terminative converb *-tala*, *-tele*, *-tolo* 'until, up to'

otolo	until
utala	so many as this
er(e)tele	up to now

ilan biya otolo kabuha	they were besieged for three months
aratala	until he does
daci dubede isitala	from beginning to end
bucetele hūsun tucike	he worked hard until he died

7. *uthai... -kini, inu...; uthai...-ci, inu...; udu bicibe; -ci geli* '(even) though...still, even if'

Ūdui uthai gamjidame yabukini inu nakabuci ojorakū	even though Ūdui acted covetously, still he should not be dismissed
Ūdui be uthai weile araci, Polat i weile be inu giyan i icihiyaci acambi	even though one punishes Ūdui, Polat's crime should also be dealt with
te udu nimeme akū oho bicibe, targabure be tuwabuci acambi	although he has now died of an illness, one still should issue a warning
fonjici geli alarakū	even though you ask, I wont' tell (you)

8. Adjective + *-kaṇ, -ken, -kon* 'rather' (final *n* is dropped)

jendu	secret	*jenduken*	rather secret
komso	few	*komsokon*	rather few
sain	good	*saikan*	rather good
hūdun	fast	*hūdukan*	rather fast
olhon	dry	*olhokon*	rather dry
akdun	strong	*akdukan*	rather strong
ujen	heavy	*ujeken*	rather heavy

9. Apprehensive verb suffix *-rahū, -rahū sembi;* sentence particle *ayoo*, and *ayoo sembi* 'it is to be feared'

Akim ini deo be ujen weile baharahū seme gelehe	Akim feared that his brother might have committed a serious crime
han manju niyalma be nikan i doro de dosirahū seme manju gisun taci sehe	because the *khan* worried that the Manchus might take up Chinese ways he ordered (people) to study Manchu
morin akū ayoo	I'm afraid there won't be any horses
hūlhai cooha hoton de dosika ayoo	it is to be feared that the rebels have entered the town
aika ishunde silhidara oci, siden i baita be tookabure ayoo	if they are envious each other, I am afraid it will delay public matters

elhe ojorakū ayoo sembikai	I am afraid there will be no peace
abka de waka ojorahu	I am afraid that one will wrong heaven

10. ***seme*** **'because, since';** ***uthai ... seme*** **'although'**

G'aopu uthai gu be udaki sehe seme	although Gaopu wanted to buy jade
cembe Yuwan gurun i Taidzu han i enen seme, gemun hecen de bibuhe	because they were the descendants of Taizu of the Mongol dynasty, one had them reside in the capital
fe hojo i omolo seme hesei jai jergi taiji obuha	because (he) was the grandson of the former *khoja*, he was made second rank *taiji* by decree
elhe ojorakū ayoo seme	because I fear there will be no peace

12. Write in Manchu script and translate into English (based on pages 115–34)**:** a) *da fungnehe gūsa i beile;* b) *wesibume jai jergi taiji fungnehe*; c) *birai amargi Gulja de tebuhebi*; d) *Ūdui dahalaki seme baiha*; e) *saišame sula amban sindaha* f) *hoton i duka be yaksifi*; g) *juwan funcere inenggi oho manggi*; h) *mukei jugūn be lashalaki*; i) *ere sidende dara cooha isinambi*; j) *jobocuka ba akū*; k) *muke mutuha erinde isinjime muterakū*; l) *geren kamni be seremšeme tuwakiyabuha*; m) *jugūn de sucunjiha be gidaha*; n) *doigonde tosome seremšeci acara dabagan;* o) *hūlha hoton de dosika be amba cooha sarkū*; p) *baita afabuci ombi*; q) *tubai bek se hoton be alibume dahaha*; r) *Ūdui geren be toktobuha be niyalma donjiha*; s) *ini sargan boso jai jibca be tucibufi seremšeme tehe cooha de aisilame buhe*; t) *hūlha amba cooha be sujame bisire turgunde*; u) *hūlhai Hotiyan hoton de sucunaha be mejigešeme safi*; v) *bek i gebu jai boigon ulha i ton be arafi Aksu de jasiha*; w) *juwe tanggū cooha be tucibufi danabume unggihe de*; x) *susai niyalma be kunesun gamabume dahalabuha;* y) *ishun aniya niyengniyeri amba cooha kaha babe efulehe*; z) *gūnin werešeme jilame gosi*; aa) *Ūdui hahilame Fude i cooha de acafi*; bb) *hūlha feksime jifi dahara be baiha*; cc) *Hojijan i uju be alibume benjihe*; dd) *hargašabufi doroi etuku šangnafi, etefi isinjiha doroi omibuhe*; ee) *ilan biya otolo kabuha*; ff) *hoise se ishunde buhiyeme silhidara tuheburengge gemu ceni fe tacin.*

13. Translate into Manchu (based on pages 115–34)**:** a) the 102nd biography; b) he exterminated Ūdui's relatives and clan; c) because he was thoroughly familiar with the conditions; d) they occupied the woods outside the town; e) (they) did not dare attack; f) the town was very strong; g) having sent selected troops there; h) they stopped it up with rocks; i) the emperor (by edict) granted silver and silk to Ūdui and his son Osman; j) let us block the escape route; k) while Ūdui's wife was helping the troops with one hundred horses; l) the letter did not go through at all; m) this time he showed still more sincerity; n) Ūdui sent the *begs* a letter asking them to defend (their towns) and resist; o) the rebels distributed a counterfeit letter; p) they opened the gates and came out; q) he quickly sent messengers to go to Aksu and report; r) you should have Ūdui rest a little; s) he was a man who stood out among the Muslims; t) waving the banner he called on them to submit; u) he followed the troops as they returned; v) his portrait was painted in the pavilion; w) for three months they were under siege in Hotien.

14. Write in Manchu script and translate into English (based on pages 135–61)**:** a) *Ūdui uthai gamjidame yabukini inu Polat i gisun de nakabuci ojorakū*; b) *nure omire de amuran*; c) *ce ele elhe baharakū de isinambi*; d) *baita firgehe turgunde fafun i gamaha*; e) *hoise sebe jobobume gejureme gaiha hacin akū*; f) *kooli obuci ojorakū*; g) *coohai kūwaran de ambula gungge ilibuha*; h) *G'aopu Osman be akim bek obureo seme baiha*; i) *bihe bihei Tang gurun i jase be tuwakiyara amban ci encu akū*; j) *hoise aiman i bek be ser sere be seremšeme badaran be sibuki sembi*; k) *se asihan ofi baita alime muterakū*; l) *Setib Aldi adali tucibume muterakū kai*; m) *i giyan i tafulame ilibuci acambi*; n) *aikabade ciralame isebume gamarakū oci bi adarame kemuni bek be baitalambini*? o) *ere gese baita inde dalji akū*; p) *Osman be dacun urehe seme wesimbuhe*; q) *Osman kunesun jufeliyen belheme bufi ekšeme jurambuha*; r) *olji be jafaha hūlha be waha gungge ilibuha*; s) *nenehe fonde coohai kūwaran de hūsun tucibure jakade*; t) *mini gūnin de yargiyan i tebcirakū*; u) *han terei ulhicun akū be jilame wara be guwebuhe*; v) *Akim ini deo be ujen weile baharahū seme gelehe*; w) *Akim sebe selei futa tabufi gemun hecen de gajifi beidehe*; x) *heni majige daldame gidaha ba akū*; y) *teni mejige bahame saka*; z) *saišame huwekiyebure be tuwabukini*; aa) *yebe ome mutehekū*; bb) *mini hoise ahasi be gosire gūnin be tuwabukini*; cc) *umesi hing seme facihiyašahai jihe*; dd) *gūsai beise kamcime sirabuha.*

15. Translate into Manchu (based on pages 135–61)**:** a) we will certainly not fall into his cunning trap; b) the emperor transferred Ūdui to the position of governor of Yarkand; c) the *akhund* must not interfere indiscriminately; d) it is to be feared that public affairs will be delayed; e) the Muslims are by nature very irresolute and suspicious; f) Ūdui will not be suspicious and Abdurayim also will not unnecessarily be on guard; g) then they will not cause trouble (impediments); h) because the matter came to light, he was executed; i) it has been a long time since they came to submit; j) it cannot be made a precedent; k) he earned great merit in military matters; l) he secretly sold public jade; m) Osman knew that his father had been on good terms with Gaopu; n) if I had made Osman governor of Yarkand; o) be grateful for my favor; p) one should deal (with it) strictly; q) this matter has nothing to do with him; r) since he has already been dismissed from the rank of *beile*, he cannot wear the two-eyed peacock feather; s) Osman prepared provisions and sent them off quickly; t) he helped the Muslims who went to till the public fields in Ili; u) Osman heard that Akim's younger brother entered into secret dealings with Samsak; v) Akim falsely accused Osman of having aided the plot; w) there were no instances of covering up and hiding anything; x) just as I was relying on him, he died of an illness; y) his rank of banner *beise* was a rank bestowed by special favor.

Reading Selection B–1

Asking for administrative leave (1874)

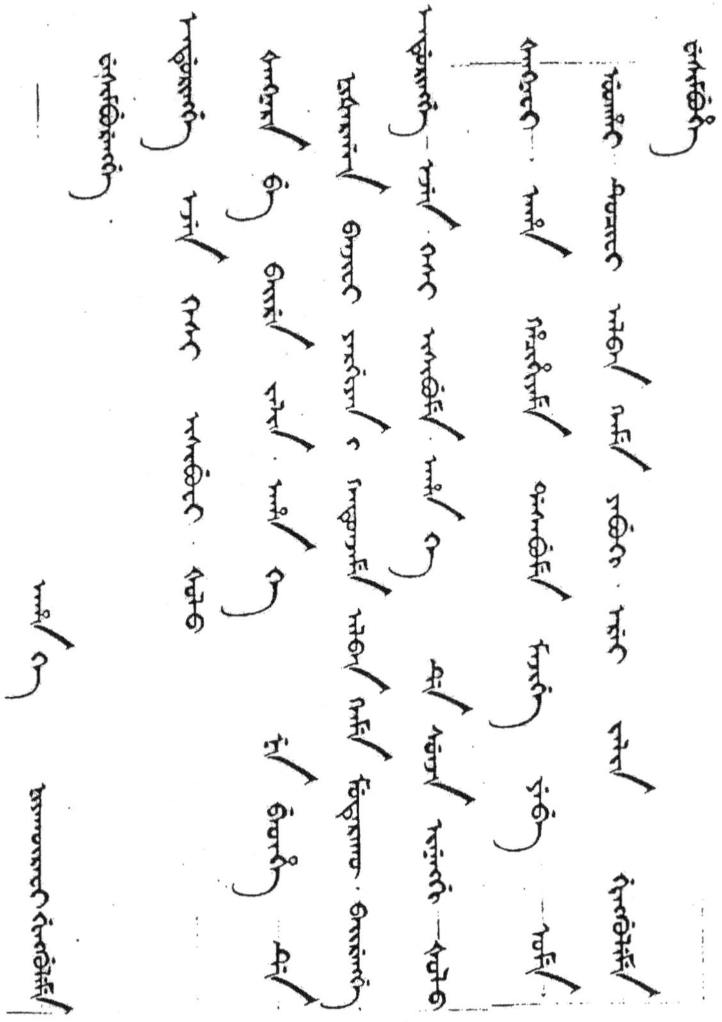

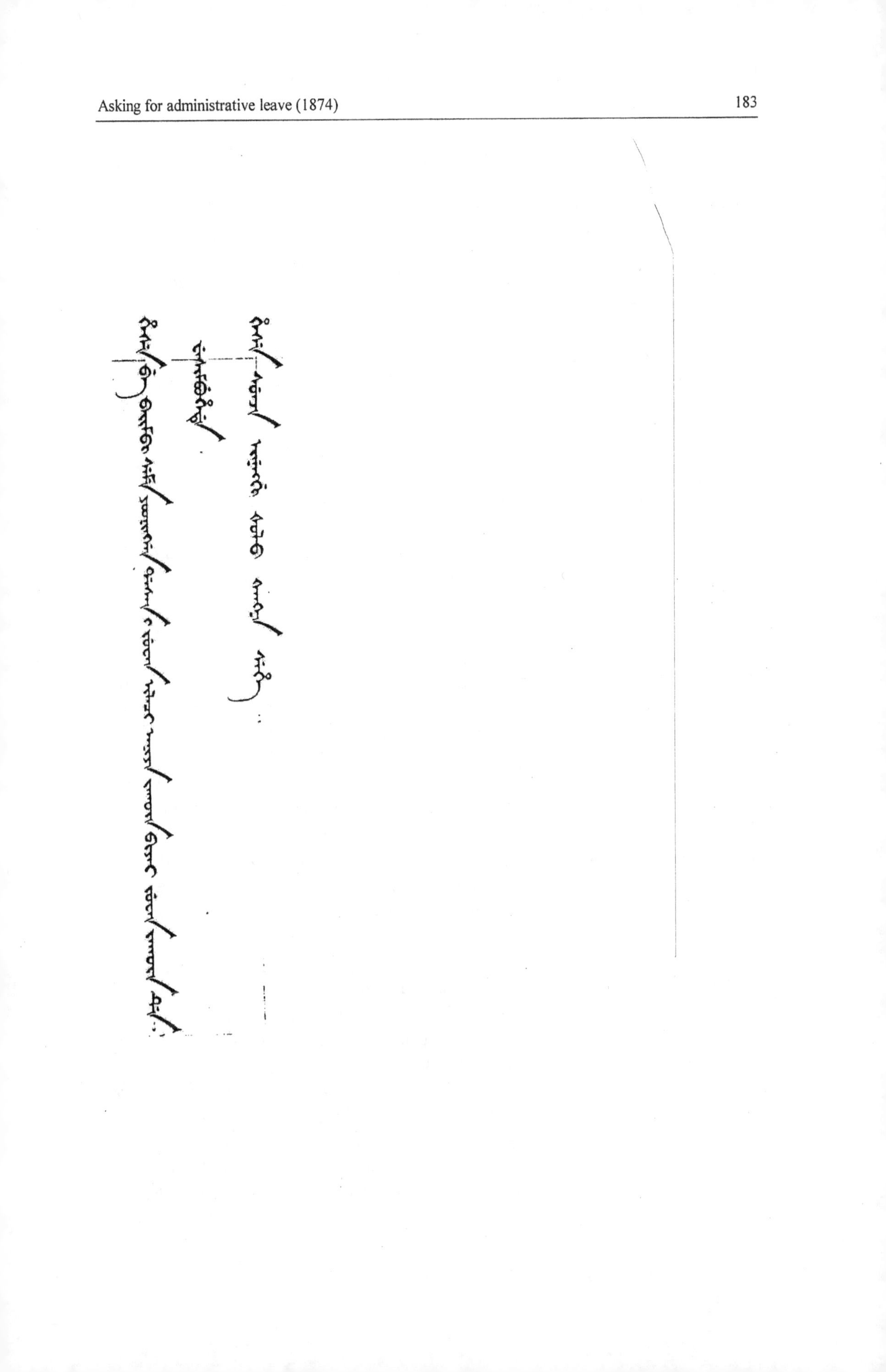

Transliteration

(182) *aha ke* [1] *niyakūrafi gingguleme wesimburengge.*[2] *enduringge ejen kesi isibufi, šolo šangnara be baire jalin. aha ke ne bethe de nišargan banjifi yargiyan i katunjame alban kame muterakū. bairengge enduringge ejen kesi isibume aha ke de sunja inenggi šolo šangnafi, aha* [1] *hacihiyame dasabume majige yebe ome, uthai tucifi alban kame yabuki. erei jalin gingguleme wesimbuhe.*

(183) *hese be baimbi seme yooningga dasan i juwan ilaci aniya jakūn biyai juwan jakūn de wesimbuhede, hese «sunja inenggi šolo šangna» sehe.*

Notes

This brief document contains all the components of a typical memorial:

Self-identification — The "who" part usually includes the title(s) and name(s) of the memorialist(s), plus a version of *wesimburengge.*
Example: *aha ke gingguleme wesimburengge* 'your servant respectfully memorializes'.

Topic — Brief announcement of the topic of the memorial, ending with *jalin.* This compares to the "Subject" line of an office memo and may be translated as 'in the matter of,' or simply with the infinitive 'to'.
Example: *enduringge ejen kesi isibufi, šolo šangnara be baire jalin* 'to request that his majesty may bestow his grace and grant a leave'.

Body of the memorial — Example: *aha ke ne bethe de nišargan banjifi yargiyan i katunjame alban kame muterakū* 'your servant now has developed a sore on his foot and cannot, even with best effort, fulfill his duties'.

Request — The request often begins with *bairengge* and concludes with a verb ending in *-ki* or *-rao, -reo, -roo.* Either the memorialist wants to do something (*-ki* 'I will,' 'let me') or he requests an action by the emperor (*-rao*, *-reo*, *-roo* 'will you please').
Example: *bairengge enduringge ejen kesi isibume aha ke de sunja inenggi šolo šangnafi...majige yebe ome, uthai tucifi alban kame yabuki* 'I beg that his majesty may bestow his grace, grant me a five-day leave and let me return to my duties upon feeling a little better'.

Conclusion This part refers back to the topic. Sometimes it is followed by another request, such as *hese be baimbi*. Example: *erei jalin ginggulеme wesimbuhe* 'for this reason I have submitted this memorial'.

Date Example: *yooningga dasan i juwan ilaci aniya jakūn biyai juwan jakūn de* 'on the eighteenth day of the eighth month of the thirteenth year of the Tongzhi reign'.

Imperial response Example: *sunja inenggi šolo šangna* 'grant a five-day leave'.

This document is taken from a 1905 collection of petitions to the emperor. In file copies, the last component is a statement from the compilers. Example: *hese be baimbi seme yooningga dasan i juwan ilaci aniya jakūn biyai juwan jakūn de wesimbuhede hese «sunja inenggi šolo šangna» sehe* 'when he memorialized requesting an edict on the eighteenth of the eighth month of the third year of the Tungzhi reign, an edict said: Grant a five-day leave'. In an original memorial the date appears without *wesimbuhede* and the imperial endorsement is a plain imperative. Compare Reading Selection B–2.

1. ***aha*:** 'your slave, your servant'. The term *aha* (Chin. *nucai* 奴才), written in small characters), is a memorialist's humble reference to himself. It was used primarily by memorialists who were Manchu, Mongol, or Chinese bannermen, though some others may also have referred to themselves in this way. Most Chinese officials, as well as some bannermen, used the term *amban* (Chin. *chen* 臣). Though the documents in this collection contain specific requests and dates, the names of the petitioners are left out. They refer to the memorialist only as *aha* or *aha ke* (in the Chinese version as *nucai ke* 奴才克). It is not clear what the word *ke* stands for in this context.

2. ***aha* (*ke*) *niyakūrafi ginggulеme wesimburengge*:** 'Your servant kneels and respectfully memorializes'. The suffix *-ngge* added to a verb stem nominalizes the verb. When it is free-standing, i.e., not followed by a finite verb, the predicate 'to be' is understood. Example: *ararangge* 'it is a case of writing.'

Memorials regularly use the free-standing *-ngge* form for an opening, either with the memorialist's name in the nominative, or in the genitive. Example: *Jaohūi wesimburengge* or *Jaohui i wesimburengge*. Both are translated as 'Jaohūi memorializes'. Grammatically, the difference stems from the fact that in *Jaohūi wesimburengge* the entire phrase—here two words—is nominalized: 'what Jaohūi memorializes is as follows'. In *Jaohūi i wesimburengge* only the verb *wesimbumbi* is nominalized: 'the memorializing (words) of Jaohūi are as follows'.

Review

1. Memorial components: Self-identification

aha wesimburengge	your servant memorializes
Jaohūi i wesimburengge	your servant Jaohūi memorializes
G'an su siyūn fu aha Ocang gingguleme wesimburengge	your servant, Ocang, governor of Gansu respectfully memorializes
aha uksun niyakūrafi gingguleme wesimburengge	your servant, a member of the royal family, kneels and respectfully memorializes
Jaohūi sei gingguleme wesimburengge	your servant Jaohūi respectfully memorializes
dorgi baita be uheri kadalara yamun i gingguleme wesimburengge	the Imperial Household Department respectfully memorializes

2. Memorial components: Topic

hese be baire jalin	to request an edict
donjibume wesimbure jalin	to inform the emperor
abkai kesi de hengkilere jalin	to prostrate to the heavenly grace
karun giyamun baicaha babe donjibume wesimbure jalin	to inform about the inspection of military posts and relay stations
Burut sei morin alibuha babe donjibume wesimbure jalin	to inform about tribute horses offered by the Kirghiz
ajige amban mini tušan be alime gaiha inenggi be gingguleme boolara jalin	to respectfully report the date of assuming my duties
alban i jeku yooni bargiyaha babe gingguleme donjibume wesimbure jalin	to respectfully inform that the collection of the grain tax has been completed
majige (or *ser sere*) *saha babe tucibume gingguleme wesimbure jalin*	to respectfully present my humble views

3. Memorial components: Request

bairengge hacihiyame tucifi alban kame yabuki	I request that you let me quickly go out and fulfill my duties
bairengge enduringge ejen kesi isibume morin be bargiyarao	we ask that his majesty grant favor and accept the horses
enduringge ejen genggiyen i bulekušefi hese wasinjiha manggi gingguleme dahame yabuki	after an edict has come down, his majesty graciously having taken note, I will respectfully follow your instructions

bairengge enduringge ejen genggiyen i bulekušereo	we ask that his majesty graciously take note
ajige amban mini tušan be alime gaiha inenggi be giyan i boolame wesimbuci acambi. bairengge enduringge ejen genggiyen i bulekušereo	it is appropriate that I, your humble servant, memorialize and report the date of having assumed my duties. I beg that the emperor graciously take note.

4. Memorial components: Conclusion

erei jalin gingguleme wesimbuhe	on this account we (have) respectfully submit(ted) a memorial
erei jalin gingguleme donjibume wesimbuhe	on this account we respectfully memorialize to inform the emperor
erei jalin gingguleme donjibume wesimbuhe. hese be baimbi	on this account we respectfully memorialize to inform the emperor and request an edict
mariha babe gingguleme donjibume wesimbuhe	we respectfully submit a memorial to inform the emperor of our return
gingguleme sakini seme wesimbuhe	I respectfully memorialize for the record

5. Memorial components: Imperial response

saha	noted
hese wasimbuha	an edict has been issued
gisurehe songkoi obu	let it be as proposed
(date) *de alime gaiha fulgiyan fi i pilehe hese saha sehe*	an edict, received on (date) and endorsed in red vermilion, said: noted
(date) *de fulgiyan fi i pilehe hese hese wasimbuha sehe*	on (date) an edict endorsed in red vermilion said: an edict has been issued
(date) *de hese gisurehe songkoi obu sehe*	on (date) an edict said: let it be as proposed

6. Translate into English and write in Manchu script: a) *aha niyakūrafi gingguleme wesimburengge*; b) *kesi isibufi šolo šangnara be baimbi*; c) *bethe de nišargan banjiha*; d) *hacihiyame dasabume majige yebe ome uthai alban kame yabuki*; e) *hese sunja inenggi šolo šangna sehe.*

Reading Selection B–2

Weather report from Mukden (1779)

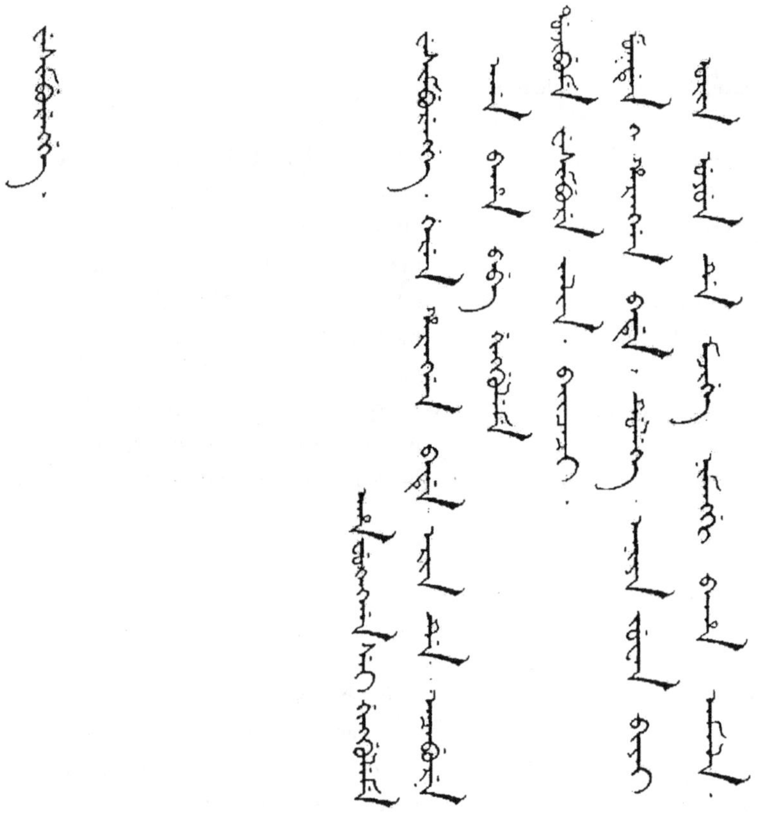

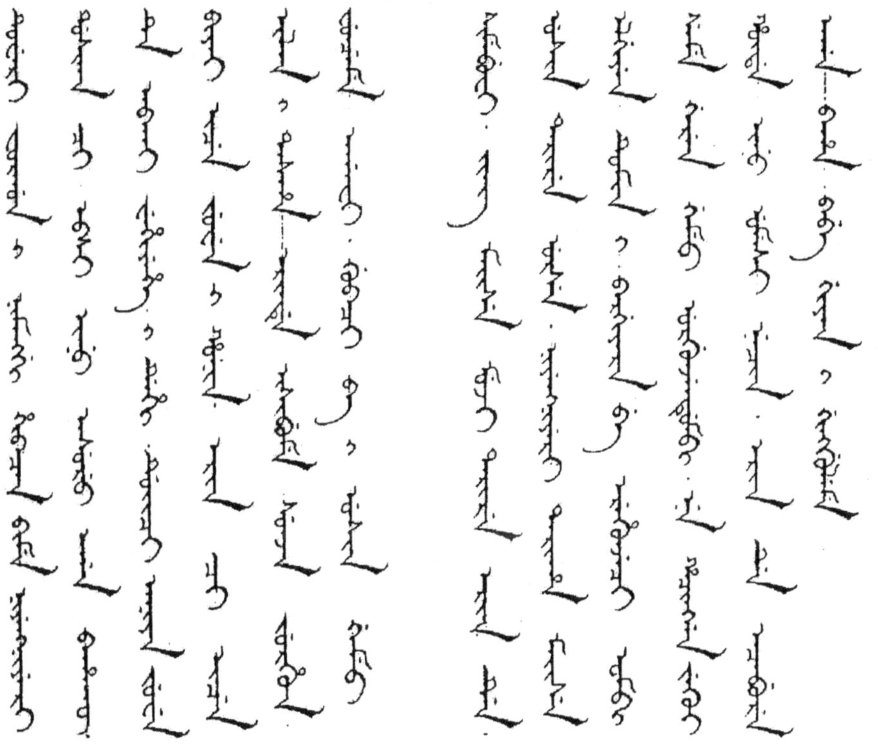

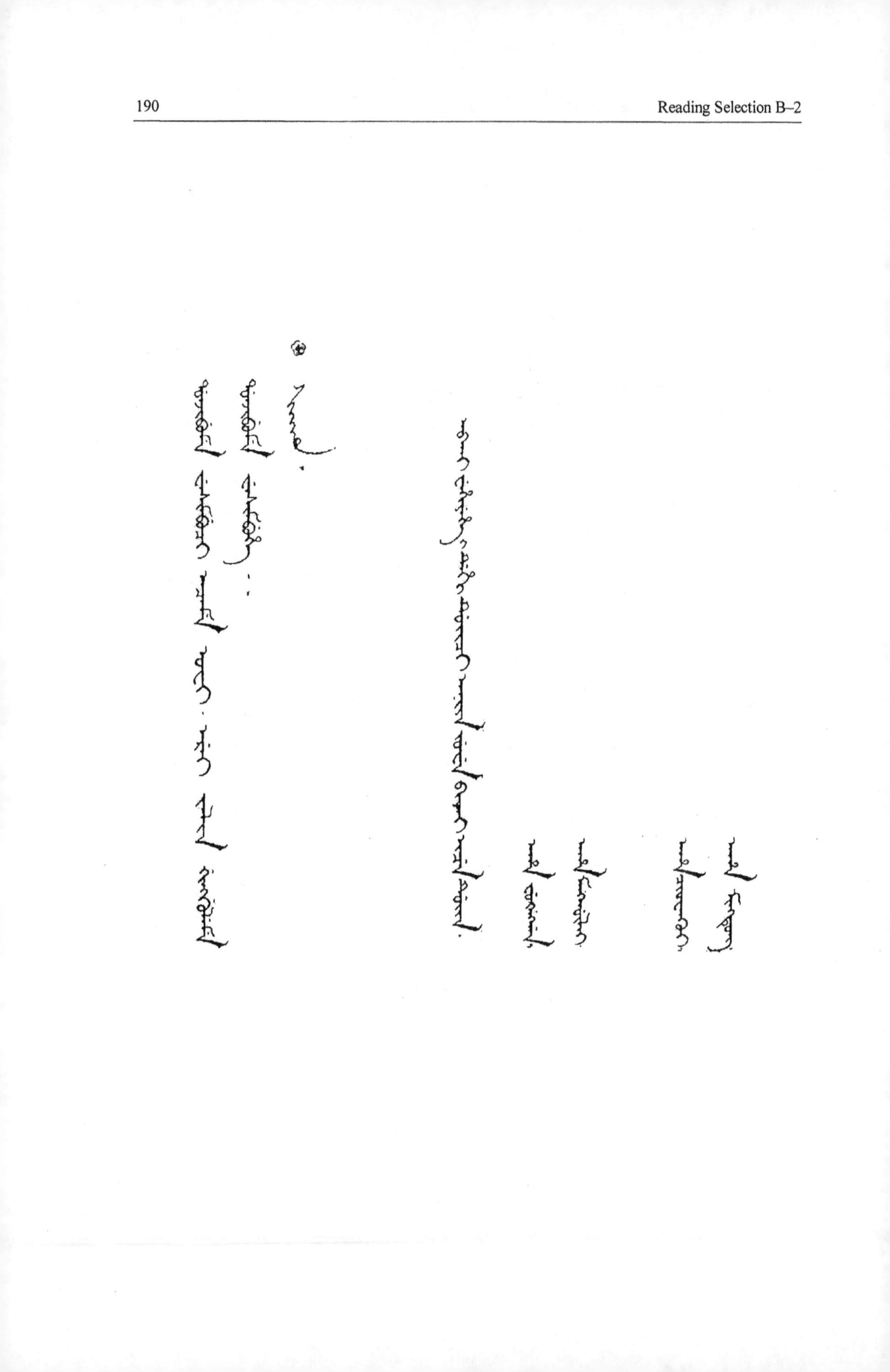

[illegible]

[illegible]

[illegible]

[illegible]

[illegible]

[illegible]

[illegible]

Transliteration

(188) *wesimburengge*[1]

aha Fuk'anggan sei gingguleme wesimburengge. geren harangga bade erin de acabure aga baha babe gingguleme donjibume wesimbure jalin. baicaci [2] *Mukden i harangga bade duleke aniya juwan biyai orin uyun de majige nimanggi baha. amala*

(189) *tuweri forgon i nimanggi hibcan bime, niyengniyeri dosika ci ebsi inu asuru aga bahakū. te abkai wehiyehe i dehi duici aniya juwe biyai ice juwe* [3] *i honin erin* [4] *ci ice ilan i tasha erinde* [4] *isibume sunja jurhun funceme agafi gubci* [5] *ba i usin gemu simebufi, jing maise muji tarire erin de usin tarire urse niyengniyeri tariha maise elgiyen tumin i bargiyara be erehunjeci ombi seme geren gemu urgunjendumbi.*[6] *ne hacingga* [7] *jekui hūda inu umesi necin. erin de acabure aga baha babe giyan i gingguleme*

(190) *donjibume wesimbuci acame ofi, erei jalin gingguleme donjibume wesimbuhe.*

(⊛ *saha*)[8]

Abkai Wehiyehe i dehi duici aniya juwe biyai ice duin

aha Fug'anggan [9]
aha Manggūlai
aha Ciowankui
aha Mingtung

Notes

1. *wesimburengge*: 'a memorial'. The word *wesimburengge*, which appears as title on the folded memorial, can refer to a routine memorial (Chin. *tiben* 題本) or to a palace memorial (*zouzhe* 奏摺). However, the Manchu *bukdari* and *jedz* usually meant *zouzhe*, and *ben* referred to a *tiben*.

2. *baicaci*: 'upon review we note that'. Commonly used in memorials, *baicaci* (Chin. *cha* 察) introduces the memorialist's comments on the matter. Often it is best left untranslated. Especially in memorials, but also in other contexts, *baicaci*, as well as *donjici* 'I hear', *gūnici* 'I think', or *tuwaci* 'we find', can be free-standing expressions which do not need to be followed by a form of *sembi*. See Review 2, and cf. Reading Selection A–6, Note 22.

3. ***ice juwe de*:** 'on the second day of the month'. As in Chinese, the number for the first ten days of a month are preceded by *ice* 'new' (Chin. *chu* 初).

4. ***honin erin*:** 'the time of the sheep', i.e., 1–3 P.M. The Manchus adopted the Chinese way of using the Twelve Branches to reckon time. For a complete table of the Manchu and Chinese Twelve Branches see Miscellaneous Information, p. 384.

5. ***gubci*:** The word *gubci* can function as an adjective or as a postposition. Examples: *gubci gurun* 'the entire country'; *booi gubci gemu saiyūn* 'everybody at home is well'.

6. ***urgunjendumbi*:** 'to rejoice together'. When the syllable *-ndu-* (or *-nu-*, *-ca-*, *-ce-*, *-co-*) is inserted between the verb stem and the verbal suffix *-mbi*, the new verb includes the meaning of togetherness or mutualness. See Review 3.

7. ***hacingga*:** 'all kinds'. Like *hacingga,* which is made up of *hacin* 'kind' and suffix *-gga*, certain adjectives are formed by adding endings *-ngga*, *-ngga*, or *-nggo* to a noun. Nouns ending in *n* drop this final consonant before adding the suffix. See Review 4.

8. The emperor's comments, called vermilion endorsements, are written onto the original memorial. They are marked in the published text with a rose symbol (❁).

9. The memorialist's name appears as Fuk'anggan and Fug'anggan in the document.

Review

1. ***donjici…sembi, tuwaci…sembi*** **'I hear, we note, etc.'**

donjici ini aciha hūlha de duribuhe sembi	I heard that his luggage was stolen by robbers
donjici fejergi hoise sebe jobobume gejureme gaiha hacin akū sembi	I hear that there are no instances of (him) making (his) Muslim subjects suffer and taking bribes
tuwaci aniyadari hūdai urse bele be asarafi hūda wesike erinde tucibufi uncambi sembi	(we note that) every year merchants hoard grain and sell it when prices are up

2. *baicaci, donjici, tuwaci* 'we find, we note, it appears'

baicaci hūdai urse udu bele be udafi asaracibe bele kemuni hecen de bimbi	(upon review we find that) even though merchants buy and accumulate grain, still there is grain in the city
baicaci Kašigar i karun tere Mergen ere aniya nadan biyade isibume ilan aniya jalukabi	(upon review we find that) Mergen, who is stationed at the sentry post of Kashgar, has completed his three-year term in the seventh month of the year
baicaci aniyadari hargašabume unggire bek se Hami de ice nadan de isinaha	(upon review we note that) every year the *begs* whom one sends for an audience arrive in Hami on the seventh day
tuwaci Oros i elcin hoton de isinahakū	it appears that the Russian envoy did not arrive in the town
donjici sini gucu isinaha	I hear your friend has arrived

3. Verb stem + *-ndu-*, *-nu-*, *-ca-*, *-ce-*, or *-co-*

urgunjembi	to rejoice	*urgunjendumbi*	to rejoice together
icihiyambi	to manage	*icihiyandumbi*	to manage together
aisilambi	to help	*aisilandumbi*	to help one another
temšembi	to quarrel, to compete	*temšendumbi* or *temšenumbi*	to quarrel with one another
acambi	to meet	*acandumbi* or *acanumbi*	to meet together
hebdembi	to discuss	*hebdenumbi*	to discuss together
dahambi	to follow	*dahacambi*	to follow together
jembi	to eat	*jecembi*	to eat together
songgombi	to weep	*songgocombi*	to weep together

4. Adjectives formed from nouns by adding *-ngga*, *-ngge*, *-nggo*

These nominal forms are often used as personal names.

baili	kindness, mercy	*bailingga*	merciful, kind
gosin	pity, mercy, love	*gosingga*	compassionate
erdemu	capability, power	*erdemungge*	virtuous, talented
elden	light, glory	*eldengge*	shining, glorious
doro	doctrine, morality	*doronggo*	moral, honest
horon	authority, awe	*horonggo*	awe-inspiring
hacin	sort, kind	*hacingga*	all kinds of

5. Some terms and phrases related to memorials

ajige amban	竊臣	I (memorialist's humble reference to himself)
amban bi	臣	I (memorialist referring to himself)
amban be	臣等	we (memorialists referring to themselves)
hese	諭	imperial edict, instruction (a separate document, based on imperial initiative)
hese	旨	imperial rescript in response to a memorial (generally shorter than an imperial edict (上諭)
tacibure hese	敕	imperial command, imperial utterance
selgiyere hese	詔	proclamation (to announce to the empire)
dergi hese	上諭	imperial edict
ulhibure hese	誥	ordinance (to manifest instructions)
hese be baimbi	請旨	to request an edict
fulgiyan fi i pilehe hese	硃批	imperial endorsement in vermilion ink
ulhibure fungnehen	誥命	patent by ordinance, used to confer titles for fifth rank and above
tacibun fungnehen	敕命	patent by command, used to confer titles below the fifth rank
unggire bithe	咨文	an official communication between two equals
hafumbume wesimbure bithe	通本	routine memorial from higher provincial authorities submitted through the Transmission Office or the Grand Secretariat
wesimbure bukdari	奏摺	memorial(routine or palace memorial)
yabure bithe	行文	despatch (to another government office)
alibure bithe	呈文	official report from lower to higher level
alibun	呈	report, petition
siden i bithe	公文	official document
enduringge tacihiyan	聖訓	sacred instructions
gisurefi wesimbumbi	議奏	to submit a discussion memorial
hacilame wesimbumbi	條陳	to submit a memorial of opinion
donjibume wesimbumbi	奏聞	to memorialize to inform
wakalame wesimbumbi	參奏	to memorialize to impeach
dahūme wesimbumbi	覆奏	to memorialize in response
akdulame wesimbumbi	保奏	to submit a memorial of recommendation
kesi de hengkilembi	謝恩	to prostrate to the imperial grace, to kowtow as an act of thanksgiving for the emperor's favor
elhe be baimbi	請安	to ask after a person's health
getuken afaha	清單	list, inventory (often enclosed as an attachment)
kesi isibumbi	加恩	to bestow favor

sehe	欽此	marks the end of an imperial utterance
sembi or *sehebi*	等因 等情 等語	marks the end of speech (by someone other than the emperor)
donjibume wesimbure jalin	爲奏聞事	to submit a memorial to inform
gingguleme wesimbure jalin	爲謹奏事	to respectfully memorialize
gisureme wesimbure jalin	爲議奏事	to submit a memorial for discussion
sakini sere jalin	爲知照事	to notify to inform, for the record
alibume boolara jalin	爲此知會	to communicate (between government offices)
erei jalin donjibume wesimbuhe	爲此謹奏	on this account I have submitted this memorial to inform
erei jalin gingguleme alibuha	爲此謹呈	on this account I have respectfully submitted this report
gingguleme sakini seme wesimbumbi	進具題知	to respectfully memorialize to inform, for the record
bairengge genggiyen i bulekušereo	伏乞皇上睿鑒	I beg your majesty's perusal
dergici toktobure be gingguleme aliyaki	請旨簡派	I respectfully await your majesty's decision
gingguleme ibebufi dele de tuwabume wesimbumbi or *gingguleme dele tuwabume ibebuhe*	恭呈御覽	I respectfully submit a memorial to the emperor for review
wesimbure bithe ibebumbi	進本	to submit a memorial
suwaliyame neneme wesimbumbi	一併先行奏呈	to forward with this memorial
gisurehe songkoi obu sehe	依議欽此	let it be as recommended
giyan i wesimbuci acambi	理合具奏	it is my duty to report/memorialize
majige saha babe gingguleme tucibume	管見恭陳	please allow me to state my humble opinion
saha	知道了	noted (imperial comment)
tuwaci...sehebi	竊見。等語	we find that

6. Write in Manchu script and translate into English: a) *baicaci erin de acabure aga baha*; b) *duleke aniya majige nimanggi baha*; c) *niyengniyeri dosika ci ebsi asuru aga bahakū*; d) *sunja jurhun funceme agaha*; e) *gubci ba i usin gemu simebuhe*; f) *tariha maise elgiyen tumin*; g) *hacingga jekui hūda umesi necin*; h) *erei jalin gingguleme donjibume wesimbuhe*.

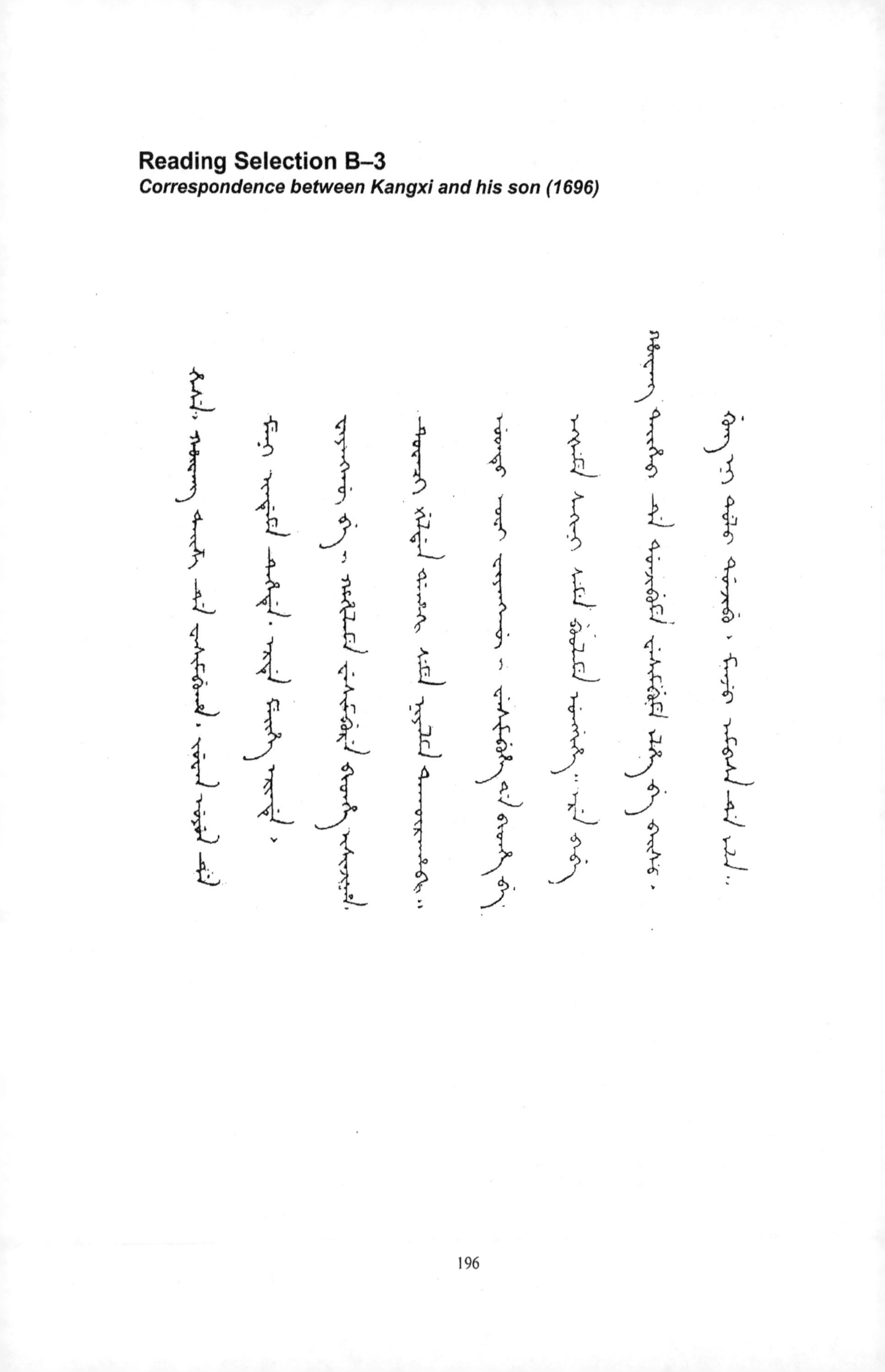

Reading Selection B–3

Correspondence between Kangxi and his son (1696)

[illegible]
[illegible]
[illegible]
[illegible]
[illegible]
[illegible]
[illegible]
[illegible]

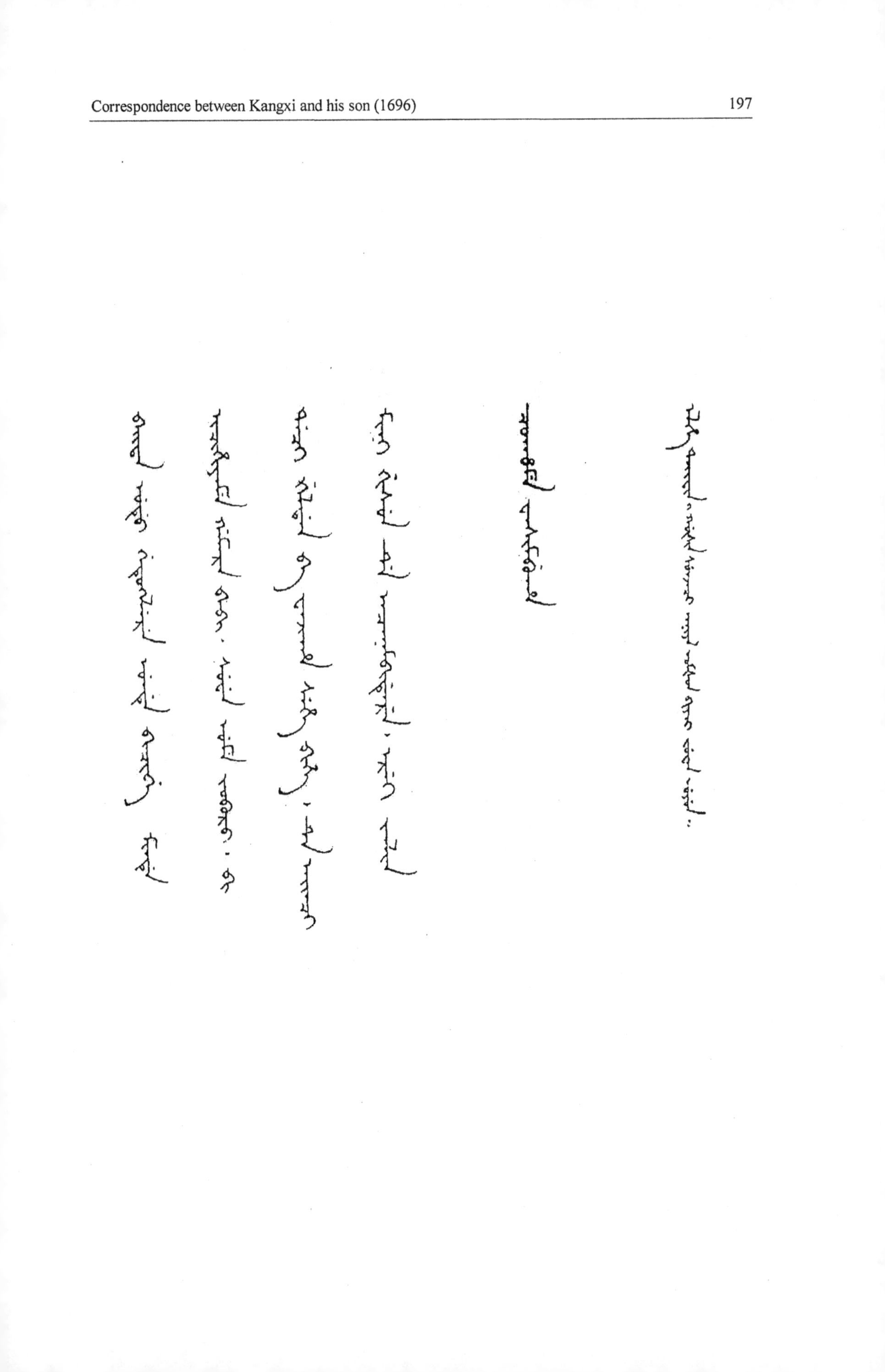

[illegible]

[illegible]

[illegible]

[illegible]

[illegible]

[illegible]

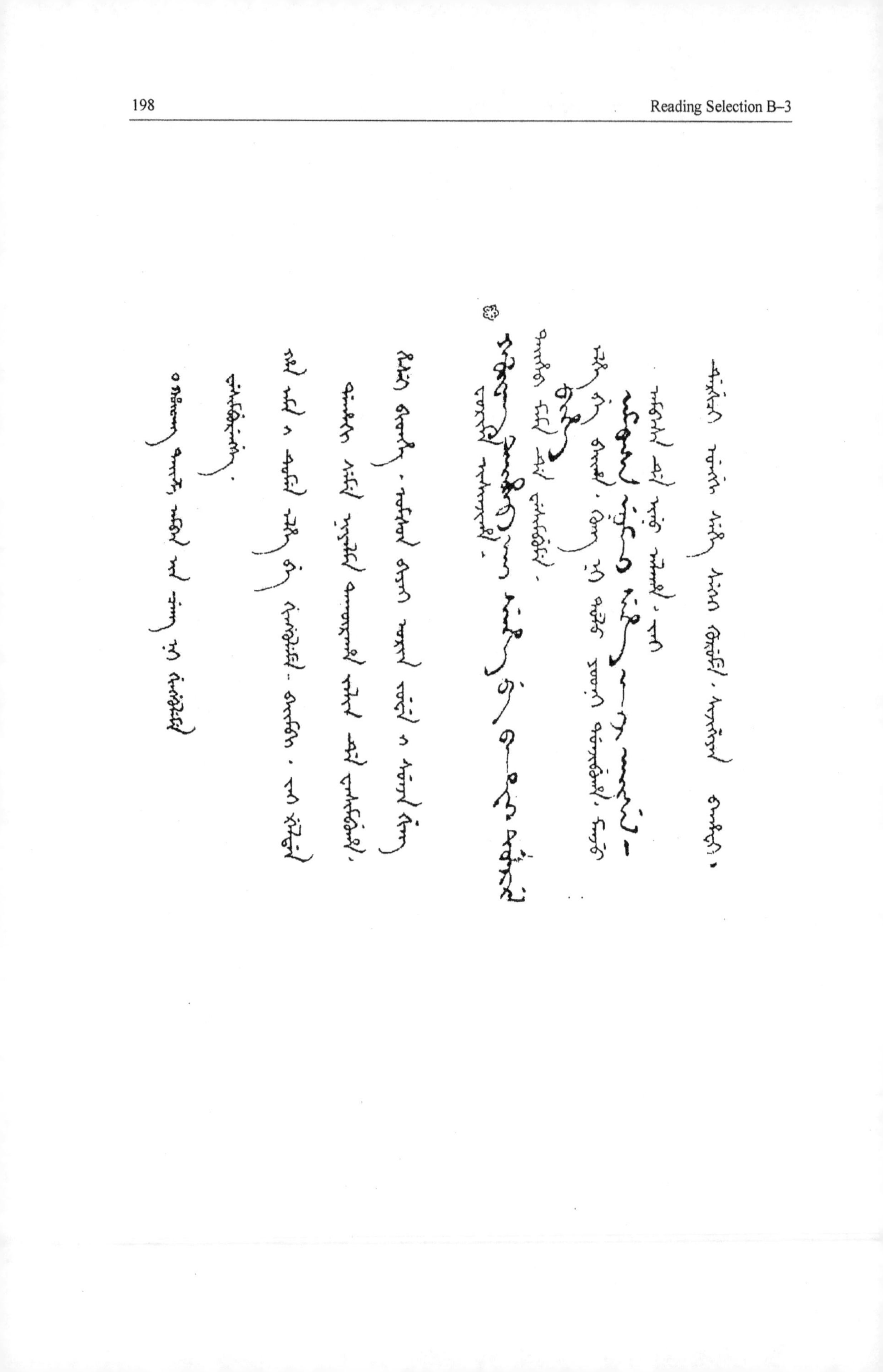

[illegible]

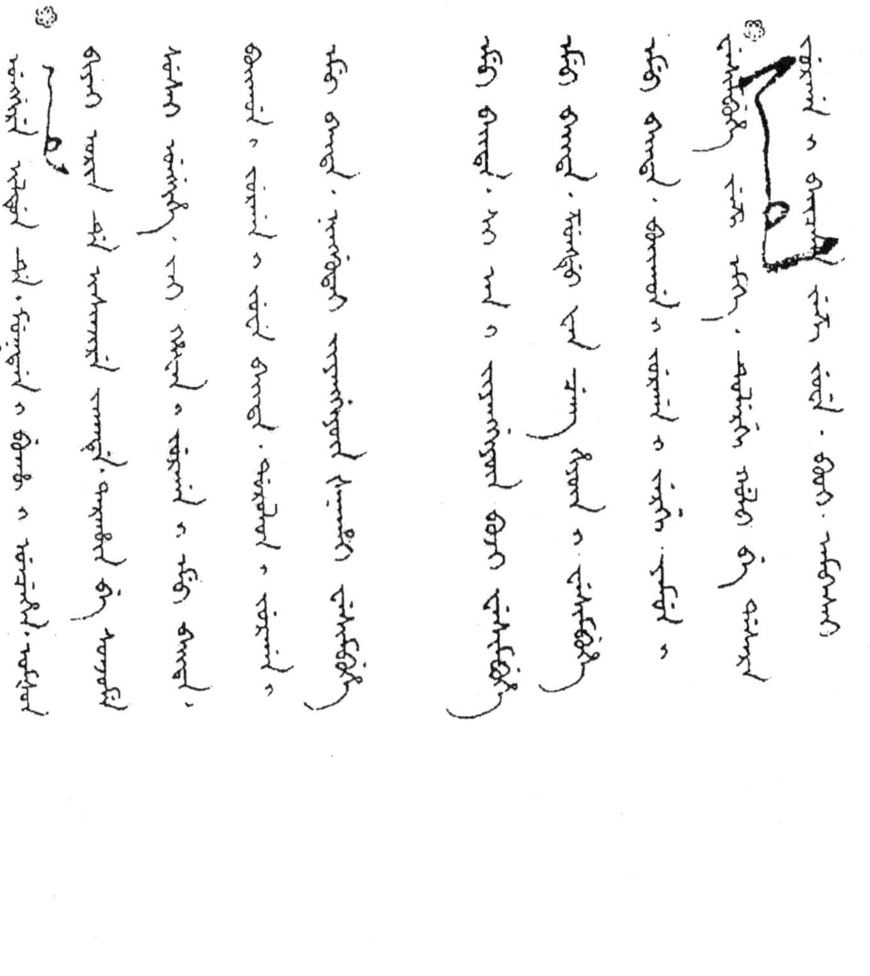

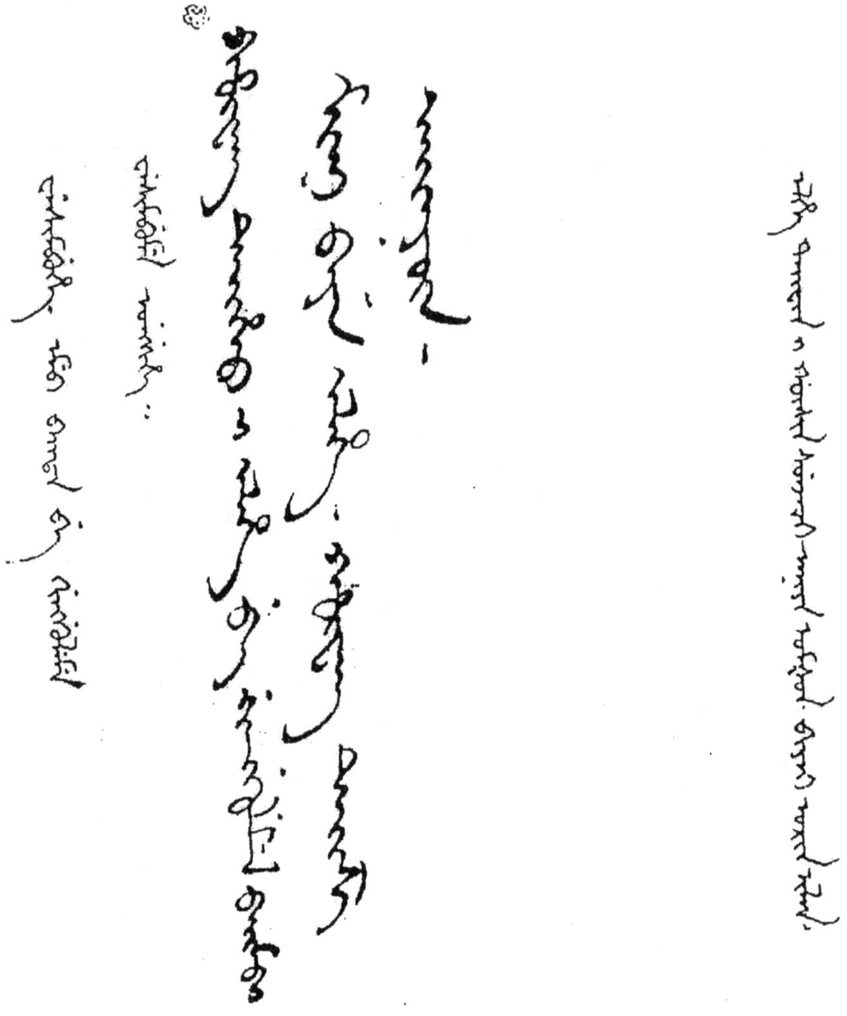

Transliteration

(196) *hese hūwang taidz de wasimbuha.*[1] *juwan uyun de meni* [2] *indeme tehede, erde meihe erinde, Fiyanggū be* [3] *i hahilame wesimbure bithe isinjiha. tuwaci G'aldan dahaki seme niyalma takūrahabi. uttu ofi Fiyanggū i wesimbuhe da bithe be, ekšeme sakini seme boolame unggihe.*[4] *ere babe hūwang taiheo de donjibume wesimbume elhe be baisu. gung ni dolo donjibu. manju ambasa de ala.*

(197) *baita udu getukelere unde bicibe minde icihiyame gamara babi.*[5] *suwe ume joboro. bi daci G'aldan ba wajiha sehe bihe, te ainci mini gisun de acanambidere,*[6] *erei jalin*

cohome wasimbuha.

elhe taifin i gūsin sunjaci aniya omšon biyai juwan uyun.

----

(198) *hūwang taidz amban In Ceng* [7] *ni gingguleme wesimburengge. han ama i tumen* [8] *elhe be gingguleme baimbi. jai G'aldan dahaki seme niyalma takūraha jalin de wasimbuha hesei bithe omšon biyai orin juwe i sunja ging forime isinjiha.*

(❁*hūwang taiheo ai sehe be bahafi* [9] *donjire bihe. ambasa umai sehe akū aise.*)[10]

taiheo mama de wesimbume, elhe be baiha. gung ni dolo yooni donjibuha, manju ambasa de inu alaha. jai dergici [11] *unggi sehe sekei kurume, sijigiyan bahafi*

(199) *unggire ildun de* [12] *Mukden i buhū i uncehen omšon*

(❁*saha*)

biyai orin de isinjire jakade, tarhūn be sonjome susai unggihe. jai hafan i jurgan i emu baita boigon i jurgan i juwe baita dorolon i jurgan i emu baita, Ninggutai jiyanggiyūn Šanahai wesimbuhe

emu baita, Si An i jiyanggiyūn Boji wesimbuhe emu baita, dzungdu Fan Ceng Hiyūn i wesimbuhe emu baita, boigon i jurgan i jergi yamun i wesimbuhe jedz emke, tulergi golo be dasara

(❁*saha*)

jurgan i baicaha jedz juwe, booi ambasai

(200) *wesimbuhe emu baita be gingguleme wesimbume unggihe.*

(*⊛hūwang taiheo i elhe be gingguleme baimbi. mini beye elhe. hūwang taidz saiyūn.*)

Elhe Taifin i gūsin sunjaci aniya omšon biyai orin ilan.

Notes

1. The two documents in this reading selection are part of an extensive correspondence between the Kangxi emperor and his son, then heir apparent, Yin Reng during the Qing campaign against the Dzungars (1696-97). At the time, Kangxi had left Yin Reng in charge of governmental affairs in Peking while he himself led his troops into the field.

2. ***meni indeme tehede*:** 'at the place where we rested'. The genitive *meni* qualifies the nominalized verb, *tehe*.

3. ***Fiyanggū be*:** Fiyanggū was a high-ranking general in charge of the westernmost division of the Qing force setting out against Galdan. The word *be* 'earl' is one of his titles, which was used at this time primarily to distinguish him from another well-known official by the same name.

4. ***sakini seme boolame unggihe*:** lit. 'I have sent it so one may know'. The expression *sakini seme* is commonly used by memorialists to report something for the record. Example: *gingguleme sakini seme wesimbuhe* 'I respectfully submit a memorial for the record'.

5. ***minde icihiyara gamara babi*:** 'I have things to take care of '. For more examples of similar expressions using *babi*, see Review 1.

6. ***te ainci mini gisun de acanambidere*:** lit. 'now it will perhaps fit my words'. Meaning: 'now my words may come true'. For more on sentence particles of probability and doubt, compare Note 10 and Review 3.

7. ***In Ceng*:** By custom, names of Manchu aristocrats were generally (but not always) written as separate syllables whereas those of non-aristocrats were linked, regardless of whether or not they were based on Chinese characters. (See Chen Jiexian [Ch'en Chieh-hsien]). "On the Romanization of Manchu Names in English Works." *Bulletin of China Border Studies*. National Cheng-chih University, Taipei, 1971). It is interesting to note the discrepancy between the Manchu name In Ceng and its Chinese equivalent Yin Reng 胤礽. According to Chen Jiexian, In Ceng's Chinese name was initially indeed Yin Cheng 胤成. It was changed later to Yin Reng (*Manchu Archival Materials* [Taipei: Linking Publishing Co., 1988]: 188).

8. ***tumen elhe be baimbi*:** This expression might be loosely translated as 'I wish you the very best'. Following Chinese practice, the word *tumen* 'ten thousand' is used to express an infinite number or an infinite amount of something. Examples: *tumen se okini* 'long live...' (Chin. *wansui* 萬歲) or *tumen de emgeri* 'just in case' (Chin. *wan i* 萬一).

9. ***hūwang taiheo ai sehe be bahafi donjire bihe*:** 'I have been able to hear what the empress dowager said'. Preceding a verb, *bahafi* takes the meaning of 'to be able', or 'to manage'. See Review 2 and compare Reading Selection A–4, Review 1.

10. ***ambasa umai sehe akū aise*:** 'I suppose the officials didn't say anything at all'. The word *aise* is a sentence particle which conveys the meaning of probability. It is similar to *dere* and, like *dere,* often occurs in conjunction with *ainci* 'perhaps'. See Review 3.

11. ***dergici unggi sehe sekei kurume*:** lit. 'the sable coat which one asked from above to send'. Meaning: 'the sable coat you, the emperor, asked me to send'. Another example: *dergici ambasa de hūdun gisurere seme afabuha* 'the emperor instructed his officials to quickly discuss (the matter)'.

12. ***ildun de*:** 'taking advantage of something to do something else'. Depending on the context, it may simply be translated with 'also'. See Review 4.

Review

1. *babi* 'there are things..., it is a case of...'

minde icihiyame gamara babi	there are I things for me to deal with
minde inu suwende fonjire babi	I also have things I want to ask you

coohai baita de ambula holbobuha babi	it has a lot to do with the military
hūda majige wasika babi	it's that the price has gone down a bit
tubai baita be mini beye isinaha manggi narhūšame wesimbure babi	after I arrive, I will memorialize (it will be a good time to memorialize) in detail about matters there

2. *bahafi* + verb 'can, to be able to'

hūwang taiheo ai sehe be bahafi donjire bihe	I have been able to hear what the empress dowager said
bahafi yabumbi	one can proceed
bahafi gisurembi	we can discuss
Mangsur bahafi Turfan de bederehekū	Mangsur was unable to return to Turfan

3. *aise* and *dere* 'perhaps, maybe, probably'

ainci mini gisun de acanambi dere	maybe what I said will come true
hono isinjihakū aise	he probably has not yet arrived
ainci šolo bahakū aise	I suppose you did not have time
ere jaka ainci efujehe dere	I suppose this thing is broken

4. *ildun de* 'taking advantage of'

sekei kurume be unggire ildun de buhū i uncehen be susai unggihe	as I was shipping the sable coat, I took the opportunity to send along fifty deer tails
booi baita be ildun de icihiyame gamambi	at the same time I'll take the opportunity to take care of some family matters
hoton tucire ildun de, bigan i tuwabun tuwambi	since we are going out of town, we'll take the opportunity to see the countryside

5. *umai* 'not at all'

umai sehe akū	they did not say anything
umai seme jaburakū	he does not answer at all
Osman umai ini ama be dahame tehengge waka	it was not (at all a fact) that Osman resided with his father
mini kesi isibume šangnaha hergen umai siraburengge waka	a rank bestowed by my grace is not something that is inherited

6. Manchu names of government ministries

boigon i jurgan	戶部	Ministry of Revenue
dorolon i jurgan	禮部	Ministry of Rites
hafan i jurgan	吏部	Ministry of Personnel
weilere jurgan	工部	Ministry of Works
beidere jurgan	刑部	Ministry of Justice
coohai jurgan	兵部	Ministry of War
dorgi yamun	內閣	Grand Secretariat
coohai nashūn i ba	軍機處	Grand Council
tulergi golo be dasara jurgan	理藩院	Court of Colonial Affairs
dorgi baita be uheri kadalara yamun	內務府	Imperial Household Department

7. Write in Manchu script and translate into English: a) *meni indeme tehede Fiyanggū be i hahilame wesimbure bithe isinjiha*; b) *da bithe be ekšeme boolame unggihe*; c) *hūwang taiheo de elhe be baisu*; d) *manju ambasa de ala*; e) *suwe ume joboro*; f) *ambasa umai sehe akū aise*; g) *dergici unggi sehe sekei kurume be unggihe*; h) *buhūi uncehen isinjire jakade tarhūn be sonjome susai unggihe*; i) *mini beye elhe.*

Reading Selection B–4

From Mampi to Fiyanggū (1697)

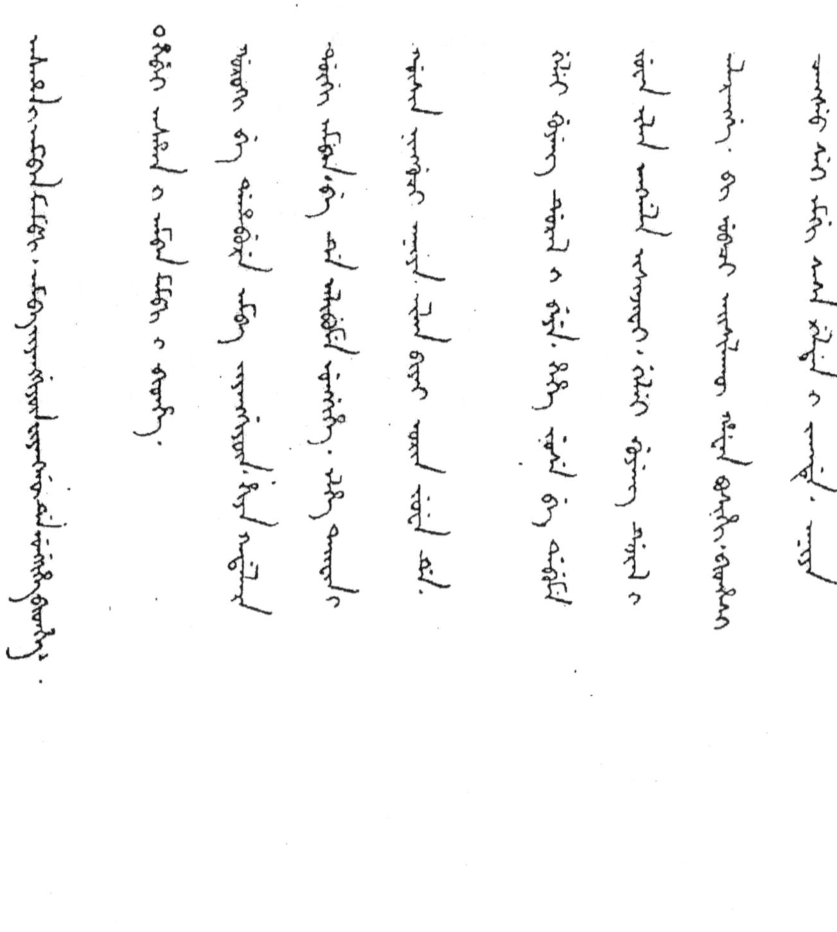

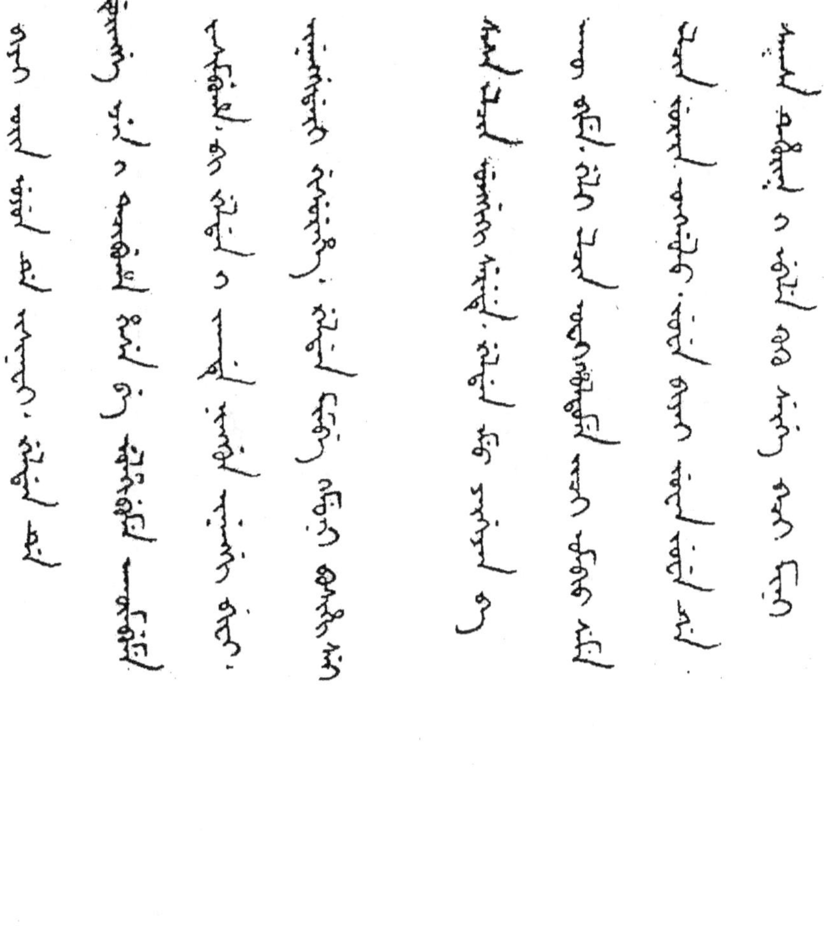

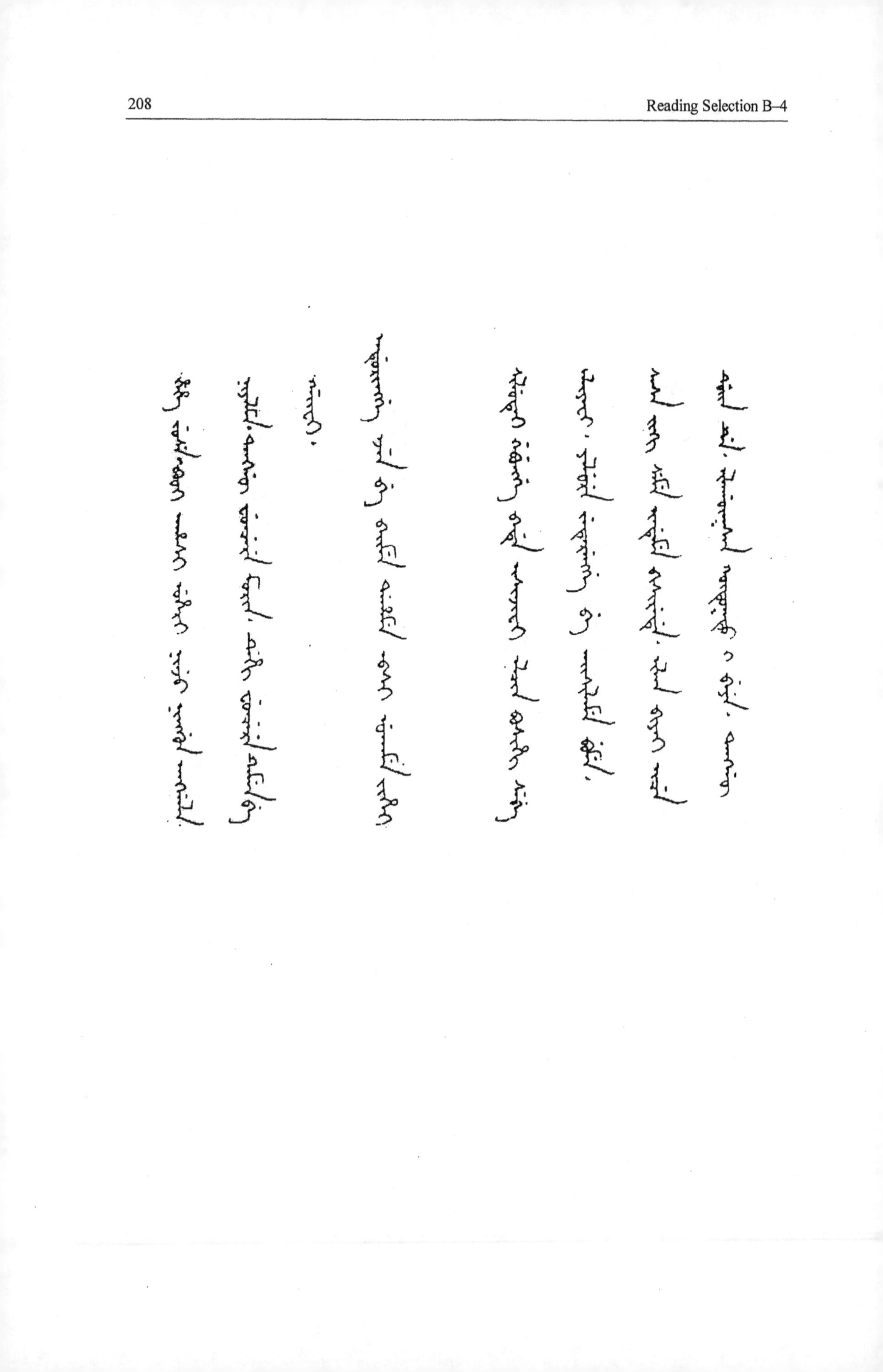

[illegible]
[illegible]
[illegible]

[illegible]

[illegible]
[illegible]
[illegible]
[illegible]

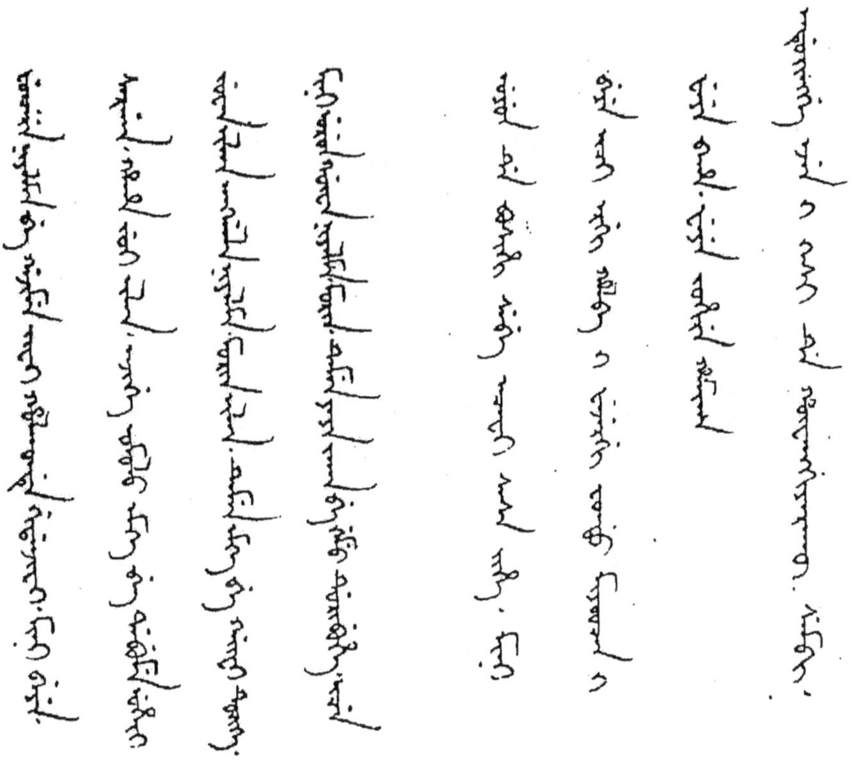

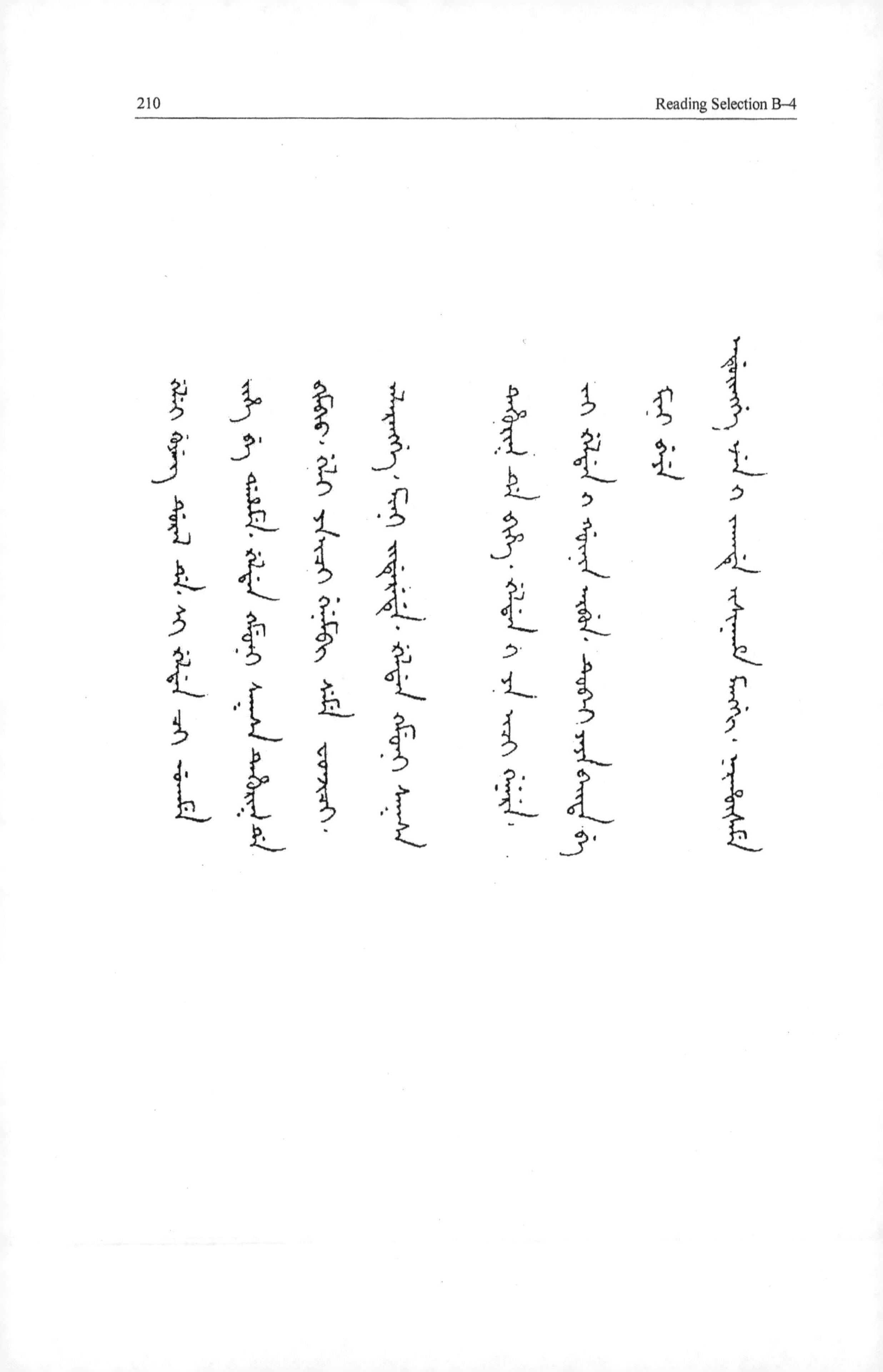

[illegible]

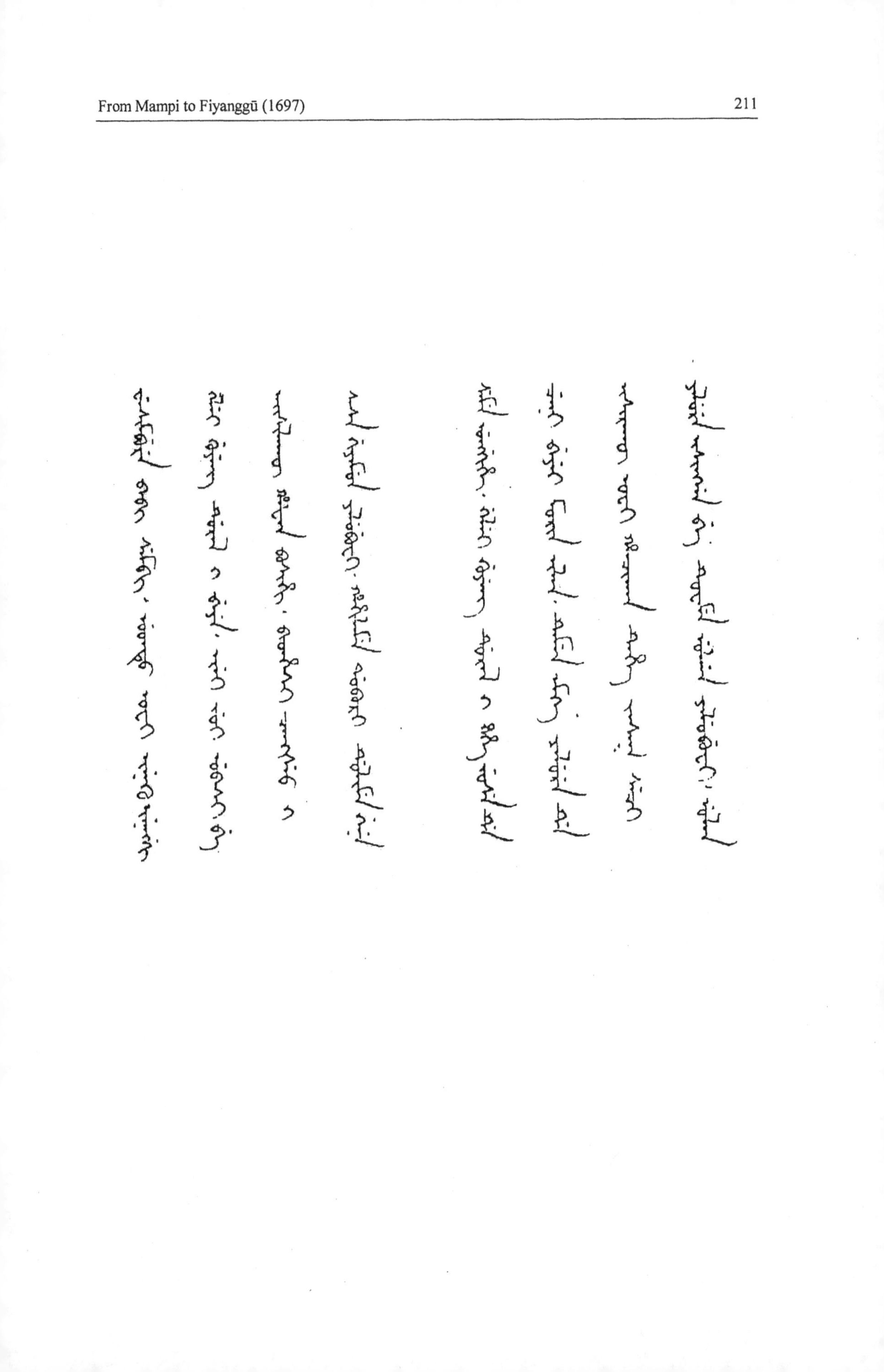

[illegible]

[illegible]

[illegible]

[illegible]

[illegible]

[illegible]

[illegible]

[illegible]

Transliteration

(206) *ashan i amban Mampi, amba jiyanggiyūn Fiyanggū de unggihe bithe*

hebei ashan i amban Mampi i bithe goroki be dahabure amba jiyanggiyūn hiya kadalara dorgi amban, be de alibume unggihe. elhe taifin i gūsin ningguci aniya ilan biyai orin juwe de

Gelei Guyeng Dural i beye, hehe juse be dabume juwan ilan anggala isinjifi, Gelei Guyeng Dural i alarangge: «bi Ubaci [1] *aisilakū hafan Bosihi, bithesi Cangšeo sei emgi sasa* [2] *G'aldan i jakade, aniya*

(207) *biyai orin uyun de isinafi, G'aldan de enduringge ejen i tacibuha hese be ulhibume akūmbume wasimbuha. bi G'aldan i jakade ninggun inenggi bifi inenggidari gisurehe. G'aldan mimbe kemuni Bosihi sei*

sasa elcin unggiki serede, G'aldan emu yargiyan ba akū bime, geli elcin ofi holtome jici ombio seme [3] *elcin jurara onggolo, juwe biyai juwan juwe de Saksa Tehurik i ebele Kuku Serge baci mini*

(208) *hehe juse, booi ahasi uheri ninju ninggun anggala niyalma, tanggū funcere morin, dehi funcere temen be gaifi, enduringge ejen be baime dahame ebsi ukame jihei* [4]

Silutei gebungge bade isinjifi elcin Bosihi sebe aliyafi, yalure jeterengge be aisilame bume, sasa jiki seme indeme bisirede, ilan biyai ice duin de Ilagūksan kūtuktu i beye, tanggū

(209) *funcere niyalma be gajime jifi holkonde gidanjifi, mini beye, sargan, haha jui ilan, ajige omolo emke be dabume uheri juwan ilan anggala niyalma morin ilan temen emke be gaifi tucike. mini urun gūwa* [5] *niyalma, morin, temen yaya jaka be gemu duribuhe. ice*

uyun de Bosihi sebe acafi sasa jihe. mini beye ici ergi halba i fejergi fondo miyoocan i feye baha. feye johire hamika.[6] *enduringge ejen i kesi de hūwanggiyarakū» sembi.*

(210) *Gelei Guyeng Dural de, «si G'aldan ci ukame jihe be dahame, G'aldan kemuni Saksa Tehurik de bimbio. geli ya ici genembi» seme fonjici, alarangge: «mini jiderede G'aldan kemuni Saksa*

Tehurik de bihe. G'aldan i ya ici genere, jai G'aldan i gūnin arbun. tubai yaya baita be mini beye enduringge ejen i jakade isinaha manggi, narhūšame

(211) *wesimbure babi» sembi. uttu ofi ineku inenggi Gelei Guyeng Dural i beye, erei jui Ubasi be aisilakū hafan Bosihi, bithesi Cangšeo i sasa giyamun yalubufi, hahilame dobori dulime gene*

seme unggihe. Gelei Guyeng Dural i hehe juse de ceni beyei morin ilan, temen emke yalure de isirakū ofi hancikan[7] *tehe jasak seci yalure isingga*[8] *be tuwame ulga yalubufi, ulan*

(212) *ulan i giyamun deri benebuhe.*[9] *erei jalin alibume unggihe.*[10]

elhe taifin i gūsin ningguci aniya ilan biyai orin juwe.

Notes

1. *Ubaci*: Mispelling for *Ubasi*. The same sequence of names appears on page 211.

2. *emgi sasa*: 'together'. Like the individual words *emgi* or *sasa* 'together', *emgi sasa* is a postposition. Both *emgi* and *sasa* may also function as adverbs. See Review 1.

3. *elcin ofi holtome jici ombio seme*: lit. 'thinking having become a messenger, can I come here to deceive?' Meaning: I did not want to become a messenger of deceit.

4. *ebsi ukame jihei Silutei gebungge bade isinjifi*: lit. 'after we arrived in Silutei as we were fleeing hither'. The durative converb *jihei* relates to *isinjifi*. It describes an action that occurs or continues at the same time another action is performed. For a review of the durative converb see Review 2 and Reading Selection A-6, Review 5.

5. *gūwa niyalma*: 'other people' or 'others'. Here the word *gūwa* functions as an adjective. As a noun *gūwa* by itself can also mean 'others, other people'.

6. *feye johire hamika*: lit. 'the healing of the wound is near'. Meaning: 'The wound is almost healed'. Cf. *amba cooha isinjire hamika* 'the imperial army will arrive soon'.

7. *hancikan*: 'somewhat near'. For a review of adjectives + *-kan, -ken, -kon* see Reading Selection A-6, Review 8.

8. ***yalure isingga be tuwame*****:** 'depending on the availability of riding animals'. Here *isingga* 'sufficient' or 'adequate' functions as a noun. See Review 3.

9. ***ulan ulan i giyamun deri benebuhe*****:** 'we had them taken by way of military post stations'.

10. ***ereci jalin alibume unggihe*****:** When this stylized conclusion of a memorial contains no additional information it may be left untranslated.

Review

1. *emgi* and *sasa* Postposition and adverb 'with, together, each other'

ini deo Hojijan i emgi fudasihūn deribuhe	together with younger brother Hojijan he started a rebellion
Hojijan Erdeni i emgi banjire sain	Hojijan and Erdeni were on good terms
Hošik teni Ming'ilha i sasa Aksu de genehe	Hošik then went with Ming Ilha to Aksu
ini sasa isinjiha	they arrived with him
sasa dosimbi	to enter together
sasa karmambi	to protect each other
emgi tembi	to live together
emgi tacire niyalma	schoolmates

2. *-hai, -hei, -hoi* Durative converb

ebsi ukame jihei ubade insijiha	fleeing in this direction, we arrived here
yasa hadahai tuwambi	to stare, to look fixedly
tehei aliyambi	to sit down and wait
bodohoi wajirakū	he kept counting endlessly

3. *isingga*

yalure isingga be tuwame	depending on the availability of riding animals
isingga gamambi	to take sufficient supplies
cooha de bure isingga be bodome werihe	they left behind sufficient supplies for the troops

4. Write in Manchu script and translate into English: a) *goroki be dahabure amba jiyanggiyūn*; b) *G'aldan de enduringge ejen i tacibuha hese be wasimbuha*; c) *G'aldan mimbe elcin unggiki serede, enduringge ejen be baime dahame ebsi ukame jihe*; d) *yalure jeterengge be aisilame buki sehe*; e) *Ilagūksan kūtuktu tanggū funcere niyalma be gajime jifi holkonde gidanjiha*; f) *ajige omolo be dabume uheri juwan ilan anggala niyalma gaifi tucike*; g) *morin, temen yaya jaka be gemu duribuhe*; h) *feye johire hamika*; i) *mini jiderede G'aldan kemuni Saksa Tehurik de bihe*; j) *ejen i jakade isinaha manggi narhūšame wesimbure babi*; k) *ceni beyei morin yalure de isirakū*; l) *yalure isingga be tuwame ulga yalubuha*; m) *ulan ulan i giyamun deri benebuhe.*

Reading Selection B–5

Fiyanggū reports on envoys from Galdan (1697)

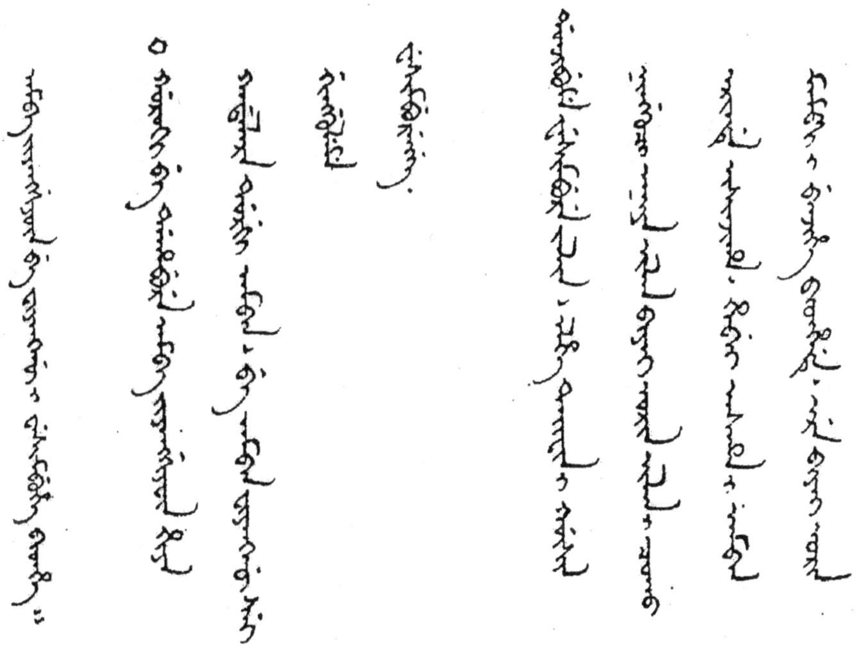

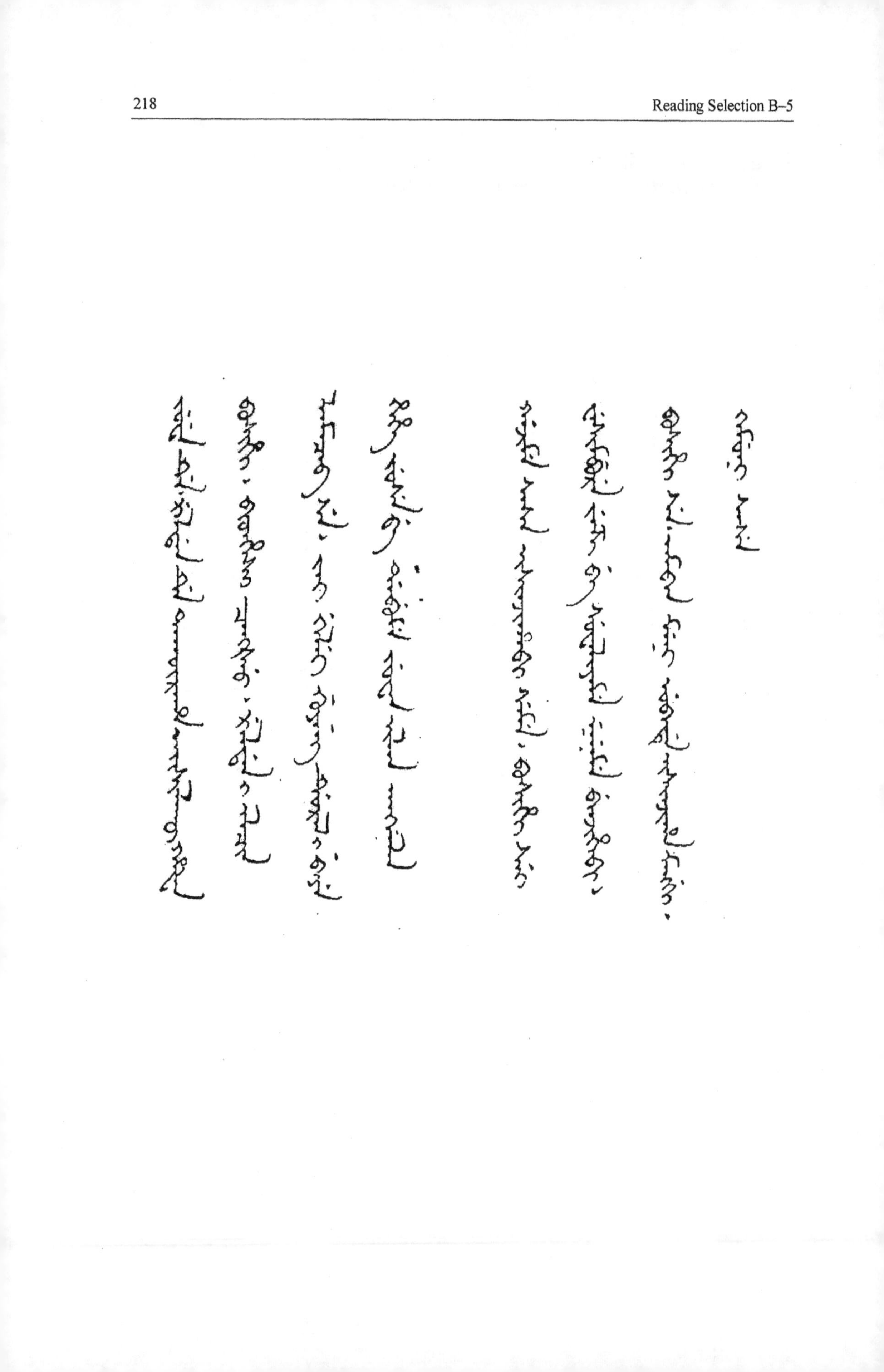

[illegible]

[illegible]

[illegible]

[illegible]

[illegible]

[illegible]

[illegible]

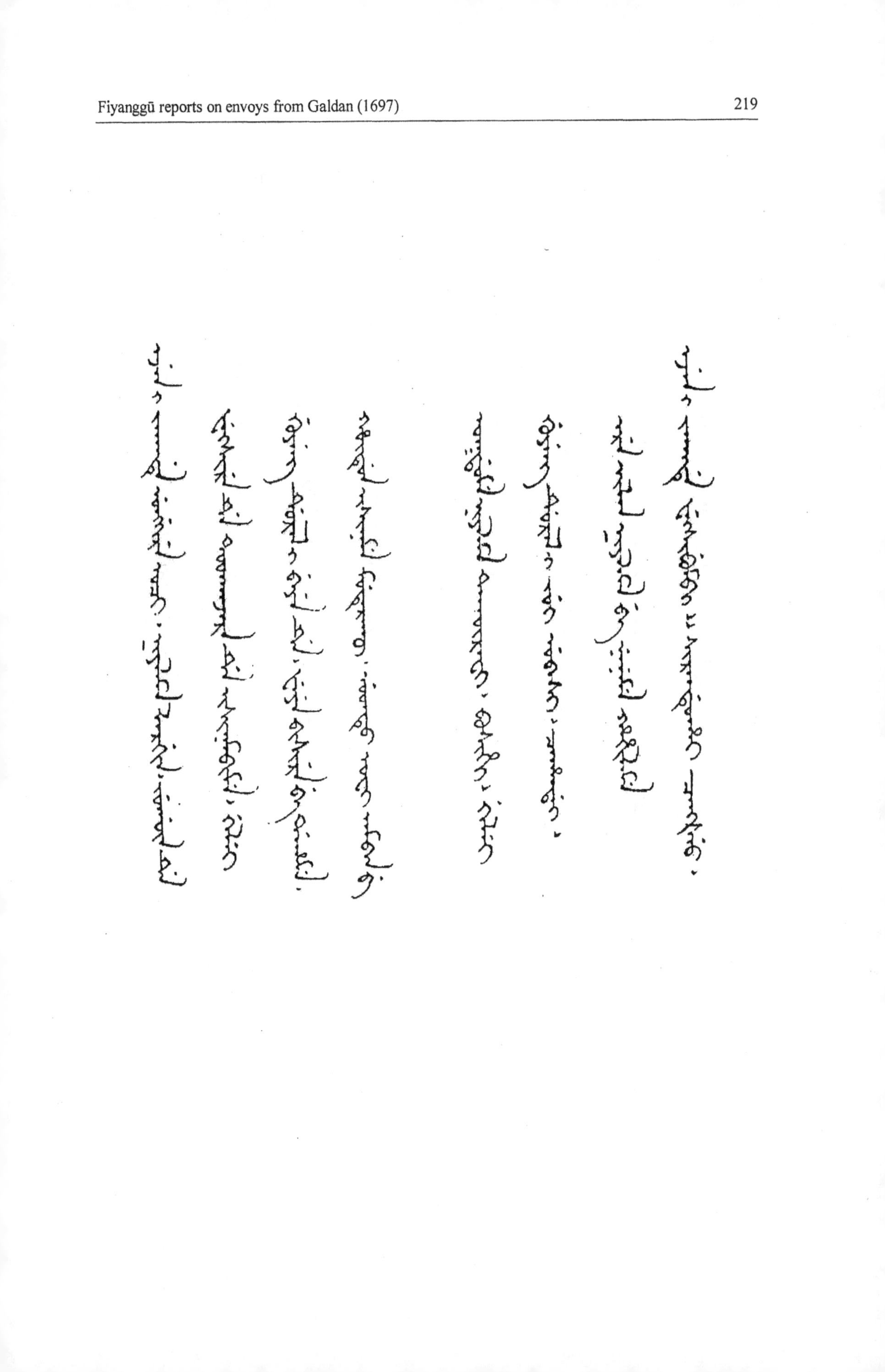

[illegible]

[illegible]

[illegible]

[illegible]

[illegible]

[illegible]

[illegible]

[illegible]

[illegible]

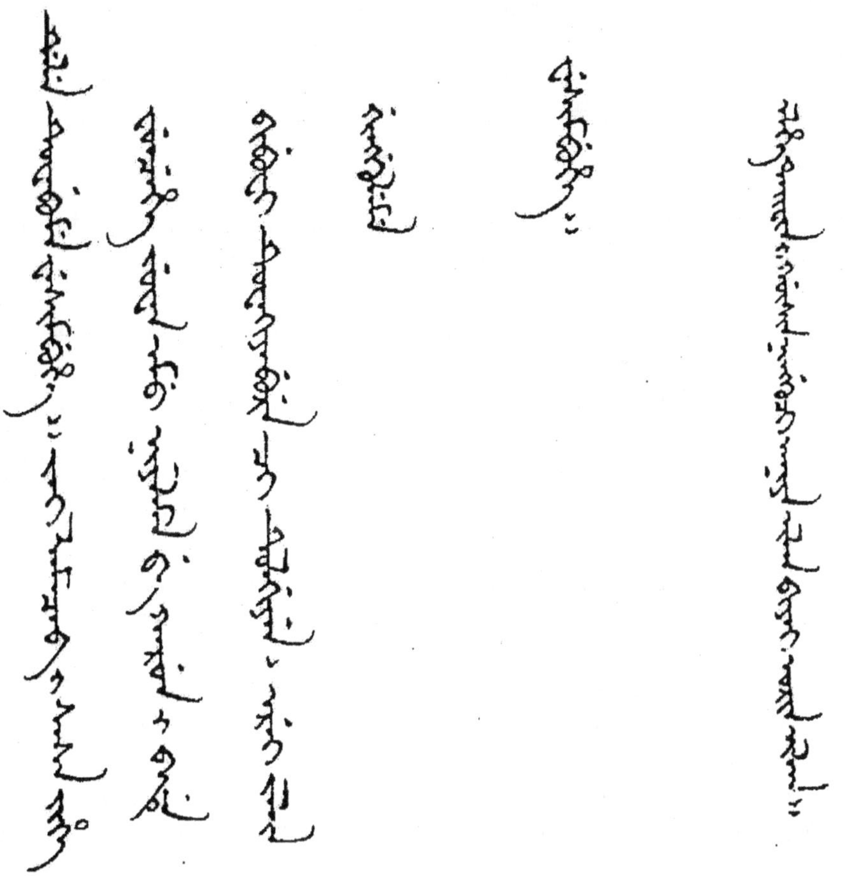

Transliteration

(217) *amba jiyanggiyūn be* [1] *Fiyanggū i wesimbuhe bithe.*

goroki be dahabure amba jiyanggiyūn hiya kadalara dorgi amban, be amban Fiyanggū sei gingguleme wesimburengge.

donjibume wesimbure jalin. elhe taifin i gūsin ningguci aniya ilan biyai orin ilan i coko erinde isinjiha hebei ashan i amban Mampi i benjihe bithede, ere biyai orin

(218) *juwe de G'aldan de takūraha aisilakū hafan Bosihi, bithesi Cangšeo, G'aldan i elcin Lamacab se, jai Gelei Guyeng Dural i beye hehe juse be dabume juwan ilan anggala*

gajime sasa isinjihabi seme, Bosihi sei wesimbure jedz be suwaliyame neneme [2] *benjihebi. Bosihi se amban meni ubade isinjiha manggi, kemuni sasa*

(219) *ejen i jakade unggire oci, niyalma largin jugūn de feksire de tookanjara de isinambime, Gelei Guyeng Dural i beye de, feye bisire be dahame, hūdun isiname muterakū. uttu ofi amban be*

okdome niyalma takūrafi, Bosihi, Gelei Guyeng Dural i jui Ubasi, Cahandai ere ilan niyalma be neneme hahilame ejen i jakade feksibumbi. siranduhai Cangšeo,

(220) *Gelei Guyeng Dural, Manji, Awangdanjin, G'aldan i elcin Lamacab, Danjila i elcin Lobdzang sebe, inu hahilame ejen i jakade feksibumbi. hebei ashan i amban*

Mampi i benjihe, G'aldan i elcin Lamacab, Gelei Guyeng Dural sede fonjiha juwe afaha bithe, Bosihi i donjibume wesimbure emu jedz be suwaliyame neneme

(221) *dele tuwabume wesimbuhe. jai Lamacab i sasa jihe funcehe juwan emu niyalma* [3] *be karun i bade bibufi tuwakiyabure ci tulgiyen, erei jalin gingguleme wesimbuhe.*

Elhe Taifin i gūsin ningguci aniya ilan biyai orin ilan.

Notes

1. *be*: Keep in mind that the word *be* has several meanings. Besides occurring as accusative particle, the meaning of *be* as 'we' or as 'earl' are common usages in documents.

2. *suwaliyame neneme wesimbuhe*: 'I am sending along', or 'I am forwarding'. (The Chinese equivalent is *yibing xianxing zouwen* 一併先行奏文.) The use of the past tense compares to the wording of *ere jalin gingguleme wesimbuhe*, which literally means 'for this reason I have respectfully memorialized'. Because this phrase marks the end of the memorial, the memorial is considered to have been written. In English one would probably prefer the present progressive tense: 'for this reason I am respectfully submitting this memorial'. Similarly, the phrase *suwaliyame neneme wesimbuhe* means that the material to be forwarded has been prepared earlier. It does not mean that it has already been sent out. In this case, this is verified by the fact that the forwarded material arrived between 5 and 7 p.m. on the twenty-third, and that the memorial is also sent on the same day.

3. *funcehe juwan emu niyalma*: 'the remaining eleven people'. Cf. *juwan funcere niyalma* 'more than ten people'.

Review

1. Write in Manchu script and translate into English: a) *hebei ashan i amban Mampi i benjihe bithede G'aldan i elcin isinjihabi sehe*; b) *hehe juse be dabume juwan ilan anggala isinjihabi*; c) *jugūn de feksire de tookanjara de isinambi*; d) *feye bisire be dahame, hūdun isiname muterakū*; e) *ilan niyalma be neneme hahilame feksibumbi*; f) *hebei ashan i amban Mampi i benjihe G'aldan i elcin sede fonjiha afaha bithe be dele tuwabume wesimbuhe*; g) *funcehe juwan emu niyalma be karun i bade bibufi tuwakiyabuha*.

Reading Selection B-6

Fiyanggū reports Galdan's death (1697)

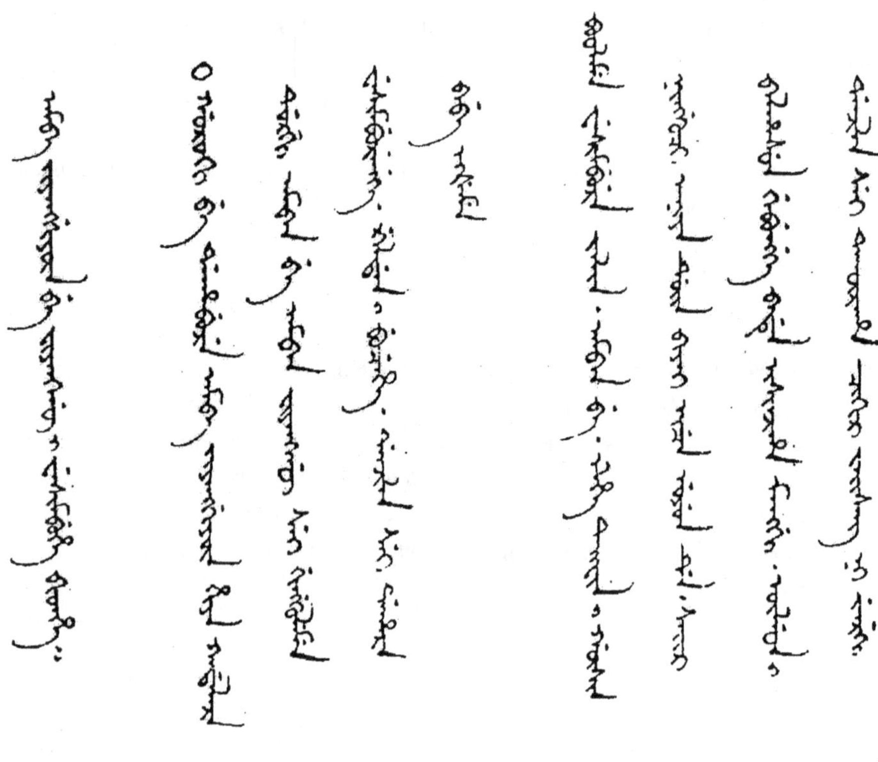

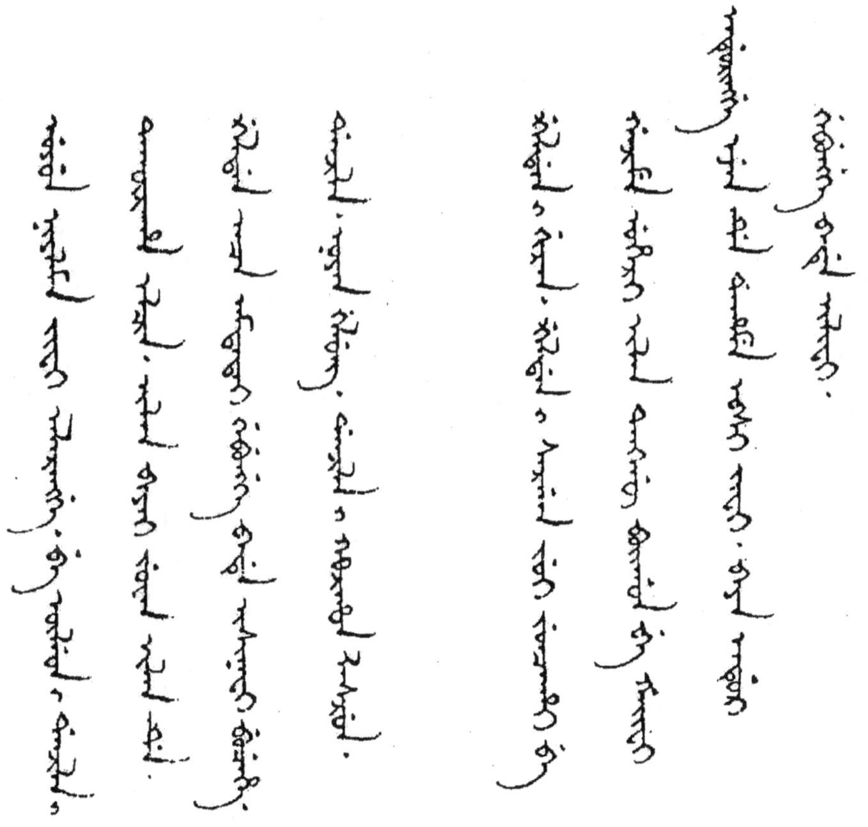

ᡤᡳᠰᡠᠨ ᠪᡝ ᡤᡳᠰᡠᡵᡝᡵᡝ ᠪᠠᡳᡨᠠ ᡨᡠᠸᠠᠮᠪᡳ᠈ ᡠᠮᡝᠰᡳᡝᠯᡝᠮᠪᡳ ᠠᠮᠪᠠᠨ᠉

ᡤᡳᠰᡠᠨ ᡤᡳᠰᡠᡵᡝᡥᡝ᠈ ᡤᡳᠰᡠᡵᡝᡥᡝ

ᠠᡥᠠᠰᡳ ᡳᠨᡳ ᠠᠨᡳᠶᠠ ᠠᠨᡳᠶᠠ

ᡤᡳᠰᡠᠨ ᠪᡝ ᠠᠰᠠᡵᠠ ᠪᡠᡨᡝ᠉

ᡠᠮᡝᠰᡳᡝᠯᡝᠮᠪᡳ ᠨᡳ ᡨᡠᠸᠠᡵᡝ ᠪᡝᠶᡝᠨᡳ᠈ ᡳᠯᡝ ᠠᠮᠪᠠᠨ᠈ ᡨᡝᡵᡝ ᠠᠮᠪᠠᠨ᠉

ᠠᡳᠰᡳᠯᠠᡵᡝ ᠠᠮᠪᠠᠨ᠈ ᡝᠮᡠ ᠨᡳᠶᠠᠯᠮᠠ ᡳᠰᡳ ᡳᠰᡳ᠈ ᡤᡳᠰᡠᠨ

ᡨᠠᡴᡡᡵᠠ ᠪᡠᡨᡝᡥᡝ ᠪᡝ ᠪᡝᠶᡝᠨᡳ᠈ ᠪᡝᠶᡝᠨ ᠠᡳᠰᡳᠯᠠᡥᠠ ᠪᡝ

ᠪᠣᠯᡤᠣ ᡩᡝᠨ᠉ ᡝᠮᡠ ᠠᠮᠪᠠᠨ᠈ ᠮᠠᠩᡤᠠ ᡨᡝᡵᡝ᠈ ᠪᠣᡥᠣᠨ

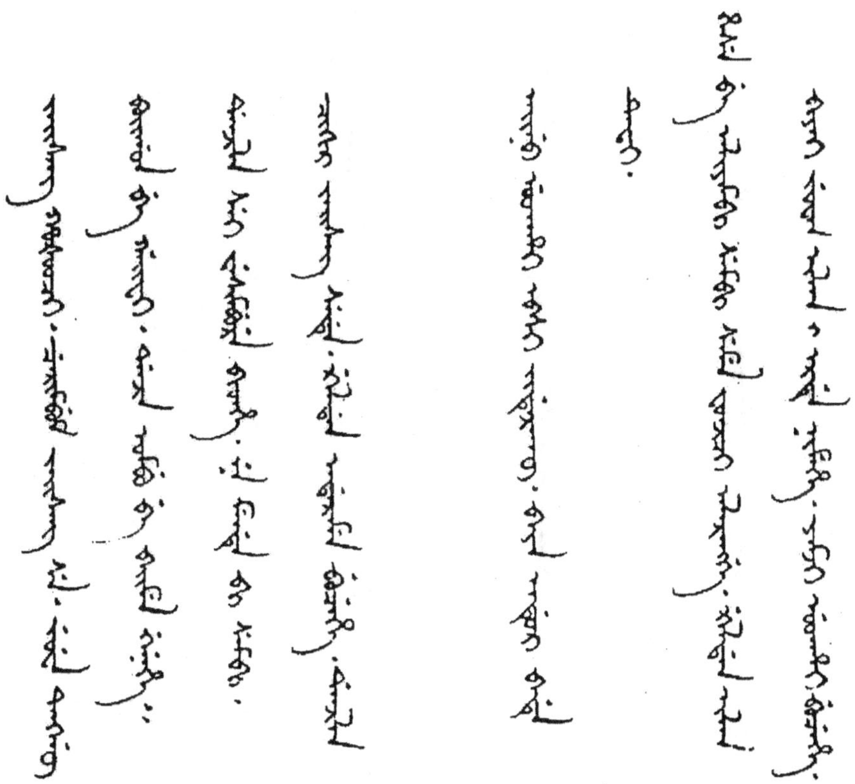

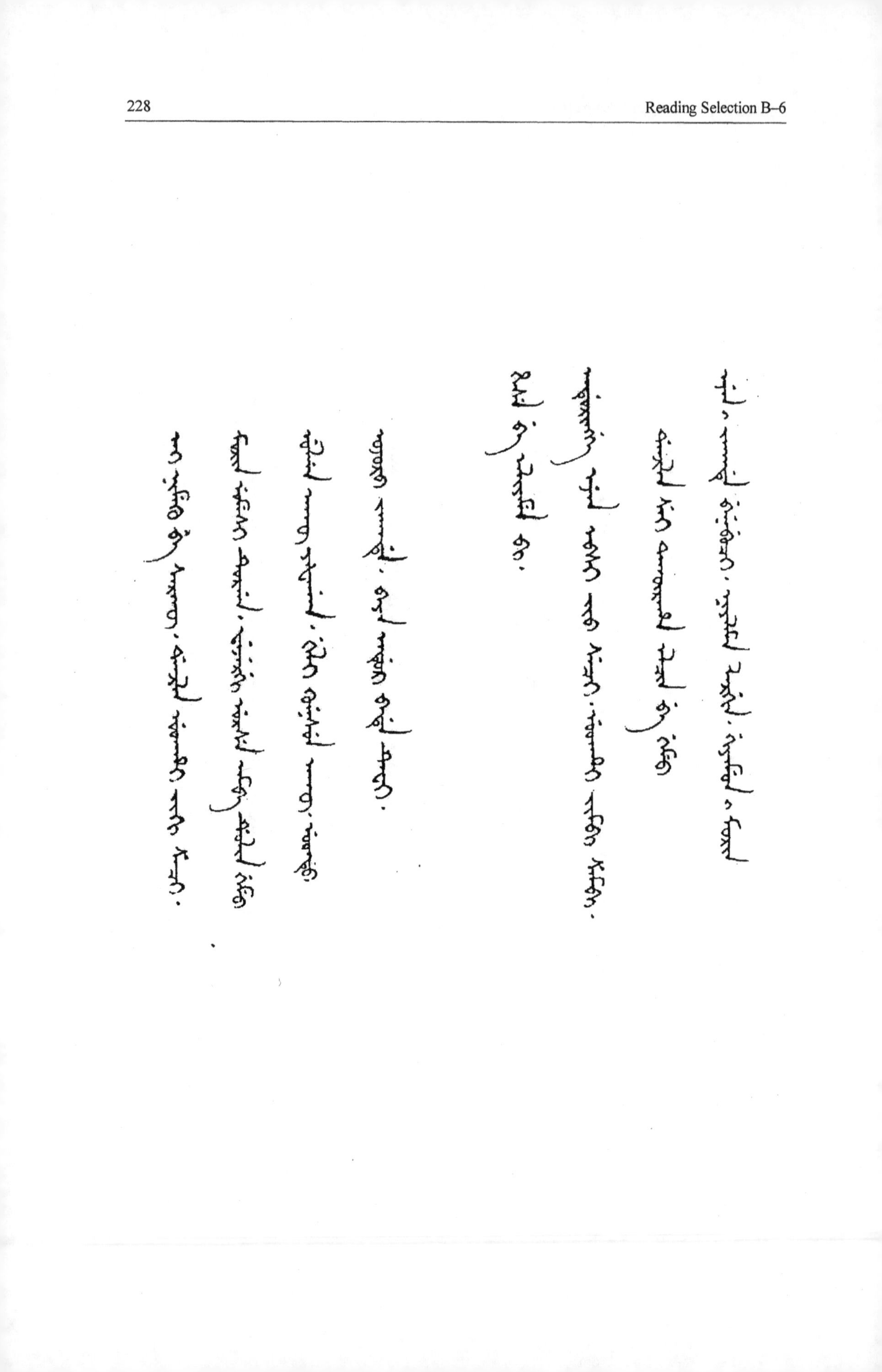

[illegible]
[illegible]
[illegible]
[illegible]

[illegible]
[illegible]
[illegible]
[illegible]
[illegible]

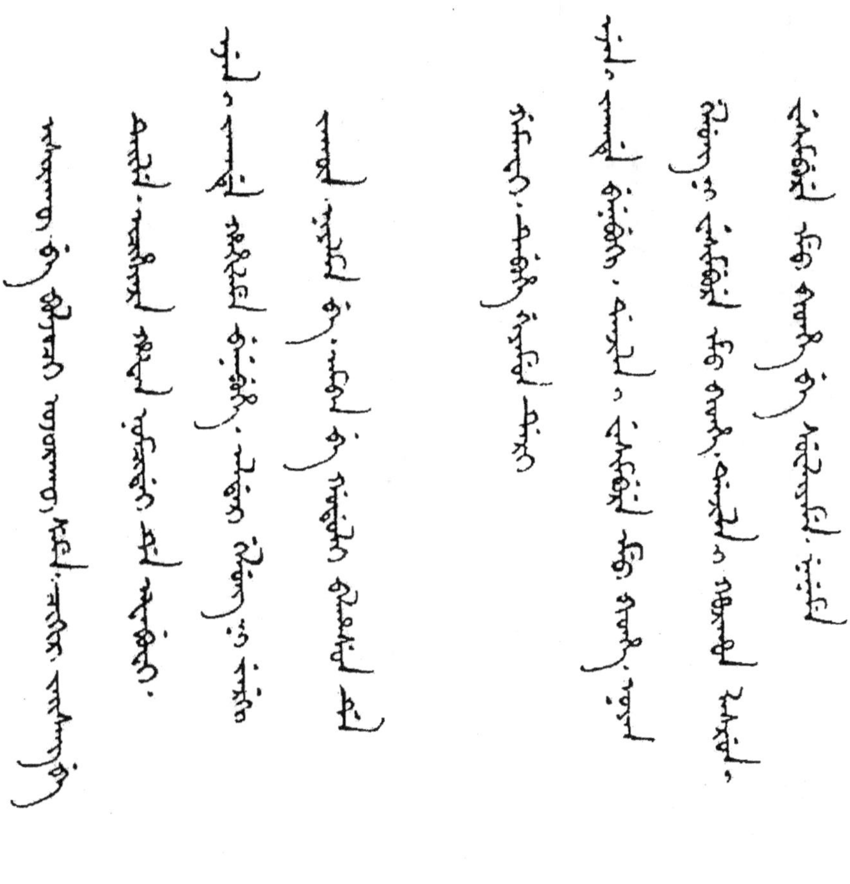

[illegible]

[illegible]

[illegible]

Transliteration

(224) *amba jiyanggiyūn be Fiyanggū i wesimbuhe bithe.*

goroki be dahabure amba jiyanggiyūn hiya kadalara dorgi amban be amban Fiyanggū sei gingguleme wesimburengge. G'aldan i bucehe, Danjila sei dahara babe ekšeme

boolame wesimbure jalin. amban be, elhe taifin i gūsin ningguci aniya duin biyai ice uyun de, Sair Balhasun gebungge bade isinjiha manggi, Ūlet i Danjila sei takūraha Cikir jaisang ni jergi

(225) *uyun niyalma* [1] *jifi alarangge. «be Ūlet i Danjila i takūraha elcin, ilan biyai juwan ilan de G'aldan Aca Amtatai gebungge bade isinafi bucehe. Danjila, Noyan gelung, Danjila i hojihon Lasrun,*

G'aldan i giran, G'aldan i sargan jui Juncahai be gajime uheri ilan tanggū boigon be gaifi enduringge ejen de dahame ebsi jifi, Baya Endur gebungge bade ilifi,

(226) *hese be aliyame tehebi. enduringge ejen adarame jorime hese wasimbuci, wasimbuha hese be gingguleme dahame jabumbi. Urjanjab jaisang,*

Urjanjab i deo Sereng, Aba jaisang, Tar jaisang, Aralbai jaisang, Erdeni Ujat lama se, juwe tanggū boigon be gaifi, Dzewang Arabtan [2] *be baime genehe. Erdeni jaisang, Usta taiji, Boroci*

(227) *jaisang Hošooci, Cerimbum jaisang se, juwe tanggū boigon be gaifi, Danjin Ombu be baime genehe. Danjila sei wesimbure bithe, ne mende bi» sembi. Cikir jaisang sede, «G'aldan adarame bucehe, Danjila*

ainu uthai ebsi jiderakū, Baya Endur bade tefi, hese be aliyambi sembi» seme fonjici alarangge: «G'aldan ilan biyai juwan ilan i erde nimehe, yamji uthai bucehe.

(228) *ai nimeku be sarkū. Danjila uthai jiki seci, morin umesi turga, fejergi urse amba dulin gemu ulga akū yafagan, geli kunesun akū, uttu ojoro jakade, Baya Endur bade tefi,*

hese be aliyame bi. enduringge ejen ebsi jio seci, uthai jimbi» sembi. Danjila sei takūraha elcin be gemu ejen i jakade benebuci, niyalma largin, giyamun i morin

(229) *isirakū be boljoci ojorakū seme,* [3] *Cikir jaisang be teile, icihiyara hafan Nomcidai de afabufi, ejen i jakade hahilame benebuhe. Aldar gelung ni jergi jakūn niyalma be, amban be Godoli Balhasun de*

gamafi, tebuhe giyamun deri ejen i jakade benebuki, Danjila i wesimbure emu bithe, Noyan gelung ni wesimbure emu bithe, Danjila i hojihon Lasrun i wesimbure emu bithe be suwaliyame, neneme 4

(230) *dele tuwabume wesimbuhe. erei jalin ekšeme gingguleme donjibume wesimbuhe.*

elhe taifin i gūsin ningguci aniya duin biyai ice uyun.

Notes

1. ***Cikir jaisang ni jergi uyun niyalma*:** lit. 'the nine people of the kind of Cikir *jaisang*'. This means there are eight people and Cikir *jaisang*.

2. ***Dzewang Arabtan*:** This document writes the name as Dzewang Arabtan, following the rule that Manchu words do not begin with the letter *r*. In Reading Selection A–3, the name occurred as Tsewang Rabtan. In Hummel's *Eminent Chinese of the Ch'ing Period* the person is listed as Tsewang Arabtan.

3. ***boljoci ojorakū*:** 'it cannot be foreseen, it is unpredictable'. This expression is usually preceded by an imperfective converb and the accusative particle *be*. Examples: *morin isirakū be boljoci ojorakū seme* 'there is no way of knowing whether there will be enough horses', or *siden i baita be tookabure be boljoci ojorakū* 'there is no telling whether it will delay public matters'.

4. ***suwaliyame neneme wesimbuhe*:** Cf. Reading Selection B–5, Note 2.

Review

1. Write in Manchu script and translate into English: a) *Danjila takūraha Cikir jaisang ni jergi uyun niyalma jihe*; b) *uheri ilan tanggū boigon be gaifi enduringge ejen de dahame ebsi jihe*; c) *Urjanjab jaisang juwe tanggū boigon be gaifi, Dzewang Arabtan be baime genehe*; d) *Danjila ainu uthai ebsi jiderakū?* e) *morin umesi turga*; f) *fejergi urse amba dulin gemu ulha akū*; g) *G'aldan erde nimehe, yamji uthai bucehe*; h) *hese be aliyame bi*; i) *niyalma largin, giyamun i morin isirakū*; j) *tebuhe giyamun deri ejen i jakade benebuki*; k) *Lasrun i wesimbure emu bithe be suwaliyame neneme dele tuwame wesimbuhe.*

Reading Selection C–1

On collective leadership (1622) **[Old Manchu]**

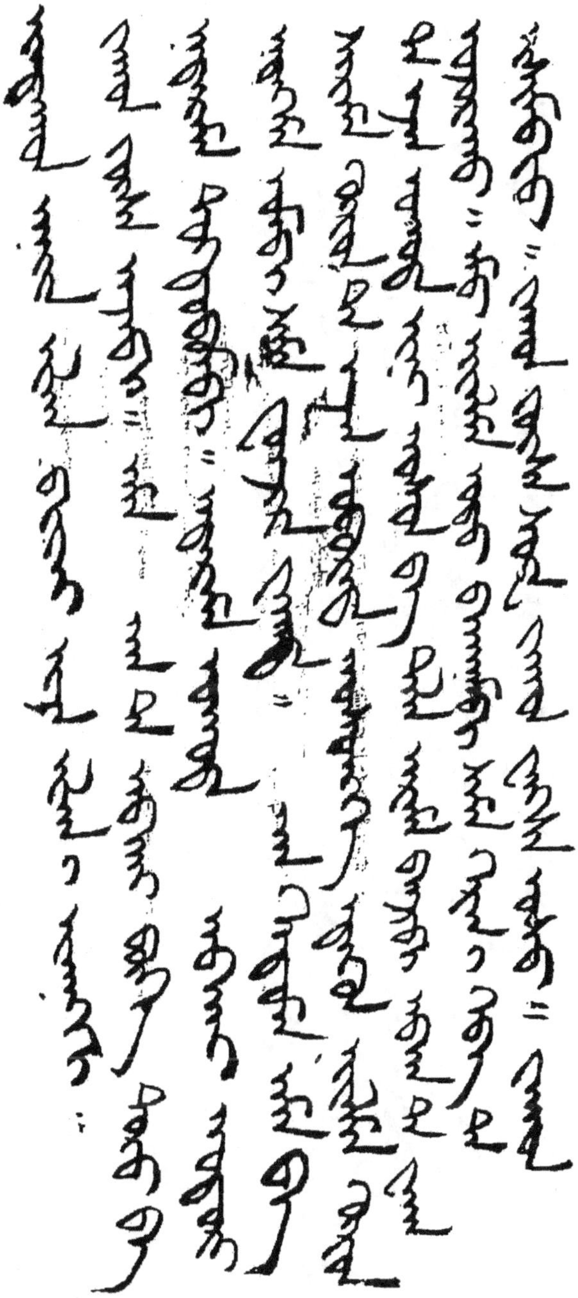

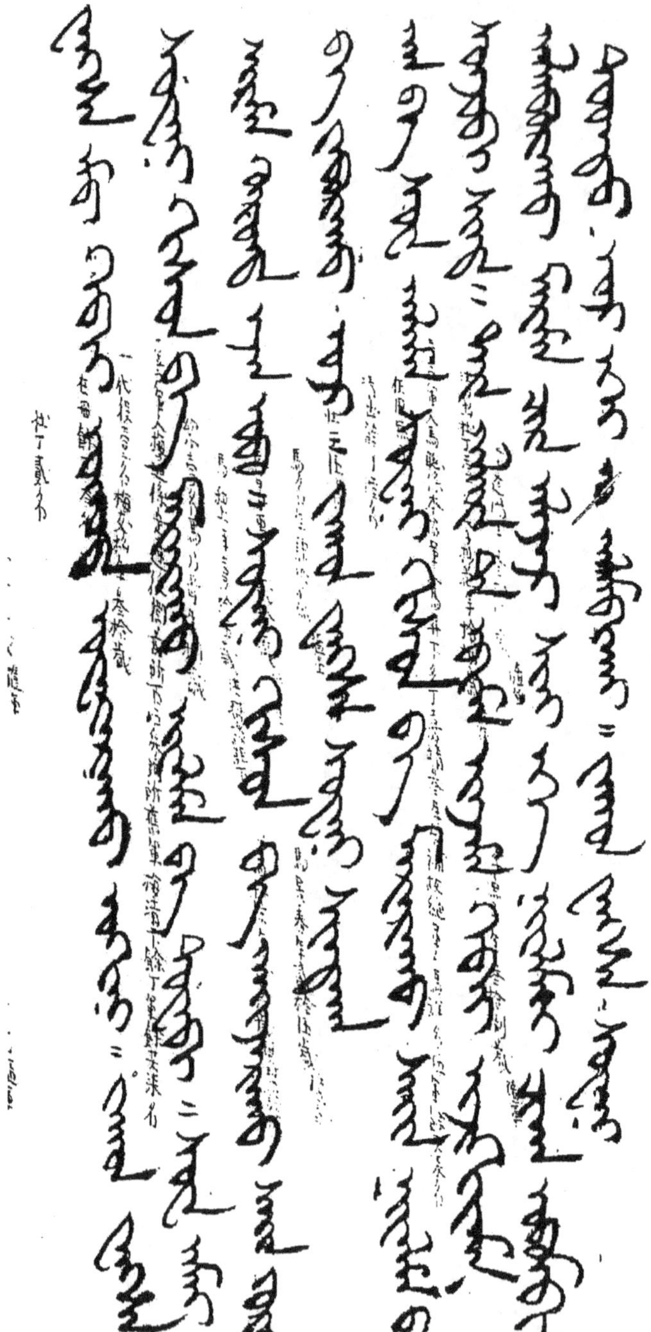

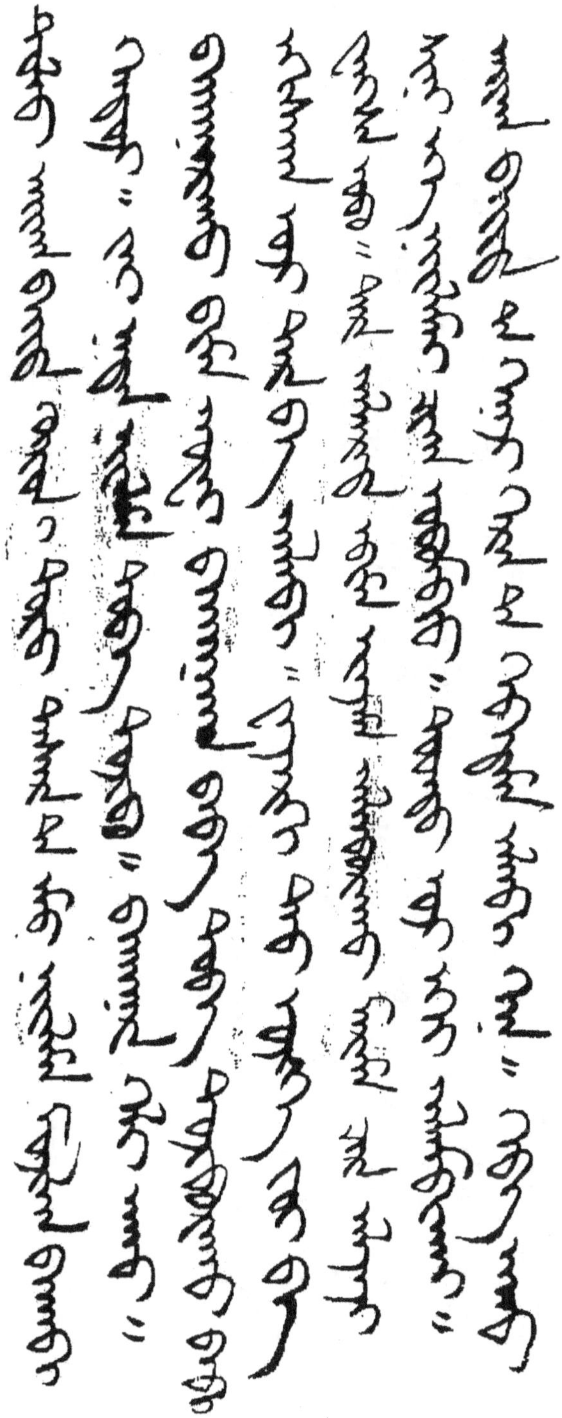

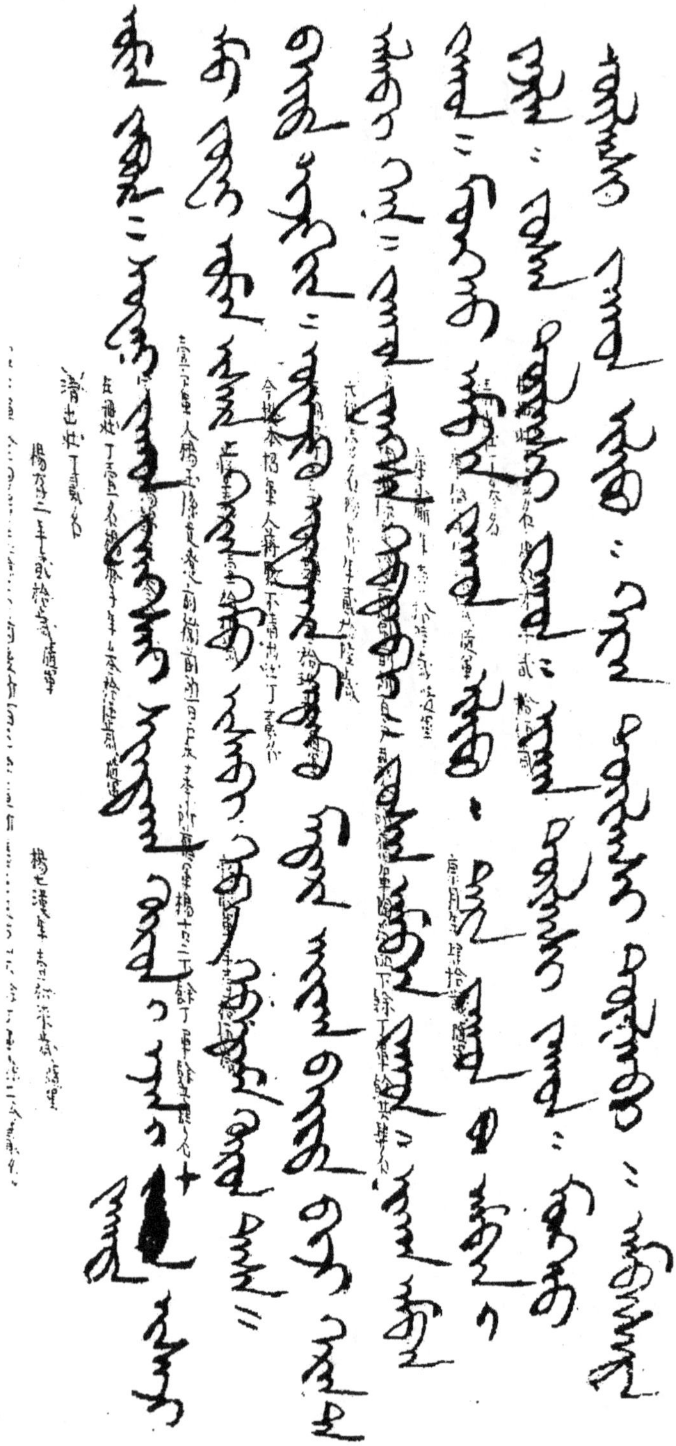

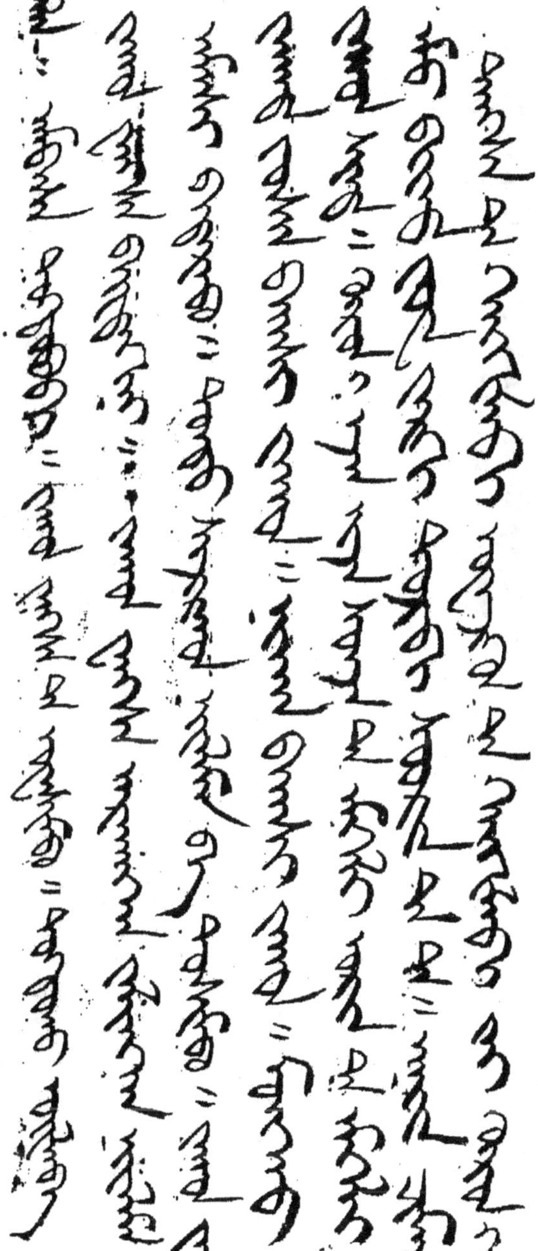

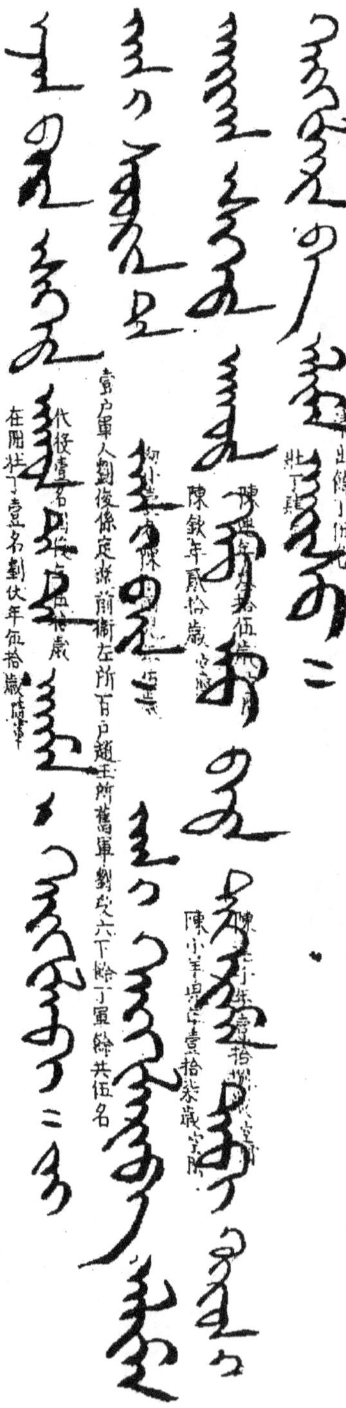
陳欽年貳拾歲
壹戶軍人劉俊係定遼前衛左所百戶趙玉所舊軍劉交六下餘丁軍餘共伍名
在閑壯丁壹名劉伏年伍拾歲

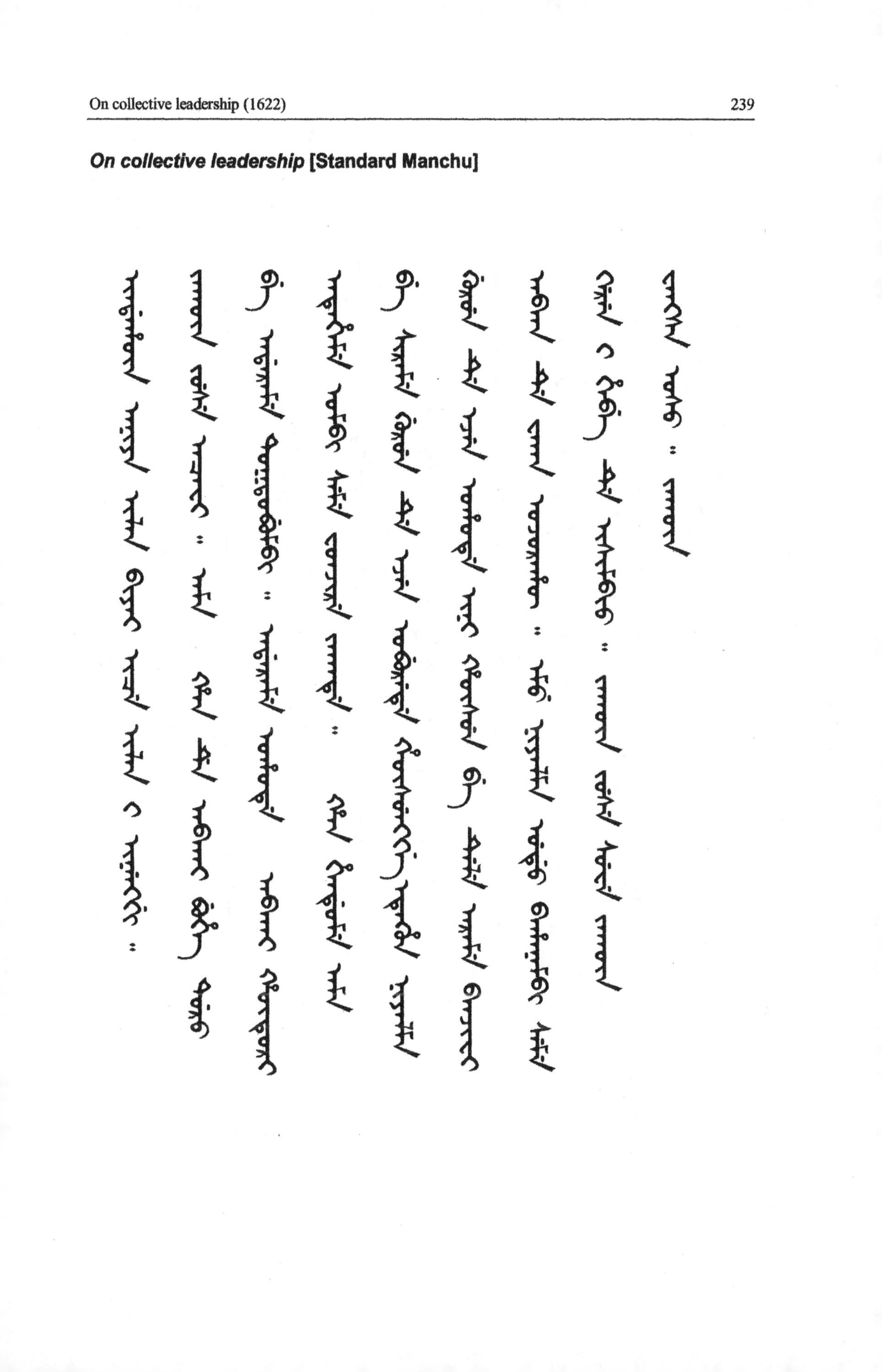

On collective leadership **[Standard Manchu]**

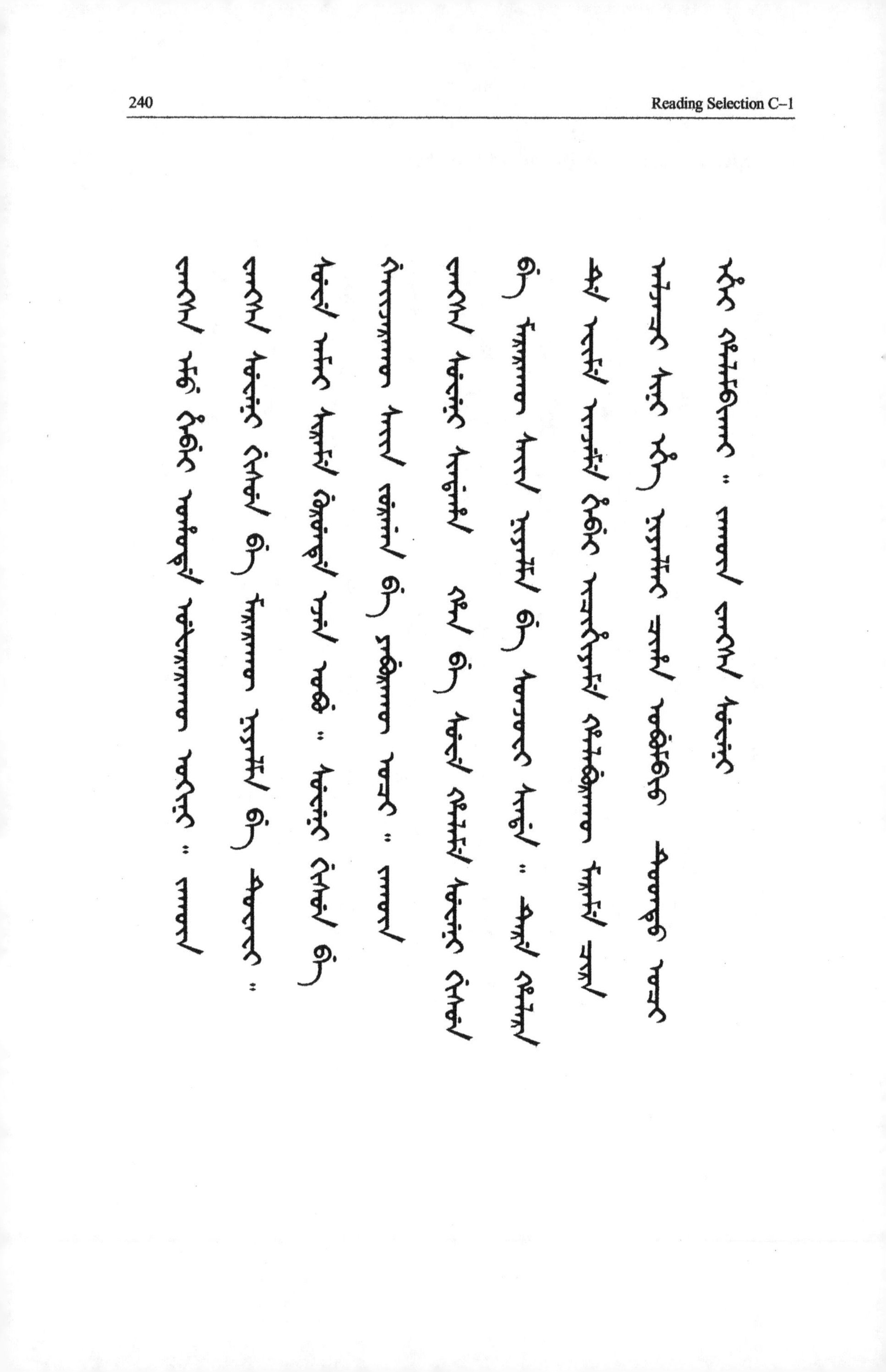

[illegible]
[illegible]
[illegible]
[illegible]
[illegible]
[illegible]
[illegible]
[illegible]
[illegible]

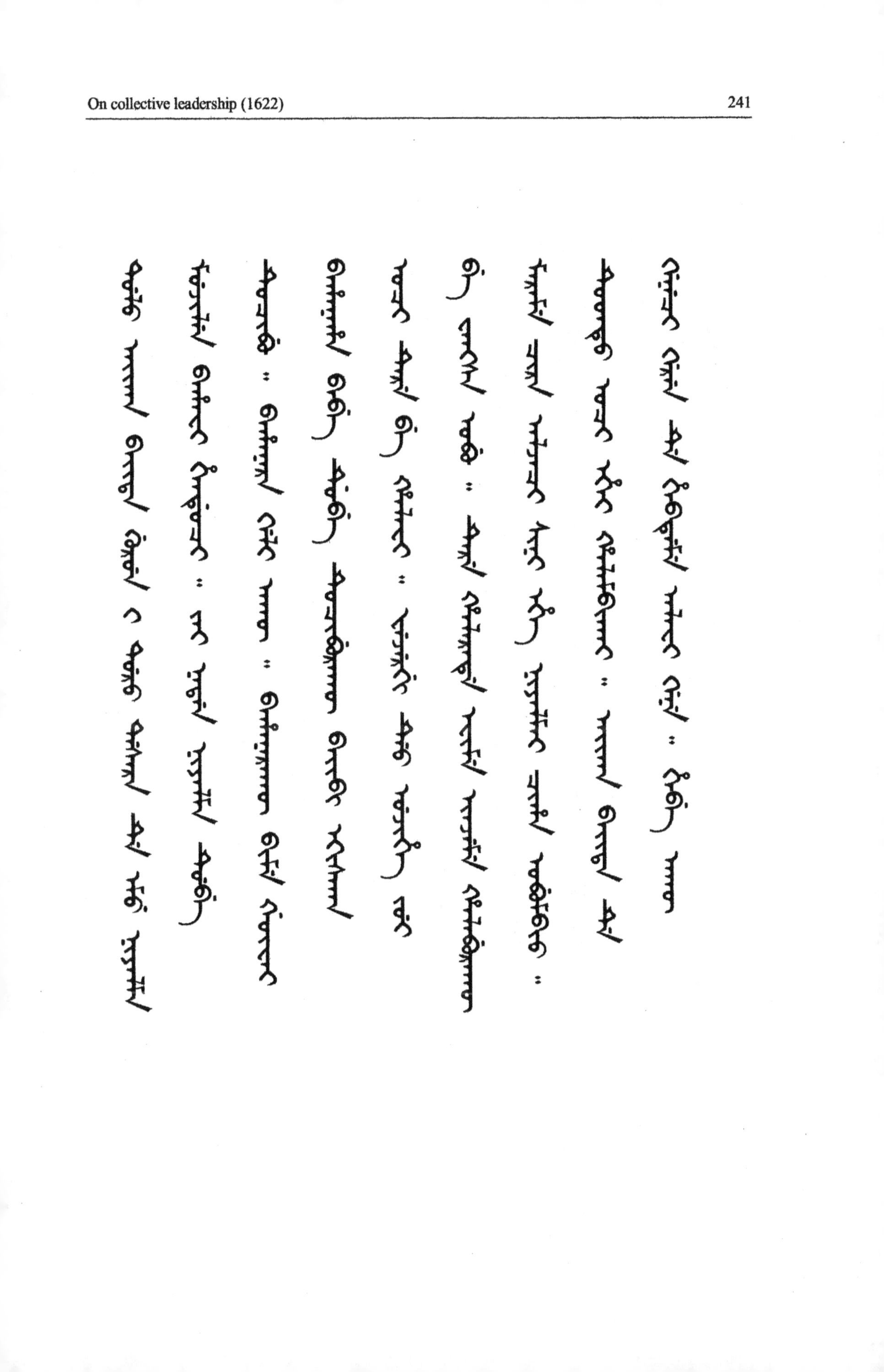

[illegible]
[illegible]
[illegible]
[illegible]
[illegible]
[illegible]
[illegible]
[illegible]
[illegible]

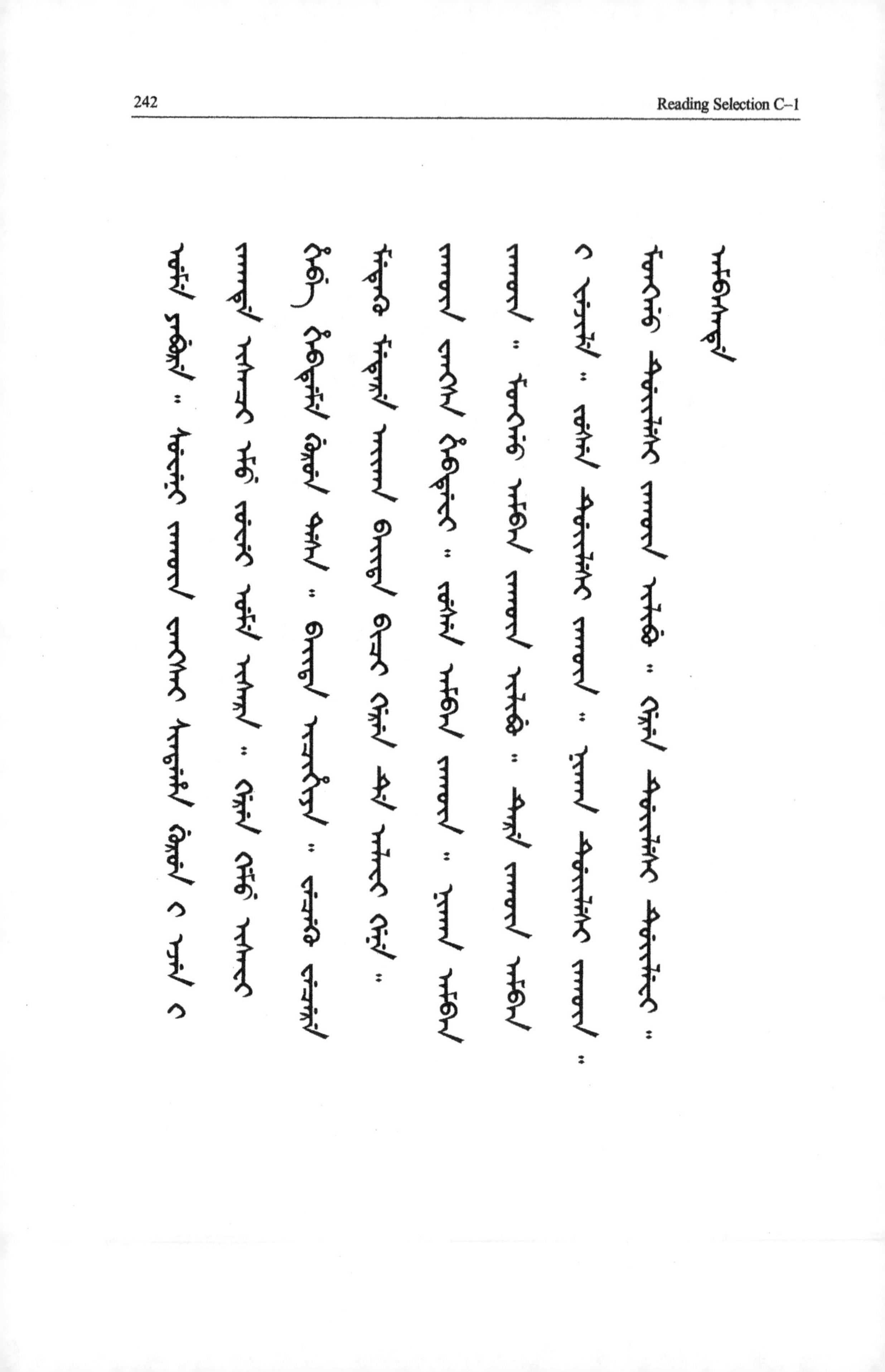

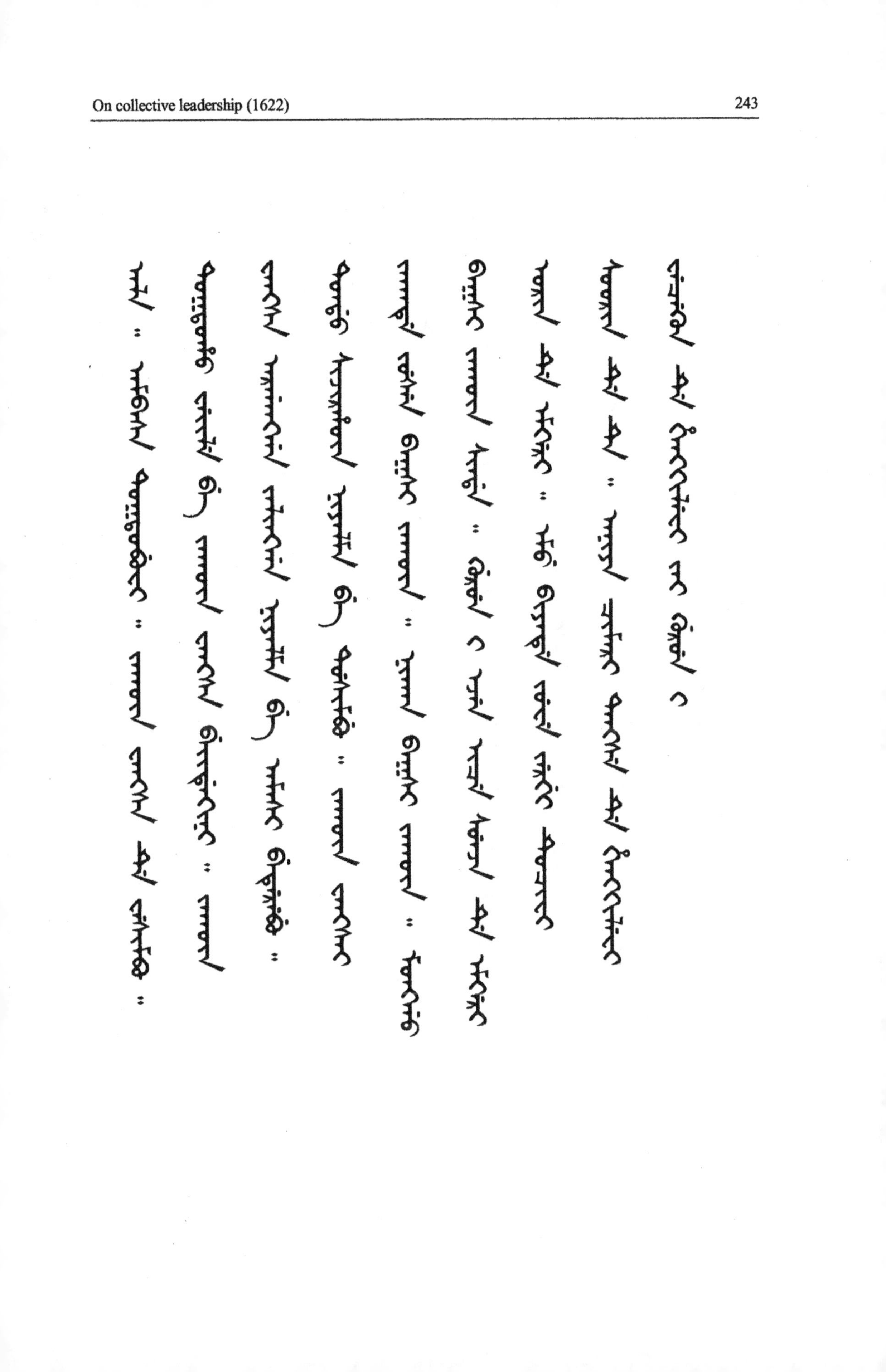

[illegible]

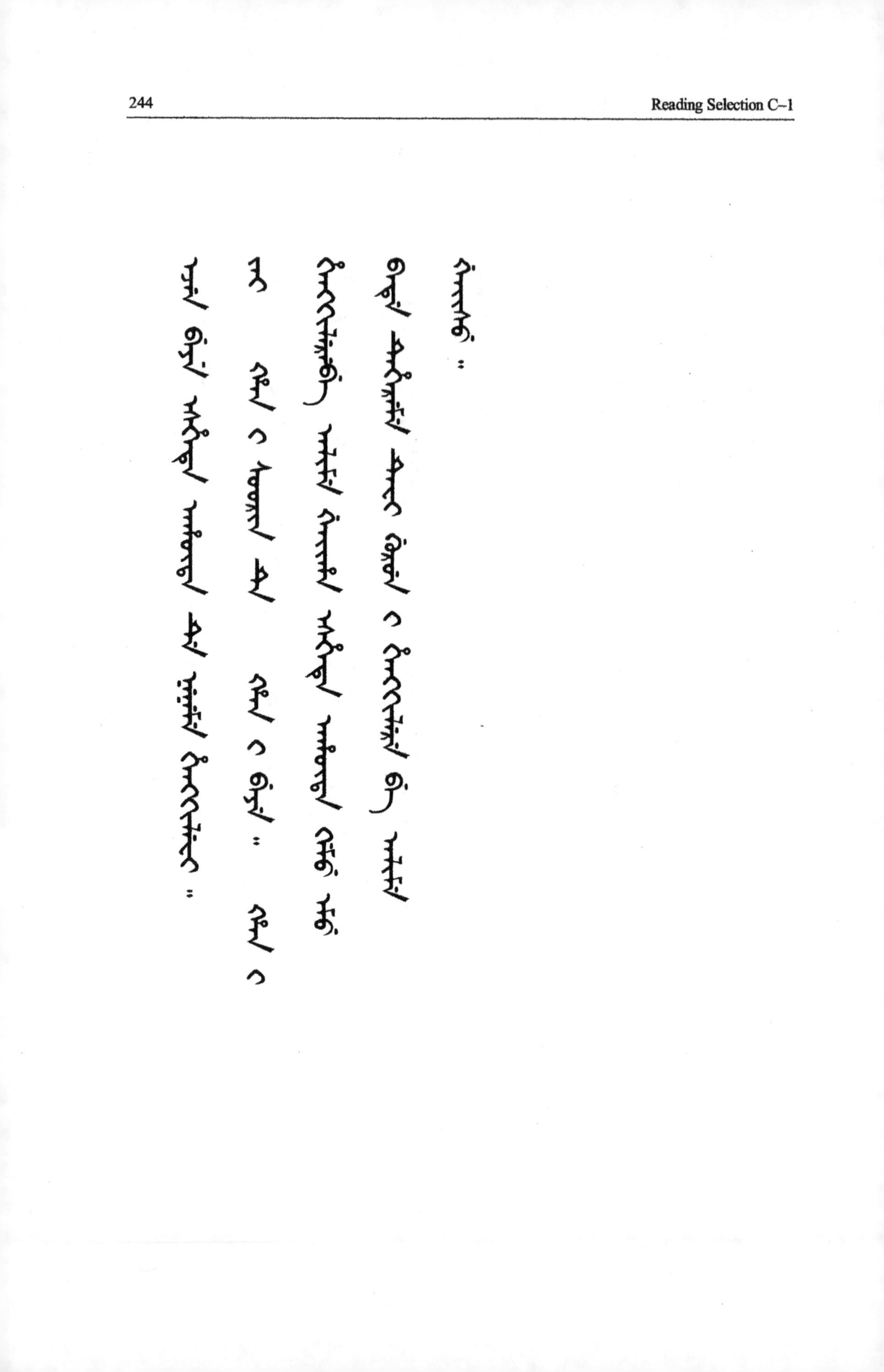

Transliteration

(233:239) *indahon [h] aniya [d] ilan biyai [d] ice [c] ilan i inenggi. jakon [h] jūse [h] acabi,[f] ama han de «abkai būhe [h] doro be adarame toktobumbi.[i] adarame ohode abkai hoturi [h] enteheme ombi» seme fonjire [e] jakade, han hendume,[2] «ama be sirame gūrun [h] de ejen oburede hosungge [h] etehun [3] niyalma [d] gūrun [h] de ejen ohode ini hosun [h] be dele arame banjibi [f] abka de waka ojoraho.[4] emu niyalma udu bahanambi seme geren i hebe de isimbio. jakon [h] jūse [h] suwe jakon [h] wangsa [5,b] oso. jakon [h]*

(234:240) *wangsa emu hebei ohode ufararako [h] okini.[6] jakon [h] wangsa suweni gisun be mararako [h] niyalma [d] be tuwabi,[f] suwe amai [7] sirame gūrunde [b,h] ejen obu. suweni gisun be gaijarako [h] sain jurgan be yaburako [h] oci, jakon [h] wangsa suweni sindaha han be suwe halame suweni gisun be mararako [h] sain niyalma [d] be sonjobi [f] sinda. tere halara de [8] ebime [f] injeme hebei icihiyame [c,d] halaburako [h] marame cira aljaci [c] sini ehe niyalmai [d] ciha obumbio.[9] tuttu oci [c] ehei [10] halambikai.[b] jakon [h] wangsa suweni*

(235:241) *dolo,[g] aika baita gūrun [h] i doro dasara de emu niyalma [d] mujilen bahabi [f] henduci,[11] jai nadan niyalma [d] dube tucibu.[c] bahanara geli ako,[h] bahanarako [h] bime gūwai [h] bahanaha babe dube tuciburako [h] babi [12] ekisaka oci tere be halabi,[f] fejergi deo ujihe [h] jui be wangsa obu. tere halarade ebime [f] injeme halaburako [h] marame cira aljaci [c] sini ehe niyalmai [d] ciha obumbio. tuttu oci ehei halambikai.[b] aika baita de geneci geren de hebdeme [13] alabi [f] gene. hebe ako [h]*

(236:242) *ūme [h] yabure.[d] suweni jakon [h] wangsai sindaha gūrun [h] i ejen i jakade [d] isaci [c] emu juwei ūme [h] isara.[14] geren gemu isabi [f] hebe hebdeme gūrun [h] dasa, baita icihiya.[d] uweciku [e] uwecere [e] meteku metere aika baita bici [15] geren de alabi [f] gene. jakon [h] wangsa hebdebi,[f] jusen [j] amban jakon,[h] nikan amban jakon,[h] monggo amban jakon [h] ilibu. tere jakon [h] amban i fejile,[e] jusen [j] duilesi jakon,[h] nikan duilesi jakon,[h] monggo duilesi jakon [h] ilibu. geren duilesi duilebi,[f] ambasade [16]*

(237:243) *ala. ambasa toktobubi,[f,i] jakon [h] wangsa de uwesimbu. toktoho [i] uilebe [e] jakon [h] wangsa beidekini. jakon [h] wangsa argangga jalingga niyalma [d] be amasi bederebu. tondo sijirhon [h] niyalma [d] be dosimbu. jakon [h] wangsai jakade jusen [j] baksi [i] jakon,[h] nikan baksi [i] jakon,[h] monggo baksi [i] jakon [h] sinda. gūrun [h] i ejen ice sunja de emgeli [17] orin de emgeli [17] emu biyade [d] juwe jergi tucibi [c,f] soorin de te. aniya [d] cimari tangse de hengkilebi,[f] uwecikun [e] de hengkilebi [f] jai gūrun [h] i*

(238:244) *ejen beye [d] eshete ahon ta [h] de neneme hengkilebi,[f] jai han i soorin te. han i beye,[d] han i hengkilerebe alime gaiha eshete ahota,[h] gemu emu bade tehereme tebi [f] gūrun [h] i hengkilere be alime gaisu.»*

Notes

1. **Differences between Old Manchu (OM) and Standard Manchu (SM) scripts:**

a) Diacritical marks (dots and circles): Except for the dot on the left side to the letter *n*, sometimes even when the letter is followed by a consonant, this document has no diacritical marks to distinguish *t* from *d*, *a* from *e*, *o* from *u*, *k* from *h* or *g*.

b) Case markers and sentence particles: More than in SM, these particles are likely to be written in an attached form. Examples: *weilebe*, *halambikai.*

c) *c* and *j*: Initial *c* and *j* are written as in SM. Mid-position c and j look alike in OM. Compare *ice*, *fonjire*, *aljaci.*

d) *y*: Initial *y* in OM is indistinguishable from initial *j* or mid-position *i*. Compare *yabure* and *jakade*. See *biya*, *niyalma*, *aniya*, *beye.*

e) *f* and *w*: OM does not have a long form of *f* to distinguish *fa* from *wa* or *fe* from *we*. Compare *waka* and *ufarakū*. However, OM words with an initial *we-* may be written as *uwe-* or *ui-*. Examples: *uwecembi* instead of *wecembi*, *uwesimbumbi* instead of *wesimbumbi*, and *uile* instead of *weile*.

f) *b* and *f*: Old Manchu frequently uses *b* when SM uses *f*. Examples: *acabi* instead of *acafi*; *ebimbi* instead of *efimbi.*

g) *t* and *d*: OM uses mostly back *d* and *t*, even before front vowels. In this document only *dolo* is written with a front *d*.

h) *ū*, *o*, and *u*: OM *ū* often appears as *u* in SM, and OM *o* appears as *ū* in SM. Moreover, OM *ū* occasionally occurs after front *k*, *g*, and *h*. Examples:

OM	SM	OM	SM	OM	SM
jūse	*juse*	*ūme*	*ume*	*hoturi*	*hūturi*
gūrun	*gurun*	*ūjihe*	*ujihe*	*ojorako*	*ojorakū*
būhe	*buhe*	*indahon*	*indahūn*	*jakon*	*jakūn*

i) ***k, g, h*****:** Generally, the use of front and back *k, g, h* follows the rules of SM where front *k, g, h* are followed by front vowels, and back *k, g, h* (*q, γ, χ*) precede back vowels *a, o*, and *ū*. There are exceptions, however, such as in *gūrun*. Also note that mid-position *k*, which is written as back *k* (*q*) in SM, is in some cases written as front *k* in this document. Examples: *toktoho* not *toqtoho; toktobumbi* not *toqtobumbi;* but: *baqsi*. (To review the relevant SM rules for end-of-syllable *q* vs. *k*, see page 22.)

j) ***s*** **vs.** ***š*****:** In OM, SM *š* is often written as plain *s*.

2. OM entries beginning an imperial quote with *wasimbuha* rarely close the quotation with a finite verb of *sembi*. In this case the quote is introduced with *han hendume*, but there is no final *sehe* at the end of the quotation.

3. ***etehun*****:** mispelling for *etuhun* 'strong, powerful'.

4. ***abka de waka ojorahū*****:** 'I am afraid one will wrong Heaven'.

5. It may be best to leave certain titles untranslated. In pre-1644 documents terms like *wang*, *amban*, *beile*, and *beise* may have had meanings different from those associated with the terms during the later Qing dynasty. The term *beise*, for example, was originally the plural of *beile*. Later it became a separate rank.

6. ***ufararakū okini*****:** 'may you not make mistakes'. The desiderative verbal suffix *-kini* can refer to either the person spoken to or to a third person. Instructions from the emperor to his officials often use this form. In these cases the meaning of *-kini* comes close to a polite causative, instructing the official 'to have something done'. For examples see Review 2.

7. ***amai*****:** 'inherited through the father'; instrumental genitive.

8. ***tere halara de*****:** 'during that change' or 'when he changes'.

9. ***sini ehe niyalmai ciha obumbio*****:** 'Will you make it become the will of your bad person?' Meaning: 'Is the bad person to prevail?'

10. ***ehei halambikai*****:** instrumental genitive in *ehei*. Meaning: 'it will change in a bad way'.

11. ***aika baita gurun i doro dasara de emu niyalma mujilen bahabi henduci*****:** 'if, when administering matters and governing the country, one person has some insight and explains it'.

12. ***babi*****:** alternate form for *baibi.*

13. OM *hebedembi* corresponds to SM *hebdembi.*

14. ***emu juwei ume isara*****:** instrumental genitive, meaning, 'don't meet in the manner of one or two'.

15. ***uweciku uwecere, meteku metere aika baita bici*****:** *uweciku uwecere* corresponds to *weceku wecere* in Standard Manchu, 'to worship the gods'. Both *wecere* and *metere* modify *baita.*

16. ***ambasa*****:** The final *n* in *amban* is dropped when adding the plural *-sa*. Compare *ahūn, ahūta* 'older brother, older brothers'; *eshen, eshete* 'uncle, uncles'. However, here we have both *ahūn ta* and *ahūta.*

17. ***emgeli*****:** corresponds to SM *emgeri* 'once, already'.

Review

1. ***-ki*** **'I will; I hope, I wish, let me; please do'**

a) Speaker's intent to do something

bi araki	I will write
bi cimari geneki	I will go tomorrow
bithe be unggiki	I will send the letter
dahaki	I will submit

b) Speaker's wish to do something

geneki	let me go, I wish to go
manju gisun i araki	let us write in the Manchu language
enteheme banjiki	I want to live forever
Hošik be Yerkiyang ni baita be daiselabuki	let us have Hošik administer Yarkand
dahaki seme baiha	he requested to submit

c) Polite command or invitation

si ubade teki	please sit here
dosiki	please come in
jeki	please eat
si juleri yarhūdaki	you lead in front

d) *-ki + semb*i 'to want'

Intensified wish or intention by the speaker to do something

Ūdui dame geneki sehe	Ūdui wanted to go and help
Hojijan Yerkiyang de bedereki serede	when Hojijan wanted to return to Yarkand
Polat akim bek oki seme Ūdui be habšabuha	wanting to become governor, Polat had Ūdui falsely accused
G'aopu gu be udaki sehe	Gaopu wanted to buy jade
Jun gar be toktobuha manggi Eseyen dahanjiki sembihe	after we pacified the Dzungars, Husayn had been wanting to submit
bi manju gisun be taciki sembi	I want to learn Manchu

For a special meaning of *-ki + seci* see below.

e) *-ki + seci* 'although, even though'

bi bithe hūlaki seci	although I want to read
bi manju gisun be taciki seci	even though I want to learn Manchu

Note: Since verbs ending in *-ki* may occur in direct speech, not all *-ki sembi* combinations have the meanings presented in d) and e). Example: *Hošik hesei icihiyame tebure be aliyaki seme wesimbuhede* 'when Hošik memorialized saying "let me wait for an edict to determine where I should reside"'.

2. *-kini*

a) 'may he, let him, may you, please do'

A desire on the part of the speaker that some action be performed by somebody else. If the person spoken to is to perform the action, the meaning is a polite command, similar to *-ki* in 1c above. Sentences with negative verbs or non-verbal predicates add the *-kini* suffix to the verb *ombi.*

tubade genekini	please go there; may he go there
ini hūncihin mukūn i urse be ujikini	let him support the people of his family
tumen aniya okini	may it last for ten thousand years
ceni booi anggala be kemuni hecen de benjikini	let them also bring the people of their households to the capital
jakūn wangsa emu hebei ohode ufararakū okini	I hope, by being of one mind, you eight *wang*s will not make mistakes

b) Have something done

In official communications the *-kini* form is often used as an indirect command to an official to have something done.

imbe jikini	let him come
imbe Aksu de baita icihiyakini	have him administer the matters of Aksu
tere baita be baicafi boolakini	have the matter investigated and reported
da an i Kašigar ba i akim bek i tušan de bibukini	have him occupy the original position of governor of Kashgar

c) *-kini + sembi* 'to want'

A strong wish by the subject that somebody else may do something. In this case the somebody else appears in the accusative form.

bi imbe genekini sembi	I want him to go
bi simbe marikini sembi	I want you to return
mini gisun be suwembe ejekini sembi	I want you to remember my words
akim bek sede tengge šangnahangge beyebe hairakini sehengge	granting the governors money reflects my wanting them to have self-respect

Note: Since verbs ending in *-kini* may occur in direct speech, not all *-kini sembi* combinations have the meanings presented in 2c. Example: *bek sede sujakini seme bithe unggihe* 'one sent a letter to the begs saying: "Resist."'

d) *-kini (inu)* 'even though'

Ūdui gamjidame yabukini inu nakabuci ojorakū	even though Ūdui acted coveteously, still one should not dismiss him
tere niyalma nikan gurun de terakū okini nikan gisun be sambi	even though he does not reside in China, he knows Chinese

3. *-cina* 'please do'

A desire that an action be performed by the person spoken to or by some other person

omicina	please drink, may you drink
nure be omire be nakacina	I hope he will stop drinking (wine)
tecina	please sit down
si te genecina	please go now

4. *-rao, -reo, -roo* Polite request

This form is more polite than *-cina.*

bairengge enduringge ejen kesi isibume morin be bargiyarao	I beg that his majesty grant favor and accept the horses
aisilara cooha be hūdun unggireo	please send relief troops quickly
enduringge ejen bulekušereo	begging his majesty's perusal (common closing phrase of a memorial)

5. Verb stem General imperative

jakūn juse suwe jakūn wangsa oso	you eight sons, you (are to) become *wang*s
baita be toktobufi wesimbu	determine the matter and memorialize
suweni gisun be marakū niyalma be gurun de ejen obu	make the person who does not oppose your words leader of the country

6. *ume…-ra* (*-re, -ro*) Negative imperative

emu juwei ume isara	don't one or two of you get together
ume onggoro	don't forget
ume sartabure	don't be late

7. Translate into Manchu: a) what should we do so that Heaven's good fortune will last forever? b) I am afraid he will wrong Heaven; c) no matter how able one person may be; d) don't make mistakes; e) select a good person who does not reject your words; f) you will have changed it badly; g) he does not grasp what others have understood; h) don't go without consultation; i) announce it to everybody and go; j) below the eight *amban*s place twenty-four judges; k) demote the traitorous and cunning people and promote loyal persons; l) the leader shall come out and sit on the throne twice per month; m) the *khan*, and his uncles and brothers shall all sit in one place and on the same level.

Reading Selection C–2

Manchu–Chinese cooperative living (1621–1622) **[Old Manchu]**

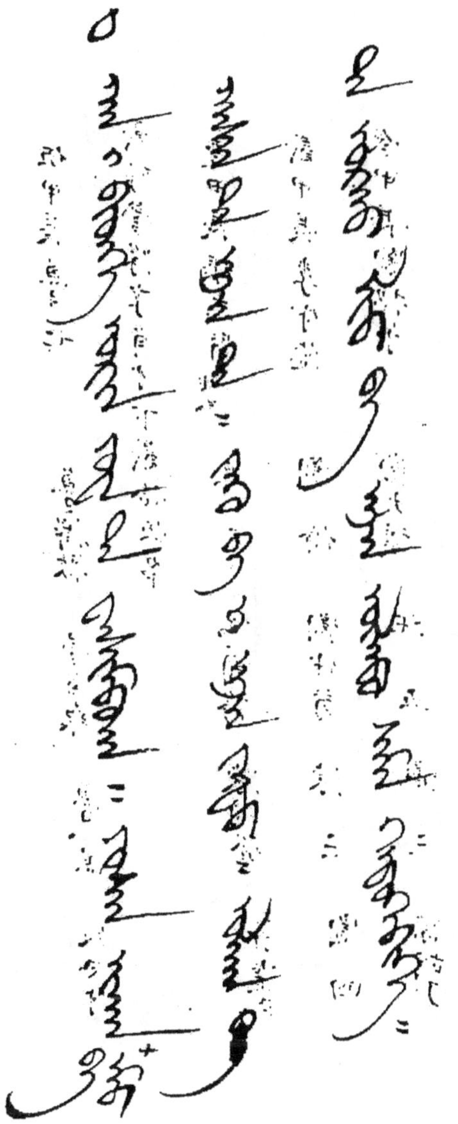

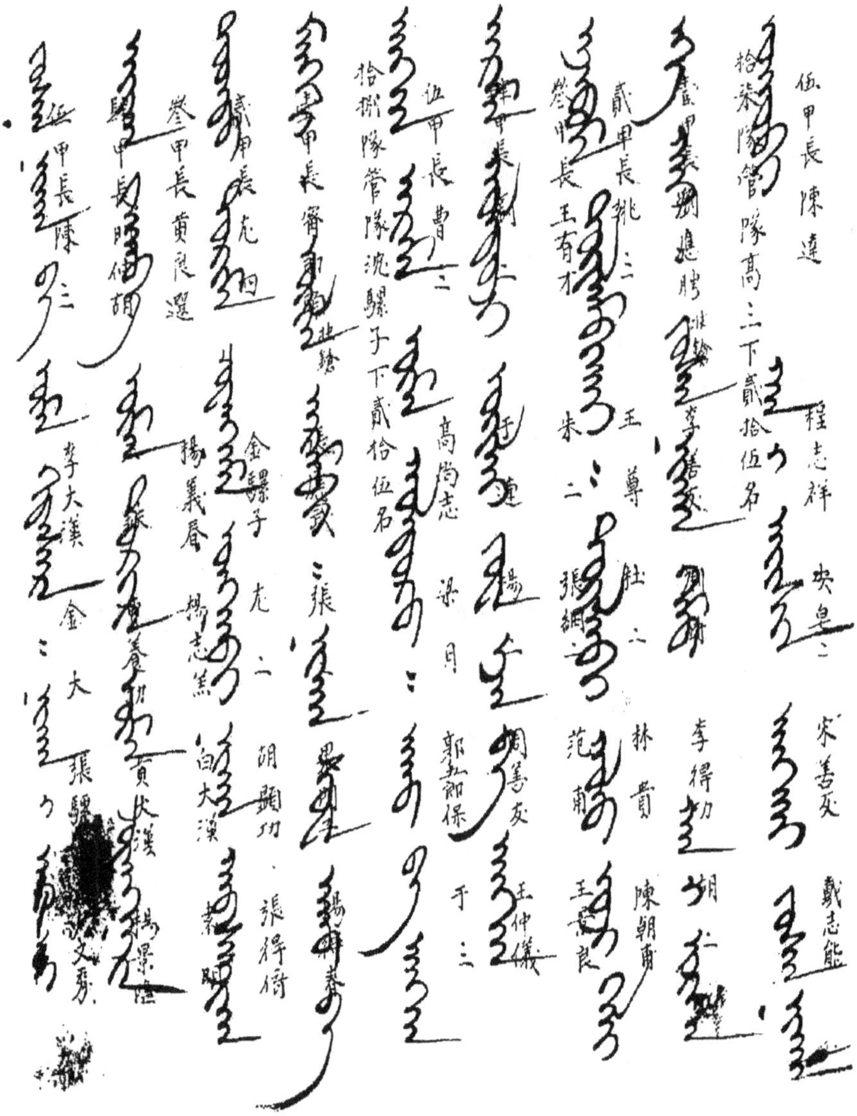

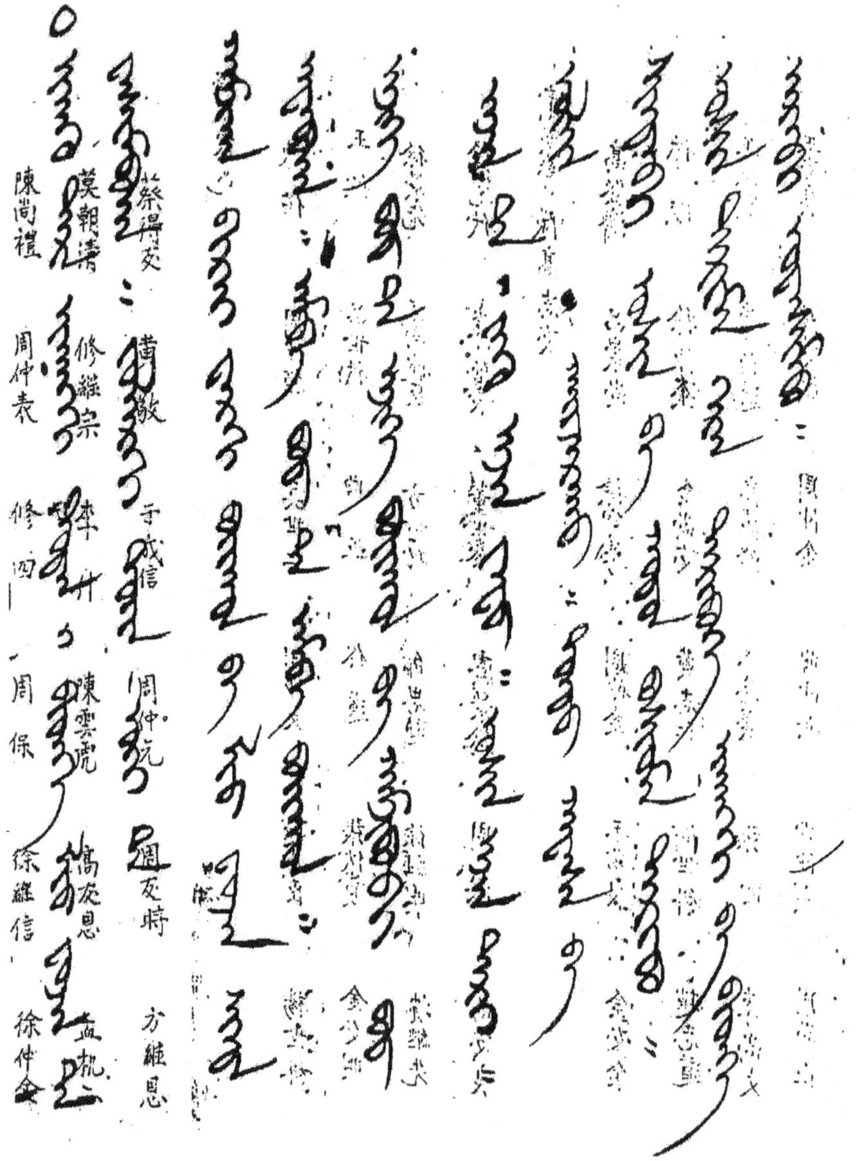

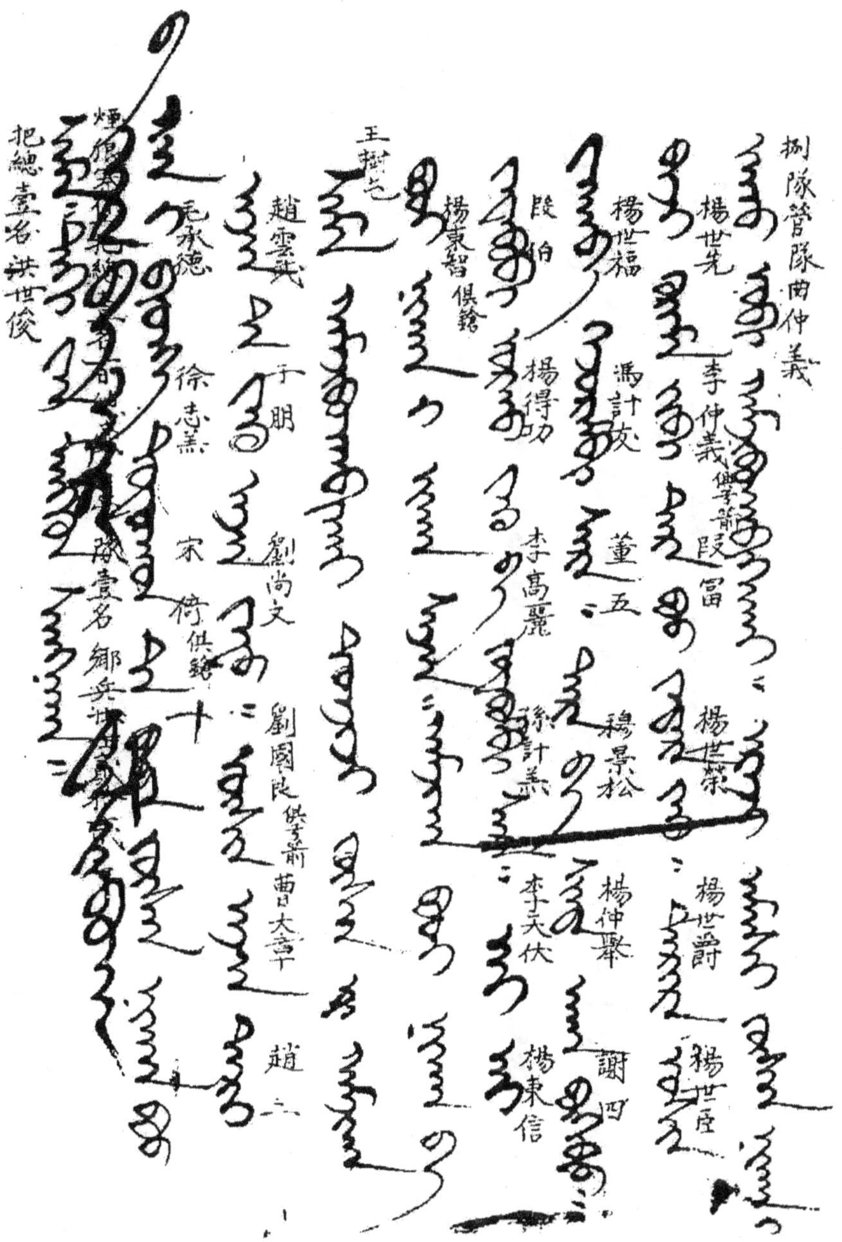

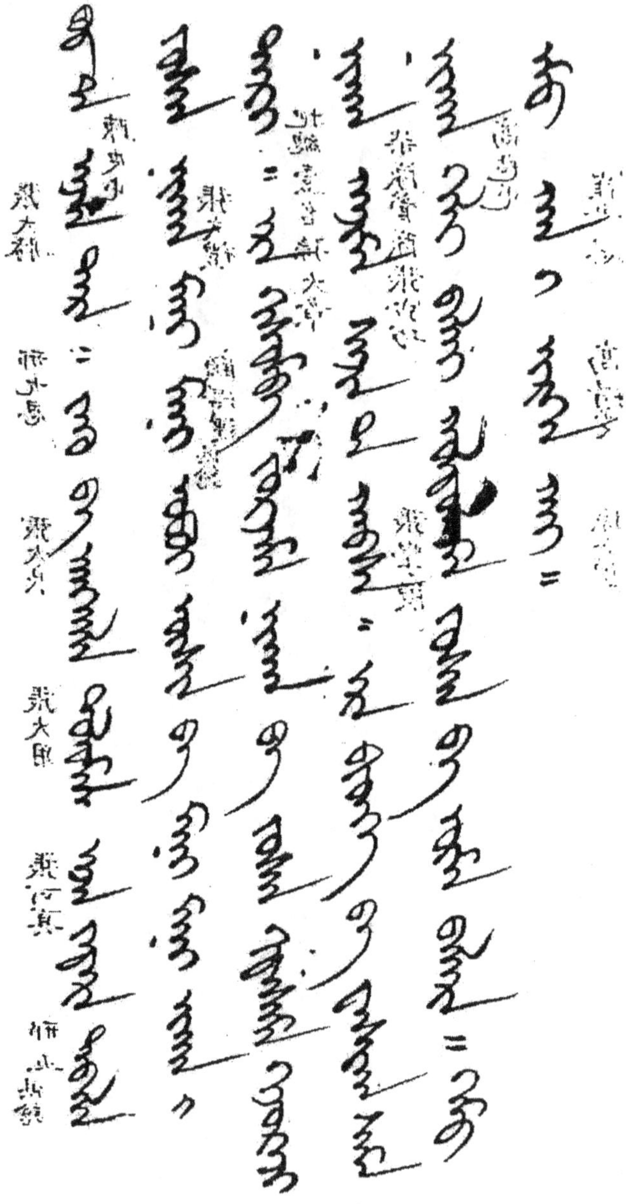

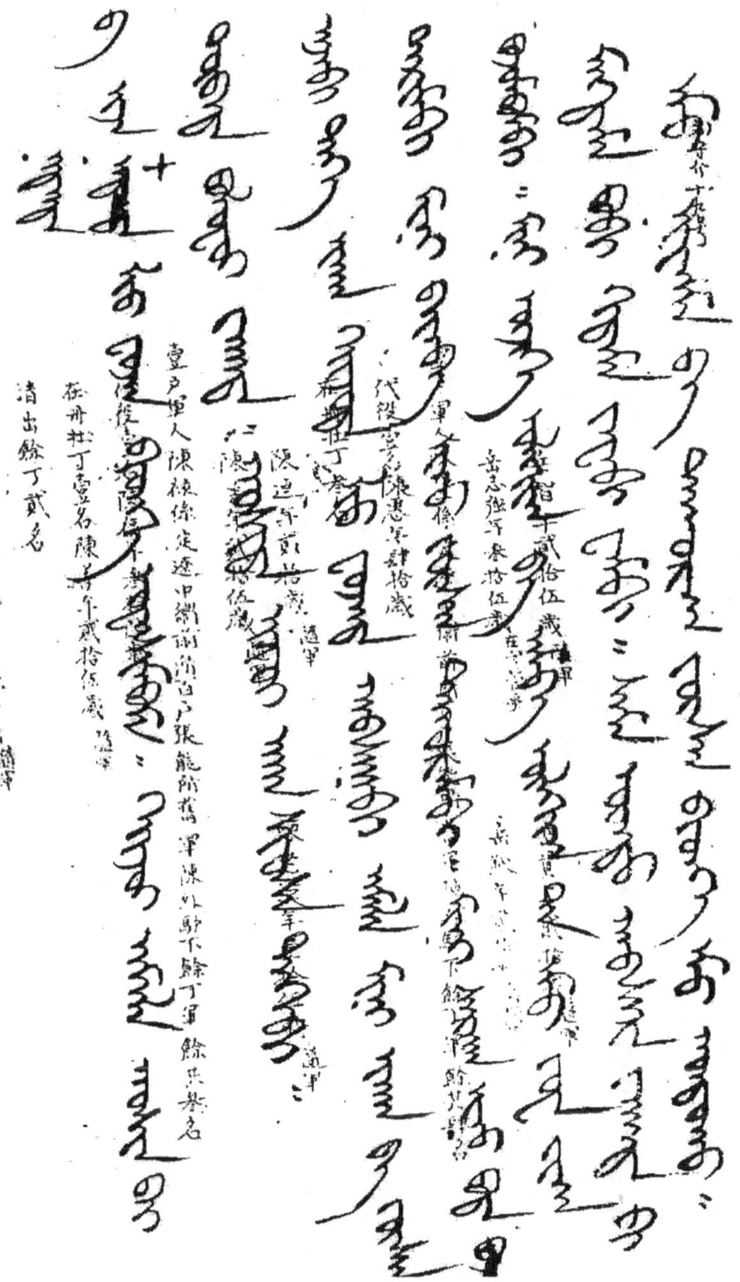

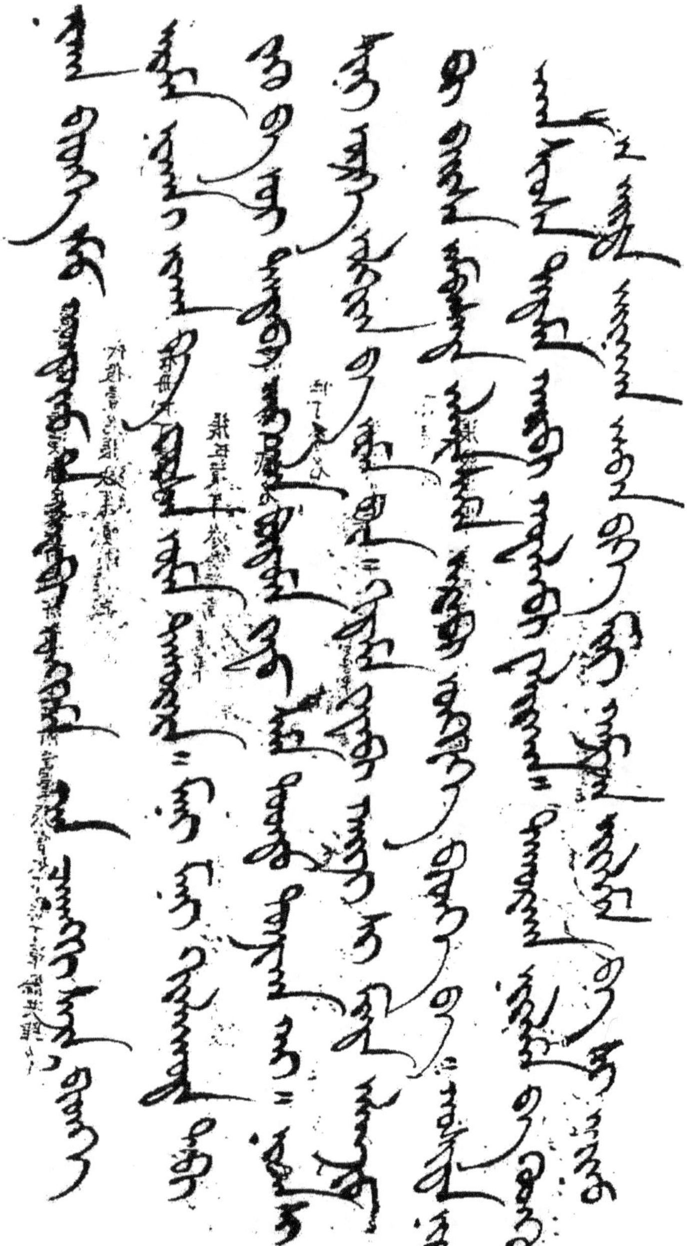

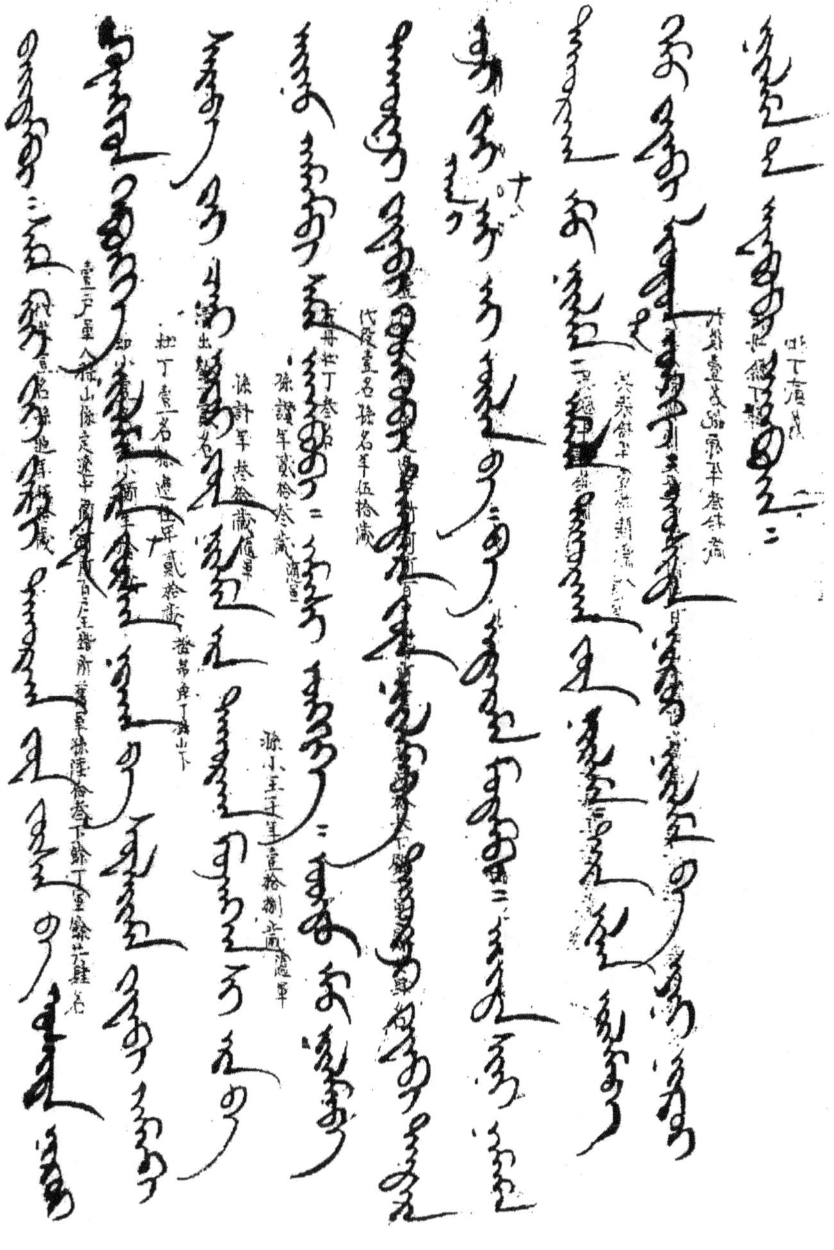

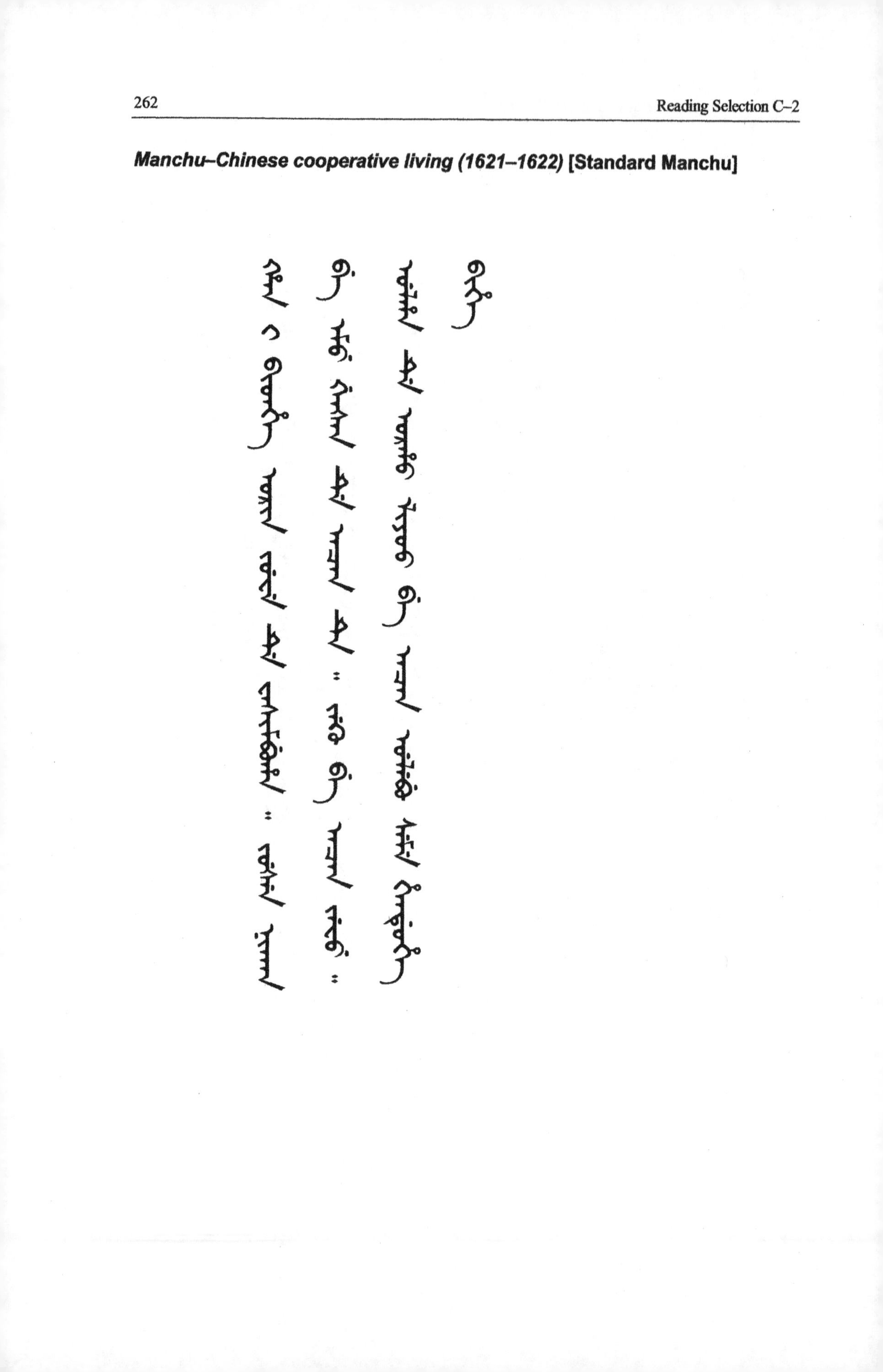

***Manchu–Chinese cooperative living (1621–1622)* [Standard Manchu]**

[illegible]

ᠵᡠᡧᡝᠨ ᠨᡳᡴᠠᠨ ᠪᡝ ᠵᡠᡧᡝᠨ [illegible] ᠉ ᠨᡳᡴᠠᠨ ᡳ [illegible] ᠪᡝ

ᠵᡠᡧᡝᠨ [illegible] ᠵᡠᡧᡝᠨ [illegible] [illegible] [illegible] [illegible]

[illegible] ᠨᡳᡴᠠᠨ [illegible] [illegible] [illegible] [illegible] ᠉

ᠨᡳᡴᠠᠨ [illegible] [illegible] ᠪᡝ [illegible] [illegible] [illegible] [illegible] ᠉ [illegible]

ᠪᡝ [illegible] [illegible] [illegible] ᡳ [illegible] [illegible] ᠪᡝ [illegible]

[illegible] [illegible] [illegible] ᠉ [illegible] [illegible] [illegible] [illegible]

[illegible] [illegible] ᠨᡳᡴᠠᠨ [illegible] [illegible] ᡳ [illegible] [illegible] ᠉ [illegible] ᡳ

[illegible] [illegible] [illegible] ᠨᡳᡴᠠᠨ

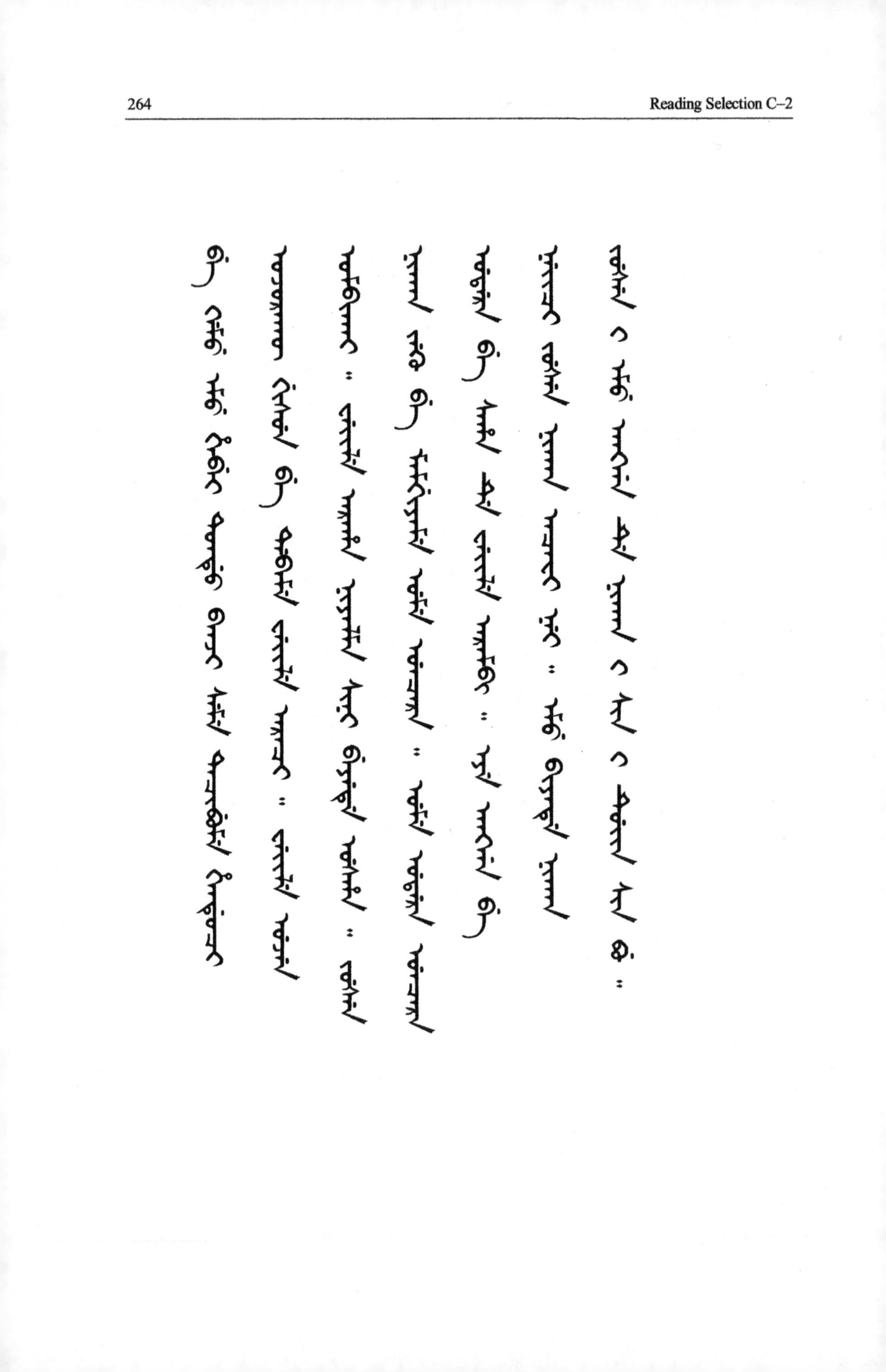

[illegible]
[illegible]
[illegible]
[illegible]
[illegible]
[illegible]
[illegible]

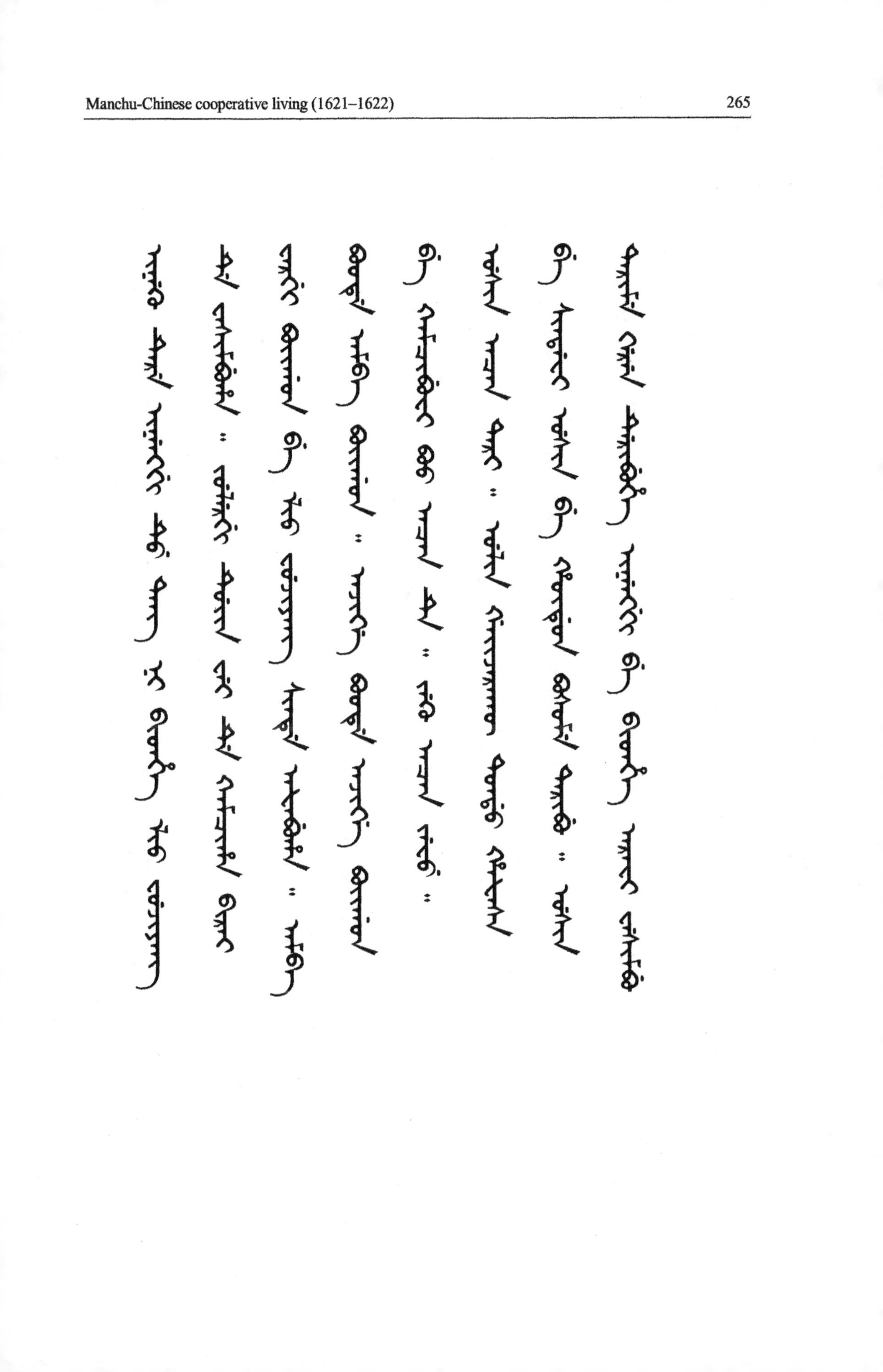

[illegible]

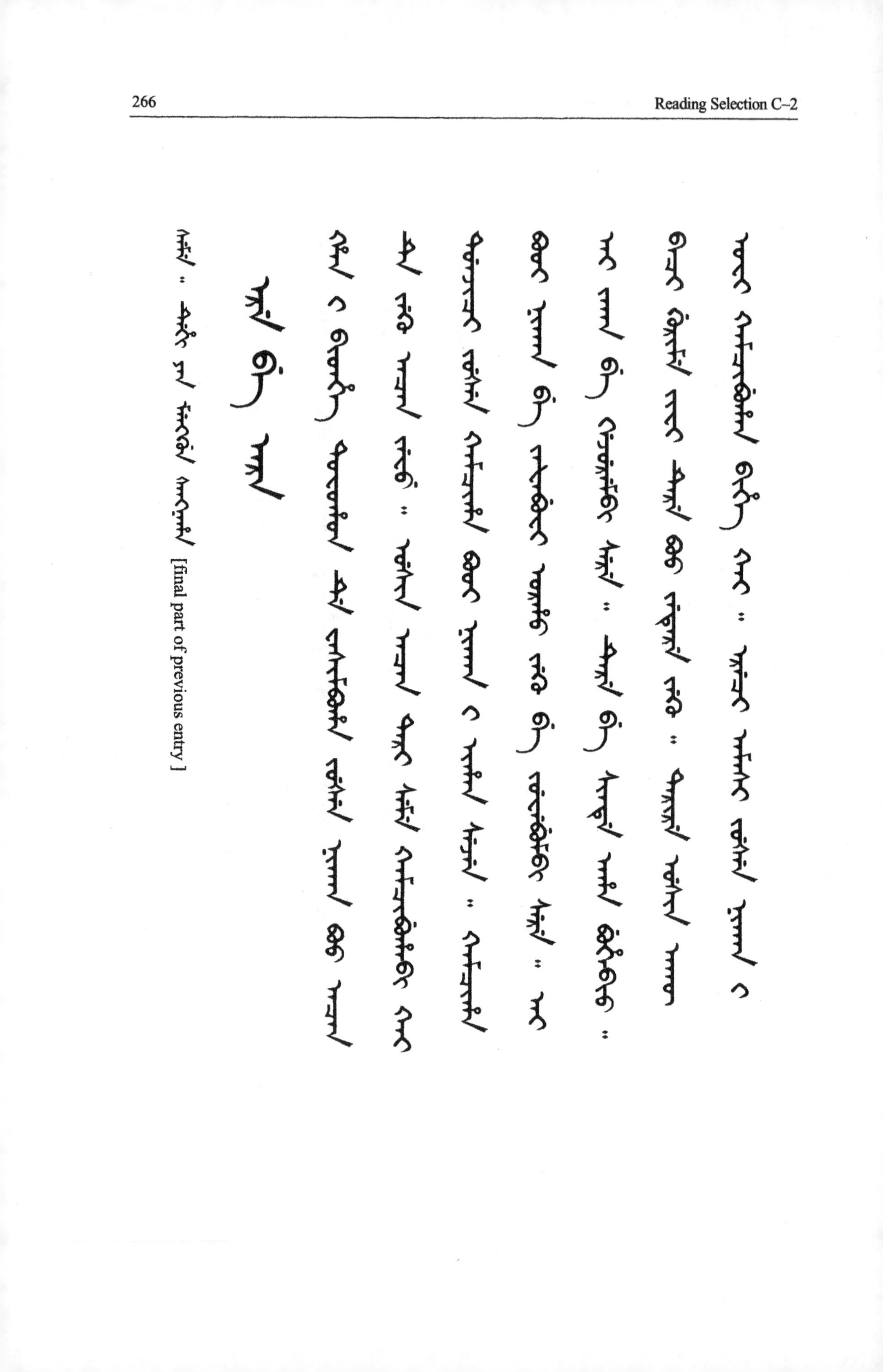

[illegible] [final part of previous entry]

[illegible]

[illegible]

[illegible]

[illegible]

[illegible]

[illegible]

[illegible]

[illegible]

ᠵᡠᡧᡝᠨ ᠪᡝ [illegible] [illegible] ᠉ ᡤᡝᠮᡠ ᡝᠮᡠ ᡥᠠᠨ ᡳ ᡳᡵᡤᡝᠨ ᡴᠠᡳ ᠉
ᡝᡵᡝ [illegible] ᠪᡝ [illegible] [illegible] ᠨᡳᡴᠠᠨ ᡴᡝᠮᡠᠨᡳ [illegible] [illegible]
[illegible] [illegible] ᠈ ᠨᡳᡴᠠᠨ [illegible] [illegible] [illegible] [illegible] ᠉
[illegible] ᡳ [illegible] ᠉ ᡝᡵᡝ ᡤᡳᠰᡠᠨ ᠪᡝ [illegible] ᠨᡳᡴᠠᠨ ᠪᡝ ᠵᡠᡧᡝᠨ
[illegible] ᠵᡠᡧᡝᠨ ᠨᡳᡴᠠᠨ ᠮᡝᠨᡳ ᠮᡝᠨᡳ [illegible] ᡠᠰᡳᠨ ᠪᡝ ᠮᡝᠨᡳ ᠮᡝᠨᡳ
[illegible] [illegible] [illegible] ᠉ [illegible] ᠪᡝ [illegible] [illegible] [illegible] [illegible]

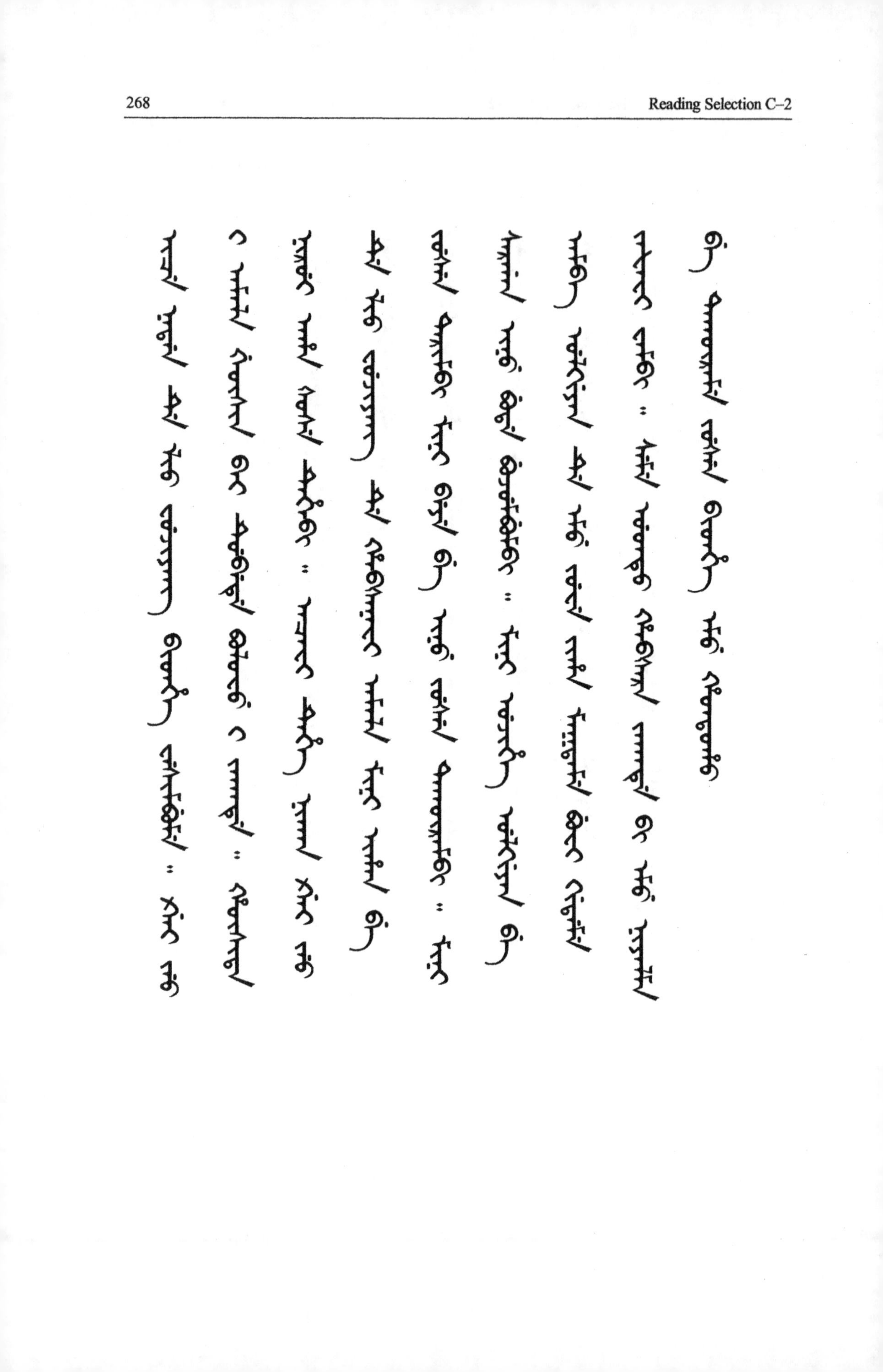

[illegible]

[illegible]

[illegible]

[illegible]

[illegible]

[illegible]

[illegible]

[illegible]

[illegible]

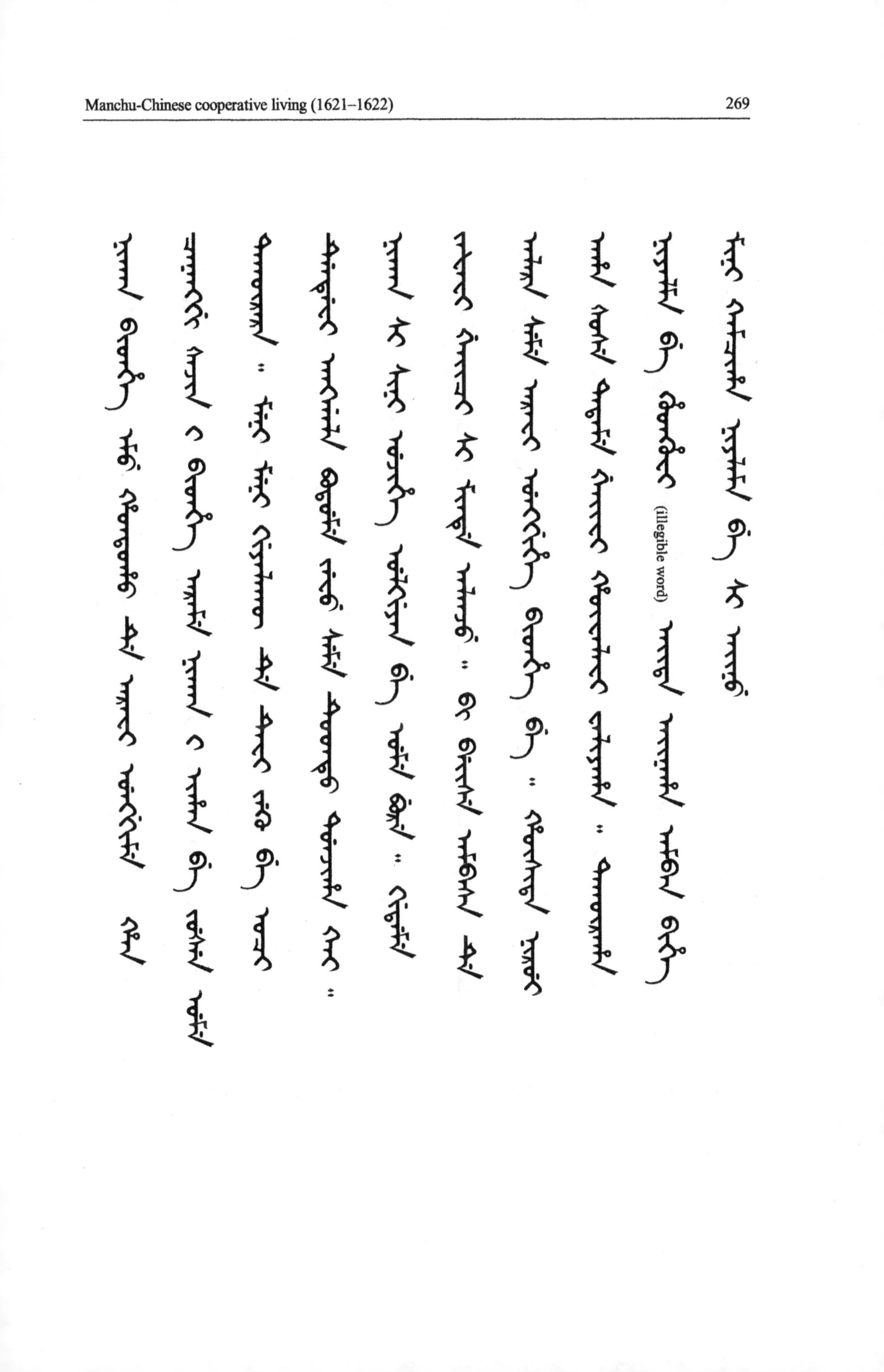

[illegible]

[illegible] (illegible word) [illegible]

[illegible]

[illegible]

[illegible]

[illegible]

[illegible]

[illegible]

[illegible]

[illegible]

ᠪᡝ [illegible] [illegible] ᠨᡳᠶᠠᠯᠮᠠ ᡩᡝ [illegible] [illegible] ᠉

ᠪᡝ [illegible] [illegible] [illegible] ᡩᡝ [illegible] ᠉ [illegible] [illegible] ᠨᡳᠶᠠᠯᠮᠠ

[illegible] ᠨᡳᠶᠠᠯᠮᠠ ᠉ [illegible] [illegible] [illegible] ᠨᡳᠶᠠᠯᠮᠠ ᠉ [illegible] [illegible] ᠨᡳᠶᠠᠯᠮᠠ

[illegible] ᠪᡝ ᠉ [illegible] [illegible] ᠉ [illegible] [illegible] [illegible] [illegible]

ᠨᡳᠶᠠᠯᠮᠠ ᠪᡝ [illegible] [illegible] [illegible] [illegible] [illegible] [illegible] [illegible] [illegible] [illegible]

[illegible] [illegible] ᠨᡳᠶᠠᠯᠮᠠ ᠪᡝ [illegible] [illegible] [illegible] ᠈ [illegible] [illegible]

[illegible] [illegible] [illegible] ᠪᡝ [illegible] [illegible] [illegible] [illegible] ᠉ [illegible] [illegible] ᠉

[illegible] [illegible] [illegible] ᠪᡝ [illegible] [illegible] [illegible] [illegible] ᠨᡳᠶᠠᠯᠮᠠ [illegible] [illegible]

[illegible] [illegible] [illegible] ᠨᡳᠶᠠᠯᠮᠠ [illegible] [illegible] [illegible] [illegible] ᠪᡝ [illegible]

[illegible] ᠉ [illegible] [illegible] [illegible] [illegible] [illegible] [illegible] [illegible] ᠪᡝ [illegible]

Transliteration

(253:262) *han i bithe, orin juwe de wasimbuha. «jusen* [h,j] *nikan be* [2] *emu gasan* [h] *de acan te. jeku be acan jefu. ulha de orho lio* [3] *be acan ulebu seme henduhebihe.*

(254:263) *jusen* [h,j] *nikan be ūme* [h] *gidasara.*[j] *nikan i aika jakabe* [b] *ūme* [h] *durire, ūme* [h] *cuwangnara. tuttu durime cuwangname nungnebi* [f] *nikan habsanjiha* [j] *manggi, uile* [e] *arambi.*[7] *nikan suwe ako* [h] *be angga arame ūme* [h] *holtoro.*[4] *ako* [h] *be angga arame holtoci uilei* [e] *juwe ejen* [5] *be angga acabume duilembikai.*[b] *duilebi* [f] *holo oci geli ehe kai. jusen* [j] *nikan gemu han i irgen ohobi. han i aisin anggai jusen* [h,j] *nikan*

(255:264) *be gemu emu hebei tondo banji seme tacibume henduci, ojorako* [h] *gisun be dabame uile araci,*[7] *uile* [e] *ujen ombikai.*[b,6] *uile* [e] *araha* [7] *niyalma sini beyede* [b] *usha. jusen* [h,j] *nikan jeku be mamgiyame ūme* [h] *uncara, ūme* [h] *udara. uncara udara be sahade uile* [e] *arambi.*[7] *eye angga be neici jusen* [h,j] *nikan acabi* [f] *nei. emu biyade* [b] *nikan jusen* [h,j] *i emu angga de nikan i sin i duin sin buu.»*[8]

(256:265) *ineku tere inenggi, dutan* [k] *i bithe, Lio fujan* [k] *de wasimbuha. «julergi duin ui* [e] *de kamciha birai wargi boigon be, Lio fujan* [k] *sinde afabuha. amba boo de amba boigon, ajige boo de ajige boigon be kamcibubi* [f] *boo acan te. jeku acan jefu. usin acan tari. ulin gaijarako* [h] *tondo hafasa be sindabi,*[f] *usin be hodun* [h] *bosiome* [j] *taribu. usin tarime geren deribuhe inenggi be bithe arabi* [f] *uwesimbu.*[e]*»*

(257:266) *ere be ara.*[9]
han i bithe tofohon de wasimbuha. «jūsen [h,j] *nikan boo acan te jeku acan jefu, ūsin* [h] *acan tari seme kamcibuhabikai.*[b] *donjici jūsen* [h,j] *kamciha booi nikan i ihan sejen, kamciha booi nikan be jafabubi* [f] *orho jeku be juwebumbi sere,*[10] *ai ai jakabe* [b] *gejurembi sere,*[10] *tere be sinde aha būhebio?*[h] *baci gurime jibi,*[f] *tere boo jetere jeku, tarire usin ako* [h] *obi,*[f] *kamcibuhabihekai.*[b] *ereci amasi jūsen* [h,j] *nikan i*

(258:267) *boo de acan tere, jeku be anggala tolome acan jetere dabala, jusen* [j] *nikan meni meni ubui ūsin* [h] *be meni meni ihan i tari. ere gisumbe* [11] *jurceme nikan be jusen* [h] *gidasame* [j] *gejureci, nikan gajime sajin* [j] *de habsa.*[j] *ere bithe be wasika seme,*[12] *nikan geli balai holtome jusen*[j] *be ūme* [h] *belere. gemu emu han i irgen kai.»*

(259:268) *ice nadande,*[b] *Lio fujan* [k] *bithe uwesimbume,*[e] *«Gaijoi* [k] *amala gosin* [h] *bai dubede, Bolofui jakade Hosita* [h] *nirui aha Siose* [j] *tehebi. acabi* [f] *tehe nikan, Gaijode* [b,k] *Lio fujan* [k] *de habsanabi* [j,f] *"amala mini ihan be jūsen* [h] *tarimbi, mini beyebe inu jusen* [h] *takorambi.*[h] *mini sargan inu buda bujumbumbi. mini ūjihe* [h] *ulgiyan* [h] *be, amba ūlgiyan* [h] *de emu juwe jiha maktame bubi,*[f] *gidame jafabi* [f] *wambi," seme uttu habsara* [j] *jakade, bi emu niyalma be takorame* [h] *jūsen* [j] *bithe emu hontoho,*

(260:269) *nikan bithe emu hontoho de arabi* [f,13] *unggime, "han cananggi sajin* [j] *i bithe arame, 'nikan i ihan be jūsen* [h,j] *ūme* [h] *takorara.*[h] *meni meni giyalakude* [b] *tebi,*[f] *jeku be oci, dendebi* [f] *anggala būdome* [h] *jefu' seme tuttu donjiha kai. nikan si sini ūjihe* [h] *ulgiyan* [h] *be ūme* [h] *bure. gidame jafabi* [f] *gaici si minde alanju. bi beise ambasade alara" seme arabi* [f] *unggihe bithe be, Husita* [h] *nirui aha Siose* [j] *tatame gaibi* [f] *howalabi* [f] *waliyaha. takoraha* [h] *niyalma be huthubi* [f]...(illegible word)... *"Aita ainaha amban bihe, mini kamciha niyalma be si ainu*

(261:270) *beidembi," seme, mini jai jergi takoraha* [h] *juwe jūsen* [h] *be, Hosita* [h] *nirui Guwanggun gebungge niyalma ere juwe jūsen* [h] *nikan be suwaliyame jafabi* [f] *gamaki serebe* [14] *jai ceni nirui juwe niyalma "ere takoraha* [h] *mujangga, si ere be ainu gamambi" seme nakabubi* [f] *amasi unggihe. uttu emu niyalmabe takoraci* [h] *jafabi* [f] *huthubi* [f] *tantara* [15] *juwe niyalmabe takoraci* [h] *jafabi* [f] *tantara oci* [15] *jai han i ai ai weile be, be adarame mutembi.»*[16] *«Aita sini nememe* [17] *takoraha* [h] *emu niyalma amala takoraha* [h] *juwe niyalma tere ilan niyalmabe gemu jafabi* [f] *Liodun* [k] *de unggi.» Hosita* [h] *nirui niyalma be ini nirui niyalma de afabubi* [f] *ganabuha.*

Notes

Even a quick glance at the documents reveals that the writing is quite untidy. Some words are started off wrong, others are crossed out entirely, suggesting that the scribe had not yet fully perfected his writing skills.

1. Orthographic differences between Old Manchu (OM) and Standard Manchu (SM):

a) Diacritical marks: No marks except for the letter *n* (in most cases).

b) Case and sentence particles: Attached forms of particles may be a bit more common than in SM, but the difference is not pronounced. Examples: *jakabe, nadande, kamcibuhabikai, kamcibuhabihekai, dulembikai.*

c) *c* and *j*: Initial *c* and *j* are written as in SM. Mid-position *c* and *j* look alike in OM. Compare *gaici* and *alanju.*

d) *y*: Initial *y* in OM is indistinguishable from initial *j*. Mid-position *y* is identical to a one-stroke mid-position *i.*

e) *f* and *w*: No long form in OM to distinguish *fa* from *wa* or *fe* from *we*. SM *weile* is written as *uile* and SM *wesimbumbi* as *uwesimbumbi.*

f) *b* and *f*: All SM *-fi* suffixes are written as *-bi.*

g) *t* and *d*: No distinction between front and back *d* and *t.*

h) *ū*, *o*, and *u*: SM *u* often appears in OM as *ū*, and SM *ū* may appear as OM *o* or *u.*

OM	SM	OM	SM
būdome	*bodome*	*howalambi*	*hūwalambi*
būre	*bure*	*Hosita*	*Hūsita*
giyalako	*giyalakū*	*takorambi*	*takūrambi*
gosin	*gūsin*	*ūjihe*	*ujihe*
hodun	*hūdun*	*ūsin*	*usin*

In the 1620s the Manchu written language was still new and in flux. Inconsistencies occur, sometimes even within the same document. In these pieces you find *ulgiyan* and *ūlgiyan, jusen* and *jūsen, bure* and *būre, usin and ūsin.*

i) *k*, *g*, *h*: The use of front and back *k, g, h* generally follows the rules of SM where front *k, g, h* precede front vowels and back *k, g, h* precede back vowels. But there are exceptions, such as *gūrun.* As in the Reading Selection B–1, the mid-position (end of syllable) *k* that is written as back *k* (*q*) in SM, may be written as front *k* in OM. Example: *maktame* instead of *maqtame*.

j) *s* vs. *š*: SM *š* occurs as *s* or *si*. Examples: *jusen, gasan, gidasambi, habsanjiha,* and *sajin* instead of *jušen, gašan, gidašambi, habšanjiha,* and *šajin*; *bosiome* and *Siose* for *bošome* and *Šose*.

k) Transcription of Chinese words: *dutan*, *fujan*, and *Liodun* are transcriptions of Chinese words ending in *-ng*. By dropping the letter *g*, these early OM adaptations abide by the traditional Manchu rule that Manchu words end either in a vowel or in the letter *n*. In SM the transcription follows the Chinese more closely: *dutang* (Chin. *tutang* 都堂), *fujiyang* (Chin. *fujiang* 副將), and *Liyoodung* (Chin. *Liaodong* 遼東).

In OM the Chinese geographical name *Gaizhou* 蓋州 is written with a front *g* before the letter *a*, a back vowel. Because certain combinations, front *g* before back vowels being one of them, did not exist in Manchu words, special letters were later created for such cases. Thus, OM *Gaijo* turns into SM *G'aijeo*.

2. *jūsen nikan be*: 'as for Jurchens and Chinese;' *be* serves as topic marker. There is no verb in the latter part of this sentence that takes the accusative. Therefore this case might show that *be* can indeed be a topic marker and is not, as some scholars have suggested, always the object to a verb. The term *manju* started to replace *jušen* after 1628 and was officially adopted in 1635.

3. *lio*: SM *liyoo* 'fodder'.

4. *nikan suwe ako be angga arame ūme holtoro*: 'You Chinese, don't lie making statements about nothing'; *ako* is nominalized and functions as object to *angga arame*.

5. *uilei juwe ejen*: SM *weile i juwe ejen*, lit. 'two leaders of the matter'. Meaning: 'two leaders with knowledge of, or responsibility over, the matter'.

6. *han i aisin anggai...uile ujen ombikai*: The grammatical structure of this sentence is as follows: a) *han i aisin...tacibume henduci* 'if one teaches through the *khan*'s highly respected mouth'; b) *ojorakū* is the negative of *ombi*, which besides the usual meaning of 'to be, to be able' also means 'to agree'. The verb *ojorakū*, 'without agreeing', is the negative parallel to *dabame* 'going against'. Both *ojorakū* and *dabame* relate to *weile araci*.

7. *uile arambi*: The dictionary meaning for *weile arambi* is 'to sentence', 'to punish', 'to accuse of'. While that meaning is possible in the first and last of the four occurrences of *weile arambi* in this piece, the contexts of the second and third occurrence strongly suggest that *weile arambi* also means 'to commit a crime'. Such meaning is reasonable since *weile* means both 'crime' and 'punishment' and *arambi* means 'to do' or 'to make'. Reading selection C–3 offers another context which suggests the meaning of 'to commit a crime' for *weile arambi*. See C–3, Note 7.

8. *buu*: The word is written as *buu* (or *boo*). It means 'give', or SM *bu*. Since the SM word *bure* 'to give' in OM occurs repeatedly as *būre*, it appears that the *uu* in *buu* stands for a final *ū*.

9. *ere be ara*: 'write this'. Certain entries in the collection of the *Old Manchu Archives* are marked *ere be ara* 'write this'; others are marked *ere be ume ara* 'don't write this'. These are notes to the copyists indicating what to include and what not to include in the copy.

10. *donjici...sere, ai ai jaka be...sere*: *donjici...sere* 'if one listens...they say', 'I hear that...and that...'. Both *sere* go with *donjici*.

11. *gisumbe*: Contracted with the particle *be*, *gisun be* becomes *gisumbe*. Before the letter *b* the letter *n* may turn into *m*. Compare *cembe*, accusative from of *ce* 'they'.

12. *ere bithe be wasika seme*: 'even though I have issued this announcement'. Compare A–6, Review 10.

13. *jusen bithe emu hontoho nikan bithe emu hontoho de arabi*: 'having written a Manchu (Jurchen) letter into one half and a Chinese letter into one half'. Meaning: 'having written the letter in both Manchu and in Chinese'.

14. *gamaki serebe*: The *-be* in *serebe* can either be seen as topic marker or as object to *nakabufi*.

15. *tantara*: The two *tantara* are parallel. The word *oci* relates to both.

16. This is the end of Liu's memorial which was introduced in line one with *wesimbume*. There is no finite verb like *sehe* marking the end of this memorial.

This section has a total of six quotes: 1) the words of Liu: from *Gaijoi* to *mutembi*, introduced by *wesimbume*; 2) Šose's accusation: from *amala* to *wambi*, framed by *habšanafi* and *seme*; 3) Liu's letter to Šose: from *han cananggi* to *alara*, framed by *unggime* and *seme arafi*; 4) within this letter Liu quotes an edict, starting with *nikan i ihan* and ending in *jefu*, framed by *arame* and *seme*; 5) Šose's response to the letter: from *Aita* to *beidembi*, framed by an illegible word and *seme*; 6) the *khan*'s response to Liu's memorial: from *Aita sini* to *unggi*, without front or end markers.

17. *nememe*: Mispelling for *neneme* 'previously', 'earlier'. The word *nememe* 'moreover, especially' is not appropriate for this context.

Review

1. Write in Manchu script and translate into English: a) *ulha de orho liyoo be acan ulebu*; b) *nikan i aika jaka be ume durire*; c) *nikan habšanjiha manggi weile arambi*; d) *duilefi holo oci geli ehe kai*; e) *gemu emu hebei tondo banji*; f) *jeku be mamgiyame ume uncara*; g) *eye angga be neici jušen nikan acafi nei*; h) *usin tarime deribuhe inenggi be bithe arafi wesimbu*; i) *tere be sinde aha buhebio?* j) *jeku be anggala tolome acan jetere*; k) *ere gisumbe jurceme nikan be gejureci*; l) *nikan geli balai holtome jušen be ume belere*; m) *jušen bithe emu hontoho, nikan bithe emu hontoho de araha*; n) *ere takūraha mujangga.*

2. Translate into Manchu: a) live in one village; b) Jurchens are not to oppress the Chinese; c) don't make false accusations; d) both the Chinese and the Jurchens are the *khan*'s people; e) eat together and work the fields together; f) appoint honest officials who do not take things; g) I hear that the Jurchens make the Chinese transport their grain; h) the Jurchens make my wife cook; i) they throw me one or two *jiha* for a fat pig; j) don't give up the pigs you have raised; k) if one takes the pigs by force, report it to me; l) if I send two people, the Jurchens seize them and beat them.

Reading Selection C–3

Manchu–Chinese inequality (1623) [Old Manchu]

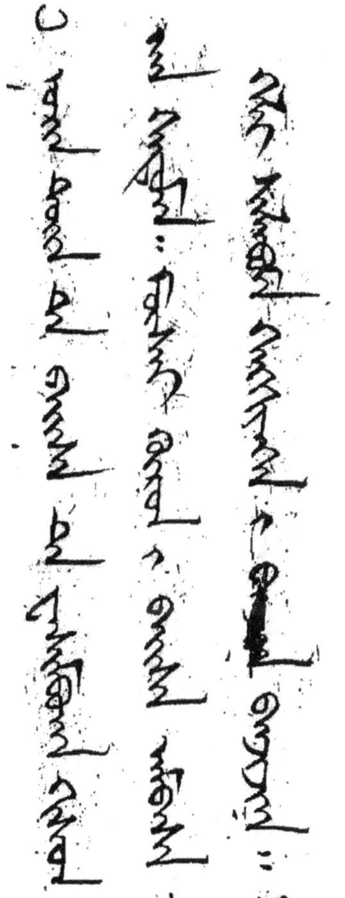

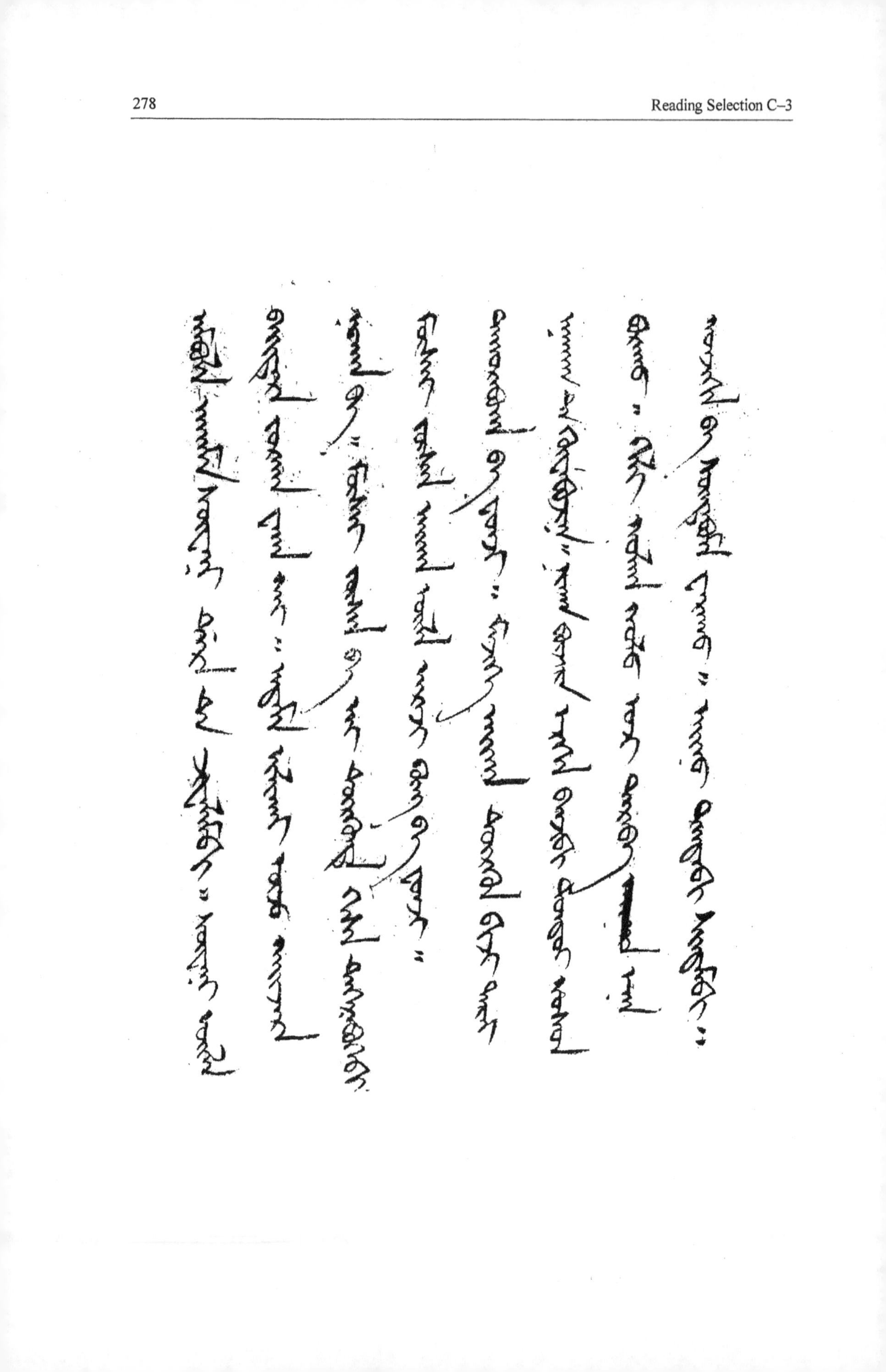

[illegible]

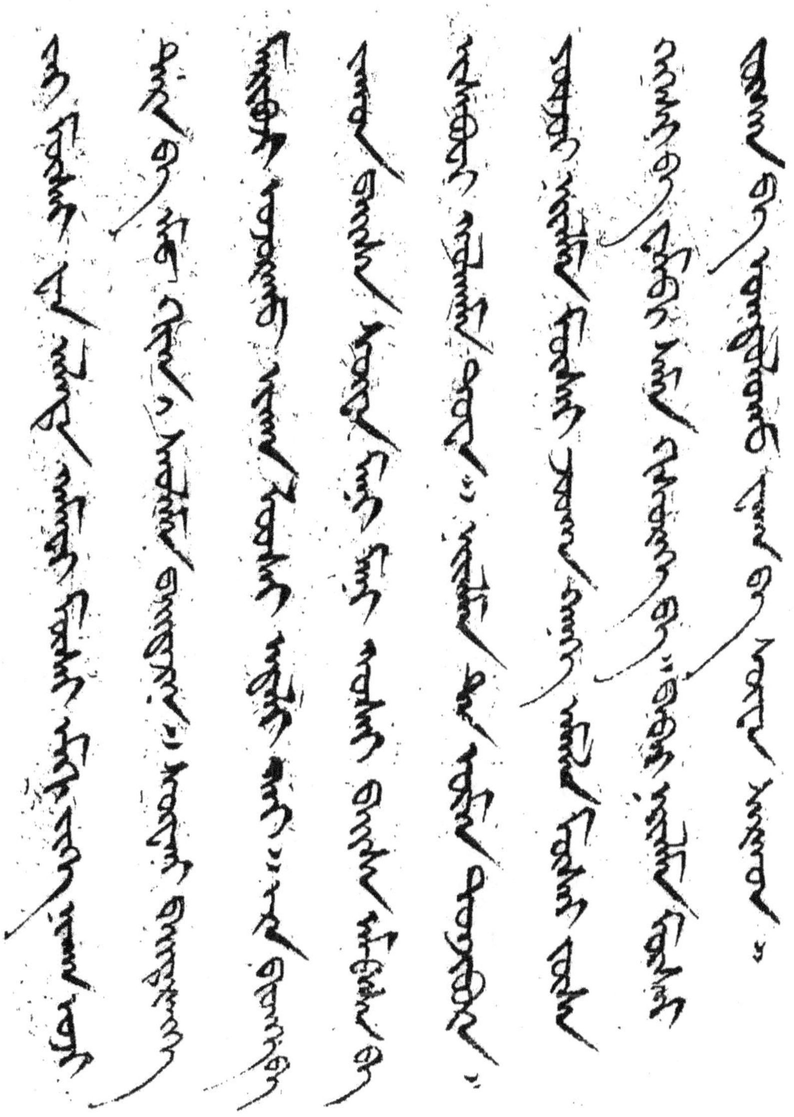

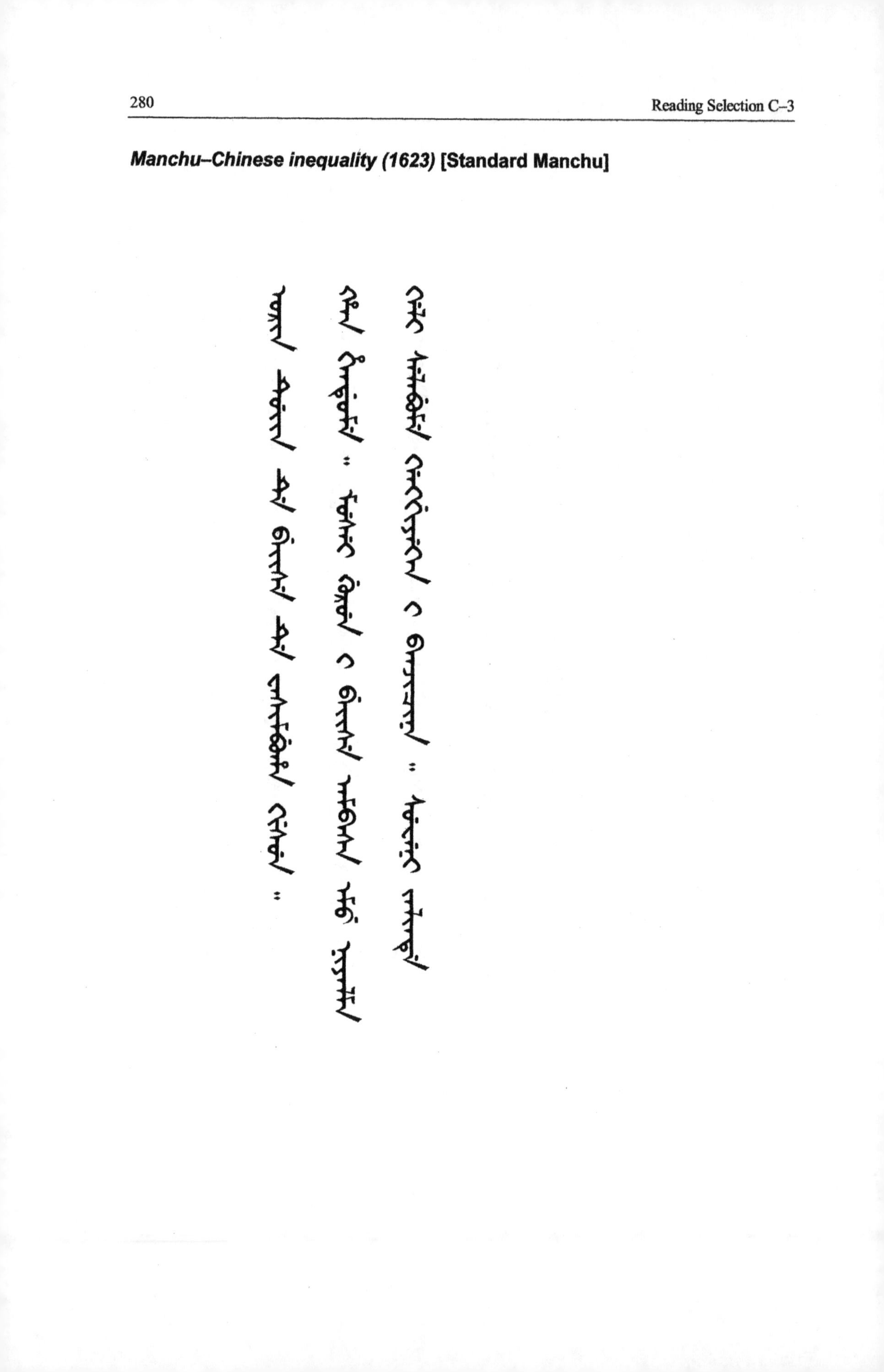

***Manchu–Chinese inequality (1623)* [Standard Manchu]**

[illegible]

[illegible]

[illegible]

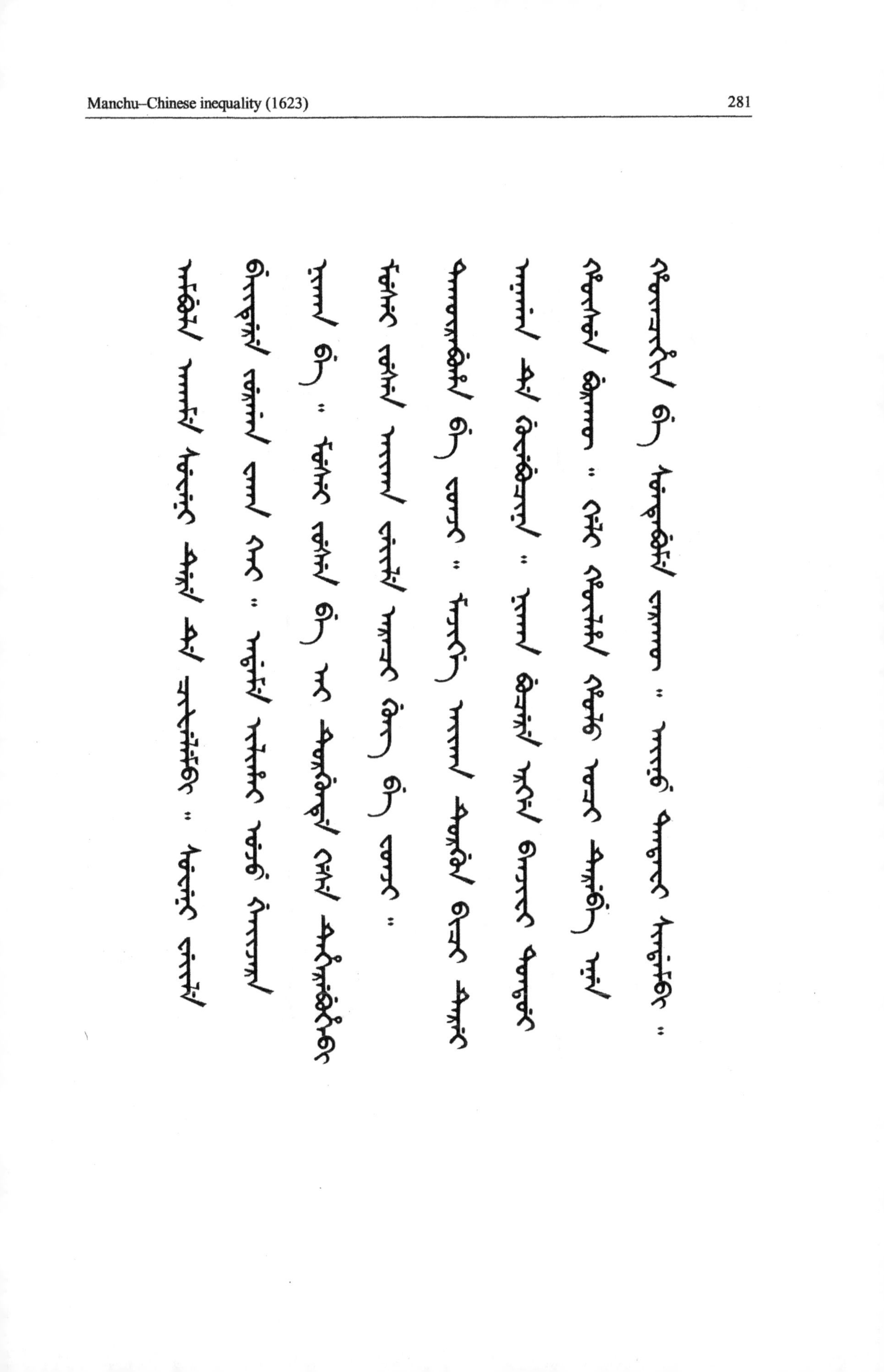

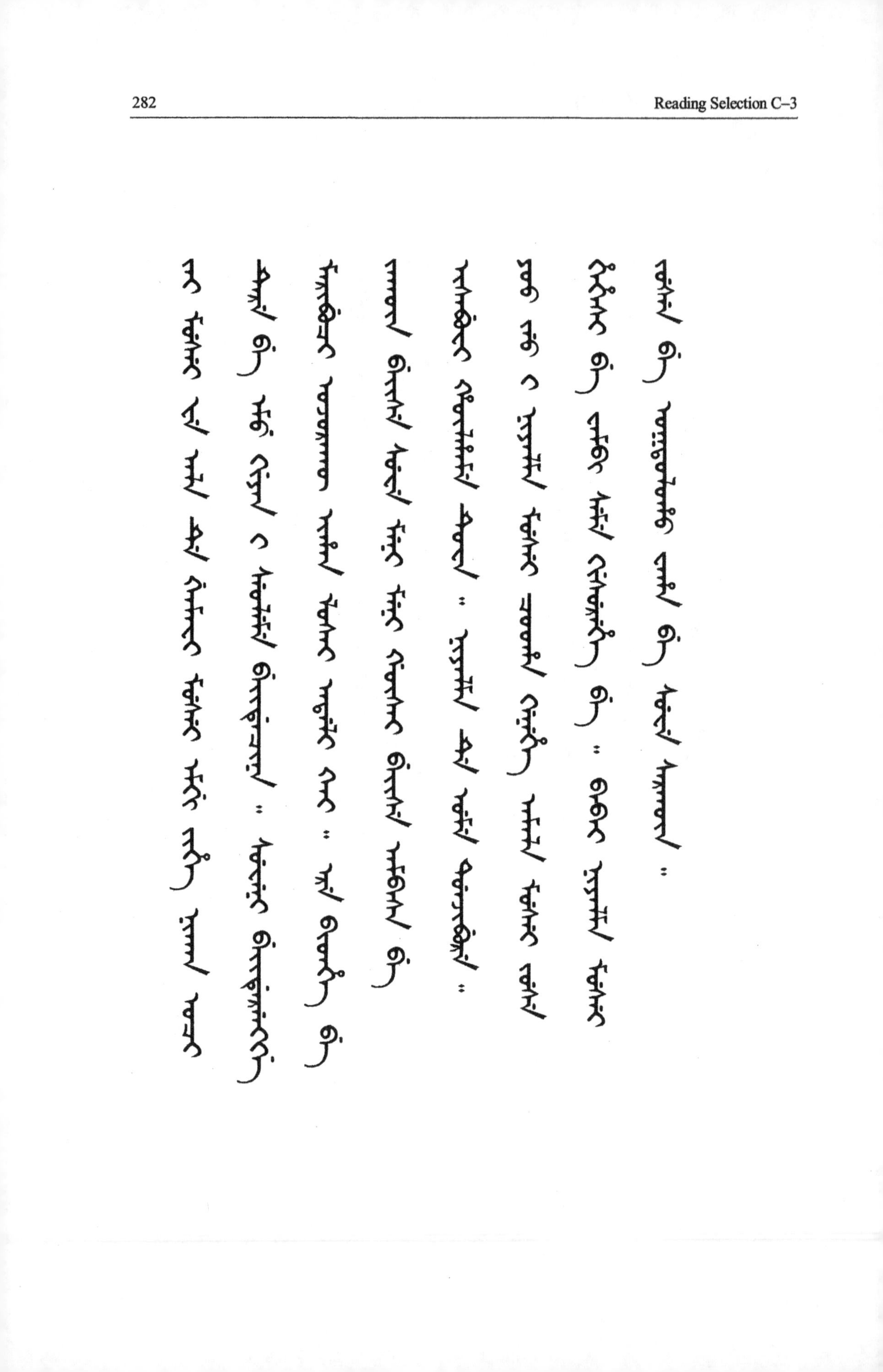

[illegible]

[illegible]

[illegible]

[illegible]

[illegible]

[illegible]

[illegible]

[illegible]

Transliteration

(277:280) *orin duin de beise de wasimbuha gisun. han hendume,*[2,a] *«mūsei* [h] *gūrun* [h] *i beise ambasa emu niyalma geli* [3] *selabume* [a] *genggiyeken i banjicina.*[c,4] *sūweni* [h] *jalinde*

(278:281) *ambula akame, sūweni* [h] *dere* [a] *de cifelembi.*[c,e] *sūweni* [h] *uile* [e] *beidere jurgan* [5] *waka kai. adame ilihai ūju* [h] *gaijara nikan* [6] *be,*[7] *mūsei* [h] *jūsen* [h] *be ai tūrgunde* [h] *gese teherebuhebi.*[7] *mūsei* [h] *jūsen* [h] *aika uile* [e] *araci* [c,8] *gūng* [h] *be fonji. takorabuha* [h] *be fonji. majige aika tūrgun* [h] *bici,*[c] *terei* [g] *anagan de gūwebucina.* [h] *nikan būcere* [c,h] *ergen banjibi* [f,9] *tondoi hosun* [h] *burako,* [h] *geli holha* [h] *holo oci* [c] *terebe* [g] *enen honcihin* [c,h] *be sūntebume* [h] *warako.*[h] *ainu tantabi* [f] *sindambi.*[10]

(279:282) *jai mūsei* [h] *Fe* [e] *Alade* [11] *gamafi* [f] *mūsei* [h] *emgi jihe nikan oci,*[c] *tere be emu giyan* [d] *i seoleme beidecina.*[c,g] *sūweni* [h] *beiderengge,*[g] *maribuci* [c] *ojorako* [h] *ihan loosai* [12] *adali* [13] *kai. ere bithe be jakon* [h] *beise sūwe* [h] *meni meni gosai* [h] *beise ambasa be isabufi* [f] *holhame* [h] *tuwa.*[g] *niyalma de ūme* [h] *donjibure. Yoojoi* [d,k] *niyalma mūsei* [h] *cooha genehe amala mūsei* [h] *jūse* [h] *hehesi be wambi seme gisurehe be, babai niyalma mūsei* [h] *jūsen* [j,h] *be oktoloho waha be suwe sarkon?* [h] *»*

Notes

1. **Orthography:** Even more than Reading Selections B–1 and B–2 (entries for 1621 and 1622), this entry for 1623 shows that the Manchu script was changing.

a) Diacritical marks: Besides the dot for the letter *n*, this selection contains one dot for the letter *e* (in *selabume*) and one for the letter *d* (in *dere*).

b) Case and sentence particles: No different from SM.

c) *c* and *j*: Initial *c* and *j* are written as in SM. Mid-position *c* looks like mid-position *j*. Examples: *cifelembi, banjicina.*

d) *y*: Initial *y* is distinguished from initial *j* with an upward curve as in SM. Mid-position *y*, on the other hand, is still identical to a one-stroke mid-position *i*. Examples: *giyan, niyalma.*

e) *f* and *w*: Initial *we* still occurs as *u*, as in *uile* for *weile*. The new long form for the letter *f* is used in *cifelembi* and *fe*.

f) *b* and *f*: Two of the four subordinate converbs in this piece use the OM ending *-bi* (*tantabi, banjibi*). The other two use SM *-fi* (*gamafi, isabufi*).

g) *t* and *d*: The SM distinction between front and back *d* and *t* is the norm. However, the words *beidecina, beiderengge, terebe, terei*, and *tuwa* use the back *t/d* even though they are followed by front vowels.

h) *ū*, *o*, and *u*: The letter *ū* in words that SM will write with *u* is still prevalent. Examples: *mūse, sūweni, ūme, gūrun, ūjen, jūsen, gūng, gūwebucina, būcere, sūntebuhe*. Similarly, various words that have *ū* in SM, are written with *o* in OM. Examples: *hosun, holha, honcihin, holhame, sarkon, burako, warako, ojorako*. Note that the last occurrence of *suwe* (next to last word) is not written as *sūwe*.

i) *k, g, h*: The use of front and back *k, g, h* follows SM rules.

j) *s* and *š*: The letter *s* still stands for *š*. Example: *jūsen* instead of *jušen*.

k) Transcription of Chinese words: *Yoojo* stands for the Chinese place name *Yaozhou* (耀州). In SM *Yoojo* will be written *Yoo Jeo*.

2. No final *sehe*.

3. *emu niyalma geli*: 'each one of you', 'every single person'.

4. *banjicina*: 'may you live'. For a review of the function of *-cina* refer to C–1, Review 3.

5. *uile beidere jurgan*: 'the way of judging crimes'. Later in the dynasty the expression *weile beidere jurgan* refers to the Ministry of Justice.

6. *adame ilihai ūju gaijara nikan*: lit. 'the Chinese, who will immediately raise [their] heads when [they] stand close to [us]'. Meaning: the Chinese who will immediately behave proudly (defiant, arrogant) when they are close (equal) to us.

7. *nikan be mūsei jūsen be gese teherebuhebi*: 'you have made the Chinese and our Jurchens equal'. Note the double accusative.

8. *uile araci*: SM *weile araci.* Though the dictionary meaning is 'to accuse, to punish', this context suggests the meaning of 'to commit a crime'. Compare C–2, Note 7.

9. *nikan bucere ergen banjibi*: lit. 'if a Chinese has lived a life that deserves to die'. Meaning: 'if a Chinese deserves the death penalty'.

10. *terebe honcihin be suntebume warako, ainu...sindambi*: 'Why do you set him free without killing him and exterminating his relatives?' Even though the Manchu text places a full stop after *warako*, *warako* is the negative converb that relates to *sindambi*.

11. *Fe Ala*: Fe Ala ('Old Hill') was Nurhaci's capital from 1587 to 1603. In 1603 he moved to nearby Hetu Ala ('Broad Hill') where he stayed until 1619. In early documents Hetu Ala is sometimes referred to as '*musei hecen*' or '*amba hecen*'. (For more information see: Giovanni Stary et al., *On the tracks of Manchu culture, 1644–1994* [Wiesbaden: Harrassowitz, 1995], pp. 1–3.) It is possible that as a time reference Fe Ala sometimes referred to the entire period of 1587 to 1619.

12. *loosa*: Stands for SM *losa* 'mule'.

13. *adali*: Here *adali* 'like, same' is a postposition taking the genitive. The word *adali* may also occur with *de,* as predicate, and after verbs. See Review 1 below.

Review

1. *adali* 'like, same'

maribuci ojorakū losai adali	like a mule which one cannot make go backwards
aisin i adali	like gold
yaya ba gemu adali	every place is the same
adali akū	it is not the same
aisin eldere adali	it shines like gold
jalan halame sirara hafan i adali be dahame	because it is just like a hereditary official
manju gisun nikan gisun de adali akū	the Manchu language is not like Chinese

2. Write in Manchu script and translate into English: a) *beise ambasa emu niyalma geli selabume genggiyeken i banjicina*; b) *suweni dere de cifelembi*; c) *nikan be jušen be ai turgunde gese teherebuhebi*; d) *takūrahabe fonji*; e) *ainu tantafi sindambi*; f) *beiderengge maribuci ojorakū losai adali kai*; g) *ere bithe be beise ambasa be isabufi hūlhame tuwa*; h) *juse hehesi be wambi seme gisurehe.*

3. Translate into Manchu: a) I feel very sorry on your behalf; b) if there is any small reason pardon them on that pretext; c) if a Chinese does not loyally do his best; d) why not kill him, his descendents and relatives? e) your way of judging is like a mule; f) don't let the people hear it; g) after our troops go back they will kill our women; h) don't you know that they have poisoned our Jurchens?

Reading Selection C–4

On maintaining the Manchu heritage (1636)

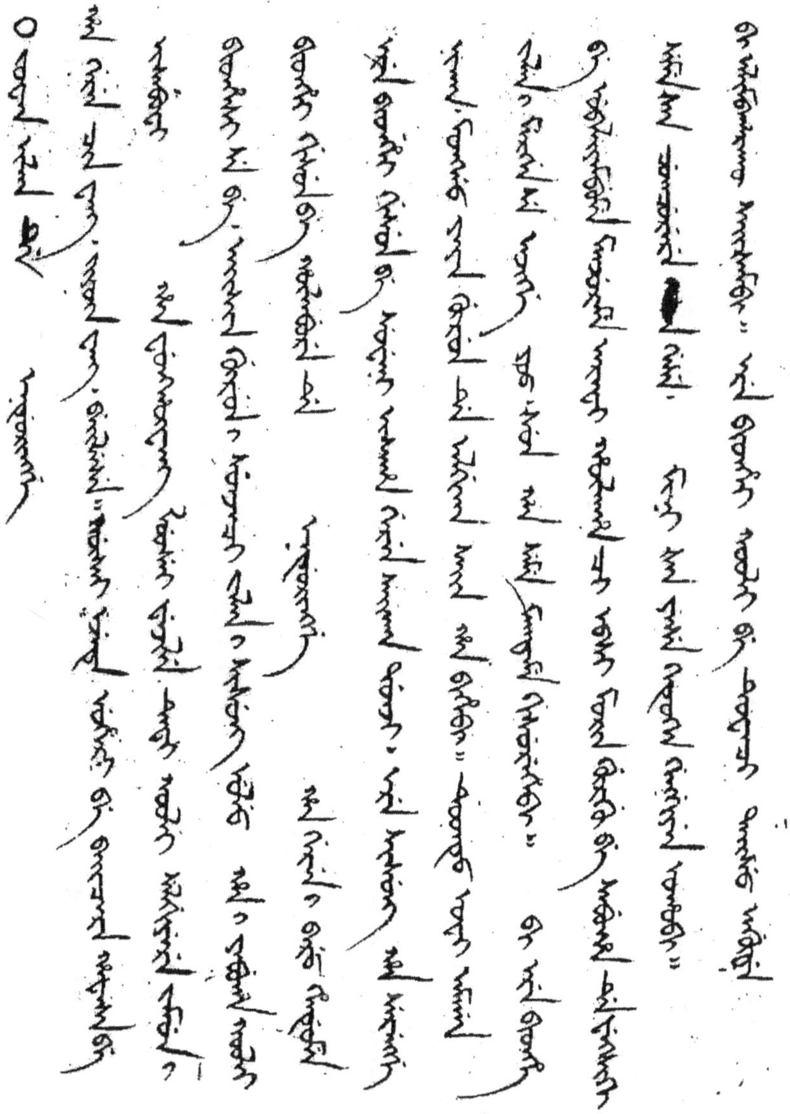

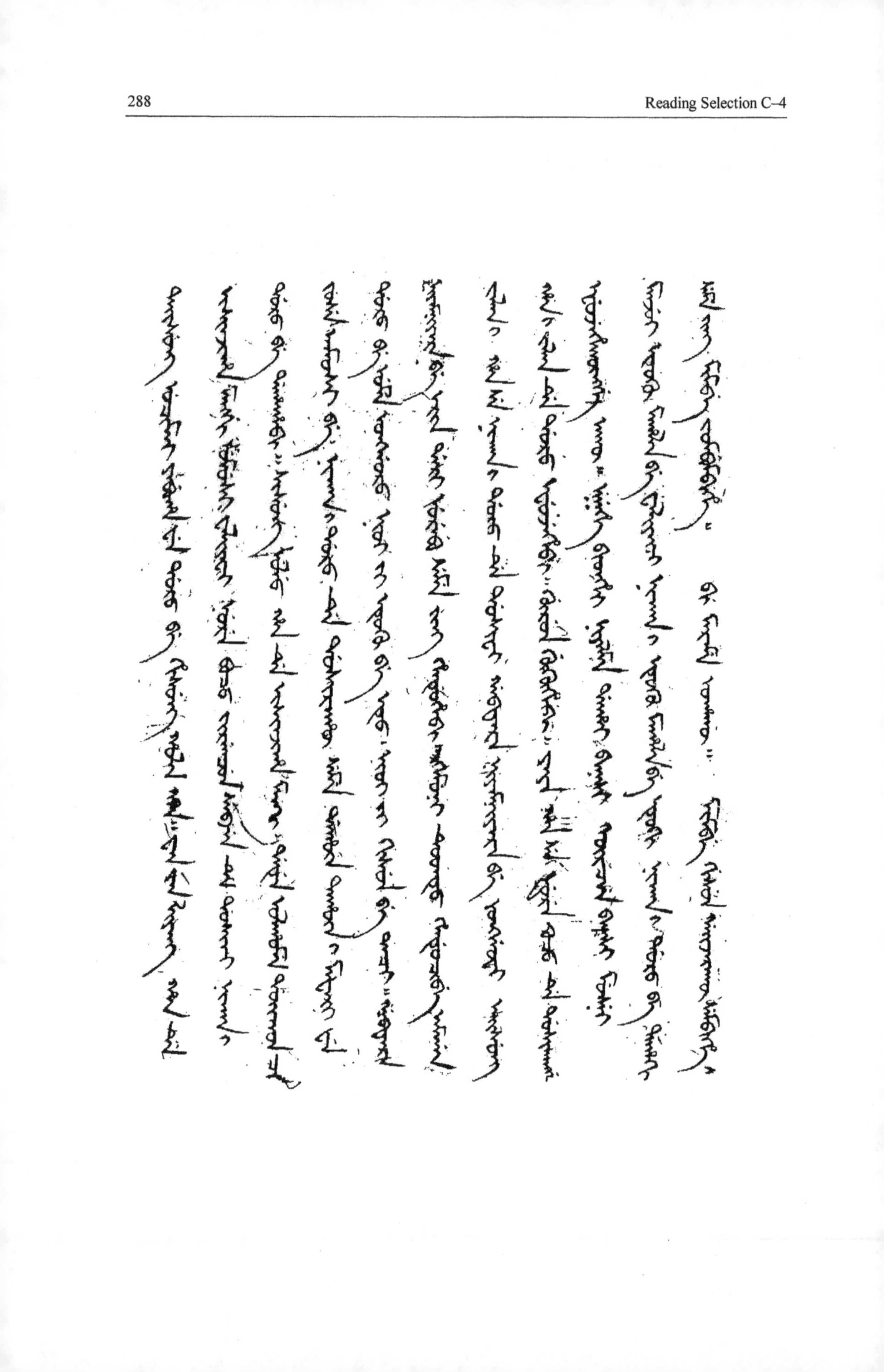

[illegible]

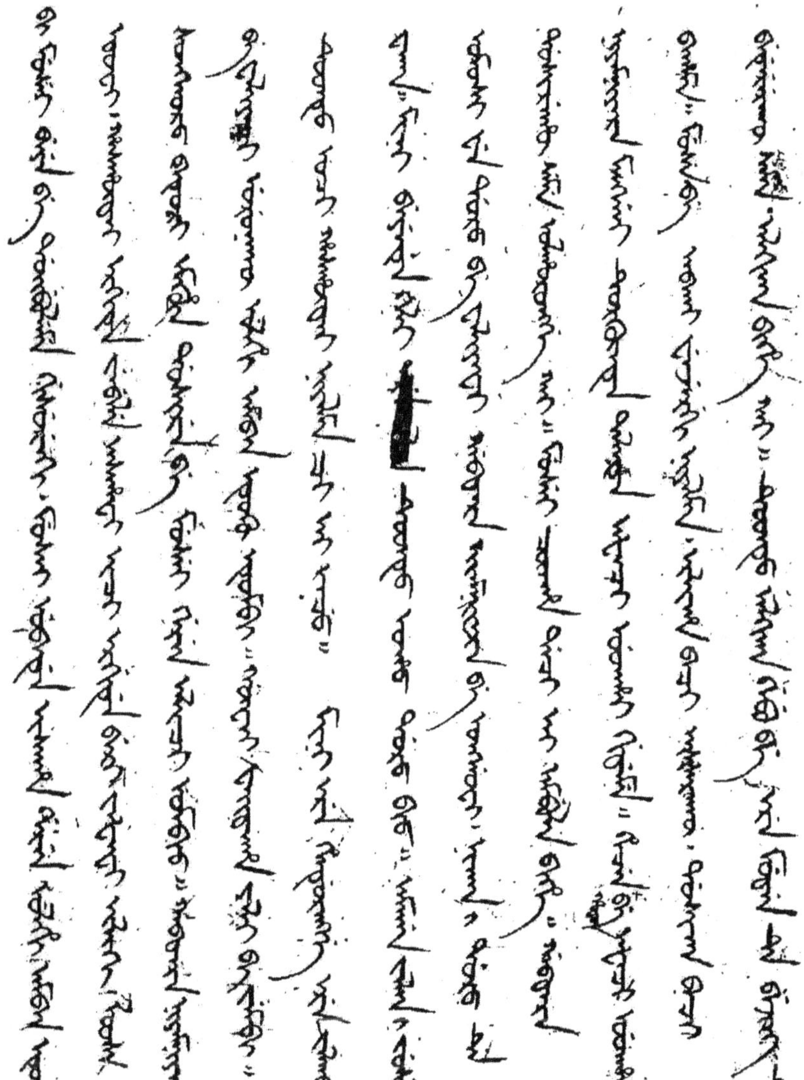

[illegible]

[illegible]

Transliteration

(287) *juwan ilan de enduringge han, geren cin wang, jiyūn* [b] *wang, beilese,*[2] *gūsai ejete, uheri be baicara hafasa be isabufi han funghūwang loosei* [b] *fejile tefi kooli selgiyere yamun i bithesi se be, aisin gūrun* [a] *i sunjaci jalan i Sisung* [b] *Ulu han i yabuha kooli bithei gisun be hūlabure de, enduringge han geren i baru hendume: «ere bithei gisun be suweni isaha geren saikan donji. ere Sisung* [b] *han serengge nikan, monggo yaya gūrun* [a] *de algika sain han bihebi. tuttu ofi amaga jalan i mergen se ajige Yoo Šun han seme maktame gisurehebi. bi ere bithe be ubaliyambume manjurame arafi hūlaha ci ebsi morin, gūrgu be sabuha de feksiki seme šan cukcurere gese,*[3] *mini šan yasa getuken genggiyen ohobi. bi alimbaharakū saišambi. ere bithei kooli be tuwaci, Taidzu* [b] *Agūda,*[a]

(288) *Taisung* [b] *Ucimai yabuha fe doro be Hisung* [b] *Hola han Wan Yan Liyang han de isinjiha manggi, umusi* [c,4] *waliyafi nure boco jirgacun sebjen de dosifi nikan i doro be dahahabi. Sisung* [b] *Ulu han de isinjiha manggi,*[c] *dade olhome doikon* [c] *ci* [c] *juse omosi be nikan i doro de dosirahū seme* [5] *dahūn dahūn i mafari* [6] *fe doro be ume onggoro, nioi ji* [b] *etuku be etu. nioi ji* [b] *gisun be taci. gabtara niyamniyara be erin dari urebu seme jing henduhebi. kemuni tuttu henducibe amaga jalan i han se nikan i doro de dosifi gabtara niyamniyara be onggofi Aisung* [b] *han i jalan de doro efujehebi. gūrun* [a] *gūkūhebi.*[a] *yaya han se nure boco de dosikangge efujehekūngge akū.*[7] *nenehe bithei niyalma Dahai baksi, Kūrcan* [b] *baksi musei manjui etuku mahala be waliyafi nikan i etuku mahala be etuki nikan i doro be dahaki seme jing mimbe jombumbihe. bi marame ohakū.*[8] *mimbe gisun gaijarakū sembihe.*

(289) *bi musei beye be duibuleme gisureki. musei ubade isaha geren ulhi amban* [9] *etuku etufi* [c] *hashūtai ergide jebele ashafi ici ergide beri jafafi iliki. Loosa Šongkoro Baturi* [c] *emhūn* [b] *dosire be* [10] *musei geren alici ombio? gabtara niyamniyara be waliyaci, urunakū ulhi amban etuku etumbi. gūwai faitaha yali be jembi.*[11] *tuttu oci, hashūtai niyalma ci ai encu? mini ere hendurengge ere jalanbe waka.*[12] *mini beyede geli tuttu oho doro bio? amaga jalan i juse omosi fe doro be waliyafi gabtara niyamniyara be onggofi nikan i doro de dosirahū seme olhorongge kai. musei cooha daci ai ambula bihe. gabtara niyamniyara manggai* [13] *turgūnde* [a] *talade afaci uthai gidame, hecen hoton be afaci uthai bahame, muse be abkai fejergi niyalma iliha baci aššarakū, dosika baci bedererakū seme alkika* [c] *bihe kai.*[14] *tuttu alkika* [c] *gebu be ere mudan de Bejing de*

(290) *cooha genefi jase tucire de mini amba gebu be suweni jakūn amban gūtubuha kai. mini gisun be suwembe ejefi bikini* [15] *serengge.»* [16]

Notes

1. Orthography: Apart from a few unclear words and some spelling errors, this 1636 piece generally conforms to SM standards.

a) Adoption of SM conventions: Soft and hard *d* and *t* are often distinguished. So are *w* and *f*, and *j* and *c*. The letter *š* occurs (*šan*, *aššarakū*) but is not yet used as *ši* to represent the Chinese syllable *shi* in *Shizong* 世宗.

Many words with *ū* and *u* are written as in SM. However, the change from *ū* to *u* in words with front *g*, *h*, *k* has not yet occurred: Thus, you still see *emhūn*, *gūrun*, *gūrgu*, *turgūnde*, *Kūrcan*, *gūkūhebi*, *Agūda* instead of *emhun*, *gurun*, *gurgu*, *turgunde*, *Kurcan*, *gukuhebi and Aguda.*

b) Transcription of Chinese sounds: The special letters created to represent certain Chinese sounds are not yet used consistently.

The word *Taidzu* (Chin. *Taizu* 太祖) is in line with SM conventions by using the letter for *dz*. However, *Šidzung*, *Taidzung*, *Hidzung*, and *Aidzung* are written as *Sisung*, *Taisung*, *Hisung*, and *Aisung*.

The Manchu transliteraton of the Chinese word *nüzhen* 女真, which is written as *nioi jy* in SM, appears as *nioi ji*. The Chinese sound *jun*, often written as *giyun* in SM, is *jiyun* in OM. OM *loose*, standing for Chinese *lou* 樓, corresponds to *leose* in SM.

c) Spelling errors: *omosi* is written as *umusi*, *doigon* as *doikon, yamun as jamun, algika* as *alkika,* one occurrence of *musei* as *musai*, and *baturu* as *baturi*. The word *etufi* erroneously uses the back *t*. The word *ci* is written as *ce*, and *manggi* appears to be written as *mangi*; *niyamnara* misses a dot for the *n*, and *juwan* lacks the dot for the *u*.

2. *beilese*: The use of *beilese* (instead of *beise*) points to the development of *beise* as a distinct (lower) rank of its own.

3. *gese*: 'like, same'. Like *adali*, the word *gese* can function as adjective, adverb, or postposition (but not as predicate). See Review 1.

4. ***umusi*:** This word is a misspelling. From the context one would assume that it stands for *omosi* 'grandsons'. The Qianlong version of the *Old Manchu Archives*, however, writes this word as *umesi* 'very', possibly making an error of its own.

5. ***dade olhome doigon ci juse omosi be nikan i doro de dosirahū seme*:** lit: 'because he feared from the beginning that the children and grandchildren would early on fall into Chinese ways'.

6. ***mafari fe doro*:** 'the old way of the ancestors'. Note that *mafari*, which is the plural of *mafa* 'ancestor', does not have a genitive *i*. Similarly, several other *mafari* compounds are established expressions: *mafari miyoo* 'ancestral temple', *mafari soorin* 'ancestral tablets', and *mafari eifu* 'ancestral grave'.

7. ***dosikangge efujehūngge akū*:** 'as for those who entered, there was not one who was not ruined'. Verbs ending in *-ngge* may have one of three meanings. The verb *ararangge*, for example, can mean:

(1) the writing, that which is written, that which one writes
(2) the act, fact, or case of writing
(3) the one who is writing, the writer

Compare Note 16 and Review 2–5.

8. ***bi marame ohakū*:** 'I remained firm and did not agree'. This is another example of *ombi* meaning 'to agree'. Compare Reading Selection C–2, Note 6, p. 274.

9. ***ulhi amban etuku*:** 'wide-sleeve clothes'. Here, the word *amban* is a variant of *amba* 'great, large, wide'.

10. ***Loosa Šongkoro Baturu emhūn dosire be*:** The particle *be* can be taken either as a topic marker, meaning 'as for Loosa entering' or as a case marker, making the entire preceding phrase object to *alici ombio* 'can we stop'.

11. *gūwai faitaha yali be jembi*: 'we will eat meat that others have cut'. This may either refer to the fact that the Manchus would no longer hunt for their own meat, or that they would become sinicized to the point of eating their meat cut into small pieces.

12. *mini ere hendurengge ere jalan be waka*: 'What I am talking about is not this generation'. *jalan be* is object to *hendurengge.* More explicitly, the phrase could read: *mini ere hendurengge ere jalan be hendurengge waka.*

13. *manggai turgunde*: The final *i* in *manggai* could be a spelling error. However, *turgunde* might also have been viewed as a postposition taking the genitive. The *i* is dropped in the Qianlong version of the document.

14. *muse be abkai fejergi niyalma iliha baci aššarakū, dosika baci bedererakū seme algika bihe kai*: 'as for us, we have become famous by people all over the world saying that once we occupy a place we do not abandon it, and that once we have entered a place we do not turn back'.

15. *ejefi bikini*: The verb form *-fi bimbi* refers to an action or event that is completed but influences the present or future. For examples see Review 6 below.

16. *...mini gisun be suwembe ejefi bikini serengge*: 'it's that I want you to remember my words'. For a review of the suffix *–ngge*, see Review 2–5 below. In the examples listed under Review 2, 3, and 4 the *-ngge* verb is a noun which functions as subject of the sentence. It is followed by a predicate to make the sentence complete. In Review 5, the *-ngge* verb is free-standing. In these cases, the predicate 'to be' is understood. In this case, *serengge* may be translated in the following ways: 'it is a case of saying', 'what one has said is as follows', or 'this is what one says'. More freely, one can also translate it as 'someone says' or ' someone said'.

Review

1. *gese* 'like, kind of'

morin šan cukcurere gese	like a horse pricking its ears
ere gese baita inde dalji akū	this kind of matter has nothing to do with him
ere gese morin be ja i bahambi	one can easily obtain this kind of horse

nikan be jušen be ai turgunde gese teherebuhebi	why do you put Chinese and Manchus on the same level
deyere gese feksime jihe	he came flying (so fast as if he flew)
talkiyan i gese	like lightening

2. *ararangge* 'the writing, that which is written, what one writes'

mini ere hendurengge ere jalan be waka	what I am talking about is not this generation
sini ere wesimbuhengge umesi inu	what you have memorialized is very correct
ere Sisung han serengge sain han bihebi	the one who is called Sisung had been a good *khan*
hese wasimbuhangge ... sehe	that which was issued as an edict said
bairengge enduringge ejen morin be bargiyarao	that which I request is that his majesty may accept the horses

3. *ararangge* 'the act of writing, the fact of writing, the instance of writing'

ja i baharangge waka	it is not something that one obtains easily
Osman umai ini ama be dahame tehengge waka	it is not at all a case of Osman residing with his father
ceni dahanjihangge inenggi goidaha	their act of submitting was a long time ago
hojo seme tukiyehengge uthai hoise mukūn i fe tacin	the way of honoring someone by using the name *khoja* is an old custom of the Muslim clans

4. *ararangge* 'he who is writing, the writer'

bisirakūngge ...	those who are not here ...
nure de dosikangge efujehekūngge akū	of all those who succumbed to alcohol there was not one who was not ruined
monggo gisun be sarkūngge bithe be ulhirakū	those who don't know the Mongolian language do not understand the script
haha hehe ere tacin de dosikangge ududu tanggū bi	the men and women who have joined the religion number several hundreds

5. ***ararangge*** **'it is a case of writing, what one has written is as follows'**

suwembe mini gisun be ejefi bikini serengge	it is that I want you to remember my words
omosi nikan i doro de dosirahū seme olhorongge kai	what I fear is that our grandchildren will succumb to Chinese ways
Jaohūi wesimburengge	Jaohūi memorializes as follows

6. ***-fi bi***

suwe mini gisun be ejefi bikini	may you keep my words in mind
gurun i doro bithe de ejefi bi	the country's Way is written in a book
jingse be ashafi bi	the button is attached, one has attached the button

7. Write in Manchu script and translate into English: a) *Ulu han i yabuha kooli bithei gisun be hūlabure de*; b) *ere Sisung han serengge yaya gurun de algika han bihebi*; c) *bi ere bithe be hūlaha ebsi ci*; d) *morin gurgu be sabuha de feksiki seme šan cukcurere gese*; e) *bi alimbaharakū saišambi;* f) *mafari fe doro be ume onggoro*; g) *gabtara niyamniyara be erin dari urebu*; h) *Aidzung han i jalan de doro efujehebi*; i) *Dahai baksi nikan i doro be dahaki seme mimbe jombumbihe*; j) *ulhi amban etuku etumbi*; k) *gūwai faitaha yali be jembi*; l) *mini beyede geli tuttu oho doro bio?*

8. Translate into Manchu: a) listen carefully (well) to the words of this document; b) like a horse that pricks its ears; c) he kept saying again and again; d) wear Nuchen clothing and learn the Nuchen language; e) I refused and did not agree; f) let me make a comparison to ourselves; g) we will wear clothing with wide sleeves; h) could all of us stand up against Losa Šongkoro? i) How great our troops used to be! j) because we were strong in mounted and dismounted archery; k) you eight high officials have put to shame our famous reputation; l) I want you to remember my words.

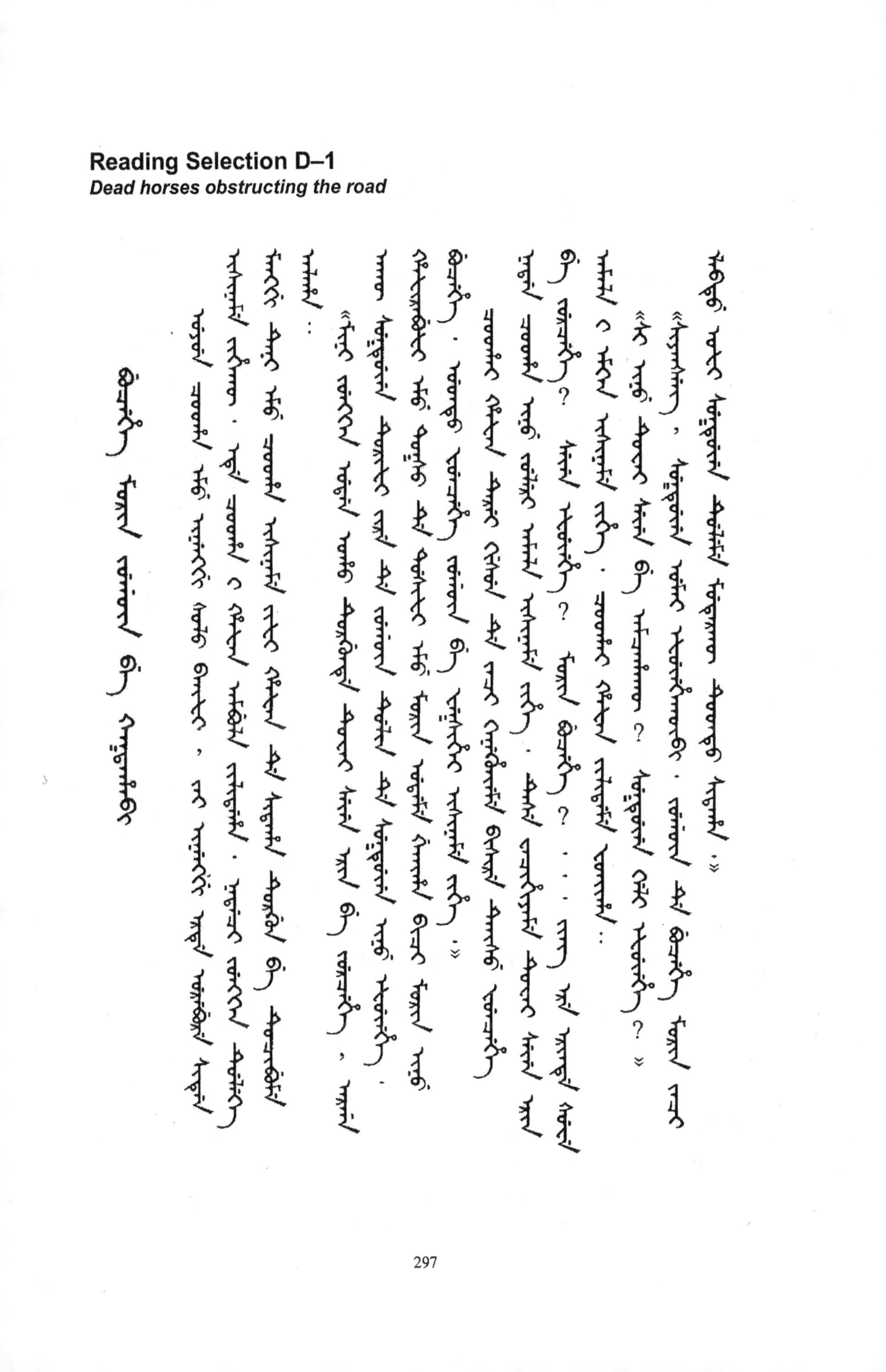

Reading Selection D–1

Dead horses obstructing the road

ᠪᡠᠴᡝᡥᡝ ᠮᠣᡵᡳᠨ ᠵᡠᡤᡡᠨ ᠪᡝ [illegible]

[illegible]

Transliteration

(297) ***Bucehe morin jugūn be kaktahabi***

uyun cooha emu inenggi šolo baifi, jai inenggi erde urebure siden [4] *isiname jihekū. ede cooha i hafan ambula jilidaha. nadaci jungken duleke manggi* [5] *teni emu cooha isiname jifi hafan de sitaha turgun be tucibume alaha:*

«mini jungken udan oho turgunde tuwai sejen erin be jurcehe. arga akū sukdujen turifi jire de jugūn dulin de sukdujen inu efujehe. hafirabufi emu tokso de dosifi emu morin udame gaiha bici morin inu bucehe. uttu funcehe jugūn be feksihei isiname jihe.»

coohai hafan terei gisun de jaci kenehunjeme bisire teisu funcehe nadan cooha inu juleri amala isiname jihe. tese wacihiyame tuwai sejen erin be jurcehe? sejen efujehe? morin bucehe? jing ere erinde šuwe amala [6] *i emken isiname jihe. coohai hafan jili dame fonjiha:*

«si inu tuwai sejen be amcahakū? sukdujen geli efujehe?»

«siyanšeng, sukdujen umai efujehekūbi. jugūn de bucehe morin jaci labdu ofi sukdujen duleme muterkū, [7] *tuttu sitaha.»*

Notes

1. Orthography: Certain letters of the Sibe script are written differently from their Manchu counterparts:

a) ***i*:** When following a vowel, mid-position *i* is written with one short and one long stroke, like the initial *i* in standard Manchu (SM). Examples: *baifi*, *baiha*, *teisu*.

b) ***j*:** Mid-position *j* is written as one down-facing stroke, like a one-stroke *i*. Examples: *sejen*, *sukdujen*, *efujehe*, *kenehunjeme*, *efujehe*, and *fonjiha*.

c) ***k*:** The letter *k* (*q*) before a consonant is written with two dots, but has only one tooth, not two. Also, in quite a few Sibe materials, including this piece, *k* before consonants is written as *k* (*q*) even when, according to SM rules (see page 22), it should be written as front *k*.
Example: *feksihei*, SM: 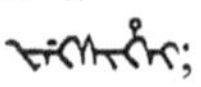; Sibe: 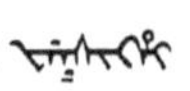 .

d) ***f*:** The letter *f* is written with the long form, even before letters *u*, *o*, and *i*. Examples: *baifi*, *efujehe*, *fonjiha*, *funcehe*, etc. Depending on the handwriting, however, the difference between an initial *f* and an initial *w* may be minimal.

Contemporary Sibe texts include modern punctuation marks, such as commas, periods, quotation and question marks.

2. Sibe Vocabulary: In general, the vocabulary of written Sibe is the same as Manchu, though Chinese influence, already considerable in standard Manchu, is still more pronounced. Vocabulary changes in modern Sibe fall into the several main categories:

a) Sound changes, but no change in meaning. Examples: *tandambi* instead of *tantambi* 'to strike'; *ufuhun* instead of *efehen* 'a large ax'; *orun* instead of *urun* 'daughter-in-law'.

b) Use of loan words instead of native words. In addition to the many Manchu/Sibe words of Mongolian origin, estimated by Nicholas Poppe to make up 20-30% of the traditional Manchu vocabulary, modern Sibe has taken expressions from other languages. The vast majority of recent loanwords in Sibe come from Chinese. For example, *wadzi* (*wazi* 襪子) instead of *fomoci* 'socks'; *si hūi* (*shihui* 石灰) instead of *doho* 'ashtray'. Some loanwords come from languages other than Chinese: *badzar* for *hūdai falga* 'market place' from Uighur; *miyeter* 'meter' and *masina* 'machine' from Russian. In some cases the native and foreign words coexist; for example: Manchu *dehetun* 'airplane' and *feiji*, from Chinese *feiji* 飛機.

c) Creation of new words based on Chinese. Examples: *pailambi* 'to send' from *pai* 派; *kaktambi* 'to obstruct' from *ka* 卡.

d) Literal translation of Chinese words and compounds. While early Manchu tended to use single words to describe a person, thing, or event, modern Sibe, even more than Standard Manchu, uses many literal translations of Chinese compounds. Examples:

bajen (*ba* + *ejen*)	Chin. *dizhu* 地主	landlord
tuwai sejen	Chin. *huoche* 火車	train
juleri amala	Chin. *qianhou* 前後	one after another
jugūn dulin	Chin. *luzhong* 路中	on the way
usin hethe	Chin. *nongye* 農業	agriculture
siden jugūn	Chin. *gonglu* 公路	highway
siden bithe	Chin. *gongwen* 公文	documentary language
gisun hergen	Chin. *yanyu* 言語	spoken language
golmin foholon	Chin. *changduan* 長短	length

A little less obvious is the increased Sibe use of converb-verb combinations. Though standard Manchu also uses this structure extensively, more of these combinations look like Chinese equivalents. Examples: *udame gaiha* for Chinese *maidao* 買到; *isiname jihe* for Chinese *daolai* 到來; or *tuwame wajifi* for *kanwan* 看完.

e) Transliteration of Chinese words and compounds.

siyanšeng	Chin. *xiansheng* 先生	Mr.
fu	Chin. *fu* 府	residence
taitai	Chin. *taitai* 太太	wife
wei yuan hūi	Chin. *weiyuanhui* 委員會	committee
gung can dang	Chin. *gongchandang* 共產黨	Communist Party
Moo jusi	Chin. *Mao zhuxi* 毛主席	Chairman Mao

Though most Chinese words in Manchu are easily recognizable to students familiar with Chinese, it is helpful to remember the most important rules that govern the transliteration of Chinese words into Manchu:

Wade-Giles	Pinyin	Sibe	Wade-Giles	Pinyin	Sibe
pao	*bao*	*boo*	*hsün*	*xun*	*siyūn*
tiao	*diao*	*diyoo*	*chün*	*jun*	*giyūn*
piao	*biao*	*biyoo*	*chou*	*zhou*	*jeo*
p'iao	*piao*	*piyoo*	*ch'ou*	*chou*	*ceo*
chuan	*zhuan*	*juwan*	*ch'üan*	*quan*	*ciowan*
tuan	*duan*	*duwan*	*hsüan*	*xuan*	*siowan*
nü	*nü*	*nioi*	*chia*	*jia*	*jiya*
yü	*yu*	*ioi*	*chien*	*jian*	*jiyan*
yuan	*yuan*	*yuwan*	*chüeh*	*jue*	*jiyo*
huang	*huang*	*hūwang*	*ch'üeh*	*que*	*ciyo*

For a complete list of Chinese syllables with their Manchu equivalents, see Part III, Miscellaneous Information, p. 377-81.

3. Structural Changes: Given that contemporary Sibe is spoken by only a small number of people who are surrounded by the Chinese majority culture and language, the Sibe language is undergoing structural changes as well, some of them the result of Chinese language influences. Quite apparent is the increased omission of sentence particles that are not necessary for the listeners' understanding. Example: *emu morin udame gaiha bicibe*: 'although I bought a horse'.

4. ***urebure siden*:** The word *siden*, originally meaning 'up to, interval, public', may be used as 'when' in Sibe. Compare Reading Selection D-2, Note 33.

5. ***nadaci jungken duleke manggi*:** 'after seven o'clock passed'. When telling time, colloquial Sibe usually uses the word *erin*, not *jungken*. It may also omit the ordinal *ci*. Examples: *te udu erin oho*? 'what time is it now?' *juwe erin oho* 'it is two o'clock'.

6. ***šuwe amala*:** 'the last'. The word *šuwe* 'very, too' can be used to express either a high degree or the highest degree. Several other words with similar meanings function in this way: *jaci* 'too, very', *umesi* 'very', *dembei* 'exceedingly, greatly', *mujakū* 'extremely, truly', *ten* 'extreme point', *nokai* 'very', *hon* 'very, most'. See Review 1 below.

7. ***muterkū*:** Standard Manchu suffix *-rakū* regularly collapses into *-rkū*.

Review

1. ***jaci, šuwe, dembei, mujakū, umesi, ten i, hon, nokai*** **'very', or superlative**

jaci amala	very much behind, last
jaci sain	very good
šuwe ujen	extremely heavy, the heaviest
dembei šahūrun	exceedingly cold, the coldest
mujakū komso	very few, the fewest
umesi mangga	very difficult, the most difficult
umesi ajige	very small, smallest
teni unenggi	very sincere, most sincere
hon ja	very easy, easiest
nokai amba	very great, greatest

2. Examples of conversational sentences

nei erin absi ohoye?	how have you been?
tere oci, šabi nio? inu, šabi inu.	is he a student? yes, he is a student.

tere oci sefu nio? waka, šabi inu.	is he a teacher? no, he is a student.
hoton de hûdai puseli bio?	are there shops in the town?
ere emu bithe oci siningge nio?	is this book yours?
ere ai turgun ni?	what is the reason?
sinde enenggi baita bio? baita akû.	are you busy today? no, I am not.
tere boode bio? akû.	is he at home? no, he is not.
aibide bi? Harbin de bi.	where is it? in Harbin.
udu aniya oho? ilan aniya oho.	how many years has it been? three years.
ai baita be arambi?	what are you doing?
te adarame?	how is it now?
i adarame? umesi sain.	how is he? very good.
sini sargan ya ba i niyalma?	where is your wife from?
ere aniya udu se oho?	how old are you this year?
si aibide genembi?	where are you going?
si ai jaka be udambi?	what are you going to buy?
sini ama ai weilen arambi?	what work does your father do?
tere oci, we? tere oci, mini gucu bi.	who is he? he is my friend.
ere oci, we i bithe bi?	whose book is this?
ere oci, sini bithe bio?	is that your book?
ere oci, ai jaka?	what is this?
suwe ai erinde genembi?	when are you going?
i ya erin de isinjimbi?	when does he arrive?
emu aniya de udu inenggi bi?	how many days are there in a year?
jihengge absi sain!	how good that he came!
si absi mentuhun!	how stupid you are!

3. Transcribe into Manchu script and translate into English: a) *uyun cooha šolo baiha*; b) *cooha i hafan ambula jilidaha*; c) *mini jungken udan oho*; d) *hafirabufi emu tokso de dosifi emu morin udame gaiha*; e) *funcehe nadan cooha juleri amala isiname jihe*; f) *tuwai sejen erin be jurcehe*; g) *sukdujen umai efuhehekūbi.*

4. Translate into Manchu: a) by early morning drill the next day the soldiers had not arrived; b) it was already after seven o'clock when one soldier arrived; c) on the way the car broke down; d) the horse also died; e) just as the officer was doubting the soldiers' explanation (words); f) the last soldier arrived; g) there were too many dead horses (lying) in the road.

Reading Selection D–2

Mr. Mouse moves

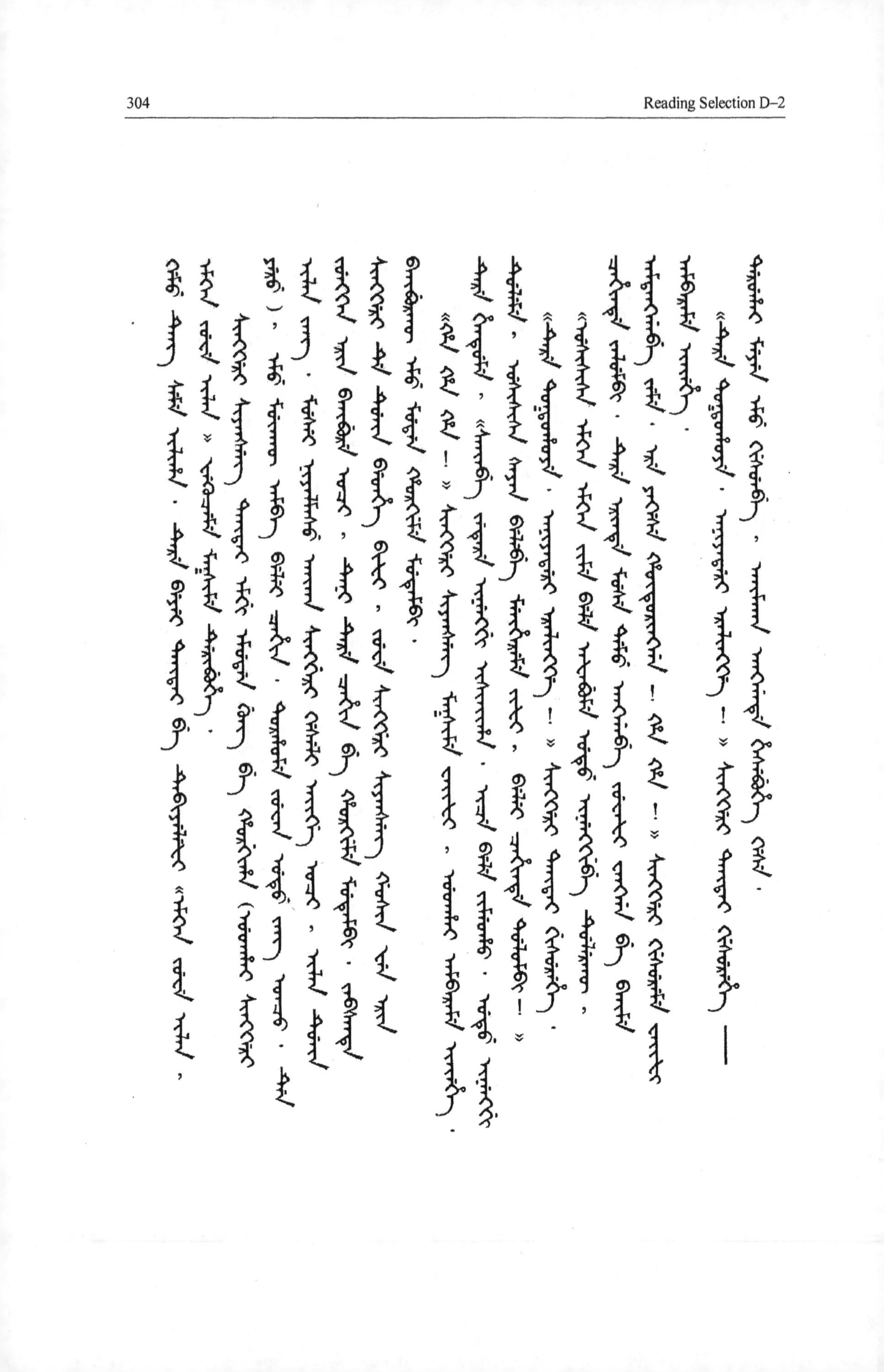

[illegible]

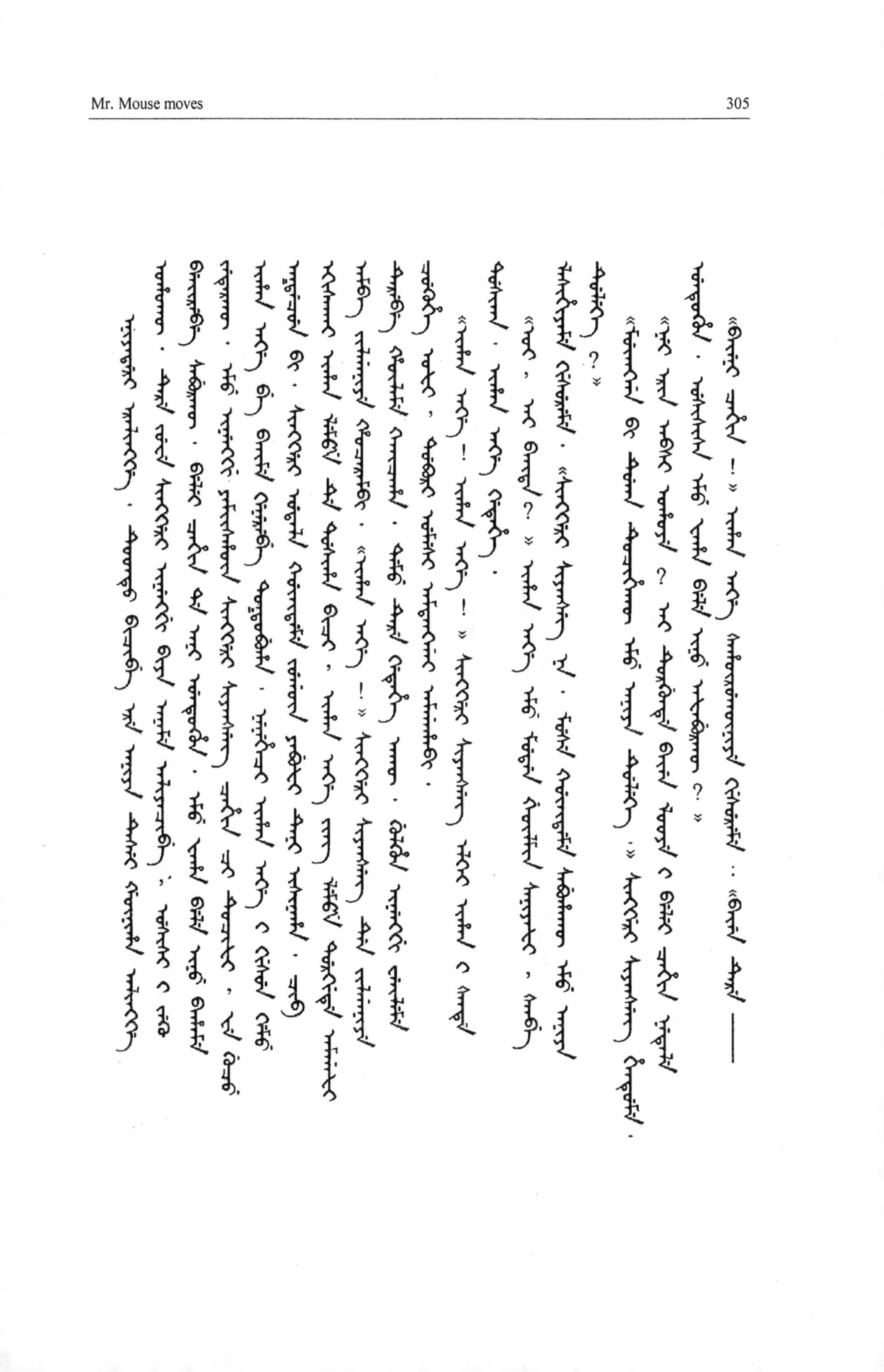

[illegible]

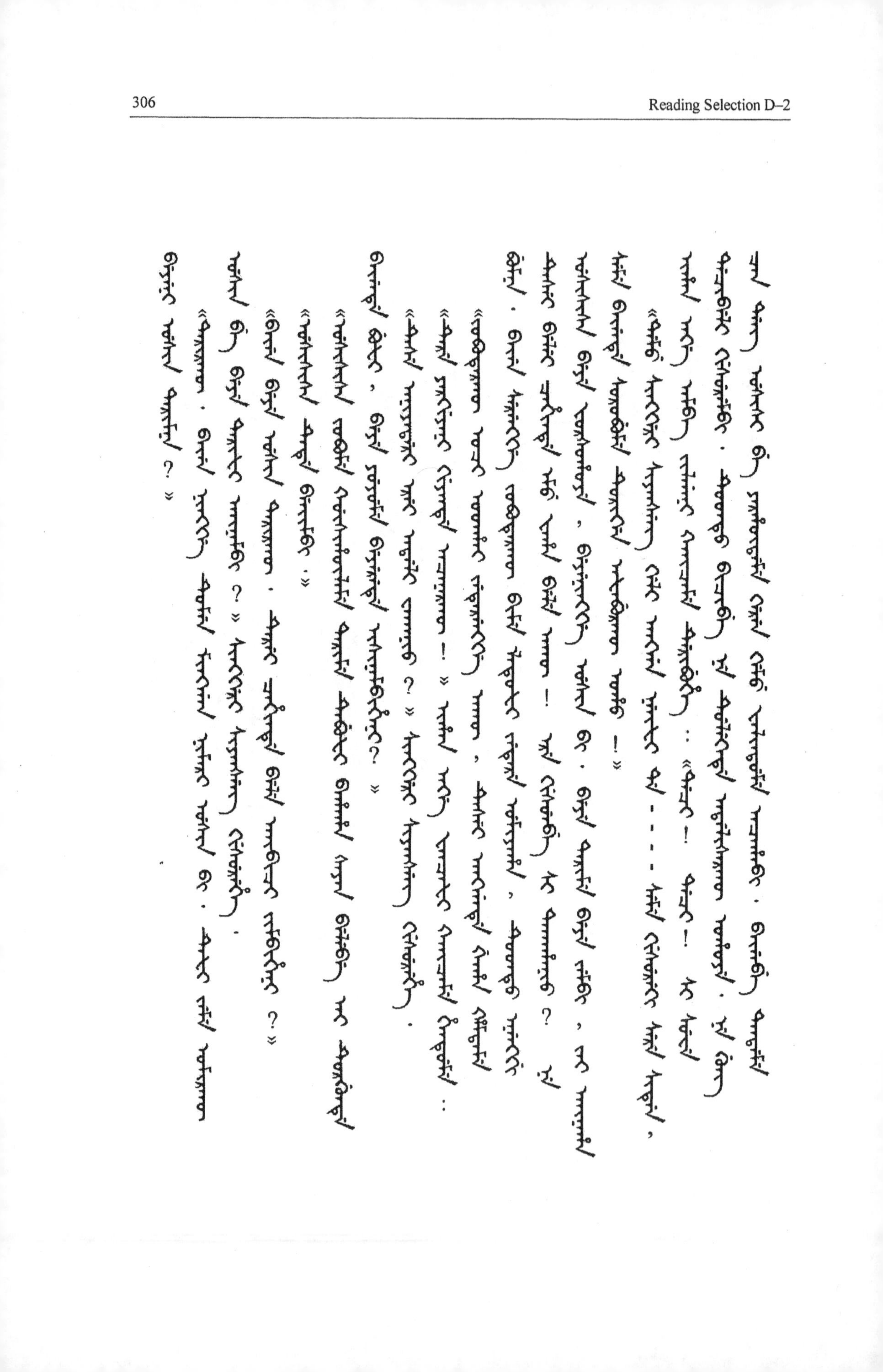

[illegible]

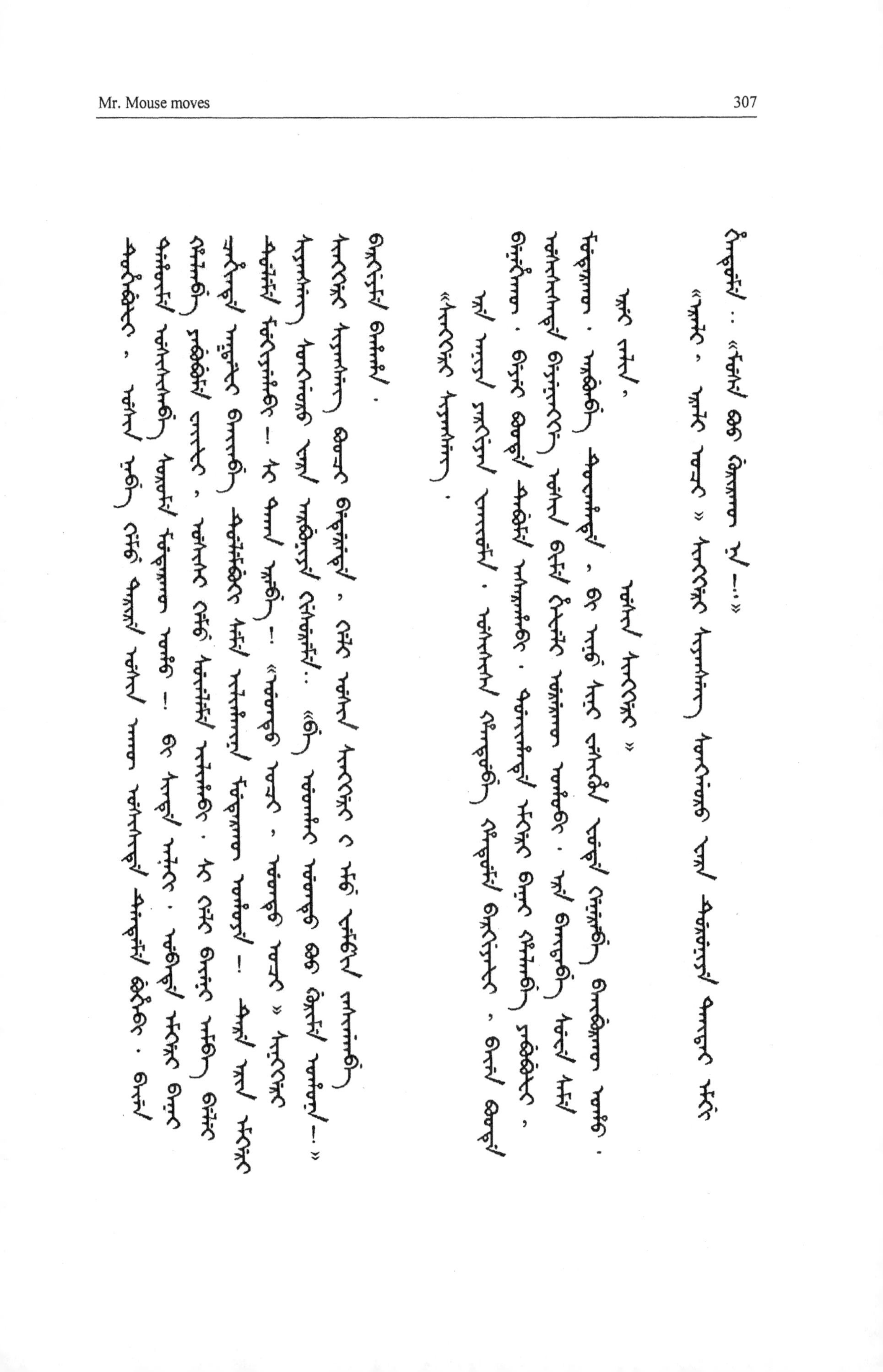

[illegible]

[illegible]

[illegible]

Transliteration

(303) ***Singgeri boo gurimbi***

emu inenggi singgeri siyanšeng emu fempin jasigan bargiyame bahaha.[1] *cohome*[2] *terei goro bai niyamangga usin singgeri i buhe jasigan inu. jasigan dolo gisurehengge*[3]

«singgeri siyanšeng:

bi sinde emu sain mejige alaki. usin dorgi handu wacihiyame urehebi, udu inenggi duleme, usisisa handu be bargiyafi, bisirele[4] *šayan belebe bajeni calude benjimbi. sinde urgulembi, hūturingge*[5] *singgeri siyanšeng, sini siyanbe*[6] *jeme omire inenggi emgeri isinjiha!*

sinde damu jasirengge: jobotengge usisisa handu be hadume bargiyaha amala, uthai tese yuyure beyerengge yasai juleri isinjimbi. tere erinde mini jemengge inu akū ome oho.[7] *ere mini aniyadari dulembun inu. ne bi suweni wesihun fude genefi udu inenggi banjimseme belhemahabi,*[8] *kemuni majige bele juwen gaifi marimbi.*

erei jalin,

elhebe baiha,[9]

sini niyamangga usin singgeri.»

singgeri siyanšeng jasiganbe tuwame wajifi, urgunjeme bayalarade[10] *šalu funiyehe*

(304) *gemu teng seme iliha. tere beyei taitai be tebiyelefi «emken juwe ilan, emken juwe ilan» fekuceme maksime deribuhe.*

singgeri siyanšeng taitai emgi[11] *emudan gung be horgiha (uthai singgeri yeru), emu mujakū amba belei cahin, torhome juwan udu jang onco. den ilan jang. musei niyalmasu*[12] *aika singgeri geseli ajige oci, ilan duin jungken erin baibure oci, teni tere cahin be horgime mutembi. jabšante*[13] *singgeri de duin bethe bifi, juwe singgeri siyanšeng gosin*[14] *fen erin baiburkū emu mudan horgime mutembi.*

«ha ha ha!» singgeri siyanšeng maksime wajifi, uthai ambarame injehe. tere hendume,[15] *«sainbe jetere inenggi isinjiha. ice bele jimeoho.*[16] *udu inenggi duleme, usisisa šayan belebe meihereme jifi, belei cahinde dolombi!»*

«tere toktohoye,[17] *aniyadari eralingge!» singgeri taitai gisurehe.*

«usisisa emken emken jime bele afabume udu inenggibe dulerkū, cahinde jalumbi, tere erinde muse damu anggabe juwafi wangga be baime amtanggabe jeme, ere yagese hūturingga![5] *ha ha!» singgeri gisureme wajifi ambarame injehe.*

«tere toktohoye, aniyadari eralingge!» singgeri taitai gisurehe—daruhai meyen emu gisunbe, aimaka anggade hesebuhe gese.[18]

(305) *aniyadari eralingge. tuttu bicibe ere aniya tesei gūniha alingge ohokū.*[19] *tere juwe singgeri inenggi biya aname aliyacibe, usisi i jeku benjirebe saburkū. belei cahin*

da ani untuhun. emu faha bele inu bahame jeterkū.[20] *emu inenggi yamjishūn singgeri siyanšeng cahin ci tucifi, fe gucu ihan age be baime generebe toktobuha. neneheci ihan age i gisun gemu akdacun bi. singggeri utala gūidame* [21] *jugūn yabufi teni isinaha. cib ekisakai ihan lempen de dosiha* [22] *bici, ihan age jing lempen dorgide amgafi amba jilganiye* [23] *hocarambi. «ihan age!» singgeri siyanšeng den jilganiye* [23] *terebe hūlame kaicaha. damu tere getehe akū. gulhun inenggi weileme cukuhe ofi, dobori umesi amtanggai amgahabi.*

«ihan age! ihan age!» singgeri siyanšeng elkei ihan i šande dosika.[22] *ihan age getehe. «oi, ai baita?» ihan age emu mudan gūlmin saniyafi,*[24] *šanbe lasihiyame gisureme.*[15] *«singgeri siyanšeng na.*[25] *muse gūidame* [21] *sabuhakū emu aniya duleke?»*[26] *«mujangga bi duka tucihekū emu aniya duleke.» singgeri siyanšeng hendume.*[15]

«nei erin absi ohoye? ai turgunde bajen looye i belei cahin netele untuhun. usisisa emu faha bele inu afaburkū?»

«bajeni cahin!» ihan age šahūrukūniye [23] *gisureme:*[15] *«bajen tere—*

(306) *beyeni usin tarimna?»*[27]

«tarirkū. bajen ningge [28] *tumen minggan nimari usin bi. tefi jeme omirkū usin be beye tarifi ainambi?* [29]*» singgeri siyanšeng gisurehe.*

«bajen beye usin tarirkū. terei cahinde bele aibici jimbiheni?»

«usisisa tede benjimbi.»

«usisisa jobome gūsihūlame tarime tebufi bahaha [1] *šayan belebe ai turgunde bajende bufi, beye yuyume beyerede isinambiheni?»*[30]

«tese aniyadari erei adali wakanio?» singgeri siyanšeng gisurehe.

«tere yargiyani giyande acanarkū!» ihan age fancafi kaicame hendume.[15]

«joboterkū oci uthai jeterengge akū, tesei anggade gaha hamtame bumna.[31] *bajen serengge* [32] *joboterkū bime latufi jetere umiyaha, tuttu enenggi tesei belei cahinde emu faha bele akū! ere gisunbe si takahanio? ne usisisa beye foršohoye, beyeningge usin bi. beye tarime beye jembi, jai ainaha seme bajende sorobume turigen afaburkū oho!»*[9]

«damu singgeri siyanšeng geli angga neifi da...seme gisureki sere siden,[33] *ihan age amba jilgani kaicame deribuhe: «daci! daci! si suwe dacibeli* [34] *gisurembi. tuttu bicibe ne dulekede adališarkū ohoye.*[17] *ne gung can dang usisisi be yarhūdame geren gemu falindume acahabi. bajenbe tandame*

(307) *tuhebufi, usin nabe gemu tarire usin akū usiside dendeme buhebi. bajen dahūme usisisabe sorome muterkū oho! bi sinde alaki. ubade emgeri banai halanbe yabubume wajifi, usisi gemu sujeleme* [35] *ilihabi. si geli bajeni amba belei cahinde akdafi banjinbe dulembuki seme ilihaina muterkū ohoye!* [36] *tere erin emgeri duleme mukiyehabi!* [37] *si taka erebe!»*[38] *«uttu oci, uttu oci» singgeri siyanšeng songgoro fara arbuniye gisureme:*[15] *«be uthai uttu boo gurime ohona!» singgeri siyanšeng booci* [39] *bedererede, geli usin singgeri i emu fempin jasiganbe bargiyame bahaha.*[1]

«singgeri siyanšeng:

ere aniya yargiyan faijuma. usisisa handube hadume bargiyafi, bajen boode benehekū. beyei boode tebume asarahabi. donjihade [40] *emgeri banai halanbe yabubufi, usisisade beyeningge usin bime hefeli urerkū* [41] *ohobi. ere baitabe suwe same muterkū. arbunbe tuwahade,*[40] *bi inu sini wesihun fude generebe baiburkū oho.*

erei jalin,

usin singgeri»

«erali, erali oci» singgeri siyanšeng songgoro fara duruniye taitai emgi hendume:[15] *«muse boo gurirkū na!»*

(308) *eiterecibe singgeri boo gurime ohobi. terei absi gurirebe daljilarkū. šošofi gisureci, enteheme nenehei alingge suitame* [42] *gūbadara, latufi jere* [43] *erin emgeri mukiyefi—tere enteheme enteheme dahūrkū.*

Notes

1. *emu fempin jasigan bargiyame bahaha*: 'he received a letter'. The dictionary perfective participle of *bahambi* is *baha*, not *bahaha*. However, one does see the latter form occasionally. The original meaning of *fempi* or *fempin* is 'sealing tape' or 'cover', but in this sentence the word *fempin* reflects the Chinese use of classifiers or measuring words, such as *feng* 封, as in *i feng xin* 一封信 'a letter' or 'one letter'. Though Manchu does have measuring words, they are less common than in Chinese. Example: *duin morin* 'four horses', *tanggū cooha* 'one hundred soldiers'.

2. *cohome*: lit. 'especially, on purpose'. Here the function is like Chinese *jiushi* 就是, translatable simply as 'it was' or 'it happened to be'.

3. *jasigan dolo gisurehengge*: lit. 'that which one said in the letter (was as follows)'. This use of the *gisurengge* compares to the opening of memorials with *wesimburengge*. However, Sibe makes extensive use of the nominalizing function of *-ngge* to represent the Chinese *de* 的 construction. Example: *si atanggi jihengge*? Chin. *ni shi shemme shihou laide* 你是什麼時候來的? See Review 1.

4. *bisirele belebe benjimbi*: 'they will bring all the rice there is'. The imperfective or perfective participle plus *-le* (and possibly *-la*) creates an adjective which denotes everything or everybody there is. See Review 2. Although both *-la* and *-le* occur, the suffix *-le* derives from *ele* 'all, whoever' and it is possible that invariable *-le* is the only grammatically correct form.

5. ***hūturingge*****:** The Manchu word is *hūturingga* 'fortunate'. Spoken Sibe does not distinguish between the syllables *-ngga*, *-ngge*, and *-nggū*, thereby lumping the three spellings into one. Such pronunciation accounts for the spelling of *hūturingge* instead of *hūturingga*. Note that the second occurrence of the word is spelled *hūturingga*.

6. ***siyanbe*****:** spoken Sibe for *sainbe* 'good things'.

7. ***akū ome oho*****:** 'it has become nonexistent, there is no more'. The verb forms *-me oho* and *-me ohobi*, or the negative form *-rkū oho* are very common in Sibe. Examples: *ice bele jime oho* 'they are about to bring the new grain'; *singgeri boo gurime ohobi* 'Mr. Mouse is about to move'; *turigen be bajen de afaburkū oho* 'they will no longer turn in rent to the landlords'; *duleke de adališarkū oho* 'it is no longer as in the past'. This type of *oho* parallels the Chinese word *le* 了 with the meaning 'to be about to' or in a negative sentence 'is no longer' or 'no more'.

8. ***banjimseme belhemahabi*****:** 'I am making preparations to stay with you'. The endings *-maha* or *-mahabi* are imperfective progressive forms. They rarely, if ever, occur in documentary Manchu, but are frequent in Sibe. See Review 3. The form *banjimseme* is a colloquial Sibe form of *banjiki seme* 'I want to stay' or 'saying let me stay'.

9. ***erei jalin elhebe baiha*****:** lit. '(having written) for this reason I wish you peace'. In the memorial section we encountered *elhebe baimbi* 'to enquire after a person' (Chin. *qing an* 請安). The expression also concludes ordinary Sibe letters, similar to 'yours sincerely' or 'with best wishes'.

10. ***bayalarade šalu funiyehe...iliha*****:** 'his whiskers bristled with happiness'. Rather than translating *de* with 'when', the *de* here is better understood as a case marker following the nominalized verb *bayalara*, giving it an instrumental meaning rather than a temporal one. For case marker *de*, see Reading Selection A–6, Review 3.

11. ***taitai emgi*:** Example of omission of the genitive case marker. This selection contains various other examples of such omissions, most noticeably with directionals: *jasigan dolo* 'in the letter', *usin dorgi* 'in the field'.

12. ***niyalmasu*:** 'human beings'. Contemporary Sibe uses *-su* to form nouns, often abstract nouns. Examples: *takasu* 'knowledge' from *takambi* 'to know'; *tucirsu* 'product' from *tucimbi* 'to come out'.

13. ***jabšante*:** *jabšande* 'fortunately'.

14. ***gosin*:** *gūsin* 'thirty'.

15. ***hendume*:** This *-me* converb stands for the *-mbi* finite verb. Spoken Sibe does not sound the letter *b* in *-mbi*, pronouncing the verb ending *-mbi* as *-me* or *-mi*. The pronunciation collapses the finite verb form *-mbi* and the converb ending *-me* into one. Other examples in this piece: *hendume*, *tarime*, *gisureme*.

16. ***jimeoho*:** *jime oho*. See Note 7 above.

17. ***ere toktohoye*:** 'that's so for sure'. The sentence particle *ye* adds emphasis, surprise or certainty. It can also function as a question particle. See Review 4.

18. ***daruhai meyen emu gisun be, aimaka anggade hesebuhe gese*:** 'as for this frequent phrase, it was as if she commanded it by saying so'. The expression *aimaka...gese* parallels the Chinese use of *haoxiang...yiyang* 好像… 一樣 'it seems like'.

Note the sequence in *daruhai meyen emu gisun*. The word *meyen* 'phrase' could serve as a measuring word as *emu meyen gisun*. However, in this case *meyen* precedes *emu*, making *daruhai meyen* a nominal phrase which, omitting genitive *i*, qualifies *gisun*. Compare *wesimbuhe emu baita* 'a matter which someone memorialized' or *gūidame sabuhakū emu aniya* in Note 26 below.

19. ***gūniha alingge ohokū*:** 'it was not as they had thought'. The word *ohokū* should be *ohakū*, negative perfective participle of *ombi* 'to be, to become'. Sibe *alingge* stands for SM *adalingga* 'similar, like'.

20. *bahame jeterkū*: 'they did not get to eat (a single kernel of grain)'. The construction appears to be a modern equivalent of SM *bahafi jeterakū* 'could not eat'. For that construction, see Reading Selection A–4, Review 1.

21. *utala gūidame jugūn yabufi*: 'having walked for a very long time'. In SM the word is *goidame*, not *gūidame*. Usually *utala* occurs before a noun, as in *utala aniya* 'so many years'.

22. *dosiha*: *dosika*. Perfective participle of *dosimbi* 'to enter'. Both versions occur in this story.

23. *amba jilganiye*: 'in a loud voice'. Besides the regular genitive/instrumental case markers *i* and *-ni*, Sibe also uses *-iye*, especially to create adverbial expressions. Examples: *songgoro fara duruniye* or *songgoro fara arbuniye* 'weeping bitterly' Also: *šahūrukūniye gisureme* 'said in a rather cold manner'.

24. *gūlmin saniyafi*: *golmin saniyafi*. The adverbial use, without as much as an adverbial genitive *i*, probably reflects the Chinese word *shenchang* 伸長 'to stretch'. SM generally uses *golmin* 'long' as an adjective.

25. *na*: The Sibe sentence particle *na* conveys emphasis, surprise, or certainty. Like *ye*, *na* can also function as a question particle. See Review 4.

26. *muse gūidame sabuhakū emu aniya duleke*: 'a year (during) which we haven't seen each other for a long time has passed'. The phrase *muse gūidame sabuhakū* qualifies *emu aniya*. Compare Note 18.

27. *beyeni usin tarimna*: 'do they till their own land?' The suffix *-mna* attached to a verb stem forms a question. Examples: *si genemna*? 'are you going?', *si tacikū de genere be cihalamna?* 'do you like going to school?'

28. *bajen ningge tumen minggan nimari bi*: 'as for the landlords, they have thousands of acres of land'. Note that there is no *de* with *bi* for 'to have'. The word *ningge* has several functions. 1) Serve as topic marker, similar to *oci*: *bajen ningge tumen minggan usin bi* 'as for landlords, they have a lot of land'. 2) Convey a possessive meaning: *usin usisiningge* 'the land is the farmers' (land); *beyeningge usin* 'land of their own'. 3) Refer back to the subject or noun: *sini ere deretu moo ningge* 'this desk of yours is a wooden one'. 4) Nominalize words, such as adjectives or numerals: *muheliyen ningge* 'the round one'. See Review 5.

29. ***tefi jeme omirkū usin be beye tarifi ainambi*****:** 'why would they live and work the land themselves suffering hunger and thirst?' The phrase *jeme omirkū* modifies *tarifi*, with the negative of *omirkū* extending to *jeme*. The verb *ainambi* 'why do something', often combines with the subordinative converb *-fi*. Example: *si urunakū bahambi. temšefi ainambi*? 'you will definitely get it. Why fight over it'?

30. ***ai turgunde beye yuyume beyerede isinambiheni*****:** 'why would they face cold and hunger?' Most questions with particle *ni*—usually translated into Chinese with *ma* 嗎 and *ni* 呢 —require a separate question word. However, *ni* may also occur with the meaning 'what about', in which case there is no need for a question word. Example: *sini age bithe be hūlamahabi. sini deo ni?* 'your older brother is studying. What about your younger brother'? See Review 6.

31. ***tesei anggade gaha hamtame bumna*****:** 'the ravens will defecate into their mouths'. Since this sentence is not a question, the *-mna* suffix as an interrogative suffix is inappropriate (see Note 27 above). Instead, *bumna* appears to be a contraction of *bumbi* with particle *na* for emphasis .

32. ***bajen serengge*****:** 'as for the landlords' or 'the so-called landlords'. As a topic marker, *serengge* follows the subject, which may be a word or a phrase. Example: *tulergi gurun i gisun be tacimbi serengge ja waka* 'learning a foreign language is not easy'.

33. ***«damu singgeri siyanšeng geli angga neifi da...seme gisureki sere siden*****:** 'when Mr. Mouse again opened his mouth wanting to say, "former..."'. It seems that the opening quotation mark is misplaced and the closing mark is missing. The sentence should read: *damu singgeri siyanšeng geli anga neifi "da..." seme....* The response from the ox tells us that the interrupted word *da...* was going to be *daci* 'formerly'.

34. ***si suwe dacibeli gisurembi*****:** 'you always say "formerly, formerly..."'. The Sibe word *beli* is a combination of the accusative case marker *be* and *li* 'only'. Other examples with *li*: *si li gene*! 'you go (alone)'; *ilan li niyalma jihebi* 'only three people came'; *juwali niyalma* 'only ten people'. The word *suwe* stands for *šuwe* 'always, very'.

35. ***usisi gemu sujeleme ilihabi*:** 'all the peasants are (rejoicing)'. Converb *-me* plus *ilihabi* is an imperfective progressive form, which is used in the same way as *-mahabi*. Compare Note 8 and Review 2. The word *sujeleme*, which is not listed in dictionaries, stands for Manchu *sebjelembi* 'to rejoice'.

36. ***ilihaina muterkū ohoye*:** 'from now on that is no longer impossible'. The word *ilihaina* consists of *ilihai* 'immediately' and *na*, a sentence particle of emphasis.

37. ***mukiyehabi*:** *mukiyehebi* 'it has expired'.

38. ***si taka erebe*:** 'you'd better know this'. This subject-verb-object structure is unusual. However, since this is direct speech, it is possible that *erebe* may have been said somewhat as an afterthought.

39. ***booci bederembi*:** 'to return home'. The case marker *ci* has two directional meanings. When referring to a point of departure it compares to *deri* 'from'; when referring to the direction of the destination it compares to *baru* 'toward'. See Review 7 below.

40. ***donjihade*:** 'people say, I have heard'. Another common Sibe expression is *arbun be tuwahade* 'it appears'. These phrases correspond to documentary Manchu *donjihaci...sembi*, or *tuwaci...sembi*, respectively.

41. ***urerkū*:** *ururkū* 'is not hungry'.

42. ***suitame*:** The dictionary meaning of *suitame* is 'to pour water, to splash'. In spoken Sibe *suitambi* stands for *suilambi* 'to work hard, to suffer hardship'.

43. ***jere*:** *jetere*. Imperfective participle of *jembi* 'to eat'.

Review

1. *-ngge* Common nominalization of verbs in Sibe

si atanggi jihengge?	when did you come?
bithe be aibide sindahangge?	where did you put the book?
si wei emgi jihengge?	with whom did you come?
si yabade bihengge?	where were you?
gairengge labdu, burengge komso	he took a lot and gave little
tere sinde buhengge ai?	what did he give you?

2. Verb + *-le* 'all (there is)'

bisirele bele be benjimbi	they will bring all the grain there is
ucarahale (*ucarahala*) *niyalma*	all the people I have met
dulekele ba	all the places they have passed through
sabuhala jaka	all the things we have seen
donjihale (*donjihala*) *mejige*	all the things one has heard
isinahale (*isinahala*) *ba*	all the places one has been to

3. Verb Stem + *-mahabi* and *-me ilihabi* Progressive tense

aga damahabi	it is raining
aga dame ilihabi	it is raining
buda jemahabi	I am eating
buda jeme ilihabi	I am eating
bi jasigan be tuwame ilihabi	I am just reading a letter
bi jasigan be tuwamahabi	I am just reading a letter

4. *ye* and *na* Particles/suffixes for emphasis and questions

tere toktohoye!	that is for sure!
usisisa beye foršohoye!	the peasants have "turned over"
dulekede adališarkū ohoye!	it is no longer as it was in the past
singgeri siyanšeng na!	Mr. Mouse!
be boo gurime ohona!	we will move!
musei boo gurirkū na!	we will not move!
absi mangga na!	how difficult!
tere ainaha bihe ye?	how was it?

nei erin absi ohoye?	what's been happening these days?
sini ama boode bina?	is your father home?
yargiyan uttu na?	is it really true?

5. Various functions of *ningge, -ningge*

bajen ningge tumen nimari usin bi	as for the landlords, they have a lot of land
ai boco ningge sain be sarkū	I don't know which color would be good
etuhun ningge sonjo	select the strong ones
ambaningge jakūn se	the older one is eight years old
usin usisiningge	the land is the farmers' (land)
tere morin juwe ejen i ningge	this horse belongs to two owners

6. Question particle *ni*

ere ai turgun ni?	what is the reason?
udu niyalma bini?	how many people are there?
sini beye ainu generkū ni?	why don't you go?
we ini mama be ujimbini?	who will take care of his grandmother?
tere baita be sara sarkū ni?	do you not know this matter?
sini ama ni?	how about your father?

7. *ci* and *deri* versus *ci* and *baru*

tere hecen ci jihe	he came from the city
tere hecen deri jihe	he came from the city
bi tacikū i baru genembi	I am going to school
bi tacikū ci genembi	I am going to school
si yabaci genembi?	where are you going?
niohe alin ci feksimbi	the wolf is running towards the mountain
mini boo ubaci goro akū	my home is not far from here
Beijing ci booci marifi uthai nimehe	after she returned home from Beijing, she fell ill

8. Write in Manchu script and translate into English: a) *goro bai niyamangga usin singgeri i buhe jasigan inu*; b) *usin dorgi handu wacihiyame urehebi*; c) *jeme omire inenggi emgeri isinjiha*; d) *singgeri siyanšeng taitai emgi maksime deribuhe*; e) *gūsin fen erin baiburkū*; f) *udu inenggi duleme usisisa jifi belei cahinde dolombi*; g) *usisi i* *jeku benjirebe saburkū*; h) *fe gucu ihan age be baime generebe toktobuha*; i) *ihan amgafi amba jilganiye hūwacarambi*; j) *singgeri elkei ihan i šande dosika*; k) *terei cahinde bele aibici jimbiheni?* l) *joboterkū oci uthai jeterengge akū*; m) *ne ususisa beye foršohoye, beyeningge usin bi*; n) *bajenbe tantame tuhebuhe*; o) *singgeri booci bederede, geli usin singgeri i emu fempin jasiganbe bargiyame bahaha*; p) *bi inu sini wesihun fude generebe baiburkū oho.*

9. Translate into Manchu: a) let me report some good news to you; b) the peasants will bring all the rice they have to the landlord's granary; c) this is my experience every year; d) I am preparing to spend a few days in your house and borrow some grain to take home with me; e) his whiskers bristled with joy; f) if we humans were as small as mice we could circle that bin in less than three hours; g) but this year it wasn't as they had thought; h) they did not get to eat a single grain of corn; i) Brother Ox had just fallen asleep in his shed; j) because he had worked hard all day he was sleeping very soundly (sweetly); k) the landlords don't work the land themselves; l) isn't it that way every year? m) the Communist Party is leading the peasants and everybody has united in solidarity; n) this year is really strange; o) I hear that land reform has already been carried out; p) the days of eating by depending on others are already a thing of the past.

Part III

Study Aids

Historical background: The Qing Dzungar campaigns

At about the same time the Manchus were establishing their new state in Manchuria in the early seventeenth century, the Western Mongols began expanding their power in Western Mongolia and Dzungaria.

At this period both the Eastern and Western Mongols consisted of several subgroups. The Western Mongols, also called Oirats or Eleuths (Ölöts), belonged to four groups: the Choros, Derbets, Khoshots, and Torghuts. Though technically the term Dzungars refers only to the Choros, the most powerful group within the confederation, it is generally used to refer to the confederation collectively. The Eastern Mongols, consisting of the Khalkas in the north and the Chahar Mongols in the southern part of Inner Mongolia, divided into several territorial units: The Tushetu Khan occupied northern Mongolia, with Urga as its center; the Zasagtu Khan had his base in western Mongolia; and the Setsen Khan was leading the eastern Khalka. In 1725 another khanate, the Sain Noyan Khanate, was carved out of the territory of the Tushetu Khan.

Important in the Manchus' political considerations was the Tibetan-Mongol relationship. Though a few Mongols had abandoned shamanism in favor of Tibetan Buddhism during the early Ming or even the Yuan dynasty, a major change came about when Altan Khan (1507–1582), along with others among the Eastern Mongol elite, converted to Buddhism during the latter sixteenth century. Altan Khan may have done so for spiritual reasons, but the conversion had obvious political implications. It gave the Tibetan church religious authority over the Mongols and created a close relationship between the political powers in Tibet and Mongolia. Collaboration between Altan Khan and a leading Tibetan *lama* from the Yellow Sect resulted in a mutual bestowal of titles. The Tibetan *lama* received from Altan Khan the title of Dalai Lama along with Mongol support in his struggle against the rival Red Sect. In return, the Dalai Lama proclaimed Altan Khan to be a reincarnation of Khubilai Khan. Bestowal of titles and political support remained hallmarks of the Mongol-Tibetan relationship for some time.

Kharakhula (d. 1635) was the first Dzungar chief who, armed with a title from the Dalai Lama for helping the Yellow Sect in Tibet, bolstered his leadership and expanded Dzungar power by conquering lands of other Mongol tribes in Western Mongolia. After his death, the Khoshots, who under their leader Gushri Khan (d. 1656) had moved south to the Kokonor region, provided Dzungar support for the Yellow Sect and for a while were the actual rulers of Tibet.

Kharakhula's son continued his father's quest for building a broad Mongol confederation, but internal dissension limited his success. A 1640 meeting held to create unity between Eastern and Western Mongols failed to bring an agreement. The murder of Kharakhula's grandson Sengge by his ambitious older brothers in 1670 provided an opportunity for

Galdan, another of Sengge's siblings, to assume the leadership position and to pursue a vigorous expansionist policy. When young, Galdan had been recognized as an incarnation of a member of an important Tibetan lineage and he had spent over ten years in Tibet studying first under the Panchen Lama and then directly under the Dalai Lama.

Soon after becoming the new Dzungar leader and receiving the Dalai Lama's blessing in the form of a title, Galdan defeated the Khoshots and annexed their territory (1677). His next move, again with encouragement from Tibet, was into Eastern Turkestan. Political power there had shifted from the earlier Chaghadai *khan*s, descendants of Chinggis Khan, to the White Mountain *khoja*s (Aqtaghlik, also Afaqiyya) and Black Mountain *khoja*s (Qarataghlik, also Ishaqiyya), two lines of Islamic leaders, both of whom traced their descent to Mohammad. When the Black Mountain *khoja* forced the White Mountain *khoja* to flee, the latter appealed to the Dalai Lama, who, in turn, urged Galdan to intervene. Galdan invaded and, with the aid of the White Mountain Khoja Afaq, conquered Kashgar, Yarkand, Hami, and Turfan, the main towns in the Tarim Basin (1679). By making Khoja Afaq his governor, Galdan shifted political power from Yarkand (the old seat of the Chaghadai *khan*s and the Black Mountain *khoja*s) to Kashgar and to the White Mountain *khoja*s.

Hoping to unify all Mongols under his rule, Galdan then sought to incorporate the Khalka *khan*s within his realm. Taking advantage of a dispute between two Khalka *khan*s he intervened in Khalka affairs. He disregarded diplomatic efforts by the Kangxi emperor to solve this intra-Khalka dispute peacefully and invaded Khalka territory in 1688. This drove over a hundred thousand Khalka Mongols into China where they sought refuge and asked for assistance.

Initially China rejected this Khalka request for assistance. The Qing had long taken note of Galdan's growing power and they realized that the Dalai Lamas gave the Dzungar leaders an aura of legitimacy among the adherents of Lamaist Buddhism. Earlier Qing forces had been preoccupied with the War of the Three Feudatories (1673–1681) in southern China, but after southern China was firmly under Manchu control, the emperor, fearing a possible alliance between Galdan and the Russians, was eager to secure Russian neutrality before engaging in a war against Galdan. The Russians had been trading with the Dzungars for some time, but at this time had little desire to ally themselves with Galdan and provoke China into denying them trade or attack their settlements in the Amur region. Therefore both countries found it to their advantage to reach an agreement through the Treaty of Nerchinsk (1689).

With Russian neutrality secured, the Qing court decided to use military action to thwart Galdan's demand that the Khalka Tushetu Khan surrender to the Western Mongols. The first encounter between the Qing and the Dzungar armies occurred in 1690 at the Battle of Ulan Butun. Even though the outcome was not decisive, it was enough to make the

Khalkas reaffirm their allegiance to the Qing. Some Dzungar groups also defected and submitted to the Manchus. Having lost one half of his forces, Galdan retreated to the Kobdo region but a serious famine in western Mongolia drove him to undertake another offensive against the Khalkha in 1695. This time the emperor personally set out against Galdan, mobilizing an army of eighty thousand men, divided into three routes (the vanguard under Fiyanggū). While away on the expedition, the emperor had his second son and designated heir apparent In Ceng (Chin. Yin-reng; 1674–1728) take care of matters in the capital.

In June 1696 the Qing defeated Galdan at Jao Modo, near the town of Urga. The defeat led to further disunity and defections among the Dzungars' subjects. Tsewang Raptan (1643–1727), Galdan's nephew, also broke with his uncle and occupied a large part of western Mongolia. Meanwhile the oasis towns of the Tarim basin tried to reassert their independence. After Galdan died in 1697, some Dzungars joined Tsewang Raptan, others joined other leaders, and others again, among them Danjila, Galdan's nephew, surrendered to the Qing.

Under Tsewang Raptan's leadership the Dzungars were primarily engaged in territorial conflicts with the Kazakhs, though they also fought the Chinese at Turfan. In 1731 a Manchu-Chinese military force suffered defeat at the hands of Galdan Tsereng, Tsewang's successor. However, unable to exploit their victory without other allies, the Dzungars entered a temporary truce with the Qing, agreeing to stay west of the Altai Mountains and not to intervene along the Chinese border.

Wedged between an expanding Russia and the Chinese empire, there now was less opportunity for Dzungar expansion. Moreover, in spite of the possibility of providing a religious bond, Tibetan Buddhism did not unify the Mongols. Neither the Dalai Lama nor the Mongol's indigenous religious authority in the person of the Jebtsundamba Khutuktu could prevent succession crises and political discord which eventually enabled the Manchus to successfully and permanently eliminate the Mongol threat to the Qing dynasty.

By 1750, dissension within the Dzungar central authority in Inner Asia caused more Mongol defections to the Qing. Among them was Amursana, a leader of the Khoits, a Western Mongol tribe that had earlier been part of the Dzungar confederation. Amursana joined the Qing army in 1754 on the promise that he would receive imperial recognition as ruler of the Khoits. Taking advantage of the unrest among the Western Mongols, the Manchus sent an expeditionary force, commanded by Bandi, to the Ili region and, with the help of Amursana, easily defeated the Dzungars. However, following their victory in 1755, the Manchus withdrew their main army leaving only a small garrison in Ili. Moreover, they did so without fulfilling Amursana's expectation for an appropriate award. Thus a dissatisfied Amursana rebelled and nearly annihilated the Qing forces who had remained behind. Bandi and his general-in-chief were surrounded in their garrison at Ili and committed suicide. Their men were killed. Subsequently another Qing expedition routed the Western Mongols for good and slaughtered most of them. In the extermination of the Dzungars the Qing campaign benefited from a smallpox epidemic amongst the Dzungars, a disease which eventually also killed Amursana, who had fled to Siberia after his defeat.

When the Qing army defeated the Dzungars in Ili, they freed two White Mountain *khoja* brothers, Hojijan (Khozi Khan) and Buranidun (Burhan-al-Din) who had been held captive by the Dzungars.[1] The two brothers returned to their home bases in Kashgar and Yarkand, recaptured the oasis towns from the Black Mountain *khoja*s, but then declared their independence, both from the Dzungars and the Manchus. Since the *khoja*s had earlier been given their freedom by the Manchus, the Manchus resented this hostile act. Therefore, as soon as Ili was secured, the Qing army turned its attention southward.

The subsequent campaigns over the control of the oasis towns in the Tarim basin form the setting for the biographies in Reading Selections A–2 through A–6. Jaohūi's forces conquered Yarkand and Kashgar, the two main strongholds of the Tarim basin, but only after the *khoja*s' forces nearly starved the Qing army during a three-month long siege near Yarkand. When the imperial force finally overcame the Muslim leaders' opposition, Hojijan and Buranidun fled to Badakshan, west of Kashgar, where that area's sultan executed them. Their heads were sent back to the imperial army.

The annexation of Ili and Kashgaria marked the final elimination of the nomad threat to China's sedentary people. Following the defeat of the Western Mongols, even the Kazakhs and the Kirghiz to the west of Ili recognized the suzerainty of China. The annexation marked a departure from Chinese traditional policy toward the western regions. Unlike the Ming which had used the tribute system to deal with Inner Asia, the Qing government spent enormous resources, financial and military, to maintain control over Eastern Turkestan. Under the new imperial administration of Chinese Turkestan, *khoja* family members and other nobles who had gone over to the Manchus were given positions of leadership, but resident imperial officials coordinated the affairs of the different oases. The overall administration of the area was entrusted to a military governor stationed at Ili and a military lieutenant governor stationed at Urumchi. This structure remained in place until the creation of Xinjiang Province in 1884.

---

[1] After Galdan had installed White Mountain Khoja Afaq as governor in Kashgar, Afaq had made an unsuccessful attempt to free himself from Dzungar rule and establish a Muslim kingdom. That act of disloyalty, followed by a leadership crisis upon Afaq's death, led the Dzungars to reconsolidate their control by holding Afaq's descendants hostage: These were Buranidun and Hojijan (also known as Yahya), the two sons of Afaq's grandson Khoja Ahmad. However, as Dzungar disunity weakened its control over the oasis towns, the Black Mountains succeeded in regaining control there.

The Qing conquest of Dzungaria precipitated a number of migrations. Some Dzungars settled on Russian territory where they were known as Kalmyks. A few Dzungars who were not slaughtered by the Qing were transported to Manchuria. To repopulate the now empty, but fertile area, the Qing brought in Chinese Muslims from the Kashgar region and Dungans (Chinese Muslims) from Kansu. They also assigned land in Dzungaria to the Torghuts who had been displaced some 150 years earlier by the Dzungars but returned in 1771 from their previous home along the Volga. The Qing also resettled various groups from Manchuria in Ili, among them about three thousand Sibe whose descendants live in what is now called the Cabcal Sibe Autonomous County and who are the only modern custodians of the Manchu language.

For more detailed information students may want to consult the following resources: James A. Millward and Laura J. Newby, "The Qing and Islam on the Western frontier," in *Empire at the Margins: Culture, Ethnicity, and Frontier in Early Modern China* by Pamela Kyle Crossley, Helen F. Siu, Donald S. Sutton (University of California Press, 2006); Peter C. Purdue, *China Marches West: The Qing Conquest of Central Eurasia* (Cambridge, Mass.: Harvard University Press, 2005); Morris Rossabi, *China and Inner Asia: From 1368 to the Present Day* (New York: Pica Press, 1975); Rene Grousset, *The Empire of the Steppes: A History of Central Asia* (New Brunswick, N.J.: Rutgers University Press, 1970); Joseph Fletcher, Jr., "The Naqshbandiyya in Northwest China," Chapter XI in *Studies in Chinese and Islamic Inner Asia*, edited by Jonathan N. Lipman (Brookfield, Vt.: Variorum, 1995); James Millward, *Beyond the Pass* (Stanford, 1998). Also of interest to students reading Manchu documents related to the Qing activities in Inner Asia might be the article "The Birth of the Oyirad Khanship," written by Junko Miyawaki, in which she discusses the origins and variations of Mongol titles, such as *khan*, *jinong*, *taiji*, etc. (*Central Asiatic Journal* 41, no. 1 [1997] 38–75).

Translations

These English translations stay fairly close to the Manchu text to help students understand how the translation came about. For their own final translations, students may want to aim for a less literal and a more polished product.

Reading selection A–1

(37) In the second month, when Taizu *Sure beile* wanted to write the Manchu language by changing the Mongol script, Erdeni Baksi and Gagai Jarguci said: "We have learned the Mongol written language, so we know it. Why now change the language that has come to us from olden times?"

Taizu said: "When the writing of the Chinese country is read aloud, the people who know the written language and those who do not know the written language all understand it. When the written language of the Mongol country is read aloud, those who do not know the written language also understand. When we read our written language in the Mongolian manner, the people of our country who do not know the written language do not understand. Why is it difficult to write in the language of our country? And why is it easy to write in Mongolian?"

(38) Gagai Jarguci and Erdeni Baksi answered: "Writing in the language of our country is good indeed." But because we don't know how to change the writing, we think it will be difficult."

Taizu *Sure beile* objected: "Write the letter *a*. If you put *ma* under the *a*, won't it be *ama*? Write the letter *e*. Then, if you write *me* under the *e*, won't it be *eme*? I have already figured it out. You try to write it. It is possible." In this way, alone resisting, he had the language that was read in the Mongolian manner changed to fit the Manchu language. After creating the Manchu written language, Taizu *Sure beile* disseminated it throughout the country.

Reading selection A–2

(52) The hundred seventeenth chapter of the imperially commissioned genealogical tables and biographies of the princes and dukes of the Mongolian and Muslim tribes of the outer entourage. The hundred and first biography. The biography of Hošik, bulwark duke, prince of the sixth degree. He was one of the Muslims residing in the capital. Hošik was a native of Khotan. Originally governor of Kashgar, he had become a subject of the Dzungars. After the imperial army defeated the Dzungars and let Buranidun return from Ili, Hošik and the various *beg*s did not receive him. But on hearing that the imperial army had arrived,

(53) they went out to meet him and let him enter. When Buranidun and his younger brother subsequently started a rebellion, Hošik escaped to the Kirghiz and put himself under the protection of Ming Ilha, the chief of the Atbash territory. In the twenty-third year of Qianlong (1758), when Hojijan fought the imperial army at Kara Usu, Bujantai, an imperial aide, went to the Kirghiz to enlist troops. Though he issued a call to arms after he arrived in the territory of Ming Ilha and showed (the letter) to him (Ming Ilha), Ming Ilha refused and did not call any troops together.

(54) In the twenty-fourth year (1759), after the imperial army broke the blockade of Kara Usu, Bujantai again went to the Kirghiz. Hošik, together with Ming Ilha, then came to Aksu where he met with Jaohūi, pacifier of the frontier, and requested to submit. When Jaohūi asked by which route the army might invade, Hošik answered: "The Hojijan brothers are on good terms with Erdeni *Beg* of Kokand. (Therefore), if the imperial army advances and puts them into a tight situation, they will escape there.

(55) On the west side of Kashgar there is a fork in the road. Let us occupy that point first." After Hošik said so, Jaohūi sent a message to Kokand alerting the people that they should not help the rebels. Since at that time Fude, right pacifier of the frontier, was encamped at Khotan, Jaohūi proposed to advance the troops along two different routes so that one detachment would attack Kashgar from Aksu, and one detachment would attack Yarkand from Khotan.

(56) Hošik then drew a map and said: "On the west side of Kashgar one road connects Opol with the Kokand Minjur mountain pass. Another road connects Yustu Artush with the Edegene and other Kirghiz tribes of Andijan. Therefore let us send them a notice to prevent the rebels from escaping. When Jaohūi entered Kashgar exactly in the way Hošik had suggested, he let Hošik be his guide. Because the Hojijan brothers abandoned the city and escaped, one subsequently pacified Yarkand and Kashgar.

(57) Jaohūi petitioned to the throne: "Let us have Hošik serve as acting governor of Yarkand. And since his father's younger brother Sulayman was formerly collector of revenues of Yarkand, let him likewise hold that original office." This was carried out by edict. In the twenty-fifth year (1760), when Hošik came for an audience, the emperor ordered him to reside in the capital, granted him the title of bulwark duke, prince of the sixth degree,

(58) and awarded him a two-eyed peacock feather. When Hošik memorialized, listing in the letter his household property in the various towns of Khotan, Hara Hash, Yarkand, and Šaguzeli, an edict was issued to have the value (of the property) appraised and have it (the equivalent value) remain in Khotan to support his relatives and family. After he died in the forty-sixth year (1781), he was succeeded by his son Ibrahim. His first successor, Ibrahim, was Hošik's eldest son,

(59) who succeeded as bulwark duke, prince of the sixth degree in the forty-sixth year of Qianlong (1781). In the forty-eighth year (1783) an edict determined: "When the position is vacated, if there has been an effort, the original rank is to be inherited. If there has been no effort, diminish the rank to the next lower grade and have the son succeed as third rank *taiji*." In the fifty-third year (1788), the emperor made his descendants succeed as Prince of the sixth degree with right to perpetual inheritance.

Reading selection A–3

(75) The biography of Husayn, bulwark duke, prince of the sixth degree. He was one of the Muslims residing in the capital. His rank was made hereditary third-degree *taiji* by decree. Husayn was a native of Yarkand. His courtesy title was Erke Khoja. The founder of his line was Paihanpar. Having been chiefs of a Muslim tribe and resided in Yarkand for generations, the family had been governing the people of their clan. Their clan's use of the honorific term *khoja* was just like the Mongol's use of the term *taiji*. After the Dzungars became strong,

(76) Tsewang Rabtan went to raid Yarkand, unseated Khoja Ahmad, took the people of his (Ahmad's) clan prisoner and made them live in Turfan. Because the people of Turfan subsequently submitted, Tsewang Rabtan forced Ahmad's clan to move to Ili. After the imperial army pacified the Dzungars, Husayn and his people had wanted to submit. When Hojijan, Ahmad's son, took advantage of Amursana's rebellion, coerced the people of his clan, and wanted to go back from Ili to Yarkand, Husayn

(77) did not go along and instead fled to the Kirghiz who lived in Khokand, Marghilan, Andijan, Namagan, and Tashkent. His younger brother Parsa and his older brother's sons Mahmut and Turdu went with him. Because Hojijan had become an enemy of the Kirghiz, the Kirghiz did not comply when he sent troops and demanded that they send the *khoja*s back. In the twenty-third year of Qianlong (1758), when Husayn heard that the imperial army had arrived in Yarkand to attack Hojijan, he together with Turdu and Narabatu, chief of the Kirghiz Hūsici tribal subdivision, took troops

(78) and went to press such towns as Yanggishar in order to fight Kashgar. Thereupon, when Hojijan fought the imperial army at Kara Usu, Hami's *jasak beise* Yusuf sent the aide Bujantai (of the imperial army) to raise troops among the Kirghiz. After he arrived in Atbash, the chief of that place, Ming Ilha, refused on the grounds that he did not have many troops. After Bujantai returned, it was discovered through spies that when Hojijan's older brother, Buranidun, had gone from Kashgar

(79) to aid Yarkand, he heard that Kirghiz troops had come to attack his city. Suspecting that they were allied with the imperial army, he did not dare strike near the

blockade of Kara Usu. One did not know which subdivision of the Kirghiz was involved. In the twenty-fourth year (1759), Mahmut went from the Kirghiz to Aksu and met with Pacifier of the Frontier Jaohūi. Informing him of the situation, he also

(80) told him that Husayn had assembled troops in Narabatu's territory and was waiting for an official communication. Through Jaohūi's office, the emperor sent an edict commending (Mahmut) and granting him silk cloth. After answering Mahmut, a letter was sent to Husayn. When Husayn took troops and came hither, he encountered over one hundred rebels on the way. He defeated them and obtained one banner which he handed over to the camp of the imperial army. When he requested to submit, Jaohūi reassured him. Because Kirghiz troops attacked the village of Bula in the region of Kashgar after Hojijan and his people had escaped,

(81) Husayn quickly dispatched one of his men, and had him go along with the aide Cengguwe with a letter to make them stop, stating: "Yarkand and Kashgar have already been pacified. If you again invade, it means you are taking on the imperial army." In response the Kirghiz troops withdrew. When Jaohūi sent Husayn to have an audience with the emperor,

(82) the emperor, noting that Husayn was a descendant of Paihanpar, bestowed on him by edict the rank of bulwark duke, prince of the sixth-degree. Husayn memorialized: "My family has been living in Yarkand for generations. After the Dzungars took me prisoner, they moved me to Turfan, and then again to Ili. When I avoided Hojijan's rebellion I went to seek refuge among the Kirghiz. As I now have the good fortune to have become a servant of his majesty's dynasty, I shall wait for you to determine where I should live."

(83) He was made to reside in the capital by edict. An edict transmitted via Jaohūi (furthermore) said: "As a member of Hojijan's clan, Husayn and his people also spent a long time in Ili. Don't make them return to Yarkand. Let him bring the members of his family also to the capital." In the forty-eighth year (1783), an(other) edict stated: "After his position is vacated, have his son likewise hold the original rank. If there is effort in the next generation, let the same princely rank be inherited. If there is no effort,

(84) diminish the rank to the next lower grade and have (the successor) succeed as third grade *taiji*. After Husayn died in the fifty-fifth year (1790), the emperor granted two hundred *taels* of silver and arranged for a mourning ceremony. An edict was issued saying: "The princely rank vacated by Husayn was not obtained through military merit. It was bestowed by my special grace. Therefore, it would be appropriate to diminish the rank upon succession. However, Husayn has served (us) for a long time. Bestowing my favor, he is to be succeeded by his son

(85) Kašahojo. Kašahojo, who was the first to succeed, was Husayn's son. In the fifty-fifth year of Qianlong (1790), he succeeded as bulwark duke, prince of sixth degree. Because he diligently fulfilled his various duties and exerted himself, the emperor by edict promoted him in the fifty-sixth year (1791) to defender general of the state, prince of the fifth degree.

Reading selection A–4

(97) The biography of Hasim, a first-rank *taiji*. He was one of the Muslims residing in the capital. His rank had been made hereditary second-degree *taiji* by decree. Hasim was a native of Turfan. Belonging to the Borjigit family, he was a descendant of the Taizu emperor of the Yuan dynasty. After Taizu of the Yuan dynasty first pacified the northwestern tribes, he divided the territories and had his princes and sons-in-law govern them. He had his second son Chaghadai reside in Ili and also govern the Muslim tribes of Turfan. Ten generations later, Tughluk Temür abandoned Mongol traditions and converted to Islam.

(98) His sons Khizr Khoja and Buhar Baimir abandoned Ili and moved to Turfan. In the twenty-fifth year of Kangxi (1686), Abul, Muzaffar, Sultan Mahamat, Emin Batur, and Hasihan came from Turfan to offer tribute on the grounds that they were descendants of the Yuan dynasty. One has dealt with this in the compilation of the biographies of the Turfan Muslim tribes. In the fifty-ninth year (1720), when the imperial army fought the Dzungars attacking Urumchi from Turfan,

(99) Hasim's older brother Mangsur went out to meet them (the imperial army) and offered them camels and horses. After the troops returned, Tsewang Raptan accused Mangsur and imprisoned him in Karashar. In the twentieth year of Qianlong (1755), when Mangsur heard that the imperial army had pacified the Dzungars, he requested to submit. General Bandi, pacifier of the north, subsequently memorialized requesting to send Mangsur to Turfan and have him govern his former subjects. Because Amursana rebelled before the request was approved,

(100) Mangsur was unable to return to Turfan. After the imperial forces pacified the Muslim cities of Yarkand in the twenty-fourth year (1759), one obtained Mangsur and Hasim. When they came for an audience in the twenty-fifth year (1760), the emperor, saying that they were descendants of Taizu of the Yuan dynasty, decreed that they both be made first-rank *taiji* and reside in the capital. After Hasim died in the thirtieth year (1765),

(101) he was succeeded by his son Abul as second-rank *taiji*, the rank having been diminished by one grade. Because Mangsur did not have any descendants, thus halting

the succession, no biography was established for him. The first successor, Abul, was Hasim's eldest son. He succeeded as second-degree *taiji* in the thirtieth year of Qianlong (1765). In the forty-eighth year (1783), an edict was issued: "After the position becomes vacant, if there has been effort, the same rank is to be inherited by the son. If there has been no effort,

(102) the rank is to be diminished by one grade and be inherited as fourth degree *taiji*. In the fifty-third year (1788), it was decreed that the rank of second-degree *taiji* should be inherited in perpetuity.

Reading selection A–5

(108) The biography of second-degree *taiji* Abdurman. He was one of the Muslim ranks residing in the capital. His rank had been made hereditary third-degree *taiji* by decree. Abdurman was a native of Yarkand. He was a descendant of Paihanpar. Originally Tsewang Raptan had dismissed the *khoja* of Yarkand, a man named Ahmad. Because he also imprisoned Ahmad's sons, Buranidun and Hojijan, after their father's death, the people of Yarkand and Kashgar set up another leader called Ike Khoja. This was Abdurman's grandfather. In the twentieth year of Qianlong (1755), after the imperial army pacified the Dzungars,

(109) Ike Khoja did not give entrance to Buranidun whom one had released and let return to Yarkand. Only when he heard that the imperial army had arrived, did he go to meet him and let him enter. Later, after Hojijan plotted a rebellion, and after he and Buranidun separately occupied Yarkand and Kashgar, they killed Ike Khoja. Hojijan captured Abdurman who had escaped to the Kirghiz and imprisoned him. After the imperial army pacified Yarkand in the twenty-fourth year (1759), one obtained Abdurman's submission.

(110) When he came for an audience in the twenty-fifth year (1760), the emperor, noting that he was the grandson of the former *khoja*, made him second-degree *taiji* by decree and had him reside in the capital. After he died in the thirty-seventh year (1772), he was succeeded by his son, Abdunidzar, at the reduced rank of third-degree. Abdunidzar, who was the first to succeed, was Abdurman's oldest son. In the thirty-seventh year (1792),

(111) he succeeded as third-degree *taiji*. In the forty-eighth year (1783), an edict decreed: "After the position is vacated, if there has been effort, the original rank is to be inherited by his son. If there has been no effort, the rank is to be reduced by one grade and inherited as fourth-degree *taiji*. In the fifty-third year (1788), it was decreed that the rank of third-degree *taiji* should be inherited in perpetuity.

Reading selection A–6

(115) The hundred-eighteenth chapter of the official genealogical tables and biographies of the outer princes and dukes of the Mongol and Muslim tribes. The hundred and second biography. The biography of the banner *beile* Ūdui, an (originally) appointed *beile*. He was one of the Muslim nobles residing in Sinkiang. After the rank was inherited as grand minister assistant commander, the emperor recently raised it to beile prince. Ūdui was a native of Kucha. His grandfather was Mardza Nimet, and his father Polat. The family had been living in Kucha for generations. After Ūdui succeeded, the Dzungars forcibly moved him to Ili and made him live north of the river at Kulja. After the imperial army pacified the Dzungars in the twentieth year of Qianlong (1755),

(116) Ūdui requested to submit. In the twenty-second year (1757), he followed Border-pacifying-general Cenggunjab, a Khalka prince, and fought the Eleuth rebels. Because Ūdui requested to accompany the Rebel-eradicating-general Yarhašan to fight the Muslim rebels, Buranidun and Hojijan, the emperor commended him, made him grand minister assistant commander and honored him with a peacock feather.

(117) At the time Abdukerem of the rebel faction became governor of Kucha, he had Ūdui's relatives killed. After the imperial army arrived in Kucha, Ūdui, having lived there for generations and therefore familiar with the local conditions, informed Vice Commander-in-chief Šundenen, who then dispatched troops and occupied the woods surrounding the town. After the rebels came, they did not dare strike. After more than ten days had elapsed since the rebels closed the city gates,

(118) Ūdui told Yarhašan: "The city of Kucha is very strong. Let us prepare ladders for scaling the walls, cut off their water supply, and lay siege. In the meantime the reinforcements are bound to arrive. Although the south-east side of the city connects with the road to Kurle and Karašar, we don't have anything to fear from there. The north side connects to Sairim, but there are the two narrow passages of Šaldalang and Osikbesh. If we sent crack troops there and have them block the defile with boulders, the rebels surely will not get through. The west side provides passage to Šayar.

(119) The Ogen river is there. When the water is high, one can get through by boat. From Yaha Tohonai and Tomulok, one reaches the towns of Sairim. Let us station troops there." Upon hearing Ūdui's report, Yarhašan sent soldiers and had them guard the narrow passages. Because the imperial army fought off an attack on the road to Tomulok which Abduhalik, Abdukerem's younger brother, had launched with over two thousand rebels, the emperor issued an edict saying: "Because Ūdui

(120) was fully aware of the important defiles that needed to be guarded through prior preparations, and as a result we have now conquered the Muslim towns, appoint him *beg*." Because our troops fought off Hojijan who once more approached Kucha from the Ogen River with over five thousand troops, the emperor rewarded Ūdui and his son with silver and silk. At the time our troops did not know that Hojijan had already entered Kucha. When the rebels opened the gates the next day

(121) and came out to resist, Ūdui requested to send troops and have them stationed around the Ogen river to block their escape route. Because Yarhašan did not take such preventive measures, Hojijan escaped. When the imperial army later took the town of Kucha, Ūdui left his son Osman to take care of matters in Kucha with Ilgar Beg and the others, and (also) had them take charge of Šayar. Ūdui himself took troops and went to Aksu. After the Border-pacifying-general Jaohūi replaced Yarhašan, he

(122) memorialized requesting to put Ūdui in charge. The emperor made Ūdui governor of Aksu and had the former *begs*, Polat and Babak, assist him. When Jaohūi subsequently invaded Yarkand, he sent Ūdui together with the aides Gabsu and Ciringjab to the six towns of Khotan. After they arrived in Elici, the local *begs* turned over the towns and submitted. When the people of Hara Hash, Yurung

(123) Hash, Tak, Cirla, and Kerya heard that Ūdui had pacified and reassured the people of Elici, they all submitted. Ūdui thereupon sent envoys of the *begs* to deliver a letter to the camp in Yarkand. He himself wrote a letter and sent it to Aksu. Because Ūdui's wife, who lived in Aksu, brought out cloth and fur to help the garrisoned soldiers there, the emperor appointed Ūdui grand minister of the imperial household.

(124) Because Hojijan at that time had taken the rebels and was resisting the imperial army at Kara Usu, the military messages from Khotan did not get through at all. Ūdui, wanting to go to the rescue, quickly sent messengers to report to Aksu after he had found out from spies that the rebels had gone to attack Khotan. Šuhede, grand minister consultant, assembled the troops of the various routes and sent them as separate units to aid the towns of Kara Usu and Khotan.

(125) At the time, while Ūdui's wife supported the army with one hundred horses, Ūdui assembled one thousand Khotanese soldiers and prepared sheep and dried grain in preparation to fight the rebels. Because of Ūdui's efforts the emperor issued an edict: "Ever since Ūdui submitted and has fought (with us), he has been acting zealously in every way. This time he has shown yet more sincerity. Therefore, bestowing my grace, reward him with the rank of duke." Afterwards, when the rebel groups with Abdukerem and others went back and forth betwen Elici and Hara Hash, Ūdui sent a letter to the *begs* telling them to firmly defend their towns. He then

(126) recorded the names of the *begs* in the six towns, along with the number of their households and livestock and sent the information to Aksu. After the relief troops arrived, one divided them and sent them to the various towns. Because the rebels coerced the people by means of circulating false information, Ūdui again sent a messenger to Aksu to report. When one dispatched two hundred troops to go to help—there were few troops in Aksu—Ūdui's wife and the *begs* had fifty of their own subordinates

(127) take provisions and go along. Ūdui sent letters to the towns informing them: "The arrival of the imperial army is near. Firmly defend the towns." After the imperial army broke the blockade of Kara Usu in the following spring, Vice Commander-in-chief Baturjigal and others went to the aid of Khotan with nine hundred soldiers. Ūdui then opened the gates of Elici and came out to meet them at Kara Hash. After he defeated the rebels at Boroci, he reassured the towns by disseminating letters. He

(128) sent his wife's older brother, Aman Beg, to quickly inform Aksu. He also sent his nephew Abdurman together with the *begs* of the six towns and had them go out a distance to meet Fude, left-pacifier-of-the-frontier, who had arrived. When one sent a memorial informing the emperor of the victory, the emperor praised the accomplishment of defending Khotan. He appointed Ūdui bulwark duke and had him return to Aksu.

(129) One appointed Abdurman third-degree imperial guardsman. Because one then proposed to divide Jaohūi and Fude's troops and have them advance along different routes, an edict came down: "Ūdui has been working zealously in military affairs for two years now. We should let him rest a little. I hear that his baggage was seized by the rebels. I am very sorry about that. Therefore give him two hundred *taels* of silver and have him administer matters in Aksu. If his request wanting to go along with the army is sincere,

(130) let him go along. But look out for him with compassion." After this edict was issued, one memorialized from Jaohūi's office, stating that Ūdui had earnestly requested to go along on the campaign. Therefore, the emperor by edict gave him double the amount of silver for expenses. When Buranidun and Hojijan heard that the imperial army had arrived, they both escaped. After Ūdui arrived in Kashgar, he quickly met up with Fude's troops and together they defeated the rebels at Alcur. The imperial army, separated into divisions, defeated the rebels who had fled to Isil Kur.

(131) When Ūdui along with Hojis, a *beg* of Khotan, and others shouted "Surrrender by waving your banners!", over ten thousand rebel partisans came running and requested submission. After Buranidun and Hojijan fled to Badakshan, Fude had Ūdui return to Kashgar, taking along the various Muslims who had surrendered. The emperor thereupon commended Ūdui for acting heroically and for having

annihilated the rebels, and appointed him *beile* prince. When people from Badakshan came to present

(132) Hojijan's head, the wife of a man by the name of Sakalsopi was among the families of the rebels who had been taken prisoner. She was Abdurman's younger sister. The emperor gave her to Ūdui. Subsequently, an edict instructed Ūdui to accompany the triumphant army on its return and come for an audience. One also promoted him and appointed him to the rank of *beile*. After Ūdui arrived in the spring of the twenty-fifth year (1760),

(133) he was announced in the Great Brilliant Bright Hall and given an audience. Having given him ceremonial clothing, one had him drink to his victorious return in the Fengzhe Garden and gave him silver and silk. His majesty also had his portrait painted in the Purple Shining Pavilion. The official laudatory speech read: "Ūdui has been with us ever since we pacified Ili and has exerted himself on behalf of the emperor. He stands out among the Muslims through his excellence.

(134) His heart is truly praiseworthy. Having gone to Khotan to pacify the people there, he was besieged for three months. Together with Gabsu he acted extremely bravely protecting and defending the towns." At the time Polat, assistant governor of Aksu, wanting to become governor, scornfully stirred up the Muslims and brought accusations against Ūdui in order so that people would recommend him (Polat) for the post. After Šuhede found misconduct and informed the emperor in a memorial, an edict was issued: "Muslims are suspicious, jealous, and bring each other to ruin. That is an old custom of theirs. We ought to prohibit this strictly.

(135) Even if Ūdui was greedy and extorted bribes, one should not dismiss him on the basis of Polat's statements. Besides, even if we punish Ūdui on this account, we should also deal with Polat's crime of trying to become governor and availing himself of this pretext and stirring up the people. There is no such thing as falling into his crafty trap and making him governor." Still, the people of Aksu brought accusations against Ūdui. Fearing that there would be no peace if one sent him back to his original post,

(136) the emperor transferred him to be governor of Yarkand. After Ūdui arrived in Yarkand, Assistant Governor Abdura'im, using the name of the *akhund* at the head of a complaint letter, accused Ūdui of being addicted to alcohol, of being irascible and reckless, and irresponsible. Following that, an edict stated: "Let it be understood by the Muslims in all the towns that from here they are to manage all matters by entrusting them to the governor. The *akhund* must not interfere indiscriminately." After Commander-in-chief Sinju sent a memorial

(137) saying that he was afraid that public matters would be delayed if Ūdui and Abdura'im were mutually suspicious and jealous of each other, the emperor determined:

"Muslims are extremely irresolute and distrustful. If we, for their sake, cover things up, there will be even less peace. I think if we bring these matters out into the open, lay them out in front of everybody by separating right from wrong, and if we teach them once, Ūdui will no longer be suspicious and Abdura'im will no longer be unnecessarily on guard.

(138) When they, after repenting their ways, administer matters in mutual harmony and in unison, then they will not hinder one another from doing their work." Because Abdura'im did not obtain the governorship, he secretly plotted with Erdeni, *beg* of Khokand, intending to start a rebellion. Because the matter came to light, he was executed. In the twenty-sixth year (1761), his majesty issued an edict saying: "It is an old custom among the Muslims for whosoever becomes *beg* to be making his subjects suffer

(139) and extort bribes. Therefore, I will bestow my grace and grant the governors of the various towns money, land, and servants as a way to say they should look out for the public good and be compassionate. Now I hear that Ūdui, governor of Yarkand, and Gadaimet, governor of Kashgar, are watching over their towns and that there are no incidents of mistreating the people and making extortions. That is very praiseworthy. Recognizing that they have been with us for a long time, show them encouragement by giving them another two hundred *tengge* in addition to the six hundred *tengge*

(140) one officially gives. This is a special favor granted by me. Don't make it a precedent." In the fortieth year (1775), an edict was issued: "Ūdui, of the rank of *beile*, and Gadaimet, of the rank of duke, both submitted in Ili, prior to our obtaining the Muslim areas. Moreover, they achieved great accomplishments in the military field. It does not compare to appointments made by grace. Let one make both of their ranks hereditary in perpetuity."

(141) After Ūdui died in the forty-third year (1778), the rank of *beile* was inherited by his son, Osman, by edict and he was given a two-eyed peacock feather. At that time Osman was governor of Aksu. When Gaopu, vice minister of Yarkand, memorialized requesting that one should make Osman succeed Ūdui as governor of Yarkand, the emperor

(142) did not have it done. (Instead) the emperor transferred Osman to Kashgar, and Setib Aldi from Kashgar to Yarkand. Yonggui, a third-degree grand minister superintendent of Uch Turfan, subsequently memorialized stating that Setib Aldi had accused Gaopu of mistreating the Muslim people and secretly selling official jade. When one found out the truth through an official investigation (examination by edict),

(143) Gaopu was put to death. An edict was issued: "After Ūdui died of an illness in the third month of this year, Gaopu memorialized requesting that Ūdui's son, Osman, be

appointed governor to administer the matters of the said place (Yarkand). However, I thought, if I thus let father and son follow each other administering matters, then the governorship of Yarkand would be just like a hereditary office of their family, and in the long run no different from the Tang dynasty frontier officials.

(144) Thus transferring Satib Aldi to Yarkand and sending Osman to Kashgar reflects my policy with regard to the Muslim tribes, a policy that protects small leaders and restrains powerful ones. If I had followed Gaopu's request and made Osman governor there, Osman aware of the good relations between his father and Gaopu would not have overcome the situation. Moreover, because he was young and could not have performed the duties of his job,

(145) he certainly would have followed along with Gaopu's activities, and they would have quietly helped each other and concealed matters. He could not have brought matters out into the open as did Setib Aldi." Having accused Ūdui for covering up for Gaopu, one stripped him of his hereditary rank. An edict was issued: "Because Ūdui until this time acted zealously in the military field, by grace I bestowed on him the rank of *beile* and made him governor of Yarkand.

(146) He should be grateful for my grace, be courageous, sincere in all matters and strive to do his best. Even if Gaopu at the time made the Muslims suffer and also wanted to secretly buy jade, Ūdui should have persuaded him not to. Or, if Ūdui had brought the matter out by accusing Gaopu, as did Setib Aldi, then he could have repaid my grace and generosity. If one looks at the fact that Ūdui actually led Gaopu astray, gave him fifty *yan* of gold and over two thousand catties of jade,

(147) and had him sell it by carrying on trade in the interior, (one recognizes) that he had earlier also made the Muslim people suffer and secretly taken jade. If we do not punish this behavior strictly, how can I continue to employ Muslim *begs*? If Ūdui were still alive, then one should execute him. Although he has now died of an illness, one should teach people not to do these things, by taking away his rank of *beile*.

(148) Because his son Osman has now succeeded him as *beile*, transmit an edict to Yonggui to have Osman expunged. However, Osman did not reside with his father and matters like these have nothing to do with him. Bestowing my grace, appoint him grand minister and let him retain the original governorship of Kashgar. Because he has already been demoted from *beile*, he should not wear the customary two-eyed peacock feather.

(149) Let one grant him a one-eyed peacock feather." Osman, the first to succeed, was Ūdui's eldest son. In the twenty-third year (1758), he was appointed governor of Kucha. When in the twenty-fourth year (1759) a memorial from Councilor Šuhede stated that

Osman was diligent, he was elevated to the third rank by edict and given a peacock feather. Subsequently, when the imperial guardsman Ciringjab took troops and moved

(150) the Dolun Muslims to guard Bugur Kurle, Osman prepared provisions and dry grain and had it delivered quickly. Commending his effort on behalf of the public, an edict was issued to have him reimbursed for a comparable value. When he went along with Ūdui for an audience in the twenty-fifth year (1760), one rewarded him with silver and silk.

(151) After he returned to Kucha, he consulted with the *beg*s of the towns of Šayar, Sairim, and Bai, and prepared over forty thousand bushels of grain to help the Muslim people who were going to Ili to cultivate the land of military colonies. For this reason the emperor commended him and rewarded him. In the thirtieth year (1765), upon hearing that the Muslims of Uch Turfan had revolted, he collected weapons and stored them in his house

(152) before quickly setting out with troops to fight the rebels. For this he was commended and decorated with second-rank insignia. After the imperial army laid siege to Uch Turfan, one divided the various routes of the army into divisions. Because Osman, when fighting the rebels, excelled in taking prisoners and killing rebels, he was commended by edict and awarded with silk. When he came for an audience in the thirty-third year (1768),

(153) he was ordered to the Gate of Heavenly Purity (audience hall in the Forbidden City in which foreign dignitaries were feasted). In the thirty-forth year (1769), he was made a second-rank *taiji*. In the fortieth year (1775), one appointed him governor of Aksu. In the forty-third year (1778), he succeeded as *beile* prince of the rank of a *beile* and transferred to the position of governor of Kashgar. Subsequently when Ūdui's crime of covering up for Gaopu was reviewed, the emperor stripped him of his hereditary rank and appointed him grand minister. In the forty-eighth year (1783),

(154) an edict was issued: "When Osman's father, Ūdui, formerly exerted himself in the military field, I bestowed my favor and granted him the rank of a *beile*. Later, after having been stripped of the *beile* rank because of the Gaopu affair, I, again bestowing my grace, granted Osman the rank of grand minister. If, after the position is vacated, one stopped it from being passed on, I could not bear it in my heart. By grace, let Osman's position of grand minister be inherited for generations in perpetuity."

(155) Previously when people came from Badakshan to turn over the three rebel sons of Buranidun, Khoja Asma, Abduhalik, and Khoja Bahadun, Buranidun's youngest son, Samsak escaped to Andijan. The emperor, having compassion for him because of his

young age, pardoned him from capture and execution. After Samsak grew up, he was poor and could not make a living. In the forty-ninth year (1784), he therefore

(156) secretly sent people to Kashgar to claim goods and assets. When Osman heard that Emur, a younger brother of the Kirghiz Grand Minister Akim, had secretly plotted with Samsak, he reported (the matter) to Booceng, grand minister superintendent of Kashgar. Akim, fearing that his younger brother might be guilty of a serious crime, bore false witness saying that Osman had aided the plot. Because of this the emperor had Akim and his accomplices put in iron chains and taken to the capital to be tried.

(157) After the truth was obtained, an edict was issued: "Governor Osman, appreciating my grace, did not hide anything at all in the matter of Samsak's secret communication with the Muslims. As soon as he had obtained the information, he reported to Booceng informing him. They then jointly conducted an honest investigation. From beginning to end he acted with determination. This is most praiseworthy.

(158) Granting favor, appoint him *beile* prince and show him encouragement by commending him." He came for an audience in the winter of the fifty-second year (1787). After he died in the first lunar month of the fifty-third year (1788) in the capital, an edict was issued: "Governor and Beile Prince Osman exerted himself with a sincere heart for many years. Always grateful for my favors, he always applied himself earnestly. Just as I was using him and depending on him, he came down with an illness after he came to the capital for an audience.

(159) Though I sent a palace guardsman to fetch a doctor to examine and treat Osman, he did not become better. Now hearing that he has died, I feel very sad. I have sent the Palace Guardsmen Fengsen and Jilun to pour a libation (in honor of Osman), and I have also granted five hundred *tael*s of silver to arrange for the funeral." Again an edict was issued: "Granting favor, let the hereditary position of grand minister which was vacated by Osman

(160) be inherited by his son Maihamet Osan. As for the title of *beile* prince, it is a rank that has been bestowed by my special grace and is not a hereditary rank. But because Osman worked hard for so many years, let the rank of *beile* prince also be inherited by Maihamet Osan by my grace. In this way, show my utmost good will and love for my Muslim subjects."

(161) Maihamet Osan, who was the second to succeed, was Osman's oldest son. When he succeeded as grand minister in the fifty-third year of Qianlong (1788), one also had him inherit the title of *beile* prince.

Reading selection B–1

(182) Your servant humbly memorializes to request that his majesty bestow his favor and grant a leave. Your servant has a sore on his foot and cannot, even with his best effort, fulfill his official duties. I beg that his majesty bestow his grace and grant his servant a five-day leave, so that I can quickly be cured and return to work immediately upon getting better. For this reason I have respectfully submitted this memorial.

(183) When he memorialized on the eighteenth day of the eighth month in the thirteenth year of Tongzhi (September 28, 1874), requesting an edict,

an edict said: "Grant a five day leave."

Reading selection B–2

(188) Memorial.

Your servant Fuk'anggan and others humbly memorialize to respectfully report that we have had the seasonal rains in our respective localities. Upon review we find that last year, on the twenty-ninth day of the tenth month, the Mukden area had little bit of snow.

(189) The winter snowfall was scant and since the beginning of spring we have not had sufficient rain either. Now, between the early afternoon (1–3 P.M.) of the second day and the early morning hours (3–5 A.M.) of the third day of the second month in this forty-fourth year of Qianlong it rained more than five inches, soaking the fields everywhere. Since this is just the time of planting wheat and barley, the farmers are all delighted because they can hope that the grain planted in the spring will result in a bountiful harvest. At this time, the price of grain is also very stable. Duty-bound to

(190) report on the seasonal rains, we respectfully memorialize on this matter.
(❁Noted.)

The fourth day of the second month in the forty-fourth year of the Qianlong reign (March 21, 1779).

Your servant Fuk'anggan, Your servant Manggūlai
Your servant Ciowankui, Your servant Mingtung

Reading selection B–3

(196) One sent an edict to the crown prince: When we were resting on the ninth, an urgent memorial from Fiyanggū arrived in the morning hours (9–11 A.M.). It appears

that Galdan has sent a messenger and wants to submit. Therefore I am sending Fiyanggū's original memorial to let everybody know immediately. Send greetings to the Empress Dowager and inform her about this matter. Also inform the people within the palace and the Manchu officials.

(197) Even though the matter is not yet clear, I have to arrange things. Do not worry. I originally said that Galdan would eventually fall. I think my words may be about to come true. Therefore I am sending this special communication.

The nineteenth day of the eleventh month in the thirty-fifth year of the Kangxi reign (December 13, 1696).

----

(198) Yin Jeng, Heir Apparent, respectfully memorializes: A thousand greetings to my father, the *khan*. Your letter about Galdan sending a messenger and wanting to submit arrived on the strike of the fifth watch on the twenty-second of the eleventh month (December 16, 1696).

I relayed your greetings to my grandmother, the Empress Dowager, and informed her. I notified everybody in the palace and also reported the matter to the Manchu officials. (❀I have heard the Empress Dowager's reaction. I suppose the officials didn't say anything.) As I am sending the sable coat and the

(199) long gown you requested, I am also sending along some deer tails from Mukden. Since they arrived on the twentieth of the month, I selected fifty fat ones for you. (❀Noted.) I am also respectfully forwarding the following: One item from the Ministry of Personnel; two items from the Ministry of Revenue; one item from the Ministry of Rites; one memorial from Šanahai, General of Ningguta; one memorial from Boji, General of Xi'an; one memorial from Governor General Fan Chengxun; one communication from departments within the Ministry of Revenue. (❀Noted.)

(200) Two investigative memorials from the Court of Colonial Affairs; and one memorial from Grand Ministers of the Imperial Household.

(❀Please send my regards to the Empress Dowager. I am well. Greetings to you.)

The twenty-third day of the eleventh month in the thirty-fifth year of the Kangxi reign (December 17, 1696).

Reading selection B–4

(206) A communication sent by Vice Minister Mampi to General-in-chief Fiyanggū.

A communication from Vice Minister Consultant Mampi, sent to the General-in-chief-Who-Pacifies-Distant-Lands, Grand Minister of the Imperial Household Department and Earl. On the twenty-second of the third month in the thirty-sixth year of Kangxi (April 13, 1697) Gelei Guyeng Dural arrived with a group of thirteen people, including his family. Gelei Guyeng Dural reported the following: "After I and Ubasi, together with Vice Director Bosihi and Clerk Cangšeo, arrived at Galdan's place

(207) on the twenty-ninth of the first month (February 20, 1697), we delivered his majesty's decree to Galdan and went to great effort to explain it to him. During the six days we were with Galdan, we had discussions every day. When Galdan kept wanting to send me as envoy to go along with Bosihi, I felt that since Galdan was not sincere I could not be his messenger and come here to deceive. So before the envoys set out, I left Kuku Serge, which is on this side of Saksa Tehurik, on the twelfth of the second month (March 4).

(208) I took along my family and servants, all together sixty-six people, over one hundred horses, more than forty camels, and escaped to submit to his majesty. After we arrived in Silutei, we stayed there to wait for Bosihi's party, wanting to assist him with provisions and transportation and come here with him. But as we were resting on the fourth of the third month (March 26), Living Buddha Ilaguksan

(209) with over one hundred people suddenly attacked us. Thirteen of us, including myself, my wife, and three sons, as well as one young grandson, got away with three horses and one camel. My daughters-in-law, the other people, our horses, camels, and everything else were taken. After meeting with Bosihi's delegation on the ninth (March 31), we came here together. I myself sustained a gunshot wound penetrating the body underneath the right shoulder blade, but the wound is almost healed now. Nothing stands in the way of his majesty's grace."

(210) We asked Gelei Guyeng Dural: "After you escaped from Galdan to come here, was he still in Saksa Tehurik? And where was he going?" The answer was: "At the time I came here Galdan was still in Saksa Tehurik. After I meet with the emperor, I will report in more detail about which direction he was going, his intentions and on the general situation there."

(211) Therefore I had Gelei Guyeng Dural and his son Ubasi go along with Vice Director Bosihi and Clerk Cangšeo, ordering them to go by military relay stations and travel quickly throughout the night. Since their own three horses and one camel were insufficient for Gelei Guyeng Dural's family, we had them taken from station to station, depending on the availability of riding animals from nearby Mongols chiefs.

(212) I have sent this communication to inform you of these matters.

The twenty-second of the third month in the thirty-sixth year of the Kangxi reign (April 13, 1697).

Reading selection B–5

(217) A memorial from the General-in-chief Earl Fiyanggū.

Fiyanggū, General-in-chief Who Pacifies Distant Lands, Grand Minister of the Imperial Household and Earl, respectfully memorializes to inform his majesty. In a letter from Vice Minister Consultant Mampi that arrived in the late afternoon of the twenty-third of the third month in the thirty-sixth year of the Kangxi reign (April 14, 1697), he says that Vice Director Bosihi and Clerk Cangšeo, whom we had sent to Galdan,

(218) arrived on the twenty-second of this month, along with Galdan's envoy Lamacab, and Gelei Guyeng Dural, who himself brought along thirteen people, including his family. The Vice Minister Consultant also forwarded a memorial from Bosihi. If, after Boshihi's arrival here, we continue to send them on together to his majesty,

(219) the number of people would be large, making for delays during travel. Since Gelei Guyeng Dural is wounded, he cannot move fast. Therefore we sent people to meet them, and will have three people, Bosihi, Gelei Guyeng Dural's son Ubasi and Cahandai rush ahead to meet with his majesty. Then later I will have Cangšeo,

(220) Gelei Guyeng Dural, Manji, Awangdanjin, Galdan's envoy Lamacab, and Danjila's envoy Lobdzang follow quickly. I am also forwarding for his majesty's perusal two lists of questions posed to Galdan's envoy Lamacab and Gelei Guyeng Dural, along with the memorial from Bosihi. These were transmitted by Vice Minister Consultant Mampi.

(221) As for the other eleven people who came with Lamacab, we will have them stay and be watched over at the sentry post.

The twenty-third day of the third month in the thirty-sixth year of Kangxi (April 14, 1697).

Reading selection B–6

(224) A memorial from General-in-chief Fiyanggū.

Fiyanggū, General-in-chief Who Pacifies Distant Lands, Grand Minister of the Imperial Household Department and Earl, respectfully memorializes and hastens to report that Galdan has died and that Danjila is about to submit. After we arrived in Sair Balhasun on the ninth of the fourth month in the thirty-sixth year of Kangxi (May 28, 1697), Cikir Jaisang heading a group of nine people sent by the Dzungar leader Danjila,

(225) came and reported: "We are envoys sent by the Dzungar leader Danjila. Galdan died at Aca Amtatai on the thirteenth of the third month (May 4, 1697). Danjila, Noyan Gelung and Danjila's son-in-law Lasrun bringing Galdan's body and Galdan's daughter, Juncahai, along with a total of three hundred households have started on their way here to submit to the emperor. They stopped at Baya Endur

(226) and are awaiting there his majesty's order. No matter what instructions his majesty may send, they will respectfully act according to the emperor's will. Urjanjab Jaisang, Urjanjab's younger brother Sereng, Aba Jaisang, Tar Jaisang, Aralbai Jaisang, and the Lama Erdeni Ujat, along with two hundred households, went to seek refuge with Tsewang Rabtan. Erdeni Jaisang, Usta Taiji, Boroci Jaisang,

(227) Hošooci, and Cerimbum Jaisang, with two hundred households, went to seek refuge with Danjin Ombu. We now have a memorial from Danjila with us." When we questioned Cikir Jaisang and his people, asking how Galdan had died, and why Danjila had not come here himself but instead wanted to stay at Baya Endur and wait for an edict, this is what was reported: "Galdan fell ill on the morning of the thirteenth of the third month and he died in the evening.

(228) One does not know what illness it was. Though Danjila wanted to come here, the horses are very thin, and the majority of his people do not have animals and have to go on foot. They also lack provisions. Therefore they stayed at Baya Endur and are awaiting the emperor's order. If his majesty orders them to come here, they will come immediately." Thinking that the number of people would be large and that there might not be enough post horses

(229) if we dispatched all of Danjila's messengers to you, we are having only Cikir Jaisang, under the care of Director Nomcidai, taken to his majesty immediately. The other eight people with Aldar Gelung, we will take to Godoli Balhasun, and then send them to you by regular post travel. I am forwarding to you one letter from Danjila, one from Noyan Gelung, and one from Danjila's son-in-law Lasrun. For this reason I am urgently and respectfully sending this memorial for your information.

(230) The ninth day of the fourth month in the thirty-sixth year of Kangxi (May 28, 1697).

Reading selection C–1

(233:239) On the third day of the third month in the year of the dog (1622), the eight sons came together and asked their father, the *khan*: "How do we solidify the heavenly mandate (the Way given by Heaven)? What should we do so that the good fortune from Heaven will last forever?" The *khan* replied: "When appointing a leader for the country to succeed the father, if a strong and powerful person becomes the leader in the country, I am afraid he will wrong Heaven by making his power supreme. No matter how able a single person may be, is he as good as the council of many? You eight sons are to be the eight *wangs*.

(234:240) When you eight *wangs* are of one mind you shall not make mistakes. After you find a person who does not reject your words, you eight *wangs* make him the leader for the country inheriting through the father. If he does not take your advice and does not follow a good path, then you eight *wangs* replace the *khan* you have appointed and select a good person who does not reject your words. If this person, when you replace him, does not let you make the change in a cheerful manner by group consensus, if he refuses and becomes angry, will you allow the desire of a bad person to prevail? If so, it will be a change for the bad. When managing the country's affairs, if amongst you eight *wangs*

(235:241) one person explains his way of thinking, then the seven others must understand clearly. If somebody does not understand and, lacking such understanding, does not grasp what others have comprehended, and merely remains quiet, replace this person and let a younger brother or a foster son become *wang*. If, during this change, the person does not let you replace him in a congenial manner, shows displeasure and objects, is the will of your bad person going to prevail? If so, it will be a change toward the bad. If you go to attend to some state affairs, go only after consulting and informing everybody. Do not go without consultation.

(236:242) When you gather around the country's leader whom you eight *wang* have appointed, don't meet with him if there are only one or two of you. Rule the country and handle all matters by everybody gathering together and consulting each other as a group. If there are matters concerning worshipping the gods or making animal sacrifices, announce it to everybody and then proceed. Upon consultation, the eight *wangs* should appoint eight Jurchen, eight Chinese, and eight Mongol *ambans*. Below these eight *ambans* place eight Jurchen judges, eight Chinese judges, and eight Mongol judges. After the judges have investigated a case, they are to

(237:243) report to the *ambans*. After the *ambans* have made their decision, they are to memorialize to the eight *wangs*. The eight *wangs* are to judge the proposed punishment. You eight *wangs*, demote the traitorous and cunning people and promote loyal and upright persons. Appoint eight Jurchen, eight Chinese, and eight Mongol learned men (*baksi*) to assist (be close to) the *wangs*. The country's leader is to make an appearance and sit on the throne twice per month, once on the fifth and once on the twentieth day of the month. On New Year's morning after prostrating himself in the imperial shrine and kowtowing to the gods

(238:244) the leader of the country should kowtow to his uncles and elder brothers before ascending the throne. The *khan*, and his uncles and elder brothers who have received his *kowtow*, shall then sit together in the same place and on an equal level and receive the *kowtow* of the people.

Reading selection C–2

(253:262) An order of the *khan* was issued on the twenty-second (Tianming 6 [1621], eleventh month): "Earlier we had said that Jurchens and Chinese should live together in the same village, eat the grain together, and raise (feed fodder to the) livestock together.

(254:263) As for you Jurchens, do not take unfair advantage of the Chinese. Do not steal any belongings of the Chinese and do not rob them. If (after) the Chinese come to accuse you for having harmed them by stealing and robbing, you will be punished. As for you Chinese, don't lie by making statements about nothing. If you lie making groundless accusations, one will judge the matter by having the two parties involved in the crime testify in court. If, after these hearings, the accusation turns out to be false, that is also bad. Both Jurchens and Chinese have become the *khan*'s people.

(255:264) Since the *khan* himself has instructed Jurchens and Chinese to all live in harmony and honestly, if someone commits the crime of disagreeing with and going against the *khan*'s words, punishment will be severe. The person who committed such a crime should blame (be angry with) himself. Jurchens and Chinese, don't squander grain by buying or selling it. If one finds out that such trading took place, there will be punishment. When you open the grain storage pits, do so only in the presence of Jurchens and Chinese. Give four Chinese *sin* to each Chinese and Jurchen person per month."

(256:265) On the same day (Tianming 7 [1622], third month, fourth day) a communication from the *dutang*'s office was sent down to Vice General Liu: "I entrust to you the families on the west side of the river who have been placed together in the four southern *wei*. After putting together large households in large houses and small households in small houses, these families should live together, eat (share the grain) together and work the fields together. Appoint officials who are honest and don't take bribes and have them urge the people to till the fields quickly. Report the dates when the people started working the fields."

(257:266) (Write this) A *khan*'s edict was issued on the fifteenth of the month (Tianming 7 [1622], third month). "Jurchen and Chinese families have been placed together and were told to live together, eat the grain together, and farm together. Now we hear that Jurchens are having the oxcarts of their Chinese cooperative households seized and the people of these households drafted, that they make the Chinese transport grass and grain and that they are pressing the Chinese for all kinds of things. Have I given them to you as slaves? Because you had no houses to live in, no grain to eat, and no land to farm after moving here from our ancestral place, I have made you live together. From here on,

(258:267) apart from living together in the houses of the Chinese and sharing the grain by allocating it according to the number of family members, Jurchens and Chinese should farm different portions of land and do so with different oxen. If a Jurchen disobeys this order and oppresses and mistreats Chinese, the Chinese should bring up the case and make an accusation before the law. Even though I have issued this order, the Chinese, on the other hand, must not lie and falsely accuse the Jurchens. You all are the people of one *khan*."

(259:268) On the seventh (Tianming 7 [1622], sixth month), Vice General Liu submitted a letter: "Thirty *li* north of Gaizhou, in the vicinity of Bolofu, lives your subject Šose, a member of the Hūsita Company. His Chinese cooperative household has gone to Vice General Liu in Gaizhou with an accusation: 'In the north the Jurchens are using my oxen to farm and they are ordering me around. They also make my wife cook for them. As for the pigs I raised, they throw me one or two *jiha* for a fat one, then take it by force and slaughter it.' Because the Chinese made these accusations, I dispatched one man with a letter, half written in Jurchen

(260:269) and half written in Chinese, telling them: 'You have heard that the *khan* earlier proclaimed a law that forbids the Jurchens to use the oxen of the Chinese, that they should live in separate quarters, and that if grain is available, it be distributed according to the number of people. You Chinese are not to give them the pigs you have raised. If they seize them, you come and report to me. I will inform the *beile* and high officials.' Subject Šose of the Hūsita Company grabbed the letter, ripped it up, and threw it away. He then tied up my messenger (*missing word in document*) and said: 'How come, you, Aita, have become a high official: Why are you

(261:270) investigating the case of the people who have been placed with me?' As for the two Jurchens I sent the second time, a man by the name of Guwanggun from the Hūsita Company wanted to seize them along with the Chinese, but two other people from their company said: 'Sending the messengers was appropriate. Why do you seize them?' They stopped him and sent the messengers back. If, when I send one person, he is seized, beaten, and tied up, and when I send two people, they are seized and beaten, then how can we do the *khan*'s work?" "Aita, summon the three people, the person you sent the first time and the two people you sent afterwards, and send them to Liaotung." One then transferred the people of the Hūsita Company to Vice General Liu's Company.

Reading selection C–3

(277:280) A communication sent to the *beile*s on the twenty-fourth (T'ien-ming 8 [1623], fifth month). The *khan* said: "May each and every one of our country's *beile*s and officials be made content and live in an enlightened manner. Grieving on your behalf, I now

(278:281) spit into your faces. Your principle for judging crimes is wrong. Why have you made the Chinese who immediately become defiant when they are close (equal) to us, and our Jurchens equal? If our Jurchens have committed a crime, look for their merits. See whether they were delegated (told to do so). If there is any small reason, pardon them on that pretext. If a Chinese deserves the death penalty because he failed to exert himself loyally or because he was a thief, why do you release him with a beating, instead of killing him and exterminating his descendants and relatives?

(279:282) Finally, those Chinese who have come with us when we took them to our Fe Ala, judge them by one principle. Your judging is like that of an ox or mule whom one cannot make go backwards. You eight *beile*s, call the *beile*s and officials of each banner together and read this letter secretly. Don't let the people hear it. Don't you know that the people of Yaozhou have said that they will kill our children and women after our troops leave, and that people everywhere have poisoned and killed our Jurchens?"

Reading selection C–4

(287) On the 13th (Chongde 1 [1636], eleventh month) the divine *khan* assembled the imperial princes, commandery princes, *beile*s, banner leaders, and censors. After the *khan* took a seat beneath the Phoenix Tower, he had the scribes from the Office for the Advancement of Literature read the statutes established by Shizong Ulu, the fifth

emperor of the Jin dynasty. The divine *khan* then addressed those present: "All of you assembled here, listen carefully to the words of this document. Emperor Shizong, he was a good *khan*, a *khan* who was famous in China, Mongolia and countries everywhere. Therefore the wise men of later generations praised him by calling him the Little Yao Shun emperor. Ever since I read this document, after one translated it into Manchu, my ears and eyes have become clear and lucid, just like a horse that pricks its ears and wants to gallop when it senses a wild animal. I hold this document in enormous esteem. If you look at these statutes, which represent the old way (*fe doro*) followed by Taizu Aguda and Taizong Ucimai,

(288) you will find that by the time of Xizong Hola Khan and Wan Yan-liang, the grandsons abandoned it. Instead, they took to drinking, lechery and comfort, and followed Chinese ways. After Shizong Ulu Khan succeeded to the throne, he feared from the very beginning that the sons and grandsons would increasingly take to Chinese ways. Therefore, he kept saying again and again: 'Don't forget the old ways of the ancestors. Wear Nuchen clothing. Learn the Nuchen language, and keep practicing mounted and dismounted archery.' Even though he often said so, the later emperors followed the Chinese ways and forgot archery. The mandate was lost during the generation of Aizong and the country perished. Among the *khan*s who succumbed to wine and lechery, there is not one who has not lost the mandate. Earlier, scholars Dahai and Kurcan kept advising me to give up Manchu dress, to wear Chinese clothing, and follow Chinese customs. Because I stood steadfast and did not agree, they said I did not accept advice.

(289) Let me compare ourselves: Let's assume all us assembled here were standing here wearing clothing with wide sleeves, carrying a case full of arrows on the left side and holding a bow on the right side. If Losa Šongkoro the Brave were to enter all by himself, could we together withstand him? Once we abandon archery, we will certainly wear clothing with wide sleeves, and we will eat meat sliced by others. If so, how would we be different from people who have taken the wrong path? I am not talking about this generation. Will this kind of way occur during my time? What one needs to fear is that the sons and grandsons of later generations will abandon the old ways, forget archery, and take up Chinese ways. How great our troops formerly were! Because they excelled in archery, they were famous for being victorious when fighting on the steppes, for capturing the towns they attacked, and for people throughout the world saying that once we had occupied a place, we would not give ground and once we had entered a place we would not turn back. Therefore, as for this reputation,

(290) you eight *amban*s have now put my great name to shame when you went outside the border on a campaign to Beijing. I want you to remember my words."

Reading selection D–1

(297) Nine soldiers took a day off and did not return for drill time the next morning. So the military officer was very angry. It was already past seven o'clock when one soldier arrived and explained the reason for his delay to the officer: "Because my clock was slow, I missed the train. I had no choice but to rent a car, but halfway on my way here the car also broke down. Finding myself in a difficult situation, I went into a village and bought a horse. But the horse too died. So I came the rest of the way running on foot." Just as the officer was extremely doubtful of this explanation, seven more soldiers arrived, one after another. Did they all miss the train? Did their cars break down? Did their horses die? Just then the last soldier arrived. The officer asked angrily: "Did you also miss the train? And the car broke down?" "Sir, it wasn't that the car broke down. There were too many dead horses in the road, so the car couldn't get through. That's why I am late."

Reading selection D–2

(303) One day Mr. Mouse received a letter. It was a letter sent by his relative Country Mouse who lived far away. The letter read:

Dear Mr. Mouse:

Let me tell you some good news. The rice in the fields is completely ripe. In a few days the farmers will harvest it and take every bit of this white rice to the landlord's granary. I am happy for you. You are fortunate, Mr. Mouse, that the days of feasting and drinking are at hand. But I am writing to you because after the long-suffering peasants harvest the rice, they will face hunger and cold. I, too, will then no longer have any food. This is my experience every year. So I am now preparing to come to your house to stay a few days and borrow a little grain to take back home with me.

With good wishes,

Your relative, Country Mouse.

After Mr. Mouse finished reading the letter, his whiskers stiffened with joy.

(304) He hugged his wife and began to jump and dance: "One, two, three, one, two, three!" Together with his wife, Mr. Mouse made a round in his palace (i.e., the mouse den), a very large grain bin, over one hundred feet around, and about thirty feet wide and high. If we humans were as small as mice, it would take us three to four hours to make the circle. But luckily mice have four legs, so the two mice could make the round in less than thirty minutes. "Ha, ha, ha," Mr. Mouse stopped dancing and laughed loudly. Then he said: "The days of feasting are here. The new grain is about to arrive. In a few days, the peasants will come carrying the white rice on their shoulders and pour it into the granary." "That's for sure. Every year it is like this," said Mrs. Mouse. "One

after another, the peasants turn in their grain and within a few days the granary will be full. Then we just open our mouths, follow the fragrant smell and eat delicious food. What bliss! Ha, ha." She kept laughing. "That's the way it is. Every year it is like that." This frequent expression of Mrs. Mouse was like an oral command.

(305) Even though every year had been like that, this year it was not as they had thought. The two mice waited for days and months but they did not see any peasants bringing grain. The granary remained as empty as before, and the mice did not get to eat a single kernel of grain. One evening, Mr. Mouse decided to leave his bin and visit his old friend, Brother Ox. Brother Ox's words had always been reliable in the past. After Mr. Mouse walked a long way, he arrived. When he entered the cow shed quietly, Brother Ox had just fallen asleep in the shed and was snoring loudly. "Brother Ox!" Mr. Mouse called him in a loud voice, but he did not wake up. Because he had been working hard all day long and was tired, he slept very soundly. "Brother Ox! Brother Ox!" Mr. Mouse nearly crawled into the ear of the ox. Brother Ox woke up: "My, what's the matter?" Brother Ox stretched, shook his ears and said: "Mr. Mouse! It's been a year since we haven't seen each other!" "Right, I haven't left the house for over a year," Mr. Mouse answered. "What's happening these days? Why has our master landlord's granary remained empty until now? And why have the peasants not turned in any grain at all?" "The landlord's granary!" the ox said coldly. "That landlord of yours—

(306) does he till his own fields?" "He does not. Being a landlord, he has a lot of land. Why would he till his fields himself, working hard without eating and drinking?" said Mr. Mouse. "If a landlord doesn't work the land himself, then where does the grain in his granary come from?" "The peasants put it there." "After being made to live a life of suffering and toiling in the fields, why would the peasants give their harvested white rice to the landlords, and starve and freeze themselves?" "Isn't that the way it is every year?" said Mr. Mouse. "That's just not right!" Brother Ox shouted angrily. "If one does not work hard, then one does not eat. Let the ravens defecate into their mouths! Those landlords, they are parasites who do not work. That's why today there isn't a kernel of grain in their granaries. Have you heard? The peasants are now liberated. The land is theirs. They work it and they eat what they grow. So they will certainly no longer be exploited and turn in rent to the landlords." When Mr. Mouse again opened his mouth and started to say "Former...," Brother Ox began to shout loudly: "Formerly, formerly...you always talk about formerly. But it's no longer like before. Now the Communist Party is leading the peasants and has organized the people. They have toppled the landlords

(307) and distributed all the fields to the landless peasants. The landlords will never again be able to exploit the peasants. Let me tell you: Here the peasants are rejoicing because the land reform has already been implemented. If you still want to rely on the landlord's large granary for your livelihood, you can no longer do so. That time is gone.

Better be aware!" "Oh, I see, I see..." Mr. Mouse wept bitterly. "Then we'd better move our home right away."

When Mr. Mouse returned home, he received another letter from Country Mouse.

Dear Mr. Mouse:
This year is truly strange. The peasants have harvested the grain but not taken it to the landlord's house. Instead they have stored it in their own homes. I hear that a land reform has already been carried out and that since the peasants now have their own land they will no longer go hungry. You cannot know this. In light of the new circumstances, I will no longer need to come to your house.
Sincerely,

Country Mouse.

"Even so," Mr. Mouse, weeping bitterly, said to his wife: "We will not move!"

(308) Nonetheless, the mice would move. Where they moved is of no concern to us. Suffice it to say that the days of depending on others for food like before are over forever. They will never, ever come again.

Grammatical Points

This section gives some summary information on various grammatical points. It does not aim to be a complete Manchu grammar, only a means to help students solidify their understanding of Manchu when working through the reading selections. The information assumes a familiarity with basic grammatical concepts and terms, but emphasizes examples over linguistic explanations.

Case markers

Case markers may be written attached as suffixes or separately. Personal pronouns usually have case markers written in the attached form. For other occurrences genitive *i* tends to be attached when it follows a noun ending in a vowel (example: *hesei*), except after proper names (example: *abkai wehiyehe i*). Genitive case markers are generally written separately when following *n* and *ng* (examples: *gurun i, wang ni*). There are, however, plenty of instances where these general rules do not hold.

Nominative: No case marker

1. as subject
2. as indefinite object
3. in compound words
4. as adverbial phrase

(1) *ama araha*	father wrote
(2) *bithe hūlambi*	to read a book
(2) *jeku jembi*	to eat (food)
(3) *nikan gurun*	Chinese country
(4) *tere inenggi*	on that day

Genitive: *i, ni* (*ni* after words ending in *-ng*).

1. possessive
2. instrumental
3. in a string of parallel nouns only the last word carries the case marker

(1) *manju gurun i gisun*	the language of the Manchu country
(1) *wang ni aha*	the slave of the king
(2) *galai jafa*	grasp it with your hand
(2) *hesei yabubuha*	it was carried out by edict
(3) *Fugiyan Taiwan i geren ba*	all the places in Fukien and Taiwan

Dative/locative: *de*

1. destination
2. indirect object
3. location in time
4. location in space
5. instrumental
6. agent in passive

(1) *Aksu de genehe*	they went to Aksu
(2) *morin be mini ama de buhe*	he gave a horse to my father
(3) *jakūn biyai ice duin de wesimbuhe*	he sent a memorial on the fourth of the eighth month
(3) *sirame jalan de faššan bici*	if there is effort in the next generation
(4) *gemun hecen de tehe hoise*	the Muslims who resided in the capital
(4) *manju gurun de selgiyehe*	he disseminated (it) in the Manchu country
(5) *ejen i hese de*	by order of the leader
(5) *tere hergen coohai gungge de bahangge waka*	this rank was not obtained through military merit
(6) *cooha de wabuha*	he was killed by soldiers

Accusative: *be*

1. direct object
2. motion through

(1) *manju bithe be fukjin deribuhe*	he created the Manchu script
(1) *monggoi bithe be taciha*	we have learned the Mongolian language
(1) *tere genere be erembi*	I hope he will go
(2) *mederi be jihe*	he came across the ocean

Ablative: *ci*

1. point of departure in space or time
2. direction of destination
3. in comparisons

(1) *mini boo ubaci goro akū*	my home is not far from here
(1) *Ili be toktobuha fon ci*	since the time we pacified Ili
(2) *sikse booci mariha*	I returned home yesterday
(2) *hūlha alin ci ukaha*	the rebels fled towards the mountains
(3) *abka ci den*	higher than the sky
(3) *manju gisun ci nikan gisun mangga*	Chinese is more difficult than Manchu

Plural

1. not expressed
2. expressed indirectly by adding adjectives, such as *geren* 'many', *eiten* 'all', *tumen* 'a myriad', or adverbially with *gemu* 'all'
3. adding suffixes, most commonly *-sa, -se*; less commonly *-so, -si*
4. some words, mostly family relationships, take suffixes *-ta, -te*, or *-ri*

Final *n* is omitted before a suffix.

(1) *hecen de tehe niyalma dahaha*	the people who lived in the town submitted
(1) *hūlha ukaha*	the rebels escaped
(2) *geren niyalma*	all people
(2) *eiten jaka, tumen jaka*	everything, all things
(2) *nikan bithe sara niyalma gemu ulhimbi*	people who know Chinese all understand
(3) *sakda, sakdasa*	old man, old men
(3) *amban, ambasa*	official, officials
(3) *faksi, faksisa*	artisan, artisans
(3) *Monggo, Monggoso*	Mongol, Mongols
(3) *Solho, Solhoso*	Korean, Koreans
(3) *aha, ahasi*	slave, slaves
(3) *haha, hahasi*	man, men
(3) *hehe, hehesi*	woman, women
(3) *omolo, omosi*	grandson, grandsons
(4) *ahūn, ahūta*	older brother, older brothers
(4) *deo, deote*	younger brother, younger brothers
(4) *non, nota*	younger sister, younger sisters
(4) *ama, amata*	father, fathers
(4) *eme, emete*	mother, mothers
(4) *sargan, sargata*	wife, wives
(4) *ejen, ejete*	leader, leaders
(4) *nakcu, nakcuta*	mother's brother, mother's brothers
(4) *mafa, mafari*	grandfather, grandfathers
(4) *mama, mamari*	grandmother, grandmothers

Plural plus case suffix

Example for *manjusa* 'Manchus':

manjusa
manjusai
manjusa de
manjusa be
manjusa ci

Personal pronouns

	Nominative	Genitive	Dat/Locative	Accusative	Ablative
I	*bi*	*mini*	*minde*	*mimbe*	*minci*
you	*si*	*sini*	*sinde*	*simbe*	*sinci*
he/she/it	*i*	*ini*	*inde*	*imbe*	*inci*
we (incl.*)	*muse*	*musei*	*musede*	*musebe*	*museci*
we (excl.*)	*be*	*meni*	*mende*	*membe*	*menci*
you	*suwe*	*suweni*	*suwende*	*suwembe*	*suwenci*
they	*ce*	*ceni*	*cende*	*cembe*	*cenci*

*The inclusive 'we' includes the person or persons spoken to, whereas the exclusive 'we' excludes them. Personal pronouns are commonly omitted.

Polite forms of referring to oneself

Based on I. Zaharov, *Grammatika man'chzhurskogo iazyka* (St. Petersburg, 1879): 108-10.

1. the emperor: *bi* or *mini beye*; his vassals in the emperor's presence: *sitahūn niyalma, emteli beye*, or *emhun beye*; Manchu officials: *aha*; non-Manchu officials: *amban*; the distinction between *aha* and *amban* was not rigidly applied.
2. higher officials, when communicating with lower officials: *adali hafan, emu ba i hafan*, or *uhei deo bi.*
3. lower officials, communicating with higher officials: *buya tušan, harangga hafan, haratu hafan*, or *fiyenten i hafan.*
4. ordinary people, communicating with officials: *irgen niyalma, ajige niyalma, fusihūn beye*, or *buya beye.*
5. people communicating with others of equal rank: *deo*; towards younger people: *mentuhun ahūn.* The word *mentuhun* 'stupid' was also used by family members; for example, *mentuhun jalahi jui* 'I, your nephew'; or *mentuhun omolo* 'I, your grandson'.

Polite forms of address

Based on I. Zaharov, *Grammatika man'chzhurskogo iazyka* (St. Petersburg, 1879): 110–12.

1. addressing the emperor: *han, ejen, abkai jui, dergi, dele, tumen se, enduringge ejen, genggiyen ejen*, or *hūwangdi.*
2. addressing higher officials: *wesihun amban, wesihun hafan.*
3. addressing other superiors: *looye* or *amba looye.*
4. addressing people of equal rank: *wesihun, wesihun beye, wesihun nofi, ahūn*; *agu, age, ahūn i beye, yekengge niyalma, aisin cira.* The word *wesihun* is commonly used for 'you' in modern letters.

Numerals

Ordinal numerals

emuci (also: *uju, ujui, tuktan*)	first
juweci (also: *jai, ilhi, jaici*)	second
gūsici	30th
nadaci	7th
juwanci	10th
juwan emuci	11th
tofohoci	15th
tanggūci	100th
minggaci	1000th

Distributive numerals

emte	one each
juwete	two each, every two
ilata	three each, every three
juwanta	ten each (ten retains the final *n*)
tofohoto	every fifteen, fifteen each
orinta, orita	twenty each
dehite	forty each
tanggūte	a hundred each

Multiplicative numerals

juwe ubu	twofold, double, two times (as much)
ilan ubu	threefold, triple, three times (as much)
nadan ubu	sevenfold
emursu	one layer
jursu	two-layered, double
ilarsu	three-layered, triple
emgeri, emu mudan, emu jergi	once (*-geri* after consonants other than *n*)
juwenggeri, juwe mudan, juwe jergi	twice (*-ggeri* after *n*)
ilanggeri, ilan mudan, ilan jergi	three times

Fractional numerals

duin i emu	1/4
duin ubu de emu ubu	1/4
duin ci emu	1/4
duin ubu de ilan ubu	3/4
minggan i emu	1/1000
hontoho	1/2

Dates

In dates, only the year and the reign take ordinal numerals. Cardinal numerals are used with months and days. The day may be followed either by *inenggi* or by *de*. When no day is mentioned, there is no *de* after *aniya*. As in Chinese, the first ten days of the month are preceded by *ice* 'new'.

Reign + *i*	ordinal + *aniya*	cardinal + *biya* + *i*	cardinal (+ *inenggi* or *de*)
abka wehiyehe i	*nadaci aniya*	*juwan biyai*	*orin emu inenggi*
abka wehiyehe i	*nadaci aniya*	*juwan biyai*	*orin emu de*
abka wehiyehe i	*nadaci aniya*	*juwan biyai*	*orin emu*

'(on) the twenty-first day of the tenth month in the seventh year of Qianlong'

aniya inenggi	(on) the first day of the year
ice sunja inenggi	(on) the fifth day (of the month)
juwe biya de	in the second month
ilan biyai orin ilan de	on the twenty-third of the third month
aniya biyai juwan uyun de	on the nineteenth of the first month
omšon biyai ice nadan de	(on) the seventh day of the eleventh month
gurun i ejen sunja de soorin de tembi	on the fifth the leader of the country sits on the throne
susai sunjaci aniya Eseyen akū oho	Husayn died in the fifty-fifth year
duleke aniya juwan biyai orin de	(on) the twentieth of the tenth month of last year
abkai wehiyehe i tofohoci aniya omšon biyai ice duin de	on the fourth day of the eleventh month in the fifteenth year of Qianlong
emu minggan uyun tanggū uyunju ningguci aniya nadan biyai tofohon de	on July 15, 1996

Adjectives

Adjectival modifiers derived from verbs

sara gisun	the language one knows
gidaha hoton	the towns one has defeated
genehekū niyalma	the people who did not go
marire cooha	the returning troops
sarkū bithe	the language one does not know
duleke baita	things of the past
bisire ulha	all one's livestock
isinjihala ba	all the places one has gone to

Adjectival suffixes with special meanings

-kan, -ken, -kon 'somewhat', 'rather'

amba	large	*ambakan*	rather large
hūdun	fast	*hūdukan*	rather fast
muheliyen	round	*muheliyeken*	somewhat round
olhon	dry	*olhokon*	somewhat dry
ujen	heavy	*ujeken*	somewhat heavy

-liyan, -liyen 'a bit'

adali	similar	*adaliliyan*	a bit similar
amba	great	*ambaliyan*	a bit large
uhuken	weak, soft	*uhukeliyen*	a bit weak, soft

-linggū, -linggu 'very'

amba	great	*ambalinggū*	huge
ehe	bad	*ehelinggu*	very bad

Derivational adjectives

noun + *-ngga, -ngge, -nggo*

baita	matter, thing	*baitangga*	useful, usable
gebu	name	*gebungge*	named
erdemu	virtue, capability	*erdemungge*	virtuous, talented
doro	morality	*doronggo*	moral, honest

verb stem + *cuka, -cuke; -hun, -hūn*

saišambi	to praise	*saišacuka*	praiseworthy
jobombi	to suffer	*jobocuka*	distressing
gelembi	to fear	*gelecuke*	frightful
olhombi	to fear	*olhocuka*	frightful, scary
wesimbi	to ascend	*wesihun*	honorable
yadambi	to be poor	*yadahūn*	poor

Comparisons

1. to be like something else
2. comparative, e.g., bigger than
3. superlative, e.g., to be biggest

(1) *loosa i adali kai*	you are like mules
(1) *aniyadari erei adali*	every year it's like this
(1) *singgeri gese ajige*	as small as a mouse
(2) *manju gisun ci nikan gisun mangga*	Chinese is more difficult than Manchu
(2) *tere ci amba*	it's bigger than that
(3) *šuwe amala i emke isinaha*	the last one arrived

Certain words that mean 'very' or 'exceedingly' (*jaci, ten i, umesi, nokai, mujakū, dembei, hon*) can also express the superlative. Example: *nikan gisun dembei mangga* or *nikan gisun mujakū mangga* 'Chinese is the most difficult'.

Adverbs

Adverbial instrumental genitive

Some nouns and adjectives can take on an adverbial function by adding the instrumental genitive *i*, in Sibe also *-iye*.

sain i arambi	to write well
yargiyan i ujen	truly heavy
cooha emke emken i isinaha	the soldiers arrived one by one
hūlha jenduken i ukaha	the bandits secretly escaped
singgeri amba jilganiye gisurehe	the mouse spoke in a loud voice

Adverbs with *seme*

Many adverbs are formed with *seme*.

šar seme	sympathetically, compassionately
teng seme	firmly, solidly
hing seme	honestly, sincerely; seriously (illness)
liyar seme	sticky, pasty
pio seme	floating, wafting
cib seme	quietly, swiftly
ainaha seme	surely, certainly
ser seme	lightly, gently

Amongst the *seme* adverbs quite a few describe sounds. They are called onomatopoetic words:

pus seme	sound of piercing something
kung cang seme	sound of drums and cymbals
pur seme	sound of birds taking flight
tuk tuk seme	pounding of the heart
hūwanggar seme	surging and roaring
tak seme	sound made by hitting something solid
kunggur seme	sound made by empty wagons, or heavy thunder
tab seme	sound of a bowstring hitting the back of the bow

Though these words appear most frequently as in their adverbial form with *seme*, they can also occur as subject (with *serengge*), as object (with *sere be*), as verb (with *sembi* or another finite form of *sembi*), or as adjective (with *sere*). Example: *hing sere mujilen i* 'with a sincere heart'.

Postpositions

There are no prepositions in Manchu. Instead Manchu has a great number of post-positions. Some of these follow nouns, some follow verbs, and some follow either nouns or verbs. Some postpositions require a specific case marker or verb form.

Examples of postpositions following nouns with genitive *i*:

adali	*aniyadari erei adali wakanio?*	isn't it like this every year?
amala	*booi amala*	behind the house
amargi	*birai amargi Gulja de tataha*	they stopped north of the river at Kulja
baru	*Hojijan Burut i baru kimulehe*	Hojijan harbored a grudge against the Burut
dolo	*arara be meni dolo bahanarakū*	we don't know how to do the writing
emgi	*bi sini emgi genembi*	I am going with you
fejile	*e i fejile me sinda*	put a *me* under the letter *e*
funde	*bi sini funde Harbin de genembi*	I'll go to Harbin for you
jakade	*cooha unggifi Ogen birai jakade tataha*	they sent troops and had them stop near the Ogen River
jalin	*tere siden i jalin faššaha*	he labored on behalf of the public (good)
juleri	*geren i fejile uru waka be tucibu*	lay out the right and wrong in front of everybody
sasa	*Lamacab i sasa jihe niyalma*	the people who came with Lamacab

Examples of postpositions following nouns with case markers other than *i*:

ebsi	*udu aniya ci ebsi*	for many years
fusihūn	*fujiyang ci fusihūn*	from the vice general down
tulgiyen	*ninggun tanggū cooha ci tulgiyen*	besides five hundred soldiers
dahame	*Osman umai ini ama be dahame tehengge waka*	Osman did not live together with his father

Examples of postpositions following verbs:

dahame	*te abkai gurun i aha oho (be) dahame*	because I have now become the subject of your country
ebsi	*ere bithe be hūlaha ci ebsi*	ever since I read this book
jakade	*Kasigar be afara jakade*	because they attacked Kashgar
manggi	*oron tucike manggi*	after the position becomes vacant
onggolo	*boode isinara onggolo*	before he arrived at home
saka	*isiname saka*	as soon as he arrived
siden	*jai inenggi erde urebure siden*	when they did their early morning drills
songkoi	*terei gisurehe songkoi Kasigar de dosika*	they entered Kashgar in the way he had told them
turgunde	*Amursana ubašaha turgunde*	because Amursana rebelled

Verbs

Manchu verbs can express past, present, and future, but they generally do so by indicating the relationship between different actions or situations rather than relating the action or situation to the time of speaking. Also, Manchu verb forms commonly occur without personal pronouns or subjects and lack distinguishing features to indicate whether the subject is the first, second, or third person. In such cases the context determines how a given verb form translates into English.

Scholars of Manchu have offered various categorizations and descriptions of Manchu verbs forms. Several decades ago Denis Sinor, in his article "La langue mandjoue" (written in 1958, and published in *Handbuch der Orientalistik.* Erste Abteilung, V. Band, Dritter Abschnitt. Edited by B. Spuler [Leiden/Köln: E.J. Brill, 1968]: 257–80), suggested that Manchu verbs designate a state or process which is either completed or awaiting completion and that it would be best to use the term aspect instead of tense. In this kind of framework the *-mbi* verb figures as neutral aspect, a form which does not commit itself to whether the process is completed or not. Sinor also entertained the possibility of considering all Manchu verbs, except *bimbi* 'to be', nouns or adjectives, words which can be turned into finite verbs with the help of the one true verb, *bimbi* (I would add *ombi* 'to become'). I find Sinor's suggestions interesting and helpful for understanding Manchu verbs, but I am not aware of other scholars having taken up this issue and developing it further.

Until we have a definitive study of Manchu verbs, preferably one in English, students may want to consult the categorizations of verb forms presented in recent Manchu grammars. (Aisin Gioro Ulasicun, p. 212; Guo Xiuchang Tong Qingfu and Zha Lu'a *Nei fon i Sibe gisun. Xiandai Xibo yu*, p. 376; Qu Liusheng, ed. *Manwen jiaocai*, pp. 131–36; and Kawachi Yoshihiro, *Manshūgo bungo bunten*, pp. 95-131. For complete information, see under References.

Tentative overview of finite verb forms

		Perfective (Past)	Imperfective (Non-perfective)
I	1	*-ha, -he, -ho*	*-mbi*
	2	*-ha bi, -he bi, -ho bi*	*-ra, -re, -ro*
II	1	*-mbihe, -me bihe*	*-me bi*
	2		*-me bimbi*
	3		*-mahabi, -me ilihabi*
III	1	*-mbihe bi*	*-habi, -hebi, -hobi*
	2	*-fi bihe*	*-fi bi*
	3	*-hai bihe, -hei bihe, -hoi bihe*	*-hai bi, -hei bi, -hoi bi*
IV		*-ha bihe, -he bihe, -ho bihe*	*-ha bihe bi, -he bihe bi, -ho bihe bi*

Perfective (Past)

I 1) an action was completed in the past (I wrote)
2) emphasis, assertive: it is a fact that...

II 1a) progressive (process) in the past (I was writing)
1b) habitual past (I used to write)
1c) hypothetical (I should have written)

III 1a) some action was completed in the past (I had written)
1b) an action occurred frequently in the past (I often wrote)
2) an action or event occurred in the past and its state continues (it is written):
baita be ejefi bihe 'one had recorded the matter', 'the matter was recorded'
3) something continued to occur in the past (I kept writing):
kemuni erehei bihe 'I had always wanted it'

IV an action or situation was ongoing for a certain period in the past (I had been writing)

Imperfective (Non-perfective)

I
1a) an action or situation is habitual or frequent (I often write)
1b) a general statement (one writes, I write)
1c) an action/event will occur (I will write)
2) same meaning as 1 but this form is rarely a finite verb

II
some action or situation is in progress (I am writing)

III
the action is completed in the past but influences the present (I have written; it is written). Examples:
tere emgeri jihebi 'he has already come'
baita be ejefi bi 'one has recorded the matter', i.e., 'the matter is recorded'
aifini ci bodohoi bi 'one planned it for a long time', 'it was planned for a long time'
kemuni erehei bi 'I've always wanted it'

IV
the action began in the past and its effect continues into the present (I have been writing)

Affirmative and negative finite verb forms. Examples for *arambi*:

araha	*arahakū (bi)*
arambihe	*ararakū bihe*
arame bihe	*ararakū bihe*
arambihebi	*ararakū bihebi*
araha bihe	*arahakū bihe*
arambi	*ararakū (bi)*
arara	*ararakū (bi)*
arame bi	*ararakū (bi)*
aramahabi	*(jing) aramahakū bi*
arame ilihabi	*(jing) aramahakū bi*
arahabi	*arahakū bi*
arafi bi	*ararakū ofi bi*
arahai bi	*ararakū ohoi bi*
araha bihebi	*arahakū bihebi*

Imperatives, desideratives, and optatives

Imperative: I want you to do something
Desiderative: somebody wants/wishes to do something
Optative: I want a third person to do something

Imperative 1. Verb stem. Informal command to a second person. Example: *ara* 'write', *ume ara* 'do not write'.

Imperative 2. Verb stem + *-rao, reo, -roo.* A more polite imperative. Example: *ararao* 'please write', *ararakū obureo* 'please, don't write'.

Imperative 3. Verb stem + *-ki.* Polite request: *teki* 'please sit down', *ararakū oki* 'please do not sit down'.

Desiderative 1. Verb stem + *-ki.* A desire or intent to do something. Example: *bi bithe araki* 'I will write a letter', 'I want to write a letter;' *bi bithe ararakū* 'I will not write a letter'.

Desiderative 2. Verb stem + *-ki sembi.* Somebody wants to do something; *araki sembi* 'I want to write', *ararakū oki sembi* 'I do not want to write'.

Optative 1. Verb stem + *-kini.* Hope or permission that somebody may do something, generally (but not always) referring to a third person. Example: *arakini* 'may he write', 'I hope he will write', *ararakū okini* 'may he not write'. This form is also used to convey permission. Example: *jikini* 'may he come', 'let him come'. In sentences with a permissive meaning, the *-kini* verb is sometimes preceded by the conditional form of the same verb. Example: *araci arakini* 'if he writes let him write', i.e., 'he may write'.

Optative 2. Verb stem + *-cina.* This optative is a polite expression of a desire to have an action performed, usually by the person spoken to. The ending *-cina* does not have a permissive meaning. Example: *aracina* 'I hope you will write', 'I would like you to write', 'please write', 'may you write', *ararakū ocina* 'may you not write'.

Optative 3. Verb Stem + *-kini sembi.* I want you or somebody else to do something. Example: *bi simbe marikini sembi* 'I want you to return', *bi simbe marirakū okini sembi* 'I want you not to return'.

Examples

I want you to do something: verb stem, *-ki, -cina, -rao (-reo, roo), -kini, -kini sembi*

tefi jefu	sit down and eat
omicina	please drink
dosiki	please come in
suwe yabuki	please go ahead
giljareo	please excuse me
tubade genekini	please go there
bi simbe marikini sembi	I want you to return
bek sede sujakini seme bithe unggihe	one sent a letter to the *beg*s asking them to resist

Somebody wants/wishes to do something: *-ki, -ki sembi*

manju gisun i araki	let us write in the Manchu language
enteheme banjiki	I want to live forever
Hošik be Yerkiyang ni baita be daiselabuki	let us have Hošik administer Yarkand
bi manju gisun be taciki sembi	I want to learn Manchu
bi bithe be hūlaki sembi	I want to read the book
ergen guweki seme ukaha	he fled wanting to save his life
tere yabuki sembi, bi unggirakū oki	he wants to go, but I will not send him

I want a third person to do something: *-kini, -kini sembi*

urse be ujikini	let him support the people
urse be ujirakū okini	don't let him support the people
bi imbe Harbin de genekini sembi	I want him to go to Harbin
imbe jikini	let him come
baita be hūdun baicakini	let them investigate the matter quickly
da an i Kašigar ba i akim bek i tušan de bibukini	have him occupy the original position of governor of Kashgar

Expressions of fear

1. verb stem + *rahū*
2. *gelhun akū* + negative verb
3. negative verb + *ayoo*
4. negative verb + *ayoo sembi*
5. verbs of fear: *gelembi, olhombi, etc.*

(1) *Akim ini deo ujen weile baharahū seme gūniha*	Akim feared that his brother might have committed a serious crime
(1) *nikan i doro dosirahū seme olhorongge kai*	one has to fear that they will fall into Chinese ways
(2) *gelhun akū generakū*	he is afraid to come
(2) *hūlha isinjifi gelhun akū Kara Usu i kaha bade hanci latunahakū*	after the rebels arrived they did not dare strike near the blockade of Kara Usu
(3) *ere ujen tušan be muterakū ayoo*	I am afraid I can't handle this difficult task
(4) *elhe ojorakū ayoo seme Yerkiyang de forgošoho*	fearing that there would be no peace one transferred him to Yarkand
(4) *jiderakū ayoo sembi*	I am afraid he will not come
(5) *bi generakū seme gelembi*	I am afraid to go
(5) *mimbe ukara de gelehe*	he was afraid I would escape

Converbs

A converb modifies another converb or a finite verb. It cannot end a sentence.

Coordinative (imperfective or nonperfective) converb *-me*

1. expresses simultaneous action
2. modifies the following verb
3. expresses purpose (especially with verbs of movement)
4. occurs with auxiliary verbs

(1) *bithe be kubulime manju gisun i araki*	let's change the script and write in Manchu
(1) *kesi isibume akim bek sindaha*	I granted favor and appointed him governor
(2) *bithe be kūbulime manju gisun i araki*	let us write in the Manchu language by changing the Mongol script
(2) *manjurame gisure*	speak in Manchu
(3) *Burut de cooha fideme genehe*	he went to the Kirghiz to enlist troops
(3) *okdome genehe*	he went to meet them
(4) *isinjime muterakū*	I could not get through (arrive)
(4) *ere jaka be baitalame bahanarakū*	I don't know how to use this thing

Watch for look-alikes: When the word *bime* 'being' connects two adjectives it means 'and'. Example: *morin amba bime akdun* 'the horse is large and strong'. There are also words other than converbs that end in *-me*. Examples:

bitume	along
dahame	after, because, according to
gojime	however, but
isime	approximately
jakarame	along
ninggureme	on top of
sirame	next
šurdeme	around

Subordinative (perfective) converb *-fi*

The subordinative converb refers to a sequence of actions. One action is completed before another action begins. A few verbs take the suffix *-pi* or *-mpi* instead of *-fi*.

suwe tefi tuwa	sit down and watch
tefi jefu cai omi	sit down, eat, and drink tea
Hošik Aksu de isinjifi Jaohūi de okdoho	after Hošik arrived in Aksu he met with Jaohūi

When following an imperfective converb, the perfective converb of *ombi*, *ofi*, means 'because'.

same ofi	because one knows
fejergi urse be jobobume ofi	because he made his people suffer

Conditional/temporal converb -*ci*

1. specifies the time when an action occurs
2. defines the condition under which an action occurs

(1)	*amba cooha ibeneci uthai ukame genembi*	when the imperial army advanced, they fled
(1)	*musei cooha talade afaci uthai gidambi*	when our soldiers fight on the plains, they are victorious
(1)	*bithe be hulaci niyalma ulhimbi*	when one reads the language out loud, people understand
(2)	*a i fejile ma sindaci ama wakao?*	if you put *ma* under *a*, isn't it *ama*?
(2)	*bithe araci acambi*	I should write a letter
(2)	*tucibuhe bici fulehun de karulaci ombi*	if he brought it into the open, he could repay my favor
(2)	*bithe ararakū bihe bici ama generakū ombihe*	if I had not written a letter, father would not have gone

Terminative converb -*tala*, -*tele*, -*tolo*

An action which occurs up to a certain time.

aratala	until he writes (wrote)
bucetele hūsun tucike	he worked hard until he died
daci dubede isitala fafuršame yabuha	from beginning to end he acted bravely
yamji de isitala teni bederehe	he returned by evening
ilan biya otolo kabuha	he was besieged for three months

Preparative (prefatory) converb -*nggala*, -*nggele*, -*nggolo*

An action has not yet started or is not yet completed.

aranggala	before I write, before I wrote
booci tucinggele buda jefu	eat before you leave the house
tese hoise babe bahara onggolo Ili i bade dahanjiha	before we conquered the Muslim places they came to submit in Ili

Concessive converb *-cibe*

An action occurs even though a certain condition is present. Sometimes *seme* is added to the affirmative converb.

ba goro bicibe tere de geneki	although the place is far, I will go there
tutto bicibe	although it is like that
sehekū bicibe	though he did not say
sehe seme bicibe	even though he said

Durative (descriptive) converb *-hai, -hei, -hoi*

An action occurs or continues at the same time another action is performed.

necimbihei yabumbi	to continuously invade
yasa hadahai tuwambi	he kept staring
dasabuhai yebe ome mutehekū	he could not be cured and get better
injehei injehei hefeli gemu nimembi	I am laughing so hard my stomach hurts

Alternative converb *-ralame, -relame, -rolame*

Two actions are performed at the same time.

bi yaburelame tuwambi	I am looking as I go along
hūlaralame araci gebsun be onggorakū	if you read and write at the same time, you won't forget the words

Instrumental converb *-tai, -tei, -toi*

An action is performed in a forced or extreme manner.

bucetei daharakū	I will not submit, even if I die
beye be waliyatai faššambi	to work oneself to death (fig.)
tere be ergeletei unggihe bi	one forced him to go

Simultaneous converb *-mbime*

One action occurs, or does not occur, while another action takes place.

si baita be sambi sembime, ainu takaraku?	while you say you know about the matter, how come you don't know?
ubade hūdašambime tubade hūdašarakū doro bio?	is there a reason for people trading here but not there?

Topic markers of emphasis

1. *oci*: marks subjects or adverbial phrases
2. *serengge*: marks only subjects and frequently implies a category; sentence often ends in *inu* or *waka*
3. *seme*: marks subjects, adverbial phrases, and objects
4. *ningge*: marks nominal subjects
5. *be*: Some scholars do not consider *be* to be a topic marker, pointing out that when *be* appears to function as a topic marker, the sentence usually also contains a verb that takes the accusative case. In that case the *be* phrase may be seen as being the accusative to that verb, placed at the beginning of the sentence.

(1) *tere oci we?*	who is he?
(1) *dergi de oci Cu de gidabuha; wargi de oci Cin de gaibuha*	on the east they were defeated by Chu, on the west they were taken by Chin
(2) *bajen serengge, latufi jetere umiyaha inu*	as for the landlords, they are parasites
(2) *niyalma seme banjifi bucerakūngge waka*	all people live and die
(3) *ereni šuwe ajige hergen be seme getukeleme takaci mutembi*	one can clearly make out even his smallest letters
(4) *bajen ningge tumen minggan nimari bi*	as for the landlords, they have thousands of acres of land
(4) *ere bithe ningge manju bithe inu*	as for this book, it is a Manchu book

Sentence particles

Sentence particles convey some abstract meaning, such as the speaker's feelings. Some particles have more than one meaning. They occur at the end of a sentence and in some cases may be written in an attached form. Some of the more commonly used particles are listed below.

Particles of emphasis

1. *dere*
2. *dabala*
3. *kai*
4. *na* (Sibe)
5. *ye* (Sibe)

(1) *tuttu oci ere uthai nure i turgun dere!*	if it's that way, it surely is because of alcohol!
(2) *damu tafulara dabala!*	I am only advising you!
(3) *ere booi dolo umesi halhūn kai!*	it's hot in this house!

(3) *tuwaha kai!*	I did see him!
(4) *absi mangga na!*	how difficult!
(5) *dulekede adališarkū ohoye!*	it is no longer as it was in the past!

Particles of encouragement or request

1. *bai* (usually with some kind of imperative)
2. *dere*

(1) *amasi bedereki bai*	please go back
(1) *ubade suwembe baitalara ba akū be dahame, gemu gene bai*	since there is no need for you here, why don't you all leave?
(2) *sinde bisirengge oci, uthai inde bumbi dere*	if you have it, why don't you give it to him?
(2) *ya jaka oci, hūdun gajifi mende bumbi dere*	if you have some things, give them to us right away

Particles of conjecture

1. *dere* 'probably, likely'
2. *aise* 'perhaps'
3. *ba* 'I suppose'
4. *ayoo* 'probably'

(1) *jasigan be bargiyame bahaha dere*	you probably have received the letter
(2) *inde yala jiha akū aise*	perhaps he truly does not have any money
(3) *tere jime muterakū ba*	I suppose he cannot come
(4) *elhe ojorakû ayoo*	there probably can be no peace

Particle of limitation

dabala 'only, merely'

bi damu si jiderakū ayoo sere dabala	I am only worried that you won't come
emu ajige hafan dabala	he is only a low official

Particle of definition

be defines a term

banin serengge uthai giyan be	what is natural is reasonable
amba ningge etuhun ojoro be kai	big means strong

Particle of astonishment

semeo forms rhetorical questions

waka semeo?	isn't that not so?
yala sain akū semeo?	isn't that truly good?

Questions

Question particles and suffixes

-o (*-bio, -mbio, -rao, -reo, -roo, -hao, -heo, -hoo, -kao, -keo*)

a i fejile ma sindaci ama wakao?	if you put *ma* under *a*, isn't it *ama*?
aika baita bio?	is anything the matter?
tereningge bio?	is it his?
nikarame bahanambio?	can you speak Chinese?
manjurame mutembio?	can you speak Manchu?
te geli majige yebeo?	are you now a bit better?

ni, -ni (*mbini, akūni*)

1. general questions
2. questions that are contrary to the speaker's belief
3. choice questions

Questions with *ni* tend to include interrogative pronouns or other questions words.

(1) *ere ai turgun ni?*	what is the reason?
(1) *si ubade tembini?*	do you live here?
(2) *si ubade terakūni?*	don't you live here?
(2) *ararakū ni?*	aren't you going to write?
(3) *Harbin de geneme generakū ni?*	are you going to Harbin or not?
(3) *tuwara tuwarakū ni?*	do you see it or not?

nio, -nio (*-mbinio*)

sefu nio?	is he (are you) a teacher?
umesi goro nio?	is it very far?
jimbinio?	is he coming?
si mini deo be sabuha nio?	have you seen my younger brother?
ere niyalma sain akū nio?	is this man not good?

-n (only with *akū*)

mutembio akūn?	can you do it (or not)?
suwe alahakūn?	did you not report [it]?
tuwarakūn?	don't you see it?

na, -na, ne, nu

generakū na?	aren't you going?
sabuhana?	did you see it?
yargiyan uttu na?	is it really true?
sini ama boode bina?	is your father home?
gisurerakū nu?	does he not say?
generakū ne?	aren't you going?

-mna (Sibe)

samna?	do you know?
si genemna?	are you going?
beyeni usin tarimna?	do they till their own fields?
si tacikū de genere be cihalamna?	do you like going to school?

ye, -ye (Sibe)

nei erin absi ohoye?	how has it been these days?
tere ainaha bihe ye?	how was he?

Question words

we	who (persons)
ai	what (things)
ya	which, what (persons or things)
ai erinde, ya erinde, atanggi	when
adarame, ai turgun (de), ai jalin	why
ainame, ainahai, ainu, adarame, antaka, absi	how
ya ba (de), aibide	where, what place
udu	how many, how much

Choice questions

These and other combinations are possible.

tuwambi tuwarakū?	do you see it or not?
tuwambio akūn?	do you see it or not?
tuwame tuwarakū?	do you see it or not?
tuwara tuwarakū?	do you see it or not?
tuwara tuwarakū ni?	do you see it or not?
tuwambio tuwarakūn?	do you see it or not?
tuwambini tuwarakūn?	do you see it or not?
tuwaha tuwahakū?	did you see it?
tuwahao akūn?	did you see it?
tuwahao undeo?	have you seen it yet?
tuwahao tuwahakū nio?	did you see it?
tuwaci ombio ojorakū?	can you see it?

Miscellaneous Information

Manchu transliteration of Chinese syllables

Some Chinese syllables are transliterated in different ways. There may be additional versions to those listed below. *W-G stands for Wade-Giles.

Pinyin	W-G*	Manchu	Pinyin	W-G	Manchu
a	*a*	*a*	*chong*	*ch'ung*	*cung*
ai	*ai*	*ai*	*chou*	*ch'ou*	*ceo*
an	*an*	*an*	*chu*	*ch'u*	*cu*
ang	*ang*	*ang*	*chua*	*ch'ua*	*cuwa*
ao	*ao*	*ao, oo*	*chuai*	*ch'uai*	*cuwai*
ba	*pa*	*ba*	*chuan*	*ch'uan*	*cuwan*
bai	*pai*	*bai*	*chuang*	*ch'uang*	*cuwang*
bao	*pao*	*boo*	*chui*	*ch'ui*	*cui*
bei	*pei*	*bei*	*chun*	*ch'un*	*cun*
ben	*pen*	*ben*	*chuo*	*ch'o*	*co*
beng	*peng*	*beng*	*ci*	*tz'u*	*tsi*
bian	*pien*	*biyan*	*cong*	*ts'ung*	*tsung*
biao	*piao*	*biyoo*	*cou*	*ts'ou*	*tseo*
bie	*pieh*	*biye*	*cu*	*ts'u*	*tsu*
bin	*pin*	*bin*	*cuan*	*ts'uan*	*tsuwan*
bing	*ping*	*bing*	*cui*	*ts'ui*	*tsui*
bo	*po*	*bo*	*cun*	*ts'un*	*tsun*
bu	*pu*	*bu*	*cuo*	*ts'o*	*tso*
ca	*ts'a*	*tsa*	*da*	*ta*	*da*
cai	*ts'ai*	*tsai*	*dai*	*tai*	*dai*
can	*ts'an*	*tsan*	*dan*	*tan*	*dan*
cang	*ts'ang*	*tsang*	*dang*	*tang*	*dang*
cao	*ts'ao*	*tsao, tsoo*	*dao*	*tao*	*dao, doo*
ce	*ts'e*	*tse*	*de*	*te*	*de*
cen	*ts'en*	*tsen*	*deng*	*teng*	*deng*
ceng	*ts'eng*	*tseng*	*di*	*ti*	*di*
cha	*ch'a*	*ca*	*dian*	*tien*	*diyan*
chai	*ch'ai*	*cai*	*diao*	*tiao*	*diyoo*
chang	*ch'ang*	*cang*	*die*	*tieh*	*diye*
chao	*ch'ao*	*cao, coo*	*ding*	*ting*	*ding*
che	*ch'e*	*ce*	*diu*	*tiu*	*dio*
chen	*ch'en*	*cen*	*dong*	*tung*	*dung*
cheng	*ch'eng*	*ceng*	*dou*	*tou*	*deo*
chi	*ch'ih*	*ci*	*duan*	*tuan*	*duwan*

Pinyin	W-G	Manchu
dui	tui	dui
dun	tun	dun
duo	to	do
e	e, eh	e, o
ei	ei	ei
en	en	en
eng	eng	eng
er	erh	el, l
fa	fa	fa
fan	fan	fan
fang	fang	fang
fei	fei	fei
fen	fen	fen, fun
feng	feng	feng, fung
fo	fo	fo
fu	fu	fu, feo
ga	ka	g'a
gai	kai	g'ai
gan	kan	g'an
gang	kang	g'ang
gao	kao	g'ao
ge	ke, ko	ge
gei	kei	gei
gen	ken	gen
geng	kêng	geng
gong	kung	gung
gou	kou	geo
gu	ku	gu
gua	kua	guwa, gūwa
guai	kuai	guwai
guan	kuan	guwan,gūwan
guang	kuang	guwang
gui	kui	gui
gun	kun	gun
guo	kuo	g'o
ha	ha	ha
hai	hai	hai
han	han	han
hang	hang	hang
hao	hao	hoo
he	he, ho	he
hei	hei	hei
hen	hen	hen
heng	heng	heng
hong	hung	hūng
hou	hou	heo
hu	hu	hu
hua	hua	hūwa
huan	huan	hūwan
huang	huang	hūwang
hui	hui	hūi
hun	hun	hūn
huo	huo	ho
ji	chi	ji, gi
jia	chia	jiya, giya
jian	chien	jiyan, giyan
jiang	chiang	jiyang, giyang
jiao	chiao	jiyoo, giyoo
jie	chieh	jiye, jiyei, giyai
jin	chin	jin, gin
jing	ching	jing, ging
jiong	chiung	jiong, giong
jiu	chiu	jio, giyu
ju	chü	jioi, gioi
juan	chüan	jiowan, giowan, giyowan
jue	chüeh	jiyo, jiyowei, jiyuwei, jiowei
jun	chün	jiyūn, giyūn
ka	k'a	k'a
kai	k'ai	k'ai
kang	k'ang	k'ang
kao	k'ao	k'ao
ke	k'e, k'o	ke
ken	k'en	ken
keng	k'eng	keng
kong	k'ung	kung
kou	k'ou	keo
ku	k'u	ku
kua	k'ua	kuwa

Pinyin	W-G	Manchu	Pinyin	W-G	Manchu
kuai	*k'uai*	*kuwai*	*miao*	*miao*	*miyoo*
kuan	*k'uan*	*kuwan*	*mie*	*mieh*	*miye*
kuang	*k'uang*	*kuwang*	*min*	*min*	*min*
kui	*k'ui*	*kui*	*ming*	*ming*	*ming*
kun	*k'un*	*kun*	*miu*	*miu*	*mio*
kuo	*k'uo*	*k'o*	*mo*	*mo*	*mo*
la	*la*	*la*	*mou*	*mou*	*meo*
lai	*lai*	*lai*	*mu*	*mu*	*mu*
lang	*lang*	*lang*	*na*	*na*	*na*
lao	*lao*	*lao, loo*	*nai*	*nai*	*nai*
le	*le*	*le*	*nan*	*nan*	*nan*
lei	*lei*	*lei*	*nang*	*nang*	*nang*
leng	*leng*	*leng*	*nao*	*nao*	*nao, noo*
li	*li*	*li*	*ne*	*ne*	*ne*
lia	*lia*	*liya*	*nei*	*nei*	*nei*
liang	*liang*	*liyang*	*nen*	*nen*	*nen*
liao	*liao*	*liyoo, lioo*	*neng*	*neng*	*neng*
lie	*lieh*	*liye, liyei*	*ni*	*ni*	*ni*
lin	*lin*	*lin*	*nian*	*nien*	*niyan*
ling	*ling*	*ling*	*niang*	*niang*	*niyang*
liu	*liu*	*lio*	*niao*	*niao*	*niyoo*
long	*lung*	*lung*	*nie*	*nieh*	*niye*
lou	*lou*	*leo*	*nin*	*nin*	*nin*
lu	*lu*	*lu*	*ning*	*ning*	*ning*
lü	*lü*	*lioi*	*niu*	*niu*	*nio*
luan	*luan*	*luwan*	*nong*	*nung*	*nung*
lüe	*lüeh*	*liyo*	*nu*	*nu*	*nu*
lun	*lun*	*luwen*	*nü*	*nü*	*nioi*
luo	*luo*	*lo*	*nüe*	*nüeh*	*niyo*
ma	*ma*	*ma*	*nuo*	*no*	*no*
mai	*mai*	*mai*	*o*	*o*	*o*
man	*man*	*man*	*ou*	*ou*	*eo*
mang	*mang*	*mang*	*pa*	*p'a*	*pa*
mao	*mao*	*mao, moo*	*pai*	*p'ai*	*pai*
me	*me*	*me*	*pan*	*p'an*	*pan*
mei	*mei*	*mei*	*pang*	*p'ang*	*pang*
men	*men*	*men*	*pao*	*p'ao*	*pao, poo*
meng	*meng*	*meng*	*pei*	*p'ei*	*pei*
mi	*mi*	*mi*	*pen*	*p'en*	*pen*
mian	*mien*	*miyan*	*peng*	*p'eng*	*peng*

Pinyin	W-G	Manchu	Pinyin	W-G	Manchu
pi	*p'i*	*pi*	*sang*	*sang*	*sang*
pian	*p'ien*	*piyan*	*sao*	*sao*	*sao*
piao	*p'iao*	*piyoo*	*se*	*se*	*se*
pie	*p'ieh*	*piye*	*sen*	*sen*	*sen*
pin	*p'in*	*pin*	*seng*	*seng*	*seng*
ping	*p'ing*	*ping*	*sha*	*sha*	*ša*
po	*p'o*	*po*	*shai*	*shai*	*šai*
pu	*p'u*	*pu*	*shan*	*shan*	*šan*
qi	*ch'i*	*ci, ki*	*shang*	*shang*	*šang*
qia	*ch'ia*	*ciya, kiya*	*shao*	*shao*	*šao*
qian	*ch'ien*	*ciyan, kiyan*	*she*	*she*	*še*
qiang	*ch'iang*	*ciyang, kiyang*	*shei*	*shei*	*šei*
qiao	*ch'iao*	*ciyoo, kiyoo*	*shen*	*shen*	*šen*
qie	*ch'ieh*	*ciye, kiye*	*sheng*	*sheng*	*šeng*
qin	*ch'in*	*cin, kin*	*shi*	*shih*	*ši*
qing	*ch'ing*	*cing, king*	*shou*	*shou*	*šeo*
qiong	*ch'iung*	*ciyung, ciong, kiong*	*shu*	*shu*	*šu*
			shua	*shua*	*šuwa*
qiu	*ch'iu*	*cio, kio*	*shuai*	*shuai*	*šuwai*
qu	*ch'ü*	*cioi, kioi*	*shuan*	*shuan*	*šuwan*
quan	*ch'üan*	*ciowan, kiowan*	*shui*	*shui*	*šui*
que	*ch'üeh*	*ciyo, kiyo*	*shun*	*shun*	*šun*
qun	*ch'ün*	*ciyūn, kiyūn*	*shuo*	*sho*	*šo*
ran	*jan*	*žan*	*si*	*ssu, szu*	*sy*
rang	*jang*	*žang*	*song*	*sung*	*sung*
rao	*jao*	*žao*	*suan*	*tsuan*	*suwan*
re	*je*	*že*	*sui*	*sui*	*sui*
ren	*jen*	*žen*	*sun*	*sun*	*sun*
reng	*jeng*	*ženg*	*suo*	*so*	*so*
ri	*jih*	*ži*	*ta*	*t'a*	*ta*
rong	*jung*	*žung*	*tai*	*t'ai*	*tai*
rou	*jou*	*žeo*	*tan*	*t'an*	*tan*
ru	*ju*	*žu*	*tao*	*t'ao*	*tao, too*
ruan	*juan*	*žuwan*	*te*	*t'e*	*te*
rui	*jui*	*žui*	*teng*	*t'eng*	*teng*
run	*jun*	*žun*	*ti*	*t'i*	*ti*
ruo	*jo*	*žo*	*tian*	*t'ien*	*tiyan*
sa	*sa*	*sa*	*tiao*	*t'iao*	*tiyoo*
sai	*sai*	*sai*	*tie*	*t'ieh*	*tiye*
san	*san*	*san*	*tong*	*t'ung*	*tung*

Pinyin	W-G	Manchu	Pinyin	W-G	Manchu
tou	*t'ou*	*teo*	*yuan*	*yüan*	*iowan, yuwan*
tu	*t'u*	*tu*	*yue*	*yüeh*	*yo, yuwei*
tuan	*t'uan*	*tuwan*	*yun*	*yün*	*yun, yūn*
tui	*t'ui*	*tui*	*za*	*tsa*	*dza*
tun	*t'un*	*tun*	*zai*	*tsai*	*dzai*
tuo	*t'o*	*to*	*zan*	*tsan*	*dzan*
wa	*wa*	*wa*	*zang*	*tsang*	*dzang*
wan	*wan*	*wan*	*zao*	*tsao*	*dzao, dzoo*
wang	*wang*	*wang*	*ze*	*tse*	*dze*
wei	*wei*	*wei*	*zei*	*tsei*	*dzei*
wen	*wen*	*wen*	*zen*	*tsen*	*dzen*
weng	*weng*	*weng*	*zeng*	*tseng*	*dzeng*
wo	*wo*	*o*	*zha*	*cha*	*ja*
wu	*wu*	*u*	*zhai*	*chai*	*jai*
xi	*hsi*	*si, hi*	*zhan*	*chan*	*jan*
xia	*hsia*	*siya*	*zhang*	*chang*	*jang*
xian	*hsien*	*siyan*	*zhao*	*chao*	*jao, joo*
xiang	*hsiang*	*siyang*	*zhe*	*che*	*je*
xiao	*hsiao*	*siyoo*	*zhei*	*chei*	*jei*
xie	*hsieh*	*siye, siyei*	*zhen*	*chen*	*jen*
xin	*hsin*	*sin*	*zheng*	*cheng*	*jeng*
xing	*hsing*	*sing*	*zhi*	*chih*	*jy*
xiong	*hsiung*	*siong, siyung*	*zhong*	*chung*	*jung*
xiu	*hsiu*	*sio, siyu*	*zhou*	*chou*	*jeo*
xu	*hsü*	*sioi*	*zhu*	*chu*	*ju*
xuan	*hsüan*	*siowan*	*zhua*	*chua*	*juwa*
xue	*hsüeh*	*siyo*	*zhuai*	*chuai*	*juwai*
xun	*hsün*	*siyūn, siyun*	*zhuan*	*chuan*	*juwan*
ya	*ya*	*ya*	*zhuang*	*chuang*	*juwang*
yan	*yen*	*yan*	*zhui*	*chui*	*jui*
yang	*yang*	*yang*	*zhun*	*chun*	*jun*
yao	*yao*	*yoo*	*zhuo*	*cho*	*jo*
ye	*yeh*	*ye*	*zi*	*tzu*	*dz*
yi	*yi*	*i*	*zong*	*tsung*	*dzung*
yin	*yin*	*in*	*zou*	*tsou*	*dzeo*
ying	*ying*	*ing*	*zu*	*tsu*	*dzu*
yong	*yung*	*yung*	*zui*	*tsui*	*dzui*
you	*yu*	*io*	*zun*	*tsun*	*dzun*
yu	*yü*	*ioi*	*zuo*	*tso*	*dzo*

Alphabetization in traditional Manchu dictionaries

Looking up a word in a traditional Manchu dictionary can be cumbersome unless one is familiar with the principle of Manchu alphabetization. The entries in such dictionaries are arranged in the sequence of the Manchu alphabet and the listings under the individual letters follow a certain sequence of syllables.

Sequence of the Manchu alphabet

a, e, i, o, u, ū, n, k(a), g(a), h(a), k(o), g(o), h(o), k(ū), g(ū), h(ū), b, p, s, š, t(a), d(a), t(e), d(e), t(i), d(i), t(o), d(o), t(u), d(u), t(ū), l, m, c, j, y, k(e), g(e), h(e), k(i), g(i), h(i), k(u), g(u), h(u), k'(a), g'(a), h'(a), k'(o), g'(o), h'(o), r, f, w, ts, dz, z, sy, cy, jy

Note that front and back *k*, *g*, *h* are listed separately and that within the back set all syllables with the letter *a* precede syllables that contain *o* or *u*. For example, *ga* follows *ka*, but it precedes *ko* and *kū*. Similarly, with the front set, *ge* comes after *ke*, but before *ki* and *ku*. Front and back *t* and *d* are treated differently. Here, front *de* also follows front *te*, and *du* comes after *tu*, but hard *ti* and *di* follow front *te* and *de*, and precede front *tu* and *du*.

Within the listings under each Manchu letter the following sequence of syllables applies:

a	*e*	*i*	*o*	*u*	*ū*
ai	*ei*	*ii*	*(i)oi*	*ui*	*ūi*
ar	*er*	*ir*	*or*	*ur*	*ūr*
an	*en*	*in*	*on*	*un*	*ūn*
ang	*eng*	*ing*	*(i)ong*	*ung*	*ūng*
ak	*ek*	*ik*	*ok*	*uk*	*ūk*
as	*es*	*is*	*os*	*us*	*ūs*
at	*et*	*it*	*ot*	*ut*	*ūt*
ab	*eb*	*ib*	*ob*	*ub*	*ūb*
ao	*eo*	*io*	*oo*	*uo*	*ūo*
al	*el*	*il*	*ol*	*ul*	*ūl*
am	*em*	*im*	*om*	*um*	*ūm*

Sample sequences

1. *na, naiman, narhun, ne, nememe, niyalma, non, nure*
2. *anambi, aha, acambi, aciha, aika, arbun, an, akdumbi, amban*
3. *takambi, tacikū, tasha, tampin, da, dari, dambi, te, deyen, den, tubihe, dulin*
4. *kai, kambi, gaha, gamambi, hada, hafan, koro, goro, holo, kūwaran, gūsa*

Qing dynasty reigns

Reign title		Personal name		Reign date
Chinese	**Manchu**	**Chinese**	**Manchu**	
Tianming 天命	*abkai fulingga*	*Nuerhachi* 努而哈赤	*Nurhaci* or *Nurgaci*	1616–1627
Tiancong 天聰	*sure han*	*Huangtaiji* 皇太極	*Hong Taiji*	1628–1636
Chongde 崇德	*wesihun erdemungge*			1636–1643
Shunzhi 順治	*ijishūn dasan*	*Fulin* 福臨	*Fulin*	1644–1661
Kangxi 康熙	*elhe taifin*	*Xuanye* 玄燁	*Hiowan Yei*	1662–1722
Yongzheng 雍正	*hūwaliyasun tob*	*Yinzhen* 胤禎	*In Jen*	1723–1735
Qianlong 乾隆	*abkai wehiyehe*	*Hongli* 弘歷	*Hung Li*	1736–1796
Jiaqing 嘉慶	*saicungga fengšen*	*Yongyan* 顒琰	*Yong Yan*	1796–1820
Daoguang 道光	*doro eldengge*	*Minning* 旻寧	*Min Ning*	1821–1850
Xianfeng 咸豐	*gubci elgiyengge*	*Yizhu* 奕詝	*I Ju*	1851–1861
Tongzhi 同治	*yooningga dasan*	*Zaichun* 載淳	*Dzai Šūn*	1862–1874
Guangxu 光緒	*badarangga doro*	*Zaitian* 載湉	*Dzai Tiyan*	1875–1908
Xuantong 宣統	*gehungge yoso*	*Puyi* 溥儀	(none)	1909–1911

Ten stems [*gan* 干]

甲	*jia*	*niowanggiyan*	green
乙	*yi*	*niohon*	greenish
丙	*bing*	*fulgiyan*	red
丁	*ding*	*fulahūn*	reddish
戊	*wu*	*suwayan*	yellow
己	*ji*	*sohon*	yellowish
庚	*geng*	*šanyan*	white
辛	*xin*	*sahūn*	whitish
壬	*ren*	*sahaliyan*	black
癸	*gui*	*sahahun*	blackish

Twelve branches [*zhi* 支] or Horary characters

子	*zi*	*singgeri*	rat	三更	third watch	11 P.M.–1 A.M.
丑	*chou*	*ihan*	ox	四更	fourth watch	1–3 A.M.
寅	*yin*	*tasha*	tiger	五更	fifth watch	3–5 A.M.
卯	*mao*	*gūlmahūn*	hare			5–7 A.M.
辰	*chen*	*muduri*	dragon			7–9 A.M.
巳	*si*	*meihe*	snake	上午	morning	9–11 A.M.
午	*wu*	*morin*	horse	正午	noon	11 A.M.–1 P.M.
未	*wei*	*honin*	sheep	下午	afternoon	1–3 P.M.
申	*shen*	*bonio*	monkey			3–5 P.M.
酉	*you*	*coko*	rooster			5–7 P.M.
戌	*xu*	*indahūn*	dog	初更	first watch	7–9 P.M.
亥	*hai*	*ulgiyan*	boar	二更	second watch	9–11 P.M.

Selected Reference Materials

Dictionaries

An Shuangcheng 安雙成 et al., eds. *Man–Han da cidian* 滿漢大辭典. Shenyang: Liaoning chubanshe, 1993. (Manchu–Chinese).

Tong Yuquan 佟玉泉, He Ling 賀靈. *Sibe Manju gisun i buleku bithe*. Urumchi: Xinjiang renmin chubanshe, 1987. (Sibe–Sibe).

Haneda Toru 羽田亨. *Man–Wa jiten* 滿和辭典. Kyoto, 1937. (Manchu–Japanese, but includes Chinese citations).

Hauer, Erich. *Handwörterbuch der Mandschusprache*. Wiesbaden: Harrassowitz, 1952–1955. (Manchu–German).

Hu Zengyi, ed. 胡增益. X*in Man–Han da cidian* 新滿漢大辭典. Urumchi: Xinjiang renmin chubanshe, 1994. (Manchu–Chinese).

Liu Housheng 劉厚生 et al. *Jianming Man–Han cidian* 簡明滿漢辭典. Kaifeng, Henan daxue chubanshe, 1988. (Manchu-Chinese).

Liu Housheng 劉厚生 & Li Leying 李樂营 eds. *Han man cidian* 漢满辭典. Beijing: Minzu chubanshe, 2005

Norman, Jerry. *A Concise Manchu–English Lexicon*. Seattle and London: University of Washington Press, 1978. (Manchu–English).

Stary, Giovanni. *Taschenwörterbuch Sibemandschurisch–Deutsch*. Wiesbaden: Harrassowitz, 1990. (Sibe–German).

Tamura Jitsuzo 田村實造, Imanishi Shunju 今西春秋, and Sato Hisashi 佐藤長. *Gotai shimbunkan yakkai* 五體清文鑒譯解. Kyoto: Kyoto University Press, 1966–1968. Indexed version of the *Wuti Qingwenjian* 五體清文鑒. (Manchu–Chinese).

Tsintsius, V.I. *Sravnitel'nyi slovar' tunguso-man'chzhurskikh iazykov*, I–II. Leningrad, 1975–1977. (Manchu–Russian).

Wujala Wenling (Wu-zha-la Wen-ling) 吳扎拉。文齡, ed. *Han-Xi jianming duizhao cidian* 漢錫簡明對照辭典. Urumchi: Xinjiang renmin chubanshe, 1989. (Chinese–Sibe).

Wuti Qingwenjian 五體清文鑑. 3 vols. Peking: Renmin chubanshe, 1957. (Manchu–Chinese).

Grammars and texts

Aisin Gioro Ulasicun (Aisinjueluo Wulaxichun) 愛新覺羅 。烏拉熙春, *Manyu yufa* 滿語語法. Huhehot: Nei Menggu chubanshe, 1983.

Clark, Larry V. "Manchu Suffix List." *Manchu Studies Newsletter* III, 1979–1980, pp. 29–40.

Gabelentz, H. C. von der. "Beiträge zur mandschurischen Konjugationslehre." *Zeitschrift der deutschen morgenländischen Gesellschaft* XVIII, 1864, pp. 202–29.

Gorelova, Liliya M. editor. *Manchu grammar*. Leiden ; Boston: Brill, 2002.

Guo Xiuchang 郭秀昌, Tong Qingfu 佟清福, and Zha Lu'a 扎魯阿. *Nei fon i Sibe gisun* [*Xiandai Xiboyu* 現代錫伯語]. Urumchi: Xinjiang Renmin chubanshe, 1995.

Haenisch, Erich. *Mandschu Grammatik mit Lesestücken und 23 Texttafeln.* Leipzig, 1961.

Harlez, Charles de: *Manuel de la Langue Mandchou. Grammaire, Anthologie et Lexique.* Paris, 1884.

Hauer, Erich. "Abriß der manjurischen Grammatik." Edited by Martin Gimm, Giovanni Stary, Michael Weiers. *Aetas Manjurica* 2. Wiesbaden: Harrassowitz, 1991.

Ji Yonghai 季永海, Liu Jingxian 劉景憲, and Qu Liusheng 屈六生. *Manyu yufa* 滿語語法. Beijing: Minzu chubanshe, 1984.

Ji Yonghai 季永海, Zhao Zhizhong 趙志忠, Bai Liyuan 白立元, eds. *Manju gisun jakūn tanggū hacin. Xiandai Manyu babaiju* 現代滿語八百句. Beijing: Zhongyang minzu chubanshe, 1989.

Kawachi, Yoshihiro 河内良弘. *Manshūgo bungo bunten* 滿洲語文語文典. Kyoto: Kyoto University Press, 1996.

Li Shulan 李樹蘭 and Zhong Qian 仲謙. *Xiboyu jianzhi* 錫伯語簡志. Beijing: Renmin chubanshe, 1986.

Liu Jingxian 劉景憲. "Zixue Manyu jiaocai" 自學滿語教材. *Manyu yanjiu* 滿語研究. Beginning with No. 1, 1985, about 20 pages in each issue.

Möllendorf, P. G. von. *A Manchu Grammar, with Analyzed Texts*. Shanghai, 1892.

Peeters, Hermes. "Manjurische Grammatik." *Monumenta Serica* V, 1940, pp. 349–418.

Qu Liusheng 屈六生. *Manju hergen tacibcen. Manwen jiaocai* 滿文教材. Urumchi: Xinjiang Renmin chubanshe, 1991.

Sinor, Denis. "La langue mandjoue." Edited by B. Spuler et al. *Handbuch der Orientalistik* I, V, Altaistik 3. Leiden-Köln, 1968, pp. 257–280.

Wylie, Alexander: *Ts'ing Wan K'e Mung (A Chinese Grammar of the Manchu Tartar Language; with Introductory Notes on Manchu Literature)*. Shanghai: London Mission Press, 1855.

Zakharov, Ivan. *Grammatika man'chzhurskogo iazyka*. St. Petersburg, 1879. Reprint. *Grammar of Manchu*. Honolulu, University of Hawaii Press, 2009.

Zhang Huake 張華克 ed. and annotator. *Qingwen xuzi zhinan jiedu* 清文虛字指南解讀. Taipei Yingyu wenhua chubanshe, 2006.

References related to the study of Altaic languages

Benzing, Johannes. *Einführung in das Studium der altaischen Philologie und der Turkologie*. Wiesbaden: Harrassowitz, 1953.

———. *Die tungusischen Sprachen; Versuch einer vergleichenden Grammatik.* Mainz: Akademie der Wissenschaften und der Literatur. Wiesbaden, In Kommission bei F. Steiner [1956].

Jin Qicong 金啓孮. *Nuzhen wen cidian* 女真文辭典. Beijing: Wenwu chubanshe, 1984.

Jin Qicong 金啓孮 and Jin Guangping 金光平. *Nüzhen yuyan wenzi yanjiu* 女真語言文字研究. Beijing: Wenwu chubanshe, 1980.

Kane, Daniel. *The Sino–Jurchen Vocabulary of the Bureau of Interpreters*. Bloomington, Ind., Indiana University, Research Institute for Inner Asian Studies, 1989.

Kiyose, Gisaburo. *A Study of the Jurchen Language and Script: Reconstruction and Decipherment*. Kyoto: Horitsubunka-sha, 1977.

Poppe, Nicholas. *Introduction to Altaic Linguistics*. Wiesbaden: Harrassowitz, 1965.

Rozycki, William. *A Reverse Index of Manchu*. With the assistance of Rex Dwyer. Bloomington, Ind., Indiana University, Research Institute for Inner Asian Studies, 1981.

———. *Mongol elements in Manchu*. Bloomington, Ind., Indiana University, Research Institute for Inner Asian Studies, 1994.

Schmidt, P. von. "Chinesische Elemente im Mandschu." *Asia Major* 7 (1931): 573–628.

Wadley, Stephen A. *Mixed-language verses from the Manchu dynasty in China*. Bloomington, Ind., Indiana University, Research Institute for Inner Asian Studies, 1991.

Reference materials for historical research

(From Jiang Qiao. "Der Lehrstoff fuer Lesung and Uebersetzung der Mandjurischen Akten." [Mainz, 1993]: 19–37. Unpublished.)

Da Qing quanshu 大清全書. *Daicing gurun i yooni bithe*. 1683. Contains about 10,000 words, among them many loanwords from Chinese as well as some older expressions from the early Qing.

Gongwen chengyu 公文成語. *Siden i bithe icihiyara de baitalara toktoho gisun*. 1889. Over 1200 entries of commonly used phrases in documents. Manchu–Chinese, arranged by categories.

Guanya mingmu 官銜名目. *Hafan hergen i gebu*. 1889. Contains over 900 titles from all levels of the bureaucracy. Manchu–Chinese equivalents. The titles are listed in the following order: titles related to royal family, to officials, civilians, and eunuchs.

Jiu Qingyu 舊清語. *Yargiyan kooli ci tukiyeme fe Manju gisun i bithe*. 1740–1780. Contains over 800 difficult words, phrases, and sentences from the early Qing. Explained in standard Manchu. Reprinted in 1987 by the Sinkiang People's Press.

Man Han hebi liubu chengyu 滿漢合璧六部成語. Urumchi: Xinjiang Renmin chubanshe, 1990.

Qingwen zonghui 清文總匯. *Manju gisun i uheri isabuha bithe.* 1897. Over 20,000 entries, arranged by Manchu syllables and explained in Chinese. The words are mostly taken from the *Qingwenjian* 清文鑒 (1708) and from the revised and expanded *Qingwenjian* (1771). A few words are taken from Manchu books and documents.

Qingwenjian 清文鑒. *Han i araha Manju gisun i buleku bithe.* 1708. Over 12,000 entries, explained in Manchu. Arranged by classification, with alphabetic index.

Wuquandian zishu 無圈點字書. *Tonki fuka akū hergen i bithe.* 1741. Difficult words from the Old Manchu Archives (1607–1636). Explained in standard Manchu.

Yashu mingmu 衙署名目. *Jurgan yamun i gebu.* 1889. Contains 1000 entries on organizations from all levels of the bureaucracy. Includes geographical names in the capital, names of palaces, and administrative units. Manchu–Chinese, arranged by categories.

Zeng ding Qingwenjian 增訂清文鑒. *Han i araha nonggime toktobuha Manju gisun i buleku bithe.* 1771. Revised and expanded *Qingwenjian.* Contains over 18,000 words. Manchu–Chinese dictionary, but with explanations in Manchu. Arranged by categories with alphabetic index.

Zhezou chengyu 摺奏成語. *Wesibure bithe icihiyara de baitalara toktoho gisun.* 1889. Over 500 entries of common idiomatic expressions used in memorials. Manchu–Chinese, arranged by categories.

Index of Grammatical Points

Vocabulary

(H): Charles O. Hucker, *A Dictionary of Official Titles in Imperial China* (Stanford, Ca.: Stanford University Press, 1985).

(BH): Brunnert, H.S. and V. V. Hagelstrom, *Present Day Political Organization in China* (Foochow, China: 1911).

Aba: (pers. name)
Abduhalik: (pers. name)
Abdukerem: (pers. name)
Abdunidzar: (pers. name)
Abdura'im: (pers. name)
Abdurman: (pers. name)
abka: heaven, emperor, sky
abkai kesi: heavenly peace
abkai wehiyehe: Qianlong reign (1736-1796)
absi: how? where to?
Abul: (pers. name)
Aca Amtatai: (geogr. name)
acabumbi: to match, to adapt to; to mix; to come together
acambi: to come together, to combine, to be in agreement, to be appropriate
acan: joined; harmony, union
acanambi: to fit, to be correct; to go to meet
aciha: baggage
adali: similar
adalingga: similar, like
adališambi: (with *de*) to resemble, to be like
adambi: to stand by, to be close to
adarame: how, why, what is to be done
adarame ohode: how, in what way
afabumbi: to entrust to, to commission, to order, to hand over
afaha bithe: list, chapter, page, sheet
afambi: to take charge of; to fight
afanambi: to go and attack
aga: rain
aga dambi: to rain
agambi: to rain
age: prince, son of emperor; polite term of address: master, sir, lord
agu: respectful term of address for men, sir, master
Aguda: (pers. name)
agūra: implement, weapon
aha: slave, servant
Ahamat: Ahmad (pers. name)
ahun: *akhund* (religious title)
ahūn: elder brother
ahūngga: eldest
ahūta: brothers (plural of *ahūn*)
ai: what? which?
ai ai: all kinds, various kinds
ai erinde: when?
ai jalin: why?
ai turgunde: why?
aibici: from where?
aibide: where?
Aidzung (Chin. *Aizong* 哀宗): ninth Jin dynasty emperor, 1224-1234
aifini: already, long ago
aika: any; if
aika... -ci: if
aikabade: if
aimaka: probably, seemingly
aimaka ... gese: it seems like
aiman: tribe
ainaha: what sort of
ainaha seme: surely, certainly, categorically
ainambi: to do what, how, why

ainame: how?
ainahai: how?
ainci: apparently, perhaps, probably
ainu: why? how?
aise: perhaps (sentence particle)
aisilakū hafan: (Chin. *yuan wailang* 員外郎) vice director of a bureau (H 8251)
aisilambi: (w/dative) to help, to provide
aisin: highly respected; gold
Aita: alias for Liu Xingzuo (劉興祚)
ajige: small
ajige amban: I (memorialist's humble reference to himself)
akambi: to be sad, to grieve
akdacuka: trustworthy, dependable
akdacun: trust, trustworthiness; what one depends on, livelihood
akdambi: to rely on
akdulambi: to defend; to confirm, to guarantee; to make strong; to recommend
akdulame tuwakiyambi: to defend resolutely
akdulame wesimbumbi: to submit a memorial of recommendation
akdun: strong
Akim: (pers. name)
akim bek: local governor (BH 863)
Aksu: (geogr. name)
akū: there is not, there are not
akū ombi: to die
akūmbumbi: to exert to the utmost, to do one's best
ala: hill with a level top
alambi: to inform
alanjimbi: to come to inform
alanju: imperative of *alanjimbi*
alba: shoulder blade
albabun: tribute
albabun jafambi: to bring tribute
alban: service, obligation (to a superior), tax, duty, tribute; official, public
alban i: official(ly)
alban i usin: public lands; lands of military colonies
alban kambi: to be on duty, to do a duty, to go out on an official errand
Alcur: (geogr. name)
Aldar: (pers. name)
algimbi (-ka): to be famous, to become known
alibumbi: causative of *alimbi*; to present, to offer (to a superior)
alibume boolara jalin: to communicate (between government offices)
alibume unggimbi: to send a communication
alibun: report, petition
alibure bithe: official report from lower to higher level
alifi icihiyambi: to handle, to deal with
alimbaharakū: greatly, exceedingly; intolerable
alimbi: to receive; to undertake; to hold up, stop up
alime gaimbi: to accept, to receive
alingge = *adalingga*: similar, same, this kind
aliyambi: to repent, to regret; to wait
aliyame gūnimbi: to regret
aljambi: to leave, to change color
ama: father
amaga: later, future, afterwards
amaga jalan: later generations, posterity
amala: after; later; behind; north
Aman: (pers. name)
amargi: north, back, behind
amargi be toktobure jiyanggiyūn (Chin. *dingbei jiangjun* 定北將軍): general for pacifying the north
amasi: backward
amasi bederembi: to demote
amba: great
amba dulin (Chin. *daban* 大半): most

amba jiyanggiyūn (Chin. *da jiangjun* 大將軍): general-in-chief (H 5897)
amban: minister, official; large, wide, great (same as *amba*)
amban be: we (memorialists referring to themselves)
amban bi: I (memorialist referring to himself)
ambarambi: to do on a large scale
ambula: very much, great(ly), widely
amcambi: to catch up to, to pursue; to take advantage of; to review a case
amcame: posthumously
amgambi: to sleep
amtangga: sweet, tasty, delicious
amtanggai: pleasurably
amuran: (with *de*) addicted
Amursana: (pers. name)
an: usual, ordinary, common
an i: original, as customary, same, continued
an i da: original, same
anagan: pretext
anambi: to move
aname: in sequence, in order, one after another
angga: mouth
angga acambi: to testify in court, to state orally
angga arambi: to acknowledge orally
anggala: person, individual, people; (postposition) in place of, instead of; not only
aniya: year
aniya biya: first lunar month of the year
aniya cimari: New Year's morning
Anjiyan: Andijan (geogr. name)
antaka: how?
ara: write (imperative)
Aralbai: (pers. name)
arambi: to do, to make; to celebrate; to write; to consider; to appoint; to pretend
arbun: condition; portrait
arga: device, plan, method
arga akū: there is nothing one can do about it
arga de dosimbi: to fall into s.o.'s trap
argangga: crafty, cunning
argiyambi: to scrape off, to expunge, to dismiss
asarambi: to collect; to put away, to store
asari: pavilion
ashambi: to wear hanging from the belt
ashan: side
ashan i amban (Chin. *shilang* 侍郎): vice minister (H 5278)
asihan: young
Asma: (pers. name)
aššambi: to move, to shake
asuru: very, exceedingly, a lot
atanggi: when
Atbaši: Atbash (geogr. name)
Awangdanjin: (pers. name)
ayoo: sentence particle of uncertainty or fear
ayoo sembi: to be afraid

ba: Chinese mile (576 meters); place; local; ancestral home; circumstances, situation; particle of conjecture
ba ba: everywhere
Babak: (pers. name)
Badakšan: Badakshan (geogr. name)
badaran: expansion, growth
baha: perf. participle of *bahambi*
Bahadun: (pers. name)
bahambi: to obtain
bahanambi: to understand, to comprehend; to be able
bai: particle of encouragement or request
Bai: (geogr. name)
baibi: simply, merely; ordinary; with no purpose

baibumbi: to require, to need, to use
baicambi: to investigate, to examine; to claim, to look for
baimbi: to request, to seek refuge, to claim, to look for
baime dahambi: to submit, to join
bairengge genggiyen i bulekešereo: I beg your majesty's perusal
baisu: imperative of *baimbi*
baita: matter
baita alimbi: to handle matters, to perform duties of the job
baita de genembi: to attend to matters
baita icihiyambi: to administer matters
baita icihiyara amban (Chin. *banshi dachen* 辦事大臣): grand minister superintendent (H 4414)
baita icihiyara ashan i amban (Chin. *banshi shilang* 辦事侍郎): vice minister (H 5278)
baita icihiyara gūsa be kadalara amban (Chin. *banshi dutong* 辦事都統): commander in chief (H 7321)
baitalambi: to use, to employ
baitalan: instrument, tool, useful things
baitalan: utilization, use
bajen: landlord
baksi (Chin. *boshi* 博士): scholar, learned man
balai: indiscriminately, falsely
balama: reckless, mad, crazy
bana i halan: land reform
Bandi (Chin. *Bandi* 班第): (pers. name)
banin: nature
banjimbi: to form, to come into existence, to be born; to live; to make a living
banjimbi sain: to be on good terms
banjin: life, livelihood
bargiyambi: to harvest, to receive; to keep, to collect; to store; to protect
baru: toward, opposite
bata: enemy
Batujirgal: (pers. name)
baturu: brave, hero
baturulambi: to act heroically
Baya Endur: (geogr. name)
bayalambi: to be happy
be: we (exclusive); accusative case marker; earl (H 4718; Chin. *bo* 伯); sentence particle (Chin. *ye* 也])
bederembi: to return
beidembi: to examine, to judge a case, to try (a court case), to sentence
beile: prince, *beile* (H 4526)
beise: plural of *beile;* later in the Qing dynasty *beise* becomes a separate rank
Bejing: Beijing
bek: *beg* (Turkish title)
bele: grain, hulled rice
belembi: to bear false witness
belhembi: to prepare
benembi: to take, to send off; to send or escort under guard
benjimbi: to bring; to send in, to transmit
beri: bow
bethe: foot, (lower) leg
beye: self; body; figure; life
beye be hairambi: to have self-respect, to behave like a gentleman
beye foršohombi (Chin. *fanshen* 翻身): to "turn over," to be liberated
beyembi: to freeze
bi: there is, there are; I (first person singular)
bibumbi: to retain
bigan: wilderness, uncultivated area
bihe bihei: in the long run
bilumbi: to calm, to soothe
bimbi: to be, to remain
bira: river
bisire: imperfective participle of *bimbi*
bisirele: all, all existing
bithe: language, book, letter

bithesi (Chin. *bitieshi* 筆帖式): scribe, clerk (H 4601)
biya: month
boco: sex, lust
boco de dosimbi: to be lustful, to be lecherous
bodombi: to calculate, to plan
boigon: household
boigon i jurgan (Chin. *hubu* 戶部): Ministry of Revenue (H 2789)
Boji (Chin. *Boji* 博濟): (pers. name)
boljoci ojorakū: it cannot be foreseen, it cannot be determined, unpredictable
boljombi: to agree on, to promise, to decide
Bolofu: (geogr. name)
boo: house, family
Booceng: (pers. name)
booi amban (Chin. *zongguan neiwufu dachen* 總管內務府大臣): grand minister of the Imperial Household Department (H 4291)
boolambi: to report
Borjigit: Borjigid (name of Chinggis Khan's clan)
Boroci: (geogr. name)
Boroci: (pers. name)
Bosihi (Chin. *Boshixi* 博什希): (pers. name)
boso: cloth
bošombi: to urge, to press
-bu-: passive, causative verbal suffix
bucembi: to die
buda: food, meal
buda jembi: to eat, to eat a meal
Bugur: (geogr. name)
Buhar Baimir: (pers. name)
buhiyembi: to suspect
buhū: deer
bujan: woods
Bujantai: (pers. name)
bujumbi: to boil, to cook
bukdari (Chin. *zouzhe* 奏摺): palace memorial
Bula: (geogr. name)
bulekušembi: to look in the mirror; to take note (by a superior)
bumbi: to give
Buranidun: Burhan ad-Din (pers. name)
burulambi: to flee
Burut: Kirghiz
buya: small, insignificant
buyembi: to love, to like, to desire

-ca-, -ce-, -co-: cooperative verbal suffix
Cahadai: Chaghadai (pers. name)
Cahandai: (pers. name)
cahin: bin, compartment for storing grain
calu: granary
cananggi: day before yesterday, previously
Cangšeo: (pers. name)
ce: they
cembe: them
Cenggunjab: (pers. name)
Cengguwe: (pers. name)
ceni: their
Cerimbum: (pers. name)
-ci: suffix for ordinals; conditional, temporal converb (if, when)
-ci acambi: if…it would be appropriate, ought, should
ci…de isibume: from…until
ci ebsi: ever since
-ci geli: even though, still
-ci ojorakū: if…it will not do, should not
-ci ombi: to be able
cib ekisaka: quiet
-cibe: concessive converb (although)
cifelembi: to spit
ciha: wish, will
cihanggai: willingly
Cikir: (pers. name)

cimari: morning, tomorrow
cin wang (Chin. *qin wang* 親王): imperial prince (designation for the sons of a reigning emperor) (H 1186)
-cina: optative verbal suffix (polite imperative)
cira: face, complexion; hard, solid; strict
cira aljambi: to change expression, to turn pale
ciralambi: to act strictly
Ciringjab: (pers. name)
Cirla: (geogr. name)
cisu: private, secret
cisui: privately, secretly
cohome: especially, exclusively
cohome wasimbumbi: to send a special communication
cohotoi: especially, particularly
coko: rooster
coko erinde: 5-7 P.M.
colgorombi: to excel
colo (Chin. *hao* 號): courtesy name, title
cooha: army
cooha de genembi: to go on a campaign
cooha dosimbi: to invade
coohai bithe: call to arms
coohalambi: to wage war
-cuka, -cuke: adjectival suffix
cukcurembi: to face forward, to protrude
cukumbi: to become tired
cuwangnambi: to seize by force, to rob

da: leader, head, origin; original, same
da an i: original, usual; as usual, as before
da bithe: original letter
dabagan: mountain pass
dabala: (postposition) besides; (sentence particle) only, merely
dabambi: to go against, to surpass
dabduri: irascible
dabume: (with *be*) including, comprising
daci: from the beginning, originally, formerly
daci dubede isitala: from the beginning to the end
dacun: sharp, clever
dacun ureme: clevery, sharply
dacun urehe: clever, diligent, sharp
dade: (adv.) in the beginning, originally; (postposition.) in addition to
Dahai: (pers. name)
dahalambi: to accompany
dahalame: jointly, at the same time
dahambi: to follow, to submit (past participle *daha* or *dahaha*)
dahame: (postposition, often with *be*) because; along
dahanduhai: subsequently
dahūmbi: to repeat, to do again
dahūme wesimbumbi: to memorialize in response
dahūn dahūn i: time after time, repeatedly
dailambi: to attack, to fight
daiselambi: to administer in an acting capacity
dalambi: to rule, to be chief
daldambi: to conceal, to cover up
dalimbi: to block off, to protect, to seal
dalji: relationship, connection
daljilakū: not to be of one's concern
daljilambi: to be of concern
dambi: to interfere, to take care of, to help, to aid
damu: but, however, nevertheless; only, just
Danjila (Chin. *Danjila* 丹濟拉): (pers. name; nephew of Galdan)
Danjin Ombu: (pers. name)
-dari: distributive nominal suffix (each, every)
daruhai: often, frequently; frequent, long-lasting

dasabumbi: to treat; to be cured, to become better
dasambi: to cure, to treat; to repair; to correct, to rule
dasame: again
dasan: good order, government
dasatambi: to repair, to put in order, to make arrangements
de: if, when, by; dative/locative case marker
de isibume: by (date)
debtelin: chapter
dedumbi: to lie down
dehi: forty
dehici: fortieth
dele: top, on top, above; supreme; on top; the emperor; after
dele tuwabume: for his majesty's information
dembei: exceedingly, greatly
den: loud; high, tall
den jilgan i: in a loud voice
dendembi: to divide
dendeme: separately, by dividing
deo: younger brother
dere: probably, likely (sentence particle); face; surface; direction; area
-dere: irregular imperfect participle ending
dere de eterakū: cannot do something for fear of hurting another's feelings
deretu: long desk, table
dergi: emperor; top, above; upper; east, eastern
dergi hese: imperial edict
dergici toktobure be gingguleme aliyaki: let me respectfully await your majesty's decision
deri: (ablative particle) from, than
deribumbi: to begin, to let begin, to conjure up
derimbi: to enter
deyembi: to fly
deyen: hall
dobori dulime: the whole night through
doigon: before, formerly, previously
doigonde: beforehand, previously
doigonci: from the beginning, early on
dolo: inside, the inside; among; within
dolo dahambi: to submit
dolo dahanjimbi: to come to submit
dolombi: to pour
donjibumbi: to inform
donjibume wesimbumbi: to memorialize to inform
donjimbi: to hear
Doolun: Dolun (people in East Turkestan)
doosidambi: to covet, to be covetous, to take bribes
dorgi amban (Chin. *nei dachen* 內大臣) grand minister of the Imperial Household Department; a general reference to members of the imperial family, nobles and other eminent persons who staffed the Imperial Household Department (H 4262).
dorgi baita be uheri kadalara yamun: the Imperial Household Department
doro: norm,Tao, way, right conduct, ceremony; government, empire
dorolon i jurgan (Chin. *libu* 禮部): Ministry of Rites (H 3631)
dosimbi: to enter
dosimbumbi: to promote; causative of *dosimbi*
dosinambi: (with *de*) to fall into
dube: end
dube tucimbi: to become clear about, to get to the bottom of something
duibulembi: to compare
duici: fourth
duilembi: to judge, to investigate the truth
duilesi: judge
duin: four
duka: gate

duleke aniya: last year
dulembi: to pass, to go by
dulembumbi: to experience, to pass through; caus. of *dulembi*; to cure
dulembun: experience
dulimbi: to stay up all night, to keep a vigil
dulin: half, middle
duribumbi: to be robbed, to lose
durimbi: to seize, to rob
durun: form, shape; model; rule, norm
dutang (Chin. *dutang* 都堂): official title for executive officer (H 7293)
duwali: faction
Dzewang Arabtan or *Dzewang Raptan*: Tsewang Raptan, nephew of Galdan
dzungdu (Chin. *zongdu* 總督): governor general (H 7158), same as Manchu term *uheri kadalara amban*

ebele: this side
eberembi: to diminish
eberembumbi: causative/passive of *eberembi*
ebsi: (w/*ci*) ever since; up till now; hither
ede: hereupon, then; therefore
Edegene: name of a Kirghiz tribe
edun: wind
efimbi: to play
efu: husband of imperial princess; husband of elder sister or of wife's elder sister; brother-in-law
efujembi: (intrans.) to be ruined; to be dismissed from a position; to break down
efulembi: (trans.) to break, to strip of (a rank)
ehe: bad
eici: or
eiten: all, everything
eiterecibe: nonetheless, in any case
ejelembi: to occupy, to rule, to establish control over
ejembi: to remember, to record
ejen: ruler, leader, master, host, emperor
ejen obumbi: to make s.b. leader
ekisaka: quiet, quietly
ekšembi: to hasten, to hurry
elcin: (plur. *elcisa*) envoy
elden: brilliance, resplendence, glory
eldengge: shining
ele: still more
elgiyen: plentiful, abundant
elgiyen tumin: plentiful, abundant
elgiyan tumin i bargiyambi: to harvest plentifully
elhe: peace
elhe be baimbi: to ask after a person's health
elhe taifin: Kangxi period
Elici: (geogr. name)
eljembi: to oppose, to resist
elkei = *elekei*: almost
elkimbi: to wave
emgeri: once, already
emgi: (w/genitive) with
emgi sasa: together
emhun: alone
Emin Batur: (pers. name)
emke: one
emke emken i: one by one
emken = *emke*: one
emteli alone, single, sole
emu: one
emu hebei ombi: to live in harmony, to be of one mind
emudan = *emu mudan*: one time
Emur: (pers. name)
encu: different, other, alone
enduringge: holy, divine, sacred
enduringge ejen: the divine lord, the emperor
enduringge tacihiyan: sacred instructions

enen: descendant
enenggi: today
enteheme: eternally, always
erali = ere adali: this way, this kind of
eralingge =ere adalingge: this way, it is like this
erde: early, early in the morning
Erdeni: (pers. name)
Erdeni Ujat: (pers. name)
ere: this
ere dade: moreover
erehunjembi: to hope for (w/acc)
ergelembi: to coerce
ergembi: to rest
ergen: life, breath
ergi: side
erin: time, season
erin akū: often
erin dari, erindari: every time, on every occasion, all the time
erin de acabure: seasonal, punctual
erin jurcembi: to miss the time
Erke: (pers. name)
ese: these
Eseyen: Husayn (pers. name)
eshen: father's younger brother
eshete: uncles (plural of *eshen*)
etembi: to overcome, to be victorious
etenggi: strong
etuhun: strong, powerful, bountiful, high
etuku: clothing
etumbi: to wear
eye: pit for storing grain or vegetables

facihiyašambi: to apply oneself; to worry, to be upset
facuhūn: rebellion
facuhūrambi: to be in disorder, to be in confusion
fafulambi: to prohibit
fafun: law
fafun i gamambi: to execute
fafuršambi: to act bravely, to act with determination
faha: kernel, grain
faidambi: to enumerate, to list
faidangga: arranged in order
faidangga ulabun (Chin. *liezhuan* 列傳): biography, collected biographies
faijuma: odd, worse
faitambi: to cut, to slice
faksalambi: to separate
falindumbi (Chin. *huxiang tuanjie* 互相團結): to unify; to be united, to achieve solidarity
fambi: to become tired; to dry up, to become very thirsty
Fan Ceng Hiyūn (Chin. *Fan Chengxun* 范承勛): (pers. name)
fancambi: to get angry
faššambi: to exert oneself, to make a great effort
faššan: effort
fe: old
Fe Ala: (geogr. name)
fejergi: under
fejile: (w/genitive) under
feksihei: at a gallop, quickly
feksimbi: to gallop, to run
fekucembi: to leap up, to skip
fempin = fempi: wrapper, cover; sealing tape
fen: minute
Fengšen: (pers. name)
feye: wound
-fi: subordinative (perfective) converb suffix (after)
fi: writing brush, pen
fidembi: to enlist
firgembi: to come to light, to be revealed, to leak out
Fiyanggū (Chin. *Feiyanggu* 費揚古): (pers. name)

fiyanggū: youngest
fiyenten: section of an official organization
foholon: short
fon: time
fondo: through, thorough, completely
fonjimbi: to ask
forgon: season
forgošombi: to transfer
forimbi: to strike, to knock
foršombi = *forgošombi*: to transfer, to change
fu (Chin. *fu* 府): residence, mansion
fudaraka be geterembure jiyanggiyūn: rebel-eradicating general
fudarambi (-ka): to rebel
fudasihūn: rebellion, rebellious
fudasihūn deribumbi: to become rebellious, to start a rebellion
Fude (Chin. *Fude* 富德): (pers. name)
fuhali: actually, completely, at all
fujiyang (Chin. *fujiang* 副將): vice general (H 2041)
fujurungga: fine, elegant
fukjin: beginning, origin
fukjin deribumbi: to originate
fulehun: alms, act of generosity
fulgiyan: red, purple, vermilion
fulgiyan fi i pilehe hese: imperial endorsement in vermilion ink
funcembi: to be in excess of, to be left over
funceme: over, in excess
funde: for the sake of, in place of
fung je yuwan (Chin. *fengzeyuan* 豐澤園): (place name)
funggala: feather
funghūwang: phoenix
funghūwang loose (Chin. *fenghuang lou* 鳳凰樓): Phoenix Tower (building on the grounds of the Shenyang Palace)
fungnembi: to appoint, to enfeoff
funiyehe: hair, fur
futa: rope

Gabšu: (pers. name)
gabtambi: to shoot an arrow
gabtara niyamniyara: dismounted and mounted archery
Gadaimet: (pers. name)
gaha: crow, raven
gaijambi: to receive; to raise
Gaijo (Chin. *Gaizhou* 蓋州): (geogr. name)
gaimbi: to take, to take away
gaisu: imperative of *gaimbi*
gajimbi: to bring
gamambi: to deal with, to take to another place
gamjidambi: to extort bribes, to act covetously
ganambi: to fetch, to gather, to go to take, to go to raise
gargan: detachment
gašan: village
gebu: name
gebungge: named
gejurembi: to seize, to force, to act cruelly toward
gejureme gaimbi: to oppress people, to extort bribes
gelecuke: frightful
Gelei Guyeng Dural: (pers. name)
gelembi: to fear
gelhun: fear
gelhun akū: dare to…, fearlessly
geli: again, then (also see *–ci geli*)
gelung (Chin. *gelong* 格隆): highest of three degrees of consecration in the Lamaist hierarchy (BH 873B)
gemu: in every case, even, all
gemun: imperial capital
gemun hecen: capital

genembi: to go, to leave
genggiyeken: rather enlightened, rather clear
genggiyen: bright, clear; smart, wise, enlightened
genggiyen i: graciously
geodebumbi: to lead s.o. astray, to be led astray
geodembi: to lead astray, to lure, to deceive
gercilembi: to accuse, to report s.o.
geren: numerous, the various; people, multitude
gese: (adj. and postposition) like, same
gese teherembi: to be even, to be equal
geseli: like this
getembi: to awaken
geterembi: to eradicate
getukelembi: to make clear, to explain
getuken: clear, lucid, understandable
getuken afaha: list, inventory (often enclosed as an attachment)
gidambi: to defeat, to suppress; to hide, to cover up, to oppress, to press
gidanjimbi: to come to raid, to come to force
gidašambi: to take unfair advantage of, to oppress
Gidzar: (pers. name)
giljambi: to pardon, to forgive
ging (Chin. *geng* 更): the watches of the night (five periods of two hours each)
ging forimbi: to strike the watch (with a wooden clapper)
ginggen (Chin. *jin* 斤): catty
ginggulembi: to respect, to honor, to act respectfully
gingguleme wesimbumbi (Chin. *jinzou* 謹奏): to respectfully memorialize
giran: corpse
giranggi: bones
gisabumbi: to wipe out, to annihilate
gisambi: to be exterminated
gisun: language, speech
gisun gaijambi: to take advice
gisurefi wesimbumbi: to submit a discussion memorial
gisurehe songkoi obu sehe: let it be as recommended
gisurembi: to discuss, to speak, to say
gisureme wesimbure jalin: to submit a memorial for discussion
giyalakū: interval, space; separation; divider
giyamun: military post station, courier station, relay station
giyamun deri benebumbi: to take via relay stations
giyamun tebumbi: to establish relay stations
giyan: reason; reasonable
giyan de acanambi: to be reasonable
giyan i: on principle, appropriately; duty-bound
giyan i ... -ci acambi: ought
giyan i wesimbuci acambi: it is my duty to report/memorialize
giyun wang (Chin. *jun wang* 郡王): commandery prince; high title of nobility normally granted to sons of imperial princes (H 1800)
gocika hiya (Chin. *yuqian shiwei* 御前侍衛): palace guardsman (H 8119)
Godoli Balhasun: (geogr. name)
goidambi: to last for a long time
golmin: long
goro: far
goroki be dahabure amba jiyanggiyūn (Chin. *fuyuan da jiangjun* 撫遠大將軍): general-in-chief who pacifies distant lands
gosimbi: to be moved with emotion, to cherish, to have mercy
gosire gūnin: concern, love

gu: jade
gubci: all, universal, entire
gucu: friend
gukumbi: to be annihilated, to perish
gulhun: entire, complete
Gulja: Kulja (geogr. name)
gung: merit; palace; duke (Chin. *gong* 公)
gung can dang (Chin. *gongchandang* 共產黨): Communist Party
gungge: merit, accomplishment
gungge ilibumbi: to accumulate merit
gurimbi: to move
gurgu: wild animal
gurun: country; people; tribe
gurun be dalire gung (Chin. *zhenguo jiangjun* 鎮國將軍): defender-general of the state (H 382)
gurun de aisilara gung (Chin. *fuguogong* 輔國公): bulwark duke, prince of the sixth degree (H 2075)
gurun de aisilara jiyanggiyūn (Chin. *fuguo jiangjun* 輔國將軍): bulwark-general of the state, noble of the tenth rank (H 2073)
gurun i doro: the way of the country, national polity, mandate of heaven
Guwanggun: (pers. name)
guwebumbi: to pardon, to forgive
guwembi: to forego, to pardon; to avoid
gūbadambi: to struggle, to squirm, to resist (when tied up)
gūidambi = *goidambi*: to last for a long time
gūnimbi: to think
gūnin: intention, thoughts, feelings, opinion, sense
gūnin arbun: intentions, inclination
gūnin werešembi: to pay attention, to be careful
gūsa: banner
gūsa be kadalara amban: lieutenant-general (of a banner) (BH 719)
gūsa beile (Chin. *gushan beile* 固山貝勒): *beile*, prince
gūsa beise (Chin. *gushan beizi* 固山貝子): *beile* prince (H 4546)
gūsici: thirtieth
gūsihūlambi = *gosiholombi*: to be miserable, to be distressed
gūsin: thirty
gūtubumbi: to be spoiled; to shame, to spoil
gūwa: other; other people, others

G'ag'ai: (pers. name)
G'aldan (Chin. *Gaerdan* 噶爾丹): Galdan (leader of the Dzungar confederation)
G'ansu: Gansu Province (geogr. name)
G'aopu: (pers. name)

-ha, -he, -ho: perfective verbal suffix
habšambi: to report; to accuse
habšanjimbi: to come to report, to come to accuse
hacihiyambi: to rush, to hurry
hacihiyame: quickly
hacilambi: to classify, to itemize
hacilame wesimbumbi: to submit a memorial of opinion
hacin: sort, kind, class, instance
hacingga: all kinds of
hadahai: fixedly (of looking)
hadambi: to affix, to fix the eyes on
hadumbi: to harvest, to reap, to cut with a sickle
hafan: an official, office, official responsibility
hafan i jurgan (Chin. *libu* 吏部): Ministry of Personnel (H 3630)
hafirabumbi: (trans.) to find or put oneself into a difficult situation; (intrans.) to be put into a difficult situation, to be pressured

hafirambi: to pinch, to pressure, to threaten
hafumbi: to go through, to penetrate; to comprehend, to thoroughly understand; to communicate, to have relations with
hafumbumbi: to give a detailed account of; to translate, to interpret; to send through, to send a message
hafumbume wesimbure bithe: routine memorial from higher provincial authorities submitted through the Transmission Office or the Grand Secretariat
hafunambi: to connect with another place
hafunjimbi: to come through
haha: man, male
haha jui: son
hahardambi: to become a man
hahilambi: to act quickly
hahilame wesimbumbi: to send an urgent memorial
-hai, -hei, -hoi: durative (descriptive) converb suffix
hairambi: to love, to cherish, to value
-hakū, -hekū, -hokū: negative perfective verbal suffix
hala: clan, family, family name
halambi: to change
halan: exchanging, reform (also see *bana i halan*)
halba: shoulder blade
halbumbi: (w/accusative) to give entrance to, to give shelter to
Hami: (geogr. name)
hamika: near
hamimbi: to approach, to be near
hamtambi: to defecate
han: emperor, khan
hanci: near
hancikan: rather near
handu: rice plant
handu bele: rice; rice plant
Hara Haši: Hara Hash (geogr. name)
harangga: the said; belonging to, subject; the appropriate
harangga ba: subordinate area
harangga niyalma: I (lower official to higher authority)
haratu: subject, subordinate, underling
hargašambi: to have an audience
haršambi: to cover up for, to be biased
hashū: left
hashūtai: depraved, heterodox
Hasihan: (pers. name)
Hasim: Hashim (pers. name)
hebdembi: to consult, to discuss; to conspire
hebedembi: old form of *hebdembi*
hebe: consultation, council, plot, plan
hebe hebdembi: to consult, to talk over
hebei amban (Chin. *canzan dachen* 參贊大臣): grand minister consultant (H 6893)
hebei ashan i amban (Chin. *yizheng shilang* 議政侍郎): vice minister consultant
hebei icihiyambi: to act in consultation, to act in unison
hebešembi: to discuss, to plot
hecen: city, town
hefeli: stomach
hehe: woman, female
hehe juse: family, dependents
hendumbi: to say, to speak, to answer
hengkilembi: to kowtow, to prostrate
heni: a little (w/neg: at all)
hergen: rank, title; alphabet letter
hese: imperial edict; fate
hese be baimbi: to request an edict
hesebumbi: to predict, to prophesy
hesei bithe: edict
hethe: property
hetu: broad, horizontal
heturembi: to block
hibcan: scarce, needy; frugal

Hidzung Hola (Chin. *Xizong* 熙宗): third Jin dynasty emperor, 1135-1150
hing seme: earnestly
hiracambi: to look with scorn, to spy on intently
hisalambi: to pour a libation in honor of the dead
hiya: guard, aide
hiya kadalara dorgi amban (Chin. *lingshiwei nei dachen* 領侍衛內大臣): grand minister of the Imperial Household Department, concurrently controlling the imperial guardsmen (H 3771)
hocarambi = *hūwacarambi*: to snore
hoise: Muslim
hojihon: son-in-law
Hojijan: Khoja Jihan (pers. name)
Hojis: (pers. name)
hojo: *khoja* (Muslim title)
hoki: accomplice
holbobumbi: to be connected with
holkon: moment, instant
holkonde: suddenly, in an instant
holo: spurious, false
holtombi: to deceive, to lie
hon: very, most, too
honin: sheep
honin erin: 1-3 P.M.
hono: still, yet
hontoho: half
Hoohan: Kokand (geogr. name)
horgimbi: to make a round, to spin
horimbi: to imprison
Hošik (Chin. *Heshike* 和什克): (pers. name)
Hošooci: (pers. name)
Hotiyan (Chin. *Hetian* 和闐): Khotan (geogr. name)
hoton: town, city
hukšembi: to be grateful for
hule: bushel
huthumbi: to tie up, to bind
huwekiyembi: to encourage
hūda: price, value; business; goods
hūda bumbi: to assess the value, to set the price
hūda salibumbi: to appraise the value
hūdai urse: merchant
hūdun: fast, quick
hūlambi: to read, to read aloud; to shout
hūlha: bandit, rebel
hūlha holo: robbers and thieves
hūlhambi: to act secretly, to rob, to steal
hūncihin: relatives by marriage
Hūsici: (pers. name)
Hūsita: (pers. name)
hūsun: power, might, strength
hūsun bumbi: to expend effort, be diligent
hūsun tucimbi: to render service, to work hard
hūsungge: strong, powerful
hūturi: good fortune
hūturingga: fortunate, lucky
hūwalambi: to break up, to cut up, to rip up
hūwaliyasun: harmony
hūwaliyasun gaimbi: to be in concord, to be in harmony
hūwang taidz (Chin. *huang taizi* 皇太子): heir apparent
hūwang taiheo (Chin. *huang taihou* 皇太后): empress dowager, mother of a reigning emperor
hūwangdi (Chin. *huangdi* 皇帝): emperor
hūwanggiyambi: (intrans.) to prevent, to stand in the way

i: genitive particle; he, she, it
Ibarayim: Ibrahim (pers. name)
ibembi: to go forward
ibenembi: to go forward, to advance
ice: new; beginning, at the beginning
Ice Jecen (Chin. *Xinjiang* 新疆): Sinkiang

ici: direction; right (not left); facing, toward
icihiyambi: to manage, to arrange, put in order; prepare a body for funeral
icihiyara hafan (Chin. *langzhong* 郎中): director of a section or bureau, e.g., the Court of Colonial Affairs (H 3565)
ihan: ox
Ike: (pers. name)
iktabumbi: (trans. and intrans.) to let s.th. pile up, to hoard; to pile up
iktambi: (trans.) to pile up, to accumulate, to hoard
ilaci: third
Ilagūksan: (pers. name)
ildun de: taking advantage of
iletulembi: to show
iletun: genealogical table, chart; elucidation, clearing up
Ilgar: (pers. name)
ilhi: next, subsequent
Ili: (geogr. name)
ilibumbi: to set up; to accumulate; to stop, to prevent
ilihai: immediately, on the spot
ilimbi: to stop (in a place); to stand (up), to set up; to recruit (troops); to serve, to occupy (a position)
ilinjambi: (intrans.) to come to a stop
imbe: him, her, it
In Ceng (Chin. *Yin Cheng* 胤成, later *Yin Reng* 胤礽): son of the Kangxi emperor
indahūn: dog
indahūn aniya: year of the dog
inde: dative/locative of *i*
indembi: to rest, to halt, to spend time
ineku: same
ineku inenggi: the same day
inenggi: day
Inggi Šar: Yanggishar (geogr. name)
ini: of him, it, her
injembi: to laugh
inu: is, was; also, too; so; correct, true
irgen: people (of a country), the common people
isambi: to assemble
isebumbi: to punish, to reprimand, to cause to fear
ishun: facing, next
ishunde: mutually
isigan bek: assistant governor (BH 863)
Isil Kur: (geogr. name)
isimbi: (with *de*) to be as good as; to reach; to suffice; to be about to
isinambi: to arrive
isingga: sufficient, adequate
isinjimbi: to arrive, to reach, to get to

ja: easy
jabšan: fortune
jabumbi: to answer; to consent
jaci: too, very; frequently
jacin: second, other
jafafi gamambi: to arrest, to capture
jafambi: to arrest, to seize, to draft, to take
jahūdai: boat
jai: second; next, again, furthermore, still; finally, as for, with respect to
jai inenggi: the next day
jailambi: to escape, to avoid, to get out of the way
jaisang (Chin. *zaisang* 宰桑): Mongolian title which replaced *taiji* for distinguishing the hereditary nobles of the Dzungar (Eleuth) tribes (BH 873A)
jaka: thing
jakade: because, when (w/imperfective); in front of, up to; near, in the neighborhood (w/genitive)
jaksaka: purple
jaksaka eldengge asari (Chin. *ziguangge* 紫光閣): Purple Brilliant Pavilion

jaksambi: to become purple
jakūci: eighth
jalahi jui: nephew
jalan: generation
jalin: for, on behalf of, because of
jalinde: (postposition) for the sake of
jalingga: traitorous, wicked
jaluka: (past participle of *jalumbi*) have become full
jalumbi: to be full; to be fulfilled, to fulfill
jang: 3.2 meters (10 Chinese feet)
janggin: official title (general term for military commander)
Jaohūi (Chin. *Zhaohui* 兆惠): (pers. name)
jargūci: judge
jasak: hereditary chief of a Mongol banner (H 35)
jasak beise: (official title)
jase: frontier
jase be tuwakiyara amban (Chin. *fanzhen* 藩鎮): military commissioner during the Tang dynasty (H 1865)
jasigan: letter
jasimbi: to mail, to send
jebele: quiver, case full of arrows
jecen: border
jecen be toktobure jiyanggiyūn (Chin. *dingbian jiangjun* 定邊將軍): pacifier of the frontier (H 6740)
jecen be toktobure hashū ergi aisilara jiyanggiyūn (Chin. *dingbian zuo-fujiangjun* 定邊佐副將軍: left pacifier of the frontier
jecen be toktobure ici ergi aisilara jiyanggiyūn (Chin. *dingbian you-fujiangjun* 定邊右副將軍): right pacifier of the frontier
jedz: memorial, same as *bukdari*
jefu: imperative of *jembi*
jeku: grain
jeku jembi: to eat
jembi (jemke, jetere): to eat; to put up with, to tolerate
jemengge: food, foodstuff
jendu: covertly
jenduken: secret, quiet, dark
jergi: grade, rank; sequence; layer; and so forth, kind of; ordinary
jergi tušan: official rank
jibca: fur (coat)
jidere: imperfect participle of *jimbi*
jiha: (monetary unit; 1/10 of an ounce of silver)
jilambi: to have compassion for
jilgan: sound, noise, voice
jilidambi or *jili dambi*: to get angry
Jilun: (pers. name)
jimbi: to come
jing: just at the time when, just; often, often, to keep on ...-ing
jingse: button (insignia of rank)
jio: (imperative of *jimbi*) come!
jirgacun: comfortable, leisurely
jirgacun sebjen: comfort
jiyanggiyūn (Chin. *jiangjun* 將軍): military general
jobocuka: distressing
jobombi: to suffer, to worry, to be in distress, to be in need
jobotembi: to do manual labor, to work hard
jobotengge: working, suffering
johimbi: to heal
jombumbi: to advise, to remind, to suggest
joombi: to cease, to stop
jorimbi: to point out, to direct; to avail o.s. of (pretext)
jufeliyen: dried grain; travel provisions (for longer excursions into the steppe)
jugūn: road
jugūn dulin: on the way

jui: son; child
julergi: front, in front
juleri: front, in front, before; south
juleri amala: one after another
julesi: forward
julge: antiquity, ancient times
Jun gar: Dzungars
Juncahai: (pers. name)
jungken: bell, clock
jungken erin: an hour's time
jurambi: to set out on a journey
jurambumbi: to send on one's way; causative of *jurambi*
jurcembi: to disobey, to go against one's word; to miss (a train, etc.)
jurgan: principle; line, row, path; duty, loyalty; ministry; board
jurhun (Chin. *cun* 寸): 1 Chinese inch, 1/10th of a foot
juse: children; sons
jušen: Jurchen [later called Manchu]
juwambi: to open the mouth
juwan: ten
juwan udu (Chin. *shiji* 十幾): in the tens
juwe: two
juwembi: to transport, to move, to transfer
juwen: loan, earnings

kadalambi: to rule, to govern
kai: sentence particle denoting emphasis
kaicambi: to shout, to yell
kaktambi: to obstruct
Kalka: Khalkha
kambi: to block, to surround
kamcimbi: to place close together; to serve concurrently; to do at the same time
kamni: narrow passage, defile
-kan, -ken, -kon: adjectival suffix indicating reduction in intensity (rather, a bit)
kanagan: pretext
Kara Šar: Karašar (geogr. name)
Kara Usu: (geogr. name)
karmambi: to protect
karulambi: to repay, to requite
karun: border guard, outpost sentry
Kašahojo: (pers. name)
Kašigar: Kashgar
katunjambi: to struggle to do something, to exert effort
kelfišembi: to be in doubt, to be irresolute
kemuni: likewise, still, yet; often
kemuni unde: not yet, still not
kenehunjembi: to doubt, to suspect
kenehunjere mangga: very distrusting
Kerya: (geogr. name)
kesi: favor, grace
kesi de hengkilembi: to prostrate to the imperial grace, to kowtow as an act of thanksgiving for the emperor's favor
kesi isibumbi: to bestow a favor
-ki: desiderative verbal suffix (let me, I will, please)
-ki seci: although
-ki sembi: desiderative verb phrase (speaker wants to do s.th.)
kicembi: (w/accusative) to strive for, to concentrate on; to be diligent
kimulembi: to harbor enmity, to seek revenge
-kini: let him, let them; may you
-kini, inu: even if, still
-kini sembi: to want s.b. to do s.th.
kiyan cing men (Chin. *qianqingmen* 前清門): Gate of Heavenly Purity
koimali: cunning, crafty
komso: few
kooli: rule, principle; law; custom; document; statute
kooli akū: there is no principle; it does not make sense
kooli bithe: document, statute

kooli selgiyere yamun (Chin. *hongwenyuan* 弘文院): Office for the Advancement of Literature (H 2912)
Kuce: Kucha (geogr. name)
kunesun: provisions (for shorter excursions or campaigns)
Kurcan: (pers. name)
Kurle: (geogr. name)
kurume: coat, garment worn over one's other garments
kūbulimbi: to change, to become altered
kūtuktu: Living Buddha (religious title)
kūwaran: camp

labdu: many
lama: lama (member of the Buddhist priesthood)
Lamacab: (pers. name)
largin: abundant, profuse, complicated
lashalambi: to cut off, to interrupt
lasihimbi: to shake
lasihiyambi = *lasihimbi*: to toss around, to shake
Lasrun: (pers. name)
latufi jetere umiyaha: parasite
latumbi: to depend on others, to stick; to provoke, to strike
-le: adjectival suffix (all there is)
lehembi: to demand
lempen: shelter
leose (Chin: *lou* 樓): tower
-linggu, linggū: adjectival suffix (very)
Lio Fujiyang (Chin. *Liu Xingzuo* 劉興祚): (pers. name)
-liyan, -liyen: adjectival suffix (a bit)
liyoo: fodder, forage
Liyoodung (Chin. *Liaodong* 遼東): (geogr. name)
Lobdzang: (pers. name)
Loosa Šongkoro Baturu: Loosa Šongkoro, the Brave (pers. name)
looye (Chin. *laoye* 老爺): master
losa: mule

mafa: ancestor, grandfather
mafari: ancestors (plural of *mafa*)
-mahabi: verbal progressive suffix
mahala: hat
Mahamat: (pers. name)
Maihamet Osan: (pers. name)
maise: wheat, grain
majige: a little; somewhat
majige saha babe gingguleme tucibume: please allow me to state my humble opinion
maksimbi: to dance
maktacun: praise, fame, eulogy
maktambi: to throw, to release; to praise
mama: grandmother
mamgiyambi: to squander, to be extravagant
Mampi (Chin. *Manpi* 滿丕): (pers. name)
Mamut: Mahmut (pers. name)
mangga: strong, firm; formidable; difficult; outstanding
manggi: after
Mangsur: (pers. name)
Manji: (pers. name)
Manju: Manchu
manjurambi: to do s.th. in the Manchu way
marambi: to refuse, to be obstinate
Margalang: Marghiland (geogr. name)
marimbi: to return, to go back
Mardza Nimet: (pers. name)
mayan: arm, elbow
mayan tatabumbi: to impede each other from doing work
-mbi: imperfective verbal suffix
-mbime: durative converb (while doing)
-me: coordinative (imperfective) converb

-me ilihabi: imperfective progressive finite verb
meihe: snake
meihe erin: (time of the snake) 9-11 A.M.
meiherembi: to carry on the shoulder
meiren: vice - (+ title); shoulder
meiren i janggin (Chin. *fu dutong* 副都統): vice commander-in-chief (H 2107)
mejige: message, news, information; military intelligence
mejigešembi: to spy
menggun: silver
meni: our
meni meni: each, every, severally, separately
mergen: wise man; wise, worthy, outstanding
meteku: animal offerings
metembi: to offer sacrifices
meyen: phrase, part, division
meyen i gisun: an expression
mimbe: me
minggan: thousand
Ming'ilha: Ming Ilha (pers. name)
mini: of me, my
Minjur: (geogr. name)
miyoocan: gun, musket, flintlock
-mna: interrogative suffix
monggo: Mongol, Mongolian
monggorombi: to act or speak Mongolian
Monggoso: Mongols
morin: horse
mudan: time, occurrence
Mudzapar: Muzaffar (pers. name)
mujakū: extremely, very
mujangga: true, correct; truly, indeed (sentence particle of emphasis)
muji: barley
mujilen: heart, mind, intention
mujilen bahambi: to understand, to comprehend
muke: water, stream
mukiyembi:
mukūn: clan, extended family
muse: we (inclusive)
mutebumbi: to achieve, to bring about (also see *tušan be mutebumbi*)
mutembi: to be able, to be possible; to be achieved
mutumbi: to grow, to be high

-n: interrogative suffix
-na, na: sentence particle for emphasis or suprise; interrogative particle
-na-, -ne-, -no-: allative verbal suffix (to go)
na: earth, land, field; local
nadaci: seventh
nakabumbi: to let go, to dismiss
nakambi: to stop, to desist, to leave a post
Namagan: (geogr. name)
Narabatu: (pers. name)
narhūšambi: to be minute, to do carefully; to do secretly
nashūn: opportunity, occasion
-ndu-: cooperative verbal suffix
ne: now; senence particle of mild interrogation
necihiyembi: to stabilize, to pacify
necimbi: to attack
necin: level, even; peaceful, calm
nei erin: nowadays
neimbi: to open
nenehe: former, previous, which went before
neneme: beforehand
nerginde: on that occasion
netele: up to now, until now
-ngga, -ngge, -nggo: adjectival suffix
-nggala, -nggele, -nggolo preparative converb suffix
-ngge: nominalizing suffix; possessive pronoun suffix

ni: genitive case marker (after *-ng*)
ni, -ni: interrogative particle or suffix
nikan: Chinese
nikembi: (w/dative) to lean on, to rely on, put oneself under the protection of; to join, to meet (said of places)
nikenjimbi: to draw near; to come to lean on
nimanggi: snow
nimari (Chin. *mu* 畝): one Chinese acre (about 1/16 of an English acre)
nimeku: sickness; pain; weakness
nimembi: to be sick
nimeme akū ombi: to die of an illness
ningge: the one which, he who
ningguci: sixth
ninggun: six
Ningguta: (geogr. name)
ninju: sixty
nio, -nio: interrogative particle or suffix
niohe: wolf
nioi ji (Chin. *nüzhen* 女真): Nuchen
niru: arrow (military unit)
nirugan: picture, sketch
nirumbi: to draw, to sketch
nišargan: a small sore
niyakūrambi: to kneel
niyalma: person, human being
niyamangga: to be related by blood
niyamniyambi: to shoot arrows from horseback; to practice mounted archery
niyengniyeri: spring
-nji-: verbal suffix (to come)
nofi: person (used after numbers larger than one)
nokai: very
Nomcidai: (pers. name)
non: younger sister
nonggimbi: to add, to increase
Noyan: (pers. name)
nu: question particle
-nu-: reciprocal verbal suffix
nukte: (nomadic) territory
nungnembi: to provoke, to harm, to murder
nure: wine

-o: interrogative and optative suffix
Ocang: (pers. name)
oci: topic marker, lit: "if it is…"
ofi: because (lit. 'having become')
Ogen: (geogr. name)
oi: exclamation used to call people's attention; sound used to call animals
ojorahū: it is to be feared
ojorakū: it will not be; it will not do, one cannot
okdombi: to go out to meet; to welcome; to engage the enemy
okto: medicine; gunpowder; poison
oktoshi: doctor
oktolombi: to poison
oktosi: doctor, physician
olhombi: to fear
olji: prisoner
oljilambi: to take prisoner
ombi: to become, to be; to be permissible, to be able; to agree
omimbi: to drink
omolo: grandson, grandchild
omosi: grandsons, grandchildren
omšon biya: the eleventh month
onco: broad, wide, generous
onggolo: before, prior to
onggombi: to forget
Opol: Opal (geogr. name)
orho: grass
orici: twentieth
orin: twenty
oron: place, vacancy; (official) position
Oros: Russian
oshodombi: to mistreat
Osikbesi: Osikbesh (geogr. name)
Osman: (pers. name)

oso: become! (imperative of *ombi*)
otok: tribal territory; tribe
otolo: until, up to
oyonggo: important

Padaimet: (pers. name)
Paihanpar: (pers. name)
Parsa: (pers. name)
pilembi: to write comments on a memorial
Polat: (pers. name)

-rakū: negative imperfective participle
-rahū: apprehensive converb suffix (fearing that)
-ralame, -relame, -rolame: alternative converb suffix
-rao, -reo, -roo: imperative verbal suffix
-re, -ra, -ro: imperfective verbal suffix

-sa, -se, -si: plural suffix
sabumbi: to see, to perceive
saha: noted (imperial comment)
saikan: carefully, well; beautiful
sain: good
Sair Balhasun: (geogr. name)
Sairim: (geogr. name)
saišacuka: praiseworthy
saišambi: to commend; to praise, to think highly of, to appreciate
saiyūn: to be well
saka: as soon as (with *-me* converb)
Sakalsopi: (pers. name)
sakini sere jalin: to inform, to notify for the record
Saksa Tehurik: (geogr. name)
salibumbi: to estimate the price
salja: branch, crossroads, fork
sambi: to know
Samsak: (pers. name)
saniyambi: to stretch
sargan: wife; woman; female
sargan jui: daughter
sarkū (= *sara*+*akū*): do *or* does not know
sasa: (w/genitive) with, together
se: year
se asihan: young
se bahambi: to grow old
sebjen: joy, gladness, pleasure
seci: although
secibe: although
sehe: marks the end of an imperial utterance
sejen: cart, vehicle
seke: sable
sekiyen: origin, source
selambi: to be content
sele: iron
selgiyembi: to disseminate
selgiyere hese: proclamation (to announce to the empire)
sembi: to say; *sembi* or *sehebi* marks the end of speech (by someone other than the emperor)
seme: because, although, no matter whether
semeo: sentence particle of astonishment
seolembi: to consider
ser sere: small, tiny
seremšembi: to guard against, to defend
Sereng: (pers. name)
sesheri: vulgar, common, lacking elegance
Setib Aldi: (pers. name)
Si An (Chin. *Xi'an* 西安): Sian (geogr. name)
siden: when; up to; interval; public
siden de: in between; in the meantime
siden i bithe: official document
sijigiyan: a long gown
sijirhūn: straight, not crooked
silhidambi: to be jealous, to envy

siliha cooha: crack troops, hand-picked troops
silimbi: to select
Silutei: (geogr. name)
simbi: to stop up, to seal
simembi: to soak, to moisten; to favor
sin: a measure equaling one Chinese bushel and eight pecks
sinagan: mourning
sinagan i baita: funeral
sindambi: to put, to release, to appoint
singgeri: mouse, rat
Sinju: (pers. name)
sirambi: to succeed, to inherit
sirame: next
siranduhai: one after another, in succession
sirentumbi: (w/dative) to enter secret dealings
sitahūn: deficient, scarce, few
sitahūn niyalma: term used by rulers to refer to themselves
sitambi: to be late, to be slow
siyanšeng (Chin. *xiansheng* 先生): Mr.
siyūn fu (Chin. *xunfu* 巡撫): provincial governor
songgombi: to weep, to cry
songgome fambi: to weep bitterly
songkoi: in accordance with
sonjombi: to select
soorin: throne
soorin de tembi: to ascend the throne; to sit on the throne
sorobumbi: to be exploited
sorombi: to exploit
sucumbi: to attack, to assault
suilambi: to suffer hardship, to be distressed; to work hard
suitambi: to pour, to spill, to splash
sujambi: to resist
suje: silk
sujelembi = *sebjelembi*: to rejoice
sukdujen (*sukdun* + *sejen*): car, vehicle
sukdun: air, breath; spirit
sula: free
sula amban (Chin. *sanzhi dachen* 散秩大臣): grand minister assistant commander of Imperial Guardsmen (H 4846)
Sulaiman: Sulayman (pers. name)
Sultan: (pers. name)
sumbi: to free, to sever
sunja: five
sunjaci: fifth
suntembi: to exterminate
sure: wise
surembi: to shout
susai: fifty
suwaliyambi: to mix, to combine; to implicate at all (w/ negative)
suwaliyame: together with, all at once, including
suwaliyame neneme wesimbumbi: to forward with this memorial
suwe: you (plural)

šabi: disciple, student
Šagudzeli: (geogr. name)
šahūrun: cold
šahūrukūn: rather cold
šajin: law, prohibition
Šaldalang: (geogr. name)
šalu = *salu*: whiskers
šan: ear
Šanahai: (pers. name)
šang bek: collector of revenues (BH 863)
šangnambi: to bestow, to grant
šar seme: sympathetic, sad, sorrowful
šayan = *šanyan*: white
Šayar: (geogr. name)
Šidzung Ulu han (Chin. *Shizong* 世宗): fifth Jin dynasty emperor, 1161-1189
šolo: leave, vacation, free time

šolo bahambi: to have time
šolo baimbi: to take time off, to ask for leave
Šose: (pers. name)
šošohon: compilation, summary
šošombi: to add together, to pull together
šošome gisurembi: to summarize
Šuhede: (pers. name)
Šundenen: (pers. name)
šurumbi: to go by boat
šusihiyembi: to agitate, to stir up
šuwe always; very, extremely; direct; totally
šuwe amala: the last

tabumbi: to tie up, to hook, to catch
tacibuha hese: imperial decree, imperial instruction (similar to *tacibure hese*)
tacibun fungnehen: patent by command, used to confer titles for fifth rank and above
tacibure hese: imperial command, imperial utterance
tacihiyan: religion; teaching, training
tacimbi: to learn
tacin: customs; religion; learning, skill
tafulambi: to advise, to counsel
-tai, -tei, -toi: instrumental converb suffix
Taidzu (Chin. *Taizu* 太祖): appellation for Nurhaci; also refers to the first emperor of the Jin dynasty, 1115-1123
Taidzung Ucimai (Chin. *Taizong* 太宗): second Jin dynasty emperor, 1123-1135
taifin: peace
taiji: (Mongolian official title)
taitai (Chin: *taitai* 太太): wife
takambi: to know, to be familiar with
takūrambi: to press into service; to employ, to send on a mission, to be in the employ of someone
takūrara niyalma: employee, messenger
tala: plain, steppe
-tala, -tele, -tolo: terminative converb (up to, until)
talkiyan: lightening; electricity
tambi: to be fastened
Tang gurun: Tang dynasty
tanggū: hundred
tangse: imperial shamanic shrine
tantambi: to beat, to hit, to strike
Tar: (pers. name)
targabumbi: to prohibit; to admonish, to warn
targambi: to abstain, to avoid, to warn
tarhūn: fat
tarimbi: to farm, to cultivate, to plow
tasha: tiger
tasha erin: (time of the tiger) 3-5 A.M.
Tašigan: Tashkent (geogr. name)
tatambi: to halt; to rip, to pull out, to strangle
te: now, recently
tebcimbi: to endure, to bear
tebiyelembi = tebeliyembi: to embrace, to hug
tebumbi: to fill up, to put in
tebuhe giyamun: established relay station
tede: therefore; dative/locative of *tere*, in this matter; up until now
teherembi: to be even, to be equal
teherebumbi: to assign equal value, to match
teile: only, just, alone
teisu: assigned responsibility, assigned place; (Sibe) when, at the same time as
tembi: to sit, to reside; to live, to occupy a position
temen: camel
temgetu: seal
temgetu bithe: certificate, manifest, license
temšembi: to contend, to quarrel, to compete

Temurtu Huluk: Tughluk Temur (pers. name)
ten: highest point, noble, basis
ten i: highest, utmost, basic
ten i gūnin: the best and sincerest intention
teng seme: solid, firm, straight
tengge: monetary unit in Eastern Turkestan
tengkimbi: to have a clear understanding of
tengkime sambi: to know clearly
teni: then
teni saka: as soon as (with coordinative converb *-me*)
tere: that; he, she, it
tere anggala: moreover
tere fonde: at that time
tereci: thereafter
tese: those
tesumbi: to be enough, to be sufficient
tob: straight, right
tob amba elden genggiyen i deyen (Chin. *zhengda guangming dian* 正大光明殿): Great Brilliant Pavilion
tofohon: fifteen
tohorombi: to calm down, to soothe
tojin: peacock
tokso: village
toktobumbi: to pacify, to fix; to decide, to determine, to solidify; passive of *toktombi*
toktofi: certainly
toktombi: to be established, to be determined; to fix, to determine
tolombi: to count
Tomulok: (geogr. name)
ton: number
tondo: upright, honest, loyal
tookambi: to delay, to interfere
tookanjambi: to procrastinate, to delay, to be slow, to be delayed
torhome: in a circle, around
tosombi: to prepare for in advance; to lie in wait, to guard against
tuba: there, that place
tubaci: from there
tubai: of that place, local
tucibumbi: to bring out; to cause to come out; to publish, to reveal
tucibume alambi: to explain
tucike: past participle of *tucimbi*
tucimbi: to come out, to go out
tugi: cloud
tugi wan (Chin. *yunti* 雲梯): ladder for scaling walls
tuhebumbi: to bring to ruin, to implicate in a crime, to topple
tuhembi: to fall down
tukiyembi: to hold up, to honor
tuktan: first; at first, originally
tulergi: outside; outer; foreign
tulergi golo be dasara jurgan (Chin. *lifanyuan* 理藩院 |): Court of Colonial Affairs (H 3603)
tulgiyen (with *ci*): in addition to, besides
tumen: ten thousand
tumen minggan (Chin. *wan qian* 萬千): myriads, numerous
tumin: thick (of soup); dense, concentrated
Turdu: (pers. name)
Turfan: (geogr. name)
turga: thin, skinny
turgun: situation; reason, motive
turgunde: because
turigen: land rent
turimbi: to rent, to lease, to hire
turun: military banner, standard
tušan: office, duty
tušan be alime gaimbi: to assume one's duties
tušan be mutebumbi: to be qualified for the job, to be competent

tušan de bibumbi: to remain in office, to retain a position
tuttu: thus, so; like that
tuwa: fire
tuwabumbi: to show
tuwabun: view; survey, review
tuwaci...sehebi: we find that
tuwai sejen: train
tuwakiyambi: to watch, to guard
tuwakiyara cooha: garrison troops
tuwambi: to see, to look; to examine, to oversee, to observe to visit; to await
tuwašatambi: to supervise, to guard, to protect
tuwelembi: to carry on trade, to deal in, to peddle
tuweri: winter

uba: this place
ubaliyambumbi: to translate
ubašambi: to rebel, to turn against
Ubasi: (pers. name)
ubu: portion, allotment, share, part; responsibility; times, -fold
ubui nonggimbi: to increase sharply, to double
ucarambi: to meet, to encounter
udambi: to buy
udan ombi: to be late, to be behind time (Chin. *wudian* 誤點)
udu: how many; although; several
udu...-cibe: although…still
udu juwan: several tens
udu...seme: no matter how much
ududu: several, many
ududu jergi: several times
ufarambi: to make a mistake; to fail; to lose; to die
uhe: mutuality, in unison
uhei: mutual, together, unified
uheri: altogether, jointly, taken as a whole; chief, main, head; outline
uheri be baicara hafan: censor
uheri be baicara yamun (Chin: *duchayuan* 都察院): censorate, chief surveillance office (H 7183)
ujen: weighty, serious
ujihe jui: foster son
ujimbi: to feed, to raise, to nurture
uju: head, first
ukambi: to flee, to run away, to desert
ukcambi: to come loose, to get free, to escape from, to elude
uksun (Chin. *zongshi* 宗室): members of the imperial family descended from Nurhaci; clan, family
ulabun: biography
ulambi: to transmit, to pass on
ulan ulan i: from hand to hand, in unbroken tradition
ulebumbi: to feed, to raise (animals)
ulga: livestock, animal (same as *ulha*)
ulgimbi: to understand
ulgiyan: pig, swine
ulha: livestock, domestic animal
ulhi: sleeve
ulhibure fungnehen: patent by ordinance, used to confer titles for fifth ranks and above
ulhibure hese: ordinance (to manifest instructions)
ulhicun: knowledge, understanding
ulhicun akū: to be young
ulhimbi: to understand
ulin: goods
ulin jaka: belongings, property, assets, valuables
umai: at all (with negative)
ume: (w/imperfective) don't
umesi: very
umesi inu: quite so, very true
umiyaha: insect

uncambi: to sell
uncehen: tail
unde: (w/imperfective) not yet, before
unenggi: sincere, sincerity
unggimbi: to send
unggire bithe: an official communication between two equals
untuhun: empty, vacant; hollow; idle; vain; space, emptiness
urebumbi: to drill, to practice
urembi: to be fully acquainted with, to be experienced; to be ripe; to be sad
urgulembi: to be joyous
urgun: joy, happiness; auspicious sign
urgunjembi: to rejoice, to be glad
urgunjendumbi: to rejoice together
Urjanjab: (pers. name)
urse: people, persons
uru: right, correct
urui: steadily, always
urumbi: to be hungry, to get hungry
Urumci: Urumchi (geogr. name)
urun: daughter-in-law
urunakū: certainly
ushambi: (with *de*) to be angry with , to resent, to be disappointed
Uši: Uch Turfan (geogr. name)
usin: field, farmland
usisi: farmer
Usta: (pers. name)
utala: so many, so much
uthai: immediately, then; it so happens; even
uthai…-ci, inu: even if…still
uthai…-kini, inu: even if…still
uttu: thus, in this manner
uttu oci: if so, if it is like this
uttu ofi: therefore, given such circumstances
uyuci: ninth
uyun: nine
Ūdui: (pers. name)
Ūlet (Chin. *Weilute* 危魯特): Eleuths, Western Mongols, Dzungars, Oirats

wacihiyambi: to complete, to finish
wacihiyame: all, completely
wajimbi: to finish, to end; to cease to exist
waka: offense, mistake; wrong; sentence particle that negates nominal predicates
waka ombi: (w/dative) to be guilty, to wrong somebody
wakalame wesimbumbi: to memorialize to impeach
wakašambi: to accuse, to blame; to deem wrong
waliyambi: to abandon
wambi: to kill
wan: ladder
wang (Chin. *wang* 王): prince, king
wangga: fragrant
Wanyan Liyang (Chin. *Wanyan Liang* 完顏亮): fourth Jin emperor (1150-1161)
wargi: west; under, underneath; right (side)
wargi amargi: northwest, northwestern
wasimbi: to issue (an order, an edict), to demote
wasimbumbi: to go down (order, edict); causative of *wasimbi*
wasinjimbi: to come down
we: who
weceku(n): god, household god
wecembi: to make offerings
wehe: stone
wehiyembi: to support
wei (Chin. *wei* 衛): Ming unit of administration; Ming: military garrison
weile: work; crime, punishment, matter
weile arambi: to sentence, to punish, to accuse of; to commit a crime, to be guilty
weile bahambi: to be guilty of a crime
weile gisurembi: to accuse, to punish

weilembi: to work; to make, to construct; to serve
werešembi: to go to the bottom of, to investigate thoroughly
werimbi: to leave (trans.), to leave behind; to retain in one's possession
wesibumbi: to raise, to promote, to select
wesihun: you, your (honorific)
wesimbi: to go up; to advance (in rank)
wesimbumbi: to memorialize, to present to the emperor; to raise; to promote
wesimbure bithe ibebumbi: to submit a memorial
wesimbure bukdari: memorial (routine or palace memorial)

ya: which?
ya ba, yaba: what place?
yabade: where? to what place?
yabubumbi: to carry out; to approve; causative of *yabumbi*
yabumbi: to go; to carry out; to be active, to serve at a post; to perform a task
yabure bithe: despatch (to another government office)
yadahūn: poor
yadambi: to be poor
yafagan: pedestrian, on foot (same as *yafahan*)
yagese: this much, so
Yaha Tohonai: (geogr. name)
yaksimbi: to shut
yali: meat
yalumbi: to ride (an animal)
yamji: evening
yamjishūn: late; late in the day
yan: tael (monetary unit)
yargiyan: true, truth
yargiyan i: truly
yargiyan i katunjame: even with best efforts
Yarhašan: Yarhašan (pers. name)
yarhūdai: guide
yarhūdambi: to guide, to lead
yasa: eye
yaya: whatsoever, ever
ye: sentence particle of emphasis or surprise
ye, -ye: interrogative particle or suffix
yebe: better
yekengge: noble, grand
Yerkiyang: Yarkand (geogr. name)
yeru: hole, den
Yonggui: (pers. name)
Yoo Jeo (Chin. *Yaozhou* 耀州): (geogr. name)
Yoo Šun (Chin. *Yao Shun* 堯舜): Yao and Shun, two model rulers during the golden age of ancient Chinese history
yooni: complete, altogether
yooningga: complete
yooningga dasan: Tongzhi reign (1862-1874)
Yurung Haši: Yurung Hash (geogr. name)
Yustu Artuši: Yustu Artush (geogr. name)
Yusub Yusuf (pers. name)
Yuwan gurun: Yuan dynasty
yuyumbi: to starve
yuyure beyere: starving and freezing

About the Author

Dr. Gertraude Roth Li, one of only a handful of experts on Manchu language and history in the U.S., began studying Manchu under Professor Joseph Fletcher at Harvard in the late 1960s. Her Ph.d. dissertation "The Rise of the Early Manchu State" (Harvard, 1975) is based on the *Jiu Manzhou dang* (Old Manchu Archives), a large collection of pre-1644 Manchu documents. While professionally engaged in international work in nongovernmental organizations and at the University of Hawai'i, Dr. Roth Li continued her scholarly work in Manchu history and Manchu language. She taught Manchu at the University of Hawai'i and at the University of California and authored a chapter titled "Manchus and Manchu State Building" for the *Cambridge History of China*, vol. 9. Dr. Roth Li lives in Honolulu, Hawai'i.

examine learner data using innovative methods of analysis and investigate issues in pragmatic development and the instruction of pragmatics.

430 pp., ISBN(10): 0–8248–3137–3, ISBN(13): 978–0–8248–3137–0 $30.

NFLRC Monographs

Richard Schmidt, series editor

Monographs of the National Foreign Language Resource Center present the findings of recent work in applied linguistics that is of relevance to language teaching and learning (with a focus on the less commonly-taught languages of Asia and the Pacific) and are of particular interest to foreign language educators, applied linguists, and researchers. Prior to 2006, these monographs were published as "SLTCC Technical Reports."

TOWARD USEFUL PROGRAM EVALUATION IN COLLEGE FOREIGN LANGUAGE EDUCATION

JOHN M. NORRIS, JOHN MCE. DAVIS, CASTLE SINICROPE, & YUKIKO WATANABE (EDITORS), 2009

This volume reports on innovative, useful evaluation work conducted within U.S. college foreign language programs. An introductory chapter scopes out the territory, reporting key findings from research into the concerns, impetuses, and uses for evaluation that FL educators identify. Seven chapters then highlight examples of evaluations conducted in diverse language programs and institutional contexts. Each case is reported by program-internal educators, who walk readers through critical steps, from identifying evaluation uses, users, and questions, to designing methods, interpreting findings, and taking actions. A concluding chapter reflects on the emerging roles for FL program evaluation and articulates an agenda for integrating evaluation into language education practice.

240pp., ISBN 978–0–9800459–3–2 $30.

SECOND LANGUAGE TEACHING AND LEARNING IN THE NET GENERATION

RAQUEL OXFORD & JEFFREY OXFORD (EDITORS), 2009

Today's young people—the Net Generation—have grown up with technology all around them. However, teachers cannot assume that students' familiarity with technology in general transfers successfully to pedagogical settings. This volume examines various technologies and offers concrete advice on how each can be successfully implemented in the second language curriculum.

240pp., ISBN 978–0–9800459–2–5 $30.

CASE STUDIES IN FOREIGN LANGUAGE PLACEMENT: PRACTICES AND POSSIBILITIES

THOM HUDSON & MARTYN CLARK (EDITORS), 2008

Although most language programs make placement decisions on the basis of placement tests, there is surprisingly little published about different contexts and systems of placement testing. The present volume contains case studies of placement programs in foreign language programs at the tertiary level across the United States. The different programs span the spectrum from large programs servicing hundreds of students annually to small language programs with very few students. The contributions to this volume address such issues as how the size of the program, presence or absence of heritage learners, and population changes affect language placement decisions.

201pp., ISBN 978–0–9800459–0–1 $40.

CHINESE AS A HERITAGE LANGUAGE: FOSTERING ROOTED WORLD CITIZENRY

Agnes Weiyun He & Yun Xiao (Editors), 2008

Thirty-two scholars examine the socio-cultural, cognitive-linguistic, and educational-institutional trajectories along which Chinese as a Heritage Language may be acquired, maintained and developed. They draw upon developmental psychology, functional linguistics, linguistic and cultural anthropology, discourse analysis, orthography analysis, reading research, second language acquisition, and bilingualism. This volume aims to lay a foundation for theories, models, and master scripts to be discussed, debated, and developed, and to stimulate research and enhance teaching both within and beyond Chinese language education.

280pp., ISBN 978–08248–3286–5 $40.

PERSPECTIVES ON TEACHING CONNECTED SPEECH TO SECOND LANGUAGE SPEAKERS

James Dean Brown & Kimi Kondo-Brown (Editors), 2006

This book is a collection of fourteen articles on connected speech of interest to teachers, researchers, and materials developers in both ESL/EFL (ten chapters focus on connected speech in English) and Japanese (four chapters focus on Japanese connected speech). The fourteen chapters are divided up into five sections:

- What do we know so far about teaching connected speech?
- Does connected speech instruction work?
- How should connected speech be taught in English?
- How should connected speech be taught in Japanese?
- How should connected speech be tested?

290 pp., ISBN(10) 0–8248–3136–5, ISBN(13) 978–0–8248–3136–3 $38.

CORPUS LINGUISTICS FOR KOREAN LANGUAGE LEARNING AND TEACHING

Robert Bley-Vroman & Hyunsook Ko (Editors), 2006

Dramatic advances in personal-computer technology have given language teachers access to vast quantities of machine-readable text, which can be analyzed with a view toward improving the basis of language instruction. Corpus linguistics provides analytic techniques and practical tools for studying language in use. This volume provides both an introductory framework for the use of corpus linguistics for language teaching and examples of its application for Korean teaching and learning. The collected papers cover topics in Korean syntax, lexicon, and discourse, and second language acquisition research, always with a focus on application in the classroom. An overview of Korean corpus linguistics tools and available Korean corpora are also included.

265 pp., ISBN 0–8248–3062–8 $25.

NEW TECHNOLOGIES AND LANGUAGE LEARNING: CASES IN THE LESS COMMONLY TAUGHT LANGUAGES

Carol Anne Spreen (Editor), 2002

In recent years, the National Security Education Program (NSEP) has supported an increasing number of programs for teaching languages using different technological media. This compilation of case study initiatives funded through the NSEP Institutional Grants Program presents a range of technology-based options for language programming that will help universities make more informed decisions about teaching less commonly taught languages. The eight chapters describe how different types of technologies are used to support language programs (i.e., Web, ITV, and audio- or video-based materials), discuss identifiable trends in elanguage learning, and explore how technology addresses issues of equity, diversity, and opportunity. This book offers many lessons learned and decisions made as technology changes and learning needs become more complex.

188 pp., ISBN 0–8248–2634–5 $25.

AN INVESTIGATION OF SECOND LANGUAGE TASK-BASED PERFORMANCE ASSESSMENTS

James Dean Brown, Thom Hudson, John M. Norris, & William Bonk, 2002

This volume describes the creation of performance assessment instruments and their validation (based on work started in a previous monograph). It begins by explaining the test and rating scale development processes and the administration of the resulting three seven-task tests to 90 university level EFL and ESL students. The results are examined in terms of (a) the effects of test revision; (b) comparisons among the task-dependent, task-independent, and self-rating scales; and (c) reliability and validity issues.

240 pp., ISBN 0–8248–2633–7 $25.

MOTIVATION AND SECOND LANGUAGE ACQUISITION

Zoltán Dörnyei & Richard Schmidt (Editors), 2001

This volume—the second in this series concerned with motivation and foreign language learning—includes papers presented in a state-of-the-art colloquium on L2 motivation at the American Association for Applied Linguistics (Vancouver, 2000) and a number of specially commissioned studies. The 20 chapters, written by some of the best known researchers in the field, cover a wide range of theoretical and research methodological issues, and also offer empirical results (both qualitative and quantitative) concerning the learning of many different languages (Arabic, Chinese, English, Filipino, French, German, Hindi, Italian, Japanese, Russian, and Spanish) in a broad range of learning contexts (Bahrain, Brazil, Canada, Egypt, Finland, Hungary, Ireland, Israel, Japan, Spain, and the US).

520 pp., ISBN 0–8248–2458–X $25.

A FOCUS ON LANGUAGE TEST DEVELOPMENT: EXPANDING THE LANGUAGE PROFICIENCY CONSTRUCT ACROSS A VARIETY OF TESTS

Thom Hudson & James Dean Brown (Editors), 2001

This volume presents eight research studies that introduce a variety of novel, non-traditional forms of second and foreign language assessment. To the extent possible, the studies also show the entire test development process, warts and all. These language testing projects not only demonstrate many of the types of problems that test developers run into in the real world but also afford the reader unique insights into the language test development process.

230 pp., ISBN 0–8248–2351–6 $20.

STUDIES ON KOREAN IN COMMUNITY SCHOOLS

Dong-Jae Lee, Sookeun Cho, Miseon Lee, Minsun Song, & William O'Grady (Editors), 2000

The papers in this volume focus on language teaching and learning in Korean community schools. Drawing on innovative experimental work and research in linguistics, education, and psychology, the contributors address issues of importance to teachers, administrators, and parents. Topics covered include childhood bilingualism, Korean grammar, language acquisition, children's literature, and language teaching methodology. [in Korean]

256 pp., ISBN 0–8248–2352–4 $20.

A COMMUNICATIVE FRAMEWORK FOR INTRODUCTORY JAPANESE LANGUAGE CURRICULA

WASHINGTON STATE JAPANESE LANGUAGE CURRICULUM GUIDELINES COMMITTEE, 2000

In recent years the number of schools offering Japanese nationwide has increased dramatically. Because of the tremendous popularity of the Japanese language and the shortage of teachers, quite a few untrained, non-native and native teachers are in the classrooms and are expected to teach several levels of Japanese. These guidelines are intended to assist individual teachers and professional associations throughout the United States in designing Japanese language curricula. They are meant to serve as a framework from which language teaching can be expanded and are intended to allow teachers to enhance and strengthen the quality of Japanese language instruction.

168 pp., ISBN 0–8248–2350–8 $20.

FOREIGN LANGUAGE TEACHING AND MINORITY LANGUAGE EDUCATION

KATHRYN A. DAVIS (EDITOR), 1999

This volume seeks to examine the potential for building relationships among foreign language, bilingual, and ESL programs towards fostering bilingualism. Part I of the volume examines the sociopolitical contexts for language partnerships, including:

- obstacles to developing bilingualism
- implications of acculturation, identity, and language issues for linguistic minorities.
- the potential for developing partnerships across primary, secondary, and tertiary institutions

Part II of the volume provides research findings on the Foreign language partnership project designed to capitalize on the resources of immigrant students to enhance foreign language learning.

152 pp., ISBN 0–8248–2067–3 $20.

DESIGNING SECOND LANGUAGE PERFORMANCE ASSESSMENTS

JOHN M. NORRIS, JAMES DEAN BROWN, THOM HUDSON, & JIM YOSHIOKA, 1998, 2000

This technical report focuses on the decision-making potential provided by second language performance assessments. The authors first situate performance assessment within a broader discussion of alternatives in language assessment and in educational assessment in general. They then discuss issues in performance assessment design, implementation, reliability, and validity. Finally, they present a prototype framework for second language performance assessment based on the integration of theoretical underpinnings and research findings from the task-based language teaching literature, the language testing literature, and the educational measurement literature. The authors outline test and item specifications, and they present numerous examples of prototypical language tasks. They also propose a research agenda focusing on the operationalization of second language performance assessments.

248 pp., ISBN 0–8248–2109–2 $20.

SECOND LANGUAGE DEVELOPMENT IN WRITING: MEASURES OF FLUENCY, ACCURACY, AND COMPLEXITY

KATE WOLFE-QUINTERO, SHUNJI INAGAKI, & HAE-YOUNG KIM, 1998, 2002

In this book, the authors analyze and compare the ways that fluency, accuracy, grammatical complexity, and lexical complexity have been measured in studies of language development in second language writing. More than 100 developmental measures are examined, with detailed comparisons of the results across the studies that have used each measure. The authors discuss the theoretical foundations for each type of developmental measure, and they consider the relationship between developmental measures and various types of proficiency measures. They also examine criteria for determining which developmental measures are the most successful and suggest which measures are the most promising for continuing work on language development.

208 pp., ISBN 0–8248–2069–X $20.

THE DEVELOPMENT OF A LEXICAL TONE PHONOLOGY IN AMERICAN ADULT LEARNERS OF STANDARD MANDARIN CHINESE

Sylvia Henel Sun, 1998

The study reported is based on an assessment of three decades of research on the SLA of Mandarin tone. It investigates whether differences in learners' tone perception and production are related to differences in the effects of certain linguistic, task, and learner factors. The learners of focus are American students of Mandarin in Beijing, China. Their performances on two perception and three production tasks are analyzed through a host of variables and methods of quantification.

328 pp., ISBN 0–8248–2068–1 $20.

NEW TRENDS AND ISSUES IN TEACHING JAPANESE LANGUAGE AND CULTURE

Haruko M. Cook, Kyoko Hijirida, & Mildred Tahara (Editors), 1997

In recent years, Japanese has become the fourth most commonly taught foreign language at the college level in the United States. As the number of students who study Japanese has increased, the teaching of Japanese as a foreign language has been established as an important academic field of study. This technical report includes nine contributions to the advancement of this field, encompassing the following five important issues:

- Literature and literature teaching
- Technology in the language classroom
- Orthography
- Testing
- Grammatical versus pragmatic approaches to language teaching

164 pp., ISBN 0–8248–2067–3 $20.

SIX MEASURES OF JSL PRAGMATICS

Sayoko Okada Yamashita, 1996

This book investigates differences among tests that can be used to measure the cross-cultural pragmatic ability of English-speaking learners of Japanese. Building on the work of Hudson, Detmer, and Brown (Technical Reports #2 and #7 in this series), the author modified six test types that she used to gather data from North American learners of Japanese. She found numerous problems with the multiple-choice discourse completion test but reported that the other five tests all proved highly reliable and reasonably valid. Practical issues involved in creating and using such language tests are discussed from a variety of perspectives.

213 pp., ISBN 0–8248–1914–4 $15.

LANGUAGE LEARNING STRATEGIES AROUND THE WORLD: CROSS-CULTURAL PERSPECTIVES

Rebecca L. Oxford (Editor), 1996, 1997, 2002

Language learning strategies are the specific steps students take to improve their progress in learning a second or foreign language. Optimizing learning strategies improves language performance. This groundbreaking book presents new information about cultural influences on the use of language learning strategies. It also shows innovative ways to assess students' strategy use and remarkable techniques for helping students improve their choice of strategies, with the goal of peak language learning.

166 pp., ISBN 0–8248–1910–1 $20.

TELECOLLABORATION IN FOREIGN LANGUAGE LEARNING: PROCEEDINGS OF THE HAWAI'I SYMPOSIUM

MARK WARSCHAUER (EDITOR), 1996

The Symposium on Local & Global Electronic Networking in Foreign Language Learning & Research, part of the National Foreign Language Resource Center's 1995 Summer Institute on Technology & the Human Factor in Foreign Language Education, included presentations of papers and hands-on workshops conducted by Symposium participants to facilitate the sharing of resources, ideas, and information about all aspects of electronic networking for foreign language teaching and research, including electronic discussion and conferencing, international cultural exchanges, real-time communication and simulations, research and resource retrieval via the Internet, and research using networks. This collection presents a sampling of those presentations.

252 pp., ISBN 0–8248–1867–9 $20.

LANGUAGE LEARNING MOTIVATION: PATHWAYS TO THE NEW CENTURY

REBECCA L. OXFORD (EDITOR), 1996

This volume chronicles a revolution in our thinking about what makes students want to learn languages and what causes them to persist in that difficult and rewarding adventure. Topics in this book include the internal structures of and external connections with foreign language motivation; exploring adult language learning motivation, self-efficacy, and anxiety; comparing the motivations and learning strategies of students of Japanese and Spanish; and enhancing the theory of language learning motivation from many psychological and social perspectives.

218 pp., ISBN 0–8248–1849–0 $20.

LINGUISTICS & LANGUAGE TEACHING: PROCEEDINGS OF THE SIXTH JOINT LSH-HATESL CONFERENCE

CYNTHIA REVES, CAROLINE STEELE, & CATHY S. P. WONG (EDITORS), 1996

Technical Report #10 contains 18 articles revolving around the following three topics:

- Linguistic issues—These six papers discuss various linguistic issues: ideophones, syllabic nasals, linguistic areas, computation, tonal melody classification, and wh-words.
- Sociolinguistics—Sociolinguistic phenomena in Swahili, signing, Hawaiian, and Japanese are discussed in four of the papers.
- Language teaching and learning—These eight papers cover prosodic modification, note taking, planning in oral production, oral testing, language policy, L2 essay organization, access to dative alternation rules, and child noun phrase structure development.

364 pp., ISBN 0–8248–1851–2 $20.

ATTENTION & AWARENESS IN FOREIGN LANGUAGE LEARNING

RICHARD SCHMIDT (EDITOR), 1996

Issues related to the role of attention and awareness in learning lie at the heart of many theoretical and practical controversies in the foreign language field. This collection of papers presents research into the learning of Spanish, Japanese, Finnish, Hawaiian, and English as a second language (with additional comments and examples from French, German, and miniature artificial languages) that bear on these crucial questions for foreign language pedagogy.

394 pp., ISBN 0–8248–1794–X $20.

VIRTUAL CONNECTIONS: ONLINE ACTIVITIES AND PROJECTS FOR NETWORKING LANGUAGE LEARNERS

MARK WARSCHAUER (EDITOR), 1995, 1996

Computer networking has created dramatic new possibilities for connecting language learners in a single classroom or across the globe. This collection of activities and projects makes use of email, the internet, computer conferencing, and other forms of computer-mediated communication for the foreign and second language classroom at any level of instruction. Teachers from around the world submitted the activities compiled in this volume—activities that they have used successfully in their own classrooms.

417 pp., ISBN 0–8248–1793–1 $30.

DEVELOPING PROTOTYPIC MEASURES OF CROSS-CULTURAL PRAGMATICS

THOM HUDSON, EMILY DETMER, & J. D. BROWN, 1995

Although the study of cross-cultural pragmatics has gained importance in applied linguistics, there are no standard forms of assessment that might make research comparable across studies and languages. The present volume describes the process through which six forms of cross-cultural assessment were developed for second language learners of English. The models may be used for second language learners of other languages. The six forms of assessment involve two forms each of indirect discourse completion tests, oral language production, and self-assessment. The procedures involve the assessment of requests, apologies, and refusals.

198 pp., ISBN 0–8248–1763–X $15.

THE ROLE OF PHONOLOGICAL CODING IN READING KANJI

SACHIKO MATSUNAGA, 1995

In this technical report, the author reports the results of a study that she conducted on phonological coding in reading kanji using an eye-movement monitor and draws some pedagogical implications. In addition, she reviews current literature on the different schools of thought regarding instruction in reading kanji and its role in the teaching of non-alphabetic written languages like Japanese.

64 pp., ISBN 0–8248–1734–6 $10.

PRAGMATICS OF CHINESE AS NATIVE AND TARGET LANGUAGE

GABRIELE KASPER (EDITOR), 1995

This technical report includes six contributions to the study of the pragmatics of Mandarin Chinese:

- A report of an interview study conducted with nonnative speakers of Chinese; and
- Five data-based studies on the performance of different speech acts by native speakers of Mandarin—requesting, refusing, complaining, giving bad news, disagreeing, and complimenting.

312 pp., ISBN 0–8248–1733–8 $15.

A BIBLIOGRAPHY OF PEDAGOGY AND RESEARCH IN INTERPRETATION AND TRANSLATION

ETILVIA ARJONA, 1993

This technical report includes four types of bibliographic information on translation and interpretation studies:

- Research efforts across disciplinary boundaries—cognitive psychology, neurolinguistics, psycholinguistics, sociolinguistics, computational linguistics, measurement, aptitude testing, language policy, decision-making, theses, dissertations;

- Training information covering program design, curriculum studies, instruction, school administration;
- Instruction information detailing course syllabi, methodology, models, available textbooks; and
- Testing information about aptitude, selection, diagnostic tests.

115 pp., ISBN 0–8248–1572–6 $10.

PRAGMATICS OF JAPANESE AS NATIVE AND TARGET LANGUAGE

Gabriele Kasper (Editor), 1992, 1996

This technical report includes three contributions to the study of the pragmatics of Japanese:

- A bibliography on speech act performance, discourse management, and other pragmatic and sociolinguistic features of Japanese;
- A study on introspective methods in examining Japanese learners' performance of refusals; and
- A longitudinal investigation of the acquisition of the particle ne by nonnative speakers of Japanese.

125 pp., ISBN 0–8248–1462–2 $10.

A FRAMEWORK FOR TESTING CROSS-CULTURAL PRAGMATICS

Thom Hudson, Emily Detmer, & J. D. Brown, 1992

This technical report presents a framework for developing methods that assess cross-cultural pragmatic ability. Although the framework has been designed for Japanese and American cross-cultural contrasts, it can serve as a generic approach that can be applied to other language contrasts. The focus is on the variables of social distance, relative power, and the degree of imposition within the speech acts of requests, refusals, and apologies. Evaluation of performance is based on recognition of the speech act, amount of speech, forms or formulæ used, directness, formality, and politeness.

51 pp., ISBN 0–8248–1463–0 $10.

RESEARCH METHODS IN INTERLANGUAGE PRAGMATICS

Gabriele Kasper & Merete Dahl, 1991

This technical report reviews the methods of data collection employed in 39 studies of interlanguage pragmatics, defined narrowly as the investigation of nonnative speakers' comprehension and production of speech acts, and the acquisition of L2-related speech act knowledge. Data collection instruments are distinguished according to the degree to which they constrain informants' responses, and whether they tap speech act perception/comprehension or production. A main focus of discussion is the validity of different types of data, in particular their adequacy to approximate authentic performance of linguistic action.

51 pp., ISBN 0–8248–1419–3 $10.

www.ingramcontent.com/pod-product-compliance
Lightning Source LLC
Chambersburg PA
CBHW080539230426
43663CB00015B/2640
9780980045956